SOMETHING ABOUT THE AUTHOR®

Something about
the Author *was named
an "Outstanding
Reference Source,"*
*the highest honor given
by the American
Library Association
Reference and Adult
Services Division.*

ISSN 0276-816X

SOMETHING ABOUT THE AUTHOR®

**Facts and Pictures about Authors
and Illustrators of Books for Young People**

volume 226

GALE
CENGAGE Learning

Detroit • New York • San Francisco • New Haven, Conn • Waterville, Maine • London

GALE
CENGAGE Learning™

Something about the Author, Volume 226

Project Editor: Lisa Kumar

Permissions: Leitha Etheridge-Sims

Imaging and Multimedia: Leitha
   Etheridge-Sims, John Watkins

Composition and Electronic Capture:
   Amy Darga

Manufacturing: Rhonda Dover

Product Manager: Mary Onorato

For product information and technology assistance, contact us at
Gale Customer Support, 1-800-877-4253.
For permission to use material from this text or product,
submit all requests online at **www.cengage.com/permissions.**
Further permissions questions can be emailed to
permissionrequest@cengage.com

Since this page cannot legibly accommodate all copyright notices, the acknowledgments constitute an extension of the copyright notice.

While every effort has been made to ensure the reliability of the information presented in this publication, Gale, a part of Cengage Learning, does not guarantee the accuracy of the data contained herein. Gale accepts no payment for listing; and inclusion in the publication of any organization, agency, institution, publication, service, or individual does not imply endorsement of the editors or publisher. Errors brought to the attention of the publisher and verified to the satisfaction of the publisher will be corrected in future editions.

EDITORIAL DATA PRIVACY POLICY: Does this publication contain information about you as an individual? If so, for more information about our editorial data privacy policies, please see our Privacy Statement at www.gale.cengage.com.

Gale, Cengage Learning
27500 Drake Rd.
Farmington Hills, MI, 48331-3535

LIBRARY OF CONGRESS CATALOG CARD NUMBER 62-52046

ISBN-13: 978-1-4144-6129-8
ISBN-10: 1-4144-6129-1

ISSN 0276-816X

This title is also available as an e-book.
ISBN-13: 978-1-4144-6458-9
ISBN-10: 1-4144-6458-4
Contact your Gale, Cengage Learning sales representative for ordering information.

Printed in Mexico
1 2 3 4 5 6 7 15 14 13 12 11

Contents

Authors in Forthcoming Volumes

Below are some of the authors and illustrators that will be featured in upcoming volumes of *SATA*. These include new entries on the swiftly rising stars of the field, as well as completely revised and updated entries (indicated with *) on some of the most notable and best-loved creators of books for children.

*Tonya Bolden ▌ In her many books, Bolden draws from history to present young readers with hopeful and positive life examples. While much of her work is nonfiction, it ranges in genre from history to biography to self-help books and draws on her knowledge and fascination with African-American history and the development of Black American culture. Bolden's award-winning books include *And Not Afraid to Dare: The Stories of Ten African-American Women, M.L.K.: Journey of a King,* and *Wake up Our Souls: A Celebration of Black Artists.*

*Floyd Cooper ▌ Winner of the Coretta Scott King Illustrator Award among many other honors, author and artist Cooper brings to life stories, poems, songs, and works of nonfiction detailing centuries of the African-American experience. "Luminous" is perhaps the word used most often by critics to describe his art, which is enriched by sunlight and life-affirming vignettes featuring families and communities. In addition to creating images to pair with works by other authors, Cooper has also illustrated his own stories featuring African-American themes and positive messages about life's possibilities.

Emily Diamand ▌ Diamand won the inaugural *Times*/Chicken House Children's Fiction Competition in her native United Kingdom with the adventure story *Flood Child,* a novel first published as *Reavers' Ransom.* A former environmental activist, she sets her tale in twentieth-third-century Britain, much of which has been turned into marshland due to climate change. *Flood and Fire,* a sequel, maintains the author's environmental focus while also adding sci-fi and fantasy adventure to the mix.

*Priscilla Galloway ▌ Galloway is both a consummate storyteller and a respected teacher whose love affair with myths, fantasy, and historical fiction has lasted almost her entire life. As a writer, she enjoys retelling fairy tales, as in *Truly Grim Tales,* and she puts ancient myths in context with the modern world in her novel *Snake Dreamer* as well as in her "Tales of Ancient Lands" series. In addition to writing nonfiction works and teaching guides, Galloway has also contributed to the "Our Canadian Girl" series with her "Lisa" books, about a young girl who travels with her family from their home in Winnipeg to the Cariboo gold fields of British Columbia in the late 1800s.

John Holyfield ▌ A painter and illustrator who works primarily in oils, Holyfield creates detailed images that evoke life in the rural South and extol strong families and faith-based traditions. Impressions from his own childhood, including family stories, are woven into his paintings of African-American characters, including his illustrations for children's books such as Ethel Footman Smothers' *The Hard-Times Jar* and Phil Bildner's *The Hallelujah Flight.* While the culture and traditions he captures with his paint brush are those of black Americans, Holyfield's body of work holds an appeal that crosses racial lines due to its inspiring depiction of life and human relationships.

*Marilyn Nelson ▌ A former poet laureate of the State of Connecticut, Nelson writes in a variety of styles about many subjects, alternating adult works with books for younger readers. She has created a poetic biography of George Washington Carver, the picture books *Snook Alone* and *Beautiful Ballerina,* as well as history-themed works such as *Sweethearts of Rhythm: The Story of the Greatest All-Girl Swing Band in the World* and *A Wreath for Emmett Till.* In addition to her poetry, Nelson teaches and mentors other writers as an educator and founder of Soul Mountain Retreat.

*Mal Peet ▌ English author and illustrator Peet has been active in children's publishing since the mid-1990s, collaborating with artist Tudor Humphries on the picture book *A Floating World* as well as producing texts for beginning readers. Despite having dozens of titles to his credit, Peet remained relatively unknown until 2004, when his first young-adult novel, *Keeper,* won two significant literary honors: the Nestlé Smarties Prize Bronze award and the Bradford Boase award. A second novel, *Tamar,* was awarded the prestigious Carnegie Medal in 2005, and Peet has continued to find success in writing for older audiences, including the highly acclaimed novels *The Penalty* and *Exposure.*

*Laura Scandiffio ▌ Born in Germany and now living in Canada, Scandiffio has harnessed her imagination into creating nonfiction children's books that feature unusual topics and creative approaches. Her thorough research and imaginative approach combine in boy-friendly titles such as *The Martial Arts Book, Escapes!: True Stories from the Edge, Evil Masters: The Frightening World of Tyrants,* as well as her contributions to the "Kids at the Crossroads" history series.

Gerry Swallow ▌ Under the pen name Dr. Cuthbert Soup, Swallow has created several witty and whimsical books for preteen readers. Mock-serious in their chronicle of events, both *A Whole Nother Story* and its sequel, *Another Whole Nother Story,* feature Soup's entertaining telling of an unfortunate family saga, full of arch humor and wordplay. Unlike Swallow—a scriptwriter and former columnist for the *Seattle Times*—the pseudonymous Soup has a substantial pedigree: founder and chief title-holder at the National Center for Unsolicited Advice, he travels the world foisting his opinions on those who least desire to hear them and regularly retires to the large secluded mansion he shares with his dog and pet garden snails.

*John Wilson ▌ Wilson focuses on historical fiction and nonfiction for both teen readers and adults in his many books. In addition to works such as *Dancing Elephants and Floating Continents: The*

Story of Canada beneath Your Feet, which focuses on his native Canada, he creates fictional stories about young people who, through circumstances beyond their control, find themselves navigating tumultuous events. Characters include the adventurous cabin boy who in the 1600s joins Henry Hudson on his voyage to discover the Northwest passage in *The Alchemist's Dream,* the young Jew who becomes trapped in Nazi Germany in *Flames of the Tiger,* and two friends who wind up on opposite sides of the religious divide in *Crusade.* War and its effects on young people are of particular interest to the author, inspiring his U.S. Civil War novels *The Flags of War* and *Battle Scars* as well as the World War I novels *And in the Morning* and *Shot at Dawn.*

Introduction

Something about the Author (*SATA*) is an ongoing reference series that examines the lives and works of authors and illustrators of books for children. *SATA* includes not only well-known writers and artists but also less prominent individuals whose works are just coming to be recognized. This series is often the only readily available information source on emerging authors and illustrators. You'll find *SATA* informative and entertaining, whether you are a student, a librarian, an English teacher, a parent, or simply an adult who enjoys children's literature.

What's Inside *SATA*

SATA provides detailed information about authors and illustrators who span the full time range of children's literature, from early figures like John Newbery and L. Frank Baum to contemporary figures like Judy Blume and Richard Peck. Authors in the series represent primarily English-speaking countries, particularly the United States, Canada, and the United Kingdom. Also included, however, are authors from around the world whose works are available in English translation. The writings represented in *SATA* include those created intentionally for children and young adults as well as those written for a general audience and known to interest younger readers. These writings cover the entire spectrum of children's literature, including picture books, humor, folk and fairy tales, animal stories, mystery and adventure, science fiction and fantasy, historical fiction, poetry and nonsense verse, drama, biography, and nonfiction. Obituaries are also included in many volumes of *SATA* and are intended not only as death notices but also as concise overviews of people's lives and work. Additionally, each edition features newly revised and updated entries for a selection of *SATA* listees who remain of interest to today's readers and who have been active enough to require extensive revisions of their earlier biographies.

Autobiography Feature

Beginning with Volume 103, many volumes of *SATA* feature one or more specially commissioned autobiographical essays. These unique essays, averaging about ten thousand words in length and illustrated with an abundance of personal photos, present an entertaining and informative first-person perspective on the lives and careers of prominent authors and illustrators profiled in *SATA*.

Two Convenient Indexes

In response to suggestions from librarians, *SATA* indexes no longer appear in every volume but are included in alternate (odd-numbered) volumes of the series, beginning with Volume 57.

SATA continues to include two indexes that cumulate with each alternate volume: the Illustrations Index, arranged by the name of the illustrator, gives the number of the volume and page where the illustrator's work appears in the current volume as well as all preceding volumes in the series; the Author Index gives the number of the volume in which a person's biographical sketch, autobiographical essay, or obituary appears in the current volume as well as all preceding volumes in the series.

These indexes also include references to authors and illustrators who appear in *Gale's Yesterday's Authors of Books for Children, Children's Literature Review,* and *Something about the Author Autobiography Series.*

Easy-to-Use Entry Format

Whether you're already familiar with the *SATA* series or just getting acquainted, you will want to be aware of the kind of information that an entry provides. In every *SATA* entry the editors attempt to give as complete a picture of the person's life and work as possible. A typical entry in *SATA* includes the following clearly labeled information sections:

PERSONAL: date and place of birth and death, parents' names and occupations, name of spouse, date of marriage, names of children, educational institutions attended, degrees received, religious and political affiliations, hobbies and other interests.

ADDRESSES: complete home, office, electronic mail, and agent addresses, whenever available.

CAREER: name of employer, position, and dates for each career post; art exhibitions; military service; memberships and offices held in professional and civic organizations.

MEMBER: professional, civic, and other association memberships and any official posts held.

AWARDS, HONORS: literary and professional awards received.

WRITINGS: title-by-title chronological bibliography of books written and/or illustrated, listed by genre when known; lists of other notable publications, such as plays, screenplays, and periodical contributions.

ADAPTATIONS: a list of films, television programs, plays, CD-ROMs, recordings, and other media presentations that have been adapted from the author's work.

WORK IN PROGRESS: description of projects in progress.

SIDELIGHTS: a biographical portrait of the author or illustrator's development, either directly from the biographee—and often written specifically for the *SATA* entry—or gathered from diaries, letters, interviews, or other published sources.

BIOGRAPHICAL AND CRITICAL SOURCES: cites sources quoted in "Sidelights" along with references for further reading.

EXTENSIVE ILLUSTRATIONS: photographs, movie stills, book illustrations, and other interesting visual materials supplement the text.

How a *SATA* Entry Is Compiled

SATA editors examine a wide variety of published sources to gather information for an entry. Biographical and bibliographic sources are consulted, as are book reviews, feature articles, published interviews, and material sometimes obtained from the biographee's family, publishers, agent, or other associates. Whenever possible, the author or illustrator is sent a copy of the entry to check for accuracy and completeness.

Entries that have not been verified by the biographees or their representatives are marked with an asterisk (*).

Contact the Editor

We encourage our readers to examine the entire *SATA* series. Please write and tell us if we can make *SATA* even more helpful to you. Give your comments and suggestions to the editor:

Editor
Something about the Author
Gale, Cengage Learning
27500 Drake Rd.
Farmington Hills MI 48331-3535

Toll-free: 800-877-GALE
Fax: 248-699-8070

Something about the Author Product Advisory Board

The editors of *Something about the Author* are dedicated to maintaining a high standard of excellence by publishing comprehensive, accurate, and highly readable entries on a wide array of writers for children and young adults. In addition to the quality of the content, the editors take pride in the graphic design of the series, which is intended to be orderly yet inviting, allowing readers to utilize the pages of *SATA* easily and with efficiency. Despite the longevity of the *SATA* print series, and the success of its format, we are mindful that the vitality of a literary reference product is dependent on its ability to serve its users over time. As literature, and attitudes about literature, constantly evolve, so do the reference needs of students, teachers, scholars, journalists, researchers, and book club members. To be certain that we continue to keep pace with the expectations of our customers, the editors of *SATA* listen carefully to their comments regarding the value, utility, and quality of the series. Librarians, who have firsthand knowledge of the needs of library users, are a valuable resource for us. The *Something about the Author* Product Advisory Board, made up of school, public, and academic librarians, is a forum to promote focused feedback about *SATA* on a regular basis. The nine-member advisory board includes the following individuals, whom the editors wish to thank for sharing their expertise:

Eva M. Davis
Director,
Canton Public Library,
Canton, Michigan

Joan B. Eisenberg
Lower School Librarian,
Milton Academy,
Milton, Massachusetts

Francisca Goldsmith
Teen Services Librarian,
Berkeley Public Library,
Berkeley, California

Susan Dove Lempke
Children's Services Supervisor,
Niles Public Library District,
Niles, Illinois

Robyn Lupa
Head of Children's Services,
Jefferson County Public Library,
Lakewood, Colorado

Victor L. Schill
Assistant Branch Librarian/Children's Librarian,
Harris County Public Library/Fairbanks Branch,
Houston, Texas

Caryn Sipos
Community Librarian,
Three Creeks Community Library,
Vancouver, Washington

Steven Weiner
Director,
Maynard Public Library,
Maynard, Massachusetts

SOMETHING ABOUT THE AUTHOR

AVI 1937-
(Edward Irving Wortis)

Personal

Born December 23, 1937, in New York, NY; son of Joseph (a psychiatrist) and Helen (a social worker) Wortis; married Joan Gabriner (a weaver), November 1, 1963 (divorced); married Coppelia Kahn (a professor of English); children: Shaun Wortis, Kevin Wortis; stepchildren: Gabriel Kahn. *Education:* Attended Antioch University; University of Wisconsin—Madison, B.A., 1959, M.A., 1962; Columbia University, M.S.L.S., 1964. *Hobbies and other interests:* Photography.

Addresses

Home—Denver, CO. *Agent*—Gail Hochman, Brandt & Hochman Literary Agents, 1501 Broadway, Ste. 2310, New York, NY 10036-5600.

Career

Writer and librarian. Author of books for children, 1960—. New York Public Library, New York, NY, librarian in performing arts research center, 1962-70; Lambeth Public Library, London, England, exchange program librarian, 1968; Trenton State College, Trenton, NJ, assistant professor and humanities librarian, 1970-86. Cofounder of "Breakfast Serials" (reading program), 1996; visiting writer in schools across the United States.

Avi (Reproduced by permission.)

Member

PEN, Authors Guild, Authors League of America.

Awards, Honors

Best Book of the Year designation, British Book Council, 1973, for *Snail Tale;* New Jersey State Council on the Arts grants, 1974, 1976, 1978; Mystery Writers of America Special Award, 1975, for *No More Magic,* 1979, for *Emily Upham's Revenge,* and 1983, for *Shadrach's Crossing;* Christopher Award, 1980, for *Encounter at Easton;* Children's Choice Award, International Reading Association (IRA), 1980, for *Man from the Sky,* and 1988, for *Romeo and Juliet—Together (and Alive) at Last;* New Jersey Authors Award, New Jersey Institute of Technology, 1983, for *Shadrach's Crossing;* Scott O'Dell Historical Fiction Award, *Bulletin of the Center for Children's Books,* 1984, for *The Fighting Ground;* Best Books for Young Adults citations, American Library Association (ALA), 1984, for *The Fighting Ground,* and 1986, for *Wolf Rider;* Library of Congress Best Books of the Year citations, 1989, for *Something Upstairs,* and 1990, for *The Man Who Was Poe;* Virginia Young Readers' Award, 1990, for *Wolf Rider;* ALA Notable Book designation, and Best Book of the Year citation, Society of Children's Book Authors and Illustrators (SCBWI), both 1990, and Newbery Honor Book designation, *Boston Globe/Horn Book* Award, and SCBWIGolden Kite Award, all 1991, all for *The True Confessions of Charlotte Doyle;* Newbery Honor Book designation, 1992, for *Nothing but the Truth; Boston Globe/Horn Book* Award for Fiction, 1996, for *Poppy;* New York Public Library Best Books of the Year citation, 1996, and National Council of Social Studies/Children's Book Council Notable Book citation, 1997, both for *Beyond the Western Sea;* Pick of the Lists designation, IRA, 1997, for *Finding Providence;* ALA Notable Book designation, 2002 for *Silent Movie;* ALA Notable Book designation, and Newbery Award, both 2003, both for *Crispin: The Cross of Lead.* Books for the Teen Age designation, New York Public Library, 2005, and Best Children's Books of the Year list, Bank Street College of Education, 2006, both for *The Book without Words;* ALA Notable Book designation, and Honor award, National Parenting Publication Awards, both 2006, both for *Crispin: At the Edge of the World;* Beacon of Liberty Award nomination, and Best Children's Books of the Year listee, Bank Street College of Education, both 2008, both for *Iron Thunder;* Best of the Best Books selection, Chicago Public Library, 2008, and Cooperative Children's Book Center Choices selection, 2009, both for *The Seer of Shadows.*

Writings

FOR CHILDREN

Things That Sometimes Happen (picture book), illustrated by Jodi Robbin, Doubleday (New York, NY), 1970, abridged edition, illustrated by Marjorie Priceman, Atheneum Books for Young Readers (New York, NY), 2001.

Snail Tale: The Adventures of a Rather Small Snail (picture book; also see below), illustrated by Tom Kindron, Pantheon (New York, NY), 1972.

No More Magic, Pantheon (New York, NY), 1975.

Captain Grey, Pantheon (New York, NY), 1977.

Emily Upham's Revenge; or, How Deadwood Dick Saved the Banker's Niece: A Massachusetts Adventure, Pantheon (New York, NY), 1978.

Night Journeys, Pantheon (New York, NY), 1979.

Encounter at Easton (sequel to *Night Journeys*), Pantheon (New York, NY), 1980.

Man from the Sky, Knopf (New York, NY), 1980.

The History of Helpless Harry: To Which Is Added a Variety of Amusing and Entertaining Adventures, Pantheon (New York, NY), 1980.

A Place Called Ugly, Pantheon (New York, NY), 1981.

Who Stole the Wizard of Oz?, Knopf (New York, NY), 1981.

Sometimes I Think I Hear My Name, Pantheon (New York, NY), 1982.

Shadrach's Crossing, Pantheon (New York, NY), 1983.

The Fighting Ground, Lippincott (Philadelphia, PA), 1984.

S.O.R. Losers, Bradbury (Scarsdale, NY), 1984.

Devil's Race, Lippincott (Philadelphia, PA), 1984.

Bright Shadow, Bradbury (Scarsdale, NY), 1985.

Wolf Rider: A Tale of Terror, Bradbury (Scarsdale, NY), 1986, Simon Pulse (New York, NY), 2008.

Devil's Race, Avon (New York, NY), 1987.

Romeo and Juliet—Together (and Alive) at Last (sequel to *S.O.R. Losers*), Avon (New York, NY), 1988.

Something Upstairs: A Tale of Ghosts, Orchard Books (New York, NY), 1988.

The Man Who Was Poe, Orchard Books (New York, NY), 1989.

The True Confessions of Charlotte Doyle, Orchard Books (New York, NY), 1990.

Windcatcher, Bradbury (Scarsdale, NY), 1991.

Nothing but the Truth: A Documentary Novel, Orchard Books (New York, NY), 1991.

"Who Was That Masked Man, Anyway?," Orchard Books (New York, NY), 1992.

Blue Heron, Bradbury (Scarsdale, NY), 1992.

Punch with Judy, Bradbury (New York, NY), 1993.

City of Light, City of Dark: A Comic Book Novel, illustrated by Brian Floca, Orchard Books (New York, NY), 1993.

The Barn, Orchard Books (New York, NY), 1994.

Shadrach's Crossing Smuggler's Island, Morrow Junior Books (New York, NY), 1994.

The Bird, the Frog, and the Light: A Fable, paintings by Matthew Henry, Orchard Books (New York, NY), 1994.

Tom, Babette, and Simon: Three Tales of Transformation, illustrated by Alexi Natchev, Macmillan Books for Young Readers (New York, NY), 1995.

Poppy (also see below), illustrated by Brian Floca, Orchard Books (New York, NY), 1995.

Beyond the Western Sea, Book One: Escape from Home, Orchard Books (New York, NY), 1995.

Beyond the Western Sea, Book Two: Lord Kirkle's Money, Orchard Books (New York, NY), 1996.

What Do Fish Have to Do with Anything?: Short Stories, Candlewick Press (Cambridge, MA), 1997.

Finding Providence: The Story of Roger Williams, Harper-Collins (New York, NY), 1997.

Poppy and Rye (also see below), illustrated by Brian Floca, Avon (New York, NY), 1998.

Perloo the Bold, Scholastic (New York, NY), 1998.

Ragweed (also see below), illustrated by Brian Floca, Avon (New York, NY), 1999.

Second Sight: Stories for a New Millennium, Philomel Books (New York, NY), 1999.

Abigail Takes the Wheel, illustrated by Don Bolognese, HarperCollins (New York, NY), 1999.

Midnight Magic, Scholastic (New York, NY), 1999.

Ereth's Birthday (also see below), illustrated by Brian Floca, HarperCollins (New York, NY), 2000.

The Christmas Rat, Simon & Schuster (New York, NY), 2000.

Prairie School, illustrated by Bill Farnsworth, HarperCollins (New York, NY), 2001.

The Secret School, Harcourt (San Diego, CA), 2001.

Don't You Know There's a War On?, HarperCollins (New York, NY), 2001.

The Good Dog, Atheneum Books for Young Readers (New York, NY), 2001.

Tales from Dimwood Forest (includes *Ragweed, Poppy, Poppy and Rye,* and *Ereth's Birthday*), illustrated by Brian Floca, HarperCollins (New York, NY), 2001.

Crispin: The Cross of Lead, Hyperion Books (New York, NY), 2002.

Silent Movie, illustrated by C.B. Mordan, Atheneum Books for Young Readers (New York, NY), 2002.

The Mayor of Central Park, illustrated by Brian Floca, HarperCollins (New York, NY), 2003.

(With Rachel Vail) *Never Mind!: A Twin Novel,* Harper-Collins (New York, NY), 2004.

The End of the Beginning: Being the Adventures of a Small Snail (and an Even Smaller Ant) (based on *Snail Tale*), illustrated by Tricia Tusa, Harcourt (Orlando, FL), 2004.

Strange Happenings: Five Tales of Transformation, Harcourt (Orlando, FL), 2005.

Poppy's Return, illustrated by Brian Floca, HarperCollins Publishers (New York, NY), 2005.

The Book without Words: A Fable of Medieval Magic, Hyperion Books (New York, NY), 2005.

Crispin: At the Edge of the World, Hyperion Books (New York, NY), 2006.

(Selector with Carolyn Shute, and contributor) *Best Shorts: Favorite Short Stories for Sharing,* illustrated by Chris Raschka, Houghton Mifflin (Boston, MA), 2006.

The Traitors's Gate, illustrated by Karina Raude, Atheneum Books for Young Readers (New York, NY), 2007.

Iron Thunder: The Battle between the Monitor and the Merrimac, Hyperion Books (New York, NY), 2007.

The Seer of Shadows, HarperCollins (New York, NY), 2008.

A Beginning, a Muddle, and an End: The Right Way to Write Writing, illustrated by Tricia Tusa, Harcourt (Orlando, FL), 2008.

Hard Gold: The Colorado Gold Rush of 1859, Hyperion Books (New York, NY), 2008.

Murder at Midnight, Scholastic (New York, NY), 2009.

Poppy and Ereth, illustrated by Brian Floca, HarperCollins (New York, NY), 2009.

Crispin: The End of Time, Balzer & Bray (New York, NY), 2010.

(Author of introduction) Rudyard Kipling, *Just So Stories,* Signet Classics (New York, NY), 2010.

Also author of numerous plays. Contributor to books, including *Performing Arts Resources, 1974,* edited by Ted Perry, Drama Book Publishers, 1975, and *Acting Out,* Simon & Schuster Books for Young Readers (New York, NY), 2008. Contributor to periodicals, including *New York Public Library Bulletin, Top of the News, Children's Literature in Education, Horn Book,* and *Writer.* Book reviewer for *Library Journal, School Library Journal,* and *Previews,* 1965-73.

Translations of Avi's books have been published in Germany, Austria, Denmark, Norway, Spain, Italy, and Japan.

Adaptations

Emily Upham's Revenge, Shadrach's Crossing, Something Upstairs, The Fighting Ground, The True Confessions of Charlotte Doyle, Nothing but the Truth, and *Read to Me* were produced on radio programs *Read to Me,* Maine Public Radio, and *Books Aloud,* WWON-Rhode Island. *The True Confessions of Charlotte Doyle, City of Light/City of Dark, Sometimes I Think I Hear My Name, Something Upstairs,* and *Night Journeys* were optioned for film. *Something Upstairs* was adapted as a play performed by Louisville (KY) Children's Theater, 1997. *Nothing but the Truth* was adapted for the stage by Ronn Smith. Many of Avi's books have been adapted as audio books.

Sidelights

During an illustrious literary career that has spanned five decades, Avi has earned both popular and critical acclaim for his inviting, intriguing novels. The inventive and versatile writer's many award-winning books, which include *The True Confessions of Charlotte Doyle, Nothing but the Truth: A Documentary Novel, Iron Thunder: The Battle between the Monitor and the Merrimac,* and the Newbery Award-winning *Crispin: The Cross of Lead,* range from mysteries and adventure yarns to historical fiction, supernatural tales, coming-of-age novels, and comic stories, some even combining several of these genres. "I take a great deal of satisfaction in using popular forms—the adventure, the mystery, the thriller—so as to hold my reader with the sheer pleasure of a good story," the author remarked in an essay on the Scholastic Web site.

While captivating even reluctant readers with his fast-paced, imaginative plots and the inclusion of plenty of action, Avi's books also offer complex, thought-provoking, and sometimes disturbingly realistic reflections of American culture. The author summed up his goals in writing young-adult novels in *Twentieth-Century Children's Writers:* "I try to write about complex issues—young people in an adult world—full of irony and contradiction, in a narrative style that relies heavily on suspense with a texture rich in emotion and imagery. I take a great deal of satisfaction in using popular forms—the adventure, the mystery, the thriller—so as to hold my reader with the sheer pleasure of a good story. At the same time I try to resolve my books with an ambiguity that compels engagement. In short, I want my readers to feel, to think, sometimes to laugh. But most of all I want them to enjoy a good read."

Born Edward Irving Wortis in New York City in 1937, Avi was raised in Boston in an artistic environment. His great grandparents and a grandmother were writers, two uncles were painters, and both parents wrote. His family was also politically active, its members aligning themselves with the radical movements spawned by the Great Depression of the 1930s. The author once explained to *SATA* that his extended family comprised "a very strong art community and what this meant for me as a child was that there was always a kind of uproari-

Cover of Avi's thought-provoking novel **Nothing but the Truth,** *featuring artwork by Peter Catalanotto.* (Illustration copyright © 1991 by Peter Catalanotto. Reproduced by permission of Orchard Books, an imprint of Scholastic, Inc.)

ous sense of debate. It was all a very affectionate sharing of ideas—arguing, but not arguing in anger, arguing about ideas."

Avi's stimulating home environment prepared the boy for the challenges of higher education. Although he was an avid reader as a child, difficulties in writing eventually caused him to flunk out of one school; these difficulties were later discovered to be the result of a dysfunction known as dysgraphia, a marginal impairment in writing abilities that causes the patient to reverse letters and misspell words. "One of my aunts said I could spell a four letter word wrong five ways," Avi once commented. Despite constant criticism at school, he kept writing, crediting his family's emphasis on the arts for his perseverance. When school assignments came back covered in red ink, he simply saved them, corrections and all. "I think there was so much criticism, I became immune to it," Avi once said. "I wasn't even paying attention to it. I liked what I wrote."

The first step on Avi's course to writing professionally was reading: everything from comic books and science magazines to histories, plays, and novels. Despite the skepticism of his teachers, he decided to make writing his career while still in high school. Throughout the summer of his junior year he "met every day with a wonderful teacher who not only taught me writing basics, but also instilled in me the conviction that I wanted to be a writer myself," he later recalled. "Perhaps it was stubbornness. It was generally agreed that was one thing I could not possibly do." Attending Antioch University, Avi enrolled in play writing rather than English courses. "That's where I really started to write seriously," he once commented. Although one of his college plays won a contest and was published in a magazine, the author admitted that of the "trunkfull of plays" he wrote, "I would say ninety-nine percent of them weren't very good."

After working at a variety of jobs, Avi found work in the theater collection of the New York Public Library, beginning his twenty-four-year career as a librarian. His determination to be a writer never flagged during this time, and he had written hundreds of pages of his "great American novel" by the time he turned his attention to children's literature. It all began with telling stories to his two sons. "My oldest would tell me what the story should be about—he would invent stuff, a story about a glass of water and so forth. It became a game, and here I had a writing background so I was telling some fairly sophisticated stories."

Along with telling stories, Avi drew pictures for fun. A friend who was writing a children's book asked Avi to provide art for his story, and although the book was rejected by a publisher, Avi was asked to illustrate other children's books. Explaining that he was a writer and not an artist, Avi agreed to illustrate if he could also write the text. After writing down all the stories he had told to his own son, Avi submitted it to the publisher.

"Of course she turned everything down," he recalled. Ultimately, Doubleday accepted the manuscript and *Things That Sometimes Happen: Very Short Stories for Very Young Readers* was published in 1970—without Avi's artwork.

Using the pen name Avi, which had been given him by his twin sister in early childhood, he continued to write children's books geared to his sons' reading levels. "At a certain point they kept growing and I didn't," the author explained. "I hit a fallow period, and then I wrote *No More Magic*. Suddenly I felt 'This is right! I'm writing novels and I love it.' From then on I was committed to writing novels."

Avi's early novels, such as *Captain Grey, Night Journeys, Encounter at Easton,* and *The Fighting Ground,* are set in colonial America. Winner of the Scott O'Dell Historical Fiction Award for children, *The Fighting Ground* presents one event-filled day in the life of Jonathan, a thirteen year old who is caught up in America's War for Independence. The novel begins as Jonathan slips away from his family's New Jersey farm in order to take part in a skirmish with a group of German Hessians, mercenary soldiers who are working for the English crown. The teen sets out for battle full of unquestioned hatred for the Hessians as well as for Tories (colonists loyal to the British) and hoping to take part in the glory of battle. He can barely carry his six-foot-long musket, and he finds it difficult trying to understand the talk among the men with whom he marches. The small group's leader is a crude individual who lies to the men and is said to be "overfond of killing." After a bloody skirmish, Jonathan is captured by three Hessians and soon learns to view them as individual human beings. Slowly, the reader, along with Jonathan, is brought to an understanding of what war means in human terms. *The Fighting Ground* was widely praised, a *Bulletin of the Center for Children's Books* critic describing Avi's novel as "a small stunner" that "makes the war personal and immediate."

"Somewhere along the line, I can't explain where, I developed an understanding of history not as fact but as story," Avi explained in an interview with Jim Roginski in *Behind the Covers:* "That you could look at a field and, with only a slight shift of your imagination, suddenly watch the battle that took place there. . . . You have to have a willingness to look beyond *things*." In *Something Upstairs: A Tale of Ghosts,* for example, a young man discovers the ghost of a murdered slave in the historic house his family has moved into in Providence, Rhode Island. The boy travels back in time to the days of slave trading, where he learns about the murder and, perhaps more importantly, about the manner in which U.S. history is collectively remembered. Like the narrator in *Something Upstairs,* Avi moved from Los Angeles to Providence; in fact, he moved into the historic house where he sets his novel.

The Man Who Was Poe, Avi's fictionalized portrait of nineteenth-century writer Edgar Allan Poe, intertwines fiction and history on several levels. Historically, Poe went through a period of severe depression and poverty, aggravated by alcoholism during the two years preceding his death in 1849. Avi, whose novel focuses on this period, said he became fascinated with Poe because he was so extraordinary and yet such "a horrible man." In the novel, a young boy named Edmund immigrates to Providence from England with his aunt and twin sister in order to look for his missing mother. When both aunt and sister also disappear, the penniless boy must elicit help from a stranger—who happens to be Edgar Allen Poe. Noticing similarities in Edmund's story to his own life and detecting material for his writing, Poe agrees to help the boy. Between maddening bouts of drunkenness, the writer ingeniously finds a trail of clues; meanwhile, Edmund alternates between feeling awe for the man's perceptive powers and despair at Poe's obvious madness. A reviewer for the *Bulletin of the Center for Children's Books* described *The Man Who Was Poe* as "a complex, atmospheric thriller" in which "Avi recreates the gloom of [the] 1840s . . . with a storyteller's ease, blending drama, history, and mystery without a hint of pastiche or calculation." According to the critic, readers "will be left in the end with both the comfort of puzzles solved and the unease of mysteries remaining."

In another unique twist on the convention of historical novels, *The True Confessions of Charlotte Doyle* presents the unlikely story of a very proper thirteen year old who, as the sole passenger and only female on a trans-Atlantic ship in 1832, becomes involved in a mutiny at sea. Holding her family's aristocratic views on social class and demeanor, Charlotte begins her voyage trusting only Captain Jaggery, whose fine manners and authoritative command remind her of her father. Shocked to find that Jaggery is a viciously brutal and inhumane shipmaster, Charlotte gradually begins to question—and discard—the values of her privileged background, revealing the strength of her true character.

The True Confessions of Charlotte Doyle received accolades from critics for its suspense, its evocation of life at sea, and particularly for the rich and believable narrative of its protagonist. The impact of Charlotte's liberation from social bonds and gender restrictions also had a powerful emotional effect on many of Avi's readers. According to the author, "many people, mostly girls, and even adults, have told me of bursting into tears" at the book's ending. In his *Boston Globe/Horn Book* award acceptance speech, Avi referenced the words of a critic who spoke of the "improbable but deeply satisfying conclusion" of the novel. "I am deeply grateful for the award you have given me today," Avi added. "But I hope you will understand me when I tell you that if the 'improbable' life I wrote lives in someone's heart as a life *possible,* then I have already been given the greatest gift a writer can receive: a reader who takes my story and endows it with life by the grace of their own desire."

In *Midnight Magic,* a magician and his servant find themselves embroiled in palace intrigue. Set in the Renaissance city of Pergamontio, the novel centers on Mangus, an illusionist believed to possess wizardly powers, and Fabrizio, his loyal ward. Summoned to the king's castle to rid Princess Teresina of her terrifying visions, the duo uncovers a deadly conspiracy revolving around Count Scarazoni, the king's nefarious advisor. According to *Booklist* critic Ilene Cooper, Avi's "combination of magic and mystery is pretty irresistible." In *Murder at Midnight,* a prequel, Mangus is suspected of printing handbills that question the king's authority. Placed under arrest, the magician must rely on young Fabrizio to prove his innocence by uncovering the identity of the true villain, a member of the king's court. *Murder at Midnight* drew praise from *Booklist* reviewer Ian Chipman, who maintained that "Avi assuredly keeps the suspense simmering right through to the end."

In the Newbery Award-winning *Crispin: The Cross of Lead,* Avi "introduces some of his most unforgettable characters," according to *Booklist* contributor Ilene Cooper. Taking place in England during the fourteenth century, as poverty, a greedy aristocracy, and the Black Plague ravage the country's peasant population, the novel finds a thirteen-year-old orphan framed for a murder he did not commit. Crispin flees from the familiar surroundings where he was raised, taking with him only the clothes on his back and his mother's lead cross, which bears an inscription he cannot decipher. Soon, Crispin falls in with a traveling juggler who, due to his burly size, is called Bear. With Bear's help the boy learns the juggler trade, and also becomes steeped in his mentor's radical politics, which include rebelling against a feudal system that keeps most people living lives of brutal poverty. As he gains in self-esteem, Crispin also learns the truth about his birth and understands his place in the world. "Avi's plot is engineered for maximum thrills, with twists, turns and treachery aplenty," noted a *Publishers Weekly* contributor, adding that the "compellingly drawn" friendship between the boy and the old juggler gives *Crispin: The Cross of Lead* its emotional heart.

A sequel to *Crispin: The Cross of Lead, Crispin: At the Edge of the World* finds Crispin and Bear fleeing from the king's authorities, funding their flight along England's coast by performing a minstrel act. After Bear is wounded, the fugitives find shelter with a wise woman and her apprentice, where Crispin finds his Catholic faith challenged. Noting the novel's realism, Vicky Smith wrote in *Horn Book* that *Crispin: At the Edge of the World* "doesn't romanticize the era; instead, it portrays England and France as places where poverty, superstition, and violence were commonplace." A *Kirkus Reviews* critic praised Avi's "swiftly paced sequel" for its "superb storytelling," dubbing *Crispin: At the Edge of the World* a "moving, history-packed adventure." In *School Library Journal* Melissa Moore had even higher praise, calling Avi's novel an "extraordinary work of lyrical simplicity, nearly flawless in its execution, and a haunting tale of love and loss."

Avi concludes his exciting trilogy with *Crispin: The End of Time,* "another rousing page-turner," according to *Horn Book* critic Jonathan Hunt. After the death of Bear, his mentor, Crispin wanders through the French countryside with his companion, Toth, a disfigured girl with a remarkable knowledge of healing herbs. On their way to Iceland, a region known to be free from strife, the duo takes refuge at a convent where Toth is befriended by the nuns and decides to stay. As Crispin continues his journey alone, he joins a band of traveling musicians who are later revealed to be murderous scoundrels, and he must risk a daring escape to save his own life. "The ending is almost unbearably intense," a contributor in *Kirkus Reviews* stated, and Cheri Dobbs, writing in *School Library Journal,* noted that Crispin's "first-person voice lends a sense of urgency to the novel, and Avi's writing style is as elegant and engaging as ever."

Other historical novels by Avi include *Prairie School* and *The Secret School,* both of which stress the importance of education. *The Secret School* takes place in Elk Valley, Colorado, in 1925, as the small town's only teacher leaves unexpectedly and a fourteen-year-old girl decides to fill the learning gap. Writing about *Prairie*

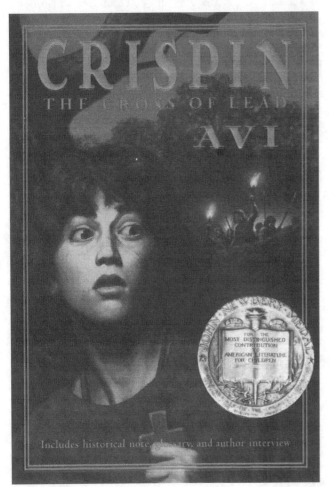

Cover of Avi's award-winning novel Crispin: The Cross of Lead *featuring artwork by Tristan Elwell.* (Illustration © 2002 by Tristan Elwell. All rights reserved. Reprinted by permission of Hyperion Books for Children.)

School in *School Library Journal,* Carol Schene noted that Avi's "gentle story" contains "a great message that is nicely woven into the daily events" in its characters' lives. Hazel Rochman, writing in *Booklist,* wrote that the author's "clear simple language never sounds condescending." In a review of *The Secret School* for *School Library Journal,* B. Allison Gray called it a "carefully plotted, enjoyable, old-fashioned tale" in which "the importance of education and dreaming of one's future are imparted in an entertaining way."

Avi returns readers to mid-nineteenth-century London in *The Traitors' Gate,* which finds fourteen-year-old John Huffam shouldering the responsibility for keeping his family safe after his father is arrested under mysterious circumstances. Soon he learns that members of his family are under surveillance by the Naval Ordinance Office, where his father works, and the teen is forced to deal with the truth of his father's character. "Avi's love of the [Victorian] period is evident" in his "charmingly told" tale, according to *School Library Journal* contributor Connie Tyrrell Burns, the critic praising *The Traitor's Gate* as an "action packed" story "from a master craftsman." Citing the references to noted novelist Charles Dickens that Avi imbeds within his storyline, a *Publishers Weekly* critic similarly dubbed the book an eventful "tale of secret identities, double-dealing and betrayal."

Set across the Atlantic in New York City over two decades later than *The Traitor's Gate, The Seer of Shadows* finds fourteen-year-old Horace Carpentine working as a photographer's apprentice. When his boss, Enoch Middleditch, decides to take advantage of the gullibility of a wealthy client and create fraudulent photographs of purported spirits, the boy accidentally releases the ghost of Eleanora. The client's dead daughter, Eleanora is determined to exact revenge upon both of her parents. Noting that Avi adopts a gothic storytelling style, a *Publishers Weekly* critic called *The Seer of Shadows* an "intriguing ghost story" that will "leave spines tingling." Phelan wrote that Avi's "engaging novel has great immediacy and strong narrative drive," and *Horn Book* critic Betty Carter deemed *The Seer of Shadows* a "dandy mystery [that] re-creates and stays within its historical period while also introducing characters confronting timeless questions of personal honor."

A U.S. Civil War tale set in 1862, *Iron Thunder* focuses on Tom Carroll, a fatherless thirteen year old who is hired to work on a secret project at the Continental Iron Works in New York City. Under the direction of Swedish inventor John Ericsson, Tom helps with the construction of the *Monitor,* an ironclad ship designed to compete with the *Merrimac,* a Confederate vessel. Threatened by rebel spies, Tom moves aboard the *Monitor* until its completion, then sails into battle with the crew when the ship leaves port. "The spectacular clash with the *Merrimac* caps this intense and action-packed account of a battle that changed the course of naval warfare," remarked a *Publishers Weekly* critic. In *Hard*

Artist Marjorie Price teams up with Avi to tell the humorous "What's Next?" story in Things That Sometimes Happen. (Illustration copyright © 2002 by Marjorie Priceman. Reprinted with the permission of Atheneum Books for Young Readers, an imprint of Simon & Schuster Children's Publishing Division.)

Gold: The Colorado Gold Rush of 1859 a young man leaves his family's struggling farm in Iowa to help protect a gold claim. After receiving word that his uncle Jesse has struck it rich in the Rocky Mountains, Early Whitcomb learns that Jesse, fearing for his safety, has disappeared, along with several hundred dollars from a local bank. Hoping to prove his uncle innocent of a robbery charge, Early heads west, joining forces with Lizzy Bunderly, the fiery daughter of a wagon-train owner. Writing in *Booklist,* Chipman applauded "the detailed, authentic touches of history and adventure" in *Hard Gold,* and *School Library Journal* reviewer Debra Banna noted that Early and Lizzy "face heartache, hardship, and loss while learning the value of endurance on this journey that takes them across the wild, unsettled territory."

Avi's *S.O.R. Losers* is a humorous contemporary novel about a group of unathletic boys who are forced by their school—one based on Avi's high school in New York City—to form a soccer team. Opposing the time-honored school ethic that triumph in sports is the American way, the boys form their own opinions about winning at something that means little to them. In a team meeting, they take stock of who they are and why it is so important to everyone *else* that they should win their games. *Horn Book* contributor Mary M. Burns called the novel "one of the funniest and most original sports sagas on record," and particularly praised Avi's skill with comedic form. "Short, pithy chapters highlighting key events maintain the pace necessary for successful comedy, Burns noted, while like "a Charlie Chaplin movie, emphasis is on individual episode—each distinct, yet organically related to an overall idea." Avi has written several other comic novels, including a sequel to *S.O.R. Losers,* titled *Romeo and Juliet—Together (and Alive) at Last,* and two well-received spoofs on nineteenth-century melodrama: *Emily Upham's Revenge* and *The History of Helpless Harry.*

Avi's other acclaimed contemporary coming-of-age novels include *A Place Called Ugly, Nothing but the Truth,* and *Sometimes I Think I Hear My Name.* Based on an actual event, the 1992 Newbery honor book *Nothing but the Truth* is the story of Philip Malloy and his battle with an English teacher, Miss Narwin. With poor grades in English keeping him off the track team, Philip repeatedly breaks school rules by humming the national anthem along with the public address system in Miss Narwin's home room. Eventually, the principal suspends Philip, but with the school in the midst of elections, various self-interested members of the community exploit the incident, describing Philip's suspension as an attack on patriotism. Much to everyone's surprise, the story snowballs into a national media event that, in its frenzied rhetoric, thoroughly overshadows the true story about a good teacher's inability to reach a student, a young man's alienation, a community's disinterest in its children's needs, and a school system's hypocrisy.

Nothing but the Truth is a book without a narrator, relating its story through school memos, diary entries, letters, dialogues, newspaper articles, and radio talk-show transcripts. Presented thus, without narrative bias, the story takes into account the differing points of view surrounding Philip's suspension, allowing the reader to root out the real problems leading to the incident. Avi once commented that he got the idea for the structure of this novel from a form of theater that arose in the 1930s called "Living Newspapers": dramatizations of issues and problems confronting American society that were presented through a "hodgepodge" of document readings and dialogues.

In addition to realistic contemporary and historical novels, Avi has also successfully penned fantasy fiction and several other unique chapter books for readers in the early elementary grades. *Poppy,* which received a *Boston Globe/Horn Book* award in 1996, tells the story of two deer mice, Ragweed and Poppy, who are about to marry when the self-proclaimed king of Dimwood Forest—an owl named Mr. Ocax—eats Ragwood, supposedly as punishment for neglecting to seek his permission to marry. Ann A. Flowers, writing in *Horn Book,* called *Poppy* "a tribute to the inquiring mind and the stout [of] heart." *Bulletin of the Center for Children's Books* critic Roger Sutton predicted of the same novel

that "sprightly but un-cute dialogue, suspenseful chapter endings, and swift shifts of perspective between Ocax and Poppy will make chapter-a-day readalouds cause for anticipation." Avi followed *Poppy* with a number of sequels, including *Poppy and Rye, Ragweed,* and *Poppy and Ereth.* In the last, the final installment in the series, Poppy is carried off to a bat colony, whereupon her porcupine friend Ereth believes she has perished and begins planning her funeral. Unconvinced, Poppy's grandson, Spruce, goes looking for the now-elderly deer mouse, who is attempting to return home to warn the forest's residents of an approaching fire. "This heart-warming fantasy is filled with fast-moving action and danger," Kira Moody reported in her *School Library Journal* review of *Poppy and Ereth.*

Avi has also created new animal-sized adventures in *The End of the Beginning: Being the Adventures of a Small Snail (and an Even Smaller Ant)* and *A Beginning, a Muddle, and an End: The Right Way to Write Writing.* Based on a beginning reader Avi authored early in his career, the first book finds friends Avon the snail and Edward the ant departing on cross-country adventures, each with his own approach to travel. Praising the artwork by Tricia Tusa, a *Publishers Weekly* reviewer wrote of *The End of the Beginning* that "bite-size chap-

Cover of Avi's historical novel **Hard Gold,** *a story that focuses on the rush to find gold in Colorado in the late 1850s.* (Map of the Nebraska Territory © Nebraska State Historical Society. Photograph of boy © Colorado Historical Society. Reproduced by permission of Hyperion Books for Children.)

ters and the clever repartee make this a charming tale," while *School Library Journal* contributor Connie Tyrrell Burns dubbed it "a wise little book" about friendship. *A Beginning, a Muddle, and an End,* which reunites Avon and Edward, finds Avon aspiring to become a writer. With Edward's help, Avon goes on a series of adventures, meeting a series of interesting creatures along the way. In this sequel, "Avi's protagonists continue to radiate plenty of unprepossessing charm," remarked a *Kirkus Reviews* contributor.

Avi turns to fantasy in *The Book without Words,* which is set in England during the eleventh century. Here Sybil is a servant of the evil alchemist Thorston, but her master perishes before he can steal the thirteen-year-old girl's vital breath. Odo, Thorston's talking raven, tells Sybil that the secret to creating the elixir of life is contained in a book that will only reveal its secret to a reader with green eyes. "Avi reigns supreme in building gothic atmosphere," concluded *Booklist* critic Jennifer Mattson, the reviewer citing the "ghastly scenes of fog-shrouded cemeteries" featured in *The Book without Words.* A *Kirkus Reviews* critic noted the "poetic, nearly comedic plays on words" that salt the novel's dialogue, and in *Kliatt* Paula Rohrlick described *The Book without Words* as an "appealingly creepy tale that features . . . a feisty heroine and a message about the dangers of greediness."

Other quirky novels for younger readers include *The Good Dog,* a tale about a malamute named McKinley who is top dog in his small town. Told from the point of view of the dog, Avi's story takes an imaginative view of the trappings of human civilization and introduces readers to a clever canine culture. Noting the dogs' emotional connection to freedom, a reviewer for *Publishers Weekly* called *The Good Dog* "reminiscent of Jack London's *The Call of the Wild.*"

Featuring striking black-and-white illustrations by C.B. Mordan, *Silent Movie* brings the drama and pathos of a silent movie of the early twentieth century to the picture-book medium. Mimicking film subtitles with his brief text, Avi spins the story of a family of Swedish immigrants whose members are separated shortly after arriving in New York harbor. While young Gustave and his mother are forced to beg on the street after being robbed, they are eventually reunited with Papa after their images are captured on film by a famous silent-movie director. Sharing the same time period—the first decade of the twentieth century—*The Mayor of Central Park* finds Big Daddy Duds, head of a gang of tough-talking city rats, determined to take over Central Park despite the objections of the park's current mayor, a long-tailed squirrel named Oscar Westerwit. When the gangster and the mayor find that they also root for opposing baseball teams, the turf battle moves to a more peaceable arena: the city ball park. In *Publishers Weekly* a contributor described *The Mayor of Central Park* as "an over-the-top romp" and added that Avi's "tough-talking prose would do an old gangster movie proud."

Although he writes full time, Avi maintains regular interaction with children by traveling around the country and talking in schools about his writing. "I think it's very important for me to hold these kids in front of my eyes," he once explained. "They're wonderfully interesting and they hold me to the reality of who they are." In *School Library Journal* he recalled a telling anecdote about his approach to children: "Being dysgraphic, with the standard history of frustration and anguish, I always ask to speak to the learning-disabled kids. They come in slowly, waiting for yet another pep talk, more instructions. Eyes cast down, they won't even look at me. Their anger glows. I don't say a thing. I lay out pages of my copy-edited manuscripts, which are covered with red marks. 'Look here,' I say, 'see that spelling mistake. There, another spelling mistake. Looks like I forgot to put a capital letter there. Oops! Letter reversal.' Their eyes lift. They are listening. And I am among friends."

Avi describes himself as a committed skeptic, yet reveals an idealistic center when he discusses young people and their role in U.S. culture. "When do you become an adult?," he once remarked to *SATA*. "Sometimes I think the difference is that psychological shift when you start to know that tomorrow is going to be the same as today. When you're a kid, there are still options, major options. For a writer like myself, a child is a kind of metaphor for regression to idealism and passionate concern: a metaphor for the ability to change or react, to be honest about all those things that as adults we tend to slide over as we make compromises to obligations and necessities." In an article for *Horn Book* he contrasted children's literature, which generally espouses values such as "sharing, nonviolence, cooperation, and the ability to love," to the adult world where power and self-interest seem to rule. "More than anything else," Avi asserted, "children's literature is about the place and role of the child in society . . . . If we—in the world of children's literature—can help the young stand straight for a moment longer than they have done in the past, help them maintain their ideals and values, those with which you and I identify ourselves, help them demand—and win—justice, we've added something good to the world."

Biographical and Critical Sources

BOOKS

Beacham's Guide to Literature for Young Adults, Volume 10, Gale (Detroit, MI), 2000.

Roginski, Jim, *Behind the Covers: Interviews with Authors and Illustrators of Books for Children and Young Adults,* Libraries Unlimited, 1985, pp. 33-41.

St. James Guide to Young-Adult Writers, St. James Press (Detroit, MI), 1999.

PERIODICALS

Booklist, January 15, 1992, Hazel Rochman, interview with Avi, p. 930; September 1, 1994, Hazel Rochman,

"Focus: How to Build a Barn," p. 40; November 15, 1997, Michael Cart, review of *Poppy*, p. 731; November 15, 1997, Michael Cart, review of *What Do Fish Have to Do with Anything?, and Other Stories*, p. 560; September 15, 1999, Ilene Cooper, review of *Midnight Magic*, p. 256; September 1, 2000, Carolyn Phelan, review of *The Christmas Rat*, p. 127; April 15, 2001, Hazel Rochman, review of *Prairie School*, p. 1568; May 15, 2002, Ilene Cooper, review of *Crispin: The Cross of Lead*, p. 1604; October 1, 2002, Gillian Engberg, review of *Things That Sometimes Happen*, p. 332; August, 2003, GraceAnne A. DeCandido, review of *The Mayor of Central Park*, p. 1976; April 1, 2004, Hazel Rochman, review of *Never Mind!: A Twin Novel*, p. 1365; September 15, 2004, Hazel Rochman, review of *The End of the Beginning: Being the Adventures of a Small Snail (and an Even Smaller Ant)*, p. 242; March 15, 2005, Jennifer Mattson, review of *The Book without Words: A Fable of Medieval Magic*, p. 1292; September 15, 2006, Carolyn Phelan, review of *Crispin: At the Edge of the World*, p. 60; August, 2007, John Peters, review of *Iron Thunder: The Battle between the Monitor and the Merrimac*, p. 75; February 15, 2008, Carolyn Phelan, review of *The Seer of Shadows*, p. 82; July 1, 2008, Thom Barthelmess, review of *A Beginning, a Muddle, and an End: The Right Way to Write Writing*, p. 69; September 1, 2008, Ian Chipman, review of *Hard Gold: The Colorado Gold Rush of 1859*, p. 95; February 15, 2009, Kay Weisman, review of *Poppy and Ereth*, p. 73; August 1, 2009, Ian Chipman, review of *Murder at Midnight*, p. 70; April 15, 2010, Carolyn Phelan, review of *Crispin: The End of Time*, p. 59.

Bulletin of the Center for Children's Books, June, 1984, review of *The Fighting Ground*, p. 180; October, 1989, review of *The Man Who Was Poe*, p. 27; January, 1996, Roger Sutton, review of *Poppy*, p. 154; February, 1996, Roger Sutton, review of *Beyond the Western Sea, Book One: The Escape from Home*, p. 183.

Horn Book, January-February, 1985, Mary M. Burns, review of *S.O.R. Losers*, p. 49; November-December, 1986, Mary M. Burns, review of *Beyond the Western Sea, Book Two: Lord Kirkle's Money*, p. 731; September-October, 1987, Avi, "All That Glitters," pp. 569-576; January-February, 1992, Avi, *Boston Globe/Horn Book* Award acceptance speech transcript, pp. 24-27; January-February, 1996, Ann A. Flowers, review of *Poppy*, p. 70; July-August, 1996, Mary M. Burns, review of *Beyond the Western Sea, Book One: The Escape from Home*, p. 461; January-February, 2002, Peter D. Sieruta, review of *The Good Dog*, p. 75; March-April, 2003, Roger Sutton, review of *Silent Movie*, p. 197; September-October, 2006, Vicky Smith, review of *Crispin: At the Edge of the World*, p. 574; May-June, 2008, Betty Carter, review of *The Seer of Shadows*, p. 305; July-August, 2009, Kitty Flynn, review of *Poppy and Ereth*, p. 416; July-August, 2010, Jonathan Hunt, review of *Crispin: The End of Time*, p. 98.

Journal of Adolescent and Adult Literacy, October, 2003, Vinnie Bonnit, review of *Crispin: The Cross of Lead*, p. 188.

Kirkus Reviews, May 15, 2002, review of *Crispin: The Cross of Lead*, p. 728; September 1, 2002, review of

Things That Sometimes Happen, p. 1302; January, 2003, review of *Silent Movie*, p. 56; May 1, 2005, review of *The Book without Words*, p. 533; August 1, 2006, review of *Crispin: At the Edge of the World*, p. 780; July 15, 2007, review of *Iron Thunder*; March 15, 2008, review of *The Seer of Shadows;* April 1, 2008, review of *A Beginning, a Muddle, and an End*; April 1, 2009, review of *Poppy and Ereth*; May 15, 2010, review of *Crispin: The End of Time*.

Kliatt, November, 2002, Maureen K. Griffin, review of *Crispin: The Cross of Lead*, p. 44; January, 2007, Paula Rohrlick, review of *The Book without Words*, p. 27; March, 2008, Paula Rohrlick, review of *The Seer of Shadows*, p. 8; September, 2008, Claire Rosser, review of *Hard Gold*, p. 6.

Publishers Weekly, September 6, 1991, review of *Nothing but the Truth*, p. 105; July 16, 2001, review of *The Secret School*, p. 181; June 3, 2002, review of *Crispin: The Cross of Lead*, p. 88; September 30, 2002, review of *Things That Sometimes Happen*, p. 70; December 16, 2002, review of *Silent Movie*, p. 66; August 11, 2003, review of *The Mayor of Central Park*, p. 280; May 10, 2004, review of *Never Mind!*, p. 60; October 25, 2004, review of *The End of the Beginning*, p. 48; June 11, 2007, review of *The Traitor's Gate*, p. 61; July 16, 2007, review of *Iron Thunder*, p. 165; April 14, 2008, review of *The Seer of Shadows*, p. 55; September 7, 2009, review of *Murder at Midnight*, p. 46.

School Library Journal, January, 1987, Avi and Betty Miles, "School Visits: The Author's Viewpoint," p. 21; December, 1997, Carol A. Edwards, review of *What Do Fish Have to Do with Anything?: Short Stories*, p. 120; September, 2000, Leda Schubert, "Breakfast Serials," p. 38; May, 2001, Carol Schene, review of *Prairie School*, p. 108; September, 2001, B. Allison Gray, review of *The Secret School*, p. 223; December, 2003, Sue Gifford, review of *The Mayor of Central Park*, p. 144; May, 2004, Eva Mitnick, review of *Never Mind!*, p. 140; October, 2004, Connie Tyrrell Burns, review of *The End of the Beginning*, p. 154; October, 2006, Melissa Moore, review of *Crispin: At the Edge of the World*, p. 147; May, 2007, Connie Tyrell Burns, review of *The Traitor's Gate*, p. 129; September, 2007, Carolyn Janssen, review of *Iron Thunder*, p. 190; February, 2008, Elizabeth Bird, review of *The Seer of Shadows*, p. 111; May, 2008, Robyn Gioia, review of *A Beginning, a Muddle, and an End*, p. 119; September, 2008, Debra Banna, review of *Hard Gold*, p. 172; August, 2009, Kira Moody, review of *Poppy and Ereth*, p. 69; October, 2009, Alana Abbott, review of *Murder at Midnight*, p. 119; June, 2010, Cheri Dobbs, review of *Crispin: The End of Time*, p. 93.

Teacher Librarian, June, 2010, "A Writer among Us: Avi," p. 74.

Voice of Youth Advocates, December, 1996, Kathleen Beck, review of *Beyond the Western Sea, Book Two*, p. 267.

ONLINE

Avi Home Page, http://www.avi-writer.com (February 23, 2011).

Scholastic Web site, http://www2.scholastic.com/ (February 23, 2011), profile of Avi.*

BACHORZ, Pam 1973-

Personal

Born 1973; married; children: one son. *Education:* Boston University, B.S. (journalism); B.A. (environmental science); M.L.S.; M.B.A.

Addresses

Home—Silver Springs, MD. *Agent*—Emily van Beek, Folio Literary, 505 8th Ave., Ste. 603, New York, NY 10018; emily@foliolit.com.

Career

Author. Presenter at schools, libraries, and conferences.

Awards, Honors

CYBILS Award finalist, 2009, Cooperative Children's Book Center Choice designation, 2010, and YALSA/ American Library Association Popular Paperbacks designation, 2011, all for *Candor.*

Writings

Candor, Egmont USA (New York, NY), 2009.
Drought, Egmont USA (New York, NY), 2010.

Sidelights

When Pam Bachorz was growing up in the Adirondack mountain region of upstate New York, theatre and music were her twin passions. Her interests expanded in college, where she earned bachelor's degrees in both journalism and environmental science before moving to graduate school and completing programs in library science and business. Despite her wide-ranging education, Bachorz revisited adolescence when she decided to embark on a writing career and produce the young-adult novels *Candor* and *Drought.*

In writing *Candor,* Bachorz was inspired by the planned suburban community in Florida where she then made her home. Praised by *School Library Journal* contributor Sharon Rawlins as "a chilling dystopian novel," *Candor* takes readers to Candor, Florida, a gated community in which even teenagers obey all the rules: They exercise and eat only healthy foods, treat their elders with respect, and do not engage in intimate physical contact outside of marriage. Although most of the town's population is regulated using subliminal mind control, one teen puts on an act in public while secretly helping other teens escape from Candor. Oscar Banks is the son of the manipulative man who founded the town, and his knowledge of his father's control systems allows him to subvert them. When Oscar falls for Nia, a new girl in town, he must decide whether to help her escape and lose her affection or find another way to

help his friend that would also help himself. While noting that Oscar is a less-than-likeable and sometimes obsessive protagonist, Rawlins dubbed Bachorz's debut novel "timely and compulsively readable." "A nicely paced plot keeps the narrative moving," asserted a *Kirkus Reviews* writer, and in *Booklist* Ian Chipman noted that "enforced conformity is . . . a potent metaphor for teenagers."

Taking place in the Adirondack Mountains, *Drought* is another dystopian novel, this time one focusing on a faith-based community that has awaited its founder for many generations. Ruby is part of a group enslaved by cruel overseers, their task to collect the liquid that gives them all prolonged life. She has been toiling for over 200 years, and when she falls in love with a kindly overseer named Ford, she realizes that escape from her life of drudgery may be possible. However, she also knows the community's unnamed secret: that it is only by intermingling with Ruby's blood that the liquid gains its power, and by leaving she will condemn all others in her Congregation to death. In *School Library Journal* Krista Hutley praised *Drought* as a "brooding, thought-provoking story" that prompts readers to ponder "powerful themes of faith and loyalty, freedom and slavery." "Tension between . . . Ruby's faith . . . and Ford's contemporary Christianity results in a complex, provocative exploration of loyalty, community, family, and belief," noted a *Publishers Weekly* critic in a similar appraisal of *Drought.*

Biographical and Critical Sources

PERIODICALS

Booklist, October 15, 2009, Ian Chipman, review of *Candor,* p. 58; December 15, 2010, Krista Hutley, review of *Drought,* p. 48.
Bulletin of the Center for Children's Books, November, 2009, Kate Quealy-Gainer, review of *Candor,* p. 101; January, 2011, Kate Quealy-Gainer, review of *Drought,* p. 255.
Kirkus Reviews, August 15, 2009, review of *Candor.*
Publishers Weekly, July 20, 2009, review of *Candor,* p. 140; November 8, 2010, review of *Drought,* p. 61.
School Library Journal, November, 2009, Sharon Rawlins, review of *Candor,* p. 100.
Voice of Youth Advocates, October, 2009, Matthew Weaver, review of *Candor,* p. 310.

ONLINE

Pam Bachorz Home Page, http://www.pambachorz.com (December 30, 2010).*

*   *   *

BARON, Kathi 1956-

Personal

Born May 23, 1956, in Fairbanks, AK; married; husband a psychiatrist; children: one son. *Education:* Ohio

Kathi Baron (Photograph by Cindy Trim. Reproduced by permission.)

State University, B.S. (occupational therapy); University of Illinois at Chicago, M.S. (occupational therapy); Vermont College of Fine Arts, M.F.A. (writing for children and young adults). *Hobbies and other interests:* Baseball (especially visiting major league parks), scrapbooking, movies, journaling, hanging out in bookstores, taking walks, reading.

Addresses

Home—Oak Park, IL. *E-mail*—kathi@kathibaron.com.

Career

Therapist and author. Occupational therapist in an outpatient behavioral health program for adults; has also worked with teens in crisis.

Member

Society of Children's Book Writers and Illustrators.

Writings

Shattered, WestSide Books (Lodi, NJ), 2009.

Contributor to scholarly journals and to books.

Sidelights

In *Shattered,* her debut novel for young adults, Kathi Baron examines the toxic effects of intergenerational abuse though the eyes of Cassie Prochazka, a talented

violinist. An occupational therapist who has worked with many teens in crisis, Baron noted on her home page that Cassie's story "was the culmination of all the voices of the abused teens I had worked with in the past." According to its author, *Shattered* is a "story about resilience."

In *Shattered* readers are introduced to fourteen-year-old Cassie, a gifted musician who plays with the Chicago Youth Symphony Orchestra. After Cassie's debut as a soloist, her father, whose behavior has become increasingly erratic, explodes into a rage, destroying his daughter's prized violin. The distraught teen runs away and finds refuge in a homeless shelter. With help from some wise and generous strangers, Cassie eventually returns home and helps her father confront some long-standing family secrets that involve the violin and painful memories of childhood abuse.

Critiquing *Shattered* in *School Library Journal,* Roxanne Myers Spencer offered praise for Baron's narrative structure, citing the book's "short chapters with staccato action and slower cadences reflective of the family's struggle to work their way through this situation." A

Cover of Baron's compelling young-adult novel Shattered, *featuring cover art by Michael Morgenstern.* (WestSide Books, 2009. Reproduced by permission of the publisher.)

critic in *Kirkus Reviews* also applauded the work, stating that "this poignant story of multigenerational abuse is a compelling read."

"Writing gives me a chance to explore relationships, the world, and to better understand what it means to be human and alive," Baron told *SATA*. "In *Shattered*, what interested me was delving into the complexity of Cassie's family; specifically, how devastating it can be for a young person to be hurt by a parent and despite that, to still yearn for that parent's love. I found it challenging to figure out how Cassie could grow and become stronger as a result of her pain. Writing *Shattered* turned into a great opportunity to experience a violinist's world as well as the magic of the creative process. I knew from the beginning that Cassie wouldn't give up playing the violin despite losing hers because I believe it's important to do what you love to do, no matter what."

Biographical and Critical Sources

PERIODICALS

Kirkus Reviews, August 15, 2009, review of *Shattered.*
School Library Journal, December, 2009, Roxanne Myers Spencer, review of *Shattered,* p. 106.

ONLINE

Cynsations Web log, http://cynthialeitichsmith.blogspot. com/ (February 25, 2010), Cynthia Leitich Smith, interview with Baron.
Kathi Baron Home Page, http://www.kathibaron.com (February 15, 2011).
Kathi Baron Web log, http://www.kathibaron.blogspot.com (February 15, 2011).
Violin and Books Web log, http://violinandbooks.wordpress. com/ (January 16, 2011), Mayra Calvani, interview with Baron.

*   *   *

BARTON, Patrice 1955-

Personal

Born 1955; married; children: one son. *Education:* University of Texas, B.F.A.

Addresses

Home and office—Austin, TX. *Agent*—Christina A. Tugeau, 3009 Margaret Jones La., Williamsburg, VA 23185; chris@catugeau.com. *E-mail*—patrice@patrice barton.com.

Career

Illustrator.

Member

Society of Children's Book Writers and Illustrators, Picture Book Artists Association.

Awards, Honors

Outstanding International Book designation, U.S. Board on Books for Young People/Children's Book Council, for *The Naming of Tishkin Silk* by Glenda Millard.

Illustrator

Carole Gerber, *Jessica McBean, Tap Dance Queen,* Blooming Tree Press (Austin, TX), 2006.
Annette Aubrey, *A Place in My Heart* ("Understanding" series), QEB Publishing (Laguna Hills, CA), 2007.
Annette Aubrey, *Flora's Family* ("Understanding" series), QEB Publishing (Laguna Hills, CA), 2007.
Annette Aubrey, *There for You* ("Understanding" series), QEB Publishing (Laguna Hills, CA), 2007.
Annette Aubrey, *The Rainbow Club* ("Understanding" series), QEB Publishing (Laguna Hills, CA), 2007.
P.K. Hallinan, *The Looking Book,* Ideals Children's Books (Nashville, TN), 2009.
Glenda Millard, *The Naming of Tishkin Silk,* Farrar, Straus & Giroux (New York, NY), 2009.
Glenda Millard, *Layla, Queen of Hearts,* Farrar, Straus & Giroux (New York, NY), 2010.
Karen Henry Clark, *Sweet Moon Baby: An Adoption Tale,* Knopf (New York, NY), 2010.
Shutta Crum, *MINE!,* Knopf (New York, NY), 2011.
Allison Wortche, *Rosie Sprout's Time to Shine,* Knopf (New York, NY), 2011.

Also contributor to educational publications, and to periodicals, including *Clubhouse Jr., Ladybug,* and *Highlights for Children.*

Sidelights

An accomplished illustrator based in Texas, Patrice Barton has provided the artwork for a number of children's books, including Glenda Millard's award-winning *The Naming of Tishkin Silk.* Barton, who illustrates both chapter books and picture books, adjusts her artistic style to fit each narrative. As she wrote in a guest post for *Cynsations* online, her approach to working on chapter books "is to create illustrations that play a supporting role. My pictures must say just enough but no more." "On the other hand," she added, "the illustrations in picture books speak volumes. They must convey the heart of the matter, honoring the author's perspective."

Barton has teamed with Annette Aubrey for four works in the "Understanding" series of picture books which focus on sensitive issues. In *The Rainbow Club,* a tale about bullying, a group of children who differentiate themselves by their choice of clothing learn a valuable lesson about inclusiveness. Reviewing the title in *Resource Links,* Carolyn Cutt observed that Barton's "large, colourful illustrations are both whimsical and emotional, adding an important perspective to the story." Aubrey examines the subject of adoption in *Flora's Family,* and here Barton's "whimsical, bright cheerful illustrations add to the happy atmosphere of the story," Cutt remarked.

In *The Naming of Tishkin Silk* Millard tells the story of a troubled youngster who learns to cope with heartache and grief though his relationship with Layla, a new classmate. *Booklist* critic Shelle Rosenfeld applauded the story's "softly rendered black-and-white drawings," and Terrie Dorio, writing in *School Library Journal,* similarly noted that Barton's "soft pen-and-ink drawings perfectly fit this quiet story." In a companion volume, *Layla, Queen of Hearts,* the lively protagonist develops a close friendship with an elderly woman who is suffering from dementia. Barton's contributions earned praise from *School Library Journal* reviewer Amy Holland, who wrote of *Layla, Queen of Hearts* that her "soft pencil drawings scattered throughout also add a sense of comfort" to Millard's tale.

Patrice Barton's illustration assignments include Glenda Millard's elementary-grade novel **The Naming of Tishkin Silk.** (Farrar, Straus & Giroux, 2009. Illustration copyright © 2009 by Patrice Barton. All rights reserved. Reproduced by permission of the illustrator.)

Biographical and Critical Sources

PERIODICALS

Booklist, November 1, 2009, Shelle Rosenfeld, review of *The Naming of Tishkin Silk,* p. 49.

Childhood Education (annual), 2008, Amanda Moretton, review of *There for You,* p. 319.

Kirkus Reviews, September 15, 2009, review of *The Naming of Tishkin Silk.*

Resource Links, April, 2008, Carolyn Cutt, reviews of *Flora's Family,* p. 1, and *The Rainbow Club,* p. 2.

School Library Journal, December, 2009, Terrie Dorio, review of *The Naming of Tishkin Silk,* p. 87; June, 2010, Amy Holland, review of *Layla, Queen of Hearts,* p. 80.

ONLINE

Cynsations Web log, http://cynthialeitichsmith.blogspot.com/ (November 18, 2010), Patrice Barton, "Guest Post: Patrice Barton on the Difference Between Illustrating Picture Books and Chapter Books."

Patrice Barton Home Page, http://www.patricebarton.com (February 15, 2011).

Patrice Barton Web log, http://pbarton.blogspot.com (February 15, 2011).

*   *   *

BECK, Andrea 1956-

Personal

Born October 25, 1956, in Montreal, Quebec, Canada; children: David, Ian. *Education:* Attended Dawson College and Ontario College of Art and Design; York University, B.A. (psychology; with honors); University of Toronto, M.S.W. *Hobbies and other interests:* Travel, gardening, pets, reading, writing, film.

Addresses

Home—Unionville, Ontario, Canada. *E-mail*—abeck@elliotmoose.ca; andrea@markhamcounselling.com.

Career

Author, illustrator, and social worker. Founder and owner of a toy company in Canada, until 1986; clinical counselor in Unionville, Ontario, Canada, 1996—. Creative consultant for *Elliot Moose* television series. *Exhibitions:* Work exhibited at Kathleen Gormley McKay Art Centre, Unionville, Ontario, Canada, 2003.

Member

Canadian Society of Children's Authors, Illustrators, and Performers, Writer's Union of Canada, Society of Children's Book Writers and Illustrators, Canadian Children's Book Centre, Ontario Association of Social Workers, Ontario College of Social Workers and Social Service Workers.

Writings

SELF-ILLUSTRATED; "ELLIOT MOOSE" SERIES

Elliot's Emergency, Kids Can Press (Toronto, Ontario, Canada), 1998.
Elliot Bakes a Cake, Kids Can Press (Toronto, Ontario, Canada), 1999.
Elliot's Shipwreck, Kids Can Press (Toronto, Ontario, Canada), 2000.
Elliot's Bath, Kids Can Press (Toronto, Ontario, Canada), 2000, Kids Can Press (Niagara Falls, NY), 2001.
Elliot Digs for Treasure, Kids Can Press (Toronto, Ontario, Canada), 2001.
Elliot's Noisy Night, Kids Can Press (Toronto, Ontario, Canada), 2002.
Elliot Gets Stuck, Kids Can Press (Toronto, Ontario, Canada), 2002.
Elliot's Great Big Lift-the-Flap Book, Kids Can Press (Toronto, Ontario, Canada), 2003.
Elliot's Christmas Surprise, Kids Can Press (Toronto, Ontario, Canada), 2003.
Elliot's Fire Truck, Orca Book Publishers (Victoria, British Columbia, Canada), 2010.

Author's works have been translated into French.

SELF-ILLUSTRATED "PIERRE LE POOF" SERIES

Pierre le Poof!, Orca Book Publishers (Victoria, British Columbia, Canada), 2009.
Pierre's Friends, Orca Book Publishers (Victoria, British Columbia, Canada), 2010.
Pierre in the Air, Orca Book Publishers (Victoria, British Columbia, Canada), 2011.

ILLUSTRATOR

Carolyn Beck, *The Waiting Dog,* Kids Can Press (Toronto, Ontario, Canada), 2003.
Carolyn Beck, *Buttercup's Lovely Day,* Orca Book Publishers (Victoria, British Columbia, Canada), 2008.

Adaptations

The "Elliot Moose" books were adapted as an animated television program, produced for Treehouse TV, 1998-2003, PBS Kids, 1998-2004, TVOntario, 1998-2010, and Qubo.

Sidelights

Canadian writer and illustrator Andrea Beck is best known for her popular "Elliot Moose" series of children's books featuring the adventures of a lovable stuffed animal and its companions. Beck's charming moose, which was also the focus of a long-running television show, grew out of her experiences as a toymaker, she noted on her home page. "I loved the days at the toy company when we had large shipments of moose going out," she explained. "They looked so funny lined up, row upon row, waiting to be inspected and beribboned and put in their boxes. Sometimes as I walked by one of those big tables, it seemed like maybe the moose were moving, or talking amongst themselves. I loved to imagine that they might alive in some way."

In addition to her "Elliot Moose" books, Beck has written and illustrated *Pierre le Poof!, Pierre's Friends,* and *Pierre in the Air,* a trilogy about a pampered show poodle and his dreams of wild adventure. She also illustrated *The Waiting Dog* and *Buttercup's Lovely Day,* both written by her sister, Carolyn Beck. Beck also serves as a family counselor in Unionville, Ontario. "I like that children who read my stories see characters who are caring and kind," she noted in a Canadian Children's Book Centre interview posted on her home page.

Beck was born in 1956 in Montreal, Quebec, and raised in nearby Rosemere. Because there were no playmates Beck's age in the neighborhood, as she recalled to *Canadian Review of Materials* interview Dave Jenkinson, "I didn't have human friends. I had toy friends. I guess that's why it's easy for me to think of toys as alive." Determined to study art, she eventually attended Dawson College and the Ontario College of Art and Design, then started her own toy company, which sold plush animals, including moose, rabbits, and beavers. After five years Beck sold her company, returned to school to study psychology, and started a family. "Reading to my children was when I truly discovered picture books," she told Jenkinson. "And I thought, 'Oh, I'd love to do this.'" Her debut title, *Elliot's Emergency,* was released in 1998 and introduces children to the engaging moose character.

Beck's "Elliot Moose" series, aimed at young readers, explores such themes as the importance of sharing and the value of self-reliance. In *Elliot's Emergency,* for instance, the gentle-hearted moose grows anxious after his plush coat tears, but then his friends arrive to patch him up. "The wonderful, warm and colourful illustrations reflect the loving, caring nature of the story and effectively enhance the storyline," stated *Resource Links* critic Betty Missett. Elliot and his sidekick, Socks the monkey, court disaster by soaking themselves just prior to their performance in a talent show in *Elliot's Bath.* According to *Booklist* reviewer Ellen Mandel, Beck's "expressive illustrations, inventively detailed in pencil crayon, will engage children in all the emotion and fun."

The "Elliot Moose" books have earned both popular and critical acclaim. *Elliot Digs for Treasure,* in which the protagonist and his pals rely on their ingenuity to escape from a deep hole, was applauded by *Resource*

Andrea Beck introduces a charming and adventurous canine hero in her self-illustrated picture book **Pierre Le Poof!** (Orca Book Publishers, 2009. Illustration copyright © 2009 by Andrea Beck. All rights reserved. Reproduced by permission.)

Links contributor Kathryn McNaughton as a tale in which Beck's "message is a very positive one, and it is presented in a light, humorous way." Liz Greenaway, writing in the *Canadian Review of Materials,* offered praise for Beck's artwork, citing especially the detailed portraits of her characters. "Beck never makes them look like actual animals as opposed to stuffed animals," Greenaway observed, "and yet her characters appear real, by virtue of their expressions and their ability to portray emotion." Reviewing *Elliot's Fire Truck* in the *Canadian Review of Materials,* Leanne Ryrie and Gre-

gory Bryan applauded the author's child-centered narrative: "Although Beck promotes the ideals of sharing, friendship, and playing together, her text is not distractingly didactic. Rather, she tells a sweet tale with an important message of inclusion and fair play."

Beck introduces a show dog who longs to roam free in *Pierre le Poof!* While preparing for the dog championships, a well-coiffed poodle named Pierre flees from his training session and heads to the park, where he makes a host of new canine friends and chases squirrels to his heart's content. Soon, however, Pierre misses his owner and struggles mightily to find his way home. *Booklist* critic Linda Perkins complimented Beck's "airy ink-and-watercolor pictures that delightfully go for the laughs." In a sequel, *Pierre's Friends,* the poodle misses his friends from the park and decides to offer them a new home in his owner's luxury apartment house. "This is a gentle story of a tender hearted pup who, in seeking to assuage his own loneliness, discovers others' greater needs and takes steps to resolve them," Alison Mews remarked in the *Canadian Review of Materials.*

Biographical and Critical Sources

PERIODICALS

Booklist, November 15, 1998, Lauren Peterson, review of *Elliot's Emergency,* p. 594; October 1, 1999, Ellen Mandel, review of *Elliot Bakes a Cake,* p. 360; March 15, 2001, Ellen Mandel, review of *Elliot's Bath,* p. 1402; November 1, 2001, Kathy Broderick, review of *Elliot Digs for Treasure,* p. 481; January 1, 2003, Carolyn Phelan, review of *Elliot's Noisy Night,* p. 904; February 1, 2010, Linda Perkins, review of *Pierre le Poof,* p. 51.

Canadian Review of Materials, January 19, 2001, Helen Arkos, review of *Elliot's Shipwreck;* April 12, 2002, Liz Greenaway, review of *Elliot Gets Stuck;* April 18, 2008, Helen Norrie, review of *Buttercup's Lovely Day;* March 26, 2010, Leanne Ryrie and Gregory Bryan, review of *Elliot's Fire Truck;* October 29, 2010, Alison Mews, review of *Pierre's Friends.*

Kirkus Reviews, October 1, 2002, review of *Elliot's Noisy Night,* p. 1463; September 1, 2009, review of *Pierre le Poof!*

Publishers Weekly, November 9, 1998, review of *Elliot's Emergency,* p. 74; February 5, 2001, review of *Elliot's Bath,* p. 90; February 3, 2003, review of *Elliot's Great Big Lift-the-Flap Book,* p. 78; September 29, 2003, review of *The Waiting Dog,* p. 65; October 26, 2009, review of *Pierre le Poof!,* p. 58.

Resource Links, December, 1998, Betty Missett Gale, review of *Elliot's Emergency,* p. 1; December, 1999, review of *Elliot Bakes a Cake,* p. 3; June, 2000, review of *Elliot's Shipwreck,* p. 1; December, 2000, review of *Elliot's Bath,* p. 2; October, 2001, Kathryn McNaughton, review of *Elliot Digs for Treasure,* p. 1; April, 2002, Gillian Richardson, review of *Elliot Gets Stuck,* p. 2; October, 2002, Sandra Tee, review of *Elliot's Noisy Night,* p. 1; June, 2003, Kathryn McNaughton, review of *Elliot's Great Big Lift-the-Flap Book,* p. 2; October, 2003, Carroll Chapman, review of *Andrea Elliot's Christmas Surprise,* p. 2.

School Library Journal, August, 2001, Kay Bowes, review of *Elliot's Bath,* p. 142; November, 2001, Cathie E. Bashaw, review of *Elliot Digs for Treasure,* p. 110; October, 2003, Susan Patron, review of *Elliot's Christmas Surprise,* p. 61; December, 2003, Linda Ludke, review of *The Waiting Dog,* p. 103; October, 2008, Shawn Brommer, review of *Buttercup's Lovely Day,* p. 129.

ONLINE

Andrea Beck Home Page, http://www.andreabeck.com (February 15, 2011).

Canadian Review of Materials Web site, http://www.umanitoba.ca/cm/ (September 8, 2002), Dave Jenkinson, "Andrea Beck."

Canadian Society of Children's Authors, Illustrators, and Performers Web site, http://www.canscaip.org/ (February 15, 2011), "Andrea Beck."

Society of Children's Book Writers and Illustrators Web site, http://www.scbwi.org/ (February 15, 2011), "Andrea Beck."

Writer's Union of Canada Web site, http://www.writersunion.ca/ (February 15, 2011), "Andrea Beck."*

*   *   *

BEIL, Michael D.

Personal

Married. *Hobbies and other interests:* Hiking.

Addresses

Office—Saint Vincent Ferrer High School, 151 E. 65th St., New York, NY 10065. *E-mail*—mbeil@saintvincentferrer.com.

Career

Writer and educator. St. Vincent Ferrer High School, New York, NY, currently teacher of English.

Writings

"RED BLAZER GIRLS" SERIES

The Ring of Rocamadour, Knopf (New York, NY), 2009.
The Vanishing Violin, Knopf (New York, NY), 2010.
The Mistaken Masterpiece, Knopf (New York, NY), 2011.

Sidelights

In addition to his day job as a high-school English teacher, Michael D. Beil entertains teen readers with his popular "Red Blazer Girls" mystery novels. Featuring a group of adventurous seventh-grade girl sleuths, the series includes *The Ring of Rocamadour, The Vanishing Violin,* and *The Mistaken Masterpiece.*

A lifelong writer, Beil began penning stories and plays as a youngster, and he even made a short horror film at the age of twelve. He was introduced to theater by his older brothers, and Thornton Wilder's classic play *Our Town* had a significant impact on his life by opening his mind to the power of storytelling. A fan of the mystery genre, Beil used his experiences as an educator at a Catholic school in New York City for *The Ring of Rocamadour,* his debut novel.

In *The Ring of Rocamadour* Beil introduces Sophia "Sophie" St. Pierre and her friends Margaret Wrobel, Leigh Ann Jaimes, and Rebecca Chen, all of whom are seventh graders at St. Veronica's on Manhattan's Upper East Side. After Sophie spots a ghostly looking woman in the window of a neighboring church, she and her friends find themselves immersed in a decades-old mystery involving the elderly woman, her estranged daughter, and an ancient ring purported to have miraculous powers. Faced with a perplexing series of clues—and donned in their school uniforms with their crimson blazers—the girls must use their knowledge of religion, literature, and math to unravel the case before a nefarious villain does. *School Library Journal* critic Danielle Serra offered praise for the work, describing *The Ring of Rocamadour* as "a clever way to combine some middle school math (graphs and grids included) with a fun mystery," and *Booklist* critic Ilene Cooper complimented the "fast and funny" narrative. Discussing his audience's reaction to the math clues sprinkled throughout the work, Biel remarked to Cooper: "Adult readers have pretty much been freaked out by it, but kids don't seem to mind. Even if they're not great math students, the difference between them and an adult is that they're exposed to it every day. There's a certain level of acceptance that it's part of their lives."

The amateur detectives make a return appearance in *The Vanishing Violin,* "a 'classic locked-room' mystery," according to Cooper. Asked by Sister Bernadette to discover the identity of a bizarre intruder who enters the school each night to clean the building, the girls stumble upon a strange message about a violin that was stolen from legendary Carnegie Hall some fifty years earlier. Soon, they begin receiving a host of cryptic, coded notes guiding them to the location of the missing instrument, but then their search is complicated by the disappearance of another violin from the shop of their good friend, Mr. Chernofsky. "Plenty of adventure is packed into one neatly solved mystery," Shannon Seglin remarked in her *School Library Journal* review of *The Vanishing Violin,* and a *Kirkus Reviews* contributor noted that the heroines act "like real tweens while tackling everything that comes their way with logic, humor and refreshing savoir faire."

Biographical and Critical Sources

PERIODICALS

Booklist, January 1, 2009, Ilene Cooper, review of *The Ring of Rocamadour,* p. 77; May 1, 2009, Ilene Cooper, "Story behind the Story: Michael D. Beil's The Red Blazer Girls: The Math behind the Mystery," p. 12.

Kirkus Reviews, May 15, 2010, review of *The Vanishing Violin.*

School Library Journal, June, 2010, Danielle Serra, review of *The Ring of Rocamadour,* p. 115; August, 2010, Shannon Seglin, review of *The Vanishing Violin,* p. 94.*

*   *   *

BELL, Hilari 1958-

Personal

Born 1958, in Denver, CO. *Education:* College graduate. *Hobbies and other interests:* Camping, reading, board and fantasy gaming.

Addresses

Home—Denver, CO.

Career

Writer. Part-time reference librarian, until 2005.

Cover of Michael D. Beil's middle-grade mystery The Red Blazer Girls: The Ring of Rocamadour, *which focuses on the adventures of three private-school sleuths.* (Jacket photographs copyright © 2009 by Lisa Predko. Reproduced by permission of Alfred A. Knopf, an imprint of Random House Children's Books, a division of Random House, Inc.)

Hilari Bell (Reproduced by permission.)

Awards, Honors

Best Books for Young Adults selection, American Library Association (ALA), and Best Book for the Teen Age selection, New York Public Library, both 2002, both for *A Matter of Profit;* Best Books for Young Adults selection, and Popular Paperbacks for Young Adults selection, both ALA, both 2004, both for *The Goblin Wood;* Best Books for Young Adults selection, ALA, 2009, for *The Last Knight.*

Writings

NOVELS

Navohar, New American Library (New York, NY), 2000.
Songs of Power, Hyperion (New York, NY), 2000.
A Matter of Profit, HarperCollins (New York, NY), 2001.
The Wizard Test, Eos (New York, NY), 2005.
The Prophecy, Eos (New York, NY), 2006.

"FARSALA" NOVEL TRILOGY

Flame, Simon & Schuster (New York, NY), 2003, published as *Fall of a Kingdom,* 2004.
Rise of a Hero, Simon & Schuster (New York, NY), 2005.
Forging the Sword, Simon & Schuster (New York, NY), 2006.

"SHIELD, SWORD, AND CROWN" NOVEL TRILOGY

Shield of Stars, Simon & Schuster (New York, NY), 2007.

Sword of Waters, Simon & Schuster (New York, NY), 2008.
Crown of Earth, Aladdin (New York, NY), 2009.

"KNIGHT AND ROGUE" NOVEL SERIES

The Last Knight, Eos (New York, NY), 2007.
Rogue's Home, Eos (New York, NY), 2008.
Player's Ruse, Harper Teen (New York, NY), 2010.

"GOBLIN" NOVEL TRILOGY

The Goblin Wood, HarperCollins (New York, NY), 2003.
The Goblin Gate, HarperTeen (New York, NY), 2010.
The Goblin War, HarperTeen (New York, NY), 2011.

"RAVEN DUET" NOVEL SERIES

Trickster's Girl, Houghton Mifflin Harcourt (Boston, MA), 2011.
Traitor's Son, Houghton Mifflin Harcourt (Boston, MA), 2012.

Sidelights

A former librarian, Hilari Bell is known for writing imaginatively plotted science-fiction and fantasy novels, among them *The Prophecy, A Matter of Profit,* and *Trickster's Girl,* as well as the books in her "Farsala" "Shield, Sword, and Crown," "Knight and Rogue," and "Goblin" novel series. In contrast to many books in her chosen genres, Bell's tales are notable for their absence of clear heroes and villains; her characters and societies are drawn using subtle shades of gray and are often motivated by political considerations rather than honor or duty. Bell is "a master at crafting distinctive societies and characters," Sally Estes wrote in *Booklist,* referencing the multiple, well-developed cultures—including goblin, alien, and even whale societies—that are explored in the author's work.

Born in 1958 in Denver, Colorado, Bell developed an interest in literature at an early age. "The first chapter book I ever read was the *Book of Three,* by Lloyd Alexander," the author stated in an interview on the HarperCollins Web site. "I was in first grade when I read it, and I spent the next few years living more in Prydain than I did in Denver, Colorado. Fantasy has been a favorite genre ever since. I got into science fiction when I read Anne McCaffrey's *The Ship Who Sang.* But I also read a lot of mysteries, and some historical fiction as well—if my first favorite book had been a mystery, I might be a mystery writer today." Bell began writing seriously after college, but it took seventeen years before she sold her first novel. "I'm the poster child for persistence," she remarked on her home page.

Bell's first published novel, *Navohar,* was written for an adult audience. The book is set in the future, after humans have successfully prevented an alien invasion of Earth with the help of a genetically engineered virus. However, this triumph turns out to be Pyrrhic: the virus has also infected the human population, causing millions of children to be born with altered genes that lead them to develop a fatal, incurable disease. One such child is Irene Olsen's nephew, Mark. These two are among the astronauts traveling the universe, searching for human populations who have not been exposed to the virus. Thus far, most of the formerly colonized planets where their crew has landed no longer have living human inhabitants, the colonizers having been wiped out by various alien diseases. However, when they land on Navohar, they discover a group of nomadic humans that has been driven out of its former colony by the Kong aliens. Now members of this group live in the deserts where the Kong do not like to venture. A cure for the virus does seem to exist on Navohar, but the descendants of the colonists worry what will happen to their planet if millions of Earth's children come there seeking it. "The story moves briskly," commented T.M. Wagner in *SF Reviews.net,* and "Bell's writing . . . is most amiable." Also citing the author's "easygoing, accessible writing style," the reviewer added that *Navohar* gains "a certain degree of light-reading appeal" and Fred Cleaver wrote in the *Denver Post* that Bell's creation of a "desert society and . . . interesting aliens are a delight."

Bell's first novel for young readers, *Songs of Power,* combines science fiction and fantasy. The story is set in a technologically advanced future, but it is the main character's ability to perform magic that drives the plot. Imina was taught some spiritual talents by her great-grandmother, an Inuit shaman, but the woman passed away when Imina was a child. Now the girl lives with her parents at a research station located at the bottom of the sea. Terrorists have released a virus that is rapidly destroying all land-based plants, so "technocrats" are working on developing a way to grow food in the oceans. The research station is plagued by technical problems, which the technocrats blame on sabotage by the terrorists, but Imina recognizes these problems as magical. Eventually, with the help of a skeptical classmate, she discovers that whales are using their magic to try to prevent humans from encroaching on their home territory. "Bell's depiction of life in the habitat and her feisty main character, Imina, make for a suspenseful read," a reviewer commented in *Publishers Weekly,* and *School Library Journal* contributor John Peters called *Songs of Power* "a whale of a debut."

Both *A Matter of Profit* and *The Goblin Wood* offer inclusive message about treating other sentient species as equals and being open to receiving their wisdom. In *A Matter of Profit* Ahvren is a young Vivitare warrior who is sickened by the battles he has seen. Tasked to serve the emperor in other ways, he is charged with discovering the source of an alleged plot on the emperor's life.

To do this, Ahvren learns to understand the way of thinking of the T'Chin Confederation, whose forty planets recently surrendered without firing a shot when the Vivitare came to conquer them. A bibliogoth—an exceptionally wise member of the T'Chin who is a scholar and happens to look something like an ant—helps Ahvren understand why the T'Chin surrendered: their philosophy is always to maximize profit, and it was more profitable to come into the Vivitare empire than to resist it. "Both the bibliogoth's wise mentorship and Ahvren's gradual and believable conversion to the T'Chin way of thinking are distinctively and engagingly handled," Anita L. Burkam wrote in *Horn Book. School Library Journal* contributor Mara Alpert praised *A Matter of Profit* as "well-written, thought-provoking, and exciting," further commenting: "It's got cool weapons and weird aliens, but it's also got some meat to it." Noting Bell's ability to create believable characters and alien cultures, Estes dubbed *A Matter of Profit* "one of the best youth sf tales to come along in many years."

In *The Goblin Wood* Bell "illuminates the sometimes spider-thin lines that prevent cultures from living together in peace," according to a *Publishers Weekly* reviewer. Makenna, the heroine of the tale, learns to respect goblins when both she and they are caught up in a decision to ban certain forms of magic. Makenna's mother, a hedgewitch, is executed, and Makenna flees into the woods. There, she allies herself with the goblins, whom the Hierarch is also trying to wipe out. For five years, these allies resist the Hierarch together, until a knight named Tobin is sent to eliminate Makenna. Instead of capturing or killing the young woman, Tobin falls in love with her and the two work together to try to make the world safe for both humans and goblins. Several reviewers praised *The Goblin Wood* for giving the Hierarch realistic, sympathetic reasons for cracking down on magic so harshly: he is only trying to stop an invasion of his realms. "The addition of political motivations to a genre mostly dominated by a good/evil dichotomy is a pleasing surprise," Burkam commented in *Horn Book,* while *School Library Journal* contributor Sharon Grover noted that Bell's exploration of "the gray areas . . . makes for some interesting and thought-provoking reading."

A sequel to *The Goblin Wood, The Goblin Gate,* transports readers to Otherworld, a place where Tobin and Makenna now live among native-born goblins. For Makenna, Otherworld is a trap: it has stolen her magic and she can no longer return to the world of the Hierarch. Hoping to save his knightly brother, Jeriah of Rovanscourt searches in the Hierarch's temple for a gate spell to free them. There he discovers a powerful and destructive secret and gains allies from among the goblins that he once despised. Recommending that readers begin with *The Goblin Wood,* Sharon Grover Hedberg added in *School Library Journal* that "the nuances of politics and the nature of good and evil are well explored" in Bell's sequel. The author "has long shown herself adept in portraying social systems and political intrigues," noted *Horn Book* contributor Anita L. Burkam, the critic praising *The Goblin Gate* as a "satisfying" fantasy.

Bell explores themes of loyalty and honor in *The Wizard Test.* Set in the walled city of Tharn, the work concerns Dayven, a warrior in training who discovers that he possesses magical powers. Raised in a society that distrusts wizardry, Dayven is apprenticed to Reddick, an apparently buffoonish master, then recruited by Lord Enar to spy on both the wizards and the neighboring Cenzars. In this office, the perceptive apprentice soon learns that the motives of his own people may not be entirely honorable. In *The Wizard Test,* remarked *Kliatt* reviewer Paula Rohrlick, Bell "asks readers to consider issues from different viewpoints, and this gives the story added depth and appeal." Writing in *School Library Journal,* Sharon Grover remarked that "hard questions are asked and answered in a . . . book that will find a wide audience and spark much discussion."

In *The Prophecy* scholarly Prince Perryn uncovers an ancient scroll that describes how to slay the black dragon that currently ravages his kingdom. According to prophecy, Perryn must locate a true bard, a unicorn, and a magical sword in order to restore peace to the land, but the prince's efforts are hindered by the king's advisor, a traitor to the crown. In *The Prophecy* Bell "layers the breathtaking action with a cast of fully realized magical creatures and universal coming-of-age questions," observed *Booklist* contributor Gillian Engberg, and Rohrlick stated that the author "blends humor and adventure effectively in this brief, fast-moving, and entertaining coming-of-age tale."

A futuristic novel with environmental themes, *Trickster's Girl* introduces Kelsa, a fifteen year old living in a world threatened with death from a bacteria unleashed by terrorists. The trees are now dying, and although Kelsa discovers that the bacteria is the cause, when she meets Raven, a shapeshifting spirit, she is told the truth: that the energy of the earth's magical underground rivers has been dissipated by man's destruction. With the help of Raven, the girl learns to tap her power over natural forces, even as other supernatural creatures hope that mankind will ultimately die out. "Bell adeptly explores the relationship between Kelsa and Raven" in *Trickster's Girl,* molding it into "a friendship based on trust," according to *School Library Journal* contributor Ragan O'Malley. The "ecological theme" and strong-minded heroine in the novel "will doubtless please the author's many fans," predicted *Booklist* contributor Michael Cart.

The "sweeping fantasy" of Bell's "Farsala" trilogy "draws its underpinnings from ancient Persian poetry . . . and the relentless march of the Roman army," Sharon Grover explained in a *School Library Journal* review of the first book in the series, *Flame.* More-recently retitled *Fall of a Kingdom, Flame* finds the Persian side of the conflict represented by the country of Farsala, which is attempting to repulse an invasion by the Hrum. The tale is told through the interlocking stories of three young Farsalans: Soraya, the fifteen-year-old daughter of the Farsalan army commander; Jiann, the illegitimate, half-peasant son of the same commander; and Kavi, a traveling peddler who is being blackmailed into spying for both sides. As in Bell's earlier books, "the cast is fully formed: the bad guys aren't entirely bad, the good guys not entirely good," commented a *Publishers Weekly* reviewer. Although the Hrum are bent on world domination, they treat their conquered subjects as citizens with full rights, while Farsala society maintains a sharp distinction between the noble deghans and the oppressed peasants. A *Kirkus Reviews* contributor praised Bell's treatment of these issues of class and culture in *Fall of a Kingdom,* commenting that they "are interwoven so well with adventure and archetypal resonance that depth arrives unannounced."

In *Rise of a Hero,* the second entry in the "Farsala" trilogy, Soraya, Jiann, and Kavi work to expel the occupying Hrum army. While Soraya disguises herself as a servant to gain access to the Hrum camp, Jiann takes command of his father's remaining forces and Kavi ignites a guerrilla resistance movement. "The characters maintain their distinctive identities here," remarked Estes, the critic also noting the "palpable sense of danger" in the narrative. "The details of military strategy and the clever, Scarlet Pimpernel-style ruses of the resistance make for entertaining reading," Burkam stated. *Forging the Sword* brings the trilogy to a conclusion. Knowing that the Hrum army will withdraw if Farsala can resist the onslaught for a year, the three protagonists evoke the memory of Sorahb, a legendary Farsalan hero, to rally the citizens of the nation. Estes described *Forging the Sword* as "an edge-of-the-seat finale," and a critic in *Kirkus Reviews* found Bell's novel to be "memorable for its individual characters and extensively detailed cultures."

Shield of Stars, the first book in Bell's "Shield, Sword, and Crown" trilogy, is set in Deorhas and concerns fourteen-year-old Weasel, a former pickpocket who now clerks for the respected Justice Holis. When his employer is arrested for plotting to overthrow a corrupt regent, Weasel joins forces with Arisa, a girl with surprising talents, to search for the Falcon, an outlaw freedom fighter. "Bell's trademark shades of gray help shift readers' perceptions of the characters and their motivations," observed *School Library Journal* contributor Beth L. Meister.

In *Sword of Waters,* the second work in the trilogy, Arisa helps her mother, a powerful military commander who shares power with Holis, maneuver through troubled political waters. Along with Weasel and young Prince Edoran, the girl uncovers a dangerous conspiracy that threatens the fragile peace that now exists in Deorthas. Prince Edoran leaves his palace to rescue Weasel from harm in *Crown of Earth,* the third volume

Cover of Bell's teen fantasy **Player's Ruse**, *a "Knight and Rogue" novel featuring artwork by Larry Rostant.* (Illustration © 2010 by Larry Rostant. Used by permission of HarperCollins Children's Books, a division of HarperCollins Publishers.)

in the "Shield, Sword, and Crown" series. As the story unfolds, the prince is joined by Arisa, and their journey involves capture and escape, a life-changing lesson, and the help of loyal friends. *Sword of Waters* "picks up speed and delicious suspense," noted a contributor in *Kirkus Reviews,* and Genevieve Gallagher concluded in *School Library Journal* that series "fans . . . will be captivated as the layers begin to unfurl and plots and deceptions are exposed." Another *Kirkus Reviews* writer noted that the "adventures" Bell weaves into *Crown of Earth* "provide plenty of interest" and lead to "a swift and surprising climax."

The exploits of a knight errant and a con artist are the subject of *The Last Knight,* the first novel in Bell's "Knight and Rogue" series. Sir Michael Sevenson and his reluctant squire, Fisk, rescue a damsel in distress only to learn she is suspected of murder. Now they must survive a number of hair-raising adventures to recapture their prisoner. "Bell's plot is nicely inventive, and she writes with a robust cheer and peppery sense of irony," Deirdre F. Baker stated in *Horn Book,* and *Kliatt* reviewer Claire Rosser deemed *The Last Knight* an "intricate, intelligent story, told for amusement."

In *Rogue's Home* Fisk helps Sir Michael and his family reclaim their honor after a mysterious villain ruins the reputation of the squire's brother-in-law. A trip to a harbor town on the trail of Michael's cousin Rosamund is the focus of *Player's Ruse,* and although Michael joins a traveling troupe of performers in the hopes of winning Rosamund's affections, her heart belongs to another. *Rogue's Home* "has the appeal of a dashing mystery-adventure," Baker observed, "but the deeper elements of friendship and family loyalty give it substance." A *Kirkus Reviews* wrote that Bell's "writing is great: lots of humor, likable people, mystery and suspense aplenty," while in *School Library Journal* Elizabeth Bird praised *Rogue's Home* for his "humor, suspense, and plot twists." *Player's Ruse* fared equally well with critics, Connie Tyrell Burns describing it in *School Library Journal* as a humorous mix of "fantasy, adventure, and mystery" that features "a large cast of characters and a fast-paced plot." "Fans of the first two books [in the "Knight and Rogue" series] will welcome this installment with enthusiasm," predicted a *Kirkus Reviews* writer in reviewing *Player's Ruse.* As it "deftly displays the deepening friendship" between Fisk and Sir Michael, Bell's portrait of "exasperation and affection provide[s] a comic foil to their ever-increasing mutual respect."

As Bell stated on the HarperCollins Web site, "I'm not sure this is a life motto, but it's what I say to myself when I tackle a novel and am contemplating how much work writing all those hundreds of pages actually entails: *If you keep pushing it, it will fall over.*"

Biographical and Critical Sources

PERIODICALS

Analog Science Fiction and Fact, February, 2001, Tom Easton, review of *Navohar,* p. 133.

Booklist, August, 2001, Sally Estes, review of *A Matter of Profit,* p. 2116; June 1, 2003, Sally Estes, review of *The Goblin Wood,* p. 1758; September 1, 2003, Sally Estes, review of *Flame,* p. 122; February 1, 2005, Jennifer Mattson, review of *The Wizard Test,* p. 957; July, 2005, Sally Estes, review of *Rise of a Hero,* p. 1922; June 1, 2006, Gillian Engberg, review of *The Prophecy,* p. 58; December 15, 2006, Sally Estes, review of *Forging the Sword,* p. 48; May 15, 2007, Jennifer Mattson, review of *Shield of Stars,* p. 62; October 1, 2007, Carolyn Phelan, review of *The Last Knight,* p. 46; August 1, 2008, Carolyn Phelan, review of *Rogue's Home,* p. 61; December 1, 2009, Carolyn Phelan, review of *Player's Ruse,* p. 41; December 15, 2010, Michael Cart, review of *Trickster's Girl,* p. 51.

Denver Post, June 25, 2000, Fred Cleaver, reviews of *Navohar* and *Songs of Power,* both p. G2.

Horn Book, January-February, 2002, Anita L. Burkam, review of *A Matter of Profit,* p. 76; May-June, 2003, Anita L. Burkam, review of *The Goblin Wood,* p. 339;

September-October, 2003, Anita L. Burkam, review of *Flame*, p. 607; July-August, 2005, Anita L. Burkam, review of *Rise of a Hero*, p. 464; July-August, Anita L. Burkam, review of *The Prophecy*, p. 435; September-October, 2007, Deirdre F. Baker, review of *The Last Knight*, p. 566; September-October, 2008, Deirdre F. Baker, review of *Rogue's Home*, p. 577; January-February, 2010, Deirdre F. Baker, review of *Player's Ruse*, p. 81; September-October, 2010, Anita L. Burkam, review of *The Goblin Gate*, p. 71.

Kirkus Reviews, September 15, 2003, review of *Flame*, p. 1171; January 15, 2005, review of *The Wizard Test*, p. 116; May 1, 2005, review of *Rise of a Hero*, p. 534; November 1, 2006, review of *Forging the Sword*, p. 1121; March 1, 2007, review of *Shield of Stars*, p. 217; August 15, 2008, review of *Rogue's Home;* October 15, 2008, review of *Sword of Waters;* September 15, 2009, review of *Crown of Earth;* December 15, 2009, review of *Player's Ruse.*

Kliatt, May, 2003, Paula Rohrlick, review of *A Matter of Profit*, p. 23; September, 2003, Paula Rohrlick, review of *Flame*, p. 6; September, 2004, Samatha Musher, review of *The Goblin Wood*, p. 27; March, 2005, Paula Rohrlick, review of *The Wizard Test*, p. 6; May, 2005, Paula Rohrlick, review of *Rise of a Hero*, p. 6; July, 2006, review of *The Prophecy*, p. 7; November, 2006, Paula Rohrlick, review of *Forging the Sword*, p. 6; July, 2007, Claire Rosser, review of *The Last Knight*, p. 8; July, 2008, Paula Rohrlick, review of *Rogue's Home*, p. 8.

Publishers Weekly, June 12, 2000, review of *Songs of Power*, p. 74; March 24, 2003, review of *The Goblin Wood*, p. 76; October 27, 2003, review of *Flame*, p. 70; March 7, 2005, review of *The Wizard Test*, p. 68; March 19, 2007, review of *Shield of Stars*, p. 63; September 24, 2007, review of *The Last Knight*, p. 74; December 6, 2010, review of *Trickster's Girl*, p. 50.

School Library Journal, May, 2000, John Peters, review of *Songs of Power*, p. 166; October, 2001, Mara Alpert, review of *A Matter of Profit*, p. 148; July, 2003, Sharon Grover, review of *The Goblin Wood*, p. 123; November, 2003, Grover, review of *Flame*, p. 134; March, 2005, Sharon Grover, review of *The Wizard Test*, p. 206; October, 2006, Sharon Grover, review of *The Prophecy*, p. 148; March, 2007, Sharon Grover, review of *Forging the Sword*, p. 203; May, 2007, Beth L. Meister, review of *Shield of Stars*, p. 129; December, 2008, Genevieve Gallagher, review of *Sword of Waters*, p. 119; October, 2009, Debra Banna, review of *Crown of Earth*, p. 119; January, 2010, Connie Tyrrell Burns, review of *Player's Ruse*, p. 96; October, 2010, Sharon Grover, review of *The Goblin Gate*, p. 106; December, 2010, Ragan O'Malley, review of *Trickster's Girl*, p. 100.

Teacher Librarian, February, 2004, Ruth Cox, review of *The Goblin Wood*, p. 37.

Voice of Youth Advocates, April, 2004, review of *Flame*, p. 20; February, 2010, Megan Lynn Isaac, review of *Player's Ruse*, p. 504.

ONLINE

BookLoons.com, http://www.bookloons.com/ (October 3, 2004), Hilary Williamson, review of *The Goblin Wood.*

Green Man Review Online, http://www.greenmanreview. com/ (February 15, 2011), Elizabeth Vail, review of *The Goblin Wood.*

HarperCollins Web site, http://www.harpercollins.com/ (November 1, 2007), "Hilari Bell."

Infinity Plus Web site, http://www.infinityplus.co.uk/ (August 4, 2001), John Grant, review of *A Matter of Profit.*

Science Fiction Writers Association Web site, http://www. sfwa.org/ (February 15, 2011), "Hilari Bell."

SF Reviews.net, http://www.sfreviews.net/ (November 1, 2007), T.M. Wagner, review of *Navohar.*

*   *   *

BLACKWOOD, Gary L. 1945-

Personal

Born October 23, 1945, in Meadville, PA; immigrated to Canada; son of Roy W. and Susie Blackwood; married Jean Lantzy, October 3, 1977; children: Gareth, Giles, Tegan. *Education:* Grove City College, B.A., 1967. *Hobbies and other interests:* Music, outdoor pursuits.

Addresses

Home—Tatamagouche, Nova Scotia, Canada. *E-mail*—gblackwood@hotmail.com.

Career

Writer of fiction and nonfiction books, playwright, and writing teacher. Missouri Southern State College, teacher of playwriting, 1989-93, 1997—; Trinidad State Junior College, teacher of writing-for-publication course, 1995. Writer in residence, Pictou-Antigonish Library System, 2009-10. *Military service:* U.S. Army, sergeant class E-5, 1968-70.

Member

Writers' Federation of Nova Scotia.

Awards, Honors

Friends of American Writers Best YA Novel, 1989, for *The Dying Sun;* Best Book for Young Adults citation, American Library Association (ALA), 1998, for *The Shakespeare Stealer,* 2000, for *Shakespeare's Scribe,* 2002, for *The Year of the Hangman;* ALA Notable Book designation, 1998, for *The Shakespeare Stealer;* Best Book designation, *School Library Journal,* 1998, for *The Shakespeare Stealer,* 2002, for *The Year of the Hangman;* Notable Book designation, *Smithsonian,* 1998, for *The Shakespeare Stealer,* 1999, for *Moonshine.*

Writings

NOVELS

The Lion and the Unicorn, Eagle Books, 1983.

Gary L. Blackwood (Reproduced by permission.)

Wild Timothy, Atheneum (New York, NY), 1987, reprinted, Puffin (New York, NY), 2002.
The Dying Sun, Atheneum (New York, NY), 1989.
Beyond the Door, Atheneum (New York, NY), 1991.
Time Masters, EPB Publishers, 1995.
The Shakespeare Stealer, Dutton (New York, NY), 1998.
Moonshine, Marshall Cavendish (Tarrytown, NY), 1999.
Shakespeare's Scribe, Dutton (New York, NY), 2000.
The Year of the Hangman, Dutton (New York, NY), 2002.
Shakespeare's Spy, Dutton (New York, NY), 2003.
Second Sight, Dutton (New York, NY), 2005.
The Just-so Woman, illustrated by Jane Manning, Harper-Collins (New York, NY), 2006.
Around the World in 100 Days, Dutton Children's Books (New York, NY), 2010.

NONFICTION

Rough Riding Reformer: Theodore Roosevelt, Benchmark (New York, NY), 1998.
Life on the Oregon Trail, Lucent (San Diego, CA), 1999.
Life in a Medieval Castle, Lucent (San Diego, CA), 1999.
The Great Race: The Amazing Round-the-world Auto Race of 1908, Abrams Books for Young Readers (New York, NY), 2008.
Mysterious Messages: A History of Codes and Ciphers, illustrated by Jason Henry, Dutton Children's Books (New York, NY), 2009.

"SECRETS OF THE UNEXPLAINED" SERIES

Alien Astronauts, Benchmark (New York, NY), 1999.
Extraordinary Events and Oddball Occurrences, Benchmark (New York, NY), 1999.
Fateful Forebodings, Benchmark (New York, NY), 1999.
Long-Ago Lives, Benchmark (New York, NY), 1999.
Paranormal Powers, Benchmark (New York, NY), 1999.
Spooky Spectres, Benchmark (New York, NY), 1999.

"BAD GUYS" SERIES; NONFICTION

Pirates, Benchmark (New York, NY), 2001.
Highwaymen, Benchmark (New York, NY), 2001.
Outlaws, Benchmark (New York, NY), 2001.
Swindlers, Benchmark (New York, NY), 2001.
Gangsters, Benchmark (New York, NY), 2001.

"UNSOLVED HISTORY" SERIES

Debatable Deaths, Marshall Cavendish (Tarrytown, NY), 2005.
Enigmatic Events, Marshall Cavendish (Tarrytown, NY), 2005.
Perplexing People, Marshall Cavendish (Tarrytown, NY), 2005.
Legends or Lies?, Marshall Cavendish (Tarrytown, NY), 2005.

STAGE PLAYS

Dark Horse, produced in repertory, 1993.
Futures: A Dining-Room Comedy-Drama in Three Acts, Players Press (Studio City, CA), 1996.
The Count of One, produced in Carmel, CA, 2001.
The Shakespeare Stealer (based on his novel), produced at Kennedy Center, 2002.
Fateville, produced in Dayton, OH, 2003.
Alien Creatures, Players Press (Studio City, CA), 2004.

Also author of other short plays, including a stage adaptation of *Ethan Frome*.

Sidelights

Gary L. Blackwood started his writing career as a teenager, and has since become a prolific author of novels and nonfiction for both young adults and middle-grade readers. Popular particularly with boys due to their western and history themes, Blackwood's novels include the alternate Revolutionary War history *The Year of the Hangman*, as well as *Second Sight* and a trio of adventure novels centering on Elizabethan playwright William Shakespeare and an orphaned teen named Widge. Turning to nonfiction, Blackwood mines intriguing facets of history to produce *Mysterious Messages: A History of Codes and Ciphers* as well as his entertaining "Bad Guys" and "Unsolved History" series. Reviewing *Mysterious Messages* in *School Library Journal*, Rebecca Donnelly deemed the book an "excellent narrative history of cryptography," and a *Kirkus Reviews* writer recommended the work, asserting that it features "the same animation that infuses his other accounts of historical enigmas and events."

Growing up in rural Cochranton, Pennsylvania, Blackwood became a book lover early on. "While I was still young enough to be sleeping in a crib," he once commented, "I struck a deal with my mother: I'd give up sucking my thumb if she bought me a series of Gene

Autry comics I'd seen advertised on the back of a cereal box." As a child, Blackwood attended one of the last remaining one-room schoolhouses in his state. The school library "consisted only of a single set of bookshelves, but it did contain a full set of the Dr. Doolittle books. I had a competition going with one of my classmates to see who could read the entire series first."

One of Blackwood's most popular books, *The Shakespeare Stealer,* was inspired by a newspaper article he first read in the mid-1960s. "It informed me that, in the sixteenth century, an English doctor named Timothy Bright had invented an early system of shorthand," he once explained. "I knew something of that time period already, from studying Shakespeare in college. The elements of shorthand and Shakespeare melded in my mind, and expanded to become my first novel."

When his manuscript was rejected by several publishers, Blackwood put it aside for several years before rewriting it as a children's book. "For a long time," Blackwood explained, "it looked as if the new improved version of the book . . . would be consigned to oblivion like its predecessor." Although the author had several other books published over the next seven years, his

manuscript was rejected sixteen different times. His persistence finally paid off when Dutton agreed to publish the revisioned novel, now titled *The Shakespeare Stealer.*

In *The Shakespeare Stealer* readers meet fourteen-year-old Widge, who was raised in a Yorkshire orphanage before becoming apprenticed to Dr. Bright. A minister, Bright teaches the teen his system of "charactery" (or shorthand) for the purpose of gaining Widge's help in stealing other ministers' sermons. After Bright sells his young apprentice to London theatrical manager Simon Bass for the sum of ten pounds, Widge is charged with using his shorthand skills to steal William Shakespeare's new play, *The Tragedy of Hamlet, Prince of Denmark,* so that Bass's own theater can produce it without having to pay royalties. When Widge is discovered hiding in a balcony of the Globe Theatre, he pretends to be stage struck and is ultimately hired as an acting apprentice for Shakespeare's acting troupe, the Lord Chamberlain's Men. At first Widge sticks to Bass's plan and tries to use his new position to steal the Globe's own copy of the play, but the "brave new world of friendship, fun, and backstage intrigue," in the words of a *Kirkus Reviews* critic, make him question his actions. His shifting loyalties enable Widge to focus on learning the arts of stagecraft and sword fighting, but he must also use these skills to evade Bass's brutal henchmen.

Cover of Blackwood's history-themed adventure novel The Shakespeare Stealer, *featuring artwork by Stephen Alcorn.* (Reproduced by permission of the illustrator.)

Appraising *The Shakespeare Stealer*, Deborah Stevens noted in her review for the *Bulletin of the Center for Children's Books* that the "pleasing air of high adventure to Widge's escapades . . . is enhanced by Blackwood's careful but never dry use of period and theatrical detail." A *Kirkus Reviews* critic called the book a "delightful and heartwarming romp through Elizabethan England," while in *Publishers Weekly* a reviewer remarked on the author's inclusion of colorful historical details and "lively depictions of Elizabethan stagecraft and street life." "It's a formula with endless appeal," asserted Sally Margolis in reviewing *The Shakespeare Stealer* for *School Library Journal,* the critic noting that "Blackwood puts a young boy in a sink-or-swim predicament in alien territory where he discovers his own strength. In *Booklist* Carolyn Phelan commented that Blackwood's "historical novel makes an exciting introduction to the period and to Shakespearean theater." Praising *The Shakespeare Stealer* in *School Library Journal*, Nancy Menaldi-Scanlan wrote that Blackwood mixes "topnotch writing with a touch of humor."

Blackwood continues Widge's adventures in *Shakespeare's Scribe* and *Shakespeare's Spy. Shakespeare's Scribe* finds the teen joining the Lord Chamberlain's Men on their travels to various towns to perform, even as rumors of the growing spread of the Black Death threaten an outbreak of the plague in London. As Widge helps transcribe a play for the injured Shakespeare, he meets a man who claims to be his father and learns a great deal about himself in the process. In *Horn Book,* Jennifer M. Brabander called *Shakespeare's Scribe* an "engaging portrayal of a young boy's coming of age in Elizabethan England," while *School Library Journal* contributor Nancy Menaldi-Scanlan lauded Blackwood's book as "extremely well structured, with . . . interesting subplots" and "realistic" dialogue. Phelan stated in her *Booklist* appraisal of the same novel that "Widge and many of the other characters emerge as memorable, complex individuals that children will want to meet again."

As stage props and costumes start to go missing in *Shakespeare's Spy,* the thefts threaten the troupe's stage success with plays such as *Hamlet* and *Measure for Measure.* Widge—now an actor—must become an undercover investigator while also finding romance with the popular playwright's beautiful daughter, Judith. In *Horn Book* Jeannine M. Chapman wrote of *Shakespeare's Spy* that, despite the many plot lines, "with its intrigues, romances, and plagues, [the novel] is an enjoyable read." A *Kirkus Reviews* writer deemed Blackwood's latest Elizabethan romp "peppered like its predecessors with hilarious wordplay and real stagecraft."

Blackwood also features fast-moving, action-filled plots and likeable characters in his standalone novels, which include *The Year of the Hangman* and *Second Sight.* In the former, he plays out an alternate history in which the British have vanquished North American colonials during the American Revolution, leaving General George Washington captive and Benjamin Franklin hiding in a New Orleans safe house. In the novel fifteen-year-old juvenile delinquent Brit Creighton Brown is sent to the colonies to gain character and winds up in the hands of the colonial underground. Joining with rebel leader Benedict Arnold, Brown attempts to rescue Washington and learns a lot about honor and loyalty in the process. A *Publishers Weekly* reviewer found *The Year of the Hangman* "adventurous, if somewhat unrealistic," but also praised the book's "clever dialogue" and "compelling questions," while in *School Library Journal* Starr E. Smith wrote: "Packed with action . . . and compelling portrayals of real-life and fictional characters," *The Year of the Hangman* "will appeal to fans of both history and fantasy."

Moving closer to the historical record, *Second Sight* focuses on a presidential assassination: the murder of Abraham Lincoln during the U.S. Civil War. The main character and narrator, teenager Joseph Ehrlich, is a struggling actor who performs a stage act with his father, Nicholas, during which he feigns clairvoyance. Then he meets Cassandra Quinn, a girl living in his family's boarding house who demonstrates a real ability to foresee the future. When Cassandra predicts Lincoln's death and states that politically radical actor John Wilkes Booth will be the killer, Joseph realizes that he must attempt to derail this tragedy. Noting that Blackwood "twist[s] history with some surprising results," Renee Steinberg praised *Second Sight* in *School Library Journal* as useful as a "springboard for some interesting

class discussions." Introducing the novel as "brilliantly re-envisioned history," a *Kirkus Reviews* writer concluded that Blackwood casts his dramatic novel with "historical people and events, sets them in the most vivid evocation" of the mid-1800s, and then "caps his mesmerizing thriller with a stunning twist."

Blackwood turns to younger readers in *The Just-so Woman,* a beginning reader illustrated by Jane Manning. In his story, he captures the way of life before electricity was available to rural farming families. The title character, a tidy woman, turns to her messy neighbor on the next farm when she runs out of butter, soap, and several other necessities, and she learns how to substitute and improvise in the process. Praising Manning's "colorful cartoon-style pictures," Hazel Rochman added that Blackwood's folksy language is "fun" and contributes to "a lively story." "Blackwood deftly integrates a sense of the rigors of homesteading life into the easy-reader format" of *The Just-so Woman,* wrote a *Kirkus Reviews* writer in reviewing the rural-themed story.

Turning to nonfiction, Blackwood's "Bad Guys" series includes such titles as *Highwaymen, Gangsters, Swindlers,* and *Outlaws,* while his "Secrets of the Unexplained" books include *Alien Astronauts, Extraordinary Events and Oddball Occurrences, Fateful Forebodings,* and *Paranormal Powers.* In his "Unsolved History" books, which include *Debatable Deaths, Enigmatic Events, Perplexing People,* and *Legends or Lies?,* Blackwood introduces readers to some of the most intriguing mysteries of the past, from questions as to who murdered Egypt's King Tutankamun and the daughters of Russia's Tsar Nicholas II to the whereabouts of El Dorado and the lost city of Atlantis. Reviewing the "Bad Guys" books, Phelan praised them as "well written and well designed," citing the author's focus on fascinating ne'er-do-wells from history. Laura Glaser wrote in *School Library Journal* that, rather than trying to excuse or explain the moral and ethical choices of past criminals, Blackwood "sticks to the facts and colorful details," making the "Bad Guys" books "simultaneously entertaining and informative reading." Praising the "Unsolved History" books, Ann G. Brouse noted in *School Library Journal* that Blackwood's "titles offer more substance than most," and Ilene Cooper wrote in *Booklist* that the series "gathers together many of history's most intriguing mysteries."

Other nonfiction titles include *The Great Race: The Amazing Round-the-World Auto Race of 1908* and *Mysterious Messages.* Sponsored by the *New York Times* and France's *Le Matin* newspaper to promote early-twentieth-century automobile manufacturers, the competition profiled in *The Great Race* was one of the first long-range motor-car races in the world. From their start in New York's Times Square, the six competitors drove across North America, up through the Alaska Territory and across the Bering Strait to Siberia, then across Asia to the finish line in Paris, France. "Blackwood's meticulous research is evident," wrote *School Library Journal* contributor Kim Dare, "and the abundant pe-

Cover of Blackwood's history-themed children's book The Great Race, *which recounts the first-ever globe-spanning motorcar competition.*
(Photographs by Frame 30 Productions (top right corner); Library of Congress (all others). Reproduced by permission of Abrams Books for Young Readers, an imprint of Harry N. Abrams, Inc.)

riod photographs [in *The Great Race*] are a pleasure to study." A *Kirkus Reviews* writer also praised the book's "lively writing . . . and abundant archival photographs," and *Booklist* critic Todd Morning predicted: "There's enough sheer adventure here, carried out by some eccentric characters, to attract almost every reader."

Biographical and Critical Sources

PERIODICALS

Booklist, June 1, 1998, Carolyn Phelan, review of *The Shakespeare Stealer*, p. 1763; September 1, 2000, Carolyn Phelan, review of *Shakespeare's Scribe*, p. 112; January 1, 2002, Carolyn Phelan, review of *Highwaymen* and *Swindlers*, p. 850; March 15, 2003, review of *Year of the Hangman*, p. 1290; September 1, 2003, Carolyn Phelan, review of *Shakespeare's Spy*, p. 119; October 1, 2005, Carolyn Phelan, review of *Second Sight*, p. 48; March 1, 2006, Ilene Cooper, review of *Enigmatic Events*, p. 87; December 1, 2006, Hazel Rochman, review of *The Just-So Woman*, p. 51; April 15, 2008, Todd Morning, review of *The Great Race: The Amazing Round-the-World Auto Race of 1908*, p. 37; October 15, 2009, Carolyn Phelan, review of *Mysterious Messages: A History of Codes and Ciphers*, p. 49.

Bulletin of the Center for Children's Books, July-August, 1998, Deborah Stevens, review of *The Shakespeare Stealer*, p. 483; December, 2002, review of *The Year of the Hangman*, p. 144.
Horn Book, June, 1998, Jennifer M. Brabander, review of *The Shakespeare Stealer*, p. 353; November, 2000, Jennifer M. Brabander, review of *Shakespeare's Scribe*, p. 752; November-December, 2003, Jeannine M. Chapman, review of *Shakespeare's Spy*, p. 739.
Kirkus Reviews, April 15, 1998, review of *The Shakespeare Stealer*, p. 576; October 15, 2003, review of *Shakespeare's Spy*, p. 1269; August 1, 2005, review of *Second Sight*, p. 844; October 15, 2006, review of *The Just-So Woman*, p. 1066; April 1, 2008, review of *The Great Race;* September 1, 2009, review of *Mysterious Messages*.
Kliatt, September, 2002, Claire Rosser, review of *The Year of the Hangman*, p. 6, and Sally M. Tibbetts, review of *Shakespeare's Scribe*, p. 15; March, 2004, Janet Julian, review of *The Year of the Hangman*, p. 59.
Publishers Weekly, June 1, 1998, review of *The Shakespeare Stealer*, p. 63; September 16, 2002, review of *The Year of the Hangman*, p. 70.
School Library Journal, June, 1998, Sally Margolis, review of *The Shakespeare Stealer*, p. 140; September, 2000, Nancy Menaldi-Scanlan, review of *Shakespeare's Scribe*, p. 225; January, 2002, Laura Glaser, reviews of *Highwaymen, Gangsters,* and *Outlaws*, p. 146; September, 2002, Starr E. Smith, review of *The Year of the Hangman*, p. 219; October, 2003, Susan Colley, review of *Shakespeare's Spy*, p. 158; February, 2004, Nancy Menaldi-Scanlan, review of *The Shakespeare Stealer*, p. 82; September, 2005, Renee Steinberg, review of *Second Sight*, p. 198; March, 2006, Ann G. Brouse, review of *Debatable Deaths*, p. 236; November, 2006, Melinda Piehler, review of *The Just-So Woman*, p. 84; December, 2006, Kathleen Baxter, review of "Unsolved History" series, p. 33; June, 2008, Kim Dare, review of *The Great Race*, p. 154; December, 2009, Rebecca Donnelly, review of *Mysterious Messages*, p. 136.
Voice of Youth Advocates, October, 2002, review of *The Year of the Hangman*, p. 269.

ONLINE

Writers' Federation of Nova Scotia Web site, http://www.writers.ns.ca/ (February 15, 2011), "Gary L. Blackwood."

*   *   *

BOASE, Susan

Personal

Born in Lansing, MI; married; husband a woodworker and furniture designer. *Hobbies and other interests:* Walking her dogs, bike riding, ceramics, listening to music, spending time with friends.

Addresses

Home—Portland, OR.

Career

Artist, illustrator, and author.

Member

Society of Children's Books Writers and Illustrators.

Awards, Honors

KIND Children's Book Award, National Association for Humane and Environmental Education, 2004, for *Lucky Boy*.

Writings

SELF-ILLUSTRATED

Lucky Boy, Houghton Mifflin (Boston, MA), 2002.

ILLUSTRATOR

Christine Graham, *Three Little Robbers,* Henry Holt (New York, NY), 2007.
Christine Graham, *Peter Peter Picks a Pumpkin House,* Henry Holt (New York, NY), 2009.
Wendy Orr, *Lost Dog Bear,* Henry Holt (New York, NY), 2011.

Sidelights

Born in Michigan and now living and working in western Oregon, Susan Boase is an artist who began focusing on book illustration in the late 1990s. Shortly after her mother died, Boase became concerned about a scruffy dog that lived in her neighborhood and was left tied outside and ignored by its busy owners. She interwove her sadness over her mom's death and her worries regarding her newly widowed father with images of the pup's imagined life to produce the story that became her first published picture book, *Lucky Boy.* Other illustration projects have more recently come Boase's way, among them *Three Little Robbers* and *Peter Peter Picks a Pumpkin House* by Christine Graham and *Lost Dog Bear* by Wendy Orr. Reviewing *Peter Peter Picks a Pumpkin House* in *Kirkus Reviews,* a critic noted that "Boase's nimble lines add necessary details, outlining facial features and family dynamics, [and] strengthening the story."

Boase works in a variety of media, including linoleum block, water color and gouache, and pencil, the last which she used to create the sepia-toned art for *Lucky Boy.* The images of the dog were based on her own fox terrier, Frida, who proved to be an engaging model. In the story, a neglected pup that is left alone by its family digs out from under its backyard fence and finds a loving friend in the elderly widower living next door. A bath, a good meal, and a loving hug transform both man and dog in a story that a *Kirkus Reviews* writer recommended "for one-on-one sharing, especially in families with lucky dogs of their own." The book's "pencil illustrations are a delight, and completely capture the nature, joy, and essence" of the dog, according to Robin L. Gibson in *School Library Journal,* and a *Publishers Weekly* contributor praised *Lucky Boy* as a "splendidly told dog story" in which the author/illustrator's "softly shaded and cross-hatched lines convey . . . innate tenderness."

In an interview for the Macmillan Web site, Boase offered the following advice to aspiring illustrators and authors: "Just to do the thing that makes you happy. Have some faith in yourself and don't think too hard about the thing you are trying to say or depict. I think the work needs to come from that place/space you inhabited as a child—a place of wonder and trust."

Biographical and Critical Sources

PERIODICALS

Kirkus Reviews, February 1, 2002, review of *Lucky Boy* p. 177; June 15, 2009, review of *Peter Peter Picks a Pumpkin House.*
Publishers Weekly, January 28, 2002, review of *Lucky Boy,* p. 290.
School Library Journal, June, 2002, Robin L. Gibson, review of *Lucky Boy,* p. 87.

ONLINE

Macmillan Web site, http://us.macmillan.com/ (February 15, 2011), "Susan Boase."
Susan Boase Home Page, http://susanboase.com/ (February 15, 2011).*

*   *   *

BONNET, Rosalinde 1978-

Personal

Born 1978, in Paris, France. *Education:* Attended École des Beaux-Arts de Versailles and Académie Charpentier; École Nationale Supérieure des Arts Décoratifs, degree, 2004.

Addresses

Home—Versailles, France.

Career

Author, illustrator, and textile and toy designer.

Writings

SELF-ILLUSTRATED

Petit girafe cherche du travail, Portes du Monde, 2004.
Quand les poules auront des dents, Portes du Monde, 2004.
Et si on aidait le petit inconnu?, Portes du Monde, 2004.
Gontran, le loup gourmand, Portes du Monde, 2005.
Moi le dragon, Portes du Monde, 2005.
La semaine de cochon, Portes du Monde, 2005.
Barnabé, le loup écolier, Portes du Monde, 2005.
La ferme des couleurs, Portes du Monde, 2005.
Hugo et Flora, Portes du Monde, 2005.
La sieste du grand méchant loup, Éditions Nathan (Paris, France), 2006.
Le bouton de la sorcière, Éditions Nathan (Paris, France), 2006.
La culotte, Des Idées y des Hommes Jeunesse, 2007.
Le noël de Louistic, Des Idées y des Hommes Jeunesse, 2007.
Un appétit de reine, Des Idées y des Hommes Jeunesse, 2007.
Deux petits dinosaures cherchent leur maman, Éditions Nathan (Paris, France), 2008.
Le petit chaperon rouge, Fleurus (Paris, France), 2010.

ILLUSTRATOR

Meryem Debladis, *Le village où il ne pleuvait plus,* Des Idées y des Hommes Jeunesse, 2007.
Fanny Joly, *Miam . . . les amis!,* Hachette Jeunesse (Paris, France), 2008.
Usborne Nursery Rhyme Picture Book, Usborne (London, England), 2008.
Usborne Very First Nursery Rhymes, Usborne (London, England), 2009.
Orianne Lallemand, *Picoti, picota!,* Casterman (Paris, France), 2009.
Barbara Barbieri McGrath, *The Little Red Elf,* Charlesbridge (Watertown, MA), 2009.
Charlotte Grossetête, *Mes histoires pour apprendree,* Fleurus (Paris, France), 2010.
Ghislaine Biondi, Bénédicte Carboneill, and Delphine Bolin, *Histoires d'animaux de la ferme,* Fleurus (Paris, France), 2010.
Ghislaine Biondi, Bénédicte Carboneill, and Delphine Bolin, *Histoires pour le soir,* Fleurus (Paris, France), 2010.
Fiona Watt, editor, *Sing-along Christmas Carols* (with CD), Usborne (London, England), 2010.
Jan Wahl, *The Art Collector,* Charlesbridge (Watertown, MA), 2011.
Orianne Lallemand, *La famille tortue,* Casterman (Paris, France), 2011.

OTHER; FOR CHILDREN

Où sont passés les princes charmants?, illustrated by Anne Simon, Milan Poche (Toulouse, France), 2007.

Un ogre à la maison, illustrated by Nathalie Polfliet, Mijade (Paris, France), 2008.
À la ferme, illustrated by Keith Furnival, Éditions Usborne, 2011.

Illustrator of paper-doll books.

Biographical and Critical Sources

PERIODICALS

Horn Book, November-December, 2009, Kitty Flynn, review of *The Little Red Elf,* p. 645.
Kirkus Reviews, September 15, 2009, review of *The Little Red Elf.*
Publishers Weekly, October 26, 2009, review of *The Little Red Elf,* p. 54.
School Library Journal, October, 2009, Eva Mitnick, review of *The Little Red Elf,* p. 82.*

*   *   *

BRALLIER, Jess M. 1953-

Personal

Born May 31, 1953, in PA; married; has children. *Education:* University of Pennsylvania, B.A.; Boston University, M.S.

Addresses

Home—MA.

Career

Publisher and author. Member of editorial staff of Little, Brown, Harcourt Brace Jovanovich, and Penguin; Addison Wesley, director of marketing for General Publishing division, then founder of Planet Dexter imprint, 1992; Family Education Network (online publisher), general manager and publisher, beginning c. 1996. Lecturer at Howard University Book Publishing Institute, Emerson College, Harvard University, and other institutions; presenter at conferences. Radcliffe Publishing Course, evaluator.

Awards, Honors

LMP Individual Achievement Award.

Writings

FOR CHILDREN

Y2Kids: Your Guide to the Millennium, illustrated by Larry Ross, Grosset & Dunlap (New York, NY), 1999.

Bouncing Science, illustrated by Bob Staake, Planet Dexter (New York, NY), 2000.

Hairy Science, illustrated by Bob Staake, Planet Dexter (New York, NY), 2000.

Shadowy Science: All You Need Is a Shadow!, illustrated by Bob Staake, Planet Dexter (New York, NY), 2000.

Thumbs Up Science, illustrated by Bob Staake, Planet Dexter (New York, NY), 2000.

Play Ball!: The World's Best Ball Games, Featuring the World's Greatest Toy, illustrated by Sammy Yuen, Price Stern Sloan (New York, NY), 2002.

Who Was Albert Einstein?, illustrated by Robert Andrew Parker, Grosset & Dunlap (New York, NY), 2002.

Tess's Tree, illustrated by Peter H. Reynolds, Harper (New York, NY), 2009.

OTHER

(Compiler with Richard P. McDonough) *The Pessimist's Journal of Very, Very Bad Days of the 1980s,* illustrated by Seth Feinberg, Little, Brown (Boston, MA), 1990.

(With Richard P. McDonough) *The Really, Really Classy Donald Trump Quiz Book: Complete, Unauthorized, Fantastic—and the Best!!,* Little, Brown (Boston, MA), 1990.

(Coauthor) Bradley E. Smith, *Write Your Own Living Will,* Crown (New York, NY), 1991.

Lawyers and Other Reptiles, Contemporary Books (Chicago, IL), 1992.

(Compiler) *Medical Wit and Wisdom: The Best Medical Quotations from Hippocrates to Groucho Marx,* Running Press (Philadelphia, PA), 1993.

The Hot Dog Cookbook: The Wiener Work the World Awaited, Globe Pequot Press (Old Saybrook, CT), 1993.

(With Sally Chabert) *Celebrate America,* Berkley (New York, NY), 1995.

(With Sally Chabert) *Cocktail Hour: A Mixer of Quips and Quotations,* Contemporary Books (Chicago, IL), 1996.

Lawyers and Other Reptiles II: The Appeal, Contemporary Books (Chicago, IL), 1996.

(With Sally Chabert) *Presidential Wit and Wisdom: Maxims, Mottoes, Sound Bites, Speeches, and Asides: Memorable Quotes from America's Presidents,* Penguin Books (New York, NY), 1996.

(With Sally Chabert) *Coach: A Treasury of Inspiration and Laughter,* Contemporary Books (Lincolnwood, IL), 2000.

Sidelights

Jess M. Brallier is general manager and publisher of the Family Educational Network, a subsidiary of educational publisher Pearson. As such, he oversees the production of books as well as the educational Web sites Factmonster.com, Infoplease.com, Funbrain.com, and Poptropica.com, the last which ranked among the top kid-focused Web sites within a few years of its 2007 start-up. Although many of his books have been collaborations with other authors, Brallier tackles biogra-

phy in his nonfiction book *Who Was Albert Einstein?* and entertains picture-book audiences in his engaging story for *Tess's Tree.* Reviewing *Who Was Albert Einstein?,* a heavily illustrated biography that presents aspects of the physicist's childhood and teen years that most young readers can relate to, Carol Fazioli noted in *School Library Journal* that Brallier gives readers "the facts and injects touches of humor into his text."

Although Brallier entered college intending to study industrial engineering, he "quickly found the students and professors playing around in literature, philosophy, writing, theology, and so on, [were] a lot more interesting and a lot more capable of making sense of life," as he noted in an interview for Teachervision.com. After majoring in creative writing, he went to work for a series of publishers, including Addison Wesley, where he initially worked as a director of marketing and then founded their Planet Dexter imprint in 1992. Allowed a great deal of latitude in determining the focus of the educational imprint, Brallier developed what he calls "stealth learning": creating appealing packaging that mixes bright colors and interactive accessories to make the learning process fun.

Brallier's first fictional story, *Tess's Tree,* was inspired by a young neighbor's love for a tree growing in her yard. In the book, Tess loves swinging from the lofty and ancient tree in her backyard, and when it is struck by lightning during a storm she feels as though she has lost a friend. To deal with her sadness, the girl organizes a funeral for the lost landscape member, and her

Jess M. Braillier's story for **Tess's Tree** *is brought to life in Peter H. Reynolds' colorful and child-friendly illustrations.* (Illustration copyright © 2009 by Peter H. Reynolds. Used by permission of HarperCollins Children's Books, a division of HarperCollins Publishers.)

action inspires others in her neighborhood to remember the important trees in their own lives. Ink-and-watercolor images by Peter H. Reynolds "poignantly convey the story's emotions," noted *School Library Journal* contributor Linda Ludke, and a *Kirkus Reviews* writer deemed *Tess's Tree* a "tender tale of love and loss." A *Publishers Weekly* critic also praised "Brallier's understated, resonant debut," adding that the "spare, emotive" art in *Tess's Tree* captures the author's "message about cycles of life and the importance of mourning."

Biographical and Critical Sources

PERIODICALS

Kirkus Reviews, August 1, 2009, review of *Tess's Tree.*
Publishers Weekly, February 6, 1995, Sally Lodge, "A World of Fun at Planet Dexter," p. 30; September 21, 2009, review of *Tess's Tree,* p. 55.
School Library Journal, June, 2002, Carol Fazioli, review of *Who Was Albert Einstein?,* p. 119; February, 2010, Linda Ludke, review of *Tess's Tree,* p. 76.

ONLINE

Family Education Network Home Page, http://fen.com/ (February 15, 2011).
Our White House Web site, http://www.ourwhitehouse.org/ (February 15, 2011), "Jess M. Brallier."
Teachervision Web site, http://www.teachervision.fen.com/ (February 15, 2011), interview with Brallier.*

*　　*　　*

BRENNA, Beverley 1962-

Personal

Born October 1, 1962, in Saskatoon, Saskatchewan, Canada; married; husband's name Dwayne; children: three sons. *Education:* University of Saskatchewan, B.Ed. (with distinction), 1984, M.Ed., 1991, special-education teacher certification, 2000, B.A. (with great distinction), 2001; University of Alberta, Ph.D. (elementary education, language, and literacy), 2010. *Hobbies and other interests:* Baking bread, nature study (especially insects), travel.

Addresses

Home—Saskatoon, Saskatchewan, Canada. *Office*—College of Education, Office ED 3121, University of Saskatchewan, 28 Campus Dr., Saskatoon, Saskatchewan S7N 0X1, Canada. *Agent*—Morty Mint and Verna Relkoff, Mint Agency; morty@mintagency.net or verna@mintagency.net. *E-mail*—beverley.brenna@gmail.com.

Beverley Brenna (Photograph by AK Photos. Reproduced by permission.)

Career

Author and educator. Elementary school teacher for Canada's Border Land School Division, Outlook School Division, Saskatchewan Valley School Division, and Saskatoon Public Schools; educational consultant for Saskatchewan Valley School Division and Saskatoon Public Schools; University of Saskatchewan, Saskatoon, assistant professor of curriculum studies.

Member

Alliance of Canadian Cinema, Television and Radio Artists, Canadian Society of Children's Authors, Illustrators, and Performers.

Awards, Honors

Saskatchewan Writers' Guild Awards for short fiction and children's literature; Saskatchewan Teachers' Federation Research Award, 1991; Young-Adult Book Award shortlist, Canadian Library Association (CLA), Saskatchewan Book Award shortlist, White Pine Award shortlist and Silver Birch Award shortlist, both Ontario Library Association, and Books for the Teen Age selection, New York Public Library, all c. 1999, all for *Wild Orchid;* Dr. Stirling McDowell Research Award, Saskatchewan Teachers' Federation, 2002; Saskatchewan Book Award shortlist, Children's Book of the Year nomination, CLA, and Silver Birch Award shortlist, Ontario Library Association, all c. 2007, all for *The Moon Children;* Dr. Marie Meyer Memorial research grant, University of Alberta, 2009-10; President's Social Sciences and Humanities Research Council grant, 2010; John Ranton McIntosh research grant, 2010; Saskatchewan Book Award shortlist, 2010, for *Something to Hang on To.*

Writings

NOVELS

Spider Summer, ITP Nelson (Scarborough, Ontario, Canada), 1998.

The Keeper of the Trees, Ronsdale Press (Vancouver, British Columbia, Canada), 1999.

Wild Orchid, Red Deer Press (Calgary, Alberta, Canada), 1999.

The Moon Children, Red Deer Press (Calgary, Alberta, Canada), 2007.

Waiting for No One, Red Deer Press (Calgary, Alberta, Canada), 2010.

Falling for Henry, Red Deer Press (Calgary, Alberta, Canada), 2011.

OTHER

Daddy Longlegs at Birch Lane, illustrated by Sandra Blair, Soundprints (Norwalk, CT), 1996.

Something to Hang on To (stories), Thistledown Press (Saskatoon, Saskatchewan, Canada), 2009.

Contributor to books, including *Horizons of Literacy,* edited by L. Wason Ellam, A. Blunt, and S. Robinson, Canadian Council of Teachers of English Language Arts (Winnipeg, Manitoba, Canada), 1995, and *Opening Tricks.* Contributor to periodicals, including *Canadian Journal of Education, Canadian Children's Book News, Language and Literacy, International Journal of Special Education,* and *Journal of the Association for Research on Mothering.* Contributor of book reviews to *Saskatoon Star Phoenix.*

Sidelights

A longtime educator and former special education teacher, Beverley Brenna is also a writer whose books include *Wild Orchid,* an award-winning young-adult novel, and the story collection *Something to Hang on To.* Brenna, a college professor who lives and works in Saskatoon, Saskatchewan, Canada, has earned praise for her sensitive portrayals of teens learning to cope with their disabilities, such as Billy, the boy with fetal alcohol spectrum disorder who stars in *The Moon Children.* Through her writing, Brenna is able to add to the body of literature about characters with disabilities. "It's not that there's a lack of characters with special needs in books," she remarked in a *Canadian Review of Materials* interview with Dave Jenkinson, "but I think that there's a lack of protagonists in central roles who live and grow as other protagonists do while having unique challenges."

Born in Saskatoon in 1962, Brenna began writing at an early age, influenced primarily by her mother. "After the supper dishes were done, she'd always sit on the couch and pull out her notebooks and do some writing," she recalled to Jenkinson. "What a powerful example in the home. It just seemed like writing was something that was OK to do, and so I've always done it." After graduating from the University of Saskatchewan, Brenna began working as an elementary school teacher and subsequently served as a coordinator of gifted programs, a reading specialist, and a special education teacher. Her interest in writing was rekindled while she took a ten-year break from her career to raise her family. "I had written adult poetry and a few adult short stories," she remarked in her interview, "but definitely the writing for children evolved after having my own kids and getting more interested in reading in the children's literature genre. I'm very appreciative of the good work that's out there, and I think that, as you encounter that good work, it just inspires you to think, 'Yah, that's the art form that I really like.'"

Cover of Brenna's short-story collection Something to Hang on To, *in which teens are seen dealing with adversity in a variety of ways.* (Thistledown Press, 2009. Cover photograph ©www.comstock.com. Reproduced by permission.)

Brenna's debut work, the nonfiction picture book *Daddy Longlegs at Birch Lane,* was released in 1996. She followed that with *Spider Summer,* a mystery novel for middle-grade readers, and *The Keeper of the Trees,* a fantasy tale in which the author "introduces the concept that all life is interrelated and interdependent," as Kathleen Kirk remarked in the *Canadian Review of Materials.*

Brenna introduces Taylor Jane Simon, an eighteen year old with Asperger's syndrome, in *Wild Orchid.* Narrated by the protagonist through a series of journal entries, the novel follows Taylor as she spends the summer following high-school graduation at Waskesiu Lake, away from the familiar comforts of home. Despite her anxieties about the sudden change, Taylor makes a host of new friends, lands her first job, and gains a newfound sense of confidence. According to *School Library Journal* contributor Wendy Smith-D'Arezzo, "Brenna has done a credible job of capturing the voice of a young woman on the brink of maturity," and Heather Lisowski noted in *Kliatt* that "the reader gets a precise view of the world as Taylor perceives it."

In a sequel, *Waiting for No One,* Taylor attempts to navigate the adult world by enrolling for a class at a local university, where she befriends Luke, a teen whose younger brother suffers from cerebral palsy. "*Waiting for No One* is not merely a continuation of *Wild Orchid,*" wrote Kristin Butcher in the *Canadian Review of Materials.* "It is the beginning of a metamorphosis. As Taylor grows into a young woman, she is beginning to see and understand how she is different from other people, and she is starting to develop strategies to help her fit in, because fit in she must if she hopes to be independent."

The Moon Children centers on the unlikely relationship between Billy, the eleven-year-old son of alcoholic parents, and Natasha, an uncommunicative neighbor who was adopted from a Romanian orphanage. When Billy's father disappears just days before a local talent show in which he and his son were to perform, Natasha breaks her silence to help her new friend enter the contest while also revealing a painful secret about her own childhood. "Once again," Jenkinson commented, "Brenna demonstrates her superb ability to present the world as it is seen through the eyes of a central character with special learning needs."

Biographical and Critical Sources

PERIODICALS

Canadian Review of Materials, December 15, 2000, Kathleen Kirk, review of *The Keeper of the Trees;* November 9, 2007, Dave Jenkinson, review of *The Moon Children;* February 4, 2011, Kristin Butcher, review of *Waiting for No One.*

Kirkus Reviews, September 15, 2009, review of *Something to Hang on To.*

Kliatt, May, 2006, Heather Lisowski, review of *Wild Orchid,* p. 17.

Resource Links, October, 2006, Joan Marshall, review of *Wild Orchid,* p. 30; December, 2009, Lindsay Schluter, review of *Something to Hang on To,* p. 29.

School Library Journal, June, 2006, Wendy Smith-D'Arezzo, review of *Wild Orchid,* p. 146.

ONLINE

Beverley Brenna Home Page, http://www.beverleybrenna. com (February 15, 2011).

Canadian Review of Materials Online, http://www. umanitoba.ca/cm/ (November, 2006), Dave Jenkinson, "Beverley Brenna."

Canadian Society of Children's Authors, Illustrators and Performers Web site, http://www.canscaip.org/ (February 15, 2011), "Beverley Brenna."

University of Saskatchewan Web site, http://www.usask.ca/ (February 15, 2011), "Beverley Brenna."

*   *   *

BROWN, Richard
See BROWN, Rick

*   *   *

BROWN, Richard E.
See BROWN, Rick

*   *   *

BROWN, Rick 1946-
(Richard Brown, Richard E. Brown)

Personal

Born 1946, in Philadelphia, PA; married; wife's name Lynne; children: three. *Education:* Philadelphia College of Art, B.F.A., 1968.

Addresses

Home—Bucks County, PA. *E-mail*—ricbrownart@ gmail.com.

Career

Illustrator. *Exhibitions:* Works included in Society of Illustrators Original Art Show, New York, NY; Bianco Gallery, Buckingham, PA, 1998; Windy Bush Gallery, New Hope, PA, 2001; Coryell Gallery, Lambertville, NJ, 2001, 2002; Phillips Mill, New Hope, 2001, 2002, 2003. *Military service:* U.S. Army, served with 101st Airborne Division in Vietnam.

Rick Brown (Reproduced by permission.)

Illustrator

Susan Pearson, *The Day Porkchop Climbed the Christmas Tree,* Prentice Hall (New York, NY), 1987.

Susan Pearson, *Porkchop's Halloween,* Simon & Schuster (New York, NY), 1988.

Pat Brisson, *Your Best Friend, Kate,* Bradbury Press (New York, NY), 1989.

David Friend, *Baseball, Football, Daddy, and Me,* Viking (New York, NY), 1990.

Pat Brisson, *Kate Heads West,* Bradbury Press (New York, NY), 1990.

Pat Brisson, *Kate on the Coast,* Bradbury Press (New York, NY), 1992.

Diane Johnston Hamm, *Rock-a-bye Farm,* Simon & Schuster (New York, NY), 1992.

Old MacDonald Had a Farm, Viking (New York, NY), 1993.

Hope Norman Coulter, *Uncle Chuck's Truck,* Bradbury Press (New York, NY), 1993.

Harriet Ziefert, *Scooter's Christmas,* HarperFestival (New York, NY), 1993.

Harriet Ziefert, *What Rhymes with Snake?: A Word-and-Picture Flap Book,* Tambourine Books (New York, NY), 1994.

Mike Thaler, *Colossal Fossil,* Scientific American Books for Young Readers (New York, NY), 1994.

Mike Thaler, *Earth Mirth: The Ecology Riddle Book,* Scientific American Books for Young Readers (New York, NY), 1994.

Wendy Cheyette Lewison, *The Princess and the Potty,* Simon & Schuster (New York, NY), 1994.

Who Built the Ark?, Viking (New York, NY), 1994.

Harriet Ziefert, *What Is Hanukkah?,* HarperFestival (New York, NY), 1994.

Charlotte Doyle, *Where's Bunny's Mommy?,* Simon & Schuster (New York, NY), 1995.

Stuart Bergen, *Fozzie's Bubble Bath,* Grosset & Dunlap (New York, NY), 1996.

Alison Inches, *Rizzo's Bike Sale,* Grosset & Dunlap (New York, NY), 1996.

Harriet Ziefert, *What Rhymes with Eel?: A Word-and-Picture Flap Book,* Viking (New York, NY), 1996.

Robert W. Wood, *Heat Fundamentals,* Learning Triangle Press (New York, NY), 1997.

Robert W. Wood, *Sound Fundamentals: Funtastic Science Activities for Kids,* Learning Triangle Press (New York, NY), 1997.

Robert S. Carrow, *Put a Fan in Your Hat!: Inventions, Contraptions, and Gadgets Kids Can Build,* Learning Triangle Press (New York, NY), 1997.

Robert S. Carrow, *Turn on the Lights—from Bed!: Inventions, Contraptions, and Gadgets Kids Can Build,* Learning Triangle Press (New York, NY), 1997.

Ann Turner, *Let's Be Animals,* HarperFestival (New York, NY), 1998.

Jane O'Connor, *Snail City,* Grosset & Dunlap (New York, NY), 2001.

Susan Kantor, *Tiny Tilda's Pumpkin Pie,* Grosset & Dunlap (New York, NY), 2002.

Harriet Ziefert, *All Dirty! All Clean!,* Sterling Publishing (New York, NY), 2005.

Harriet Ziefert, *Old MacDonald Had a Cow,* Sterling Publishing (New York, NY), 2005.

Grace Maccarone, *Graduation Day Is Here!,* Scholastic (New York, NY), 2006.

Rabbi Joe Black, *Boker Tov!: Good Morning!,* Kar-Ben Publishing (Minneapolis, MN), 2009.

Jacqueline Jules, *Going on a Hametz Hunt,* Kar-Ben Publishing (Minneapolis, MN), 2010.

AS RICHARD E. BROWN

Franklyn M. Branley, *The Great Moon Hoax,* Ginn (Lexington, MA), 1987.

Peter Lerangis, *A Kid's Guide to New York City,* Harcourt Brace Jovanovich (San Diego, CA), 1988.

Karen Grove, *A Kid's Guide to Florida,* Harcourt Brace Jovanovich (San Diego, CA), 1989.

Diane C. Clark, *A Kid's Guide to Washington, D.C.,* Harcourt Brace Jovanovich (San Diego, CA), 1989, revised edition, Harcourt (Orlando, FL), 2008.

AS RICHARD BROWN

Valerie Stalder, reteller, *Even the Devil Is Afraid of a Shrew: A Folktale of Lapland,* Addison-Wesley (Reading, MA), 1972.

Patty Wolcott, *The Marvelous Mud Washing Machine,* Addison-Wesley (Reading, MA), 1974, reprinted, Random House (New York, NY), 1991.

Deborah Kovacs, *Frazzle's Fantastic Day,* Western Publishing/Children's Television Workshop (New York, NY), 1980.

Emily Perl Kingsley, *I Can Do It Myself,* Western Publishing/Children's Television Workshop (New York, NY), 1980.

Valjean McLenighan, *Special Delivery,* Western Publishing/Children's Television Workshop (New York, NY), 1980.

Ellen Weiss, *The Tool Box Book,* Western Publishing/Children's Television Workshop (New York, NY), 1980.

Linda Hayward, *Sesame Seasons,* Western Publishing/Children's Television Workshop (New York, NY), 1981, published as *A Big Year on Sesame Street,* 1989.

Deborah Kovacs, *When Is Saturday?*, Western Publishing/Children's Television Workshop (New York, NY), 1981.

Elisabeth Burrowes, *A Sleepy Story*, Golden Press (New York, NY), 1982.

Sesame Street Good Time to Eat!, Golden Press (New York, NY), 1982.

Jeffrey Moss, *People in Your Neighborhood*, Western Publishing/Children's Television Workshop (New York, NY), 1983.

Kathy S. Kyte, *Play It Safe: The Kids' Guide to Personal Safety and Crime Prevention*, Knopf (New York, NY), 1983.

Earlene Long, *Gone Fishing*, Houghton Mifflin (Boston, MA), 1984.

Brenda Nelson, *Mud fore Sale*, Houghton Mifflin (Boston, MA), 1984.

Kathy S. Kyte, *The Kids' Complete Guide to Money*, Knopf (New York, NY), 1984.

Harriet Ziefert, *Birthday Card, Where Are You?*, Puffin Books (New York, NY), 1985.

Dina Anastasio, *Count All the Way to Sesame Street*, Western Publishing/Children's Television Workshop (New York, NY), 1985.

Linda Hayward, *Look What I Can Do*, Western Publishing/Children's Television Workshop (New York, NY), 1985.

Harriet Ziefert, *Nicky's Christmas Surprise*, Puffin Books (New York, NY), 1985.

Harriet Ziefert, *Where Is My Easter Egg?*, Puffin Books (New York, NY), 1985.

Harriet Ziefert, *Where's the Halloween Treat?*, Puffin Books (New York, NY), 1985.

Harriet Ziefert, *Nicky's Friends*, Puffin Books (New York, NY), 1986.

Harriet Ziefert, *Nicky's Noisy Night*, Puffin Books (New York, NY), 1986.

Harriet Ziefert, *Nicky's Picnic*, Puffin Books (New York, NY), 1986.

Harriet Ziefert, *The Small Potatoes and the Snowball Fight*, Dell (New York, NY), 1986.

One Hundred Words about Animals, Harcourt Brace Jovanovich (San Diego, CA), 1987.

One Hundred Words about Transportation, Harcourt Brace Jovanovich (San Diego, CA), 1987.

Harriet Ziefert, *Nicky Upstairs and Down*, Puffin Books (New York, NY), 1987.

Harriet Ziefert, *Pet Day*, Little, Brown (Boston, MA), 1987.

Harriet Ziefert, *Trip Day*, Little, Brown (Boston, MA), 1987.

Harriet Ziefert, *Where Is Nicky's Valentine?*, Puffin Books (New York, NY), 1987.

Harriet Ziefert, *Worm Day*, Little, Brown (Boston, MA), 1987.

One Hundred Words about My House, Harcourt Brace Jovanovich (San Diego, CA), 1988.

One Hundred Words about Working, Harcourt Brace Jovanovich (San Diego, CA), 1988.

Harriet Ziefert, *Don't Cry, Baby Sam*, Puffin Books (New York, NY), 1988.

Harriet Ziefert, *Egg-drop Day*, Little, Brown (Boston, MA), 1988.

Harriet Ziefert, *Mystery Day*, Little, Brown (Boston, MA), 1988.

Harriet Ziefert, *Thank You, Nicky!*, Puffin Books (New York, NY), 1988.

Stephanie Calmenson, *All about Me*, Western Publishing/Children's Television Workshop (New York, NY), 1989.

Linda Hayward, *Cars and Planes, Trucks and Trains*, Western Publishing/Children's Television Workshop (New York, NY), 1989.

Linda Hayward, *People in My Neighborhood*, Western Publishing/Children's Television Workshop (New York, NY), 1989.

Amy Valens, *Jesse's Daycare*, Houghton Mifflin (Boston, MA), 1990.

Alison Inches, *Christmas in Snowy Forest*, Puffin Books (New York, NY), 1996.

Alison Inches, *Halloween at Creepy Castle*, Puffin Books (New York, NY), 1996.

Alison Inches, *Happy Birthday, Miss Piggy!*, Puffin Books (New York, NY), 1996.

Alison Campbell, *It's Bedtime!*, Puffin Books (New York, NY), 1996.

Jennifer Dussling, *Kermit's Teeny Tiny Farm*, Grosset & Dunlap (New York, NY), 1996.

Lara Rice, *Miss Piggy Camps Out*, Grosset & Dunlap (New York, NY), 1996.

Alison Inches, *Monster Market*, Puffin Books (New York, NY), 1996.

Harriet Ziefert, *Baby Buggy, Buggy Baby*, Houghton Mifflin (Boston, MA), 1997.

Kate Foster, *Backstage with Miss Piggy*, Puffin Books (New York, NY), 1997.

Ellen Weiss, *Muppet Manners*, Puffin Books (New York, NY), 1999.

Harriet Ziefert, *Surprise!*, Sterling Publishing (New York, NY), 2006.

Sidelights

A highly regarded illustrator, Rick Brown has contributed artwork to dozens of picture books in his decades-long career. Brown consistently earns praise for his colorful, cartoon-like pictures, which have appeared in such works as Jane O'Connor's *Snail City* and Rabbi Joe Black's upbeat picture book *Boker Tov!: Good Morning!* In the words of *Booklist* reviewer Gillian Engberg, Brown creates "bright, color-saturated pictures, with plenty of visual clues," to bring to life *Snail City*, which follows a fast-paced creature that must adapt to a slow-paced world. In *Boker Tov!* "Brown's deeply colored acrylic paintings offer secular scenes of a multicultural and multiracial neighborhood," according to a *Kirkus Reviews* critic.

In *Rockabye Farm* Brown aslo brings to life Diane Johnston Hamm's story about a farmer who personally attends to each of his animals as nighttime approaches. A *Publishers Weekly* contributor praised the combination of art and narrative in this work stating that the "simple, rhythmic text is perfectly accompanied by Brown's reassuring illustrations." A youngster helps care for a relative's cows in *Uncle Chuck's Truck,* a story by Hope Norman Coulter that also features Brown's art. "Fields and furrows are landscaped in clear, skillfully blended watercolors, then delineated in black ink," wrote a critic for *Publishers Weekly* in describing Coulter's picture book.

Wendy Cheyette Lewison offers a humorous look at a universal rite of passage in *The Princess and the Potty.* Here Brown's princess "trots out an engaging range of facial expressions," according to a *Publishers Weekly* reviewer. In Charlotte Doyle's *Where's Bunny's Mommy?* readers observe a young rabbit's daily routine at day care while his mother takes care of business at her office. "Outlined in bold, black lines, the water color illustrations show up well," observed Carolyn Phelan in a *Booklist* review of *Where's Bunny's Mommy?*

Biographical and Critical Sources

PERIODICALS

Booklist, April 15, 1994, Mary Harris Veeder, review of *The Princess and the Potty,* p. 1541; April 1, 1995, Carolyn Phelan, review of *Where's Bunny's Mommy?,* p. 1424; December 15, 1998, Carolyn Phelan, review of *Let's Be Animals,* p. 756; April 15, 2001, Gillian Engberg, review of *Snail City,* p. 1568.
Kirkus Reviews, August 15, 2009, review of *Boker Tov! Good Morning!*
Publishers Weekly, February 9, 1990, review of *Baseball, Football, Daddy and Me,* p. 59; June 22, 1992, review of *Rockabye Farm,* p. 60; February 1, 1993, review of *Uncle Chuck's Truck,* p. 93; January 17, 1994, review of *The Princess and the Potty,* p. 430; May 23, 1994, review of *What Rhymes with Snake?: A Word-and-Picture Flap Book,* p. 86; August 30, 1999, reviews of *Where Do You Live?* and *What Do You Eat?,* both p. 77.
School Library Journal, August, 2001, Maura Bresnahan, review of *Snail City,* p. 156.

ONLINE

Rick Brown Home Page, http://www.rickbrownillustration. net (February 15, 2011).

* * *

BROWNING, Tom 1949-

Personal

Born 1949, in Ontario, OR.

Addresses

Home—Eugene, OR. *E-mail*—tom@tombrowning.com.

Career

Fine-art painter, illustrator, and muralist. Professional painter beginning 1972. *Exhibitions:* Work exhibited in group and solo shows at Clagget Rey Gallery, Vail, CO; Insight Gallery, Fredericksburg, TX; National Cowboy and Western Heritage Museum; Wilcox Gallery, Jackson, WY; Eiteljorg Museum of American Indian and Western Art, Indianapolis, IN; Settler's West Gallery, Tucson, AZ; and Phoenix Art Museum, 2010. Work included in permanent collections at William S. and Ann Atherton Art of the American West Gallery.

Member

Cowboy Artists of America, Portrait Painters Society of America, Northwest Rendezvous Group.

Awards, Honors

Northwest Rendezvous Group Award of Excellence, 1994, and four merit awards; Portrait Painters Society of America Award finalist, 2000; Prix de West Award, Prix de West Show, 2009.

Illustrator

Bill Maynard, *Santa's Time Off: Poems,* Putnam (New York, NY), 1997.
Elvis Presley and Vera Matson, *Elvis Presley's Love Me Tender* (song lyrics), HarperCollins (New York, NY), 2003.
Stormie Omartian, *Prayers and Promises for My Little Boy,* Harvest House (Eugene, OR), 2008.
Clement C. Moore, *The Night before Christmas,* Sterling (New York, NY), 2009.

Contributor to periodicals, including *Art of the West, Focus Santa Fe, Rainbow, Santa Fe Magazine, Southwest Art, Skywest,* and *U.S. Art.*

OTHER

Timeless Techniques for Better Oil Paintings, North Light Books (Cincinnati, OH), 1994.

Sidelights

A professional painter who focuses on Western and wildlife subjects, Tom Browning works in a variety of artistic media, including acrylics and oils. He is a member of several prestigious art organizations, including the Portrait Painters Society of America and Cowboy Artists of America, and his evocative paintings have been exhibited in galleries and juried shows throughout the United States. As an illustrator, Browning's work has appeared in several books for children, among them *Santa's Time Off: Poems* by Bill Maynard and *Prayers and Promises for My Little Boy* by Stormie Omartian. In an unusual picture-book offering, he also creates a fresh interpretation of a classic song popularized by the king of Rock and Roll in *Elvis Presley's Love Me Tender.*

In *Timeless Techniques for Better Oil Paintings,* which was published in 1994, Browning shares his technique, creating a valuable resource for both intermediate and advanced artists.

In *Elvis Presley's Love Me Tender* Browning revisions the popular '50s ballad as a loving ode from a parent to a child. His detailed oil paintings focus on a father and daughter as they share special times over the course of a year, from sharing storybooks and playing croquet to lessons on bike riding, ice skating, and other outdoor activities. Bound with a CD of Presley singing his song, the book serves as a "tribute of a father's love for his daughter," observed Jane Marino in *School Library Journal.* In *Publishers Weekly* a writer addressed the appropriateness of pairing a romantic love song like "Love Me Tender" with visions of a parent and child, assuring adults that "children should have no such qualms" about the book's merger of lyrics and art. "Who would have thought that the King's classic song could have made such a lovely read-aloud for children?," exclaimed a *Kirkus Reviews* writer, the critic also praising Browning's "beautifully loose and fluid brushwork" and the "sunlit colors" that appear throughout his picture book.

Biographical and Critical Sources

PERIODICALS

Kirkus Reviews, March 1, 2003, review of *Elvis Presley's Love Me Tender,* p. 396.
Publishers Weekly, April 21, 2003, review of *You Gotta Have Art,* p. 64.
School Library Journal, July, 2003, Jane Marino, review of *Elvis Presley's Love Me Tender,* p. 116; October, 2009, Anne Connor, review of *The Night before Christmas,* p. 82.

ONLINE

Tom Browning Home Page, http://tombrowning.com (December 30, 2010).*

* * *

BYRD, Robert 1942-
(Robert John Byrd)

Personal

Born January 11, 1942, in Atlantic City, NJ; son of Robert and Phoebe Byrd; married; wife's name Ginger; children: Robby, Jennifer. *Education:* Attended Trenton Junior College, 1963; Philadelphia Museum College of Art, B.F.A., 1966.

Addresses

Home—Haddonfield, NJ. *E-mail*—rbyrdart@yahoo.com.

Career

Illustrator and author. Philadelphia College of Art, Philadelphia, PA, instructor in illustrating, 1976-77; Moore College of Art, Philadelphia, instructor in illustrating, 1977—. *Exhibitions:* work included in shows for Society of Illustrators, New York, NY, 1971-77; Graphis Press, Zurich, Switzerland, 1974-77; Philadelphia Art Alliance, Philadelphia, PA, 1974; Bologna Children's Book Fair, Bologna, Italy, 1975; Rosenfeld Gallery, Philadelphia, 1982; University of the Arts, Philadelphia; and Art Institute of Chicago, Chicago, IL. Work held in permanent collections at Free Library of Philadelphia and Philadelphia College of Art. *Military service:* U.S. Navy, 1961-62.

Member

Graphic Artists Guild, Philadelphia Children's Reading Round Table, Philadelphia College of Art Alumni Association.

Awards, Honors

Children's Book Showcase, Children's Book Council, 1975, for *The Pinchpenny Mouse;* Citation of Merit, Society of Illustrators, 1976; Golden Kite Award, Society of Children's Book Writers and Illustrators, Orbis Pictus Award Honor Book designation, Norman A. Sugarman Biography Award, and Notable Social Studies Trade Books for Young People selection, National Council for the Social Studies/Children's Book Council (NCSS/CBC), all 2004, all for *Leonardo;* Newbery Medal, 2008, Notable Children's Books designation, American Library Association, Best Children's Book of the Year selection, Bank Street College of Education, Notable Children's Book selection, National Council of Teachers of English, Cooperative Children's Book Center Choices listee, Notable Social Studies Trade Books for Young People selection, NCSS/CBC, Best Books for Children and Teens selection, Chicago Public Library, Parents' Choice Gold Award, and One Hundred Titles for Reading and Sharing selection, New York Public Library, all 2007, all for *Good Masters! Sweet Ladies!* by Laura Amy Schlitz.

Writings

SELF-ILLUSTRATED

Marcella Was Bored, Dutton (New York, NY), 1985.
(Reteller) *The Bear and the Bird King,* Dutton (New York, NY), 1995.
(Reteller) *Finn MacCoul and His Fearless Wife: A Giant of a Tale from Ireland,* Dutton (New York, NY), 1999.
Saint Francis and the Christmas Donkey, Dutton (New York, NY), 2000.
Leonardo: Beautiful Dreamer, Dutton (New York, NY), 2003.

(Reteller) *The Hero and the Minotaur: The Fantastic Adventures of Theseus,* Dutton (New York, NY), 2005.

ILLUSTRATOR

Jack Stokes, adaptor, *Wiley and the Hairy Man,* Macrae Smith Co. (Philadelphia, PA),1970.

I.G. Edmonds, adaptor, *The Possible Impossibles of Ikkyu the Wise,* Macrae Smith Co. (Philadelphia, PA), 1971.

Vicki Cobb, *Heat,* F. Watts (New York, NY), 1973.

Robert Kraus, *Poor Mister Splinterfitz!,* Springfellow Books, 1973.

Ida Scheib and Carole E. Welker, *The First Book of Food,* revised edition, F. Watts (New York, NY), 1974.

Robert Kraus, The *Pinchpenny Mouse,* Windmill Books (New York, NY), 1974.

Robert Kraus, *Rebecca Hatpin,* Windmill Books (New York, NY), 1974.

Robert Kraus, *The Gondolier of Venice,* Windmill Books (New York, NY), 1976.

Robert Kraus and Bruce Kraus, *The Detective of London,* Windmill Books (New York, NY), 1978.

Susan Saunders, *Charles Rat's Picnic,* Dutton (New York, NY), 1983.

Stephanie Calmenson, selector and reteller, *The Children's Aesop,* Doubleday Book and Music Club (New York, NY), 1988.

Riki Levinson, reteller, *The Emperor's New Clothes,* Dutton Children's Books (New York, NY), 1991.

Kathleen Kain, *All about How Things Are Made: With Inspector McQ,* World Book (Chicago, IL), 1992, published as *Inspector McQ Presents All about How Things Are Made,* 1995.

Marilyn Jager Adams, *The Market,* Open Court, 1995.

Paula Fox, *The Little Swineherd and Other Tales,* Dutton (New York, NY), 1996.

Laura Amy Schlitz, *The Hero Schliemann,* Candlewick Press (Cambridge, MA), 2006.

Laura Amy Schlitz, *Good Masters! Sweet Ladies!: Voices from a Medieval Village,* Candlewick Press (Cambridge, MA), 2007.

Steven Kroll, *Barbarians!,* Dutton Children's Books (New York, NY), 2009.

Kathleen Krull, *Kubla Khan: Emperor of Everything,* Viking Children's Books (New York, NY), 2010.

Sidelights

An accomplished illustrator, Robert Byrd has created artwork for dozens of picture books, among them such highly regarded tales as and *Good Masters! Sweet Ladies!: Voices from a Medieval Village* by Laura Amy Schlitz and *Kubla Khan: Emperor of Everything* by Kathleen Krull. Byrd has also drawn praise for his narrative skills in his original, self-illustrated books, which include the award-winning *Leonardo: Beautiful Dreamer.* "The most important thing is to have the small world I create in a picture perfectly match the words of the story," Byrd stated in an essay on his home page.

Byrd penned his first solo effort, *Marcella Was Bored,* in 1985. In this humorous debut he tells the story of a cat that, bored with her usual activities, runs away from home only to discover that the sympathy and attention she receives from her family are what she really wants after all. A reviewer for *Growing Point* noted that in this telling of a familiar story, the cat stands in for the usual portrait of a dissatisfied child, and the humor created by the switch from human to cat sheds a new light on "an all too familiar family situation." *School Library Journal* contributor Lorraine Douglas dubbed Byrd's illustrations "charming" and declared: "Filled with details, these gently colored scenes are filled with activity and portray Marcella as a childlike and expressive feline."

After taking time out to illustrate books by Stephanie Calmenson and Riki Levinson, Byrd returned for his next solo effort, a retelling of the Grimm Brothers *The Bear and the Bird King.* This little-known fable highlights how easily and how foolishly wars get started. *School Library Journal* critic Linda Boyles described Byrd's successful adaptation as "an easy narrative" with "bright watercolor washes [that] are filled with humor and movement" and "complement the text." Other reviewers found the book's intricately designed illustrations equally enjoyable, noting that the author/illustrator's detailed drawings ground the story in the eighteenth century, with birds in frock coats, top hats, and bustled costumes. A reviewer for *Publishers Weekly* wrote that the "verve and humor that infuse" Byrd's retelling "are reflected and multiplied in wonderfully detailed artwork."

Byrd's picture books draw on stories and legends from history. In *Saint Francis and the Christmas Donkey* he features Byzantine-styled artwork, while his adaptation of a Celtic myth in *Finn MacCoul and His Fearless Wife: A Giant of a Tale from Ireland* draws on the stylized imagery of the story's origins. In *Finn MacCoul and His Fearless Wife* the giant Finn and his wife Oonagh possess magical powers that they use to outsmart their enemy, the bully Cucullin, whose loss of a golden finger means the end of his power. The story, filled with historical and cultural details, attracts children because of its combination of humor and suspense. Karen Morgan, writing in *Booklist,* praised Byrd for his creative partnering of text and illustration, while a *Kirkus Reviews* writer dubbed the illustrations for *Finn MacCoul and His Fearless Wife* "elegant" and praised the author's inclusion for of historical detail. Byrd's intricate watercolor renderings "spur interest" in the story's plot and also "convey a palpable sense of the Celtic past," according to the same critic.

Saint Francis and the Christmas Donkey presents what *Horn Book* contributor Mary M. Burns praised as a "loving and reverent tribute to the saint who was perhaps the first documented ecologist," and relates the story of a lowly beast's important role in the story of the Nativity, complete with what a *School Library Journal* contributor described as Byrd's "wonderfully colorful, humorous pen-and-ink pictures of a multitude of animals."

***Robert Byrd's detailed artwork brings to life his retelling of a traditional Irish story in* Finn MacCoul and His Fearless Wife.** (Illustration copyright © 1999 by Robert Byrd. All rights reserved. Used by permission of Dutton, a division of Penguin Young Readers Group, a member of Penguin Group (USA) Inc., 345 Hudson Street, New York, NY 10014.)

In his self-illustrated *The Hero and the Minotaur: The Fantastic Adventures of Theseus* Byrd offers a retelling of tales from Greek myth, interweaving the stories of Theseus, a king of Athens, with those of Icarus, Ariadne, and Heracles. According to *School Library Journal* critic Nancy Menaldi-Scanlan, "Byrd tells the tales simply and clearly, including important details and tying up all loose ends so that everything blends together seamlessly." Writing in *Booklist*, Gillian Engberg offered praise for *The Hero and the Minotaur*, noting that Byrd's "beautiful ink-and-watercolor artwork will easily draw children into the action."

Byrd also combines his interest in historic detail and his artistic talents in *Leonardo.* In "as thorough an exploration of Leonardo's achievements as can be wrought in picture-book format," according to a *Kirkus Reviews* critic, *Leonardo* tells the story of one of the most creative geniuses of the Renaissance world. Tracing Leonardo da Vinci's many accomplishments thematically rather than chronologically, Byrd is able to convey a vast amount of information yet not overwhelm young readers. In his book's layout, he copies the style of da Vinci's famous notebooks, which include sketches of futuristic flying machines and notes about perspective along with shopping lists and other miscellaneous information. Praising the author's creation of "finely detailed tableaux, brimming with content," *Horn Book* contributor Peter D. Sieruta dubbed *Leonardo* "a celebration" of its subject's "inquiring spirit and creative vision." Christine E. Carr, writing in *School Library Journal*, described the same book as "a gorgeous biography suitable for group sharing," while *New York Times Book Review* contributor Daria Donnelly maintained that *Leonardo* "exudes an energy that mimics Leonardo's own restless creativity."

Among Byrd's notable picture-book collaborations is his work for Schlitz's *The Hero Schliemann* and *Good Masters! Sweet Ladies!*, the latter which earned a Newbery medal. In *The Hero Schliemann* Schlitz presents a biography of Heinrich Schliemann, the nineteenth-century German businessman and archaeologist who discovered the actual location of the remains of the legendary city of Troy. "Byrd's wry illustrations match the breeziness of the text and add verve to the whole," a *Kirkus Reviews* contributor observed. Engberg also praised the illustrator's contributions, noting that "Byrd's detailed drawings extend the dramatic story."

Schlitz brings a late-thirteenth-century English village to life in *Good Masters! Sweet Ladies!*, a work composed of monologues and dialogues from a host of intriguing characters, including a knight's son, a mud-slinger, and an eel-catcher. In his arwork for this book, Byrd "does not channel a medieval style; rather, he mutes his palette and angles some lines to hint at the period," a contributor in *Publishers Weekly* reported, and a *Kirkus Reviews* critic similarly noted that "Byrd's watercolor-and-ink pictures add lovely texture and evoke medieval illustration without aping it."

Byrd's illustrations for Laura Amy Schlitz's **Good Masters! Sweet Ladies!** *captures the animation of Medieval life.* (Illustration copyright © 2007 by Robert Byrd. Reproduced by permission of Candlewick Press, Somerville, MA.)

In Steven Kroll's *Barbarians!*, a work of nonfiction, the author examines the history of four warlike peoples: the Goths, Huns, Vikings, and Mongols. Kroll discusses not only their famed military leaders, including Attila and Genghis Khan, but also the farming methods, trading policies, and religious practices of these cultures. Although Byrd had little reference material to draw on for his illustrations, he fills the pages of *Barbarians!* "with colorful details, energetic figures and artfully composed reconstructions of historical and mythological scenes," a contributor in *Kirkus Reviews* maintained. Carolyn Phelan, critiquing *Barbarians!* in *Booklist*, similarly noted that Byrd's "many detailed, energetic ink-and-watercolor illustrations show the barbarians at home and at war."

Krull explores the life of the thirteenth-century Mongol ruler who founded the Yuan dynasty in China in *Kubla Khan,* focusing on the political, cultural, and social aspects of the great leader's regime. "The grandiosity of his reign is well depicted in Byrd's Eastern-style artwork," Ian Chipman stated in *Booklist*. "Byrd's tapestry-like ink and watercolor illustrations reflect the broad scope of the Khan's reach," Christine M. Heppermann declared in her *School Library Journal* review of Krull's book.

Byrd once told *SATA:* "To me, illustrating means making pictures. That is all I really ever wanted to do with my ability. I always drew as a child, but oddly enough never thought of it as a profession, or what you did when you grew up.

"I could always draw, but I never took art courses in high school. After a stint in the Navy I went to Trenton

Junior College for a year, trying to 'find myself' academically and otherwise. I did well in the art courses and switched to the Philadelphia Museum School of Art. I wanted to be an illustrator from the very beginning of my studies there.

"Out of all my creative work, illustrating children's books gives me the greatest satisfaction. It is my 'fine art.' It keeps me going aesthetically. The books have permanence and a quality of something meaningful."

Biographical and Critical Sources

PERIODICALS

Booklist, January 1, 1999, Karen Morgan, review of *Finn MacCoul and His Fearless Wife: A Giant of a Tale from Ireland;* July, 2005, Gillian Engberg, review of *The Hero and the Minotaur: The Fantastic Adventures of Theseus,* p. 1928; June 1, 2006, Gillian Engberg, review of *The Hero Schliemann: The Dreamer Who Dug for Troy,* p. 100; August, 2007, Carolyn Phelan, review of *Good Masters! Sweet Ladies!: Voices from a Medieval Village,* p. 69; May 1, 2009, Carolyn Phelan, review of *Barbarians!,* p. 76; July 1, 2010, Ian Chipman, review of *Kubla Khan: The Emperor of Everything,* p. 54.

Growing Point, May, 1987, review of *Marcella Was Bored,* p. 4806.

Horn Book, November, 2000, Mary M. Burns, review of *Saint Francis and the Christmas Donkey,* p. 744; September-October, 2003, Peter D. Sieruta, review of *Leonardo: Beautiful Dreamer,* p. 625; July-August, 2006, Kathleen Isaacs, review of *The Hero Schliemann,* p. 469; November-December, 2007, Deirdre F. Baker, review of *Good Masters! Sweet Ladies,* p. 699; November-December, 2010, Christine M. Heppermann, *Kubla Khan,* p. 115.

Kirkus Reviews, January 1, 1994, p. 67; December 15, 1998, review of *Finn MacCoul and His Fearless Wife;* June 15, 2003, review of *Leonardo,* p. 857; June 15, 2005, review of *The Hero and the Minotaur,* p. 678; July 15, 2006, review of *The Hero Schliemann,* p. 730; July 15, 2007, review of *Good Masters! Sweet Ladies!;* June 1, 2009, review of *Barbarians!*

New York Times Book Review, November 16, 2003, Daria Donnelly, review of *Leonardo,* p. 20; December 16, 2007, John Schwartz, review of *Good Masters! Sweet Ladies!,* p. 21.

Publishers Weekly, December 13, 1993, review of *The Bear and the Bird King,* p. 69; September 25, 2000, Elizabeth Devereaux, review of *Saint Francis and the Christmas Donkey,* p. 69; August 27, 2007, review of *Good Masters! Sweet Ladies!,* p. 90.

School Library Journal, January, 1986, Lorraine Douglas, review of *Marcella Was Bored,* p. 55; May, 1994, Linda Boyles, review of *The Bear and the Bird King,* p. 108; October, 2000, review of *Saint Francis and the Christmas Donkey,* p. 57; September, 2003, Christine E. Carr, review of *Leonardo,* p. 227; August, 2005, Nancy Menaldi-Scanlan, review of *The Hero and the Minotaur,* p. 112; September, 2006, Rita Soltan, review of *The Hero Schliemann,* p. 236; August, 2007, Alana Abbott, review of *Good Masters! Sweet Ladies!,* p. 138; August, 2009, Lucinda Snyder Whitehurst, review of *Barbarians!,* p. 123; October, 2010, Barbara Scotto, review of *Kubla Khan,* p. 100.

ONLINE

Robert Byrd Home Page, http://www.robertbyrdart.com (February 15, 2011).*

*   *   *

BYRD, Robert John
See BYRD, Robert

C

CASTRO L., Antonio 1941-
(Antonio Castro Lopez)

Personal

Born 1941, in Zacatecas, Mexico; married; children: Antonio.

Addresses

Home—Juarez-El Paso metropolitan area.

Career

Illustrator and muralist. *Exhibitions:* Work exhibited at galleries and museums in Mexico City and Oaxaca, Mexico, as well as in Texas, Spain, and Italy. Commissioned mural installation in government palace in State of Chihuahua, Mexico.

Awards, Honors

Independent Publishers IPPY Award for Best Children's Book, and Aesop Accolade selection, both 2002, both for *Pájaro verde* by Joe Hayes; Southwest Book Award, Texas Institute of Letters Children's Book Award finalist, and Paterson Poetry Center Children's Book Award, all 2004, all for *The Treasure on Gold Street* by Lee Merrill Byrd; *Storytelling World* Resource Award Young Listeners Honor Book award, 2011, for *The Gum-chewing Rattler* by Joe Hayes.

Illustrator

Bea Bragg, *The Very First Thanksgiving: Pioneers on the Rio Grande,* Harbinger House (Tucson, AZ), 1989.

Candice M. DeBarr and Jack A. Bonkowske, *Saga of the American Flag: An Illustrated History,* Harbinger House (Tucson, AZ), 1990.

Katherine S. Talmadge, *The Life of Charles Drew,* Twenty-first Century Books (Frederick, MD), 1992.

Julie Fromer, *Jane Goodall, Living with the Chimps,* Twenty-first Century Books (Frederick, MD), 1992.

Lynn Hall, *Barry, the Bravest Saint Bernard,* Random House (New York, NY), 1992.

Marcia Newfield, *The Life of Louis Pasteur,* Twenty-first Century Books (Frederick, MD), 1992.

Elizabeth Schleichert, *The Life of Dorthea Dix,* Twenty-first Century Books (Frederick, MD), 1992.

Elizabeth Schleichert, *The Life of Elizabeth Blackwell,* Twenty-first Century Books (Frederick, MD), 1992.

Jennifer Bryant, *Margaret Murie: A Wilderness Life,* Twenty-first Century Books (Frederick, MD), 1993.

Debby Anker and John de Graaf, *David Brower: Friend of the Earth,* Twenty-first Century Books (Frederick, MD), 1993.

Katherine S. Talmadge, *John Muir: At Home in the Wild,* Twenty-first Century Books (Frederick, MD), 1993.

Susan DeStefano, *Theodore Roosevelt, Conservation President,* Twenty-first Century Books (Frederick, MD), 1993.

Julie Dunlap, *Aldo Leopold: Living with the Land,* Twenty-first Century Books (Frederick, MD), 1993.

Joe Hayes, *Pájaro verde/The Green Bird,* Cinco Puntos Press (El Paso, TX), 2002.

Lee Merrill Byrd, *The Treasure on Gold Street/El tesoro en la calle Oro,* Cinco Puntos Press (El Paso, TX), 2003.

Joe Hayes, reteller, *The Day It Snowed Tortillas/El día que nevaron tortillas,* Cinco Puntos Press (El Paso, TX), 2003.

Joe Hayes, *The Gum-chewing Rattler,* Cinco Puntos Press (El Paso, TX), 2006.

Arna Bontemps and Langston Hughes, *Boy of the Border,* Sweet Earth Flying Press (El Paso, TX), 2009.

Joe Hayes, *The Love-sick Skunk,* Cinco Puntos Press (El Paso, TX), 2010.

Sidelights

Antonio Castro L. is a Mexican-born artist whose detailed pencil and water-color illustrations have appeared in numerous books for young children, among them Katherine S. Talmadge's biography *John Muir: At Home in the Wild,* Lynn Hall's *Barry, the Bravest Saint Bernard,* Lee Merrill Byrd's *The Treasure on Gold Street/El*

Antonio Castro L. created the detailed art that captures the tall-tale themes in storyteller Joe Hayes' **The Gum-chewing Rattler.** (Cinco Puntos Press, 2006.
Illustration copyright © 2006 by Antonio Castro L. Reproduced by permission.)

tesoro en la calle Oro, and *The Gum-chewing Rattler* and *Pájaro verde/The Green Bird,* two books by southwestern storyteller Joe Hayes. Castro L.'s work as a fine artist has been exhibited in both Mexico and the United States, as well as in galleries in Spain and Italy. In 2005, he completed a commission for the government of the Mexican State of Chihuahua: a mural for the state palace that commemorates the 1892 Battle of Tomochic, which was ended in the destruction of the village that bears its name and also helped to ignite the Mexican Revolution.

Praising Castro L.'s work on *The Treasure on Gold Street,* an award-winning story about a child's loving relationship with a mentally challenged woman, a *Kirkus Reviews* writer called the book's illustrations "a fascinating combination of the vivid portraiture of Castro L. laid upon . . . cheery, Sunday-comics-style backgrounds." Working with Hayes, a professional storyteller who is known for his original tall tales, on *Pájaro verde,* he also created illustrations with almost photographic detail. In Hayes' fanciful story, Mirabel is one sister in a family of nine. After she accepts a proposal of marriage from a green bird, her sisters and mother make fun of the girl. Mirabel's strange choice proves to be a good one, however, when the bird reveals itself to be something other than what it seems in a story that contains such classic fairy-tale elements as a vengeful mother, an amazing transformation, and a long and difficult journey. "The illustrations are large, detailed, and imaginative," wrote *School Library Journal* critic Ann Welton, while in *Booklist* Hazel Rochman cited Castro L. for contributing "lush, romantic paintings that are both realistic and magical" to Hayes' "great read-aloud."

Another story by Hayes, *The Gum-chewing Rattler,* features a modern-day story that is based on the author's childhood in Arizona. In his double-page spreads, the illustrator uses "varying perspectives" to "depict the exaggerations of this tall tale perfectly," according to Judith Constantinides in *School Library Journal,* and a *Kirkus Reviews* contributor wrote that Castro L.'s "warmly humorous, photographically exact scenes" capture the humorous drama of the contemporary tall tale. "An upbeat and playful story," *The Gum-chewing Rattler* is "perfectly accentuated by the wry yet realistic art," concluded a critic for *Children's Bookwatch.*

Biographical and Critical Sources

PERIODICALS

Booklinks, January-February, 2006, Margaret Read MacDonald, review of *Pájaro verde/The Green Bird,* p. 57.

Booklist, October 15, 2002, Hazel Rochman, review of *Pájaro verde,* p. 408.

Childhood Education (annual), 2007, Ursula Adams, review of *The Gum-chewing Rattler,* p. 326.

Children's Bookwatch, February, 2007, review of *The Gum-chewing Rattler.*

Kirkus Reviews, November 1, 2003, review of *The Treasure on Gold Street/El tesoro en la calle Oro,* p. 1309; November 15, 2006, review of *The Gum-chewing Rattler,* p. 1174.

School Library Journal, November, 2002, Ann Welton, review of *Pájaro verde,* p. 152; December, 2003, Ann Welton, review of *The Treasure on Gold Street,* p. 142; April, 2004, Ann Welton, review of *The Day It Snowed Tortillas/El día que nevaron tortillas,* p. 146; January, 2007, Judith Constantinides, review of *The Gum-chewing Rattler,* p. 97; October, 2009, Kathleen Isaacs, review of *Boy of the Border,* p. 120.

ONLINE

Cinco Puntos Press Web site, http://www.cincopuntos.com/ (February 15, 2011), "Antonio Castro Lopez."*

* * *

CHANG, Grace 1961-
(Grace Chang Venner)

Personal

Born 1961, in Beijing, China; daughter of Chang Bao Ting (a radio and stage performer); married children: a son. *Hobbies and other interests:* Bicycling.

Addresses

Home—Brooklyn, NY. *E-mail*—gracechangdiscovery@yahoo.com.

Career

Storyteller, performer, and author. Circus entertainer and illusionist in China; actress in films, including *The Joy Luck Club.* Adoptions from the Heart (philanthropic organization), adoption agent and director of China program. Presenter at school.

Awards, Honors

Pioneer award, 2007, for work with Chinese-American adoptions.

Writings

Jin Jin the Dragon, illustrated by Chong Chang, Enchanted Lion Books (Brooklyn, NY), 2007.

Jin Jin and Rain Wizard, illustrated by Chong Chang, Enchanted Lion Books (Brooklyn, NY), 2009.

Biographical and Critical Sources

PERIODICALS

Children's Bookwatch, March, 2008, review of *Jin Jin the Dragon.*

Kirkus Reviews, September 1, 2009, review of *Jin Jin and Rain Wizard.*

School Library Journal, July, 2008, Grace Oliff, review of *Jin Jin the Dragon,* p. 67; December, 2009, Margaret A. Chang, review of *Jin Jin and Rain Wizard,* p. 78.

ONLINE

Authors and Illustrators Who Visit Schools Web site, http://www.authorsillustrators.com/ (February 15, 2011), "Grace Chang."

Grace Chang Home Page, http://www.changimagination.com (February 15, 2011).*

* * *

CHIMA, Cinda Williams

Personal

Married; husband a scientist; children: Eric, Keith. *Education:* University of Akron, B.A. (philosophy); Case Western Reserve University, M.A. (nutrition). *Hobbies and other interests:* Cooking, hand weaving and spinning.

Addresses

Home and office—Cleveland, OH. *Agent*—Christopher Schelling, Ralph M. Vicinanza, Ltd., 303 W. 18th St., New York, NY 10011. *E-mail*—cinda@cindachima.com.

Career

Author of fantasy fiction. Formerly worked as an advertising copy typist; professional dietician; University of Akron, Akron, OH, assistant professor. Presenter at schools and workshops; speaker at writers' conferences.

Member

Society of Children's Book Writers and Illustrators, Science Fiction and Fantasy Writers of America, The Lit—Cleveland.

Awards, Honors

Booksense Summer Reading Pick, American Library Association (ALA) Popular Paperbacks listee, and Great Lakes Book Award finalist, all 2006, and South Carolina Young Adult Book Award nominee, Abe Award nominee (IL), Garden State Teen Book Award nominee (NJ), and Isinglass Teen Book Award nominee (NH), all 2009, all for *The Warrior Heir;* Cleveland Lit Award for Fiction, and New York Public Library Books for the Teen Age designation, both 2008, both for *The Wizard Heir; Voice of Youth Advocates* Best Science-Fiction, Fantasy, and Horror selection, 2008, for *The Dragon Heir,* 2009, for *The Demon King;* ALA Best Fiction for Young Adults selection, 2009, and Volunteer State Book Award nomination, and South Carolina Book Award nomination in Junior Books category, both 2011, all for *The Demon King.*

Writings

"HEIR" FANTASY NOVEL SERIES

The Warrior Heir, Hyperion Books for Children (New York, NY), 2006.

The Wizard Heir, Hyperion Books for Children (New York, NY), 2006.

The Dragon Heir, Hyperion Books for Children (New York, NY), 2008.

"SEVEN-REALMS" FANTASY NOVEL SERIES

The Demon King, Disney/Hyperion Books (New York, NY), 2009.

The Exiled Queen, DisneyHyperion (New York, NY), 2010.

The Gray Wolf Throne, Disney/Hyperion Books (New York, NY), 2011.

OTHER

Contributor to books, including *A Cup of Comfort for Christmas,* edited by Coleen Sell, Adams Media (Avon, MA), 2003; *A Cup of Comfort for Courage,* edited by Sell, Adams Media, 2004; *The World of the Golden Compass: The Otherworldly Ride Continues,* edited by Scott Westerfeld, BenBella Books, 2007; *Flirtin' with the Monster,* edited by Ellen Hopkins, 2009; and *The Way of the Wizard,* edited by JohnJoseph Adams, Prime Books, 2010. Contributor of nutrition column to Cleveland, OH, *Plain Dealer,* 2004-07.

Adaptations

Audiobook adaptations of Chima's novels include *The Wizard Heir,* Recorded Books, 2008, *The Dragon Heir,* Recorded Books, 2009, *The Demon King,* Recorded Books, 2010, and *The Exiled Queen,* Recorded Books, 2011.

Sidelights

Although trained as a nutritionist, Ohio resident Cinda Williams Chima has channeled her curiosity and her many interests into a second career as a fantasy novelist. In addition to her three-volume "Heir" series, which includes *The Warrior Heir, The Wizard Heir,* and *The Dragon Heir,* Chima treats fans to another saga of wizards, warriors, powerful talismans, and compelling heroes in her "Seven Realms" novel sequence. Chima "is adept with teen culture" wrote a reviewer for the Cleveland, Ohio, *Plain Dealer,* and her efforts to reference both "slasher-film references" and "the works of Shakespeare" in her fantasy novels "strengthens both her narrative voice and . . . adds subtly to the moral subtext" of her fiction.

"I've spent a lot of time prowling through graveyards and digging through dusty old records, uncovering family stories," Chima explained to *Cynsations* online interviewer Cynthia Leitich Smith. "My roots are in the Appalachians of southern Ohio, and there's a strong history of magic there. My grandmother was supposed to have had the 'second sight'—she read the cards for people. When I was in college, I took an English literature tour to England: went to Stratford and the Lake District and the theatres in London. I incorporated elements of all of those things into [my fantasy novel] *The Warrior Heir,* and its sequel, *The Wizard Heir.*"

In *The Warrior Heir* Chima takes readers to Ohio, where high-school student Jack Swift lives in a small Midwestern town. When the teen neglects to take the medicine he has been given since he can remember, the magic within him is exposed. Now a group of wizards recognizes Jack as a Warrior Heir, a rare being capable of helping a wizard amass power and gain supremacy above all others by fighting to the death in tournaments designed to allocate such power within the secret wizard community known as Weirland. Now Jack's friends and relatives are revealed to be equally magical creatures—enchantresses, soothsayers, wizards, enchanters, and the like—and they help the teen gain the fighting and magical skills that will help him meet his destiny. Noting that Jack's maturation is well portrayed in *The Warrior Heir, Kliatt* contributor Michele Winship added that Chima "cleverly entwines ancient magic and contemporary adolescence in a coming-of-age story that works on both levels." Because "many details about the Weir are initially hidden from readers," the author is able to reveal her story's intricacies in a way that is "involving and often surprising," observed *School Library Journal* reviewer Steven Engelfried, the critic dubbing Chima's first novel "suspenseful and entertaining."

In *The Wizard Heir* Chima turns her focus to a teen wizard-in-training as he attempts to take control of his growing magical powers. Orphaned as an infant, Seph McCauley is sixteen years old when the sorcerer who has guarded him from the world of magic dies. Now alone, Seph is increasingly frightened by his growing power, power that proves destructive and even deadly because of his inability to control it. After causing a destructive fire, Seph is sent to a school for troubled teens located in a remote area of Maine, and there he comes under the tutelage of the school's wizard headmaster. However, Seph soon begins to question his mentor's motives, and when he encounters several other powerful creatures, including Warrior Heir Jack Swift, he realizes that the powers he possesses may also lead to his demise.

In *School Library Journal* Sharon Rawlings observed of *The Wizard Heir* that Chima's "exciting page-turner is darker than *The Warrior Heir* due to the introduction of several violent characters." A *Kirkus Reviews* contributor had a similar reaction to the novel, concluding that the fantasy "sequel improves on the original, leaving fans eager for the foreshadowed resolution." In *Booklist* Krista Hutley called Seph an "appealing" and resourceful protagonist and deemed *The Wizard Heir* an "absorbing, suspenseful" installment in Chima's Weirland saga.

Seph's story continues in *The Dragon Heir,* in which the power struggle among the wizard houses forces many to seek sanctuary in Jack's hometown of Trinity, where he and his friends will provide protection. Meanwhile, the search for a magical opal called the Dragonheart forces Seph and Jack, as well as several powerful friends, into a battle with those who would usurp all power. Chima's "finely structured tale . . . roars to a satisfying conclusion," wrote Sue Giffard in her *School Library Journal* review of *The Dragon Heir,* and a *Kirkus Reviews* writer noted that "centuries of wizardly scheming, slavery and slaughter reap apocalyptic fallout" in the author's "superlative" story.

Chima's first "Seven Realms" novel, *The Demon King,* draws readers into a new fantasy that is set in another mythical world. Sixteen-year-old Han Alister has left his life as a street tough in the city of Felsmarch, and now he prefers to escape into the mountains with his friend Fire Dancer. When they meet three young wizards bent on destruction, Han confiscates a magic amulet from one of them. Only later, he learns that the amulet was once the property of the evil and destructive Demon King. Meanwhile, Princess Raisa, the fifteen-

Cover of Cinda Williams Chima's fantasy novel The Demon King, *part of her "Seven Realms" series.* (Copyright © 2009 by Cinda Chima. Reproduced by permission of Hyperion, an imprint of Disney Book Group.)

year-old daughter of the queen of the Grey Wolf clan, is forced to return to court and an arranged marriage, although she would rather be out among her clanfolk, who are suffering hardships. Although war and rebellion threaten, the queen is preoccupied by the advances of power-hungry High Wizard Gavan Bayar, leaving the Grey Wolf clan in need of a new leader, a warrior queen like the legendary Hanalea who killed the Demon King.

The adventures of Han and Raisa continue in *The Exiled Queen,* as Han works to evade the relentless Bayar family while also gaining the skills to ultimately fight their magical power. Joining Fire Dancer, he travels south to Oden's Ford, where a bargain with the mystical Crow builds his talent for wizardry. For Raisa, disguised as a gentlewoman and traveling with a friend, Oden's Ford also provides knowledge, as well as safety. The teens' paths cross when Raisa becomes Han's tutor, although her identity must remain secret as she prepares for her future as a Gray Wolf queen.

"Chima shows a sure hand with details and history, and readers will be drawn into the lives" of her teen protagonists, predicted Beth Meister in her *School Library Journal* review of *The Demon King.* A *Kirkus Reviews* writer cited the "rich characterization and exquisite world building" of the "Seven Realms" series opener, adding that its pantheon of characters, "complex and distinct in personality, are placed with jewel-like precision, [and] set off by dark glints of villainy." "Whether reveling in . . . fairy-tale-romance . . . , or inventing a complex clan culture, Chima delivers a high-interest, high-action story" in *The Demon King,* wrote *Horn Book* contributor Anita L. Burkam, and a *Publishers Weekly* contributor cited the novel's "elegant prose" and the "complex and comprehensible world" that Chima establishes in her "Seven Realms" series.

Biographical and Critical Sources

PERIODICALS

Booklist, April 1, 2006, Holly Koelling, review of *The Warrior Heir,* p. 31; May 15, 2007, Krista Hutley, review of *The Wizard Heir,* p. 59; May 15, 2010, Mary Burkey, review of *The Demon King,* p. 58.

Horn Book, January-February, 2010, Anita L. Burkam, review of *The Demon King,* p. 83.

Kirkus Reviews, April 1, 2006, review of *The Warrior Heir,* p. 344; May 15, 2007, review of *The Wizard Heir.*

Kliatt, March, 2006, Michele Winship, review of *The Warrior Heir,* p. 8; July 15, 2008, review of *The Dragon Heir;* September 15, 2009, review of *The Demon King.*

Plain Dealer (Cleveland, OH), August 10, 2008, review of *The Dragon Heir.*

Publishers Weekly, September 28, 2009, review of *The Demon King,* p. 65.

School Library Journal, July, 2006, Steven Engelfried, review of *The Warrior Heir,* p. 98; December, 2006, Heather Dieffenbach, review of *The Warrior Heir,* p. 73; December, 2007, Sharon Rawlins, review of *The Wizard Heir,* p. 120; October, 2008, Sue Giffard, review of *The Dragon Heir,* p. 140; April, 2009, Jo-Ann Carhart, review of *The Wizard Heir,* p. 62; November, 2009, Cynde Suite, review of *The Dragon Heir,* p. 59; December, 2009, Beth L. Meister, review of *The Demon King,* p. 108.

Voice of Youth Advocates, June, 2007, Melissa Moore, review of *The Wizard Heir,* p. 157; October, 2008, Melissa Moore, review of *The Dragon Heir,* p. 347; October, 2009, Melissa Moore, review of *The Demon King,* p. 328.

ONLINE

Cinda Williams Chima Home Page, http://www.cindachima.com (February 15, 2011).

Cinda Williams Chima Web log, http://cindachima.blogspot.com (February 15, 2011).

Cynsations Web site, http://cynthialeitichsmith.blogspot.com/ (September 26, 2006), Cynthia Leitich Smith, interview with Chima.

* * *

CLELAND, Janet

Personal

Female. *Education:* University of Texas at Austin, B.F.A. *Hobbies and other interests:* Singing and performing with women's chorus, photography, hiking.

Janet Cleland (Reproduced by permission.)

Addresses

Home—San Anselmo, CA. *E-mail*—janet@janetcleland.com.

Career

Illustrator. Clients include Hallmark Cards, J.P. Morgan, AT& T, Purina, Public Heath Institute, Putnam Penguin, and Public Broadcast System (PBS).

Illustrator

Dean Koontz, *Christmas Is Good!: Trixie Treats and Holiday Wisdom,* Yorkville Press (New York, NY), 2005.
Dean Koontz, *I, Trixie, Who Is Dog,* G.P. Putnam's Sons (New York, NY), 2009.
Dean Koontz, *Trixie and Jinx,* G.P. Putnam's Sons (New York, NY), 2010.

Sidelights

After graduating from the University of Texas, Janet Cleland spent three years as an artist for Hallmark Cards in Kansas City, Missouri, before moving to the San Francisco Bay Area to start her own illustration business. Cleland's whimsical illustrations have been commissioned for both editorial and advertising work including an advertising campaign to promote public funding of Public Television's Boston affiliate WGBH. In addition, her work has appeared on numerous greeting cards, calendars, puzzles and other merchandising products. Cleland's artwork has also been introduced to young readers in the pages of a series of picture books written by popular thriller author Dean Koontz that include *Christmas Is Good!: Trixie Treats and Holiday Wisdom, I, Trixie, Who Is Dog,* and *Trixie and Jinx.*

Hints for a perfect doggie Christmas are shared by Koontz and Trixie in *Christmas Is Good,* which pairs Cleland's loosely drawn art with photographs of the actual Trixie, an elderly golden retriever. Although Koontz's beloved pet eventually passed away, he has also honored her memory in *I, Trixie, Who Is Dog* and *Trixie and Jinx.* In the first story, Trixie explains that only the especially fortunate are destined to be born as dogs; unlucky are the cats, birds, and humans. The humorous doggie narrative that details the bliss of living as a canine continues in *Trixie and Jinx,* which finds Trixie lonely when best friend Jinx the dachshund is taken away on his human family's vacation. Her search for a new companion is captured in Cleland's amusing

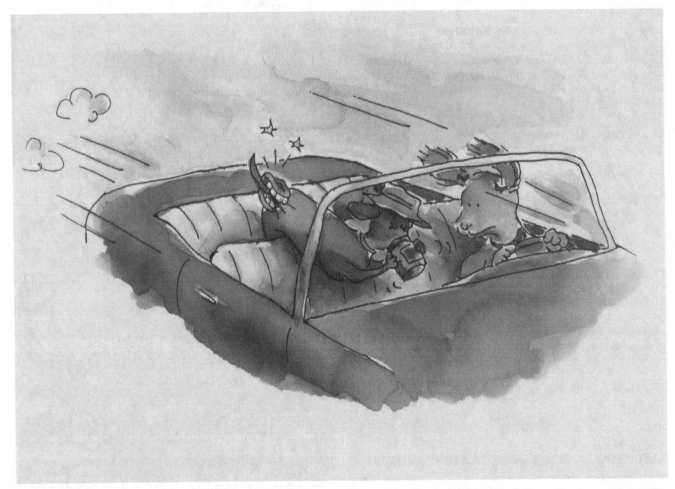

Cleland helps thriller writer Dean Koontz tell a story based on the antics of his own beloved pet in **I, Trixie, Who Is Dog.** (Illustration copyright © 2009 by Janet Cleland. All rights reserved. Used by permission of G.P. Putnam's Sons, a division of Penguin Young Readers Group, a member of Penguin Group (USA) Inc., 345 Hudson Street, New York, NY 10014. In the U.K. and British Commonwealth by Broadthink.)

pen-and-ink and water-color art, which "mixes full-bleed spreads and single pages with spot art to add interest and movement," according to *School Library Journal* contributor Amy Lilien-Harper. "Cleland's watercolor and pen-and-ink spreads lend cheerful color to the vignettes" in *I, Trixie, Who Is Dog,* commended Meg Smith in *School Library Journal,* and a *Kirkus Reviews* writer noted that her illustrations for Koontz's "canine fantasy" "are filled with hilarious details."

Biographical and Critical Sources

PERIODICALS

Bulletin of the Center for Children's Books, October, 2009, Deborah Stevenson, review of *I, Trixie, Who Is Dog,* p. 70.
Children's Bookwatch, January, 2010, Putnam/Philomel, review of *I, Trixie, Who Is Dog.*
Kirkus Reviews, September 1, 2009, review of *I, Trixie, Who Is Dog.*
School Library Journal, April, 2010, Meg Smith, review of *I, Trixie, Who Is Dog,* p. 132; November, 2010, Amy Lilien-Harper, review of *Trixie and Jinx,* p. 74.

ONLINE

Janet Cleland Home Page, http://janetcleland.com (February 15, 2011).
Ispot Web site, http://www.stock-illustration-portfolios.com/ (February 15, 2011).

*   *   *

COLATO LAÍNEZ, René 1970-

Personal

Born May 23, 1970, in San Salvador, El Salvador; son of Fidel Colato and Juana Laínez. *Ethnicity:* "Latino-Hispanic-Salvadoran-American." *Education:* California State University Northridge, B.A. and teaching credential, 1993; Vermont College of Fine Arts, M.F.A. (writing for children and young adults), 2005.

Addresses

Home—Sun Valley, CA. *Agent*—Stefanie Von Borstel, Full Circle Literary, 7676 Hazard Center Dr., Ste. 500, San Diego, CA 92108; stefanie@fullcircleliterary.com. *E-mail*—rcolato@earthlink.net.

Career

Educator and author. Fernangeles Elementary School, Sun Valley, CA, bilingual teacher, 1993—.

Member

Authors Guild, Society of Children's Book Writers and Illustrators, U.S. Board on Books for Young People, California Association for Bilingual Education, California Readers, Children's Literature Council of Southern California.

Awards, Honors

Orgullo Salvadoreño Honor designation, El Salvador Consulate Texas, and Southwest Books of the Year selection, both 2005, Tejas Star Book Award finalist, 2007-08, and Best Children's Book designation, New Mexico Book Award, 2008, all for *Playing Lotería/El juego de la lotería;* special recognition, Los Angeles Unified School District, 2006; Best Bilingual Picture Book selection, International Latino Book Award, and special recognition, Paterson Prize for Books for Young People, both 2006, and Tejas Star Book Award finalist, 2008-09, all for *I Am René, the Boy/Soy René, el niño;* honorable mention, International Latino Book Award, and Américas Book Award commended title, both 2010, and Tejas Star Book Award finalist, 2010-11, all for *René Has Two Last Names/René tiene dos apellidos.*

Writings

FOR CHILDREN

Waiting for Papá/Esperando a Papá, illustrated by Anthony Accardo, Arte Público Press (Houston, TX), 2004.
Playing Lotería/El juego de la lotería, illustrated by Jill Arena, Luna Rising (Flagstaff, AZ), 2005.
I Am René, the Boy/Soy René, el niño, illustrated by Fabiola Graullera Ramírez, Arte Público Press (Houston, TX), 2005.
René Has Two Last Names/René tiene dos apellidos, illustrated by Fabiola Graullera Ramírez, Piñata Books (Houston, TX), 2009.
My Shoes and I, illustrated by Fabricio Vanden Broeck, Boyds Mills Press (Honesdale, PA), 2010.
The Tooth Fairy Meets El Ratón Pérez, illustrated by Tom Lintern, Tricycle Press (Berkeley, CA), 2010.
From North to South/Del norte al sur, illustrated by Joe Cepeda, Children's Book Press (San Francisco, CA), 2010.

Contributor of poems and articles to children's magazine *Revista Iguana.* Columnist for Web logs *Labloga* and *Los Bloguitos.*

Sidelights

A native of El Salvador, writer and educator René Colato Laínez is the author of several bilingual picture books, including *I Am René, the Boy/Soy René, el niño,* winner of the International Latino Book Award. "I write from my own personal experiences, which seem to mirror those of many immigrant children in the United States," Colato Laínez remarked to Aline Pereira in a *PaperTigers.org* interview. "Identity issues, separation from a loved one, fear of speaking/learning a new language, embarrassment of speaking their native language in their new country: these are all problems that immigrant children deal with all the time. I write from my heart, and always try to send a message of hope to my readers."

René Colato Laínez's bilingual and family-themed story in **René Has Two Last Names** *features artwork by Fabiola Graullera Ramírez.* (Arte Público Press—University of Houston. Illustration copyright © 2009 by Fabiola Graullera Ramírez. Reprinted with permission from the publisher.)

Colato Laínez's debut title, *Waiting for Papá/Esperando a Papá,* centers on the long-distance relationship between a young boy and his father. While living in the United States with his mother, eight-year-old Beto writes a stirring tribute to his Papá, who remains in El Salvador. When Beto's letter is read on the radio, it jumpstarts a school fundraiser to purchase a much-needed gift for Beto's father. "Laínez's child-centered words make the concept of refugees more approachable and sympathetic," a critic in *Kirkus Reviews* remarked, and Ann Welton similarly noted in *School Library Journal* that the work "offers a sound introduction to the many issues surrounding immigration and its impact on families."

In *Playing Lotería/El juego de la lotería,* another of Laínez's original self-illustrated stories, an American youngster bonds with his Mexican grandmother while playing lotería, a form of bingo. "This is a warm and reassuring story of a boy's involvement not only with his family but also his culture," Welton commented.

A semi-autobiographical tale, *I Am René, the Boy/Soy René, el niño* concerns a Salvadoran immigrant who discovers, somewhat embarrassingly, that his first name is pronounced the same as that of a female classmate. According to Welton, Colato Laínez's story "will prompt discussion and empathy for students struggling with language acquisition and cultural change." In a companion volume, *René Has Two Last Names/René tiene dos apellidos,* a youngster completes a family tree to explain his heritage to his disapproving schoolmates. A contributor in *Kirkus Reviews* praised the author's "sincere, earnest voice" and described the tale as an "easily understood example of cultural differences."

Another work based on the author's childhood experiences, *My Shoes and I,* describes a boy's difficult journey from El Salvador to the United States. "This inspiring tale soars with real emotions, even as it celebrates the resiliency of children," Marilyn Taniguchi maintained in *School Library Journal.* In a lighter vein, *The Tooth Fairy meets El Ratón Pérez* focuses on a confrontation between the Tooth Fairy and her Latin-American counterpart, a brash rodent. Laínez's story introduces the "topic of cultural identity with humor and grace," in the words of a *Publishers Weekly* critic.

Colato Laínez once told *SATA:* "I was born in El Salvador. When I was a boy, every Saturday my mom and I went to her uncle's house to wash his clothes. It was in this house, the house of Jorge Buenaventura Laínez, where I learned the word 'escritor' (writer). My mom's uncle was a famous writer whose poetry and prose is popular in Central America. I wanted to be like him. He is still my inspiration.

"I have been writing all my life. As a child I wrote about my toys and school. As I grew older, El Salvador was involved in a civil war. My father and I had to leave the country and come to the United States. We had hard times on our way to Mexico City. My father lost all his money. He had to work to get more money and I was left alone in an old trailer that became our home. In that old trailer, I wrote and wrote in notebooks about my dreams, desires, adventures, etc. It was there that I realized that I could be a writer. Four months later, we reached the city of Los Angeles.

"In Los Angeles High School, my Spanish teacher read one of my short stories and invited me to participate in the Spanish-language school newspaper *La Voz Estudiantil* ('The Student's Voice'). My articles and poems were published for three years. During high school and college, I wrote seven novels for adults, intending them for my friends and relatives.

"While earning a bachelor's degree in liberal studies from California State University Northridge, I read my short story 'Lágrima de sangre' ('Blood Tears') to a group of theatre students. One of the students approached me after my reading and told me that she had been looking for a story to perform for high-school students, and that mine was perfect. It was a great sensation to watch my own story on stage. Later on, another group of college students performed my story 'Black Sheep among White Lambs.'

"I have been a teacher for many years in a bilingual classroom at Fernangeles Elementary School. I have written many books for my students. Children at school know me as 'the teacher full of stories/el maestro lleno de cuentos.'

"My goal as a writer is to write good multicultural children's literature. Stories where minority children are represented in a positive way. Stories where they can see themselves as heroes. Stories where children can dream and have hopes for the future. I want to show readers authentic stories of Latin-American children living in the United States."

Biographical and Critical Sources

PERIODICALS

Booklist, February 1, 2010, Linda Perkins, review of *My Shoes and I,* p. 46.

Kirkus Reviews, November 15, 2004, review of *Waiting for Papá/Esperando a Papá,* p. 1091; April 15, 2005, review of *I Am René, the Boy/Soy René, el niño,* p. 476; October 1, 2009, review of *René Has Two Last Names/René tiene dos apellidos;* February 15, 2010, review of *The Tooth Fairy Meets El Ratón Pérez.*

Publishers Weekly, March 15, 2010, "Cultural Explorations," review of *The Tooth Fairy Meets El Ratón Pérez,* p. 52.

School Library Journal, January, 2005, Ann Welton, review of *Waiting for Papá,* p. 120; May, 2005, Ann Welton, review of *I Am René, the Boy,* p. 118; October, 2005, Ann Welton, review of *Playing Lotería/El juego de la lotería,* p. 148; October, 2009, Diana Borrego Martinez, review of *René Has Two Last Names,* p. 116; March, 2010, Marilyn Taniguchi, review of *My Shoes and I,* p. 122, and Mary Landrum, review of *The Tooth Fairy Meets El Ratón Pérez,* p. 124.

ONLINE

California Readers Web site, http://californiareaders.org/interviews/ (February 15, 2011), Bonnie O'Brian, "Meet René Colato Laínez."

Criticas Online, http://www.criticasmagazine.com/ (March 1, 2007), interview with Colato Laínez.

PaperTigers.org, http://www.papertigers.org/ (September, 2006), Aline Pereira, interview with Colato Laínez.

René Colato Laínez Home Page, http://www.renecolatolainez.com (February 15, 2011).*

*   *   *

COMBRES, Élisabeth 1967-

Personal

Born 1967, in France. *Education:* Earned college degree.

Addresses

Home—France. *E-mail*—elisabeth.combres@free.fr.

Career

Author and journalist.

Awards, Honors

Prix Sorcières, 2002, for *Mondes rebelles junior;* Prix de la Presse des Jeunes, 2003, for *Les 1000 mots de l'info;* Prix Nouvelle Revu Pédagogique, and National Books for a Global Society listee, both 2010, both for *Broken Memory.*

Writings

NONFICTION

(With Florence Thinard) *Mondes rebelles junior,* Michalon (France), 2001.

(With Florence Thinard) *Les 1000 mots de l'info: pour mieux comprendre et décrypter l'actualité,* illustrated by Clément Oubrerie, Gallimard jeunesse (Paris, France), 2004.

Élisabeth Combres (Reproduced by permission.)

(With Sophie Lamoureux and Florence Thinard) *Le clés de l'info: pour mieux comprendre le médias et l'actualité,* new edition, Gallimard jeunesse (Paris, France), 2005.

(With Florence Thinard) *Le terrorisme,* illustrated by Diego Aranega, Documentation Française (France), 2007, new edition, 2010.

(With Florence Thinard) *Le réchauffement climatique,* illustrated by Diego Aranega, Documentation Française (France), 2007, new edition, 2010.

(With Florence Thinard) *Élections et démocratie,* illustrated by Diego Aranega, Documentation Française (France), 2007.

(With Florence Thinard) *L'Union européenne,* illustrated by Diego Aranega, Documentation Française (France), 2007.

(With Florence Thinard) *Le pétrole,* illustrated by Diego Aranega, Documentation Française (France), 2007, new edition, 2010.

(With Florence Thinard) *La mondialisation économique,* illustrated by Diego Aranega, Documentation Française (France), 2007, new edition, 2010.

L'Islam, illustrated by Diego Aranega, Documentation Française (France), 2008.

La Chine, illustrated by Diego Aranega, Documentation Française (France), 2008.

NOVELS

La mémoire trouée, Gallimard jeunnesse (Paris, France), 2007, translated by Shelley Tanaka as *Broken Memory:*

A Novel of Rwanda, Groundwood Books (Toronto, Ontario, Canada), 2009.

Le monde en chiffres, Gallimard jeunesse (Paris, France), 2009.

Contributor to anthologies, including *Nouvelles vertes,* Thierry Magnier, 2005.

Sidelights

In addition to working as a journalist in her native France, Élisabeth Combres has also collaborated with fellow author Florence Thinard on a sequence of nonfiction books that draw on her knowledge of world politics and culture. Beginning with *Mondes rebelles junior,* which focuses on revolutionaries around the world, their other collaborations include *Les 1000 mots de l'info: pour mieux comprendre et décrypter l'actualité, Le clés de l'info: pour mieux comprendre le médias et l'actualité,* and a series of shorter profiles with an European slant that include artwork by Diego Aranega. Beginning in the mid-2000s, Combres has also written several novels for middle-grade readers. Published in the original French as *La mémoire trouée,* her first published novel, *Broken Memory: A Novel of Rwanda* was also her first book to be translated into English.

In *Broken Memory* Combres takes as her backdrop the Rwandan genocide of 1994, in which the government-sponsored Hutu military set about eradicating the Tutsi people. Emma, a Rwandan girl, is five years old in 1994, and she hides from the soldiers who murder her mother. Emma being hidden by Mukecuru, a local Hutu peasant, the girl is also helped by a new friend to confront the terror of her past. Slowly, with a determination to survive that was willed by her mother, she returns to her home and completes the education she needs to build a successful adult life. Combres' novel gains vivid and sometimes tragic detail from interviews the author had with survivors of the Rwandan genocide. Her use of "stark, clipped prose" makes *Broken Memory* a "short, spare novel" which Hazel Rochman recommended in *Booklist* as "an excellent addition" to high-school-level Holocaust studies. While a *Kirkus Reviews* writer cited the book's lack of an explanatory preface, the critic went on to recommend *Broken Memory* as "approachable and evocative," adding that "the dearth of materials on the Rwandan genocide" for middle-grade readers makes Combres' novel a "stand out." In *School Library Journal* Kelly McGorray found *Broken Memory* to be "a challenging read" that is also "a testament to the struggles of those who survived these unspeakable atrocities."

Biographical and Critical Sources

PERIODICALS

Booklist, September 1, 2009, Hazel Rochman, review of *Broken Memory: A Novel of Rwanda,* p. 80.

Bulletin of the Center for Children's Books, December, 2009, Hope Morrison, review of *Broken Memory,* p. 148.

Canadian Review of Materials, September 25, 2009, Joan Marshall, review of *Broken Memory.*

Kirkus Reviews, September 1, 2009, review of *Broken Memory.*

Library Media Connection, November-December, 2009, Ellen Wickham, review of *Broken Memory,* p. 81.

Resource Links, February, 2010, Margaret Mackey, review of *Broken Memory,* p. 28.

School Library Journal, December, 2009, Kelly McGorray, review of *Broken Memory,* p. 110.

ONLINE

Charte Repertoire Web site, http://charte.repertoir.free.fr/ (February 15, 2011), "Élisabeth Combres."*

*   *   *

CONROY, Melissa 1969-

Personal

Born 1969, in Beaufort, SC; daughter of Joseph (a Marine fighter pilot) and Barbara (a teacher and attorney) Jones; adopted daughter of Pat Conroy (a writer); married; children: one daughter, one son. *Education:* Rhode Island School of Design, B.F.A., 1987; University of Georgia, M.F.A. (painting), 1998; Philadelphia University, M.S. (textile design), 2006.

Addresses

Home—Philadelphia, PA. *E-mail*—info@melissaconroy.com.

Career

Sculptor, textile designer, and author/illustrator. Creator of Wooberry dolls; teacher and adjunct professor at Philadelphia University.

Awards, Honors

Pulpwood Queens Book Club Children's Book of the Year award, 2010, for *Poppy's Pants.*

Writings

(Self-illustrated) *Poppy's Pants,* Blue Apple Books (Maplewood, NJ), 2009.

(Self-illustrated) *My Grandma Is an Author,* Blue Apple Books (Maplewood, NJ), 2011.

Sidelights

Artist and author Melissa Conroy grew up in a large, talkative, story-telling family. "I was the quiet one," she admitted to *SATA.* "My dad was an author and my mother was an assistant district attorney. As a kid, I loved to draw. I didn't think I would become an author.

Melissa Conroy (Photograph by Benjamin J. Shermeta. Reproduced by permission.)

How could I do something my dad did so well, when I was always quiet? But, I listened closely to all of the family stories. Without realizing it, I was learning how to be a storyteller through listening. For a long time, I thought my dad had no job, because he didn't leave the house to go to work. I liked that about my dad and wanted to grown up to do something I loved too.

"After graduating from art school with a degree in painting, I worked many jobs, from wax chaser at an art foundry to executive assistant. Eventually I settled on teaching art and creative writing. All the while I explored painting, sculpture, and textile design in my studio. Soon, I began exhibiting my artwork in New York City. After my first child was born, I began making dolls inspired by my daughter's drawings. I named the dolls Wooberry dolls and began creating my own characters. The Wooberry dolls led to my first opportunity to write and illustrate a picture book.

"*Poppy's Pants* revisits an event from childhood, when my dad asked me to sew up a pair of his pants. Sewing can be an exciting challenge for a second grader. Penelope, the main character in the book, discovers that sewing up a hole is more challenging than it seems, but she is able to come up with her own solution. The illustrations for *Poppy's Pants* combine drawings with photographs of Melissa's dolls.

"*My Grandma Is an Author,* another of my stories, is about a grandson who helps his grandmother find her story. Problem solving and the creative process are themes throughout both my stories. As a visual artist, I see a natural connection between drawing and writing. Through drawing, the world reveals itself. You get to look at things with fresh eyes and that helps to write with fresh eyes as well."

Biographical and Critical Sources

PERIODICALS

Kirkus Reviews, September 1, 2009, review of *Poppy's Pants.*

Conroy's unique mixed-media photographs are a feature of her illustrations featuring her Wooberry characters. (Reproduced by permission.)

Publishers Weekly, September 14, 2009, review of *Poppy's Pants,* p. 46.

School Library Journal, October, 2009, Linda Staskus, review of *Poppy's Pants,* p. 88.

ONLINE

Melissa Conroy Home Page, http://www.melissaconroy.com (February 15, 2011).

Reading Tub Web site, http://www.thereadingtub.com/ (July, 2009), "Melissa Conroy."

Wooberry Web site, http://www.wooberry.com (February 15, 2011).

* * *

COOPER, Michelle 1969-

Personal

Born 1969, in Sydney, New South Wales, Australia. *Education:* Earned college degree (speech pathology).

Addresses

Home—Sydney, New South Wales, Australia. *E-mail*—michelle@michellecooper-writer.com.

Career

Author and speech pathologist; specialist in learning disabilities for fifteen years.

Awards, Honors

Ethel Turner Prize for Young People's Literature, and Parent's Choice Book Award Recommended selection, both 2009, and Best Books for Young Adults selection, American Library Association, 2010, all for *A Brief History of Montmaray.*

Writings

The Rage of Sheep, Random House Australia (Milsons Point, New South Wales, Australia), 2007.

"MONTMARAY JOURNALS" SERIES

A Brief History of Montmaray, Random House Australia (North Sydney, New South Wales, Australia), 2008, Alfred A. Knopf (New York, NY), 2009.
The FitzOsbornes in Exile, Random House Australia (North Sydney, New South Wales, Australia), 2010, Alfred A. Knopf (New York, NY), 2011.

Contributor to periodicals, including *Reading Time* and *Viewpoint.*

Adaptations

Cooper's novels *A Brief History of Montmaray* and *The FitzOsbornes in Exile* were adapted as audiobooks by Louis Braille Audio, 2010 and 2011 respectively.

Sidelights

Although her primary career is as a speech pathologist, Australian author Michelle Cooper has also established a second career writing for teens. Cooper's first novel, *The Rage of Sheep,* focuses on a young teen learning to tolerate differences, while the books in her ongoing "Montmaray Journals" series take readers to a tiny island in the Bay of Biscay, off the coast of France and Spain, as World War II threatens to sweep Europe.

Cooper went to school in Fiji and rural Australia before attending college in the large city of Sydney, her plan to major in pharmacy. She took a break after her junior year and worked odd jobs before returning to school. With a degree in speech pathology, Cooper now works with students with language and learning challenges. She began her first novel, *The Rage of Sheep,* after September 11 prompted discussions among her students regarding religious intolerance and cultural differences, and she completed the work with the assistance of Alyssa Brugman, an author and a mentor assigned through the Children's Book Council of Australia. Set in the mid-1980s, Cooper's epistolary story focuses on a fifteen year old whose attempts to fit in with the popular crowd seem threatened when she is assigned to work with a student whose fundamentalist Christian beliefs spark a debate between creationism and evolution during their science project. In *Aussie Reviews* online, Claire Saxby praised Cooper's debut novel, dubbing *The Rage of Sheep* "a lightly-handled, funny and entertaining story."

In *A Brief History of Montmaray* Cooper introduces Sophie FitzOsborne, who lives with her younger sister, her cousin Veronica, and her uncle on the tiny island of Montmaray. The family's ancestral home is as crumbling as the sanity of Uncle John, who holds himself as king of the island. The novel is framed as Sophie's diary, which she begins in 1936, on her sixteenth birthday. The observant teen captures the changes in her family fortunes as the once-wealthy FitzOsbornes dwell amid

Michelle Cooper (Reproduced by permission.)

the tattered remnants of their past while holding onto the vestiges of their nobility. Sophie's own worries—about her upcoming society debut, their annoying housekeeper, and the madness of King John—slowly become overshadowed by the growing threat of Germany's Nazi government, as island residents leave and Nazi soldiers arrive to disrupt the island's small, insular world.

A sequel to *A Brief History of Montmaray, The FitzOsbornes in Exile,* finds the FitzOsborne family living in England, where they have taken asylum to escape the war. The excitement of her first ball is diminished by Sophie's fears over her family's straitened finances, and her aunt Charlotte seems determined to solve the problem by marrying both Sophie and Veronica off as quickly as possible. Citing the novel's "highly atmospheric setting," a *Publishers Weekly* contributor added that "the revelation of long-hidden family secrets adds additional gothic undertones" to Cooper's "powerful historical novel." *A Brief History of Montmaray* "has a bit of everything: romance, betrayal, a haunting, espionage, . . . and murder," noted Kimberly Monaghan in *School Library Journal,* and a *Kirkus Reviews* critic predicted that Cooper's "winning heroine . . . will touch the heart." Writing in *Booklist,* Ian Chipman recommended *A Brief History of Montmaray* as "a smart and stirring choice to usher fans of the Brontës into the twentieth century."

Biographical and Critical Sources

PERIODICALS

Booklist, September 15, 2009, Ian Chipman, review of *A Brief History of Montmaray,* p. 66.

Bulletin of the Center for Children's Books, November, 2009, Karen Coates, review of *A Brief History of Montmaray,* p. 106.

Horn Book, November-December, 2009, Deirdre F. Baker, review of *A Brief History of Montmaray,* p. 665.

Kirkus Reviews, October 1, 2009, review of *A Brief History of Montmaray.*

Publishers Weekly, October 19, 2009, review of *A Brief History of Montmaray,* p. 53.

School Library Journal, December, 2009, Kimberly Monaghan, review of *A Brief History of Montmaray,* p. 110.

ONLINE

Aussie Reviews Online, http://www.aussiereviews.com/ (February 15, 2011), Claire Saxby, review of *The Rage of Sheep.*

Cover of Cooper's evocative young-adult novel **A Brief History of Montmaray,** *which draws readers into a family living a different kind of life.* (Jacket photograph copyright © 2009 by Jupiter Images. Used by permission of Alfred A. Knopf, an imprint of Random House Children's Books, a division of Random House, Inc.)

Michelle Cooper Home Page, http://www.michellecooper-writer.com (December 30, 2010).

Michelle Cooper Web log, http://michellecooper-writer.com/blog (February 15, 2011).

*　　*　　*

COX, Paul 1957-

Personal

Born July 31, 1957, in London, England; married. *Education:* Attended Camberwell School of Art; Royal College of Art, degree, 1982.

Addresses

Home and office—East Sussex, England. *Agent*—Richard Solomon, Richard Solomon Artists Representative, 149 Madison Ave., Ste. 708, New York, NY 10016; richardrichardsolomon.com. *E-mail*—paulwcox@gmail.com.

Career

Painter and book illustrator. *Exhibitions:* Work exhibited at Chris Beetles Gallery, London, England, 1989, 1993, 2001 (major retrospective), 2006, and 2009 (major retrospective). Mural installations include Royal College of Surgeons, London.

Awards, Honors

Folio Society competition prize.

Illustrator

Rick Ball, *Low Tech: Fast Furniture for Next to Nothing,* Century (London, England), 1982.

Dylan Thomas, *The Outing,* Dent (London, England), 1985.

Lance Salway, compiler, *The Vain Teddy and Other Teddy Bear Stories,* Piccadilly (London, England), 1985.

Peter Terson, *The Offcuts Voyage,* Oxford University Press (Oxford, England), 1988.

Gabriel Alington, *The Evacuee,* Walker (London, England), 1988.

Jerome K. Jerome, *Three Men in a Boat,* Pavilion (London, England), 1989.

John Cotton and Fred Sedgwick, *The Biggest Riddle in the World,* Mary Glasgow, 1990.

Allan Frewin Jones, *Tommy and the Sloth,* Simon & Schuster Young Books (Hemel Hempstead, England), 1992.

Tim Heald, *Honourable Estates: The English and Their Country Houses,* Pavilion (London, England), 1992.

Kenneth Grahame, *The Wind in the Willows,* Reader's Digest Association (London, England), 1993.

Louise Nicholson, *Look out London!,* Riverswift (London, England), 1995.

Jeanne Willis, *Tinkerbill,* Collins (London, England), 1999.

Wilma Horsbrugh, *The Train to Glasgow,* Clarion (New York, NY), 2004.

Gerald Durrell, *My Family and Other Animals,* Folio Society (London, England), 2006.

Stanley Trachtenberg, *The Elevator Man,* Eerdmans Books for Young Readers (Grand Rapids, MI), 2009.

Also illustrator of *Dino's Day in London* by Stephen Rabley; *The Cricket Match* by Hugh de Selincourt; *Some Experiences of an Irish RM* by E.Œ. Somerville and Martin Ross; *Leave It to PSmith* by P.G. Wodehouse; and eleven volumes of Wodehouse's "Jeeves and Wooster" series. Contributor to periodicals, including the *Atlantic Monthly,* London *Daily Telegraph, Country Life, Spectator,* London *Sunday Times Magazine, Punch,* London *Times,* and *Esquire.*

Sidelights

A highly regarded British watercolorist, Paul Cox has provided illustrations for a number of children's books, including *The Elevator Man,* the debut picture book by Stanley Trachtenberg. Often praised for his distinctive artistic style, which is noted for its charm and whimsy, the prolific Cox also contributes work to such publications as *Vanity Fair* and *Punch,* and his art has been featured on stamps for the Royal Mail and a mural at the Royal College of Surgeons, among other projects. According to Paul Alm, writing in a *Watercolor* profile of the artist, "Cox's commissioned work bears the indelible stamp of his signature style. Each piece seems to seize a single fleeting moment of life—as unstaged as a snapshot and yet executed with such precision that no mark appears out of place."

Born in 1957, in London, England, Cox studied illustration at the Camberwell School of Art and the Royal College of Art, from which he graduated. During his time there, Cox garnered recognition for his entry in a

Folio Society contest to illustrate Kingsley Amis's famed novel *Lucky Jim.* "The illustrations were never published," Alm noted, "but they established Cox as an artist whose talents in caricature and capturing a moment are met by an equally vivacious imagination." In 1982 Cox began his career as a freelance artist, dividing his time between studio work and projects done on location. Cox works quickly, he remarked to Alm, "to generate a sense of urgency and pace that suits my style. I'm essentially drawing with color, rather than just painting a line drawing."

Cox's illustrations have graced the pages of a wide range of literary works, including *The Wind in the Willows,* a children's classic by Kenneth Grahame, *Some Experiences of an Irish RM,* a collection of tales by E.Œ. Somerville and Martin Ross, and *Leave It to Psmith* a comic novel by twentieth-century British humorist P.G. Wodehouse. Based on a 1954 poem by Wilma Horsbrugh, *The Train to Glasgow* describes a youngster's humorously chaotic journey aboard a steam train overrun by squawking chickens. "Cox reinforces the antique flavor of this droll bit of verse," a contributor in *Kirkus Reviews* noted, and Hazel Rochman, writing in *Booklist,* applauded the "exuberant, detailed watercolors" in the cumulative tale.

Trachtenberg's *The Elevator Man* centers on a boy's fascination with his apartment building's old-fashioned elevator and the man who operates the machinery. When young Nathan learns that the building's renovations include an automated elevator, however, he begins to worry about his friend's livelihood. "Swirling watercolor illustrations capture fast-paced urban activity," a critic stated in *Kirkus Reviews,* and a reviewer in *Publishers Weekly* observed that Cox's "radiant palette, balletic ink line and cosmopolitan aesthetic bring a buoyant spirit to this metropolitan fable."

Paul Cox's illustration projects includes creating the artwork for Wilma Horsbrugh's entertaining **The Train to Glasgow.** (Illustration copyright © 2004 by Paul Cox. Reproduced by permission of Houghton Mifflin Company.)

Cox plays with perspective to add levity to his artwork for Stanley Tra-chtenberg's story in **The Elevator Man.** (Illustration © 2009 by Paul Cox. Reproduced by permission of Eerdmans Books for Young Readers, an imprint of Wm. B. Eerdmans Publishing Co.)

Biographical and Critical Sources

PERIODICALS

Booklist, June 1, 2004, Hazel Rochman, review of *The Train to Glasgow,* p. 1742.

Kirkus Reviews, March 15, 2004, review of *The Train to Glasgow,* p. 271; August 15, 2009, review of *The Elevator Man.*

Publishers Weekly, September 21, 2009, review of *The Elevator Man,* p. 57.

School Library Journal, May, 2004, Grace Oliff, review of *The Train to Glasgow,* p. 114; October, 2009, Judith Constantinides, review of *The Elevator Man,* p. 106.

Watercolor, September 1, 2005, David Alm, "Stilled Life: The Illustrations of Paul Cox."

ONLINE

Paul Cox Home Page, http://www.paulcoxartist.com (February 15, 2011).*

*   *   *

CREECH, Sharon 1945-
(Sharon Rigg)

Personal

Born July 29, 1945, in South Euclid, OH; daughter of Ann and Arvel Creech; married (divorced); married Lyle D. Rigg (a school headmaster), 1982; children: Rob, Karin. *Education:* Hiram College, B.A.; George Mason University, M.A.

Addresses

Home—The Pennington School, 112 W. Delaware Ave., Pennington, NJ 08534. *Agent*—Amy Berkower, Writers House, 21 W. 26th St., New York, NY 10010.

Career

Affiliated with Federal Theater Project Archives, Fairfax, VA; *Congressional Quarterly,* Washington, DC, editorial assistant; The American School in Switzerland (TASIS), Surrey, England, teacher of American and British literature, 1979-82, 1984-94, teacher of American and British literature in Lugano, Switzerland, location, 1983-85.

Awards, Honors

Billee Murray Denny Poetry Award, Lincoln College (IL), 1988, for "Cleansing"; Best Books designation, *School Library Journal,* 1994, Notable Children's Book designation, American Library Association (ALA), Children's Book Award (England), U.K. Reading Association Award, and Newbery Medal, ALA, all 1995, W.H. Smith Award, 1996, and Young Readers Award, Virginia State Reading Association, Heartland Award, Sequoia Award, and Literaturhaus award (Austria), all 1997, all for *Walk Two Moons;* Whitbread Award shortlist, 1997, for *Chasing Redbird;* Christopher Award, 2000, and Newbery Honor Book designation, 2001, both for *The Wanderer;* Christopher Award, 2002, for *Love That Dog;* Carnegie Medal, 2003, and Rebecca Caudill Young Readers' Book Award second place, 2005, both for *Ruby Holler;* Carnegie Medal nomination, 2005, for *Heartbeat.*

Writings

FOR YOUNG PEOPLE

Absolutely Normal Chaos, Macmillan (London, England), 1990, HarperCollins (New York, NY), 1995.

Walk Two Moons, HarperCollins (New York, NY), 1994.

Pleasing the Ghost, illustrated by Stacey Schuett, HarperCollins (New York, NY), 1996, published as *The Ghost of Uncle Arvie,* illustrated by Simon Cooper, Macmillan (London, England), 1996.

Chasing Redbird, HarperCollins (New York, NY), 1997.

Bloomability, HarperCollins (New York, NY), 1998.

The Wanderer, illustrated by David Diaz, HarperCollins (New York, NY), 2000.

Love That Dog: Learning about Poetry from Miss Stretchberry, HarperCollins (New York, NY), 2001.

Ruby Holler, Joanna Cotler Books (New York, NY), 2002.

Heartbeat, HarperCollins (New York, NY), 2004.

Replay, Joanna Cotler Books (New York, NY), 2005.

Hate That Cat, Joanna Cotler Books (New York, NY), 2008.

The Unfinished Angel, Joanna Cotler Books (New York, NY), 2009.

PICTURE BOOKS

Fishing in the Air, illustrated by Chris Raschka, Joanna Cotler Books (New York, NY), 2000.
A Fine, Fine School, illustrated by Harry Bliss, Joanna Cotler Books (New York, NY), 2001.
Granny Torrelli Makes Soup, Joanna Cotler Books (New York, NY), 2003.
Who's That Baby?: New-Baby Songs, illustrated by David Diaz, Joanna Cotler Books (New York, NY), 2005.
The Castle Corona, illustrated by David Diaz, Joanna Cotler Books (New York, NY), 2007.

OTHER

(Under name Sharon Rigg) *The Recital* (novel), Pan-Macmillan (London, England), 1990.
(Under name Sharon Rigg) *Nickel Malley,* Pan-Macmillan (London, England), 1991.
The Center of the Universe: Waiting for the Girl (play), produced in New York, NY, 1992.

Short plays included in anthology *Acting Out: Six One-Act Plays! Six Newbery Stars!,* edited by Justin Chanda, Atheneum (New York, NY), 2008.

Adaptations

Walk Two Moons was adapted for the stage by Julia Jordan in 2005; several of Creech's titles have been recorded as audiobooks.

Sidelights

Sharon Creech's second novel for young adults, *Walk Two Moons,* brought its author instant celebrity in the United States when it won the 1995 Newbery Honor Medal. Interestingly, her first novel for teens, *Absolutely Normal Chaos,* had not yet been published in America. The reason? The Ohio-born author had been living in England for several years and made her publishing debut there. Creech's name is no longer unknown, however, and more recent novels such as *Heartbeat, Replay,* and *The Unfinished Angel,* as well as picture books such as *Granny Torrelli Makes Soup* and *Who's That Baby?: New-Baby Songs* have earned her a loyal readership.

Creech was born and raised in a suburb of Cleveland, Ohio, as a member of a close-knit extended families full of stories. She was an enthusiastic writer throughout grade school and high school, and was an equally enthusiastic reader. After receiving her bachelor's degree from Hiram College, Creech went on to George Mason University in Washington, DC, for her master's degree. She then worked at the Federal Theater Project Archives and was an editorial assistant at the *Congressional Quarterly.* She eventually married, had two children, and then got divorced. In 1979, Creech moved to Thorpe, England, and got a job as an English teacher at The American School in Switzerland's English campus.

Three years later she married fellow school staffer Lyle D. Rigg. Rigg had been hired as assistant headmaster—the British equivalent of a school principal—and soon after he and Creech were married, they transferred to the school's Swiss campus.

In 1984, Rigg returned to Thorpe as headmaster of the English branch, where he and Creech would make their home until they moved to the United States in 1994. "As a teacher of American and British literature to American and international teenagers," Rigg recalled in a *Horn Book* article, "Sharon . . . shared her love both of literature and of writing. She'd open up Chaucer's world in *The Canterbury Tales* and then head off to Canterbury with her students so that they could make the pilgrimage themselves. She'd offer *Hamlet,* and then off they would all go to Stratford-upon-Avon."

For many years Creech devoted her time almost exclusively to her teaching and her family. "In 1980, when my children and I had been in England for nine months," she recalled in *Horn Book,* "my father had a stroke. Although he lived for six more years, the stroke left him paralyzed and unable to speak. . . . Think of all those words locked up for six years." Creech started her first novel a month after her father's death in 1986, "and when I finished it," she continued, "I wrote another, and another, and another. The words rushed out."

Absolutely Normal Chaos, Creech's first book for young readers, deals with a variety of themes, some specific to adolescence, such as first love, growing up, and schoolwork, and others more universal, such as dealing with relatives and friends, learning compassion, and gaining understanding. The novel is the fictional journal of one summer in the life of thirteen-year-old Mary Lou Finney of Easton, Ohio, and as it starts Mary Lou is begging her English teacher not to read the writing that follows. The girl's summer, it becomes apparent, is more bizarre than usual for a teen. "Her life is disrupted in more ways than one by the arrival of a gangling, uncommunicative cousin, Carl Ray, from West Virginia, by his curious relationship with Charlie Furtz, the genial neighbour from across the road, who subsequently dies of a heart attack, and by her own budding romance," explained Joan Zahnleiter in *Magpies.* These circumstances force Mary Lou to confront issues in her own life and to come to terms with her family and issues such as death and illegitimacy.

"Mary Lou is a typical teen whose acquaintance with the sadder parts of life is cushioned by a warm and energetic family," stated Cindy Darling Codell in her *School Library Journal* review. The narrator's "entertaining musings on Homer, Shakespeare, and Robert Frost are drawn in nifty parallels to what is happening in her own life," Codell continued. Nancy Vasilakis wrote in *Horn Book* that Mary Lou "grows in a number of important ways throughout the summer, and the metaphors she now recognizes in the *Odyssey* could, she realizes, very well apply to her own life."

SHARON CREECH
WINNER OF THE NEWBERY MEDAL FOR WALK TWO MOONS

the
unfinished
Angel

Cover of Sharon Creech's engagingly imaginative story The Unfinished Angel, *featuring artwork by Alex Eben Meyer.* (Illustration © 2009 by Alex Eben Meyer. Used by permission of HarperCollins Children's Books, a division of HarperCollins Publishers.)

Themes of growth and self-actualization also appear in Creech's novel *Walk Two Moons*. In this story, thirteen-year-old Salamanca "Sal" Tree Hiddle relates the plight of her friend Phoebe, whose mother has left home. What makes Phoebe's story particularly relevant to Sal is the fact that Sal's mother Sugar also left home and never returned. "Sal finds that recounting Phoebe's story helps her understand the desertion of her own mother," explained Deborah Stevenson in the *Bulletin of the Center for Children's Books*. "Creech skillfully keeps these layers separate but makes their interrelationship clear, and the plot moves along amid all this contemplation with the aid of a mysterious note-leaver, a local 'lunatic,' an eccentric English teacher, and Sal's budding romance." The author's Native-American references are "the best things about this book," asserted *New York Times Book Review* contributor Hazel Rochman, "casual, contemporary and mythic, not an exotic thing apart. Sal . . . loves the Indian stories her mother told her," with their "celebration of the sweeping natural world and our connectedness with it." "For once in a children's book," Rochman concluded, "Indians are people, not reverential figures in a museum diorama. Sal's Indian heritage is a natural part of her finding herself in America."

Themes common to both *Absolutely Normal Chaos* and *Walk Two Moons* included dealing with death and the feelings of grief and loss that follow. These themes are also linked to Creech's life. "When I read Salamanca's story now, with some distance," the author revealed in *Horn Book*, "I hear such longing in her voice—for her mother, for her father, for the land—and I know that her longing is also my longing . . . for my children, my larger family, and for my own country."

Directed to a younger readership, *Pleasing the Ghost* also deals with death and loss, but with a lighter touch. Nine-year-old Dennis is visited in his bedroom by a parade of ghosts, although he never encounters the ghost of his late father. Instead, the boy meets up with his late Uncle Arvie, who asks for the boy help in assisting his widow, Dennis's Aunt Julia, in locating the gifts and money Arvie has left for her. Mystery blends with comedy in Creech's tale as Dennis must first decipher his late uncle's messages, jumbled due to the speech impairment caused by a stroke Arvie suffered before his death. *Pleasing the Ghost* "has several mythical elements: three wishes, magic, ghosts, a lonely young boy whose father has died, a quest and a satisfactory conclusion," asserted *School Librarian* contributor Ann Jenkin. A *Publishers Weekly* reviewer observed that "Arvie's earnest affection for Julia and Dennis makes him a role model as well as a clown, and Creech's attention to nuances of feeling grounds this light tale in emotional truth." In *Booklist* Michael Cart called *Pleasing the Ghost* an "engaging story that manages to deal lightheartedly with emotional loss by offering [Creech's] readers the enduring promise of hope."

Creech returns readers to the hills of Kentucky in *Chasing Redbird*, another story of grief, loss, and discovery. Thirteen-year-old Zinnia Taylor, the third of seven siblings, enjoys escaping to the "Quiet Zone" of her neighboring aunt and uncle's home. The death of Zinny's aunt, however, causes her despondent uncle to engage in increasingly eccentric behavior as he succumbs to unrelenting grief, leaving Zinny to find solace elsewhere. The teenager soon becomes obsessed with her discovery of a long, winding trail near her home—a trail once used by trappers and Native Americans. As Zinny works to clear the trail, occasionally interrupted by the attentions of an older boy, she unearths markers and other indications of her ancestors' presence in the region. "Creech has written a striking novel, notable for its emotional honesty," declared Ethel L. Heins in a *Horn Book* review of *Chasing Redbird*. "In her Newbery Medal acceptance speech," Heins added, "the author spoke of her predilection for mystery and for metaphorical journeys; she has worked both into the novel and, in addition, once again bridges the gap between the generations and binds them together." A *Kirkus Reviews* commentator, who also had high praise for the book, maintained that "Creech crams her novel full of wonderful characters, proficient dialogue, bracing descriptions, and a merry use of language." A *Publishers Weekly* reviewer called *Chasing Redbird* "Creech's best yet," while Deborah Stevenson concluded in the *Bulletin of the Center for Children's Books* that the novelist "again demonstrates her expertise at evoking physical and emotional landscapes and the connections between the two."

Dinnie Doone has lived in thirteen states in twelve years, but nothing prepares her to be whisked away to the American School in Lugano, Switzerland, in Creech's novel *Bloomability*. Dinnie's Uncle Max is the headmaster at the school, and the girl now finds herself learning to ski and speak Italian as she gradually overcomes feelings of being a stranger. Recognizing the opportunity that the move affords her—it is a year of "bloomabilities"—Dinnie welcomes the diversity and new ideas she had previously protected herself from while moving from place to place. Nancy Bond, writing in *Horn Book,* praised *Bloomability,* writing that "Creech surrounds [Dinnie] with a lively, sympathetic, often amusing cast of adult and adolescent characters, and Dinnie herself is an appealing narrator." Dinnie's coming-of-age story is "a story to stimulate both head and heart," commented John Peters in *Booklist*.

The title of Creech's award-winning novel *The Wanderer* is also the name of the sailboat in which thirteen-year-old Sophie sets sail with her three uncles and two cousins. The story of their journey from Connecticut to England is told through cousins Sophie and Cody's journal entries. Sophie is excited about sailing across the ocean and anxious to visit her grandfather, who has returned to his childhood home in England. During the voyage, she regales her cousins and uncles with the many stories her grandfather told her when she was young, despite the fact that she has never met the man. When they face a dangerous storm, the group must pull together in order to keep the boat afloat. The story, particularly the ocean voyage, is a metaphor for self-discovery. In Cody's journal entries, readers learn that Sophie's parents are dead and she lives with an adoptive mother; meanwhile, the girl's journey helps her deal with the painful secrets of her past. "Presented directly," wrote Carolyn Phelan in her *Booklist* review of *The Wanderer*, "the weight and force of such revelations might have swamped the . . . [narrative], but here, handled obliquely, they simply lift and carry the whole story." *Kliatt* contributor Paula Rohrlick considered Creech's novel "an exciting and touching story of adventure on the high seas and of emotional discoveries."

In her novel *Love That Dog: Learning about Poetry from Miss Stretchberry* Creech tells the story of fourth grader Jack, whose teacher introduces her students to poetry via the works of Robert Frost, William Blake, and other well-known writers. Jack resists his teacher's attempts to make students write their own poetry, however, and his fledgling efforts at versifying form the story, told through Jack's writing journal. Many of his early free-verse poems take the form of complaints over having to write them, sometimes in the style of William

Carlos Williams. Eventually, Jack comes to understand the need for poetry and the talent it takes to write it. In his final poem to appear in the book, he discusses the fate of his beloved dog, Sky. Jack eventually becomes a fan of poetry and invites his favorite poet, Walter Dean Myers, to visit his school. The real poems Miss Stretchberry uses in her lessons are printed at the back of the book, further blurring the line between fact and fiction. Praising *Love That Dog* in the *New York Times Book Review,* Meg Wolitzer asserted of Creech: "Not only has she shown young readers what a poem can do, she's also shown them what a novel can do." Hazel Rochman wrote in *Booklist* that "the story shows how poetry inspires reading and writing with everyday words that make personal music." "By exposing Jack and readers to the range of poems that moves Jack," wrote a *Publishers Weekly* critic, "Creech conveys a life truth: pain and joy exist side by side."

A sequel to *Love That Dog, Hate That Cat,* takes readers into the next grade, where Miss Stretchberry is again the teacher. Favoring more traditional writing over free verse, Jack's professorial Uncle Bill introduces the boy to structured poetic forms and techniques such as metaphor and alliteration, as well as encouraging him to ponder more abstract themes. Jack's feelings about Sky's death, worries about his mom, and even his animus toward an aggressive neighborhood cat, are sidelined when his new kitten goes missing, and all these elements ultimately find an outlet in verse. The fifth grader's "growing excitement as he discovers the delights of sound . . . and expression is palpable," wrote *School Library Journal* contributor Marie Orlando in a review of *Hate That Cat,* while a *Kirkus Reviews* writer predicted of the book that "teachers will welcome both Jack's poems and Creech's embedded writing lessons." Dubbing *Hate That Cat* "a worthy companion piece to *Love That Dog,*" Thom Barthelmess added in *Booklist* that the author uses "observant sensitivity and spare verse" in her portrait of "a boy who discovers the power of self-expression."

Ruby Holler, another novel by Creech, finds orphaned twins Dallas, a boy, and Florida, a girl, taking a three-month leave from the orphanage where they live in order to accompany Sairy and Tiller Morey, an older couple from Ruby Holler, on their separate vacations. Florida and Tiller are scheduled to go canoeing, and Dallas and Sairy are going birdwatching. Florida and Dallas prove to be trouble wherever they go, but as they prepare for their respective journeys in the rural confines of Ruby Holler, they slowly learn to respect the Moreys and learn more about themselves. A writer for *Kirkus Reviews* noted that "charm and humor is encapsulated in this romp with its melodramatic elements of treasure and orphans." *Ruby Holler* "celebrates the healing effects of love and compassion," wrote a reviewer for *Publishers Weekly,* the critic adding that the novel "evokes a feeling as welcoming as fresh-baked bread." In *Booklist* Phelan deemed Creech's novel "a stylized yet solid story," and *Kliatt* reviewer Paula Rohrlick noted that "younger YAs . . . will appreciate the happy ending of this sweet, deliberately rather old-fashioned tale." *Horn Book* critic Joanna Rudge Long complimented Creech's use of "brief chapters, swift action, . . . generous doses of humor, engagingly quirky characters, and a lively, kid-friendly voice." With *Ruby Holler,* Creech became the first American to win the United Kingdom's top children's prize, the Carnegie Medal.

Twelve-year-old Annie and Annie's friend Max love running together in *Heartbeat.* However, Annie soon begins noticing some changes in Max: he now runs to win, instead of just for the joy of it. As tension grows between the two due to Max's insistence that Annie join his track team, Annie's grandfather, a former champion runner and Annie's inspiration, becomes ill and develops dementia. *Heartbeat* is told in verse from Annie's point of view and reveals the girl's feelings of joy about her mother's pregnancy, as well as her worries about both her grandfather and her friend Max. "This is vintage Creech, and its richness lies in its sheer simplicity," stated Luann Toth in her *School Library Journal* review of *Heartbeat.* Annie's "pondering is realistic for a bright, sensitive twelve-year-old," commented Susan Dove Lempke in *Horn Book,* while a *Publishers Weekly* reviewer deemed *Heartbeat* "a wholly satisfying emotional journey."

In *Replay* Leonardo feels invisible amid his siblings, although he has dreams of achieving great things. When he does not get the hoped-for role in a school play, he is nonetheless thrilled about being cast in the production, and wants to share that excitement with his sometimes unappreciative family. When Leo discovers a journal written by his father when the man was about Leo's age, the boy realizes that he is not the only one in the family with big dreams. Creech tells her story in *Replay* using a variety of formats, including journal entries and play-script dialogue. "In this warm, funny, philosophical novel, Creech cleverly juxtaposes life and stage life," noted a *Kirkus Reviews* contributor. "Though the subjects are serious, they are played out with humor," commented Lempke in *Horn Book,* and *Kliatt* reviewer Rohrlick dubbed *Replay* "another tour-de-force" from Creech. Rochman, writing in *Booklist,* called the novel "both uproarious and tender," and praised Creech's use of a "pitch-perfect dialogue that will sweep readers right to the end of the story." A *Publishers Weekly* contributor noted that *Replay* is "written with the kind of warmth, understanding, and economical prose that has characterized Creech's previous novels."

A snippet of a story told by her two-year-old granddaughter combined with Creech's experiences returning to Switzerland while her husband worked there during the 2007-08 school year to produce her novel *The Unfinished Angel.* In an Italian-speaking village located in the Swiss Alps there stands an ancient stone tower, and this tower is the home of a spunky angel who looks out for the local villagers. Only the children can sense An-

gel's presence, and they enjoy her humorous antics. When Zola arrives from America, she has a sense of fun that matches that of the village guardian, and soon she and Angel team up to enliven village life and also make the future brighter for a group of unhappy orphans. "Some books are absolute magic, and this is one of them," asserted Alyson Low in her *School Library Journal* review of *The Unfinished Angel,* praising the story's "tender, comical celebration of the human spirit" as well as Angel's humorous tendency to invent words to fill in the holes in her vocabulary. A *Kirkus Reviews* writer also cited the levity in Angel's dialogue, describing it as a string of "phonemic mix-ups, word coinage, inverted grammar and nonsense that soars and fizzes." "As adept at writing fantasy as she is creating slice-of-life novels, Newbery medalist Creech . . . again works her magic," concluded a *Publishers Weekly* contributor, while in *School Library Journal* Marzena Currie described *The Unfinished Angel* as "a delightful story which will bring smiles and laughter all around."

Described by *Booklist* contributor Jennifer Mattson as "a departure for Creech," *The Castle Corona* draws on the author's fascination with the ruined remains of castles that she explored during her years spent in England and Europe. Illustrated by David Diaz, the story reads like a fairy tale although whimsy replaces standard fantasy elements. Orphaned siblings Pia and Enzio make their home in a feudal Italian village in the shadow of Castle Corona, and they are captivated by the royal family living nearby. When the children discover a pouch containing a cache of stolen objects, they decide to return them to King Guido and Queen Gabriella, even though they might be accused of the theft. Their decision proves to be a good one for both the orphans and the royal family, resulting in what *School Library Journal* contributor Barbara Scotto described as a "good-natured, rollicking romp" in which Diaz evokes the Medieval-esque setting in intricate "illustrations [that] capture the feeling of medieval illuminations." For Mattson, the high points of the novel included its "engaging, puzzlelike plot," while a *Publishers Weekly* critic cited Creech's "playful tone and gently criticism of aristocracy." Rohrlick described *The Castle Corona* as "a charming read" with "a gentle sense of humor," and a *Kirkus Reviews* writer praised Creech's "original fairy tale" as "immensely satisfying both in its telling and its presentation."

Although best known for her novels for middle-graders and young adults, Creech is also the author of several picture books, including *A Fine, Fine School, Granny Torrelli Makes Soup,* and *Who's That Baby?* An enthusiastic educator named Mr. Keene (inspired by Creech's husband) decides to keep school open on Saturdays in *A Fine, Fine School.* Not surprisingly, his plan does not please the students, especially Tillie. Tillie's time for climbing trees and playing with her dog is even more seriously curtailed when the principal takes his radical plan further, and requires school attendance on Sundays, holidays, and even during the summer. When

Tillie confronts Mr. Keene and persuasively argues that learning takes place outside the classroom as well, he comes to understand that having time to teach a pet dog some new tricks is as valuable as time in the classroom. "This book has it all," wrote Ilene Cooper in her *Booklist* review of *A Fine, Fine School:* "a fine, fresh idea [and] a witty text that's fun to read aloud."

Granny Torrelli Makes Soup introduces friends Rosie and Bailey. Bailey, the boy who lives next door to Rosie, is blind, and the two have been friends for a very long time. The friendship is threatened, however, when Rosie unwittingly usurps the one thing that makes Bailey feel special: reading Braille. Fortunately, Granny invites Bailey over to help make soup, and the three of them are able to work through misunderstandings during their time in Granny's kitchen. "Rosie's present-tense voice is fresh and young, with an ingenuous turn of phrase," wrote a *Kirkus Reviews* contributor. *School Library Journal* critic Maria B. Salvadore noted that Creech's "authentic voice gradually reveals what has happened and the accompanying emotions ranging from anger and angst to happiness and contentment."

The poems in *Who's That Baby?* are geared toward the adults who read them aloud as much as to their young audience. Inspired by the birth of Creech's granddaughter, the collection includes poem-songs about babies doing baby things, or looking like burritos wrapped up in their quilts. All of the poems are told in the first-person, from the perspective of the baby. "The often-rhythmic, short-lined poem-songs are perfect for reading aloud to baby burritos," wrote Karin Snelson in her review of *Who's That Baby?* for *Booklist.*

Despite her successful career writing for younger readers, Creech never intended to be a children's writer; in fact, her first novel, *Absolutely Normal Chaos,* was written with adults as the intended audience. After her publishers decided to market it for young adults, the writer did some research in order to find out how children's books are made, and she soon discovered that she had a knack for writing for a young audience. As Creech later joked to *Time* magazine interviewer Andrea Sachs, "If you came up and tapped me on the shoulder when I was in one of my writing trances, I suppose I would maybe talk like a seventh grader."

Biographical and Critical Sources

BOOKS

Beacham's Guide to Literature for Young Adults, Volumes 9, 11, 12, Gale (Detroit, MI), 2001.

Children's Literature Review, Volume 42, Gale (Detroit, MI), 1997.

St. James Guide to Young-Adult Writers, 2nd edition, St. James Press (Detroit, MI), 1999, pp. 195-197.

PERIODICALS

Booklist, September 15, 1998, John Peters, review of *Bloomability,* p. 226; April 1, 2000, Carolyn Phelan, review of *The Wanderer,* p. 1456; August, 2001, Ilene Cooper, review of *A Fine, Fine School,* p. 2116, and Hazel Rochman, review of *Love That Dog: Learning about Poetry from Miss Stretchberry,* p. 2118; March 15, 2002, review of *Love That Dog,* p. 1234; April 1, 2002, Carolyn Phelan, review of *Ruby Holler,* p. 1328; February 1, 2004, Jennifer Mattson, review of *Heartbeat,* p. 976; August, 2005, Karin Snelson, review of *Who's That Baby?: New-Baby Songs,* p. 2032; September 1, 2005, Hazel Rochman, review of *Replay,* p. 124; September 1, 2007, Jennifer Mattson, review of *The Castle Corona,* p. 113; August 1, 2008, Thom Barthelmess, review of *Hate That Cat,* p. 70; July 1, 2009, Andrew Medlar, review of *The Unfinished Angel,* p. 61.

Bulletin of the Center for Children's Books, March, 2004, Timnah Card, review of *Heartbeat,* p. 267.

Five Owls, fall, 2004, Susie Wilde, review of *Granny Torrelli Makes Soup,* p. 22.

Horn Book, September-October, 1998, Nancy Bond, review of *Bloomability,* p. 605; November-December, 2001, Betty Carter, review of *Love That Dog,* p. 743; May-June, 2002, Joanna Rudge Long, review of *Ruby Holler,* p. 327; November-December, 2003, Betty Carter, review of *Granny Torrelli Makes Soup,* p. 741; May-June, 2004, Susan Dove Lempke, review of *Heartbeat,* p. 326; November-December, 2005, Susan Dove Lempke, review of *Replay,* p. 714; November-December, 2007, Susan Dove Lempke, review of *The Castle Corona,* p. 675; November-December, 2008, Susan Dove Lempke, review of *Hate That Cat,* p. 699.

Journal of Adolescent & Adult Literacy, May, 2002, Jennifer Anstiss, review of *Love That Dog,* p. 794.

Kirkus Reviews, March 15, 2002, review of *Ruby Holler,* p. 408; July 1, 2003, review of *Granny Torrelli Makes Soup,* p. 908; August 15, 2005, review of *Who's That Baby?,* p. 911; September 1, 2007, review of *The Castle Corona;* September 1, 2008, review of *Hate That Cat;* September 15, 2009, review of *The Unfinished Angel.*

Kliatt, May, 2002, Paula Rohrlick, review of *Ruby Holler,* p. 6, and review of *The Wanderer,* p. 18; September, 2004, Mary Purucker, review of *Heartbeat,* p. 61; March, 2005, Claire Rosser, review of *Granny Torrelli Makes Soup,* p. 18; September, 2005, Paula Rohrlick, review of *Replay,* p. 7; September, 2007, Paula Rohrlick, review of *The Castle Corona,* p. 9.

New York Times Book Review, October 21, 2001, Meg Wolitzer, review of *Love That Dog,* p. 30; January 11, 2009, Julie Just, review of *Hate That Cat,* p. 13.

Publishers Weekly, July 20, 1998, review of *Bloomability,* p. 220; June 18, 2001, review of *Love That Dog,* p. 82; July 16, 2001, Jason Britton, interview with Creech, p. 153; July 23, 2001, review of *A Fine, Fine School,* p. 75; March 4, 2002, review of *Ruby Holler,* p. 80; April 19, 2004, Claire Kirch, "A New Moon for Sharon Creech," p. 26; May 10, 2004, review of

Heartbeat, p. 19; January 10, 2005, review of *Granny Torrelli Makes Soup,* p. 58; September 5, 2005, review of *Replay,* p. 63; September 17, 2007, review of *The Castle Corona,* p. 54; September 28, 2009, review of *The Unfinished Angel,* p. 64.

School Librarian, spring, 2010, Marzena Currie, review of *The Unfinished Angel,* p. 33.

School Library Journal, August, 2001, Grace Oliff, review of *A Fine, Fine School,* p. 144, Lee Bock, review of *Love That Dog,* p. 177; September, 2001, interview with Creech, p. 21; August, 2003, "Sharon Creech Wins Carnegie Medal," p. 20, and Maria B. Salvadore, review of *Granny Torrelli Makes Soup,* p. 158; February, 2004, Luann Toth, review of *Heartbeat,* p. 142; November, 2004, Alison Follos, review of *Love That Dog,* p. 65; February, 2005, Joyce Adams Burner, review of *Granny Torrelli Makes Soup,* p. 58; September, 2005, Maria B. Salvadore, review of *Replay,* p. 203; October, 2005, Bina Williams, review of *Who's That Baby?,* p. 136; October, 2007, Barbara Scotto, review of *The Castle Corona,* p. 146; October, 2008, Marie Orlando, review of *Hate That Cat,* p. 142; September, 2009, Alyson Low, review of *The Unfinished Angel,* p. 154.

Time, August 27, 2001, Andrea Sachs, "A Writer Who's Thirteen at Heart," p. F17.

ONLINE

Sharon Creech Home Page, http://www.sharoncreech.com (February 15, 2011).*

*　　*　　*

CROSSINGHAM, John 1974-

Personal

Born 1974, in Canada.

Addresses

Home—Toronto, Ontario, Canada.

Career

Singer, songwriter, and writer. Performer with indie rock bands ThanatoPop, Raising the Fawn, beginning 1997, and Broken Social Scene, beginning 1999. Recordings include: (with Raising the Fawn) *Raising the Fawn,* 2001, *By the Warmth of Your Flame,* 2004, *The Maginot Line,* 2006, (with Broken Social Scene) *Broken Social Scene,* 2005, and *Forgiveness Rock Record.* 2010.

Writings

NONFICTION

(With Bobbie Kalman) *The Earth from A to Z* ("AlphaBasiCs" series), Crabtree (New York, NY), 1999.

(With Bobbie Kalman) *Colonial Home* ("Historic Communities" series), Crabtree (New York, NY), 2000.

(With Bobbie Kalman) *Endangered Pandas* ("Earth's Endangered Animals" series), Crabtree (New York, NY), 2005.

(With Bobbie Kalman) *Seashore Food Chains* ("Food Chains" series), Crabtree (New York, NY), 2005.

(With Bobbie Kalman) *Seals and Sea Lions* "Living Ocean" series), Crabtree (New York, NY), 2006.

(With Bobbie Kalman) *Insect Homes* ("World of Insects" series), Crabtree (New York, NY), 2006.

(With Bobbie Kalman) *Land Habitats* ("Introducing Habitats" series), Crabtree (New York, NY), 2007.

Learn to Speak Music: A Guide to Creating, Performing, and Promoting Your Songs, illustrated by Jeff Kulak, Owlkids (Berkeley, CA), 2009.

Author's work has been translated into French and Spanish.

"SPORTS IN ACTION" NONFICTION SERIES

(With Sarah Dann) *Basketball in Action,* Crabtree (New York, NY), 2000.

(With Sarah Dann) *Baseball in Action,* Crabtree (New York, NY), 2000.

(With Sarah Dann) *Volleyball in Action,* Crabtree (New York, NY), 2000.

Lacrosse in Action, Crabtree (New York, NY), 2001.

Football in Action, Crabtree (New York, NY), 2001.

Cycling in Action, illustrated by Bonna Rousa, Crabtree (New York, NY), 2002.

Snowboarding in Action, illustrated by Bonna Rousa, Crabtree (New York, NY), 2002.

Skateboarding in Action, illustrated by Bonna Rousa, Crabtree (New York, NY), 2002.

Tennis in Action, illustrated by Bonna Rousa, Crabtree (New York, NY), 2002.

(With Niki Walker) *Swimming in Action,* illustrated by Bonna Rousa, Crabtree (New York, NY), 2003.

(With Bobbie Kalman) *Gymnastics in Action,* illustrated by Bonna Rousa, Crabtree (New York, NY), 2003.

In-line Skating in Action, illustrated by Bonna Rousa, Crabtree (New York, NY), 2003.

Wrestling in Action, illustrated by Bonna Rousa, Crabtree (New York, NY), 2003.

Cheerleading in Action, illustrated by Bonna Rousa, Crabtree (New York, NY), 2003.

(With Bobbie Kalman) *Skiing in Action,* Crabtree (New York, NY), 2005.

(With Bobbie Kalman) *Track Events in Action,* Crabtree (New York, NY), 2005.

(With Bobbie Kalman) *Judo in Action,* Crabtree (New York, NY), 2006.

Author's work has been translated into French and Spanish.

"SCIENCE OF LIVING THINGS" NONFICTION SERIES; WITH BOBBIE KALMAN

What Are Camouflage and Mimicry?, Crabtree (New York, NY), 2001.

What Is a Bear?, Crabtree (New York, NY), 2001.
What Is an Elephant?, Crabtree (New York, NY), 2001.
What Is Migration?, Crabtree (New York, NY), 2002.
What Is Hiberation?, Crabtree (New York, NY), 2002.

"LIFE CYCLE" NONFICTION SERIES; WITH BOBBIE KALMAN

The Life Cycle of a Snake, Crabtree (New York, NY), 2003.
The Life Cycle of a Raccoon, Crabtree (New York, NY), 2003.
The Life Cycle of a Shark, Crabtree (New York, NY), 2006.

"EXTREME SPORTS; NO LIMITS!" NONFICTION SERIES; WITH BOBBIE KALMAN

Extreme Skateboarding, Crabtree (New York, NY), 2004.
Extreme Surfing, Crabtree (New York, NY), 2004.
Extreme In-line Skating, Crabtree (New York, NY), 2004.
Extreme Motocross, Crabtree (New York, NY), 2004.
Extreme Climbing, Crabtree (New York, NY), 2004.
Extreme Sports, Crabtree (New York, NY), 2004.
Extreme Skydiving, Crabtree (New York, NY), 2006.

"SPORTS STARTERS" NONFICTION SERIES

(With Bobbie Kalman) *Kick It Soccer*, Crabtree (St. Catherine's, Ontario, Canada), 2007.
(With Bobbie Kalman) *Slam Dunk Basketball*, Crabtree (St. Catherine's, Ontario, Canada), 2007.
(With Bobbie Kalman) *Huddle up Football*, Crabtree (St. Catherine's, Ontario, Canada), 2007.
Spike It Volleyball, Crabtree (St. Catherine's, Ontario, Canada), 2008.
Pass It Lacrosse, Crabtree (St. Catherine's, Ontario, Canada), 2008.
Slap Shot Hockey, Crabtree (St. Catherine's, Ontario, Canada), 2008.
High Flying Martian Arts, Crabtree (St. Catherine's, Ontario, Canada), 2008.

Sidelights

Canadian singer and songwriter John Crossingham started his musical career with the Ontario band ThanatoPop before cofounding Toronto-based Raising the Fawn in 1997. While continuing to record with Raising the Fawn, he also teamed up with the members of another band in the city, Broken Social Scene, in 1999, and has performed and recorded with both bands in the years since. To support his musical career, Crossingham also worked as a freelance writer for Crabtree Publishing, where he created dozens of nonfiction books for elementary-grade readers. In 2009 he combined his experience as a working musician with his talent for writing in *Learn to Speak Music: A Guide to Creating, Performing, and Promoting Your Songs.*

Featuring mid-mod-styled illustrations by Jeff Kulak, *Learn to Speak Music* helps young musicians and garage-band wannabes develop the skills needed to share their creative talent with audiences. From deciding which instrument to learn to mastering basic musical terms, writing songs, jamming with friends, and working with other musicians in a band, Crossingham's book also provides practical advice on finding gigs and recording and promoting one's band locally. His text is augmented with advice from a number of Canadian musicians, such as Emily Haines, Kevin Drew, and Andrew Whiteman, who share their own experiences working in bands and building a following.

In appraising *Learn to Speak Music*, a *Kirkus Reviews* writer characterized Crossingham's guide as full of "general advice of the commonsense variety," while Ann Ketcheson wrote in *Resource Links* that the veteran musician "speaks from experience" in conveying "a great deal of practical information." The author's "easy tone . . . doesn't talk down to the reader," according to *Booklist* contributor Ilene Cooper, and in *Macleans* Michael Barclay asserted that his "clear, plain language [is] devoid of the drab bafflegab that drags down other how-to books for any age." Praising *Learn to Speak Music* as "incredibly readable" and featuring a "comfortable, conversational tone," Tracy Weiskind added in *School Library Journal* that Crossingham's book is also inspirational: it "will wow anyone who is ready to recognize that creative spark within," according to the critic.

Biographical and Critical Sources

PERIODICALS

Booklist, November 1, 2009, Ilene Cooper, review of *Learn to Speak Music: A Guide to Creating, Performing, and Promoting Your Songs*, p. 57.
Kirkus Reviews, September 15, 2009, review of *Learn to Speak Music*.
Macleans, October 29, 2009, Michael Barclay, review of *Learning to Speak Music*.
Publishers Weekly, November 2, 2009, review of *Learn to Speak Music*, p. 53.
Resource Links, February, 2010, Ann Ketcheson, review of *Learn to Speak Music*, p. 37.
School Library Journal, November, 2009, Tracy Weiskind, review of *Learn to Speak Music*, p. 128.

ONLINE

AllMusic Web site, http://www.allmusic.com/ (February 15, 2011), "John Crossingham."*

D

DEWAN, Ted 1961-

Personal

Born 1961, in Boston, MA; immigrated to England, 1988; married Helen Cooper; children: Pandora. *Education:* Brown University, degree (engineering and electronic music); studied art with author/illustrator David Macaulay. *Hobbies and other interests:* Music.

Addresses

Home—Oxford, England. *E-mail*—ted.dewan@worm works.com.

Career

Writer and artist. Milton Academy, Boston, MA, physics instructor for five years; freelance artist, 1988—.

Member

Society of Authors (former chairman, Children's Writers and Illustrators Group).

Awards, Honors

Mother Goose Award, and *Times Educational Supplement* Information Award shortlist, both 1992, both for *Inside the Whale and Other Animals;* Kurt Maschler Award shortlist, 1997, for *The Sorcerer's Apprentice;* Blue Peter Award, and Kate Greenaway Award Honorable Mention, both 2002, both for *Crispin, the Pig Who Had It All; Publishers Weekly* Ten Best Books of the Year selection, 2004, for *Bing Bunny.*

Writings

SELF-ILLUSTRATED; FOR CHILDREN

(Reteller) *Three Billy Goats Gruff,* Andre Deutsch (London, England), 1994, Scholastic (New York, NY), 1995.

Top Secret, Andre Deutsch (London, England), 1996, Doubleday (New York, NY), 1997.

(Reteller) *The Sorcerer's Apprentice, and Music of Magic and Electricity* (based on *Der Zauberhling* by Johann Wolfgang von Goethe; includes audiotape), Corgi (London, England), 1997, Doubleday (New York, NY), 1998.

The Weatherbirds (nonfiction), Puffin (London, England), 1999.

Crispin, the Pig Who Had It All, Doubleday (New York, NY), 2000.

Baby Gets the Zapper, Transworld (London, England), 2001, Random House (New York, NY), 2002.

Crispin and the Three Little Piglets, Transworld (London, England), 2002, Doubleday (New York, NY), 2003.

Crispin and the Best Birthday Surprise Ever, Transworld (London, England), 2007.

One True Bear, Bloomsbury (New York, NY), 2009.

"BING BUNNY" SERIES: SELF-ILLUSTRATED; FOR CHILDREN

Get Dressed, David Fickling Books (New York, NY), 2003.

Paint Day, David Fickling Books (New York, NY), 2003.

Bed Time, David Fickling Books (New York, NY), 2003.

Something for Daddy, David Fickling Books (New York, NY), 2003.

Go Picnic, David Fickling Books (New York, NY), 2004.

Make Music, David Fickling Books (New York, NY), 2004.

Swing, David Fickling Books (New York, NY), 2004.

Yuk!, David Fickling Books (New York, NY), 2004.

ILLUSTRATOR; FOR CHILDREN

Grace L. Mitchell and Harriet Chmela, *I Am, I Can: A Preschool Curriculum,* Telshare, 1977.

Steve Parker, *Inside the Whale and Other Animals,* Doubleday (New York, NY), 1992.

Steve Parker, *Inside Dinosaurs and Other Prehistoric Creatures,* Dorling Kindersley (London, England), 1993, Doubleday (New York, NY), 1994.

Kit Wright, *Rumpelstiltskin,* Hippo (London, England), 1998.

Helen Cooper, *Sandmare,* Corgi (London, England), 2001, Farrar, Straus & Giroux (New York, NY), 2004.

Elizabeth Kay, *The Divide,* Chicken House (Frome, England), 2003.

Elizabeth Laird, *The Ice Cream Swipe,* Oxford University Press (Oxford, England, 2003.

Elizabeth Kay, *Back to the Divide,* Scholastic (New York, NY), 2004.

Elizabeth Kay, *The Half Twist,* Chicken House (Frome, England), 2005.

Elizabeth Kay, *Jinx on the Divide,* Scholastic (New York, NY), 2007.

Sophie Masson, *Thomas Trew and the Flying Huntsman,* Hodder Children's (London, England), 2007.

ILLUSTRATOR; FOR ADULTS

Robert Ornstein, *The Evolution of Consciousness,* Prentice-Hall (Englewood Cliffs, NJ), 1991.

Robert Ornstein, *The Roots of the Self: Unraveling the Mystery of Who We Are,* HarperCollins (San Francisco, CA), 1993.

James Burke and Robert Ornstein, *The Axemaker's Gift,* Putnam (New York, NY), 1995.

Marc D. Hauser, *Wild Minds,* Henry Holt (New York, NY), 1999.

John Lloyd and John Mitchinsun, *The Book of Animal Ignorance: Everything You Think You Know Is Wrong,* Faber & Faber (London, England), 2007, Harmony, 2008.

Robert Ornstein, *MindReal: How the Mind Creates Its Own Virtual Reality,* Malor Books (Boston, MA), 2008.

Dewan's illustrations have appeared in British newspapers, including as regular features in the London *Times, Daily Telegraph, Independent,* and *Guardian.*

Sidelights

An American-born artist who now makes his home in England, Ted Dewan has been praised for creating book illustrations that feature his characteristic quirky, engaging style. Using his artistic skills, timely approach, and creative concepts, Dewan encourages readers to find new appreciation for familiar material. *Books for Keeps* contributor Pam Harwood admired the author's "'cool' language" and "bright, lively pictures," which bring Dewan's adaptation of the time-honored story *Three Billy Goats Gruff* back to life. Among original tales, Dewan has also authored such self-illustrated picture books as *Baby Gets the Zapper, One True Bear,* and *Crispin and the Three Little Piglets,* in addition to the toddler-friendly tales in his "Bing Bunny" series. Praising the spunky black bunny character who stars in *Paint Day, Get Dressed, Make Music,* and several other tales, Ilene Cooper wrote in *Booklist* that "it's hard to know what's more fun" in a "Bing Bunny" book: "the computer-collage art or the satisfying way Dewan captures a child's world."

After studying engineering at Brown University and teaching physics at Milton Academy in Boston, Massachusetts, Dewan decided to make a career change. He began illustrating nonfiction books for both children and adults, including several volumes by science writer Steve Parker. Published in 1992, *Inside the Whale* showcases Dewan's pen-and-ink and watercolor drawings alongside Parker's examination of the morphology of the world's largest mammals. Similar in format, *Inside Dinosaurs and Other Prehistoric Creatures* investigates the processes used by modern scientists to recreate detailed models of dinosaurs. *School Library Journal* contributor Cathryn A. Camper praised both books for using "humor and imagination, instead of knives" to examine the anatomy of these creatures.

With the success of his illustrations for Parker, Dewan moved on to create his own stories for children, and he attempts to explain one of the great mysteries of childhood in *Top Secret.* Published in 1996, *Top Secret* reveals, in a comic-book format, the complex technology and heroic bravery responsible for the legend of the tooth fairy. In Dewan's book, the "new kid"—one of seven turtle-like creatures—describes the dangerous mission with which his crew has been charged. Their goal: undetected tooth extraction from beneath the pillow of a sleeping girl and replacement of said tooth with a shiny coin. *School Library Journal* contributor Karen James noted Dewan's humorous peppering of technical jargon, such as "zip cable" and "Slumber Zone," to augment the text. Citing the combination of "catchy lingo of the narration and the Lego-like machines," a *Kirkus Reviews* critic called *Top Secret* "adventurous fun, especially for the mechanically inclined,"

The star of Ted Dewan's slyly humorous picture book Crispin, the Pig Who Had It All *acts truly piggy when Santa delivers a far-too-lightweight Christmas package.* (Copyright © 2000 by Ted Dewan. Used by permission of Doubleday, an imprint of Random House Children's Books, a division of Random House, Inc.)

while *Booklist* reviewer Carolyn Phelan predicted that "children will enjoy the visual wit and pizzazz that characterizes this original picture book."

The Sorcerer's Apprentice, and Music of Magic and Electricity, which Dewan based on a ballad by eighteenth-century German writer Johann Wolfgang von Goethe, features an unusual character—a robot—in the title role. In a workplace that *School Librarian* contributor Anne Rowe described as "a cross between a metal workshop and Dr. Frankenstein's laboratory," Dewan's modern-day sorcerer puts together gears, wires, bulbs, transistors, and other mechanical things to create new inventions. Because his workshop has becoming cluttered with bits of left-over stuff, the sorcerer wires together a savvy robot apprentice to clean up after him. The first robot, who quickly becomes addicted to technology in the form of television, accumulates enough stuff to build a successor to perform the cleanup; this new robot does the same. So it goes, until all the robots revolt against the sorcerer, forcing the inventor to flip the "off" switch on his entire mechanical crew, all except his original apprentice. A *Publishers Weekly* contributor called *The Sorcerer's Apprentice* a "post-modern melodrama" that "cautions against cloning, environmental depletion and television," while a *Kirkus Reviews* writer dubbed the work a "rollicking remake of the classic tale." Drawing on his interest in electronic music, Dewan also created a musical accompaniment to his visual story, arranging compositions by Paul-Abraham Dukas and Camille Saint-Saëns and including his own, titled "The March of the Robots."

Wealthy young porker Crispin Tamworth is introduced in Dewan's self-illustrated *Crispin: The Pig Who Had It All,* which focuses on what *Booklist* reviewer Ilene Cooper called "a familiar theme, made fresh and funny thanks to a witty yet heartfelt text and eye-popping art." Getting anything and everything he wants, Crispin values next to nothing, and his room soon becomes a dumping ground for broken and discarded toys of all sorts. Still, there is always something new to want, and when Santa leaves him nothing but an empty box one Christmas, the pig is more than a little petulant. Fortunately, with the help of resourceful new friends Penny and Nick, he learns that a toy's real value is having someone to share it with.

Another sort of sharing—sharing his family with a new sibling—is the focus of *Crispin and the Three Little Piglets,* which finds Crispin out of the limelight when his mother brings home three new siblings. In *School Library Journal* Barbara Buckley praised Dewan's "cleverness," noting that the illustrations of Crispin and his endlessly exercising mother in their upper-middle-class home "give real personalities to all of the characters." Also enjoying Dewan's humorous twist on the classic story about the three little pigs, Julie Cummins wrote in *Booklist* that *Crispin and the Three Little Pig-*

Dewan retells a traditional story and pairs it with updated artwork in **The Sorcerer's Apprentice.** (Copyright © 1997 by Ted Dewan. Used by permission of Doubleday, an imprint of Random House Children's Books, a division of Random House, Inc.)

lets is enlivened by "puckish, humorous illustrations . . . burst[ing] with details that reflect real life with a twist."

In *One True Bear* Damien is a little boy who takes out his anger on his toys, especially teddy bears. Most bears in the Bear Force know they are not up to the challenge, even though every child should have a special teddy. Then a brave bear named Darcy Brewster volunteers to become Damien's teddy bear, and after a period of time the patient toy is able to help Damien form his first friendship. In *School Library Journal* Catherine Callegari praised Dewan's "wonderfully rich and detailed illustrations," and in *Booklist* Diane Foote wrote that his depiction of "a realistic, high-energy boy" is a feature of this "particularly satisfying" picture book. *One True Bear* "brings to mind Margery Williams' *The Velveteen Rabbit*," a *Kirkus Reviews* writer maintained, the critic adding that Dewan's "old-fashioned tale is sweet and charming and will bring enjoyment to many a child."

Each of Dewan's books takes up to eight months to create, from idea to finished art, and most of that time is spent on the illustrations. Noting on his home page that he chose not to major in art during college because "I didn't think I was groovy enough to fit in with the other art students (I didn't have any black clothes)," he offered this encouragement to aspiring illustrators: "The best way to become good at drawing is to do a lot of it. Too many people stop drawing when they're ten because suddenly they get worried that they're not good enough. You have to keep practicing if you want to get better."

Book illustration is only one of Dewan's creative endeavors; he also works occasionally as an installation artist creating unique environments. One of his three-dimensional works, "King of Instruments," was exhibited in Oxford, England, in 2003 and featured a Steampunk home cinema that screened a homemade faux-educational filmstrip concerning a takeover plot by pipe organs (the film was collaboration with Dewan's brother, New York-based artist Brian Dewan). A year later he was commissioned by the Oxford City Council to create the "Cyclemas Tree," a holiday sculpture constructed from the city's surplus of derelict bicycles. Interestingly, this project started something of a holiday tradition among local artists. In 2007, as lead artist for Luminox, Oxfordshire's Millennium celebration, in 2007, Dewan worked closely with the French fire-installation group Carabosse to transform Oxford's central piazza, Broad Street, into a wonderland of fire; his own contribution was a seventy-foot bamboo structure from which hung a fiery pendulum that was gently propelled by members of the public, swinging 1,000 times every evening for the duration of the celebration.

In 2010 Dewan was lead designer and the primary energy behind the creation of Britain's first-ever resident-designed-and-built "DIY Street," sponsored by Sustrans

Dewan creates art that brings to life his captivating story in the picture book **One True Bear.** (Walker & Company, 2009. Copyright © 2009 by Ted Dewan. Reproduced by permission.)

as well as by private donations. The in-street installation took four years of planning and consultation with Dewan's neighbors. Inspired by the idea of two young residents, the imaginative streetscape features an enormous Cheshire Cat planter that is only visible under the light of car headlamps. As the first artist-in-residence for the Oxford-based Story Museum, he also created lamps and door hardware, as well as an installation presenting itself as a household goods shop catering exclusively to the city's prestigious "fictional community."

Biographical and Critical Sources

PERIODICALS

Booklist, April 1, 1997, Carolyn Phelan, review of *Top Secret,* p. 1337; November 15, 2000, Ilene Cooper, review of *Crispin: The Pig Who Had It All,* p. 638; April 1, 2003, Julie Cummins, review of *Crispin and the Three Little Piglets,* p. 1401; May 1, 2003, Diane Foote, review of *Sandmare,* p. 1591; February 15, 2004, Ilene Cooper, review of *Get Dressed,* p. 1062; May 1, 2005, Jennifer Mattson, review of *Go Picnic,* p. 1589; July 1, 2008, Nancy Bent, review of *The Book of Animal Ignorance: Everything You Think You Know Is Wrong,* p. 22; December 1, 2009, Diane Foote, review of *One True Bear,* p. 52.

Books for Keeps, September, 1995, Pam Harwood, review of *Three Billy Goats Gruff,* p. 10.

Kirkus Reviews, January 15, 1997, review of *Top Secret,* p. 140; December 1, 1997, review of *The Sorcerer's Apprentice,* p. 1774; January 1, 2002, review of *Baby Gets the Zapper,* p. 43; December 15, 2002, review of *Crispin and the Three Little Piglets,* p. 1849; September 15, 2009, review of *One True Bear.*

Publishers Weekly, February 24, 1997, review of *Top Secret,* p. 90; January 12, 1998, review of *The Sorcerer's Apprentice,* p. 59; January 19, 2004, reviews of *Get Dresses* and *Paint Day,* both p. 74; October 25, 2004, review of *Something for Daddy,* p. 49; January 17, 2005, review of *Go Picnic* and *Make Music,* p. 38.

School Librarian, November, 1997, Anne Rowe, review of *The Sorcerer's Apprentice,* p. 185.

School Library Journal, April, 1994, Cathryn A. Camper, review of *Inside Dinosaurs and Other Prehistoric Creatures,* p. 144; March, 1997, Karen James, review of *Top Secret,* p. 150; March, 2003, Barbara Buckley, review of *Crispin and the Three Little Piglets,* p. 191; July, 2004, Olga R. Kuharets, review of *Get Dressed,* p. 69; July, 2003, Shara Alpern, review of *Sandmare,* p. 89; September, 2003, Bruce Anne Shook, review of *The Divide,* p. 215; July, 2004, Olga R. Kuharets, review of *Get Dressed,* p. 69; September, 2004, Steven Engelfried, review of *Back to the Divide,* p. 209; February, 2005, Martha Topol, review of *Go Picnic,* p. 96; January, 2006, Lisa Marie Williams, review of *Jinx on the Divide,* p. 135; November, 2009, Catherine Callegari, review of *One True Bear,* p. 76.

ONLINE

Ted Dewan Home Page, http://www.wormworks.com (February 15, 2011).

*   *   *

DITCHFIELD, Christin 1973-

Personal

Born 1973. *Education:* Southwestern University, M.A. (biblical theology). *Religion:* Christian.

Addresses

Home—Sarasota, FL. *Office*—Take It to Heart Ministries, P.O. Box 1000, Osprey, FL 34229. *E-mail*—Christin@takeittoheartradio.com.

Career

Christian speaker, radio personality, and writer. *Take It to Heart* (internationally syndicated two-minute daily devotional radio program), host; guest on radio and television programs; speaker at conferences.

Writings

FOR CHILDREN

Cowlick!, illustrated by Rosalind Beardshaw, Random House (New York, NY), 2007.

Christin Ditchfield (Reproduced by permission.)

"Shwatsit!": No One Knows Just What It Means, illustrated by Rosalind Beardshaw, Golden Books (New York, NY), 2009.

Bible Stories of Boys and Girls, illustrated by Jerry Smath, Golden Books (New York, NY), 2010.

Little Golden Book Bible Favorites, illustrated by Pamela Broughton, Random House (New York, NY), 2011.

SERIES NONFICTION; FOR CHILDREN

Sports Great Michael Chang, Enslow Publishers (Springfield, NJ), 1999.

Kayaking, Canoeing, Rowing, and Yachting, Children's Press (New York, NY), 2000.

Swimming and Diving, Children's Press (New York, NY), 2000.

Top Ten American Women's Olympic Gold Medalists, Enslow (Berkeley Heights, NJ), 2000.

Wrestling, Children's Press (New York, NY), 2000.

Gymnastics, Children's Press (New York, NY), 2000.

Cycling, Children's Press (New York, NY), 2000.

Martina Hingis, introduction by Hannah Storm, Chelsea House (Philadelphia, PA), 2001.

Wood, Children's Press (New York, NY), 2002.

Water, Children's Press (New York, NY), 2002.

Soil, Children's Press (New York, NY), 2002.

Coal, Children's Press (New York, NY), 2002.

Joseph E. Johnston: Confederate General, Chelsea House (Philadelphia, PA), 2002.

Oil, Children's Press (New York, NY), 2002.

Condoleezza Rice: National Security Advisor, Franklin Watts (New York, NY), 2003, revised as *Condoleezza Rice: America's Leading Stateswoman,* 2007.

Johnny Appleseed, Children's Press (New York, NY), 2003.

Golf, Children's Press (Danbury, CT), 2003.

Ice Hockey, Children's Press (New York, NY), 2003.

Memorial Day, Children's Press (New York, NY), 2003.

Presidents' Day, Children's Press (New York, NY), 2003.

The Shoshone, Children's Press (New York, NY), 2003.

Tennis, Children's Press (New York, NY), 2003.

Volleyball, Children's Press (New York, NY), 2003.

Bible Heroes of the Old Testament, illustrated by Ande Cook, Golden Books (New York, NY), 2004.

Knowing Your Civil Rights, Children's Press (New York, NY), 2004.

Serving Your Community, Children's Press (New York, NY), 2004.

Freedom of Speech, Children's Press (New York, NY), 2004.

Clara Barton: Founder of the American Red Cross, Franklin Watts (New York, NY), 2004.

The Comanche, Children's Press (New York, NY), 2005.

Louisa May Alcott: Author of Little Women, Franklin Watts (New York, NY), 2005.

The Choctaw, Children's Press (New York, NY), 2005.

The Blackfoot, Children's Press (New York, NY), 2005.

The Chippewa, Children's Press (New York, NY), 2005.

The Arapaho, Children's Press (New York, NY), 2005.

The Crow, Children's Press (New York, NY), 2005.

The Lewis and Clark Expedition, Children's Press (New York, NY), 2006.

Spanish Missions, Children's Press (New York, NY), 2006.

Bono, Cherry Lake Pub. (Ann Arbor, MI), 2008.

Northeast Indians, Heinemann-Raintree (Mankato, MN), 2011.

Plateau Indians, Heinemann-Raintree (Mankato, MN), 2011.

The Story of Plastic, Heinemann-Raintree (Mankato, MN), 2011.

The Story of Soap, Heinemann-Raintree (Mankato, MN), 2011.

The Story of Water, Heinemann-Raintree (Mankato, MN), 2011.

The Story of Wool, Heinemann-Raintree (Mankato, MN), 2011.

North Carolina ("Thirteen Colonies" series), Heinemann-Raintree (Mankato, MN), 2011.

South Carolina ("Thirteen Colonies" series), Heinemann-Raintree (Mankato, MN), 2011.

Virginia ("Thirteen Colonies" series), Heinemann-Raintree (Mankato, MN), 2011.

OTHER

A Family Guide to Narnia: Biblical Truths in C.S. Lewis's The Chronicles of Narnia, Crossway (Wheaton, IL), 2003.

Take It to Heart: Sixty Meditations on God and His Word, Crossway Books (Wheaton, IL), 2005.

The Three Wise Women: A Christmas Reflection, Crossway Books (Wheaton, IL), 2005.

A Family Guide to The Lion, the Witch, and the Wardrobe, Crossway Books (Wheaton, IL), 2005.

A Family Guide to Prince Caspian, Crossway Books (Wheaton, IL), 2007.

A Family Guide to the Bible, Crossway Books (Wheaton, IL), 2009.

A Way with Words: What Women Should Know about the Power They Possess, Crossway (Wheaton, IL), 2010.

First Place 4 Health: A New Beginning, Gospel Light (Ventura, CA), 2011.

First Place 4 Health: Living for Christ, Gospel Light (Ventura, CA), 2011.

Author of gospel tracts for Good News Publishers. Contributor to periodicals, including *Focus on the Family, Today's Christian Woman, Sports Spectrum,* and *Power for Living.* Author of column "Everyday Theology" for *Today's Christian* magazine for three years.

Sidelights

Christin Ditchfield is known to many as the host of *Take It to Heart!,* a daily Christian radio program that airs throughout the United States and Canada as well as in Central and South America. A popular speaker, Ditchfield is also a writer who has published widely in Christian periodicals as well as written dozens of books for children. Many of her books are nonfiction titles that are part of book series that range in focus from sports to biographies to Native-American cultures to books about the earth's natural resources. Ditchfield has also written several fictional stories, among them a pair of humorous picture books and the faith-based story collections *Bible Stories of Boys and Girls* and *Little Golden Book Bible Favorites.*

Discussing Ditchfield's book *Condoleezza Rice: America's Leading Stateswoman,* Hazel Rochman wrote in *Booklist* that Ditchfield does "a good job of relating the personal life story to the history of the times." Noting the author's obvious admiration for her subject, *School Library Journal* reviewer Mary Mueller cited the em-

Rosalind Beardshaw creates the images that bring to life Ditchfield's whimsical family-centered tale in "**Shwatsit!**" (Farrar, Straus & Giroux, 2009. Illustration copyright © 2009 by Patrice Barton. All rights reserved. Reproduced by permission of the illustrator.)

phasis placed on Rice's "intellect, integrity, and hard work" as she left her native Birmingham, excelled at Stanford University, and rose to the position of Secretary of State under President George W. Bush. Ditchfield's texts for the book series that includes *Oil, Water,* and *Soil* are "simply written, informative, and well organized," according to *Booklist* critic Gillian Engberg, and in *School Library Journal* Kate Kohlbeck deemed the author's "brief, yet quite thorough" prose in *Golf* and *Tennis* to be "just the thing for eager young sports fans."

Ditchfield turns to fiction in her entertaining picture books *Cowlick!* and *"Shwatsit!": No One Knows Just What It Means,* both of which are brought to life in entertaining illustrations by Rosalind Beardshaw. In *Cowlick!* an overly affectionate cow creeps into a bedroom and gives slurpy kisses to each of the two children sleeping there. The next morning the youngsters awaken to find that the cow's tongue has created the hair-style of the book's title. Calling *Cowlick!* a "charming bovine comedy," *Booklist* contributor Stephanie Zvirin concluded that "even very young children will get the joke" in Ditchfield's amusing story. In *School Library Journal* Julie Roach praised the book's "short, lively text" and "appealing rich and textured paintings," while a *Kirkus Reviews* writer insisted that "brevity and true whimsy imbue this breezy bedtime rhyme."

Ditchfield brings a similar lighthearted humor to her rhyming text in *"Shwatsit!"* The title refers to the favorite exclamation of a feisty toddler who uses the term throughout her busy day, as she waves her big brother goodbye, plays at the park, and helps her mother do the weekly laundry. It is up to everyone in the family to determine what *"Shwatsit!"* actually means. In *School Library Journal* Debbie S. Hoskins praised Beardshaw's "cheerful and colorful art," and a *Kirkus Reviews* writer recommended Ditchfield's humorous story as "a winning choice for all those older siblings wanting to help out with the baby."

Several of Ditchfield's books serve as companion volumes to the popular faith-based fiction of British writer C.S. Lewis. Lewis's "Chronicles of Narnia" books are full of biblical themes, and in *A Family Guide to Narnia: Biblical Truths in C.S. Lewis's The Chronicles of Narnia,* as well as several related titles, Ditchfield provides a reader's guide that identifies and discusses the Christian roots of the series that includes *The Lion, the Witch, and the Wardrobe, Prince Caspian,* and *A Horse and His Boy.* In addition to providing the location of Scriptural references, the author also expands on the Christian themes running through Lewis's literary classic, making *A Family Guide to Narnia* useful to students as well as general readers.

Biographical and Critical Sources

PERIODICALS

Booklist, March 15, 1999, review of *Sports Great Michael Chang,* p. 1339; August, 2000, Ilene Cooper, review

of *Swimming and Diving,* p. 2143; October 15, 2002, Gillian Engberg, review of *Oil,* p. 420; December 15, 2003, Hazel Rochman, review of *Condoleezza Rice: America's Leading Stateswoman,* p. 747; January 1, 2007, Stephanie Zvirin, review of *Cowlick!,* p. 113.

Kirkus Reviews, December 1, 2006, review of *Cowlick!,* p. 1218; August 15, 2009, review of *"Shwatsit!": No One Knows Just What It Means.*

Publishers Weekly, January 1, 2007, review of *Cowlick!,* p. 48.

School Library Journal, June, 2003, Kate Kohlbeck, reviews of *Golf* and *Tennis,* both p. 125; January, 2004, Pamela K. Bomboy, review of *President's Day,* p. 113; January, 2007, Julie Roach, review of *Cowlick!,* p. 90; February, 2007, Mary Mueller, review of *Condoleezza Rice,* p. 134; November, 2009, Debbie S. Hoskins, review of *"Shwatsit!",* p. 76.

Today's Christian, November-December, 2006, Eugene Pratt, review of *The Three Wise Women: A Christmas Reflection,* p. 10.

ONLINE

Outreach Speakers Web site, http://www.outreachspeakers. com/ (May 1, 2008), "Christin Ditchfield."

Take It to Heart Radio Web site, http://www.takeittoheart radio.com/ (February 15, 2011), "Meet Christin."

* * *

DONALDSON, Julia 1948-

Personal

Born September 16, 1948, in London, England; daughter of James (a geneticist) and Elizabeth (a secretary) Shields; married Malcolm Donaldson (a pediatrician), September 30, 1972; children: Hamish (deceased), Alastair, Jesse. *Education:* Bristol University, earned degree (drama and French), 1970. *Politics:* Tory. *Hobbies and other interests:* Walking, cycling, playing the piano, singing, flowers and fungi.

Addresses

Home—Glasgow, Scotland.

Career

Children's book author and playwright. Former songwriter for children's television; performer at book festivals and theatres; director of storytelling workshops. Patron of Artlink Central charity.

Awards, Honors

Smarties Gold Medal for picture books, and Kate Greenaway Medal nomination, both 1999, and Blue Peter Award for Best Book to Read Aloud, and Experian Big Three Book Prize, both 2000, all for *The Gruffalo;*

Blue Peter Award for Best Book to Read Aloud, Children's Book Award shortlist, Sheffield Children's Book Award shortlist, and Scottish Children's Book Award, all 2002, all for *Room on the Broom;* Booktrust Early Years Award, 2004, Blue Peter Award for Best Book to Read Aloud, 2005, and Giverny Award, 2007, all for *The Snail and the Whale;* Blue Peter Book Award shortlist, and Scottish Royal Mail Book Award shortlist, both 2005, both for *Charlie Cook's Favourite Book;* W.H. Smith Children's Book of the Year honor, 2005, for *The Gruffalo's Child.*

Writings

FOR CHILDREN

A Squash and a Squeeze, illustrated by Axel Scheffler, Margaret K. McElderry (New York, NY), 1993.

Birthday Surprise (play), Ginn (Aylesbury, England), 1994.

Names and Games (play), Ginn (Aylesbury, England), 1995.

(Reteller) *Turtle Tug* (play), Ginn (Aylesbury, England), 1995.

(Reteller) *The Three Billy Goats Gruff* (play), Ginn (Aylesbury, England), 1995.

(Reteller) *The Boy Who Cried Wolf* (play), Ginn (Aylesbury, England), 1995.

(Reteller) *The Magic Twig* (play), Ginn (Aylesbury, England), 1995.

Space Girl Sue, illustrated by Clive Scruton, Ginn (Aylesbury, England), 1996.

(Reteller) *Town and Country Mouse,* illustrated by Nick Schon, Ginn (Aylesbury, England), 1996.

Mr. Snow, illustrated by Celia Canning, Ginn (Aylesbury, England), 1996.

(Reteller) *Counting Chickens,* illustrated by Jeffrey Reid, Ginn (Aylesbury, England), 1996.

The King's Porridge, Ginn (Aylesbury, England), 1996.

The Wonderful Smells (play), illustrated by Jan Nesbitt, Ginn (Aylesbury, England), 1997.

Top of the Mops (play), Ginn (Aylesbury, England), 1997.

The Brownie King, illustrated by John Eastwood, Heinemann (Oxford, England), 1998.

Books and Crooks (plays), Stanley Thornes (Cheltenham, England), 1998.

The False Tooth Fairy (plays), Ginn (Aylesbury, England), 1998.

Waiter! Waiter!, illustrated by Jim Kavanagh, Heinemann (Oxford, England), 1998.

All Gone!, illustrated by Alexa Rutherford, Ginn (Aylesbury, England), 1998.

The Gruffalo, illustrated by Axel Scheffler, Dial Books for Young Readers (New York, NY), 1999, tenth anniversary edition, Macmillan (London, England), 2009.

Steve's Sandwiches, Ginn (Aylesbury, England), 1999.

Clever Katya, Ginn (Aylesbury, England), 1999.

The Noises Next Door, Ginn (Aylesbury, England), 1999.

Monkey Puzzle, illustrated by Axel Scheffler, Macmillan (London, England), 2000.

(Reteller) *The Strange Dream,* illustrated by Thomas Sperling, Oxford University Press (Oxford, England), 2000.

Problem Page (play), illustrated by David Mostyn, Heinemann (Oxford, England), 2000.

The Boy Who Talked to Birds, illustrated by Suzanne Watts, Oxford University Press (Oxford, England), 2000.

One Piece Missing, Rigby Heinemann (Oxford, England), 2000.

Jumping Jack, Rigby Heinemann (Oxford, England), 2000.

The Giant Jumperee, Rigby Heinemann (Oxford, England), 2000.

Follow the Swallow, illustrated by Martin Ursell, Mammoth (London, England), 2000, Crabtree (New York, NY), 2002, new edition illustrated by Pam Smy, Egmont (London, England), 2007.

(Reteller) *The King's Ears,* illustrated by Lisa Berkshire, Oxford University Press (London, England), 2000.

The Monsters in the Cave, Ginn (Aylesbury, England), 2001.

Stop, Thief!, Ginn (Aylesbury, England), 2001.

Room on the Broom, illustrated by Axel Scheffler, Dial Books for Young Readers (New York, NY), 2001.

The Dinosaur's Diary, illustrated by Debbie Boon, Puffin (London, England), 2002.

Night Monkey, Day Monkey, illustrated by Lucy Richards, Egmont (London, England), 2002.

The Smartest Giant in Town, illustrated by Axel Scheffler, Macmillan Children's (London, England), 2002, published as *The Spiffiest Giant in Town,* Dial Books for Young Readers (New York, NY), 2003.

The Trial of Wilf Wolf, illustrated by Martin Ursell, Longman (Harlow, England), 2003.

Princess Mirror-Belle, illustrated by Lydia Monks, Macmillan (London, England), 2003.

The Head in the Sand: A Roman Play, illustrated by Ross Collins, Hodder Wayland (London, England), 2003.

The Magic Paintbrush, illustrated by Joel Stewart, Macmillan (London, England), 2003.

Conjure Cow, illustrated by Nick Sharratt, Puffin (London, England), 2003.

Brick-a-breck, illustrated by Philippe Dupasquier, A. & C. Black (London, England), 2003.

Bombs and Blackberries: A World War II Play, illustrated by Philippe Dupasquier, Hodder Wayland (London, England), 2003.

The Snail and the Whale, illustrated by Axel Scheffler, Macmillan Children's Books (London, England), 2003, Dial Books for Young Readers (New York, NY), 2004.

One Ted Falls out of Bed, illustrated by Anna Currey, Macmillan (London, England), 2004, Holt (New York, NY), 2006.

The Wrong Kind of Bark, illustrated by Garry Parson, Egmont (London, England), 2004, Crabtree (New York, NY), 2005.

Wriggle and Roar!: Rhymes to Join in With, illustrated by Nick Sharratt, Macmillan (London, England), 2004.

Crazy Mayonnaisy Mum: Poems, illustrated by Nick Sharratt, Macmillan (London, England), 2004.

Sharing a Shell, illustrated by Lydia Monks, Macmillan (London, England), 2004.

The Gruffalo's Child, illustrated by Axel Scheffler, Macmillan (London, England), 2004, Dial Books for Young Readers (New York, NY), 2005.

Rosie's Hat, illustrated by Anna Currey, Macmillan (London, England), 2005.

Chocolate Moose for Greedy Goose, illustrated by Nick Sharratt, Macmillan (London, England), 2005.

The Gruffalo's Song, and Other Songs (includes compact disk), illustrated by Axel Scheffler, Macmillan (London, England), 2005.

Princess Mirror-Belle and the Magic Shoes, illustrated by Lydia Monks, Macmillan (London, England), 2005.

The Giants and the Joneses, illustrated by Greg Swearingen, Holt (New York, NY), 2005.

Charlie Cook's Favorite Book, illustrated by Axel Scheffler, Macmillan (London, England), 2005, Dial Books for Young Readers (New York, NY), 2006.

(With John Henderson) *Fly, Pigeon, Fly!,* illustrated by Thomas Docherty, Little Tiger (London, England), 2006.

Hippo Has a Hat, illustrated by Nick Sharratt, Macmillan (London, England), 2006.

Princess Mirror-Belle and the Flying Horse, illustrated by Lydia Monks, Macmillan (London, England), 2006.

The Mermaid and the Octopus, illustrated by Anni Axworthy, Collins (London, England), 2006.

The Pot of Gold, illustrated by Sholto Walker, Collins (London, England), 2006.

No Milk Today, illustrated by Jenny Williams, Oxford University Press (Oxford, England), 2006.

Play Time, Macmillan (London, England), 2006.

Bricks for Breakfast, illustrated by Philippe Dupasquier, Picture Window Books (Minneapolis, MN), 2006.

Spinderella, illustrated by Liz Pichon, Crabtree (New York, NY), 2006.

The Quick Brown Fox Cub, illustrated by Lucy Richards, Crabtree (New York, NY), 2006.

Tyrannosaurus Drip, illustrated by David Roberts, Macmillan (London, England), 2007, Feiwel &' Friends (New York, NY), 2008.

Tiddler, the Story-telling Fish, illustrated by Axel Scheffler, Alison Green (London, England), 2007, published as *The Fish Who Cried Wolf,* Arthur A. Levine Books (New York, NY), 2008.

Where's My Mom?, illustrated by Axel Scheffler, Dial Books for Young Readers (New York, NY), 2008.

The Gruffalo Pop-up Theatre Book, illustrated by Axel Scheffler, Macmillan (London, England), 2008.

The Princess Mirror-Belle Collection, (contains *Princess Mirror-Belle, Princess Mirror-Belle and the Magic Shoes,* and *Princess Mirror-Belle and the Flying Horse*), illustrated by Lydia Monks, Macmillan (London, England), 2008.

One Mole Digging a Hole, illustrated by Nick Sharratt, Macmillan (London, England), 2008.

Stick Man, illustrated by Axel Scheffler, Alison Green (London, England), 2008, Arthur A. Levine Books (New York, NY), 2009.

Tabby McTat, illustrated by Axel Scheffler, Alison Green (London, England), 2009.

Running on the Cracks (novel), Holt (New York, NY), 2009.

The Troll, illustrated by David Roberts, Macmillan (London, England), 2009.

Toddle Waddle, illustrated by Nick Sharratt, Macmillan (London, England), 2009.

What the Ladybug Heard, illustrated by Lydia Monks, Macmillan (London, England), 2009, Holt (New York, NY), 2010.

Also author of educational materials for Oxford University Press and Walker Books.

Author's work has been published in over twenty languages.

"TALES FROM ACORN WOOD" SERIES; ILLUSTRATED BY AXEL SCHEFFLER

Postman Bear, Campbell (London, England), 2000.
Fox's Socks, Campbell (London, England), 2000.
Hide and Seek Pig, Campbell (London, England), 2000.
Rabbit's Nap, Campbell (London, England), 2000.

OTHER

Also author of songs, scripts, and stories for British Broadcasting Corporation television and radio (mainly children's programs). Author of *Cat Whispers,* Rigby. Author of unpublished musicals *King Grunt's Cake* and *Pirate on the Pier.* Contributor of poetry and plays to anthologies.

Adaptations

The Gruffalo was adapted as a board book, an oversized-format book, an audiobook, as a musical stage production produced in Chester, England, in 2001, and as an animated television show produced by the British Broadcasting Corporation in 2009. Several of Donaldson's works, including *The Giants and the Joneses, The Snail and the Whale,* and *Stick Man,* were adapted as audiobooks.

Sidelights

A British storyteller and songwriter, Julia Donaldson is the author of such critically acclaimed children's books as *Room on the Broom, Stick Man,* and *The Gruffalo* the last which is considered to be a contemporary classic. Donaldson's stories are noted for their humor and lyricism and reflect her interest in folk tales and fables. "I really enjoy writing verse, even though it can be fiendishly difficult," the author noted on her home page. "I used to memorise poems as a child and it means a lot to me when parents tell me their child can recite one of my books." As Nick Duerden wrote in the London *Independent,* Donaldson's stories "are as entertaining to read as they are to listen to, and thus she has made bedtime routines so much less protracted and painful than they otherwise could so easily be. Parents everywhere are terribly grateful."

Donaldson retells the well-known story about an elderly woman who wishes for a larger house in *A Squash and a Squeeze,* the first of many books she would create with frequent collaborator Axel Scheffler, a German illustrator. Dubbed a "jolly version" of the traditional folk tale by *Books for Keeps* reviewer Liz Waterland, Donaldson's retelling finds the woman frustrated over the lack of room in her tiny home. Taking the advice of a wise man, she invites all her farm animals into the house, one by one until no more creatures will fit. After ousting the cumbersome creatures, the woman realizes that her home is quite large enough after all. Donaldson's songwriting skills are put "to creative use in this bouncy, rhyming tale," according to a *Publishers Weekly* critic.

Donaldson continues in the same humorous vein in many of her other picture books, including *The Gruffalo,* a work illustrated by Scheffler. Inspired by a Chinese folk tale and told in rhyming verse, *The Gruffalo* introduces an imaginary creature invented by a frightened mouse as a means of scaring off potential predators. After the mouse avoids becoming the tasty snack of, in turn, a hungry fox, owl, and snake by warning of the approach of a large, lumbering, long-toothed creature, it comes upon the very Gruffalo it has described, complete with fangs, claws, and a healthy appetite. Donaldson continues her story in a sequel, *The Gruffalo's Child,* which finds the daughter of the Gruffalo determined to search out the fearsome but tiny creature her father warned her about. In a *Publishers Weekly* review of *The Gruffalo* a contributor wrote that Donaldson "manipulates the repetitive language and rhymes to good advantage," and London *Observer* reviewer Sam Taylor dubbed the book "a modern classic." In *Booklist* Stephanie Zvirin praised Donaldson's rhymes, noting that its "bouncy, humorous text flows smoothly," while *Books for Keeps* reviewer Clive Barnes called *The Gruffalo* "cleverly constructed." Praising Scheffler's "humorous, cartoonlike illustrations" for *The Gruffalo's Child, Horn Book* contributor Jennifer M. Brabander noted of the sequel that the images "work well with Donaldson's pleasingly repetitive" rhyming text, resulting in "a story that . . . is clever rather than truly scary."

More than a decade after its initial publication, *The Gruffalo* remains as popular as ever. Translated into forty languages, the work has sold more than four million copies and was voted Great Britain's favorite bedtime story by BBC radio listeners. *The Gruffalo* has also been adapted for the stage as a musical and as an animated television special featuring the voices of Robbie Coltrane and Helena Bonham-Carter. Reflecting on her story's immense popularity, Donaldson told London *Times* contributor Amanda Craig that it was quite a struggle to get the book published. "I was a bit worried that *The Gruffalo* was too weird, but Axel read it and showed it to his editor at Macmillan," the author recalled. "Things are a bit changed now, but in those days, picture books had become almost like medicine with which anxious parents could dose their children. Whereas I believe that if children are having a tough time what they need is the stuff you get in ancient myths and classics."

With *Room on the Broom* Donaldson uses a folktale format to tell the story of how helpful animals hitch a ride on the broomstick of a generous witch. A striped cat, spotted dog, green parrot, and hopping frog each help the witch out of a jam, and in return they are given a ride on what ends up being a very comfortable conveyance. Noting that Donaldson's "rhythm and rhyme are lively and quick," *Booklist* reviewer GraceAnne A. DeCandido added that Scheffler's illustrations for *Room on the Broom* "partake equally of silly and spooky." While the storyline's "metrical rhyme and goofy suspense aren't groundbreaking," according to a *Publishers Weekly* contributor, young readers will "find it refreshing" to see a witch cast in a new role in Donaldson's entertaining story. Pamela K. Bomboy, writing in *School Library Journal,* predicted that because *Room on a Broom* is "full of fun, and not at all scary," it will be a "surefire read-aloud hit" at story hours.

The Snail and the Whale follows the journey of a tiny snail and the fast-swimming whale that helps the diminutive creature along. Noting the story's environmental subtext, a *Publishers Weekly* reviewer added that *The Snail and the Whale* "lightly demonstrates that friendships come in all shapes and sizes." A stuffed animal stars in *One Ted Falls out of Bed,* a counting picture book featuring art by Anna Currey. In Donaldson's tale, after a teddy bear is nudged out of his child's bed and onto the floor in the middle of the night, he enlists the help of three mice in waking the sleeping child and returning to his place under the covers. Noting that Currey's illustrations "capture the giddy, magical fun" of Donaldson's story, a *Publishers Weekly* reviewer added that *One Ted Falls out of Bed* gives pre-readers ample opportunities to elaborate on the story's rhyming text. In *Kirkus Reviews,* a critic dubbed the book "a sweet addition to any bedtime routine."

Giants figure in a number of Donaldson's books. *The Spiffiest Giant in Town* follows George the giant as he attempts a clothing make-over, and its rhyming text inspired a *Publishers Weekly* reviewer to write that "joie de vivre and the characters' droll camaraderie will almost certainly prove infectious." *The Giants and the Joneses* moves readers into a fairy-tale realm, as Donaldson puts a new spin on the story about Jack and the beanstalk. In this tale, a giant child named Jumbeelia lives up above the clouds. Fascinated with human children, she grows a beanstalk down to earth and kidnaps the three young Jones siblings: Colette, Poppy, and Stephen. Trapped in Jumbeelia's playhouse in the sky, where they are the victim of the giant's brother's teasing, the children must find a way to escape the misguided young giantess and return to earth. In her novel story Donaldson even includes a glossary of Groilish terms, Groil being the language spoken by giants. Praising the author's ability to create a dual narrative mixing human English and giant Groilish, *School Library Journal* reviewer Elaine E. Knight called *The Giants and the Joneses* "an exciting story with a subtle message about respect and cooperation."

Along with *The Snail and the Whale* and *The Spiffiest Giant in Town,* Donaldson and Scheffler have collaborated on several other titles. *Charlie Cook's Favorite Book,* for instance, captures the magic of reading in eleven linking stories that were praised by a *Kirkus Reviews* writer as "masterfully rhymed" and "clever" in their approach. Donaldson offers an aquatic take on a children's classic in *The Fish Who Cried Wolf,* about a tiny sea creature with a propensity for telling whoppers. "Donaldson's rhyming text is crisp and clean," a *Publishers Weekly* critic stated in a review of this book.

In *Where's My Mom?,* a helpful but easily confused butterfly assists a little lost monkey find his way home. "The bouncy rhyming couplets will charm children," remarked Julie Roach in *School Library Journal.* The idea for Donaldson's holiday tale *Stick Man* came from a drawing by Scheffler, who once pictured the Gruffalo's child holding a doll made from sticks. In the work, a small, wooden figure finds itself at the mercy of a frolicsome dog, a group of energetic children, and an industrious swan until it is rescued by a special Christmas Eve visitor. "It's a touching tale, more fearful and melancholy than the rumbustious Gruffalo," Craig noted, and *Horn Book* reviewer Kitty Flynn maintained of *Stick Man* that "Donaldson's lively rhyme and Scheffler's comical illustrations . . . help temper worries about our hero's fate."

Donaldson joined forces with illustrator David Roberts on *Tyrannosaurus Drip,* a humorous tale of mistaken identity. Safe from the dim-witted carnivores that live across the raging river, the duckbills loudly champion their vegetarian lifestyle. When a duckbill egg is carried away and deposited in the T. Rex camp, however, the peace-loving hatchling—dubbed "Drip" by his nest mates—finds himself in the middle of the simmering rivalry. "Children will enjoy the repetitive lilt" in *Tyrannosaurus Drip,* Kim T. Ha remarked in *School Library Journal,* "and adults will appreciate how naturally it reads." A tiny insect rallies her barnyard friends to stop an attempted robbery in *What the Ladybug Heard,* a work "full of slapstick action, animal noises, and repeated phrases that invite participation," according to a *Publishers Weekly* critic.

Donaldson's young-adult novel *Running on the Cracks* offers a "sensitive treatment of mental illness," according to *Booklist* reviewer Michael Cart. The work centers on Leonora "Leo" Watts-Chan, an orphaned teen who flees her aunt and uncle's unhappy home and ventures to Scotland to locate the paternal grandparents she has never met. Arriving in Glasgow, Leo is befriended by Finlay, a goth wannabe, and Mary, a mentally ill woman. They assist the teen in her search, even when their efforts are complicated by the appearance of Leo's disagreeable uncle. "Fast-paced, [and] richly characterized," according to a *Kirkus Reviews* critic, *Running on the Cracks* is a personal story for the author, whose eldest son Hamish suffered from a schizoaffective disorder and committed suicide in 2003 at the age of twenty-

five. Donaldson now serves as a patron of Artlink Central, a charity that connects artists and individuals with special needs.

Biographical and Critical Sources

BOOKS

Howell, Gill, *Julia Donaldson: A Biography,* Oxford University Press (Oxford, England), 2006.

PERIODICALS

Booklist, April 26, 1993, review of *A Squash and a Squeeze,* p. 78; July, 1999, Stephanie Zvirin, review of *The Gruffalo,* p. 1950; September 1, 2001, GraceAnne A. DeCandido, review of *Room on the Broom,* p. 120; March 1, 2003, Carolyn Phelan, review of *The Spiffiest Giant in Town,* p. 1201; May 1, 2006, Carolyn Phelan, review of *Charlie Cook's Favorite Book,* p. 88; June 1, 2006, Kathy Broderick, review of *One Ted Falls out of Bed,* p. 80; July 1, 2009, Michael Cart, review of *Running on the Cracks,* p. 56.

Books for Keeps, May, 1995, Liz Waterland, review of *A Squash and a Squeeze,* p. 8; May, 1999, Clive Barnes, review of *The Gruffalo,* p. 21.

Childhood Education, fall, 1999, Kelly Krawczyk, review of *The Gruffalo,* p. 44.

Children's Book Review Service, August, 1993, review of *A Squash and a Squeeze,* p. 158.

Daily Mail (London, England), January 1, 2010, Jenny Johnston, "*The Gruffalo* Creator Julia Donaldson Reveals the Story behind Britain's Best-loved Bedtime Story."

Guardian (London, England), December 19, 2009, Susanna Rustin, "A Life in Children's Books: Julia Donaldson."

Horn Book, January-February, 2005, Jennifer M. Brabander, review of *The Gruffalo's Child,* p. 75; July-August, 2006, Kitty Flynn, review of *One Ted Falls out of Bed,* p. 424; November-December, 2009, Kitty Flynn, review of *Stick Man,* p. 640.

Independent (London, England), November 29, 2009, Nick Duerden, "I Created a Monster: Julia Donaldson on How *The Gruffalo* Has Taken over Her Life."

Kirkus Reviews, June 1, 1999, review of *The Gruffalo,* p. 882; August 1, 2001, review of *Room on the Broom,* p. 1121; January 1, 2003, review of *The Spiffiest Giant in Town,* p. 60; February 15, 2004, review of *The Snail and the Whale,* p. 176; August 15, 2005, review of *The Giant and the Joneses,* p. 912; May 1, 2006, review of *Charlie Cook's Favorite Book,* p. 455; May 15, 2006, review of *One Ted Falls out of Bed,* p. 516; January 15, 2008, review of *Where's My Mom?*; April 15, 2008, review of *The Fish Who Cried Wolf*; May 15, 2008, review of *Tyrannosaurus Drip*; August 1, 2009, review of *Running on the Cracks*; September 15, 2009, review of *Stick Man*; April 15, 2010, review of *What the Ladybug Heard.*

Los Angeles Times Book Review, May 2, 1993, review of *A Squash and a Squeeze,* p. 7.

Observer (London, England), April 4, 1999, Sam Taylor, "When You've Been Traumatized by a Teddy, There's Only One Way Out. . . ."

Publishers Weekly, April 26, 1993, review of *A Squash and a Squeeze,* p. 78; June 21, 1999, review of *The Gruffalo,* p. 67; September 10, 2001, review of *Room on the Broom,* p. 92; January 6, 2003, review of *The Spiffiest Giant in Town,* p. 59; February 23, 2004, review of *The Snail and the Whale,* p. 75; December 13, 2004, review of *The Gruffalo's Child,* p. 68; May 15, 2006, review of *Charlie Cook's Favorite Book,* p. 71; May 22, 2006, review of *One Ted Falls out of Bed,* p. 50; March 3, 2008, review of *Where's My Mom?,* p. 45; May 19, 2008, review of *The Fish Who Cried Wolf,* p. 53; June 16, 2008, review of *Tyrannosaurus Drip,* p. 48; September 7, 2009, review of *Stick Man,* p. 43; September 28, 2009, review of *Running on the Cracks,* p. 66; May 10, 2010, review of *What the Ladybug Heard,* p. 41.

School Librarian, spring, 2010, Peter Andrews, review of *Tabby McTat,* p. 27.

School Library Journal, April, 1993, Nancy Seiner, review of *A Squash and a Squeeze,* pp. 95-96; August, 1999, Marianne Saccardi, review of *The Gruffalo,* pp. 132-133; September, 2001, Pamela K. Bomboy, review of *Room on the Broom,* p. 187; March, 2003, Bina Williams, review of *The Spiffiest Giant in Town,* p. 191; February, 2004, Kathleen Kelly MacMillan, review of *The Snail and the Whale,* p. 111; March, 2005, Marge Loch-Wouters, review of *The Gruffalo's Child,* p. 170; October, 2005, Elaine E. Knight, review of *The Giants and the Joneses,* p. 112; June, 2006, Marge Loch-Wouters, review of *One Ted Falls out of Bed,* p. 110; July, 2006, Jill Heritage Maza, review of *Charlie Cook's Favorite Book,* p. 71; May, 2008, Julie Roach, review of *Where's My Mom?,* p. 94; June, 2008, Grace Oliff, review of *The Fish Who Cried Wolf* and Kim T. Ha, review of *Tyrannosaurus Drip,* p. 100; October, 2009, Eva Mitnick, review of *Stick Man,* p. 79; December, 2009, Shawna Sherman, review of *Running on the Cracks,* p. 114; April, 2010, Kara Schaff, review of *What the Ladybug Heard,* p. 124.

Times (London, England), November, 1993, review of *A Squash and a Squeeze,* p. 45; May 11, 2008, Gillian Bowditch, "The Gruffalo's Unhappy Child: Julia Donaldson, Author of the Children's Bestseller, Talks Frankly about Her Son Hamish's Suicide"; October 3, 2008, Amanda Craig, interview with Donaldson.

ONLINE

Gruffalo Gang Web site, http://www.gruffalo.com/ (February 23, 2011).

Julia Donaldson Home Page, http://www.juliadonaldson. co.uk (February 23, 2011).

Northern Children's Book Festival Web site, http://www. ncbf.org.uk/ (July 13, 2010), "Julia Donaldson."*

G

GAMMELL, Stephen 1943-

Personal
Born February 10, 1943, in Des Moines, IA; son of a magazine art editor and a homemaker; married; wife's name Linda (a photographer). *Education:* Attended college in Des Moines, IA. *Hobbies and other interests:* American history; playing the guitar, banjo, mandolin, and piano—"anything with strings"; outdoor activities, including backpacking, bicycling, camping, and canoeing, especially in the American West; movies, especially comedies featuring Laurel and Hardy; eating big breakfasts and chocolate chip cookies.

Addresses
Home—St. Paul, MN.

Career
Author and illustrator of books for children. Freelance illustrator, beginning 1960s. *Exhibitions:* Work included in exhibition "Beyond the Book: The Fine Art of Book Illustrators," Bloomington Theatre and Art Center, Bloomington, MN, 2011.

Awards, Honors
Notable Book citation, American Library Association (ALA), 1976, for *The Kelpie's Pearls* by Molly Hunter; Best Books for Young Adults citation, ALA, 1978, for *The Hawks of Chelney* by Adrienne Jones; Outstanding Book of the Year citation, *New York Times,* 1979, *Boston Globe/Horn Book* Award Honor Book designation, and ALA Notable Book citation, both 1980, all for *Stonewall* by Jean Fritz; Children's Choice citation, International Reading Association/Children's Book Council, 1980, for *Meet the Vampire* by Georgess McHargue; *Boston Globe/Horn Book* Award Honor Book designation for illustration, *New York Times* Best Illustrated Book citation, *New York Times* Outstanding Book of the Year citation, and Parents' Choice Award, Parents' Choice Foundation, all 1981, Caldecott Award Honor Book designation, ALA, and American Book Award nomination for Best Picture Book nomination, 1982, all for *Where the Buffaloes Begin* by Olaf Baker; Children's Choice Award citation, 1982, for *Wake up, Bear . . . It's Christmas!; New York Times* Best Illustrated Book citation, and Child Study Association of America's Children's Books of the Year citation, both 1985, and Caldecott Medal Honor Book designation, and *Boston Globe/Horn Book* Award Honor Book designation, both 1986, all for *The Relatives Came* by Cynthia Rylant; Children's Books of the Year citation, Child Study Association of America, 1985, for *Thanksgiving Poems* by Myra Cohn Livingston; *Boston Globe/Horn Book* Award Honor Book citation, 1987, and Golden Sower Award nomination, Nebraska Library Commission, 1990, both for *Old Henry* by Joan W. Blos; Caldecott Medal, 1989, for *Song and Dance Man* by Karen Ackerman; Minnesota Picture Book Award, Minnesota Center for the Book, 1993, for *Old Black Fly* by Jim Aylesworth, and 1998, for *Is That You, Winter?;* numerous best book and notable book citations by local and state library associations; numerous child-selected awards.

Writings

SELF-ILLUSTRATED

Once upon MacDonald's Farm, Four Winds (New York, NY), 1981, revised edition, Simon & Schuster (New York, NY), 2000.

Wake up, Bear . . . It's Christmas!, Lothrop (New York, NY), 1981.

(Reteller) *The Story of Mr. and Mrs. Vinegar,* Lothrop (New York, NY), 1982.

Git Along, Old Scudder, Lothrop (New York, NY), 1983.

Is That You, Winter?, Harcourt (San Diego, CA), 1997.

Twigboy, Harcourt (San Diego, CA), 2000.

Ride, Harcourt (San Diego, CA), 2001.

Mudkin, Carolrhoda Books (Minneapolis, MN), 2011.

ILLUSTRATOR

Ida Chittum, *A Nutty Business,* Putnam (New York, NY), 1973.

Sara Newton Carroll, *The Search: A Biography of Leo Tolstoy,* Harper (New York, NY), 1973.

Paul Zindel, *Let Me Hear Your Whisper* (play), Harper (New York, NY), 1974.

Ramona Maher, *The Glory Horse: A Story of the Battle of San Jancinto and Texas in 1836,* Coward (New York, NY), 1974.

Patricia Lee Gauch, *Thunder at Gettysburg,* Coward (New York, NY), 1974, reprinted, Boyds Mills Press (Honesdale, PA), 2003.

Miriam Anne Bourne, *Nabby Adams' Diary,* Coward (New York, NY), 1975.

Seymour Simon, *Ghosts,* Lippincott (Philadelphia, PA), 1976.

Georgess McHargue, *Meet the Werewolf,* Lippincott (Philadelphia, PA), 1976.

Mollie Hunter, *The Kelpie's Pearls,* Harper (New York, NY), 1976.

Mollie Hunter, *A Furl of Fairy Wind: Four Stories,* Harper (New York, NY), 1977.

Ramona Maher, *Alice Yazzie's Year* (poetry), Coward (New York, NY), 1977.

Ellen Harvey Showell, *The Ghost of Tillie Jean Cassaway,* Four Winds (New York, NY), 1978.

Marietta Moskin, *Day of the Blizzard,* Coward (New York, NY), 1978.

Adrienne Jones, *The Hawks of Chelney,* Harper (New York, NY), 1978.

Dilys Owen, *Leo Possessed,* Harcourt (San Diego, CA), 1979.

Michael Fox, *Whitepaws: A Coyote-Dog,* Coward (New York, NY), 1979.

Jean Fritz, *Stonewall,* Putnam (New York, NY), 1979.

Margaret Greaves, *A Net to Catch the Wind,* Harper (New York, NY), 1979.

Georgess McHargue, *Meet the Vampire,* Lippincott (Philadelphia, PA), 1979.

David Seed, *Stream Runner,* Four Winds (New York, NY), 1979.

Eve Bunting, *Yesterday's Island,* Warne (New York, NY), 1979.

Eve Bunting, *Terrible Things: An Allegory of the Holocaust,* Harper (New York, NY), 1980.

Eve Bunting, *Blackbird Singing,* Macmillan (New York, NY), 1980.

Malcolm Hall, *And Then the Mouse . . .: Three Stories* (folktales), Four Winds (New York, NY), 1980.

Helen Reeder Cross, *The Real Tom Thumb,* Four Winds (New York, NY), 1980.

Ann Brophy, *Flash and the Swan,* Warne (New York, NY), 1981.

Olaf Baker, *Where the Buffaloes Begin,* Warne (New York, NY), 1981.

Nathaniel Benchley, *Demo and the Dolphin,* Harper (New York, NY), 1981.

Maggie S. Davis, *The Best Way to Ripton,* Holiday House (New York, NY), 1982.

Dennis Haseley, *The Old Banjo,* Macmillan (New York, NY), 1983.

Cynthia Rylant, *Waiting to Waltz: A Childhood* (poetry), Bradbury (Scarsdale, NY), 1984.

Alison C. Herzig and Jane L. Mali, *Thaddeus,* Little, Brown (Boston, MA), 1984.

Cynthia Rylant, *The Relatives Came,* Bradbury (New York, NY), 1985.

Myra Cohn Livingston, editor, *Thanksgiving Poems,* Holiday House (New York, NY), 1985.

Larry Callen, *Who Kidnapped the Sheriff?; or, Tales from Tickflaw,* Atlantic Monthly Press (New York, NY), 1985.

George Ella Lyon, *A Regular Rolling Noah,* Bradbury (Scarsdale, NY), 1986.

Joan W. Blos, *Old Henry,* Morrow (New York, NY), 1987.

Janet Taylor Lisle, *The Great Dimpole Oak,* Franklin Watts (New York, NY), 1987.

Karen Ackerman, *Song and Dance Man,* Knopf (New York, NY), 1988.

Tom Birdseye, *Airmail to the Moon,* Holiday House (New York, NY), 1988.

Virginia Driving Hawk Sneve, editor, *Dancing Teepees: Poems of American Indian Youth* (poetry), Holiday House (New York, NY), 1989.

Rafe Martin, *Will's Mammoth,* Putman (New York, NY), 1989.

Myra Cohn Livingston, editor, *Halloween Poems* (poetry), Holiday House (New York, NY), 1989.

Lyn Littlefield Hoopes, *Wing-a-Ding,* Little, Brown (Boston, MA), 1990.

George Ella Lyon, *Come a Tide,* Orchard Books (New York, NY), 1990.

Elvira Woodruff, *The Wing Shop,* Holiday House (New York, NY), 1991.

Jim Aylesworth, *Old Black Fly,* Holt (New York, NY), 1992.

Liz Rosenberg, *Monster Mama,* Putnam (New York, NY), 1993.

Jim Aylesworth, *The Burger and the Hot Dog* (poetry), Atheneum (New York, NY), 2001.

Jennifer Donnelly, *Humble Pie,* Atheneum (New York, NY), 2002.

(With Cheng-Khee Chee, Mary GrandPre, and Janice Lee Porter) Barbara Juster Esbensen, *Swing around the Sun,* Carolrhoda Books (Minneapolis, MN), 2002.

Tamson Weston, *Hey, Pancakes!,* Harcourt (San Diego, CA), 2003.

Robert Kinerk, *Timothy Cox Will Not Change His Socks,* Simon & Schuster (New York, NY), 2005.

Judy Sierra, *The Secret Science Project That Almost Ate the School,* Simon & Schuster (New York, NY), 2006.

Anne Bowen, *I Know an Old Teacher,* Carolrhoda Books (Minneapolis, MN), 2008.

George Ella Lyon, *My Friend, the Starfinder,* Atheneum (New York, NY), 2008.

C.K. Williams, *How the Nobble Was Finally Found,* Harcourt (Boston, MA), 2009.

ILLUSTRATOR; "SCARY STORIES" FOLKTALE SERIES; RETOLD BY ALVIN SCHWARTZ

Scary Stories to Tell in the Dark: Collected from American Folklore (also see below), Lippincott (Philadelphia, PA), 1981.

More Scary Stories to Tell in the Dark: Collected and Retold from Folklore (also see below), Lippincott (Philadelphia, PA), 1984.

Scary Stories Three: More Tales to Chill Your Bones (also see below), HarperCollins (New York, NY), 1991.

Scary Stories Fright Pack (includes *Scary Stories to Tell in the Dark, More Scary Stories to Tell in the Dark,* and *Scary Stories Three*), HarperCollins (New York, NY), 1997, published as *Scary Stories Boxed Set,* 2001.

OTHER

Author's books have been translated into Dutch, French, German, Italian, and Spanish, among other languages.

Gammell's papers are housed in permanent collections at the Mazza Collection, University of Findlay, Findlay, OH, and the de Grummond Collection, University of Southern Mississippi.

Adaptations

Filmstrip/cassette adaptations by Random House/Miller-Brody include *Where the Buffaloes Begin,* 1982, *The Old Banjo,* 1984, and *The Relatives Came,* 1986. *Song and Dance Man* was adapted as a video with teacher's guide by Miller-Brody, 1990, and as a puzzle book, JTG, 1991. Live Oak Media issued a combination book, cassette, and teacher's guide of *The Relatives Came,* 1999, and Books on Tape released it on cassette, 2000. PIM released a video of *Come a Tide,* read by Dixie Carter. The "Scary Stories" series were adapted for audiocassette. Filmstrip adaptations were made of *Old Henry, Will's Mammoth, Song and Dance Man,* and *Monster Mama.*

Sidelights

An author and illustrator of books for children and young adults, Stephen Gammell has received numerous honors for his work, including the prestigious Caldecott Medal for his contributions to *Song and Dance Man* by Karen Ackerman. The prolific Gammell has created art for everything from humorous tales, fantasies, and picture books to realistic and historical fiction, poetry collections, a play, and an alphabet book. His illustrations, which range from precise pencil drawings to wildly extravagant full-page watercolors, have graced the works of such authors as Eve Bunting, Georgess McHargue, George Ella Lyon, Jim Aylesworth, and Judy Sierra. "Gammell's art is known for its exuberance," declared Ilene Cooper in *Booklist.*

Gammell's self-illustrated picture books fall into two categories: works of pure fantasy and works that blend reality and fantasy. Generally humorous in tone, they feature unconventional protagonists—such as Mac-Donald, the farmer of the children's song of the same name; Scudder, a mountain man; Old Man Winter, a crusty, pint-size geezer; and Twigboy, an anthropomorphic stick—and surprise endings. Gammell is also the creator of a Christmas story about a bear who meets Santa Claus, a semi-autobiographical picture book about two siblings stuck in the back seat during a car trip, and a retelling of an old English folktale. Asked to name the biggest influence on his writing and art, Gammell told a *BookPage* online interviewer: "My imagination, and lots of papers and pencils."

As an illustrator, Gammell often uses pencil, pastel, and watercolor, and his mixed-media approach results in gleaming images—sometimes defined, sometimes impressionistic—done in scratchy line and swirling, spattered colors. He is celebrated for the variety, energy, expressiveness, and distinctiveness of his art, and he is often praised for complementing, extending, and even surpassing the texts that he illustrates. Describing his illustrations in Jennifer Donnelly's *Humble Pie,* for example, a *Publishers Weekly* contributor observed that Gammell's "interpretations add dramatic punch and leavening along with a healthy dash of humor."

Considered an interpretive artist whose pictures successfully capture the moods and emotions of the texts that he illustrates, Gammell's images range in effect

Stephen Gammell's illustration projects include creating the colorful artwork for Karen Ackerman's **Song and Dance Man.** (Illustration copyright © 1988 by Stephen Gammell. Used by permission of Alfred A. Knopf, an imprint of Random House Children's Books, a division of Random House, Inc.)

Liz Rosenberg's overly rambunctious youngster comes to life in Gammell's energetic art for **Monster Mama.** (Illustration copyright © 1993 by Stephen Gammell. All rights reserved. Used by permission of Philomel Books, a division of Penguin Young Readers Group, a member of Penguin Group (USA) Inc., 345 Hudson Street, New York, NY 10014.)

rett noted that "every line in Stephen Gammell's distinctive illustrations is imbued with emotion. Every color and change of value creates mood."

Born in Des Moines, Iowa, Gammell grew up in a family that fostered his artistic pursuits. His father was an art editor at Meredith Publishing, the company that produced popular magazines such as *Better Homes & Gardens.* As the author/illustrator once told *SATA,* "A big part of my childhood was spent drawing. Practically every night my father would bring home a variety of pencils and paper. These great piles of paper of many thicknesses and colors were better than any toy. Father also supplied me with magazines like *Collier's* and *Saturday Evening Post.* I remember being impressed by their illustrations and cutting them up to make scrapbooks. While I had no notion of what an artist was, I did have an awareness of illustration from an early age. I knew these magazine illustrations were with a story, but I never read them. I was only interested in the art." As a small boy, Gammell used to lie on his stomach on the floor of the solarium in the family house; there, he would draw airplanes, semaphores, soldiers, and trains, as well as "the usual cowboys and Indians. Now that I'm older, I stand up, use a drawing board, have better paper and pencils, and throw more drawings away than I used to, but it's still just as much fun as ever. Drawing, that is."

At the time, Gammell's favorite illustrations were of cowboys and Native Americans. Although he did not know it then, he was appreciating the works of artists

from sensitive, haunting, and poignant to unrestrained, exaggerated, and surreal; his pictures in the latter vein have inspired favorable comparisons with those of popular English artist Ralph Steadman. In some of his illustration projects, especially those dealing with the supernatural such as the "Scary Stories" series of tales, poems, and songs collected by Alvin Schwartz, he creates art that is considered particularly macabre and gruesome. Noted for the excellence of his work in books of American history and folklore, especially those relating to the American West, Gammell is often acknowledged for creating panoramic landscapes as well as for the accuracy of his details.

As a writer, Gammell characteristically uses brief texts in both prose and poetry to act as the jumping-off points for his illustrations. He also favors hand-lettered texts, a feature that he sometimes incorporates into images for books by others. Although his writing is sometimes considered less effective than his illustrations, his work has been heralded as a pairing of enjoyable stories with entertaining twists and beautiful art. A reviewer in *Publishers Weekly* called Gammell "one of the most gifted illustrators working today," while in *Horn Book* Annie Schwartz called his work "down-to-earth, spontaneous, warm, energetic, [and] seriously playful." Writing in *Children's Books and Their Creators,* Mary Brigid Bar-

Jennifer Donnelly's story of a young, well-diapered adventurer is the subject of Gammell's humorous artwork in **Humble Pie.** (Illustration copyright © 2002 by Stephen Gammell. Reprinted by permission of Atheneum Books for Young Readers, an imprint of Simon & Schuster Children's Publishing Division.)

such as Frederic Remington, Charles Marion Russell, and Frank Schoonover. "I also remember liking the paintings and romantic illustrations of Robert Fawcett," he told *SATA.* "I was interested in the detail of his work, the particular way he drew a dress, a window curtain, a chair." As a child, Gammell rarely went to art museums. However, he did visit the historical museums that were located near his home in Des Moines. "I loved the stuffed animals, the American Indian artifacts, and memorabilia of the West. The exhibitions about the settling of Iowa were fascinating to me." He continued, "As years go by, you retain what is interesting from childhood and toss out the rest. Somehow the memorabilia and romance of Western history has always stayed with me. I suppose part of the lasting appeal is that artifacts are just plain fun to draw. I like the line and the form of the objects. An arrowhead, for instance, is fun to pick up, to play with, to touch, to draw. Tomahawks, hatchets, old revolvers, boots, and leather all have a certain sensual, visual appeal for me, and they, consequently, turn up in my illustrations."

Gammell received a great deal of support from his parents. "My father," he recalled, "was very encouraging. He would help me draw, supply the paper and pencils, but he would never coach me or tell me how to work. I picked up the interest on my own; my parents never pushed me. It got me through elementary school. If you could draw, the big kids were more hesitant about beating you up. I tried to make this work for me." He attended grade school, high school, and college in Iowa. "I tried to get through high school by drawing, too," he also admitted to *SATA.* "I'd turn in book reports with illustrations, thinking the teachers would be impressed, but, of course, they weren't. After college, I drifted about for nine years. All through the 1960s, I did odd jobs and continued to draw, but I never thought of myself as an artist. I wasn't intelligent enough to think about making a living or anything, much less art. I just fooled around."

During the late sixties Gammell moved to his current home state of Minnesota. While living in Minneapolis, he began to draw small ads for friends who ran neighborhood book and record stores; these ads were published in local magazines and newspapers. Gammell also created posters for music stores and signs for regional colleges and illustrated articles for local magazines. He told *SATA:* "I fell into this by accident and can't imagine what would be better suited to my personality and abilities than doing this for a living—stuck away safely in a second floor studio, out of public view and bothering no one, doing harmless drawings and paintings. Everyone's happy. Or relieved."

In the early 1970s Gammell made a pivotal trip to New York City. "My roommate was an actor in a local theater company which was about to put on a play in New York City. This friend asked whether I'd like to tag along, and I agreed. I knew there were publishing companies in New York and that children's books, which

were beginning to interest me, came out of major New York publishers. I put together some of my drawings and sketches as well as the ads and illustrations I had been doing in Minneapolis. My thought was to contact some people in publishing. I didn't want or expect to find a job. I was simply interested in getting a professional opinion of my work." Gammell visited several publishers of children's literature and asked the editors for some criticism. An editor at G.P. Putnam's Sons liked his work and gave him a sample manuscript. "She suggested I take it home and make two or three drawings," Gammell recalled. "She could see I knew how to draw, but was interested in whether I could maintain a sense of consistency and continuity from page to page. I made some drawings and brought them back several days later. To my surprise, she offered me a contract for that very book, *A Nutty Business.*" Featuring a humorous story by Ida Chittum, *A Nutty Business* was published in 1973 and describes how the local squirrels declare war on Farmer Flint when he gathers nuts in order to pay for the calico cloth desired by his wife and daughter.

Gammell created pencil drawings for another early illustration project, *Thunder at Gettysburg,* Patricia Lee Gauch's fictionalized account of the U.S. Civil War battle that describes a young girl's experiences helping wounded soldiers. A reviewer in *Publishers Weekly*

In his colorful art, Gammell captures the unique fantasy spirit in C.K. Williams' picture book **How the Nobble Was Finally Found.** (Illustration copyright © 2009 by Stephen Gammell. Reproduced by permission of Houghton Mifflin, an imprint of Houghton Mifflin Harcourt Publishing Company.)

stated that "Gauch's dramatic, verse-like text and Gammell's somber black-and-white drawings evoke the horror of war with startling but not overpowering clarity." Writing in another issue of the same periodical, a reviewer called Gammell's drawings for Bunting's 1980 picture book *Terrible Things: An Allegory of the Holocaust* "superb."

Gammell considers *And Then the Mouse . . .: Three Stories,* a collection of folktales by Malcolm Hall, to be a turning point in his career. "With it, I was finally able to get silly and free myself from inhibitions," he told *SATA.* "*And Then the Mouse . . .* loosened me up; I quit taking myself so seriously. As a result, I felt better about my attitude, my drawings, *myself.* From then on, I only accepted books that I really wanted to illustrate, books I could enjoy. I stopped trying to make an 'artistic statement,' and freed myself from the restrictive, self-imposed seriousness."

Where the Buffaloes Begin, a picture book by Olaf Baker, is the first of the books illustrated by Gammell to receive major awards for its art. A Native American legend that was originally published in 1915 in the children's magazine *St. Nicholas,* the story describes how ten-year-old Little Wolf travels to a legendary lake to see the sacred spot where the buffaloes begin. The boy guides the buffaloes back to his village, where the thundering herd tramples the members of an enemy tribe, thus saving Little Wolf's people from annihilation. Writing in the *New York Times Book Review,* George A. Woods commented: "As legends go, [this] is better than most . . . . It is Stephen Gammell, however, who deserves the honors for his black-and-white illustrations. Working on a larger scale than customary for him, he provides spectacular scenes" and "conveys the hulking, surging, rampaging strength of the shaggy buffaloes as they rise out of a shadowy mist, the mist of legend or dream." Kate M. Flanagan, writing in *Horn Book,* called the full-and double-page pencil drawings "magnificent." *Where the Buffalo Begin* was named both a Caldecott Award honor book and a *Boston Globe/Horn Book* Award honor book; it was also nominated for an American Book Award for best picture book.

Gammell produced his first original book, *Once upon MacDonald's Farm,* in 1981. In this picture book, which is illustrated with shaded pencil drawings and silhouettes, Gammell relates the "true" story behind the farmer of the beloved traditional song. At one time, MacDonald did not have any animals on his farm. He buys an elephant, a baboon, and a lion to help him restock his land. During the day, MacDonald uses the elephant for plowing, tries to milk the lion, and attempts to get eggs from the baboon; that night, the outraged animals leave. The next day, a kindly neighbor—another farmer—gives MacDonald a horse, a cow, and a chicken. MacDonald starts again, singing the song's noted refrain while plowing with . . . his chicken! A reviewer commented in *Publishers Weekly* that *Once upon MacDonald's Farm* owes its charm "to Gammell's

drawings, rendered with the precision and charm that have made his illustrations distinguished additions to many books on Americana." Noting the book's "funny, slightly surrealistic mood," *New York Times Book Review* critic Karla Kuskin called Gammell's words "as silly as they are choice, and they are perfectly matched in his poker-faced, expertly penciled drawings."

Since the publication of *Once upon MacDonald's Farm,* Gammell has continued to create his own works while providing the pictures for stories by other authors. In *Wake up, Bear . . . It's Christmas!,* his first full-color picture book, a bear that has hibernated through seven Christmases is determined to be awake for this one. Waking to his alarm on Christmas Eve, he is visited by a white-bearded man with a sleigh pulled by reindeer. The bear invites the visitor to come in and get warm; in thanks, the visitor takes the bear for a ride in his sleigh. Writing in *Horn Book,* Ethel L. Heins commented that, with its "brief text alternating between prose and verse and its luminous paintings conveying both the ingenuousness of the characters and the festivity of the season, [*Wake up, Bear . . . It's Christmas!*] is fresh and inviting."

Gammell shares his interest in the American West in *Git Along, Old Scudder,* in which an old mountain man gets lost and finds his way by drawing a map of the landmarks that he sees. He comes down from a mountain, goes to a fort for some rest, then heads off into the wilderness to finish his map. Spouting colorful comments in folksy dialect, the man gives names such as "Sneaky Tree Road" and "Two Nose Pass" to the landmarks on the trail and asks young readers if they agree with his choices. However, readers see—before Scudder does—that the map leads the old codger in a big circle. Writing in *Booklist,* Denise M. Wilms stated that *Git Along, Old Scudder* "is set off by masterful watercolor paintings that capture the arid western landscape and startling blue skies," while Clarissa Erwin asserted in *School Library Journal* that "a sense of the rich, western landscape and true grit, along with Old Scudder's drawled narrative make this a gem." Writing in *Horn Book,* Mary M. Burns called *Git Along, Old Scudder* "a handsome book that not only suggests the lure of the frontier but also offers young audiences an insight into the process by which many American landmarks acquired their colorful names."

Gammell's fourth self-illustrated picture book, *Is That You, Winter?,* depicts Old Man Winter as a grumbling, pint-size character sporting a droopy, white mustache and wearing a ten-gallon hat. He spreads snow across the land from the back of his truck, a vehicle that, though battered, can fly. When he takes a tumble into the snow, he is picked up by a little girl, who defends him from the name-calling of her playmates and assures Old Man Winter that he is special. Gammell illustrates *Is That You, Winter?* in pencil, pastel, and watercolor with multicolored splatters and swirls; the dialogue of his text is hand-lettered, while the narrative is set in regular type. Calling the book "an ebullient tour de force," Marigny Dupuy noted in the *New York Times Book Review* that Gammell's illustrations are "a festival of color and image," and *Booklist* critic John Peters predicted that "children will turn back to savor the sudden shifts of scale" in his engaging art. A reviewer for *Publishers Weekly* advised: "Forget those icy-looking fellows like Jack Frost" before calling the protagonist of *Old Man Winter* Gammell's "latest addition to his unforgettable cast of characters."

In his picture book *Ride* Gammell draws on his childhood memories in addressing the theme of sibling rivalry. In this work a brother and sister are riding in the back seat of the family car during a Sunday outing. The siblings go to war with each other, setting turf limits and struggling for power, and as the battle escalates so do their imaginations. Just as the two, now dinosaurs dressed in sneakers, are ready to make each other extinct, their mother—who remains oblivious to all off the goings-on—brings out sandwiches from the picnic basket. Sporting hand-lettered text and written totally in dialogue, *Ride* is illustrated in watercolor, pastel, and pencil with touches of bright aqua and chartreuse. Writing in the *New York Times Book Review,* Scott Veale called Gammell's book "a quirky, gently subversive view of life in the rearview mirror," and added that the author/illustrator;s "wildly fanciful, swooshing illustrations . . . are the main attraction in a narrative that pulls no punches, so to speak." As a *Horn Book* critic observed, the illustrator's "signature art expresses the erupting anger with panache," and in *Booklist* Hazel Rochman concluded that "kids will recognize the anger and frustration, and they will laugh, not only with one another, but also with the adults who make the decisions and trap the kids together."

In addition to original stories, Gammell has continued to create pictures for books by other writers, among them *Waiting to Waltz: A Childhood,* a collection of thirty autobiographical poems by Cynthia Rylant about growing up in a small Appalachian town during the 1960s. Another collaboration with Rylant, *The Relatives Came,* describes how the lives of an Appalachian family are made more joyous by the arrival of relatives from Virginia. The parents, grandparents, and children of the visiting family fill up the house; in fact, there are so many people that meals have to be eaten in rotation. The cheerful, loving relatives picnic, garden, play music, and fix things around the house, among other activities. When they leave, the family is lonely, but they know that their relatives will return the next summer. Writing in the *New York Times Book Review,* Anne Tyler stated, "If there's anything more charming than the tone of voice in this story, it's the drawings that go with it. Stephen Gammell fills the pages with bright, crayony pictures teeming with details that children should enjoy poring over for hours." Calling *The Relatives Came* a "picture book as good as country music," Ann A. Flowers noted in *Horn Book* that the illustrations "are exuberant, untidy depictions of country life

and down-home people in lively primary colors and quirky outlines." Gammell and Rylant received honor book designations from both the Caldecott Award and *Boston Globe/Horn Book* Award committees for *The Relatives Came.*

In 1989 Gammell won the Caldecott Medal for his illustrations for *Song and Dance Man* by Karen Ackerman. Based partly on the author's childhood, this picture book features Grandpa, a retired vaudevillian who delights his three grandchildren by recreating his act for them. Grandpa goes into the attic, dons a bowler hat and tap shoes, and picks up a gold-tipped cane to demonstrate some of the songs, dances, jokes, and banjo-playing he used to do on stage. As he performs for them, the young narrators learn what it was like to be a real song-and-dance man. *School Library Journal* critic Gratia Banta asserted that Gammell's "animated, crisp, colored pencil line drawings enhance" *Song and Dance Man* and "complement the text tenderly."

Come a Tide, a picture book by Lyon, is among Gammell's most popular illustrated works. Set in the hills of rural Kentucky, the story takes place in March, when the springtime combination of snow and rain brings on a natural disaster. Grandma, a feisty woman whose house is on higher ground than everyone else in the town, watches as a flood washes away parts of houses and barnyard animals. Four families on the hillside—including that of the narrator, Grandma's young granddaughter—drive to Grandma's house to wait out the flood, and the woman's reassurance, wisdom, and wry wit help them cope with the tragedy. Writing in the *New York Times Book Review,* Kathleen Krull called *Come a Tide* "a complete success," adding that its "shimmering artwork goes a long way toward making the book such pure fun." According to Krull, Lyon and Gammell "have produced a weather-wise work of art that resonates—and exhilarates," while a *Publishers Weekly* critic dubbed *Come a Tide* "a gem of a picture book, [and] a seamless collaboration between author and artist."

A host of furry, scaly, and slimy creatures invade an educator's house in *I Know an Old Teacher,* Anne Bowen's silly take on the childhood favorite "I Know an Old Lady Who Swallowed a Fly." Writing in *Kirkus Reviews,* a critic stated that "Gammell's gleefully messy illustrations" for Bowen's story "give children an original view of teachers' private lives."

Gammell reteamed with Lyon for the lyrical picture book *My Friend, the Starfinder,* a story based on the author's childhood memories. Centering on the relationship between a young girl and an elderly neighbor, the book celebrates the power of imagination. According to Cooper, "Gammell's energetic art, a mix of precise lines and hue-soaked swirls and shapes, captures both the everyday and the otherworldiness of the story."

A humorous alphabet book in rhyme by Jim Aylesworth, *Old Black Fly* outlines the twenty-six horrible things done by the pesky title character—a villain with bulging red eyes, in Gammell's interpretation—as it turns a household upside down before receiving its comeuppance. Writing in *Booklist,* Carolyn Phelan wrote that while "another artist might have depicted the fly irritating the inhabitants of the house, . . . in Gammell's interpretation, mere irritation gives way to frenzy as Old Black Fly unleashes page after page of household pandemonium." Margaret A. Bush observed in *Horn Book* that Gammell "spatters all of his crudely sketched watercolor scenes, creating an energetic chaos sure to invite giggles from many children." Describing the book's art as "spattery, jumpy . . . , splashed with color, alive with movement, line, and humor," *School Library Journal* critic Gail C. Ross called *Old Black Fly* "a book that's sure to become a classic."

With a story by Liz Rosenberg, *Monster Mama* features young Patrick Edward and his mother, a roaring, spell-casting woman "with a bad hair day and needing a manicure," as described by a reviewer in *Publishers Weekly.* In addition to her other talents, Monster Mama, who lives in a cave behind the family home, paints, bakes, gardens, and nurses Patrick Edward when he is sick. When three bullies capture him, tie him up, and taunt him about his mother, Patrick Edward roars and breaks his bonds. Monster Mama hears her son, chases the bullies home, and makes them bake a new cake to replace one that they destroyed. The reviewer in *Publishers Weekly* concluded of *Monster Mama* that "Gammell's trademark electric palette and airy, spattered paint technique make for illustrations that crackle with childlike energy." Writing in *Horn Book,* Nancy Vasilakis noted that "the startling contrast between the benign, often lyrical text and Gammell's extravagant illustrations . . . produce the impish dynamics that are at the heart of this original book."

Gammell also contributed the illustrations to *The Burger and the Hot Dog,* a collection of poems by Aylesworth that feature such imaginative food characters as Barb Brownie, Tex Tater, and Frankie Fish Stick. The artist "has cooked up a batch of humorous, mixed-media illustrations in a loose, washy style," observed a contributor to *Kirkus Reviews* in reviewing the book. A terribly spoiled child learns a valuable lesson about compassion from his wise and clever grandmother when he is sealed in a giant pastry crust in Jennifer Donnelly's *Humble Pie.* A critic in *Kirkus Reviews* noted of this book that Gammell's pictures, "full of mischief and all of his splattery details, hold just the right amount of waggish exaggeration and expression, and suit the antic wit of the telling perfectly."

In Tamson Weston's *Hey, Pancakes!,* a work told in verse, a trio of energetic youngsters prepares a special breakfast while their parents snooze. "Gammell's exuberant, paint-splattered artwork creates a sense of topsy-turvy movement," a *Publishers Weekly* reviewer commented, and in *Booklist* Gillian Engberg also praised the artwork, noting that "its explosions of color and texture are so visceral that children may test the pages for spilled syrup." *Timothy Cox Will Not Change His Socks,* a work by Robert Kinerk, focuses on the odiferous aftermath of a youngster's decision to forgo washing his footwear for an entire month. "The pages become more and more spattered with color as the stench increases," Marianne Saccardi observed in *School Library Journal.*

Gammell's "signature spattery artwork," in the words of a *Publishers Weekly* critic, also graces the pages of Judy Sierra's *The Secret Science Project That Almost Ate the School.* The work, which concerns a young girl who accidentally unleashes a batch of mutant slime upon her family, features "skew-angled, paint-splotched illustrations, which explode with fantasy and the familiar, messy details of a child's world," as Engberg noted. In *How the Nobble Was Finally Found,* a fanciful tale by C.K. Williams, an impish creature leaves his solitary home in search of friendship. Here the artist Gammell "uses his delicious transparent colors, lightening his dark splatters, shadows and tangles, to great effect," as a contributor maintained in *Kirkus Reviews.*

Discussing his work as an illustrator, Gammell once told *SATA:* "The first time I read a manuscript, I can immediately tell whether I want to illustrate it. I may not know how the illustrations will look, but I get a certain feeling from the text. I respond to the words and, if I can respond to a story, I can illustrate it. My first concern is to serve the story. That is an illustrator's job. I don't research unless I have to because I prefer to draw from my imagination. I need to know whether a detail is anatomically correct before I can take liberties, however. If I must find out how something looks—what comes out of an animal's little paws, for instance, or which side of the face the trunk is on—I'll go to the library. But if I can get away with making up my own version, I will. It is more fun to work this way, and the illustrations are more expressive. Whatever I draw, whether it's a buffalo or a chair, I try to make it my own to satisfy myself." He continued, "I am inspired by a text which gives me the freedom to interpret. I don't like being tied to a specific historical time period, style of architecture, or costume. I like texts which take place anytime, anywhere. For this reason, I enjoy elements of fantasy in a story and turn down anything that is too literal. A careful look at my work tells the way I *interpret* a text. I take a poetic approach. The events I depict could easily be portrayed in a number of different ways."

"Much of my early work," Gammell added, "is done in pen and ink because I wasn't trained in color media. Watercolor is still difficult for me. My interest in book design has evolved over the years. I like to keep artistic control over design, especially type placement, and I often make suggestions concerning overall design, quality of paper, and format." Regarding his working habits, Gammell commented, "I prefer to work alone, without feedback from the author. I believe that once a manuscript is written and accepted, the writer's work is over. . . . When I illustrate a story, I want to work with my ideas and my perception of the work, not with the author."

Gammell keeps to a regular schedule when he is working on a book. "I work in my studio every day. Whether I accomplish my work or not, I am there. It's my job to show up, and because I like my work, I wouldn't have it any other way. I don't like to split my focus, and prefer to work on one book at a time. I would like to have the time to draw or paint outside of my illustration, but I'm at the mercy of a good manuscript. As long as they continue to come in, I will continue to work on them. I remember times when I would finish a book, turn it in, and have weeks of free time, but was so nervous about not having another book to do that I had a hard time relaxing enough to do my own drawings.

"I think of myself as an artist—admittedly a basic term that can mean almost anything. One of the forms that my art takes is book illustration. It is very fulfilling to me. I don't feel a need to get away from my studio to rejuvenate. I love my work. I love drawing, painting, and making books. In a deep sense, I *am* my work—what is seen on the page is really me."

Biographical and Critical Sources

BOOKS

Silvey, Anita, editor, *Children's Books and Their Creators*, Houghton (Boston, MA), 1995.

PERIODICALS

Booklist, April 1, 1983, Denise M. Wilms, review of *Git Along, Old Scudder,* p. 1033; February 15, 1992, Carolyn Phelan, review of *Old Black Fly,* p. 1106; September 1, 1997, John Peters, review of *Is That You, Winter?,* p. 132; May 1, 2001, Hazel Rochman, review of *Ride,* p. 1689; July, 2002, Ilene Cooper, review of *Humble Pie,* p. 1857; August, 2003, Gillian Engberg, review of *Hey, Pancakes!,* p. 1981; May 1, 2005, Gillian Engberg, review of *Timothy Cox Will Not Change His Socks,* p. 1591; October 15, 2005, Gillian Engberg, review of *Kids in the Kitchen,* p. 59; August 1, 2006, Gillian Engberg, review of *The Secret Science Project That Almost Ate the School,* p. 94; January 1, 2008, Ilene Cooper, review of *My Friend, the Starfinder,* p. 92.

Horn Book, June, 1981, Kate M. Flanagan, review of *Where the Buffaloes Begin,* p. 298; December, 1981, Ethel L. Heins, review of *Wake up, Bear . . . It's Christmas!,* p. 653; April, 1983, Mary M. Burns, review of *Git Along, Old Scudder,* p. 150; March, 1986, Ann A. Flowers, review of *The Relatives Came,* p. 197; July-August, 1989, Annie Schwartz, "Stephen Gammell," pp. 456-459; March-April, 1990, Mary M.

Burns, review of *Come a Tide,* p. 104; May-June, 1992, Margaret A. Bush, review of *Old Black Fly,* p. 325; March-April, 1993, Nancy Vasilakis, review of *Monster Mama,* p. 200; May, 2001, Joanna Rudge Long, review of *Ride,* p. 310; March-April, 2008, Susan Dove Lempke, review of *My Friend, the Starfinder,* p. 207.

Kirkus Reviews, October 1, 2001, review of *The Burger and the Hot Dog,* p. 1418; August 15, 2002, review of *Humble Pie,* p. 1221; April 15, 2005, review of *Timothy Cox Will Not Change His Socks,* p. 476; February 15, 2008, review of *My Friend, the Starfinder;* August 15, 2008, review of *I Know an Old Teacher;* August 1, 2009, review of *How the Nobble Was Finally Found.*

New Yorker, December 7, 1981, Faith McNulty, review of *Wake up, Bear . . . It's Christmas!,* p. 227.

New York Times Book Review, February, 15, 1981, George A. Woods, review of *Where the Buffaloes Begin,* p. 22; June 26, 1981, Karla Kuskin, "Seeing and Reading," p. 54; November 10, 1985, Anne Tyler, "Disorder at 4 A.M.," p. 37; October 14, 1990, Kathleen Krull, review of *Come a Tide,* p. 33; February 15, 1998, Marigny Dupuy, review of *Is That You, Winter?,* p. 26; June 3, 2001, Scott Veale, "Back-Seat Warriors," p. 49.

Publishers Weekly, May 5, 1980, review of *Terrible Things: An Allegory of the Holocaust,* p. 77; April 24, 1981, review of *Once upon MacDonald's Farm,* p. 75; January 23, 1987, review of *Old Henry,* p. 88; January 12, 1990, review of *Come a Tide,* p. 60; June 8, 1990, review of *Thunder at Gettysburg,* p. 54; January 25, 1993, review of *Monster Mama,* p. 87; August 11, 1997, review of *Is That You, Winter?,* p. 401; April 1, 2001, review of *Ride,* p. 63; November 5, 2001, review of *The Burger and the Hot Dog,* p. 67; July 8, 2002, review of *Humble Pie,* p. 49; December 23, 2002, review of *Swing around the Sun,* p. 69; August 18, 2003, review of *Hey, Pancakes!,* p. 77; October 16, 2006, review of *The Secret Science Project That Almost Ate the School,* p. 53; January 28, 2008, review of *My Friend, the Starfinder,* p. 67; July 27, 2009, review of *How The Nobble Was Finally Found,* p. 62.

School Library Journal, August, 1983, Clarissa Erwin, review of *Git Along, Old Scudder,* pp. 50-51; January, 1989, Gratia Banta, review of *Song and Dance Man,* p. 58; April, 1992, Gail C. Ross, review of *Old Black Fly,* p. 88; May, 2001, Wendy Lukehart, review of *Ride,* p. 115; January, 2002, Caroline Ward, review of *The Burger and the Hot Dog,* p. 116; September, 2003, Laurie Edwards, review of *Hey, Pancakes!,* p. 193; June, 2005, Marianne Saccardi, review of *Timothy Cox Will Not Change His Socks,* p. 118; November, 2006, Susan Lissim, review of *The Secret Science Project That Almost Ate the School,* p. 113; September, 2008, Mary Elam, review of *I Know an Old Teacher,* p. 140; September, 2009, Barbara Elleman, review of *How the Nobble Was Finally Found,* p. 137.

ONLINE

BookPage Online, http://www.bookpage.com/ (June, 2000), "Meet the Author: Stephen Gammell."

Children's Literature Network, http://www.childrenslitera turenetwork.org/ (March 11, 2011), "Stephen Gammell."*

* * *

GEORGE, Jean
See GEORGE, Jean Craighead

* * *

GEORGE, Jean Craighead 1919-
(Jean George)

Personal

Born July 2, 1919, in Washington, DC; daughter of Frank Cooper (an entomologist) and Mary Carolyn Craighead; married John Lothar George (a sociologist), January 28, 1944 (divorced, 1963); children: Carolyn Laura, John Craighead, Thomas Luke. *Education:* Pennsylvania State University, B.A., 1941; attended Louisiana State University, Baton Rouge, 1941-42, and University of Michigan. *Politics:* Democrat. *Hobbies and other interests:* Painting; field trips to universities and laboratories of natural science, modern dance, whitewater canoeing.

Addresses

Home—Chappaqua, NY. *E-mail*—jeangeorge1@verizon. net; jeangeorgemail@aol.com.

Career

Writer and journalist. International News Service, Washington, DC, reporter, 1941-43; Washington Post and Times-Herald, Washington, DC, reporter, 1943-46; *Pageant* magazine, New York, NY, artist, 1946-47; Newspaper Enterprise Association, New York, NY, artist and reporter, 1946-47; teacher in Chappaqua, NY, 1960-68; Reader's Digest, Pleasantville, NY, staff writer, 1969-74, roving editor, 1974-80.

Member

PEN, League of Women Voters, Duchess County Art Association.

Awards, Honors

Aurianne Award, American Library Association (ALA), 1956, for *Dipper of Copper Creek;* Newbery Honor Book, and Notable Book citation, both ALA, both 1960, International Hans Christian Andersen Award honor listee, International Board on Books for Young People (IBBY), 1962, Lewis Carroll Shelf citation, 1965, and George G. Stone Center for Children's Books Award, 1969, all for *My Side of the Mountain;* named Woman of the Year, Pennsylvania State University, 1968; Clare-

Jean Craighead George (Photograph by Ellan Young Photography. Reproduced by permission.)

mont College award, 1969; Eva L. Gordon Award, American Nature Study Society, 1970; *Book World* First Prize, 1971, for *All upon a Stone;* Newbery Medal, National Book Award finalist, American Association of Publishers, German Youth Literature Prize, West German section of IBBY, and Silver Skate award, Netherlands Children's Book Board, all 1973, and named among ten best American children's books in 200 years, Children's Literature Association, 1976, all for *Julie of the Wolves;* School Library Media Specialties of Southeastern New York Award, 1981; Irvin Kerlan Award, University of Minnesota, 1982; University of Southern Mississippi Award, 1986; Grumman Award, 1986; Washington Irving Award, Westchester Library Association, 1991; Reading Is Fundamental Award, 1995; Knickerbocker Award for Juvenile Literature, School Library Media Section of New York Public Library Association; Children's Book Guild Award for Nonfiction, Children's Book Guild/*Washington Post,* 1998, for body of work; Notable Children's Books listee, *New York Times,* 1999, for *Frightful's Mountain;* Jeremiah Ludington Award, 2003; Key Award nomination, 2005; *My Side of the Mountain* selected to represent the state at National Book Festival, 2005; One Hundred Titles for Reading and Sharing selection, *New York Times,* 2009, for *The Cats of Roxville Station.*

Writings

SELF-ILLUSTRATED JUVENILE FICTION

(With husband, John Lothar George) *Vulpes, the Red Fox,* Dutton (New York, NY), 1948.

(With John Lothar George) *Vison, the Mink,* Dutton (New York, NY), 1949.

(With John Lothar George) *Masked Prowler: The Story of a Raccoon,* Dutton (New York, NY), 1950.

(With John Lothar George) *Meph, the Pet Skunk,* Dutton (New York, NY), 1952.

(With John Lothar George) *Bubo, the Great Horned Owl,* Dutton (New York, NY), 1954.

(With John Lothar George) *Dipper of Copper Creek,* Dutton (New York, NY), 1956.

The Hole in the Tree, Dutton (New York, NY), 1957.

Snow Tracks, Dutton (New York, NY), 1958.

My Side of the Mountain, Dutton (New York, NY), 1959.

The Summer of the Falcon, Crowell (New York, NY), 1962.

Red Robin, Fly Up!, Reader's Digest (Pleasantville, NY), 1963.

Gull Number 737, Crowell (New York, NY), 1964.

Hold Zero!, Crowell (New York, NY), 1966.

Water Sky, Harper (New York, NY), 1987.

On the Far Side of the Mountain, Dutton Children's Books (New York, NY), 1990.

The Tarantula in My Purse; and 172 Other Wild Pets, HarperCollins (New York, NY), 1996.

Tree Castle Island, HarperCollins (New York, NY), 2002.

Charlie's Raven, Dutton (New York, NY), 2004.

JUVENILE FICTION

Coyote in Manhattan, illustrated by John Kaufmann, Crowell (New York, NY), 1968.

All upon a Stone, illustrated by Don Bolognese, Crowell (New York, NY), 1971.

Who Really Killed Cock Robin?: An Ecological Mystery, Dutton (New York, NY), 1971.

Julie of the Wolves, illustrated by John Schoenherr, Harper (New York, NY), 1972.

All upon a Sidewalk, illustrated by Don Bolognese, Dutton (New York, NY), 1974.

Hook a Fish, Catch a Mountain: An Ecological Spy Story, Dutton (New York, NY), 1975, published as *The Case of the Missing Cutthroats: An Ecological Mystery,* HarperCollins (New York, NY), 1996.

Going to the Sun, Harper (New York, NY), 1976.

The Wentletrap Trap, illustrated by Symeon Shimin, Dutton (New York, NY), 1978.

The Wounded Wolf, illustrated by John Schoenherr, Harper (New York, NY), 1978.

River Rats, Inc., Dutton (New York, NY), 1979.

The Cry of the Crow, Harper (New York, NY), 1980.

The Grizzly Bear with the Golden Ears, illustrated by Tom Catania, Harper (New York, NY), 1982.

The Talking Earth, Harper (New York, NY), 1983.

Shark beneath the Reef, Harper (New York, NY), 1989.

The Missing Gator of Gumbo Limbo: An Ecological Mystery, HarperCollins (New York, NY), 1992.

The First Thanksgiving, illustrated by Thomas Locker, Philomel Books (New York, NY), 1993.

The Fire Bug Connection: An Ecological Mystery, HarperCollins (New York, NY), 1993.

Dear Rebecca, Winter Is Here, illustrated by Loretta Krupinski, HarperCollins (New York, NY), 1993.

Julie, illustrated by Wendell Minor, HarperCollins (New York, NY), 1994.

Animals Who Have Won Our Hearts, illustrated by Christine Herman Merrill, HarperCollins (New York, NY), 1994.

To Climb a Waterfall, illustrated by Thomas Locker, Philomel Books (New York, NY), 1995.

There's an Owl in the Shower, illustrated by Christine Herman Merrill, HarperCollins (New York, NY), 1995.

Julie's Wolf Pack, illustrated by Wendell Minor, HarperCollins (New York, NY), 1997.

Look to the North: A Wolf Pup Diary, illustrated by Lucia Washburn, HarperCollins (New York, NY), 1997.

Arctic Son, illustrated by Wendell Minor, Hyperion Books for Children (New York, NY), 1997.

Dear Katie, the Volcano Is a Girl, Hyperion Books for Children (New York, NY), 1998.

Elephant Walk, Disney Press (New York, NY), 1998.

Giraffe Trouble, Disney Press (New York, NY), 1998.

Gorilla Gang, Disney Press (New York, NY), 1998.

Rhino Romp, Disney Press (New York, NY), 1998.

Frightful's Mountain, Dutton Children's Books (New York, NY), 1999.

Incredible Animal Adventures, Harper Trophy (New York, NY), 1999.

Morning, Noon, and Night, HarperCollins (New York, NY), 1999.

Snow Bear, Hyperion Books for Children (New York, NY), 1999.

Nutik, the Wolf Pup, illustrated by Ted Rand, HarperCollins (New York, NY), 2000.

Nutik and Amaroq Play Ball, illustrated by Ted Rand, HarperCollins (New York, NY), 2000.

Lonesome George, illustrated by Wendell Minor, HarperCollins (New York, NY), 2001.

Frightful's Daughter, illustrated by Daniel San Souci, Dutton (New York, NY), 2002.

Luck: The Story of a Sandhill Crane, illustrated by Wendell Minor, HarperCollins (New York, NY), 2006.

Frightful's Daughter Meets the Baron Weasel, illustrated by Daniel San Souci, Dutton Children's Books (New York, NY), 2007.

Goose and Duck, illustrated by Priscilla Lamont, Laura Geringer Books (New York, NY), 2008.

The Wolves Are Back, illustrated by Wendell Minor, Dutton Children's Books (New York, NY), 2008.

The Cats of Roxville Station, illustrated by Tom Pohrt, Dutton Children's Books (New York, NY), 2009.

The Last Polar Bear, illustrated by Wendell Minor, Laura Geringer Books (New York, NY), 2009.

The Buffalo Are Back, illustrated by Wendell Minor, Dutton Children's Books (New York, NY), 2010.

Galapagos George, illustrated by Wendell Minor, Dutton Children's Books (New York, NY), 2011.

NONFICTION

Spring Comes to the Ocean (juvenile), illustrated by John Wilson, Crowell (New York, NY), 1966.

(Self-illustrated) *Beastly Inventions: A Surprising Investigation into How Smart Animals Really Are* (juvenile),

McKay, 1970, published as *Animals Can Do Anything,* Souvenir Press, 1972.

Everglades Wildguide, illustrated by Betty Fraser, National Park Service, 1972.

(With Toy Lasker) *New York in Maps, 1972/73,* New York Magazine, 1974.

(With Toy Lasker) *New York in Flashmaps, 1974/75,* Flashmaps, 1976.

The American Walk Book: An Illustrated Guide to the Country's Major Historical and Natural Walking Trails from New England to the Pacific Coast, Dutton (New York, NY), 1978.

The Wild, Wild Cookbook: A Guide for Young Foragers (juvenile), illustrated by Walter Kessell, Crowell (New York, NY), 1982.

Journey Inward (autobiography), Dutton (New York, NY), 1982.

(Self-illustrated) *How to Talk to Your Animals* (also see below), Harcourt (New York, NY), 1985.

(Self-illustrated) *How to Talk to Your Dog* (originally published in *How to Talk to Your Animals*), Warner (New York, NY), 1986, illustrated by Sue Truesdell, Harper-Collins (New York, NY), 2000.

(Self-illustrated) *How to Talk to Your Cat* (originally published in *How to Talk to Your Animals*), Warner (New York, NY), 1986, illustrated by Paul Meisel, Harper-Collins (New York, NY), 2000.

Acorn Pancakes, Dandelion Salad, and 38 Other Wild Recipes, illustrated by Paul Mirocha, HarperCollins (New York, NY), 1995.

Everglades (juvenile), illustrated by Wendell Minor, HarperCollins (New York, NY), 1995.

"THIRTEEN MOONS" SERIES; JUVENILE NONFICTION

The Moon of the Owls (also see below), illustrated by Jean Zallinger, Crowell (New York, NY), 1967, revised edition illustrated by Wendell Minor, 1993.

The Moon of the Bears (also see below), illustrated by Mac Shepard, Crowell (New York, NY), 1967, revised edition illustrated by Max Shepherd, 1993.

The Moon of the Salamanders (also see below), illustrated by John Kaufmann, Crowell (New York, NY), 1967, revised edition illustrated by Marlene Hill Werner, 1992.

The Moon of the Chickarees (also see below), illustrated by John Schoenherr, Crowell (New York, NY), 1968, revised edition illustrated by Don Rodell, 1992.

The Moon of the Monarch Butterflies (also see below), illustrated by Murray Tinkelman, Crowell (New York, NY), 1968, revised edition illustrated by Kam Mak, 1993.

The Moon of the Fox Pups (also see below), illustrated by Kiyoaki Komoda, Crowell (New York, NY), 1968, revised edition illustrated by Norman Adams, 1992.

The Moon of the Wild Pigs (also see below), illustrated by Peter Parnall, Crowell (New York, NY), 1968, revised edition illustrated by Paul Mirocha, 1992.

The Moon of the Mountain Lions (also see below), illustrated by Winifred Lubell, Crowell (New York, NY), 1968, revised edition illustrated by Ron Parker, 1991.

The Moon of the Deer (also see below), illustrated by Jean Zallinger, Crowell (New York, NY), 1969, revised edition illustrated by Sal Catalano, 1992.

The Moon of the Alligators (also see below), illustrated by Adrina Zanazanian, Crowell (New York, NY), 1969, revised edition illustrated by Michael Rothman 1991.

The Moon of the Gray Wolves (also see below), illustrated by Lorence Bjorklund, Crowell (New York, NY), 1969, revised edition illustrated by Sal Catalano, 1991.

The Moon of the Winter Bird (also see below), illustrated by Kazue Mizumura, Crowell (New York, NY), 1969, revised edition illustrated by Vincent Nasta, 1992.

The Moon of the Moles (also see below), illustrated by Robert Levering, Crowell (New York, NY), 1969, revised edition illustrated by Michael Rothman, 1992.

Autumn Moon (includes *The Moon of the Deer, The Moon of the Alligators,* and *The Moon of the Gray Wolves The Moon of the Winter Bird,* and *The Moon of the Moles*), HarperTrophy (New York, NY), 2001.

Winter Moon (includes *The Moon of the Owls* and *The Moon of the Bears,*), HarperTrophy (New York, NY), 2001.

Spring Moon (includes *The Moon of the Salamanders, The Moon of the Chickarees,* and *The Moon of the Monarch Butterflies*), HarperTrophy (New York, NY), 2002.

Summer Moon (includes *The Moon of the Fox Pups, The Moon of the Wild Pigs,* and *The Moon of the Mountain Lions*), HarperTrophy (New York, NY), 2002.

"ONE DAY" SERIES; JUVENILE NONFICTION

One Day in the Desert, illustrated by Fred Brenner, Harper (New York, NY), 1983.

One Day in the Alpine Tundra, illustrated by Walter Gaffney-Kessell, Harper (New York, NY), 1984.

One Day in the Prairie, illustrated by Bob Marstall, Harper (New York, NY), 1986.

One Day in the Woods, illustrated by Gary Allen, Harper (New York, NY), 1988, released with CD, 2008.

One Day in the Tropical Rain Forest, illustrated by Gary Allen, Crowell (New York, NY), 1990.

"OUTDOOR ADVENTURES" PICTURE-BOOK SERIES

Cliff Hanger, illustrated by Wendell Minor, HarperCollins (New York, NY), 2002.

Fire Storm, illustrated by Wendell Minor, HarperCollins (New York, NY), 2003.

Snowboard Twist, illustrated by Wendell Minor, Harper-Collins (New York, NY), 2004.

OTHER

(Author of introduction and contributor) *Marvels and Mysteries of Our Animal World,* Reader's Digest Association, 1964.

(Illustrator) John Johnson Craighead, *Hawks, Owls, and Wildlife,* 1969.

(Editor with Ann Durell and Katherine Paterson) Aliki, *The Big Book for Our Planet,* Dutton Children's Books (New York, NY), 1993.

(With Twig C. George) *Pocket Guide to the Outdoors: Based on "My Side of the Mountain,"* Dutton Children's Books (New York, NY), 2009.

Also author of play *Tree House,* music by Saul Aarons. Contributor of articles on natural history and children's literature to periodicals, including *Horn Book, Audubon, Reader's Digest, National Wildlife,* and *International Wildlife.* Consultant for science books.

George's manuscripts are held in the Kerlan Collection at the University of Minnesota, Minneapolis.

Adaptations

My Side of the Mountain was adapted as a film starring Teddy Eccles and Theodore Bikel, Paramount, 1969. *Julie of the Wolves* was adapted as a recording, read by Irene Worth, Caedmon, 1977; as a film; and as a musical with music by Chris Kubie. *One Day in the Woods* was adapted as a musical video, with music by Fritz Kramer and Kubie, Kunhardt Productions, 1989; and as a musical, with music by Kubie, HarperCollins Audio, 1997. *On the Far Side of the Mountain* and *Frightful's Mountain* were recorded as an audiocassette by Recorded Books, 1995. Other books adapted for audiocassette include *Charlie's Raven,* Recorded Books, 2004.

Sidelights

Newbery Medal winner Jean Craighead George has made nature the center of her fiction and nonfiction work in a prolific career spanning over half a century of writing and illustrating. In her novels, picture books, and books of fact, George treats readers to fascinating glimpses into the natural world, earning recognition as "our premier naturalist novelist," according to *New York Times Book Review* contributor Beverly Lyon Clark. Writing first with her husband and more recently alone, she has penned animal studies such as *Dipper of Copper Creek* and *Luck: The Story of a Sandhill Crane* as well as adventure tales such as *My Side of the Mountain, Julie of the Wolves,* and *Charlie's Raven,* in which young people learn to survive in the wilderness. George's books are distinguished by authentic detail and a blend of scientific curiosity, wonder, and concern for the natural environment, all expressed in a manner critics have described as both unsentimental and lyrical. As Karen Nelson Hoyle observed in the *Dictionary of Literary Biography,* George "elevates nature in all its intricacies and makes scientific research concerning ecological systems intriguing and exciting to the young reader."

Although George illustrated her own stories early in her writing career, by the mid-1960s she began teaming up with talented artists such as Wendell Minor, Paul Mirocha, Symeon Shimin, Thomas Locker, Ted Rand, and Daniel San Souci in producing her nature-filled books. One of her most frequent collaborators, Minor, has created the detailed paintings in dozens of George's picture books, among them *Arctic Son,* which was dubbed

Cover of George's picture book Arctic Theme, *which describes life in the far north and features artwork by Wendell Minor.* (Illustration copyright © 1997 by Wendell Minor. Reprinted by permission of Hyperion Books for Children.)

a "picture-book ode to the Arctic" by a *Publishers Weekly* critic. A chronicle of the birth and early years of George's grandson, the book is a "warm, positive story of life in the Far North," wrote Mollie Bynum in her *School Library Journal* review of *Arctic Son.*

Born in Washington, DC, to a family of naturalists, George was destined to develop an early love of nature. Her father was an entomologist, her mother was a lover of nature and of storytelling, and her twin brothers were also drawn to the outdoors and contributed articles to major magazines about falconry while still in high school. Her twin brothers were a hard act for George to follow, and while growing up she became as adept on the softball field as she was on a mountain trail. She graduated from Pennsylvania State University in 1941, studying science and English. Thereafter she studied art at Louisiana State University and pursued graduate work at the University of Michigan.

George met her future husband, John Lothar George, during World War II, and they were married four months later. John completed his academic studies and taught at various colleges, including Vassar, while his wife worked as a newspaper reporter. Once her three children were born, she began writing books, the first of which benefited from John's field notes. In *Meph the Pet Skunk, Vulpes the Red Fox,* and *Dipper of Copper Creek* George profiles different wild creature; for example, *Dipper of Copper Creek* introduces young children to the Rocky Mountain water ouzel, a bird that nests behind waterfalls, through its story about an old prospector and his grandson. Winner of the Aurianne Award in 1956, *Dipper of Copper Creek* set the tone for much of George's literary output through its informed and entertaining blend of fact and fiction.

One of George's best-known books, as well as her first major solo effort, *My Side of the Mountain* developed in her mind for some time before it was put on paper. Using the backwoods lore she had learned during camping trips with her father and brothers along the Potomac River, she crafted a story about a teenage boy who runs away to the Catskill Mountains and lives off the land for a year. In a first-person account, thirteen-year-old Sam Gribley describes his self-sufficient wilderness life in detail. Equipped with a pen knife, a ball of cord, an ax, and forty dollars, Sam whittles a fish hook out of a green twig, constructs a tent from hemlock boughs, and makes snowshoes from ash saplings and deer hide. Shared by Frightful, a female peregrine falcon that the boy captures and trains, Sam's year in the woods is considered by some critics to be the ultimate survival tale for youngsters. On the fiftieth anniversary of the novel, Barbara Bader viewed *My Side of the Mountain* from a different perspective. "Sam Gribley's escape from the confines of a New York apartment to ancestral land in the Catskills is more in the tradition of Daniel Boone and Henry David Thoreau than of the castaway Crusoe," Bader asserted in *Horn Book*. "Sam comes to the woods equipped—with a few basic tools and a lot of heavy reading."

My Side of the Mountain won a number of awards, including a Newbery honor, in addition to being adapted for film in 1969. The novel also inspired two highly popular sequels as well as the nature guide *Pocket Guide to the Outdoors: Based on "My Side of the Mountain."* In *On the Far Side of the Mountain* Frightful is seized by a conservation officer as an endangered species, and Sam's sister Alice then goes missing. In *Frightful's Mountain* the point of view shifts from humans to wildlife as Frightful concentrates on only one thing while she is held captive by poachers: returning somehow to Sam. Fortunately, Alice is instrumental in freeing the captive peregrine, allowing the falcon to find its way back to the boy it knows as its home. "George builds the suspense in a third-person narration that most often takes the falcon's perspective," noted a *Publishers Weekly*, the critic adding that details such as peregrine migratory, mating, and nesting habits "are seamlessly woven into the plot" of *Frightful's Mountain*. Praising George's story in the *New York Times Book Review*, Mary Harris Russell predicted that *Frightful's Mountain* "will change the way you look at the world."

In addition to novels, George follows the adventures of the peregrine falcon in the picture books *Frightful's Daughter* and *Frightful's Daughter Meets the Baron Weasel*. Enhanced by San Souci's detailed paintings, *Frightful's Daughter* recounts the plight of peregrine

Another collaboration with Minor, The Last Polar Bear, *allows George to share her love of the Arctic with young readers.* (Illustration copyright © 2009 by Wendell Minor. Used by permission of HarperCollins Children's Books, a division of HarperCollins Publishers.)

eyas (chick) Oksi as it learns the ways of the wild and the dangers posed by some humans. Almost caught by poachers, Frightful's independent-minded offspring is cared for by Sam until it is time for the creature to return to the wild, resulting in a book that a *Kirkus Reviews* writer cited as an effective "means of introducing children to Sam Gribley's intriguing world." Readers revisit Sam in his forest home in *Frightful's Daughter Meets the Weasel*, as a woodland weasel considers Frightful's two eyases as potential food for its own young now that winter is approaching. "Without anthropomorphizing, both the author and San Souci] . . . make this nature tale and its animal participants accessible and inviting to young readers," noted *Booklist* critic John Peters, and in *Kirkus Reviews* a critic praised *Frightful's Daughter Meets the Baron Weasel* as a "visually splendid" story that "introduces young readers to the realities of wilderness survival."

The popularity of *My Side of the Mountain* could not have come at a better time for George, who divorced in 1963 and set about earning a living as a single parent by her writing. She also pursued her love of nature, turning her home in Chappaqua, New York, into something of a zoo with hundreds of wild animals living in her house and backyard, among them owls, robins, mink, seagulls, and even tarantulas. The success of *My Side of the Mountain* helped, as did a job with *Reader's Digest* from 1969 to 1982. Several other juvenile novels followed, including *Gull Number 737, Hold Zero!,* and *Coyote in Manhattan,* as well as the popular nonfiction series "Thirteen Moons," which features a different animal for each of the new moons of the year's lunar calendar. Sutherland noted in a *Bulletin of the*

Center for Children's Books review of series install-ment *The Moon of the Fox Pups* that George "writes of the animal world with knowledge and enthusiasm, her descriptions of wild life untainted by melodrama or an-thropomorphism." The thirteen books in the "Thirteen Moons" series were reissued beginning in 1991 with re-vised texts and new illustrations, and have been more-recently re-released in the four volumes *Spring Moon, Summer Moon, Autumn Moon,* and *Winter Moon.*

One summer in the late 1960s George and her younger son, Luke, made a journey to Alaska, and this trip strongly shaped her novel *Julie of the Wolves.* The two had gone to Barrow to learn about wolf behavior from a scientist doing a study there. They received some un-planned lessons in native Inuit culture after George met a young Inuit woman and learned a great deal about na-tive life. The young woman would also inspire the char-acter of the novel's heroine. From the scientists study-ing wolves, George learned that humans are able to communicate with wolves and learn wolf language. One female wolf actually communicated back to the author. "When she answered back," George recalled on her home page, "I knew that I wanted to write a book about a little girl who is lost on the tundra and saves her life by communicating with wolves. So I did."

Julie of the Wolves records the adventures of an Inuit teen who becomes lost on the tundra while running away from an unhappy marriage. When her father dis-appears on a hunting expedition, Miyax—also known by the English name Julie—is adopted by relatives. At age thirteen she marries so she can leave her foster home. Although her husband is slow-witted and the marriage is little more than a formality, Miyax is con-tent to live with his family. His forceful attempt to have sex with her, however, frightens her and she leaves him. Remembering her California pen pal's repeated in-

George and Minor take readers to life on the Western plains in the picture book **The Buffalo Are Back.** (Illustration copyright © 2010 by Wendell Minor. All rights reserved. Used by permission of Dutton Children's Books, a division of Penguin Young Readers Group, a member of Penguin Group (USA) Inc., 345 Hudson Street, New York, NY 10014.)

vitations to visit, Miyax sets out across the tundra. When she loses her way in the barren land, she survives by learning to communicate with a wolf pack and is befriended by the lead wolf, whom she names Amaroq. Julie's knowledge of Inuit ways is also crucial to her survival, although gradually she begins to understand that the old ways are dying.

Writing that the novel's "plot, character development, and setting are epic in dimension," Hoyle called *Julie of the Wolves* "George's most significant book" to date. In *School Library Journal* Alice Miller Bregman described the novel as "compelling" and commented that "George has captured the subtle nuances of Eskimo life, animal habits, [and] the pain of growing up, and combines these elements into a thrilling adventure which is, at the same time, a poignant love story." Reviewing *Julie of the Wolves* for the *New York Times Book Review,* James Houston observed that the novel "is packed with expert wolf lore, its narrative beautifully conveying the vastness of tundra as well as many other aspects of the Arctic." Although Houston questioned the reality of such a connection between human and wolf, he concluded that readers "slowly come to think of these wolves as dear friends." Writing in *Horn Book,* Virginia Haviland lauded George's novel as a "book of timeless, perhaps even of classic dimensions." Awards committees took a similar view, nominating *Julie of the Wolves* for many prizes and bestowing upon it the prestigious Newbery Medal among other honors.

George revisits her characters in *Julie,* a sequel that begins only minutes after the ending of *Julie of the Wolves,* as well as in *Julie's Wolf Pack,* a story told almost totally from the perspective of the wolves. In *Julie* the Inuit girl returns to her family's village, Kangik, only to discover that her long-estranged father, Kapugen, has married a white woman and left the old ways behind. As Julie struggles to save her beloved wolves, she also falls in love with a young Siberian man, Peter Sugluk. "This one will go like hotcakes, both to new readers and old fans of the prequel," commented Susan Dunn in a *Voice of Youth Advocates* review of *Julie,* the critic praising George's story as both "an excellent adventure" and a novel that supplies a "delicious taste of a nontraditional lifestyle and personality." Writing in the *New York Times Book Review,* Hazel Rochman observed that "what's glorious is the lyrical nature writing. . . . George's sense of the place is so instinctive and so physically precise that the final Edenic vision of natural world order restored . . . is like a ringing song of triumph."

With *Julie's Wolf Pack* the focus shifts to the pack, now led by Kapu, the new alpha male. Constantly challenged by a loner wolf named Raw Bones, Kapu must prove himself to the pack while rabies looms as another enemy. Although many reviewers felt that *Julie's Wolf Pack* lacks the dramatic tension of *Julie of the Wolves* and *Julie,* largely because Julie is peripheral to the plot, Carrie Eldridge, wrote in *Kliatt* that George's "obvious

knowledge of her subject matter is admirable and resonates throughout the story." Speaking with Karen Williams in the *Christian Science Monitor,* George explained her affinity for wolves: "I am intrigued that their society is very much like ours—with leaders (alphas), vice presidents (betas), and cabinet members. They all have talents, and the wolf pack recognized them. I love their devotion to each other. They stay together partly for economic reasons, but mainly because of their deep affection and loyalty."

As she did with *My Side of the Mountain,* George teamed with illustrator Ted Rand to produce several picture-book adaptations of *Julie's Wolf Pack.* In *Nutik, the Wolf Pup* and *Nutik and Amaroq Play Ball* Julie's younger brother Amaroq is put in charge of a hungry wolf pup that has been orphaned in the wild. While the two quickly become the best of friends, Amaroq realizes that at some point his new playmate will have to be returned to the pack. Praising Rand's paintings in *Nutik, the Wolf Pup* for their ability to "capture the affection between boy and pup," *Booklist* contributor Linda Perkins also cited George's work in "skillfully telescop[ing]" a subplot of her novel "into a picture book with heart-tugging appeal."

Featuring detailed paintings by Minor, *Tree Castle Island* returns to George's characteristic themes in its focus on a resourceful young person able to survive in the wild. The novel finds fourteen-year-old Jack staying with his uncle Hamp in Florida while Jack's parents travel to Europe. Building his own canoe, he explores the Okefenokee Swamp near his uncle's house. After several days of exploring, Jack discovers that he cannot return home because of a blockage that has formed in the river; the current is now running the wrong way. Deciding to wait the situation out, the teen makes his way to an island in the middle of the swamp, where he builds a makeshift tree house for protection. A stray dog named Dizzy wanders onto the scene and becomes the boy's companion, followed by a local boy named Jake who, in a twist of fate, ultimately changes Jack's life forever. Carolyn Phelan, writing in *Booklist,* praised George's choice of the Okefenokee Swamp as "a well-developed, original setting." The ending of *Tree Castle Island*, wrote a critic for *Kirkus Reviews,* is "a pleasant and satisfying surprise."

George researched *Tree Castle Island* by exploring the 700-square miles of the Okefenokee Swamp with her fourteen-year-old nephew and two granddaughters. She based Jack's island tree house on an old legend about Paradise Island, a beautiful island deep in the swamp where the mysterious "Sun Daughters" are said to live. "Although Jack doesn't find Paradise Island," George told Deborah Hopkinson in an online interview for *BookPage,* "he does make an important discovery about his own past."

Another story inspired by the author's trips with family members is *Charlie's Raven.* Thirteen-year-old Charlie worries about his naturalist grandfather as the man recovers from a debilitating heart attack. After learning from his Teton Sioux friend Singing Bird that ravens have the ability to help the sick heal Charlie captures a young raven chick he names Blue Sky. Hiding his true motives and unsure whether a bird with such a bad reputation can actually work for good, he declares that the bird is part of a research project. As Charlie's grandfather teaches the teen how to care for and observe the bird, he truly does seem to heal, and the experience also creates a strong bond between the man and his grandson. As Charlie learns about the bird, he begins to understand the duality of nature; as a *Kirkus Reviews* writer noted, "there aren't true dividing lines between good and bad in the natural world." Kay Weisman, reviewing *Charlie's Raven* in *Booklist,* praised it as "a satisfying family story," while in *Publishers Weekly* a critic wrote that George "weaves threads of Native American lore and scientific fact into a moving story." While noting that *Charlie's Raven* contains an overabundance of not-quite-believable occurrences, Ellen Fader wrote in *School Library Journal* that young readers "will close the book with a healthy respect for the natural world."

George's fascination with the Arctic has continued to inspire her, producing the novels *Water Sky* and *The Wounded Wolf.* She has also framed her study of nature in the continental United States as ecological mysteries in the books *Hook a Fish, Catch a Mountain: An Ecological Spy Story* (republished as *The Case of the Missing Cutthroat*), *Who Really Killed Cock Robin?: An Ecological Mystery, The Fire Bug Connection: An Ecological Mystery,* and *The Missing 'Gator of Gumbo Limbo.* Wilderness themes are threaded with adventures in novels such as *Going to the Sun,* set in the Rocky Mountains; *River Rats, Inc.,* dealing with white-water rafting; *The Wentletrap Trap,* set on the island of Bimini; and *The Cry of the Crow,* which takes place in the Florida Everglades.

In *Morning, Noon, and Night,* another of her collaborations with Minor, George portrays the activities of a variety of animals from dawn on the East Coast to sundown on the West. In *Luck* the artist's "skilled paintings provide richly varied perspectives" on the journey of a sandhill crane during its migration from Texas north to Siberia and back, producing what *School Library Journal* critic Margaret Bush recommended as a "pleasant tale [that] will be enjoyable shared reading for birdwatchers." The Arctic spring is captured in *Snow Bear,* in which an Inuit girl goes out on a hunt and encounters a bear cub. Patricia Manning, reviewing *Snow Bear* for *School Library Journal,* commented that "the simple, pleasing text is accompanied by luminous watercolors [by Minor] that faithfully record this charming (if improbable) chance meeting."

Environmental issues are at the core of several books by George, among them *There's an Owl in the Shower,* in which an out-of-work logger's son takes in a baby owl only to discover that it is the species of spotted owl

that has cost his father his job. *The Wolves Are Back* focuses on what can happen when man interferes with the natural balance of nature, in this case the elimination of wolves from Yellowstone National Park. Through the successful efforts of western ranchers, who feared the loss of livestock, the wolf population of the "Lower 48" was essentially nil by the mid-1920s. Within a half century it became clear to naturalists that these natural predators were a crucial element in preserving the environment, as the increased populations of deer and other species began to erode the environment. In George's story, readers follow the re-introduction of ten Canadian wolves into Yellowstone, an event that took place in 1995 as a first step to restoring the region's natural balance. Noting that "George has always represented anti-Bambi realism," Bader cited the author for including the often-brutal "kill-or-be-killed" aspects of the cycle of life in her book, adding that she weaves within her story "clear, succinct information about how the wolves were eliminated and how they were brought back." In *School Library Journal* Esther Moberg praised the "uplifting, lyrical story" in *The Wolves Are Back,* adding that "it is full of facts that children will enjoy." Citing the "lush, naturalistic paintings and gentle, carefully chosen words," a *Kirkus Reviews* writer recommended George's picture book as "a splendid way to share an appreciation for the natural world."

Similar in focus to *The Wolves Are Back, The Buffalo Are Back* reunites George and Minor, this time to recount how the buffalo that once roamed the Plains states were almost made extinct by the late nineteenth century. George describes the role of buffalo in the culture of the region's native peoples, and then recounts how the rise of railways and the government's efforts to develop the West transformed the large, lumbering buffalo into a barrier to progress. Following the environmental disaster that has been commemorated in history as the Dust Bowl of the 1930s, buffalo were reintroduced into their native areas, along with the native grasses that both sustain and are sustained by the grazing beasts. *The Buffalo Are Back* "provides a unique perspective on an integral time in American history," wrote Jody Kopple, the *School Library Journal* contributor adding that Minor's watercolor images "are rich with detail." In *Booklist* Carolyn Phelan praised the same work as "succinctly and gracefully written," and in *Horn Book* Bader dubbed the book a "compact ecodrama" that, with paintings by Minor "that both document and dramatize," serves as "another small triumph from a seasoned team."

While many of her stories focus on life in the wild, George's *The Cats of Roxville Station* helps readers to realize that wild animals can live in surprising places. Illustrated by Tom Pohrt, the story takes place in a suburban New York train station, where abandoned animals survive alongside raccoons, chipmunks, squirrels, snakes, skunks, and other creatures that have adapted to human communities. Rachet the cat survives being tossed into the river near Roxville Station and is adopted by a pack of wild cats that live nearby. As the former house cat learns to protect itself against foxes and other animals that would harm it, it also finds a human protector in Mike, a foster teen who feels a bond with the timid orange-furred tabby. As with her nature books, George avoids giving her animal characters human characteristics; "when Ratchet and the other cats 'talk' it is with scent and body language," according to a *Kirkus Reviews* writer. "Simply and directly, George weaves the whys and wherefores of cats' lives . . . into a smooth narrative," noted *Booklist* critic Ilene Cooper, and in *Horn Book* Bader commended *The Cats of Roxville Station,* writing that George's readers "may also want to investigate the four-footed society, unsuspected by humans, in their own backyards."

Throughout her writing career, George has blended scientific accuracy with her love of nature and her ability to convey that love through telling detail, dramatic narrative, and likeable, realistic characters. As she noted on her home page, despite the distractions of modern culture, "Children are still in love with the wonders of nature, and I am too. So I tell them stories about a boy and a falcon, a girl and an elegant wolf pack, about owls, weasels, foxes, prairie dogs, the alpine tundra, the tropical rain forest. And when the telling is done, I hope they will want to protect all the beautiful creatures and places." Discussing her life as a writer during an online chat posted at the New York Public Library Web site, George exclaimed: "I just love it. I have a perfect life where I read, I go out into the wilderness and camp. I meet scientists and learn about their studies of wild animals and then I come home and I sit at my computer, close my eyes and start creating the world I have seen. Then I get up and make supper!"

Biographical and Critical Sources

BOOKS

Beacham's Guide to Literature for Young Adults, Volumes 2, 4, Beacham Publishing (Osprey, FL), 1990.

Cary, Alice, *Jean Craighead George,* Learning Works (Santa Barbara, CA), 1996.

Children's Literature Review, Volume 1, Gale (Detroit, MI), 1976.

Contemporary Literary Criticism, Volume 35, Gale (Detroit, MI), 1985.

Dictionary of Literary Biography, Volume 52: *American Writers for Children since 1960: Fiction,* Gale (Detroit, MI), 1986.

Gallo, Donald R., editor, *Speaking for Ourselves: Autobiographical Sketches by Notable Authors of Books for Young Adults,* National Council of Teachers of English (Urbana, IL), 1990.

George, Jean Craighead, *Journey Inward,* Dutton (New York, NY), 1982.

St. James Guide to Young-Adult Writers, 2nd edition, St. James Press (Detroit, MI), 1999.

Viguers, Ruth Hill, *A Critical History of Children's Literature,* revised edition, Macmillan (New York, NY), 1969.

Writers for Young Adults, Scribner (New York, NY), 1997.

PERIODICALS

Booklist, November 15, 1996, Carolyn Phelan, review of *The Tarantula in My Purse; and 172 Other Wild Pets,* p. 581; September 1, 1999, Linda Perkins, review of *Frightful's Mountain,* p. 132; February 1, 2001, Linda Perkins, review of *Nutik, the Wolf Pup,* p. 1055; May 15, 2001, Carolyn Phelan, review of *Nutik and Amaroq Play Ball,* p. 1757; March 15, 2002, Carolyn Phelan, review of *Tree Castle Island,* p. 1255; September, 2002, Julie Cummins, review of *Frightful's Daughter,* p. 136; December 1, 2003, Ilene Cooper, review of *Fire Storm,* p. 684; August, 2004, Kay Weisman, review of *Charlie's Raven,* p. 1933; October 15, 2004, GraceAnne A. DeCandido, review of *Snowboard Twist,* p. 410; September 1, 2007, John Peters, review of *Frightful's Daughter Meets the Baron Weasel,* p. 114; December 1, 2007, Carolyn Phelan, review of *Goose and Duck,* p. 48; April 1, 2008, Todd Morning, review of *The Wolves Are Back,* p. 49; March 15, 2009, Ilene Cooper, review of *The Cats of Roxville Station,* p. 57; August 1, 2009, Andrew Medlar, review of *The Last Polar Bear,* p. 79; April 15, 2010, Carolyn Phelan, review of *The Buffalo Are Back,* p. 44.

Bulletin of the Center for Children's Books, June, 1960, Zena Sutherland, review of *My Side of the Mountain,* p. 161; July-August, 1968, Zena Sutherland, review of *The Moon of the Fox Pups,* p. 174; July, 2001, review of *Nutik, the Wolf Pup,* p. 408.

Christian Science Monitor, September 25, 1997, Karen Williams, "Talking with Wolves, Then Writing about Them," p. 82.

Horn Book, January-February, 1973, Virginia Haviland, review of *Julie of the Wolves,* pp. 54-55; July-August, 1989, Karen Jameyson, "A Second Look: *My Side of the Mountain,*" pp. 529-531; May-June, 2008, Danielle J. Ford, review of *The Wolves Are Back,* p. 337; January-February, 2009, Barbara Bader, "Jean of the Wolves," p. 43; July-August, 2009, Barbara Bader, review of *The Cats of Roxville Station,* p. 423; July-August, 2010, Barbara Bader, review of *The Buffalo Are Back,* p. 131.

Kirkus Reviews, May 1, 2002, review of *Tree Castle Island,* p. 654; May 15, 2002, review of *Cliff Hanger,* p. 732; August 15, 2002, review of *Frightful's Daughter,* p. 1223; August 15, 2003, review of *Fire Storm,* p. 1972; September 1, 2004, review of *Charlie's Raven,* p. 865; April 15, 2006, review of *Luck: The Story of a Sandhill Crane,* p. 406; September 1, 2007, review of *Frightful's Daughter Meets the Baron Weasel;* December 15, 2007, review of *Goose and Duck;* March 1, 2008, review of *The Wolves Are Back;* April 1, 2009, review of *The Cats of Roxville Station;* October 1, 2009, review of *The Last Polar Bear.*

Kliatt, July, 1999, Carrie Eldridge, review of *Julie's Wolf Pack,* p. 16; May, 2003, Claire Rosser, review of *Tree Castle Island,* p. 16.

New York Times Book Review, January 21, 1973, James Houston, review of *Julie of the Wolves,* p. 8; May 10, 1987, Beverly Lyon Clark, review of *Water Sky,* p. 26; November 13, 1994, Hazel Rochman, review of *Julie,* p. 27; November 21, 1999, Mary Harris Russell, review of *Frightful's Mountain,* p. 28.

Publishers Weekly, July 21, 1997, review of *Arctic Son,* p. 200; October 18, 1999, review of *Frightful's Mountain,* p. 83; April 29, 2002, review of *Cliff Hanger,* p. 69; September 15, 2003, review of *Fire Storm,* p. 67; October 4, 2004, review of *Charlie's Raven,* p. 88; May 1, 2006, review of *Luck,* p. 62.

School Library Journal, January, 1973, Alice Miller Bregman, review of *Julie of the Wolves,* p. 75; May, 1996, Edith Ching, audio review of *On the Far Side of the Mountain,* p. 75; November, 1997, Mollie Bynum, review of *Arctic Son,* pp. 81-82; September, 1999, Patricia Manning, review of *Snow Bear,* p. 182; January, 2001, Debra Bogart, review of *Frightful's Mountain,* p. 74; March, 2001, Catherine T. Quattlebaum, review of *Nuttik the Wolf Pup,* p. 208; May, 2002, Faith Brautigam, review of *Tree Castle Island,* p. 152; September, 2002, Margaret Bush, review of *Frightful's Daughter,* p. 192; December, 2002, Dorian Chong, review of *Frightful's Daughter,* p. 96; November, 2003, Linda Ludke, review of *Fire Storm,* p. 94; September, 2004, Ellen Fader, review of *Charlie's Raven,* p. 205; November, 2004, Rebecca Luhman, review of *Snowboard Twist,* p. 103; June, 2006, Margaret Bush, review of *Luck,* p. 112; February, 2008, Kelly Roth, review of *Goose and Duck,* p. 90; March, 2008, Esther Moberg, review of *The Wolves Are Back,* p. 184; June, 2009, Kara Schaff Dean, review of *The Cats of Roxville Station,* p. 124; December, 2009, Grace Oliff, review of *The Last Polar Bear,* p. 82; March, 2010, Christine Markley, review of *Pocket Guide to the Outdoors: Based on "My Side of the Mountain,"* p. 176; July, 2010, Jody Kopple, review of *The Buffalo Are Back,* p. 74.

Teaching PreK-8, May, 1994, Diane Winarski, "The Dynamic Environment of Jean Craighead George."

Voice of Youth Advocates, December, 1994, Susan Dunn, review of *Julie,* p. 272; March, 2001, Catherine T. Quattlebaum, review of *Nutik, the Wolf Pup,* p. 208; July, 2001, Sally R. Dow, review of *Nutik and Amaroq Play Ball,* p. 81.

ONLINE

BookPage.com, http://www.bookpage.com/ (May 15, 2006), Deborah Hopkinson, interview with George.

Jean Craighead George Home Page, http://www.jeancraigheadgeorge.com (February 15, 2011).

New York Public Library Summer Reading Web site, http://summerreading.nypl.org/ (August 17, 2004), transcript of Live Chat with George.

OTHER

All about the Book!: A Kid's Video Guide to "Julie of the Wolves" (DVD), Tim Podell Productions, 2002.

A Talk with Jean Craighead George (DVD), Tim Podell Productions, 1991.

Storyteller: A Year with Jean Craighead George (DVD), Craighead Environmental Research Institute, 2005.*

*   *   *

GOLDS, Cassandra 1962-

Personal
Born 1962, in Sydney, New South Wales, Australia.

Addresses
E-mail—cassandragolds@yahoo.com.

Career
Writer.

Awards, Honors
Aurealis Award shortlist, 2004, and Notable Book designation, Children's Book Council of Australia, and White Ravens Catalogue selection, both 2005, all for

Cassandra Golds (Photograph by Jo Negrine-Aiello. Reproduced by permission.)

Clair-de-Lune; Patricia Wrightson Prize for Children's Literature shortlist, New South Wales Premier's Literary Awards, 2006, for *The Mostly True Story of Matthew and Trim;* Aurealis Award shortlist, 2009, and Best Children's Books of the Year selection, Bank Street College of Education, Notable Book designation, Children's Book Council of Australia, and Prime Minister's Literary Award shortlist in young-adult fiction section, all 2010, all for *The Museum of Mary Child.*

Writings

Michael and the Secret War, Angus & Robertson (Sydney, New South Wales Australia), 1985, Atheneum (New York, NY), 1989.

Clair-de-Lune, Puffin Books (Camberwell, Victoria, Australia), 2004, Knopf (New York, NY), 2006.

The Mostly True Story of Matthew and Trim, illustrated by Stephen Axelsen, Puffin Books (Camberwell, Victoria, Australia), 2005.

The Museum of Mary Child, Kane Miller (Tulsa, OK), 2009.

The Three Loves of Perimmon, Penguin (Camberwell, Victoria, Australia), 2010.

Contributor of serialized graphic novels, illustrated by Stephen Axelsen, to *School Magazine.*

Sidelights

An award-winning Australian writer, Cassandra Golds has garnered both popular and critical acclaim for works that combine fantasy, horror, and mystery, including *Clair-de-Lune* and *The Museum of Mary Child.* Born in Sydney, Golds began writing stories at an early age, influenced by such favorite authors as Hans Christian Andersen, C.S. Lewis, and Nicholas Stuart Gray. Her first published novel, *Michael and the Secret War,* a fantasy tale about a young man's strange encounters with beings from an alternate reality, was written when she was nineteen years old.

Clair-de-Lune centers on the title character, a gifted but solitary young girl who lives in an old, enchanted building. Clair-de-Lune has not spoken since her mother, a famed ballerina, died on stage years earlier, yet she possesses an extraordinary talent for dance and is forced by her despotic grandmother to practice relentlessly. One day, however, Clair-de-Lune meets Bonaventure, a talking mouse with a love of ballet who introduces her to a magical otherworld and helps the girl finally discover her own voice. The novel drew strong praise from London *Times* critic Amanda Craig, who stated that "Golds writes with a profound sympathy for lonely, sensitive children that I have come across only in Joan Aiken's *The Wolves of Willoughby Chase* and Elizabeth Goudge's *The Little White Horse.*" Adèle Geras, writing in the London *Guardian,* described *Clair-de-Lune* as "a story that conveys both the beauty and

Cover of Golds' novel Clair-de-Lune, *featuring artwork by Sonia Kretschmar.* (Illustration © 2006 by Sonia Kretschmar. Used by permission of Random House Children's Books, a division of Random House, Inc.)

glamour of the dance and also the sacrifices you have to make for its sake. Very importantly, too, it's a book about the power of love. The touching relationship between Clair-de-Lune and her little mouse friend makes a tale (pun intended) that will move even the youngest reader."

A troubled, isolated girl is also the focus of *The Museum of Mary Child,* an "enthralling moral fable," according to a *Kirkus Reviews* writer. Under the stern control of her coldhearted godmother, Heloise endures a life of austerity and mind-numbing routine until she discovers a doll hidden beneath the floorboards of their cottage. When her godmother finds out, the woman takes Heloise to the adjoining Museum of Mary Child, a horrifying building dedicated to the memory of a madwoman. The terrified Heloise runs away, embarking on a bizarre and wondrous journey. "This story reads like a fairy tale with elements of mystery, romance, Gothic horror, fantasy, and all parts terrific," Jessica Miller commented in *School Library Journal.* A *Publishers Weekly* reviewer also applauded *The Museum of Mary Child,* remarking that, "Gothic and wonderfully creepy, Golds's . . . atmospheric story delights, offering meditations on the nature and power of love."

Biographical and Critical Sources

PERIODICALS

Booklist, January 1, 2006, Jennifer Mattson, review of *Clair-de-Lune,* p. 83.

Guardian (London, England), April 15, 2006, Adèle Geras, review of *Clair-de-Lune.*

Kirkus Reviews, January 1, 2006, review of *Clair-de-Lune,* p. 41; August 15, 2009, review of *The Museum of Mary Child.*

Publishers Weekly, September 28, 2009, review of *The Museum of Mary Child,* p. 65.

School Library Journal, July, 2006, Carol Schene, review of *Clair-de-Lune,* p. 102; December, 2009, Jessica Miller, review of *The Museum of Mary Child,* p. 118.

Times (London, England), April 8, 2006, Amanda Craig, review of *Clair-de-Lune.*

ONLINE

Cassandra Golds Home Page, http://www.cassandragolds. com.au (February 15, 2011).

H

HARLOW, Joan Hiatt 1932-

Personal

Born July 25, 1932, in Malden, MA; daughter of Albert E. (a singer) and Marguerite (a registered nurse) Hiatt; married Richard Lee Harlow (a banker and auditor), August 17, 1951 (deceased, 2002); children: Deborah Balas, Lisa Harlow, Kristan Delphia, Scott, Jennifer Lichtenberg. *Ethnicity:* "English, Scots, and Welsh descent." *Education:* Stenotype Institute of Boston, certificate, 1951. *Hobbies and other interests:* Astronomy, traveling, history, swimming, music.

Addresses

Home—Venice, FL.

Career

Children's book author. Redevelopment Authority, Wilmington, MA, administrative assistant, 1967-73; special-needs secretary of public schools in Littleton, MA, 1977-78; Institute of Children's Literature, instructor, 1981-2002.

Member

Society of Children's Book Writers, Author's Guild, Authors League of America, Westford Players (secretary and member of board of directors).

Awards, Honors

Magazine Merit Award for fiction, Society of Children's Book Writers and Illustrators, 2000, for short story; Disney Adventures Book Award, 2000, Henry Bergh Companion Animals Award, American Society for the Prevention of Cruelty to Animals, Michigan Reading Association Readers' Choice Award, International Reading Association/Children's Book Council Children's Choice designation, Capitol Choice selection, Iowa Readers' Choice nomination, and Sunshine State Book Award, all 2002, and Sasquatch Reading Award nomination, 2003, all for *Star in the Storm;* Best Children's Book of the Year selection, Children's Book Committee at Bank Street College, William Allen White Children's Book Award nomination, and Rhode Island Reader's Choice nomination, all 2003, and Nutmeg Book Award nomination (CT), 2004, all for *Joshua's Song;* Best Children's Book of the Year selection, 2004, and Edgar Award nomination, Mystery Writers of America, and Best Children's Books of the Year designation, Bank Street College of Education, all for *Shadows on the Sea;* Best Children's Books of the Year designation, Bank Street College of Education, 2004, for *Thunder from the Sea;* Best Children's Books of the Year designation, Bank Street College of Education, 2007, for *Blown Away!;* Parents' Choice Recommended selection, 2009, for *Secret of the Night Ponies.*

Writings

JUVENILE

(With daughter, Kristan Harlow) *Poems Are for Everything,* Christopher, 1973.
The Shadow Bear, Doubleday (New York, NY), 1980.
Star in the Storm, Margaret K. McElderry Books (New York, NY), 2000.
Joshua's Song, Margaret K. McElderry Books (New York, NY), 2001.
Shadows on the Sea, Margaret K. McElderry Books (New York, NY), 2003.
Thunder from the Sea, Margaret K. McElderry Books (New York, NY), 2004.
Midnight Rider, Margaret K. McElderry Books (New York, NY), 2005.
Blown Away!, Margaret K. McElderry Books (New York, NY), 2007.
Secret of the Night Ponies, Margaret K. McElderry Books (New York, NY), 2009.
Firestorm!, Margaret K. McElderry Books (New York, NY), 2010.

Also author of *The Wishing Sky, The Creatures of Sand Castle Key, The Dark Side of the Creek,* and *The Mysterious Dr. Chen,* Wright Group/McGraw-Hill. Contributor of stories and articles to periodicals, including *Cricket, Child Life, Ranger Rick's, Cobblestone, Humpty Dumpty's, ChickaDee, Your Big Backyard,* and *Young World.*

Adaptations

Shadows on the Sea was adapted as an audiobook by Recorded Books, 2003.

Sidelights

Joan Hiatt Harlow is the author of several novels for children that focus on U.S. and Canadian history, among them the Revolutionary War-era historical mystery *Midnight Rider, Blown Away!,* a novel set in the Florida Keys, and *Secret of the Night Ponies,* a tale from Newfoundland. Taking place during World War II, Harlow's award-winning *Shadows on the Sea* finds fourteen-year-old Jill suspicious that a Nazi U-boat submerged off the Maine coast may be in contact with someone living near her grandmother's house, where Jill is spending the summer. *Shadows on the Sea* was praised by a *Publishers Weekly* contributor, who cited Harlow for her "excellent job of describing the hardships of war on those back home" in a mystery novel that "offers an enjoyable slice-of-life" portrait of a wartime childhood. Harlow includes an afterword to *Shadows on the Sea* that discusses the submarine and spy activity that actually took place along the northern New England coast.

Harlow's first novel, *Star in the Storm,* features Sirius, a large black dog with a white star on his chest who lives with Maggie's family in 1912 Newfoundland. When a new law bans all dogs except those used in sheep herding, Sirius risks being shot, so young Maggie hides her beloved dog in a cave. When a steamer runs into trouble offshore, Sirius is called upon to swim to the foundering ship with a rope, thereby saving the passengers. Debbie Carton, reviewing *Star in the Storm* for *Booklist,* wrote that "the relationship between the girl and her beloved dog is beautifully drawn" in Harlow's engaging novel. A *Horn Book* contributor found that "Maggie is a likable, self-reliant protagonist; and dog-lovers will revel in the many exploits of the gentle giant she loves so dearly." Renee Steinberg noted in *School Library Journal* that "Harlow's descriptive prose clearly evokes images of the Newfoundland coast and life in 1912, and she carefully incorporates folklore of the region into her story." *Star in the Storm* won the American Society for the Prevention of Cruelty to Animals' Henry Bergh Companion Animals Award, as well as a Disney Adventures book award and a Michigan Reading Association Readers' Choice award.

Moving ahead a decade to 1929, *Thunder from the Sea* finds orphaned, thirteen-year-old Tom Campbell working at the Newfoundland home of childless couple Enoch and Fiona Murray. During a fishing trip with Enoch, a sudden storm comes up and Tom spots a Newfoundland pup floundering in the rough waters. Rescuing the dog and naming his new friend Thunder, Tom gains the dog he always wanted, but is soon disheartened when another family, the Bosworths, attempt to claim his new companion. Ultimately, several close encounters with danger and a shooting convince the Bosworths that Tom and Thunder should remain together, in a dog-and-boy story that *School Library Journal* contributor Shawn Brommer described as "fast paced" and *Booklist* reviewer Linda Perkins dubbed "nonstop action for dog lovers."

Joshua's Song is set in 1918 Boston, where young Joshua must quit school and earn a living after the death of his wealthy father during an influenza epidemic. Working as a newsboy in the streets, Joshua comes into conflict with a gang of young toughs who control the city's newspaper distribution. He also witnesses and describes the Great Molasses Flood, an event triggered by an explosion in a tank storing tons of molasses that killed twenty-one people. Chris Sherman, writing in *Booklist,* predicted that "even readers who don't usually like historical fiction will enjoy Harlow's vivid depiction of early-twentieth-century working-class life and conditions," while Sally Bates Goodroe concluded in *School Library Journal* that the author "skillfully integrates historical fact to make a colorful setting believable."

Drawing comparisons to *Johnny Tremain,* a classic tale by Esther Forbes, Harlow's *Midnight Rider* concerns Hannah Andrews, a fourteen-year-old orphan who plays a key role in a series of tumultuous events occurring on the eve of the American Revolution. An indentured servant at the home of General Thomas Gage, a powerful British officer stationed in Massachusetts Colony, Hannah learns of a secret passage that allows her to leave the compound at night and ride her beloved horse, Promise. When the young woman, whose sympathies lie with the rebels, overhears British officers plotting to confiscate munitions from a nearby town, she decides to warn the villagers despite the danger to herself. According to Bruce Anne Shook, writing in *School Library Journal,* Harlow's narrative in *Midnight Rider* "has enough adventure and suspense to hold the interest of readers."

The notorious Labor Day Hurricane of 1935 is the focus of *Blown Away!* While working for Sharkey, a crusty and eccentric fisherman, thirteen-year-old Jake Pitney begins an unlikely friendship with Mara, a sensitive newcomer who babysits Jake's young sister, Star. When a powerful hurricane bears down on the region, Jake and his family are forced to weather the storm, which devastates the Keys, killing hundreds. After the storm passes, Jake begins a frantic search for Sharkey and Mara, assisted by Sharkey's mischievous mule and its canine sidekick. *Blown Away!* "has a strong sense of time and place," noted a *Kirkus Reviews* contributor.

"The palpable sense of unease about the approaching storm . . . and the sense of loss and disorientation are described in detail," observed *School Library Journal* critic Nancy P. Reeder.

A Newfoundland teen finds adventure and peril in Harlow's *Secret of the Night Ponies,* a work containing "interesting characters, an empathetic heroine, and a fast-paced plot," according to Carol Schene in *School Library Journal.* The novel centers on Jessie Wheller, whose efforts to rescue an abused girl and a herd of wild ponies is aided by a group of shipwreck survivors. "The seemingly separate adventures are actually tightly linked by the characters and the unusual setting," Carolyn Phelan reported in her *Booklist* review of the novel.

Harlow once confessed to an interviewer with Massachusetts's *Lowell Sun* that writing children's books is "very easy, if you can think like a child." Still, she added, the craft itself requires passion, dedication, hard work, and the ability to deal with rejection. For Harlow, the pleasure of writing comes from "escaping into another time realm with characters who wait patiently for my return. I love sharing this experience with children I've never met who enjoy my stories and feel affection for my characters. E-mails and letters from fans help me to realize how universal my books have become, and the responsibility that my stories may affect the lives of children. I want my books to portray courage, clean morals, good choices, and hope for the future." Harper's career as a writer has transformed many a family vacation into a research trip. "It's difficult not to get carried away at times," she once remarked. "I must be strange, because I really enjoy research!"

Biographical and Critical Sources

PERIODICALS

Booklist, January 1, 2000, Debbie Carton, review of *Star in the Storm,* p. 922; December 15, 2001, Chris Sherman, review of *Joshua's Song,* p. 731; September 15, 2003, Hazel Rochman, review of *Shadows on the Sea,* p. 231; August, 2004, Linda Perkins, review of *Thunder from the Sea,* p. 1934; November 1, 2009, Carolyn Phelan, review of *Secret of the Night Ponies,* p. 49; November 15, 2010, Ryan Donovan, review of *Firestorm!,* p. 48.
Horn Book, March, 2000, review of *Star in the Storm,* p. 195; July-August, 2004, Joanna Rudge Long, review of *Thunder from the Sea,* p. 452.
Kirkus Reviews, August 15, 2003, review of *Shadows on the Sea,* p. 1073; June 1, 2005, review of *Midnight Rider,* p. 637; July 1, 2007, review of *Blown Away!;* October 1, 2009, review of *Secret of the Night Ponies.*
Kliatt, January, 2007, Claire Rosser, review of *Midnight Rider,* p. 23.
Library Journal, September, 2003, Cheri Estes Dobbs, review of *Shadows on the Sea,* p. 214

Lowell Sun (Lowell, MA), June 10, 1979, interview with Harlow.
New York Times Book Review, April 26, 1981, Karla Kuskin, review of *Shadow Bear,* p. 54.
Publishers Weekly, February 21, 2000, review of *Star in the Storm,* p. 88; August 27, 2001, review of *Star in the Storm,* p. 87; October 29, 2001, review of *Joshua's Song,* p. 64; September 15, 2003, review of *Shadows on the Sea,* p. 66.
Sarasota Herald-Tribune Style, November, 2002, interview with Harlow, pp. 34-37.
School Library Journal, January, 1982, review of *Shadow Bear,* p. 64; April, 2000, Renee Steinberg, review of *Star in the Storm,* p. 134; November, 2001, Sally Bates Goodroe, review of *Joshua's Song,* p. 158; September, 2004, Shawn Brommer, review of *Thunder from the Sea,* p. 207; August, 2005, Bruce Anne Shook, review of *Midnight Rider,* p. 128; July, 2007, Nancy P. Reeder, review of *Blown Away!,* p. 103; November, 2009, Carol Schene, review of *Secret of the Night Ponies,* p. 108.

ONLINE

Joan Hiatt Harlow Home Page, http://mysite.verizon.net/sevenjays1 (February 15, 2011).
Simon & Schuster Web site, http://www.simonandschuster.com/ (February 15, 2011), "Joan Hiatt Harlow Revealed."*

*   *   *

HARPER, Charise
See HARPER, Charise Mericle

*   *   *

HARPER, Charise Mericle
(Charise Harper)

Personal

Born in Vancouver, British Columbia, Canada; married; children: one daughter, one son. *Education:* College degree (marketing).

Addresses

Home—Mamaroneck, NY. *E-mail*—charise@chariseharper.com.

Career

Author, illustrator, and cartoonist.

Writings

SELF-ILLUSTRATED

When I Grow Up, Chronicle Books (San Francisco, CA), 2001.

Imaginative Inventions: The Who, What, Where, When, and Why of Roller Skates, Potato Chips, Marbles, and Pie and More!, Little, Brown (Boston, MA), 2001.

There Was a Bold Lady Who Wanted a Star, Little, Brown (Boston, MA), 2002.

The Trouble with Normal, Houghton Mifflin (Boston, MA), 2003.

Itsy Bitsy the Smart Spider, Dial Books for Young Readers (New York, NY), 2003.

Yes, No, Maybe So, Dial Books for Young Readers (New York, NY), 2004.

The Monster Show: Everything You Never Knew about Monsters, Houghton Mifflin (Boston, MA), 2004.

(Under name Charise Harper) *Baby Time: A Fast, Fun Keepsake Album,* Chronicle Books (San Francisco, CA), 2004.

The Invisible Mistakecase, Houghton Mifflin (Boston, MA), 2005.

The Little Book of Not So, Houghton Mifflin (Boston, MA), 2005.

Flush!: The Scoop on Poop throughout the Ages, Little, Brown (New York, NY), 2006.

Amy and Ivan: What's in That Truck?, Tricycle Press (Berkeley, CA), 2006.

When Randolph Turned Rotten, Knopf (New York, NY), 2007.

Good Night, Leo: A Swashbuckling Bedtime Adventure, Robin Corey Books (New York, NY), 2008.

Milo's Special Words: A Well-behaved Little Book, Robin Corey Books (New York, NY), 2009.

Mimi and Lulu: Three Sweet Stories, One Forever Friendship, Balzer & Bray (New York, NY), 2009.

Cupcake: A Journey to Special, Disney/Hyperion (New York, NY), 2010.

Pink Me Up, Alfred A. Knopf (New York, NY), 2010.

Gigi in the Big City, Robin Corey Books (New York, NY), 2010.

The Best Birthday Ever, Hyperion (New York, NY), 2011.

Henry's Heart, Holt (New York, NY), 2011.

The Power of Cute, Robin Corey Books (New York, NY), 2011.

SELF-ILLUSTRATED; "FASHION KITTY" SERIES

Fashion Kitty (graphic novel), Hyperion (New York, NY), 2005.

Fashion Kitty versus the Fashion Queen (graphic novel), Hyperion (New York, NY), 2007.

Fashion Kitty and the Unlikely Hero, Hyperion Paperbacks for Children (New York, NY), 2008.

SELF-ILLUSTRATED; "JUST GRACE" SERIES

Just Grace, Houghton Mifflin (Boston, MA), 2007.

Still Just Grace, Houghton Mifflin Company (Boston, MA), 2007.

Just Grace Walks the Dog, Houghton Mifflin (Boston, MA), 2008.

Just Grace Goes Green, Houghton Mifflin Books for Children (Boston, MA), 2009.

Just Grace and the Snack Attack, Houghton Mifflin Books for Children (Boston, MA), 2009.

Just Grace and the Terrible Tutu, Houghton Mifflin Harcourt (Boston, MA), 2011.

ILLUSTRATOR

Amy Krouse Rosenthal, *Spoken Gems: A Journal for Recording the Funny, Odd, and Poignant Things Your Child Says,* Andrews McMeel (Kansas City, MO), 2000.

Kathleen O'Dell, *Agnes Parker . . . Girl in Progess,* Dial Books (New York, NY), 2003.

Kathleen O'Dell, *Agnes Parker . . . Happy Camper?,* Dial Books (New York, NY), 2005.

Sandra Markle, *Chocolate: A Sweet History,* Grosset & Dunlap (New York, NY), 2005.

Ralph Covert, *Ralph's World Rocks!* (with CD), Henry Holt (New York, NY), 2008.

OTHER

Flashcards of My Life (middle-grade novel), Little, Brown (Boston, MA), 2006.

Contributor of illustrations to *New York Times, Chicago Tribune, Village Voice,* and *San Francisco Examiner.* Creator of "Eye-Spy," weekly alternative syndicated comic strip, beginning 1996.

Adaptations

Just Grace was adapted as an audiobook, Recorded Books (Prince Frederick, MD), 2008.

Sidelights

Charise Mericle Harper is the author of numerous self-illustrated picture books for children, producing her self-illustrated debut work, *When I Grow Up,* in 2001. With their brightly colored illustrations, in styles that vary in every book, Harper's works range from the lighthearted to the factual, and her whimsical humor can be gleaned from their titles: *There Was a Bold Lady Who Wanted a Star, Cupcake: A Journey to Special, The Little Book of Not So, Flush!: The Scoop on Poop throughout the Ages,* and *The Power of Cute.* Her imaginative storytelling also finds an outlet in the graphic novels in her "Fashion Kitty" series, the middle-grade novel *Flashcards of My Life* and the books in her "Just Grace" reader series.

Born in Vancouver, British Columbia, Canada, Harper enjoyed drawing as a child, but her parents' practical counsel prompted her to major in marketing in college. The opportunity to create album-cover designs encouraged her to pursue her art, and with a self-made marketing strategy Harper soon saw her illustrations and a cartoon strip called "Eye-Spy" appearing in Chicago periodicals. A suggestion from a literary agent led to her decision to write her first self-illustrated children's book, *When I Grow Up.*

In Harper's picture-book debut, the titular phrase "When I grow up. . ." is repeated on each double-page spread, paired with a positive attribute and an illustration to highlight that particular personality characteristic. "Every page [of *When I Grow Up*] is framed and the textured, vibrant illustrations have a tactile element," noted *School Library Journal* contributor Shawn Brommer. "Most memorably," wrote a *Publishers Weekly* critic, "Harper uses black-and-white photos of children's faces, seemingly snipped from a grade school yearbook, as collage elements."

Since *When I Grow Up* was published, Harper has crafted a steady stream of imaginative books, both fictional stories and books filled with interesting snippets of real-life facts. In *Imaginative Inventions: The Who, What, Where, When, and Why of Roller Skates, Potato Chips, Marbles, and Pie and More!* she explores, in verse, the origins of everyday items such as chewing gum and piggy banks, pairing her text with illustrations that exhibit what *Booklist* contributor GraceAnne A. DeCandido described as "puckish and offbeat visual imagery." *There Was a Bold Lady Who Wanted a Star,* Harper's take on the folk song "I Know an Old Lady Who Swallowed a Fly," follows an adventurous woman's efforts to capture a star for her young son using up-to-date modes of transportation that include a colorful convertible automobile and a small airplane. "Acrylic cartoons in bright colors lend a zany feel" to Harper's story, noted Leslie Barban in *School Library Journal,* and a *Kirkus Reviews* critic stated that "the repetitive pattern and cumulative effect follow that of the original and the jaunty illustration style fits the tale."

Inspired by her own daughter's love of a favorite nursery rhyme, Harper's *Itsy Bitsy the Smart Spider* presents a "spirited take on a much-loved classic," according to a *Kirkus Reviews* critic. In this picture book, Itsy tires of being washed out by the rain and goes to great lengths to stay dry. Focusing on familiar daily activities such as eating, sharing, and getting dressed, *Yes, No, Maybe So* features "a clever, discussion-opening" story "about acceptable and unacceptable behavior—and the gray areas in between," according to *Horn Book* reviewer Martha V. Parravano. In the words of a *Kirkus Reviews* critic, "the concept is explored with giggle-inducing humor."

Harper treats readers to a recipe for fun in *Cupcake,* as various ingredients hop into a bowl and create dapper Vanilla Cupcake, who promptly joins its family of icing-topped relatives. With fancy flavors and decorative toppings, the other cupcakes seem more appealing until plain Vanilla Cupcake is topped by the talented Candle. Another inventive story plays out in Harper's *Pink Me Up,* as a little bunny named Violet gets ready to join Mother Bunny at a special party. Not just any party, this one is an all-pink party: everything they wear, everything they see, and everything they eat will be pink! Although Mother gets sick and cannot go, plucky Father Bunny agrees to go, as long as Violet will help

make him the appropriate color. In *School Library Journal* Tanya Boudreau deemed Harper's colorful acrylic art both "humorous and lively," and Jennifer Brabander wrote in *Horn Book* that *Pink Me Up* "will perhaps inspire kids, pink-lovin' or not, to think creatively when faced with a change in plans." Describing *Cupcake* in *Booklist,* Ilene Cooper concluded that the author/illustrator's "mix of black lines, patterned backgrounds, and swirly sweetness, makes the simple moral about being special quite palatable."

In her "Fashion Kitty" books "Harper brings her comedic sense and flat, droll cartoons together in a graphic novel for young girls," noted a contributor in *Kirkus Reviews.* The first book in the series, *Fashion Kitty,* concerns Kiki Kittie, an eight-year-old feline whose superhero secret identity incorporates a flair for style. Kiki's adventures continue in several other illustrated stories: *Fashion Kitty versus the Fashion Queen* find the stylish cat in competition, while the threat of dowdy school uniforms prompts Fashion Kitty to come to the rescue of Kiki and her classmates in *Fashion Kitty and the Unlikely Hero.* According to Jennifer Feigelman, reviewing *Fashion Kitty* in *School Library Journal,* Harper's "pictures are artistically appealing and visually spectacular."

Starring a spunky third grader, Harper's "Just Grace" books include *Just Grace, Still Just Grace, Just Grace Walks the Dog, Just Grace Goes Green, Just Grace and the Snack Attack,* and *Just Grace and the Terrible Tutu.* "Grace is not an easy child to bring up, but she's a thinking child," Harper told *California Kids!* interviewer Patricia Newman. "I like to celebrate the kid that thinks outside the box." In the easy-reading series opener, Grace becomes concerned when a neighbor's cat runs away, but her plan to track down the missing kitty may require the help of school bully Sammy Stringer. Competition over a new boy in the neighborhood makes things tense in *Still Just Grace,* especially when a family vacation takes the girl out of town during the crucial "getting to know you" phase. The imaginative Grace makes the most of a cardboard pet in *Just Grace Walks the Dog,* while the trend to recycle hits Grace and her third-grade friends in *Just Grace Goes Green.* Everyday food becomes more interesting when the class studies food around the world, although student projects inspire a bit of jealousy in *Just Grace and the Snack Attack,* a book *School Library Journal* contributor Jackie Partch described as characteristic of the series due to its "short sections" of text interspersed "with small, cartoon sketches, diagrams, and lists." In the same periodical, Michele Sealander recommended *Just Grace Goes Green* as "an appealing book for early chapter-book readers," while Harper's "smoothly" flowing text and "endearing character" make *Just Grace Walk the Dog* a story in which "everything rings true," according to *School Library Journal* contributor Anne Knickerbocker.

A newly minted teen in junior high school records her thoughts about friends, boys, dreams, self-image, and the future in Harper's middle-grade novel *Flashcards of My Life*. After Emily receives an unusual birthday gift from her Aunt Chester, she begins chronicling the trials and triumphs of her middle-school world, including her encounters with catty girlfriends and unrequited love. "Full of early teen angst," according to Diana Pierce in *School Library Journal*, *Flashcards of My Life* has elements that will appeal to both preteens and high-school freshmen. "Harper's tale will elicit nods of recognition—and a few chuckles," observed a *Publishers Weekly* critic, while a *Kirkus Reviews* writer predicted that "Emily's search for the truth about friendship, romance and identity will appeal to 'tween fans of conversational chick-lit."

Biographical and Critical Sources

PERIODICALS

Booklist, December 15, 2001, GraceAnne A. DeCandido, review of *Imaginative Inventions: The Who, What, Where, When, and Why of Roller Skates, Potato Chips, Marbles, and Pie and More!*, p. 734; November 15, 2002, Diane Foote, review of *There Was a Bold Lady Who Wanted a Star*, p. 605; May 1, 2003, Connie Fletcher, review of *The Trouble with Normal*, p. 1605; February 1, 2006, Jennifer Hubert, review of *Flashcards of My Life*, p. 50; May 15, 2006, Jennifer Mattson, review of *Amy and Ivan*, p. 49; January 1, 2007, Connie Fletcher, review of *Flush!: The Scoop on Poop throughout the Ages*, p. 108; March 1, 2007, Kay Weisman, review of *Just Grace*, p. 84; September 15, 2007, Kay Weisman, review of *Still Just Grace*, p. 66; November 15, 2007, Jesse Karp, review of *When Randolph Turned Rotten*, p. 52; February 15, 2009, Hazel Rochman, review of *Just Grace Goes Green*, p. 92; November 15, 2009, Hazel Rochman, review of *Mimi and Lulu: Three Sweet Stories, One Forever Friendship*, p. 43; March 1, 2010, Ilene Cooper, review of *Cupcake: A Journey to Special*, p. 76; March 15, 2010, Kay Weisman, review of *Just Grace and the Snack Attack*, p. 45; April 15, 2010, Karen Cruze, review of *Pink Me Up*, p. 52.

Bulletin of the Center for Children's Books, November, 2002, review of *There Was a Bold Lady Who Wanted a Star*, p. 109; December, 2005, review of *Fashion Kitty*, p. 183.

California Kids!, August, 2010, Patricia Newman, interview with Harper.

Horn Book, May-June, 2004, Martha V. Parravano, review of *Yes, No, Maybe So*, p. 313; March-April, 2007, Kitty Flynn, review of *Flush!*, p. 213; January-February, 2008, Christine M. Heppermann, review of *When Randolph Turned Rotten*, p. 72; March-April, 2009, Robin L. Smith, review of *Just Grace Goes Green*, p. 196; November-December, 2009, Jennifer M. Brabander, review of *Just Grace and the Snack Attack*, p. 674; March-April. 2010, Jennifer M. Brabander, review of *Cupcake*, p. 44; May-June, 2010, Jennifer M. Brabander, review of *Pink Me Up*, p. 68.

Kirkus Reviews, August 1, 2001, review of *Imaginative Inventions*, p. 1123; August 15, 2002, review of *There Was a Bold Lady Who Wanted a Star*, p. 1224; February 1, 2003, review of *The Trouble with Normal*, p. 230; February 1, 2004, review of *Itsy Bitsy the Smart Spider*, p. 134; March 15, 2004, review of *Yes, No, Maybe So*, p. 270; July 15, 2004, review of *The Monster Show: Everything You Never Knew about Monsters*, p. 686; February 1, 2005, review of *Agnes Parker . . . Happy Camper?*, p. 179; August 1, 2005, review of *Fashion Kitty*, p. 848; January 1, 2006, review of *Flashcards of My Life*, p. 41; January 15, 2007, review of *Flush!*, p. 73; August 1, 2007, review of *Still Just Grace*; March 15, 2008, review of *Just Grace Walks the Dog*; July 15, 2008, review of *Ralph's World Rocks!*; August 1, 2009, review of *Mimi and Lulu*.

Publishers Weekly, February 12, 2001, review of *When I Grow Up*, p. 209; August 20, 2001, review of *Imaginative Inventions*, p. 79; September 16, 2002, review of *There Was a Bold Lady Who Wanted a Star*, p. 67; February 10, 2003, review of *The Trouble with Normal*, p. 186; August 9, 2004, review of *The Monster Show*, p. 250; October 3, 2005, review of *Fashion Kitty*, p. 71; January 9, 2006, review of *Flashcards of My Life*, p. 54; May 29, 2006, review of *Amy and Ivan*, p. 61; April 30, 2007, review of *Just Grace*, p. 161; November 12, 2007, review of *When Randolph Turned Rotten*, p. 55; August 17, 2009, review of *Mimi and Lulu*, p. 60; December 7, 2009, review of *Cupcake*, p. 46.

School Library Journal, July, 2001, Shawn Brommer, review of *When I Grow Up*, p. 82; October, 2001, Lynda Ritterman, review of *Imaginative Inventions*, p. 140; September, 2002, Leslie Barban, review of *There Was a Bold Lady Who Wanted a Star*, p. 213; February, 2003, Susan Patron, review of *Agnes Parker . . . Girl in Progress*, p. 146; April, 2003, Wanda Meyers-Hines, review of *The Trouble with Normal*, p. 122; March, 2004, Wendy Woodfill, review of *Itsy Bitsy the Smart Spider*, p. 169; July, 2004, Kathleen Kelly MacMillan, review of *Yes, No, Maybe So*, p. 77; September, 2004, Mary Elam, review of *The Monster Show*, p. 161; March, 2005, Debbie Whitbeck, review of *Agnes Parker . . . Happy Camper?*, p. 216; June, 2005, Margaret Bush, review of *The Little Book of Not So*, p. 116; November, 2005, Jennifer Feigelman, review of *Fashion Kitty*, p. 174; December, 2005, Lisa S. Schindler, review of *The Invisible Mistakecase*, p. 114; January, 2006, Diana Pierce, review of *Flashcards of My Life*, p. 133; September, 2006, Catherine Threadgill, review of *Amy and Ivan*, p. 173, and Julie Roach, review of *Flush!*, p. 192; October, 2007, Terrie Dorio, review of *Still Just Grace*, p. 116; December, 2007, Carolyn Janssen, review of *When Randolph Turned Rotten*, p. 90; March, 2008, Anne Knickerbocker, review of *Just Grace Walks the Dog*, p. 164; October, 2008, Jane Marino, review of *Ralph's World Rocks*, p. 130; March, 2009, Michele Sealander, review of *Just Grace Goes Green*, p. 114; May, 2009, Mari Pongkhamsing, review of *Fashion Kitty and the Unlikely Hero*, p. 132; December 1, 2009, review of *Cupcake*; December, 2009, Jackie Partch, review of *Just*

Grace and the Snack Attack, p. 84; April, 2010, Tanya Boudreau, review of *Pink Me Up,* p. 126; June, 2010, Linda Ludke, review of *Cupcake,* p. 72.

Voice of Youth Advocates, February, 2006, Kelly Czarnecki, review of *Flashcards of My Life,* p. 485.

ONLINE

Book Page Web site, http://www.bookpage.com/ (February 15, 2011), Linda M. Castellitto, interview with Harper.

Charise Mericle Harper Home Page, http://www.charise harper.com (February 15, 2011).

Charise Mericle Harper Web log, http://drawingmom.blog spot.com (February 15, 2011).

*   *   *

HARTMAN, Carrie

Personal

Born in ND; married; husband's name Craig; children: Sophia, Abigail, Jack. *Education:* Minneapolis College of Art and Design, B.F.A. (illustration).

Addresses

Home—Woodbury, MN. *E-mail*—studio@carriehartman. com.

Career

Illustrator, animator, and educator. Minneapolis College of Art and Design, Minneapolis, MN, instructor in illustration. Speaker at schools and conferences.

Member

Society of Children's Book Writers and Illustrators, Children's Literature Network.

Awards, Honors

Award from Society of Illustrators, Los Angeles; Educational Press Association Award nomination; Award for Best Illustrated Picture Book for the Educational Industry, Association of Educational Publishers, 2006, for *My Mouth Is a Volcano!* by Julia Cook.

Writings

SELF-ILLUSTRATED

Child of Mine, Maren Green Pub. (Oak Park Heights, MN), 2007.

ILLUSTRATOR

Gloria Gaither and Shirley Dobson, *Making Ordinary Days Extraordinary: Great Ideas for Building Family Fun and Togetherness,* Multnomah Kidz (Colorado Springs, CO), 2004.

Gloria Gaither and Shirley Dobson, *Creating Family Traditions: Making Memories in Festive Seasons,* Multnomah Kidz (Colorado Springs, CO), 2004.

Gloria Gaither and Shirley Dobson, *Celebrating Special Times with Special People,* Multnomah Kidz (Colorado Springs, CO), 2005.

Gloria Gaither and Shirley Dobson, *Hide It in Your Heart: Creative Ways for Families to Explore God's Word,* Multnomah Kidz (Colorado Springs, CO), 2005.

Julie Cook, *My Mouth Is a Volcano,* National Center for Youth Issues (Chattanooga, TN), 2006.

Personal Space Camp, National Center for Youth Issues (Chattanooga, TN), 2007.

Todd Snow and Peggy Snow, *Feelings to Share from A to Z,* Maren Green Pub. (Oak Park Heights, MN), 2007.

Todd Snow, *Manners Are Important,* Maren Green Pub. (Oak Park Heights, MN), 2007.

Julia Cook, *It's Hard to Be a Verb!,* National Center for Youth Issues (Chattanooga, TN), 2008.

Trudy Harris, *The Clock Struck One: A Time-telling Tale,* Millbrook Press (Minneapolis, MN), 2009.

Rebecca Eckler and Erica Ehm, *Mischievous Mom at the Art Gallery,* Key Porter (Bolton, Ontario, Canada), 2010.

Contributor to periodicals, including *Baltimore Sun, Hartford Courant, Minnesota Parent, Minneapolis Star Tribune, New York, Shine, Threads,* and *The Rake.*

Sidelights

Based in Minnesota, Carrie Hartman is a professional illustrator whose work includes editorial and advertising art, animation and character development, poster graphics, and art for greeting cards. An instructor at the Minneapolis College of Art and Design, where she earned her degree, Hartman also creates art for children's picture books. In addition to illustrating stories such as Todd Snow's *Manners Are Important* and Trudy Harris's *The Clock Struck One: A Time-telling Tale,* she also created the original self-illustrated *Child of Mine,* a book inspired by its own experiences as a mother and designed to build bridges between parents and children struggling with attention and learning difficulties.

Hartman grew up in North Dakota, where the Sunday comics became learning tools that taught her to draw Mickey Mouse, Charlie Brown, Garfield, and other favorite characters. Her love of cartoons, as well as of animated films, comes through in her illustrations, which "capture the comical bedlam" in *The Clock Struck One* "with flair," according to *Booklist* critic Shelle Rosenfeld. In *School Library Journal* Kirsten Cutler also praised the "expressive mixed-media illustrations" Hartman creates to bring to life Harris's text, and a *Kirkus Reviews* writer described the story's engagingly drawn animal characters as "full of personality."

Biographical and Critical Sources

PERIODICALS

Booklist, August 1, 2009, Shelle Rosenfeld, review of *The Clock Struck One: A Time-telling Tale,* p. 78.

Childhood Education, summer, 2010, Amy Murphy Eberle, review of *The Clock Struck One,* p. 276.

Kirkus Reviews, August 15, 2009, review of *The Clock Struck One.*

Publishers Weekly, August 24, 2009, review of *The Clock Struck One,* p. 60.

School Library Journal, September, 2009, Kirsten Cutler, review of *The Clock Struck One,* p. 122.

ONLINE

Carrie Hartman Home Page, http://www.carriehartman.com (December 31, 2010).

Carrie Hartman Web log, http://carriehartman.blogspot.com (February 11, 2011).*

*   *   *

HERRERA, Diego
See YAYO

*   *   *

HIATT, Shelby

Personal

Born in Evansville, IN. *Education:* Rollins College, B.A. (political science); graduate study at University of Geneva.

Addresses

Home—Los Angeles, CA. *E-mail*—shelbyhiatt@shelbyhiatt.net.

Career

Author and actor. Worked at United Nations Office of Public Information; actor in stage works, including *Sign of Affection* and *The Sweet Enemy;* television roles include Jane Dawson on *General Hospital.* KTWV Radio, sketch writer; NBC-TV, staff writer for *Santa Barbara* (series).

Writings

Panama, Houghton Mifflin (Boston, MA), 2009.

Also author of screenplays.

Sidelights

A writer and actress based in Southern California, Shelby Hiatt was inspired to begin her first novel during a visit with friends living on an hacienda in El Valle, Panama. From there she could view the Panama Canal, a key trading route that links the Atlantic and Pacific oceans, and she decided to weave the sights, sounds, and culture around her into a fictional story. While soaking up the setting of the region, Hiatt also began researching the personal narratives of the men and women who lived and worked in the Canal Zone during the waterway's construction from 1904 to 1914. In 2009 her novel *Panama* was published.

In *Panama* readers meet a fifteen-year-old girl whose father, an engineer, is hired to work on the Panama Canal. Because he will be living in South America for three years, his family accompanies him, leaving their home in Dayton, Ohio, and adapting to a new life in the humid tropical climate. Living in the jungle, an exotic place where nature seems uncontrollable, Hiatt's narrator realizes that there is a new world to explore outside the canal-worker community, which mirrors life in the American Midwest. Then she meets Federico, a handsome and educated Spanish activist who is working as a canal laborer while also advocating on behalf of the canal workers. When the young woman embraces her

Cover of Shelby Hiatt's novel Panama, *which finds a young woman hoping to create a new life after a family move.* (Jacket photo of young woman © 2009 Veer. Photo of Chagres River © 2009 by Blaine Harrington III. Reproduced by permission of Houghton Mifflin, an imprint of Houghton Mifflin Harcourt Publishing Company.)

time in Panama as a new adventure, she begins a physical relationship that moves her from childhood to adulthood. Calling *Panama* an "impressive debut," a *Kirkus Reviews* writer praised Hiatt's narrator as "intelligent and forthright," adding that the "wonderfully detailed backdrop . . . never overpowers the human story." In *Booklist* Hazel Rochman noted the "steamy" depiction of teen romance in the novel and predicted that "both the romance and questions of social justice will grab teens."

Biographical and Critical Sources

PERIODICALS

Booklist, July 1, 2009, Hazel Rochman, review of *Panama,* p. 56.
Bulletin of the Center for Children's Books, November, 2009, Elizabeth Bush, review of *Panama,* p. 113.
Kirkus Reviews, August 15, 2009, review of *Panama.*
School Library Journal, December, 2009, Emma Burkhart, review of *Panama,* p. 120.
Voice of Youth Advocates, December, 2009, Matthew Weaver, review of *Panama,* p. 406.

ONLINE

Authors Unleashed Web log, http://authorsunleashed. blogspot.com/ (February, 2010), Jen Wardrip, interview with Hiatt.
Shelby Hiatt Home Page, http://www.shelbyhiatt.net (December 31, 2010).

* * *

HO, Jannie

Personal

Born in Hong Kong; immigrated to United States. *Education:* Parsons, the New School of Design, B.F.A. (illustration).

Addresses

Home—Ann Arbor, MI. *Agent*—Mela Bolinao, MB Artists, 775 6th Ave., Ste. 6, New York, NY 10001. *E-mail*—jannie@chickengirldesign.com.

Career

Illustrator. Worked as a graphic designer and art director; freelance illustrator.

Writings

SELF-ILLUSTRATED

Light the Menorah, Price Stern Sloan (New York, NY), 2009.

Jannie Ho (Reproduced by permission.)

The Great Matzoh Hunt, Price Stern Sloan (New York, NY), 2010.

ILLUSTRATOR

Tish Rabe, *The Penguins' Perfect Picnic,* Innovative Kids, 2007.
Steve Metzger, *The Mixed-up Alphabet,* Scholastic (New York, NY), 2007.
Lisa Trumbauer, *The Haunted Ghoul Bus,* Sterling Pub. Co. (New York, NY), 2008.
Cari Meister, *Lily's Lucky Leotard,* Stone Arch Books (Mankato, MN), 2009.
Cari Meister, *T-Ball Trouble,* Stone Arch Books (Mankato, MN), 2009.
Lisa Trumbauer, *The Great Reindeer Rebellion,* Sterling (New York, NY), 2009.
Light the Menorah, Price Stern Sloan (New York, NY), 2009.
Matt Bruning, *You Can Draw Monsters and Other Scary Things,* Picture Window Books (Mankato, MN), 2010.
Matt Bruning, *You Can Draw Zoo Animals,* Picture Window Books (Mankato, MN), 2010.
The Great Matzoh Hunt, Price Stern Sloan (New York, NY), 2010.
Joan Holub, *What Does Cow Say?,* Cartwheel Books (New York, NY), 2011.

Creator of mini-comics. Contributor to periodicals, including *High Five* and *Highlights for Children.*

Biographical and Critical Sources

PERIODICALS

Kirkus Reviews, September 15, 2009, review of *The Great Reindeer Rebellion.*

School Library Journal, November, 2008, Martha Simpson, review of *The Haunted Ghoul Bus,* p. 102; October, 2009, Mara Alpert, review of *The Great Reindeer Rebellion,* p. 84.

ONLINE

Jannie Ho Home Page, http://www.chickengirldesign.com (February 15, 2011).

* * *

HOF, Marjolijn 1956-

Personal

Born 1956, in Amsterdam, Netherlands; father a psychologist; married; husband's name Otto; children: Jotte. *Education:* Bibliothek-und Dokumentationsakademie (the Hague, Netherlands), degree (library science).

Addresses

Home—Krommenie, Netherlands.

Career

Author. Wormerveer Library, Amsterdam, Netherlands, children's librarian, c. 1979-99.

Awards, Honors

Gouden Uil Jeugendliteratuurprijs, and Gouden Griffel award, both 2007, and Deutscher Jugendliteraturpreis (Germany), and Prix des jeunes lecteurs de gironde (France), both 2009, and U.S. Board on Books for Young People Outstanding International Books selection, 2010, all for *Een kleine kans;* Gouden Uil long-list selection, 2009, for *Moeder nummer hul;* Nederlands Letterenfonds grant, 2010.

Writings

De bloem van de buurt, illustrated by Kees de Boer, Hilversum, 1999.

Het panterfeestje, illustrated by Natalie Kuypers, Hilversum, 2000.

Toeter, illustrated by Pauline Oud, Hilversum, 2001.

Bing wil slapen, illustrated by Fransje Smit, Gottmer (Haarlem, Netherlands), 2003.

Kleuren speuren, Centraal Museum Utrecht (Utrecht, Netherlands), 2003.

Maks moet!, illustrated by Fransje Smit, Gottmer (Haarlem, Netherlands), 2004.

Stockstaartjes, illustrated by Mylo Freeman, Leopold (Amstersam, Netherlands), 2006.

Een kleine kans, Querido (Amsterdam, Netherlands), 2006, translated by Johanna R. Prins and Jehanna W. Prins as *Against the Odds,* Groundwood Books (Toronto, Ontario, Canada), 2009.

Oversteken, Querido (Amsterdam, Netherlands), 2007.

Assepoester (musical dramatization of "Cinderella" based on Opus 87 by Sergei Prokofiev), illustrated by Martijn van der Linden, produced by Russian National Orchestra, Universal Music, 2007.

Moeder nummer nul, Querido (Amsterdam, Netherlands), 2008.

(With Iris Kuijpers) *Als niemand kijkt,* Querido (Amsterdam, Netherlands), 2009.

Contributor to educational series *Leeshuis,* 2004-06, and to anthologies, including *Nergens bang voor,* 2006, and *Privacy,* illustrated by Els van Egeraat and Albo Helm, Kwintessens (Hilversum, Netherlands), 2006.

Author's work has been translated into Arabian, Basque, Catalan, French, German, Icelandic, Japanese, Korean, Norwegian, Polish, Portuguese, Slovenian, Spanish, and Turkish.

"KOE EN MUS" BOARD-BOOK SERIES

Tsjoeken—Ziek, illustrated by Fransje Smit, Gottmer/Becht (Bloemendaal, Netherlands), 2002.

Modder—Dromen, illustrated by Fransje Smit, Gottmer/Becht (Bloemendaal, Netherlands), 2002.

Vliegen—Verstoppen, illustrated by Fransje Smit, Gottmer/Becht (Bloemendaal, Netherlands), 2002.

IJs—Logeren, illustrated by Fransje Smit, Gottmer/Becht (Bloemendaal, Netherlands), 2002.

Alleen—Donker, illustrated by Frasje Smit, Gottmer/Becht (Bloemendaal, Netherlands), 2002.

Dansen—Regen, illustrated by Fransje Smit, Gottmer/Becht (Bloemendaal, Netherlands), 2002.

Jarig—Fluiten, illustrated by Fransje Smit, Gottmer/Becht (Bloemendaal, Netherlands), 2002.

Adaptations

Een kleine kans was adapted for film by Lotte Tabbers and directed by Nicole van Kilsdonk, Lemming Film, 2011.

Sidelights

A Dutch author, Marjolijn Hof worked as a children's librarian for almost twenty years before shifting into a writing career. Her books, which are geared toward toddlers and children in elementary school, include the children's novels *Het panterfeestje, Toeter,* and *Moeder nummer nul,* as well as the seven-book "Koe en Mus" series of toddler-friendly stories featuring artwork by Fransje Smit. First published in Danish as *Een kleine kans,* the novel *Against the Odds* was Hof's first book to appear in English translation.

Hof was born in Amsterdam in 1956. and grew up in The Hague. As a child she was exposed to art and books due to her psychologist father's love of collecting. While attending Montessori school, Hof's math and science grades were lackluster but she made up for them through her success in both drawing and Dutch. She dreamed of pursuing a career as an artist, but she found writing to be a viable creative outlet while studying at the city's Library and Documentation Academy. A move to Amsterdam and a job at Wormerveer Library, where she was surrounded by books, fueled Hof's desire to write. She eventually married and began raising her daughter, and while working part time she began writing adult poems and stories for children. In 1999, after attending a writer's school, Hof resigned from the library and began writing full time.

In *Against the Odds* Hof introduces a likeable girl named Kiki. Although her parents are married and her home is secure, Kiki spends most of her time with her mother because her father works overseas as a doctor for a humanitarian organization. Now her father is stationed in a region of the world where violence is common, and she can sense her mother's concern. When

days pass with no word as to his whereabouts Kiki decides to ensure her father's safety by stacking the odds in her family's favor. She has never known anyone to have both a dead parent and a dead pet, so she brings home a tiny pet mouse that is not long for this world. "Kiki's thought processes may be shocking, but the delivery is anything but sensational," wrote Heather Booth in her *Booklist* review of *Against the Odds.* A *Kirkus Reviews* writer noted that Hof's "simple, childlike language" effectively captures the girl's efforts to "comprehend and interpret" the adult world around her. "The little girl's desperate reasoning is spot on in terms of developmental level and worldview," asserted Elissa Gershowitz in *Horn Book,* and the role of Kiki's mother in determining how to best share information with her child is "heartrendingly realistic." In *School Library Journal* Sharon R. Pearce found Hof's writing style to be "a bit old-fashioned, yet comforting" and praised *Against the Odds* as an "engaging" story that crystalizes a young girl's world-view and "emotional journey."

Biographical and Critical Sources

PERIODICALS

Booklist, October 15, 2009, Heather Booth, review of *Against the Odds,* p. 63.

Horn Book, January-February, 2010, Elissa Gershowitz, review of *Against the Odds,* p. 87.

Kirkus Reviews, September 1, 2009, review of *Against the Odds.*

New York Times Book Review, October 11, 2009, Julie Just, review of *Against the Odds,* p. 13.

School Library Journal, November, 2009, Sharon R. Pearce, review of *Against the Odds,* p. 82.

ONLINE

Marjolijn Hof Home Page, http://marjolijnhof.nl (February 15, 2011).*

*   *   *

HOLLYER, Beatrice 1957-

Personal

Born 1957, in South Africa; immigrated to England, c. late 1980s; married; children: one daughter. *Education:* University of Cape Town, B.A. (English and philosophy. *Hobbies and other interests:* SCUBA diving, white-water rafting, tennis, cooking.

Addresses

Home—London, England. *E-mail*—beatricehollyer@ stantonmarris.com.

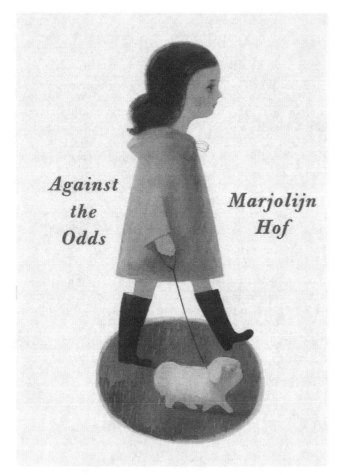

Cover of Marjolijn Hof's novel **Against the Odds,** *which features artwork by Isabelle Arsenault and was the author's first work to be translated into English.* (Cover illustration copyright © 2009 by Isabelle Arsenault. Reproduced by permission of Allen & Unwin. In North America by permission of Groundwood Books.)

Career

Journalist and author. British Broadcasting Corporation, London, England, foreign correspondent and newscaster until 1994; Stanton Marris (consultancy), London, partner, organizational consultant, and executive coach, beginning 2000.

Member

European Mentoring and Coaching Council.

Awards, Honors

Teachers' Choice selection, International Reading Association, 1998, for *Wake up, World!*, 2004, for *Let's Eat.*

Writings

FOR CHILDREN

Wake up, World!: A Day in the Life of Children around the World, Henry Holt/Oxfam (New York, NY), 1999.
Let's Eat!: Children and Their Food around the World, Frances Lincoln/Oxfam (London, England), 2003, published as *Let's Eat!: What Children Eat around the World,* Henry Holt/Oxfam (New York, NY), 2004.
Our World of Water: Children and Water around the World, photographs by Zadie Smith, Frances Lincoln (London, England), 2008, Henry Holt/Oxfam (New York, NY), 2009.

OTHER

(With Lucy Smith) *Sleep: The Secret of Problem-free Nights,* Sterling Pub. (New York, NY), 1996, published as *Sleep: The Easy Way to Peaceful Nights,* Cassell (London, England), 2002.
(With Lucy Smith) *Feeding: The Simple Solution,* Ward Lock (London, England), 1997.

Contributor to periodicals, including *Inside Track* and *Management Today/Entrepreneur Weekly.*

Sidelights

In her books *Wake up, World!: A Day in the Life of Children around the World* and *Let's Eat!: What Children Eat around the World* London-based writer Beatrice Hollyer shares her experiences talking to children around the world. Before she started her own family, Hollyer worked as a foreign correspondent and television newscaster for the British Broadcasting Corporation, reporting on political upheaval in the Middle East, the former Yugoslavia, and her native South Africa. Now based in London, England, she has written several guides for parents of young children and also works as a business consultant. "When I was a journalist I traveled the world," Hollyer noted in an interview for the Macmillan Books Web site. "I've always liked school, and sometimes I used to photograph the school children I saw on my travels. I enjoyed the way they looked so different, and yet I knew that the experience of school itself would be very similar. So when I was asked to write a book about the lives of children in different countries around the world, it seemed like a perfect fit."

Readers meet children from eight very different countries—Russia, Australia, Vietnam, Brazil, India, England, Ghana, and the United States—in *Wake up, World!,* which tracks each child from morning to night as he or she embarks on a typical day. A companion volume, *Let's Eat,* shows the cultural, economical, and geographical differences that are mirrored in regional diets. Here Hollyer introduces five children and illustrates the unique food preferences, cooking techniques, and celebratory menus that are unique to each as well as those they share. Capturing the eating traditions of South Africa, Mexico, Thailand, rural France, and India, *Let's Eat* features a "clearly written text" that gives readers "a better understanding of differences and similarities among people aroun d the world," according to *Booklist* contributor Carolyn Phelan. "A map and food glossary are useful aids," noted Anne L. Tormohlen in her *School Library Journal* review of the same book, while in *Booklist* Lauren Peterson deemed *Wake up, World!* "good inspiration for children to chronicle a typical day in their own lives."

Hollyer turns to the environment in *Our World of Water: Children and Water around the World,* and here her text is accompanied by photographs by award-winning English novelist Zadie Smith. Water is needed everywhere that life exists on earth, and all people need it in equal amounts in order to survive. In her characteristic approach, Hollyer focuses on children living in such distinct places as Bangladesh, Ethiopia, Peru, Mauritania, Tajikistan, and the United States, showing how their water is collected, cleaned, transported, and used by humans, livestock, and agriculture. In *School Library Journal* Carol S. Sturges dubbed *Our World of Water* a "revealing look at the status of water in the world," and a *Kirkus Reviews* writer noted that Hollyer's "simple narrative is punctuated by. . . [quoted] observations both poignant . . . and eye-openingly mundane." As she did with her first two books for children, Hollyer directed a portion of the profits of *Our World of Water* to the international charity Oxfam.

Biographical and Critical Sources

PERIODICALS

Booklist, September 15, 1999, Lauren Peterson, review of *Wake up, World!: A Day in the Life of Children around the World,* p. 264; November 15, 2004, Carolyn Phelan, review of *Let's Eat!: What Children Eat around the World,* p. 576; November 1, 2009, Kathleen Isaacs, review of *Our World of Water: Children and Water around the World,* p. 41.

Kirkus Reviews, September 1, 2009, review of *Our World of Water.*

School Library Journal, February, 2005, Anne L. Tormohlen, review of *Let's Eat!,* p. 122; August, 2009, Carol S. Surges, review of *Our World of Water,* p. 90.

ONLINE

Macmillan Web site, http://us.macmillan.com/ (February 15, 2011), interview with Hollyer.

Stanton Marris Web site, http://www.stantonmarris.com/ (February 15, 2011), "Beatrice Hollyer."

* * *

HUMPHRIES, Tudor 1953-

Personal

Born 1953, in England.

Addresses

Home—North Devon, England.

Career

Illustrator, painter, sculptor, and photographer. Former theatre designer.

Writings

SELF-ILLUSTRATED

Hiding, Orchard Books (New York, NY), 1997.
Maxinaboxboy, Ragged Bears (Andover, England), 1999.
Otter Moon, Boxer Books (London, England), 2009.

ILLUSTRATOR

Michael Harrison, *The Doom of the Gods,* Oxford University Press (Oxford, England), 1985.
Michael Harrison, *The Curse of the Ring,* Oxford University Press (Oxford, England), 1986.
Judy Allen, *Worlds Apart,* Walker Books (London, England), 1988.
Patricia MacLachlan, *Seven Kisses in a Row,* MacRae, 1989.
D.K. Swan, adaptor, *Dr Jekyll and Mr Hyde* (based on the story by Robert Louis Stevenson), Longman (Harlow, England), 1991.
Sandy Shepherd, *Myths and Legends from around the World,* Evans (London, England), 1994.
Jinny Johnson, *How Fast Is a Cheetah?,* Rand McNally (Skokie, IL), 1995.
Bram Stoker, *Dracula* (abridged version), DK Pub. (New York, NY), 1997.

(With Michael Woods) Jinny Johnson, *Animal Superstars,* Marshall (London, England), 1997.
Rosalind Kerven, *King Arthur* ("Eyewitness Classics" series), DK Pub. (New York, NY), 1998.
Mal Peet, *A Floating World,* Ragged Bears (Andover, England), 1998.
Hiawyn Oram, reteller, *The Lion, the Witch and the Wardrobe,* based on the book by C.S. Lewis, HarperCollins (New York, NY), 2004.
Hiawyn Oram, *The Giant Surprise: A Narnia Story,* HarperCollins (New York, NY), 2005.

ILLUSTRATOR; "UP THE GARDEN PATH"/"BACKYARD BOOKS" SERIES BY JUDY ALLEN

Are You a Butterfly?, Kingfisher (New York, NY), 2000.
Are You a Ladybug?, Kingfisher (New York, NY), 2000, published as *Are You a Ladybird?,* Kingfisher (London, England), 2000.
Are You a Snail?, Kingfisher (New York, NY), 2000.
Are You a Spider?, Kingfisher (New York, NY), 2000.
Are You a Bee?, Kingfisher (New York, NY), 2001.
Are You a Dragonfly?, Kingfisher (New York, NY), 2001.
Are You an Ant?, Kingfisher (New York, NY), 2002.
Are You a Grasshopper?, Kingfisher (New York, NY), 2002.

ILLUSTRATOR; "ANIMALS AT RISK" SERIES BY JUDY ALLEN

Tiger, Walker Books (London, England), 1992, Candlewick Press (Cambridge, MA), 1992.
Elephant, Walker Books (London, England), 1992, Candlewick Press (Cambridge, MA), 1993.
Panda, Walker Books (London, England), 1992, Candlewick Press (Cambridge, MA), 1993.
Whale, Walker Books (London, England), 1992, Candlewick Press (Cambridge, MA), 1993.
Seal, Walker Books (London, England), 1993, Candlewick Press (Cambridge, MA), 1994.
Eagle, Candlewick Press (Cambridge, MA), 1994.

Sidelights

British wildlife painter Tudor Humphries earned an education in theatrical design before shifting his focus to book illustration. Worked primarily in water color, Humphries' detailed images reflect his fascination for plants and animals and the rural surroundings near his home in North Devon, England. The skilled use of light in bringing to life his many subjects is a characteristic of the artist's contribution to books by writers that include Judy Allen, Michael Harrison, Patricia MacLachlan, Jinny Johnson, Mal Peet, and Hiawyn Oram. In addition, Humphries has also created the original self-illustrated books *Hiding, Otter Moon,* and *Maxinaboxboy.* Reviewing *Hiding,* in which a little girl avoids a scolding by avoiding her mom, Stephanie Zvirin noted in *Booklist* that Humphries' "sing-songy" prose teams well with his "large, delicately colored" and "appealing" art.

In *Otter Moon* Humphries uses a realistic woodland setting to ground his fanciful story about a playful young otter that is charged with catching a fish for the Otter King's breakfast. While the search for a suitable fish is aided by a friendly heron, the king's demand that the fish be served on a silver dish presents more of a challenge in the lushly illustrated bedtime tale. In *School Library Journal* Margaret Bush praised the "sweeping watercolor views" that appear in many of the story's double-page images and concluded that "Humphries has a way with words and a good hand with a paintbrush." The agile young otter in *Otter Moon* has "the soul of a poet," according to a *Kirkus Reviews* writer, and the author/illustrator's "lyrical prose . . . is perfectly matched to his beautiful, dusky watercolors." "The watery world Humphries depicts is quiet and pleasant," wrote *Booklist* contributor Karen Cruze, while a *Publishers Weekly* contributor predicted that children "whose imaginations are fired by the secret lives of wild creatures will treasure" Humphries' book. Reviewing *Otter Moon* for *Children's Book Review Online*, Phoebe Vreeland wrote that Humphries' "watercolor palette is masterfully used to take us from the pink hues of dusk, far into the inky blue nighttime and velvety depths of the river and finally back again to the warmth of sunrise." *Otter Moon* "has all the elements of a perfect bedtime story," added Vreeland: "transition from day to night, a loveable animal hero . . . on a magical journey and of course a victorious ending."

Allen has been one of Humphries' frequent collaborators, and his artwork appears in her nonfiction series "Up the Garden Path" and "Animals at Risk." Known in the United States as the "Backyard Books" series, the "Up the Garden Path" books include *Are You a Butterfly?*, *Are You a Snail?*, and several other similarly titled stories. In their pages, readers are given a view of life from a tiny creature as they follow it through its early stages of growth and sometimes metamorphosis. In her text, Allen addresses the creature itself with an engaging familiarity, while Humphries' "colorful and precise" paintings are "just right for sharing," according to Carolyn Phelan in her *Booklist* review of *Are You a Butterfly?* *School Library Journal* contributor Patricia Manning recommended the "Up the Garden Path" books as "attractive introductions to creatures likely to be found in backyards and empty lots."

In their "Animals at Risk" books Allen and Humphries continue their successful collaboration, this time turning to animals that may be unfamiliar to most readers. In *Seal,* for example, Allen describes the plight of the rare monk seal through a story of a girl vacationing with her family near the sea's Mediterranean home. Humphries' art for the book features "a distinguished handling of color and light and shadow," wrote *Booklist* critic Julie Corsaro, and in her review of *Eagle,* which is set in the Philippines and describes a boy's encounter with a giant raptor, Mary Harris Veeder maintained that the book's water-color illustrations "make the setting specific, and . . . suggest . . . a serious story rather than a brisk bright one."

Tudor Humphries' illustration projects include creating the nature-themed art in his own picture-book story, **Otter Moon.** (Boxer Books, 2009. Illustration copyright © 2009 Tudor Humphries. Reproduced by permission of the illustrator.)

Biographical and Critical Sources

PERIODICALS

Booklist, May 1, 1994, Julie Corsaro, review of *Seal,* p. 1606; September 1, 1994, Mary Harris Veeder, review of *Eagle,* p. 47; December 1, 1997, Stephanie Zvirin, review of *Hiding,* p. 641; May 15, 2000, Carolyn Phelan, review of *Are You a Snail?,* p. 1745; May 15, 2000, Carolyn Phelan, review of *Are You a Ladybug?,* p. 1745; October 15, 2000, Carolyn Phelan, review of *Are You a Butterfly?,* p. 441; October 15, 2000, Carolyn Phelan, review of *Are You a Spider?,* p. 441; December 1, 2009, Karen Cruze, review of *Otter Moon,* p. 52.

Childhood Education, winter, 2001, Jill Quisenberry, review of *Are You a Bee?,* p. 109.

Kirkus Reviews, August 15, 2009, review of *Otter Moon.*

Publishers Weekly, March 20, 2000, reviews of *Are You a Ladybug?* and *Are You a Snail?,* both p. 94; August 31, 2009, review of *Otter Moon,* p. 55.

School Librarian, spring, 2010, Becky Carter, review of *Otter Moon,* p. 27.

School Library Journal, September 15, 1997, Michael Rogers, review of *Dracula,* p. 108; September, 2000, Karey Wehner, review of *Are You a Ladybug?,* p. 213; April, 2001, Patricia Manning, review of *Are You a Butterfly?,* p. 128; April, 2001, Patricia Manning, review of *Are You a Spider?,* p. 128; October, 2009, Margaret Bush, review of *Otter Moon,* p. 96.

ONLINE

Children's Book Review Online, http://www.thechildrens bookreview.com/ (August 10, 2010), Phoebe Vreeland, review of *Otter Moon.**

J

JOHNSTON, Tony 1942-

Personal

Born January 30, 1942, in Los Angeles, CA; daughter of David Leslie (a golf professional) and Ruth Taylor; married Roger D. Johnston (a banker), June 25, 1966; children: Jennifer, Samantha, Ashley. *Education:* Stanford University, B.A. (history), 1963, M.Ed., 1964. *Hobbies and other interests:* Archaeology, collecting dance masks and Latin American textiles, collecting children's books and children's book art, Western history, especially of California.

Addresses

Home—San Marino, CA.

Career

Children's book author. Fourth-grade teacher in public elementary school, Altadena, CA, 1964-66; McGraw-Hill Publishing Company, New York, NY, editing supervisor, 1966-68; Harper & Row Publishers, Inc., New York, NY, copy editor of children's books, 1969. University of California—Los Angeles Extension, teacher of picture-book writing. Active member, Friends of the Adobes.

Awards, Honors

Children's Choice Award, Harris County Public Library, 1979, for *Four Scary Stories;* Children's Choice designation, 1986, for *The Quilt Story;* Outstanding Literary Quality in a Picture Book honor, Southern California Council on Literature for Children and Young People, 1989, for *Yonder;* Parents' Choice Award for Children's Books, 1992, for *Slither McCreep and His Brother, Joe;* named Honorary Texan, 1993, for *The Cowboy and the Black-eyed Pea;* Southern California Council on Literature for Children and Young People award (now California Literature Council), 1997, for body of work; Simon Wiesenthal Once upon a World Award, and City of

Los Angeles plaque, both 1997, both for *The Wagon;* Henry Bergh Honor designation, American Society for the Prevention of Cruelty to Animals, 2000, for *It's about Dogs;* John and Patricia Beatty Award, and Golden Dolphin Award, both Southern California Booksellers Association, both 2003, both for *Any Small Goodness;* Best Children's Book of the Year selection, Bank Street College of Education, for *The Ancestors Are Singing;* Sigurd F. Olson Nature Writing Award, Sigurd Olson Environmental Institute, 2004, for *Isabel's House of Butterflies;* Best Book for Young Adults designation, American Library Association, for *Bone by Bone by Bone.*

Writings

FOR CHILDREN

The Adventures of Mole and Troll, illustrated by Wallace Tripp, Putnam (New York, NY), 1972.

Fig Tale, illustrated by Giulio Maestro, Putnam (New York, NY), 1974.

Mole and Troll Trim the Tree, illustrated by Wallace Tripp, Putnam (New York, NY), 1974.

Odd Jobs, illustrated by Tomie dePaola, Putnam (New York, NY), 1977.

Five Little Foxes and the Snow, illustrated by Cyndy Szekeres, Putnam (New York, NY), 1977.

Night Noises, and Other Mole and Troll Stories, illustrated by Cyndy Szekeres, Putnam (New York, NY), 1977.

Four Scary Stories, illustrated by Tomie dePaola, Putnam (New York, NY), 1978.

Little Mouse Nibbling, illustrated by Diane Stanley, Putnam (New York, NY), 1979.

Dedos de luna (title means "Moon Fingers"), illustrated by Leonel Maciel, Secretaría de Educación Pública (Mexico City, Mexico), 1979.

Conchas y caracoles (title means "Shells and Snails"), Secretaría de Educación Pública (Mexico City, Mexico), 1979.

Animales fantásticas (title means "Fantastic Animals"), Secretaría de Educación Pública (Mexico City, Mexico), 1979.

Happy Birthday, Mole and Troll, illustrated by Cindy Szekeres, Putnam (New York, NY), 1979.

Odd Jobs and Friends, illustrated by Tomie dePaola, Putnam (New York, NY), 1982.

The Vanishing Pumpkin, illustrated by Tomie dePaola, Putnam (New York, NY), 1983.

Mi regalo (title means "My Present"), Secretaría de Educación Pública (Mexico City, Mexico), 1984.

The Witch's Hat, illustrated by Margot Tomes, Putnam (New York, NY), 1984.

The Quilt Story, illustrated by Tomie dePaola, Putnam (New York, NY), 1985.

Farmer Mack Measures His Pig, illustrated by Megan Lloyd, Harper (New York, NY), 1986.

Whale Song, illustrated by Ed Young, Putnam (New York, NY), 1987.

Yonder, illustrated by Lloyd Bloom, Dial Books for Young Readers (New York, NY), 1988, reprinted, Gibbs Smith (Salt Lake City, UT), 2002.

Pages of Music, illustrated by Tomie dePaola, Putnam (New York, NY), 1988.

My Friend Bear, Ladybird Books (London, England), 1989.

The Badger and the Magic Fan: A Japanese Folktale, illustrated by Tomie dePaola, Putnam (New York, NY), 1990.

The Soup Bone, illustrated by Margot Tomes, Harcourt (San Diego, CA), 1990.

I'm Gonna Tell Mama I Want an Iguana (poems), illustrated by Lillian Hoban, Putnam (New York, NY), 1990.

Grandpa's Song, illustrated by Brad Sneed, Dial Books for Young Readers (New York, NY), 1991.

Goblin Walk, illustrated by Bruce Degen, Putnam (New York, NY), 1991.

Little Bear Sleeping, illustrated by Lillian Hoban, Putnam (New York, NY), 1991.

The Promise, illustrated by Pamela Keavney, Harper (New York, NY), 1992.

The Cowboy and the Black-eyed Pea, illustrated by Warren Ludwig, Putnam (New York, NY), 1992.

Slither McCreep and His Brother, Joe, illustrated by Victoria Chess, Harcourt (San Diego, CA), 1992.

Lorenzo, the Naughty Parrot, illustrated by Leo Politi, Harcourt (San Diego, CA), 1992.

The Last Snow of Winter, illustrated by Friso Henstra, Tambourine (New York, NY), 1993.

The Tale of Rabbit and Coyote, illustrated by Tomie dePaola, Putnam (New York, NY), 1994.

(Translator) *My Mexico/Mexico mío,* illustrated by F. John Sierra, Putnam (New York, NY), 1994.

Three Little Bikers, illustrated by G. Brian Karas, Knopf (New York, NY), 1994.

The Old Lady and the Birds, illustrated by Stephanie Garcia, Harcourt (San Diego, CA), 1994.

Little Rabbit Goes to Sleep, illustrated by Harvey Stevenson, HarperCollins (New York, NY), 1994.

Amber on the Mountain, illustrated by Robert Duncan, Dial Books for Young Readers (New York, NY), 1994.

Alice Nizzy Nazzy: The Witch of Santa Fe, illustrated by Tomie dePaola, Putnam (New York, NY), 1995.

The Iguana Brothers, illustrated by Mark Teague, Blue Sky Press (New York, NY), 1995.

Very Scary, illustrated by Douglas Florian, Harcourt (San Diego, CA), 1995.

How Many Miles to Jacksonville?, illustrated by Bart Forbes, Putnam (New York, NY), 1995.

Little Wild Parrot, Tambourine Books (New York, NY), 1995.

The Bull and the Fire Truck, illustrated by R.W. Alley, East West Books (New York, NY), 1996.

Fishing Sunday, illustrated by Barry Root, Tambourine Books (New York, NY), 1996.

The Ghost of Nicholas Greebe, illustrated by S.D. Schindler, Dial Books for Young Readers (New York, NY), 1996.

The Magic Maguey, illustrated by Elisa Kleven, Harcourt (San Diego, CA), 1996.

Once in the Country: Poems of a Farm, illustrated by Thomas B. Allen, Putnam (New York, NY), 1996.

The Wagon, illustrated by James E. Ransome, Tambourine Books (New York, NY), 1996.

Day of the Dead, illustrated by Jeanette Winter, Harcourt (San Diego, CA), 1997.

We Love the Dirt, illustrated by Alexa Brandenberg, Cartwheel Books (New York, NY), 1997.

Sparky and Eddie: The First Day of School, illustrated by Susannah Ryan, Scholastic Press (New York, NY), 1997.

The Chizzywink and the Alamagoozlum, illustrated by Robert Bender, Holiday House (New York, NY), 1998.

Boo!: A Ghost Story That Could Be True, Cartwheel Books (New York, NY), 1998.

Sparky and Eddie: Trouble with Bugs, illustrated by Susannah Ryan, Scholastic (New York, NY), 1998.

Sparky and Eddie: Wild, Wild Rodeo!, illustrated by Susannah Ryan, Scholastic (New York, NY), 1998.

Bigfoot Cinderrrrella, illustrated by James Warhola, Putnam (New York, NY), 1998.

An Old Shell: Poems of the Galápagos, illustrated by Tom Pohrt, Farrar, Straus (New York, NY), 1999.

Big Red Apple, illustrated by Judith Hoffman Corwin, Cartwheel Books (New York, NY), 1999.

It's about Dogs, illustrated by Ted Rand, Harcourt (San Diego, CA), 2000.

Uncle Rain Cloud, illustrated by Fabricio Vanden Broeck, Charlesbridge (Watertown, MA), 2000.

The Barn Owls, illustrated by Deborah Kogan Ray, Charlesbridge (Watertown, MA), 2000.

Any Small Goodness: A Novel of the Barrio, illustrated by Raúl Colón, Blue Sky Press (New York, NY), 2000.

Desert Song, illustrated by Ed Young, Sierra Club Books for Children (San Francisco, CA), 2000.

Alien and Possum: Friends No Matter What, illustrated by Tony DiTerlizzi, Simon & Schuster Books for Young Readers (New York, NY), 2001.

Cat, What Is That?, illustrated by Wendell Minor, HarperCollins (New York, NY), 2001.

My Best Friend Bear, illustrated by Joy Allen, Rising Moon (Flagstaff, AZ), 2001.

Clear Moon, Snow Soon, illustrated by Guy Porfirio, Rising Moon (Flagstaff, AZ), 2001.

Desert Dog, illustrated by Robert Weatherford, Sierra Club Books for Children (San Francisco, CA), 2001.

Gopher up Your Sleeve, illustrated by Trip Park, Rising Moon (Flagstaff, AZ), 2001.

That Summer, illustrated by Barry Moser, Harcourt (San Diego, CA), 2002.

Sunsets of the West, illustrated by Ted Lewin, Putnam (New York, NY), 2002.

Alien and Possum Hanging Out, illustrated by Tony DiTerlizzi, Simon & Schuster (New York, NY), 2002.

Go Track a Yak!, illustrated by Tim Raglin, Simon & Schuster (New York, NY), 2003.

The Mummy's Mother, Sky Blue Press (New York, NY), 2003.

A Kenya Christmas, illustrated by Leonard Jenkins, Holiday House (New York, NY), 2003.

Isabel's House of Butterflies, illustrated Susan Guevara, Sierra Club Books for Children (San Francisco, CA), 2003.

The Ancestors Are Singing, illustrated by Karen Barbour, Farrar, Straus (New York, NY), 2003.

The Worm Family, illustrated by Stacy Innerst, Harcourt (San Diego, CA), 2004.

The Harmonica, illustrated by Ron Mazellan, Charlesbridge (Watertown, MA), 2004.

Ten Fat Turkeys, illustrated by Rich Deas, Cartwheel Books (New York, NY), 2004.

The Spoon in the Bathroom Wall, Harcourt (San Diego, CA), 2005.

Noel, illustrated by Cheng-Khee Chee, Carolrhoda (Minneapolis, MN), 2005.

Chicken in the Kitchen, illustrated by Eleanor Taylor, Simon & Schuster (New York, NY), 2005.

The Whole Green World, illustrated by Elsa Kleven, Farrar, Straus (New York, NY), 2005.

Angel City, illustrated by Carole Byard, Philomel Books (New York, NY), 2006.

Sticky People, illustrated by Cyd Moore, HarperCollins (New York, NY), 2006.

Off to Kindergarten, illustrated by Melissa Sweet, Cartwheel Books (New York, NY), 2007.

Bone by Bone by Bone, Roaring Brook Press (New Milford, CT), 2007.

Cat, What Is That?, illustrated by Wendell Minor, David R. Godine (Boston, MA), 2008.

P Is for Piñata: A Mexico Alphabet, illustrated by John Parra, Sleeping Bear Press (Chelsea, MI), 2008.

Voice from Afar: Poems of Peace, illustrated by Susan Guevara, Holiday House (New York, NY), 2008.

My Abuelita, illustrated by Yuyi Morales, Harcourt (Boston, MA), 2009.

First Grade, Here I Come!, illustrated by Melissa Sweet, Cartwheel Books (New York, NY), 2012.

Contributor to textbooks and poetry anthologies. Contributor to periodicals, including *Cricket.*

Author's papers are housed in the Tony Johnston Collection, Huntington Library, San Marino, CA.

Adaptations

The Last Snow of Winter and *Fishing Sunday* were adapted as electronic books by iPictureBooks (New York, NY), 2001.

Sidelights

Tony Johnston, a prolific author of books for children and young adults, has earned numerous honors and critical acclaim for her works of fiction and nonfiction, picture books, poetry, and early readers. A number of her titles, which include *Go Track a Yak!* and *The Worm Family* as well as the middle-grade Arthurian spoof *The Spoon in the Bathroom Wall,* feature quirky characters—both human and animal—in a variety of unusual situations. Other books, such as *The Quilt Story,* focus on historical or contemporary themes, while *My Abuelita* and similar works feature bilingual texts in which Spanish words intermingle with a largely English text. In appraising the many books to her credit, it is difficult to pin Johnston down to a specific focus, in part due to her wide-ranging interests. As she remarked in an interview on the Harcourt Web site, "I have no typical style. If you read a bunch of my books, you'd probably think they were written by a bunch of different people. Every story is different. It starts as something that needs to get out from inside of you; it shows you the best way to say it."

Johnston was born in Los Angeles and grew up in nearby San Marino. As a child, she loved reading and books and was most impressed by the fantasies of J.R.R. Tolkien. Johnston's fascination with T.H. White's novel

Tony Johnston depicts family life in the early 1800s in* The Quilt Story, *a picture book featuring illustrations by award-winning artist Tomie dePaola. (Illustration copyright © 1985 Tomie dePaola. All rights reserved. Used by permission of G.P. Putnam's Sons, a division of Penguin Young Readers Group, a member of Penguin Group (USA) Inc., 345 Hudson Street, New York, NY 10014.)

quartet about King Arthur inspired her own novel *The Spoon in the Bathroom Wall,* in which fourth grader Martha Snapdragon discovers that her science teacher is raising dragons. As the school bully takes on the role of Martha's arch nemesis and school principal Mr. Klunk sets his evil designs on ruling the world (at least, the world of Horace E. Bloggins Elementary School), Martha discovers that her destiny is set forth in the prophecy surrounding a spoon that is wedged in the tile wall of the school's boy's bathroom. In *School Library Journal,* Terrie Dorio dubbed *The Spoon in the Bathroom Wall* an "entertaining story," and a *Publishers Weekly* critic concluded that, "with duly preposterous pomp," Johnston's "comically written caper builds to a crowning scene of glory."

After graduating from Stanford University, Johnston taught for two years at a public school in Altadena, California. When her husband's job required them to relocate, she moved east to New York City, where she worked for a number of years as an editing supervisor and a copy editor for children's books. While working at Harper & Row, Johnston benefited from her job as private secretary to legendary editor Ursula Nordstrom. In 1972 Putnam published her first children's book, *The Adventures of Mole and Troll.*

Everyday childhood situations were the inspiration for the first of Johnston's popular "Mole and Troll" stories, while the second, *Mole and Troll Trim the Tree,* was based on the author's memories of her own real-life Christmases. Other books in the series include *Night Noises, and Other Mole and Troll Stories* and *Happy Birthday, Mole and Troll.* A *Booklist* reviewer, describing Johnston's endearing protagonists as "two of the more worthwhile recurring easy-reader actors," went on to call Mole and Troll "ingenious and distinct, and they regularly show evidence of a remarkable likeness-of-soul to their audience."

Animals are also cast in the title role of Johnston's *Five Little Foxes and the Snow,* which was inspired by a Christmas the author spent in New Hampshire. In *Little Mouse Nibbling* she introduces a very shy mouse who stays inside nibbling at this and that until a cricket brings Christmas carolers to its door, while *The Worm Family* finds a squirmy seven-member family proud of their worminess, despite the disdain of their less-twisty neighbors. A *Publishers Weekly* contributor wrote of *Little Mouse Nibbling* that Johnston's "unabashedly sentimental Christmas fantasy should find its way under many a Yuletide tree for years to come," while *School Library Journal* writer John Sigwald praised *The Worm Family* as "a unique take on prejudice."

In her picture-book texts, Johnston often uses a rhythmic, poetic style. *Whale Song,* which a *Kirkus Reviews* contributor deemed "a stunningly beautiful evocation of the gentle giants of the deep," is a paean to Nature; the numbers only represent the song that travels from whale to whale. Children will "respond to the chanting beat"

Johnston takes readers on a fantastic journey in her middle-grade adventure The Spoon in the Bathroom Wall, *featuring a cover illustration by Brett Helquist.* (Cover illustration © 2005 by Brett Helquist. Copyright © 2005 by the Johnston Family Trust. Reproduced by permission of Houghton Mifflin Harcourt Publishing Company. This material may not be reproduced in any form or by any means without the prior written permission of the publisher.)

of *Chicken in the Kitchen,* predicted *Booklist* contributor Gillian Engberg, the reviewer adding that Johnston's "folksy language is appealing." *Yonder* is based on a Johnston family tradition in which trees are planted to commemorate the births and deaths of family members. "With the eloquent simplicity of a Shaker hymn, Tony Johnston's words capture the cyclical pattern of a farming way of life," Hanna B. Zeiger stated in a review of *Yonder* for *Horn Book.*

The author's other poetry books include *I'm Gonna Tell Mama I Want an Iguana,* which includes mostly humorous poems on such diverse subjects as sunset, frogs' eggs, skeletons, and jellyfish. *I'm Gonna Tell Mama I Want an Iguana* was described by Tiffany Chrisman in *Children's Book Review Service* as a collection that "does much to stretch the imaginative powers" of its readers.

It's about Dogs collects forty short poems, including rhymed quatrains, haiku, and blank verse, while *Cat, What Is That?* finds Johnston taking a similar poetic look at felines. According to Margaret Bush in *School Library Journal, It's about Dogs* brings to life "poignant . . . as well as funny" moments, resulting in a "richly rendered tribute" to man's best friend. "Johnston's compact rhymes [are] often astonishingly apt," a *Publishers Weekly* critic wrote in a review of *Cat, What Is That?*

Johnston profiles a fascinating creature in *The Barn Owls,* which focuses on a family of owls living in an old barn in California, while *An Old Shell: Poems of the Galápagos* presents young readers with a poetic look at the remarkable creatures of these isolated islands. Johnston offers over thirty very short poems in *Gopher up Your Sleeve,* a verse collection that features all manner of creatures: from caterpillars and parrots to quetzals and sloths. Citing the "outlandish, computer-generated illustrations" by Trip Park, *School Library Journal* contributor Kathleen Kelly MacMillan wrote that in *Gopher up Your Sleeve* Johnston "plays with language and rhyme in a way that will draw kids in."

Not all of Johnston's stories cast animals as main characters. For example, *Odd Jobs* focuses on an enter-

Cover of Johnston's coming-of-age novel Any Small Goodness, *featuring a cover illustration by Raúl Colón.* (Cover illustration © 2005 by Brett Helquist. Copyright © 2005 by the Johnston Family Trust. Reproduced by permission of Houghton Mifflin Harcourt Publishing Company. This material may not be reproduced in any form or by any means without the prior written permission of the publisher.)

prising young man who will take on any job that is offered, including washing the dirtiest dog in town, standing in for a friend at dance class, and guarding a balloon from a bratty child brandishing a sharp pin. A critic for *Booklist* praised the fact that in *Odd Jobs* Johnston has "created a resilient, inventive character and put him into laughable situations." *Any Small Goodness: A Novel of the Barrio* is set in Los Angeles and finds Arturo and his family working to diminish the impact of gang violence on their lives. "The characters are likable and warm," according to Sharon McNeil in her *School Library Journal* review of Johnston's story.

In what *Booklist* contributor Gillian Engberg described as "moving lines that read like free-verse poetry," *Angel City* tells a poignant story about an elderly man who discovers an infant abandoned in a dumpster. "A quieter exploration of the toll inner-city violence takes on the innocent is hard to imagine," remarked a *Kirkus Reviews* critic. In another sobering work, *Voice from Afar: Poems of Peace,* Johnston "offers thoughtful responses to war's senseless violence," wrote *School Library Journal* Marilyn Taniguchi. The twenty-six selections in the book, ranging from haiku to free verse, examine topics such as grief, faith, poverty, combat, and renewal. "A moving invitation to hope," observed a critic in *Kirkus Reviews.*

In the humorous picture book *Slither McCreep and His Brother, Joe* two siblings deal with the usual problems of fighting and sharing. Rather than human children, however, Slither and Joe are boa constrictors, and they go around squeezing, swallowing, and otherwise ruining each other's possessions. *Wilson Library Bulletin* reviewers Donnarae MacCann and Olga Richard commented that *Slither McCreep and His Brother, Joe* "offers family realism plus one of the most zany, surreal settings imaginable." Similarly, *The Chizzywink and the Alamogoozlum*—a story prominently featuring the letter "z"—presents the tale of a marauding giant mosquito whose intentions are foiled by a healthy dose of maple syrup. Writing in *Booklist,* Susan Dove Lempke complimented Johnston's use of "rich language and a rhythm" in the book, adding that *The Chizzywink and the Almagoozlum* is amply suited to reading aloud.

In the equally lighthearted *The Vanishing Pumpkin* a seven-hundred-year-old woman and an 800-year-old man meet a ghoul, a rapscallion, and a varmint as they search for their missing Halloween pumpkin. The headgear featured in *The Witch's Hat*—a tale *School Library Journal* contributor Kay McPherson dubbed "fresh and funny"—falls into the witch's magic pot and turns into a bat, a rat, and a cat before Johnston's entertaining Halloween tale winds to a close, while a less-helpful witch send a frustrated father on a foolish errand in *Go Track a Yak!*

According to *Horn Book* contributor Ann A. Flowers, *The Ghost of Nicholas Greebe* is a "not too spooky story" about a man whose bones are dug up by a dog and how, as a ghost, he must retrieve them. *Bigfoot Cinderrrrrella* follows Ella the Bigfoot and her romance with a prince, presenting youngsters with a "silly twist on a favorite fairy tale" that deals with the romance question "with humor and style," according to a *Publishers Weekly* contributor. Also praising Johnston's quirky tale, Ellen Mandel, in her *Booklist* review, deemed *Bigfoot Cinderrrrrella* a "howlingly funny take on the original." Johnston looks at a universal childhood experience—attending the first day of school—in *Off to Kindergarten,* a work told in verse. Here the author's "simple, playful rhyme expresses every kid's fear and excitement about leaving home," Hazel Rochman stated in *Booklist.*

Readers are introduced to life during different periods of history in several books by Johnston. She takes readers back to ancient Egypt in *The Mummy's Mother,* a humorous story that finds a boy mummy determined to track down his mummy mother after she is stolen by grave robbers. Including art by award-winning illustrator Tomie dePaola, *The Quilt Story* introduces readers to Abigail, a young girl who finds comfort and companionship in the midnight-blue appliquéd quilt her mother made especially for her. Abigail and her family travel West via covered wagon and make a new home on the American frontier. As the girl grows up, her treasured quilt is eventually stored away in the attic, where, a century later, it is discovered by another little girl, who also finds it a comfort when her family moves. The true-life experience of Holocaust survivor Henryk Rosmaryn is the focus of *The Harmonica,* in which a Polish boy shares his musical gifts with others during a dark time.

Johnston's Halloween-themed story pairs up with Douglas Florian's colorful art in **Very Scary.** (Voyager Books, 1999. Illustration copyright © 1995 by Douglas Florian. Reproduced by permission of the illustrator.)

Setting is an important component of *Amber on the Mountain,* a novel for older elementary-grade readers. Amber lives in an isolated mountain community that has no school or teacher; she has never even learned to read. However, when a man comes to build a mountain road (a seemingly impossible task), his daughter sets herself the just-as-impossible task of teaching Amber to read. When the road is completed and the man and his daughter leave, Amber teaches herself to write so that she can keep in touch with her new friend. A *Kirkus Reviews* critic stated that "Johnston's beautifully honed narrative glows with mountain imagery and the warmth of the girls' friendship," and a reviewer in *Publishers Weekly* called the novel a "heartwarming story" with "lyrical images and picturesque and convincing dialogue."

The setting for several of Johnston's books, including *Lorenzo, the Naughty Parrot, Uncle Rain Cloud, Isabel's House of Butterflies,* and *My Abuelita,* reflects the fact that the author and her family lived in Mexico for fifteen years. Featuring a bilingual text, *My Mexico/ Mexico mío* contains eighteen short poems in both English and Spanish versions, while *Uncle Rain Cloud* and *Day of the Dead* insert Spanish vocabulary within a mostly English text. In *Uncle Rain Cloud* Johnston introduces a man who needs his nephew to translate for him, even though this dependency causes him embarrassment. *Booklist* reviewer Hazel Rochman called *Uncle Rain Cloud* "funny" and "touching," adding that "Johnston's text is clear and poetic." "Brisk pacing, sympathetic characters, and clear prose . . . effectively make a winner," concluded Ann Welton in her *School Library Journal* of the same book. In *Day of the Dead* the customs surrounding a well-known Mexican tradition of celebrating long-time ancestors are incorporated into a "dazzling little volume," according to a *Publishers Weekly* reviewer, while *Isabel's House of Butterflies* introduces children to the annual monarch butterfly migration into the mountains of Mexico.

In *P Is for Piñata: A Mexico Alphabet* Johnston introduces young readers to the landforms, traditions, and people of that nation, covering subjects from the Ballet Folklórico, a celebrated dance ensemble, to Diego Rivera, a world renowned muralist, to the Usumacinta River. Johnston's sidebars, which accompany her verse summaries of each topic, "are clearly written, often lively, and well worth reading," in the words of *Booklist* reviewer Carolyn Phelan.

The relationship between a young boy and his grandmother is at the heart of *My Abuelita,* "a charming tribute to family and the joys and inspiration that storytelling can bring," according to Shelle Rosenfeld in *Booklist.* Illustrated with digitally-enhanced photographs of polymer-clay sculptures by Yuyi Morales, the work follows a child as he helps his beloved caretaker prepare for her job as a professional storyteller. "Johnston conjures up a senior citizen of enormous creativity and

Johnston teams up with artist Yuyi Morales to create the multigenerational picture book **My Abuelita**. (Illustration © 2009 by Yuyi Morales. Reproduced by permission of Houghton Mifflin Harcourt Publishing Company.)

indomitable spirit," a *Publishers Weekly* critic noted, and Mary Landrum, writing in *School Library Journal,* called *My Abuelita* "the universal story of a loving intergenerational relationship."

In addition to picture books, Johnston has also written beginning readers such as *Alien and Possum: Friends No Matter What* and the works in the "Sparky and Eddie" series. In *Alien and Possum* a possum sees a spaceship crash near his home, and then befriends his alien visitor and learns about tolerance. The characters return in *Alien and Possum Hanging Out,* which follows the growing friendship between the unlikely duo in three short stories. According to a *Publishers Weekly* contributor, the "springy pace, lively dialogue and Alien's silly sound effects" in *Alien and Possum* will appeal to the younger set. In *Booklist,* Carolyn Phelan cited Johnston's "ready wit and understanding of a child's perspective" in the two books, while a *Kirkus Reviews* writer noted that Johnston's "droll and expressive language helps to add a little humor" to each story.

In *Sparky and Eddie: The First Day of School* two close friends are looking forward to the first day of school until they learn they will be in different classrooms, while *Sparky and Eddie: Wild, Wild Rodeo,* find the siblings competing in the class rodeo. In *Booklist,* Rochman described Johnston's text in the series opener as "exuberant," while Phelan judged *Sparky and Eddie: Wild, Wild Rodeo* a "highly entertaining entry in a fine series."

A decided change of pace for the author, Johnston's young-adult novel *Bone by Bone by Bone* concerns the powerful friendship between David, the son of a white

racist, and Malcolm, an African-American youth. Set in small-town Tennessee during the 1950s, the novel focuses on David's growing concerns for Malcolm's safety after David becomes convinced that his father has joined the Ku Klux Klan. "Readers . . . will feel haunted by this powerful story of a child awakening to family secrets and violence," Gillian Engberg commented in her review of *Bone by Bone by Bone* for *Booklist.*

"My goal in writing is simply to entertain—myself and someone else," Johnston once explained to *SATA.* "If I manage to stir up a little love of language or make someone laugh or feel good about himself or go back to the library for another book along the way, well, that's all pink frosting on the cake."

Biographical and Critical Sources

BOOKS

Authors of Books for Young People, Scarecrow Press (Metuchen, NJ), 1990.

PERIODICALS

Booklist, October 15, 1974, review of *Mole and Troll Trim the Tree,* p. 244; March 15, 1977, review of *Night Noises and Other Mole and Troll Stories,* p. 1097; November 15, 1977, review of *Odd Jobs,* p. 559; May 15, 1996, Kay Weisman, review of *Fishing Sunday,* p. 1592; July, 1996, Stephanie Zvirin, review of *The Ghost of Nicholas Greebe,* p. 1829; October 15, 1996, Annie Ayres, review of *The Magic Maguey,* pp. 435-436, and Michael Cart, review of *How Many Miles to Jacksonville?,* p. 435; January 1, 1997, Carolyn Phelan, review of *The Wagon,* p. 869; February 1, 1997, Carolyn Phelan, review of *The Bull and the Fire Truck,* p. 949; August, 1997, Carolyn Phelan, review of *Sparky and Eddie: The First Day of School,* p. 1910; September 15, 1997, Hazel Rochman, review of *Day of the Dead,* p. 242; February 1, 1998, Hazel Rochman, review of *Sparky and Eddie: The First Day of School,* p. 926; May 1, 1998, Carolyn Phelan, review of *Sparky and Eddie: Wild, Wild Rodeo,* p. 1524; June 1, 1998, Susan Dove Lempke, review of *The Chizzywink and the Alamagoozlum,* pp. 1779-1780; December 1, 1998, Ellen Mandel, review of *Bigfoot Cinderrrrrella,* p. 668; December 1, 1999, GraceAnne A. DeCandido, review of *An Old Shell: Poems of the Galápagos,* p. 700; February 15, 2000, Todd Morning, review of *The Barn Owls,* p. 1118; March 15, 2000, John Peters, review of *It's about Dogs,* p. 1383; October 1, 2000, Gillian Engberg, review of *Desert Song,* p. 336; January 1, 2004, Hazel Rochman, review of *The Harmonica,* p. 857; February 15, 2001, Hazel Rochman, review of *Uncle Rain Cloud,* p. 1134; July, 2001, Carolyn Phelan, review of *Alien and Possum:*

Friends No Matter What, p. 2023; November 1, 2001, Ilene Cooper, review of *Clear Moon, Snow Soon,* p. 482; April 1, 2003, Gillian Engberg, review of *The Ancestors Are Singing,* p. 1406; September 1, 2003, Hazel Rochman, review of *A Kenyan Christmas,* p. 134; November 1, 2003, Ed Sullivan, review of *The Mummy's Mother,* p. 497, and Carolyn Phelan, review of *Isabel's House of Butterflies,* p. 600; January 1, 2005, Gillian Engberg, review of *Chicken in the Kitchen,* p. 870; June 1, 2006, Gillian Engberg, review of *Angel City,* p. 84; August, 2007, Gillian Engberg, review of *Bone by Bone by Bone,* p. 68, and Hazel Rochman, review of *Off to Kindergarten,* p. 83; December 15, 2008, Carolyn Phelan, review of *P Is for Piñata: A Mexico Alphabet,* p. 42 and Gillian Engberg, review of *Voice from Afar: Poems of Peace,* p. 43; August 1, 2009, Shelle Rosenfeld, review of *My Abuelita,* p. 80.

Bulletin of the Center for Children's Books, December, 1974, review of *Mole and Troll Trim the Tree,* p. 64; November, 2003, Deborah Stevenson, review of *A Kenya Christmas,* p. 109; January, 2004, Elizabeth Bush, review of *The Mummy's Mother,* p. 195; September, 2004, Deborah Stevenson, review of *The Worm Family,* p. 23.

Catholic Library World, March, 1973, review of *Mole and Troll,* p. 512.

Children's Book Review Service, December 19, 1990, Tiffany Chrisman, review of *I'm Gonna Tell Mama I Want an Iguana,* p. 39.

Horn Book, July-August, 1988, Hanna B. Zeiger, review of *Yonder,* p. 480; May-June, 1996, Nancy Vasilakis, review of *My Mexico/Mexico mío,* p. 345; November-December, 1996, Ann A. Flowers, review of *The Ghost of Nicholas Greebe,* pp. 725-726; January-February, 1997, Anne Deifendeifer, review of *Once in the Country: Poems of a Farm,* p. 74.

Junior Bookshelf, April, 1975, review of *Mole and Troll Trim the Tree,* p. 98.

Kirkus Reviews, December 15, 1974, review of *Mole and Troll Trim the Tree,* p. 1302; August 15, 1987, review of *Whale Song,* p. 1241; June 15, 1994, review of *Amber on the Mountain,* p. 847; August 1, 2001, review of *Alien and Possum: Friends No Matter What,* p. 1126; March 15, 2003, review of *The Ancestors Are Singing,* p. 469; June 15, 2003, review of *Go Track a Yak!,* p. 860; September 1, 2003, review of *Isabel's House of Butterflies,* p. 1126; October 1, 2003, review of *The Mummy's Mother,* p. 1225; November 1, 2003, review of *A Kenya Christmas,* p. 1317; December 15, 2003, review of *The Harmonica,* p. 1451; October 1, 2004, review of *The Worm Family,* p. 963; January 1, 2005, review of *Chicken in the Kitchen,* p. 53; March 15, 2005, review of *The Whole Green World,* p. 353; April 15, 2005, review of *The Spoon in the Bathroom Wall,* p. 475; November 1, 2005, review of *Noel,* p. 1194; May 1, 2006, review of *Sticky People,* p. 461; October 15, 2008, review of *Voice from Afar;* August 1, 2009, review of *My Abuelita.*

Publishers Weekly, May 7, 1979, review of *Little Mouse Nibbling,* p. 83; June 16, 1994, review of *Amber on the Mountain,* p. 63; October 9, 1995, review of *Little*

Wild Parrot, p. 85; October 21, 1996, review of *The Magic Maguey,* p. 82; September 1, 1997, review of *Day of the Dead,* p. 103; March 30, 1998, review of *The Chizzywink and the Alamogoozlum,* p. 81; November 2, 1998, review of *Bigfoot Cinderrrrella,* p. 81; October 4, 1999, review of *The Ghost of Nicholas Greebe,* p. 77; November 8, 1999, review of *An Old Shell,* p. 67; January 31, 2000, review of *The Barn Owls,* p. 105; September 11, 2000, review of *Day of the Dead,* p. 93; September 25, 2000, review of *Desert Song,* p. 118; October 30, 2000, review of *Bigfoot Cinderrrrrella,* p. 78; February 26, 2001, review of *My Best Friend Bear,* p. 84; July 30, 2001, review of *Cat, What Is That?,* p. 83; September 24, 2001, review of *Clear Moon, Snow Soon,* p. 52, review of *Alien and Possum: Friends No Matter What,* p. 93; June 23, 2003, review of *Go Track a Yak!,* p. 66; September 22, 2003, review of *A Kenya Christmas,* p. 70; November 24, 2003, review of *The Mummy's Mother,* p. 65; May, 2004, Cris Riedel, review of *The Harmonica,* p. 116; December 6, 2004, review of *The Worm Family,* p. 58; February 28, 2005, review of *Chicken in the Kitchen,* p. 66; May 23, 2005, review of *The Spoon in the Bathroom Wall,* p. 79; September 26, 2005, review of *Noel,* p. 89; November 3, 2008, reviews of *P Is for Piñata,* p. 58, and *Voice from Afar,* p. 59; August 31, 2009, review of *My Abuelita,* p. 55.

School Library Journal, October, 1978, review of *Four Scary Stories,* p. 135; December, 1984, Kay McPherson, review of *The Witch's Hat,* p. 72; March, 2000, Sue Sherif, review of *The Barn Owls,* p. 208; June, 2000, Margaret Bush, review of *It's about Dogs,* p. 167; December, 2000, Daryl Grabarek, review of *Desert Song,* p. 112; April, 2001, Ann Welton, review of *Uncle Rain Cloud,* p. 113; August, 2001, Susan Marie Pitard, review of *My Best Friend Bear,* p. 154; September, 2001, Sharon McNeil, review of *Any Small Goodness,* p. 226; October, 2001, review of *Clear Moon, Snow Soon,* p. 66; November, 2001, Ruth Semaru, review of *Desert Dog,* p. 126; August, 2002, Kristin de Lacoste, review of *Alien and Possum Hanging Out,* p. 158; November, 2002, Kathleen Kelly MacMillan, review of *Gopher up Your Sleeve,* p. 127; April, 2003, Sharon Korbeck, review of *The Ancestors Are Singing,* p. 183; October, 2003, Virginia Walter, review of *A Kenya Christmas,* p. 64, and Jennifer Ralston, review of *Any Small Goodness,* p. 98, and Angela J. Reynolds, review of *The Mummy's Mother,* p. 168; November, 2003, Catherine Threadgill, review of *Go Track a Yak!,* p. 102; December, 2003, Ann Welton, review of *Isabel's House of Butterflies,* p. 117; February, 2005, John Sigwald, review of *The Worm Family,* p. 104; April, 2005, Nina Lindsay, review of *The Ancestors Are Singing,* p. 56, and Bethany L.W. Hankinson, review of *The Whole Green World,* p. 99; May, 2005, Corrina Austin, review of *Chicken in the Kitchen,* p. 86; June, 2005, Terrie Dorio, review of *The Spoon in the Bathroom Wall,* p. 117; June, 2006, Wendy Lukehart, review of *Angel City,* p. 120; July, 2006, Julie Roach, review of *Sticky People,* p. 79; July, 2007, Rachel G. Payne, review of

Off to Kindergarten, p. 78; December, 2008, Marilyn Taniguchi, review of *Voice from Afar,* p. 150; January, 2009, Sandra Welzenbach, review of *P Is for Piñata,* p. 92; August, 2009, Mary Landrum, review of *My Abuelita,* p. 78.

Teacher Librarian, March, 1999, Shirley Lewis, review of *Bigfoot Cinderrrrella,* p. 44.

Wilson Library Bulletin, September, 1992, Donnarae Mac-Cann and Olga Richard, review of *Slither McCreep and His Brother, Joe,* p. 90.

ONLINE

Harcourt Web site, http://www.harcourtbooks.com/ (February 23, 2011), interview with Johnston.

Penguin Group Web site, http://us.penguingroup.com/ (February 23, 2011), "Tony Johnston."

Stanford University Web site, http://www.stanford.edu/ (July-August, 2007), Sonja Bolle, "Children Will Listen: In Four Decades of Writing for Kids, Tony Johnston Has Learned That Nothing Trumps the Voice."*

K

KOHLER, Dean Ellis 1947-

Personal

Born January 25, 1947, in VA.

Addresses

Home—Hampton Roads, VA. *E-mail*—musicmill1@aol.com.

Career

Author and copywriter. Worked variously as a graphic designer, photographer, sound engineer, and television and radio broadcaster; owner of advertising and public relations company; works as a mobile disc jockey. Musician, performing solo and with bands including Dean and the Mustangs, Electric Banana, the Satellites, Spectrum, Mad Wax, Mousey Brown, and Big Bubba and the Blockbusters. *Military service:* U.S. Army; served in Vietnam as part of 127th M.P. Company, 1967.

Awards, Honors

Cybil Award nomination for Best Nonfiction, 2009, for *Rock 'n' Roll Soldier.*

Writings

(With Susan VanHecke) *Rock 'n' Roll Soldier: A Memoir,* foreword by Graham Nash, HarperTeen (New York, NY), 2009.

Sidelights

Dean Ellis Kohler has always loved music, and as a young teen he kept busy organizing bands that he fronted, guitar in hand. By the time he was in high school, Kohler and his band the Satellites had lined up a recording contract and were performing gigs in and around their Portsmouth, Virginia, home town. Kohler's teenage dreams of playing for larger audiences came to an end in the mid-1960s when he received notice that he was being drafted to fight for the U.S. Army in Vietnam. His experiences overseas, and his determination to share his music with others, are the focus of *Rock 'n' Roll Soldier: A Memoir,* which he coauthored with professional writer Susan VanHecke.

With a foreword by noted rock performer Graham Nash, *Rock 'n' Roll Soldier* takes readers back to 1967, the year Kohler completed basic training and joined the U.S. Army as part of the 127th Military Police Company. At the encouragement of the commander at his base near Qui Nhon, South Vietnam, he scouted out some instruments in town and taught fellow M.P.'s Jon Sugden, Mike Ioli, and Ben Jessen the rudimentary skills necessary to perform in a rock band. When the group—called the Electric Banana after a lyric in a pop song by Donovan—established a respectable play list of cover songs, they performed for G.I. audiences, their performances alternating with days of relentless guerilla fighting in the war's combat zone. "What started as a lark . . . ultimately became a lifeline for me and the band . . . ," Kohler recalled on his home page. "One moment we were going toe to toe with the Vietcong. The next we were crossing the deadly An Khe Pass to play 'We Gotta Get Outta This Place' for a crowd of cheering GIs." Through their sideline as rock musicians—the Electric Banana even cut a recording in Qui Nohn—Kohler and his bandmates "created our own bit of order out of the chaos of Vietnam, bringing some sense of normalcy to the surreal hell of war."

Reviewing Kohler's compelling memoir in *School Library Journal,* Dylan Thomarie wrote that *Rock 'n' Roll Soldier* "reads like an action-packed novel" on the strength of Kohler's conversational narrative style. "Scenes of panic and carnage alternate with the wild cheering of weary soldiers" in the author's war-era chronicle, observed Daniel Kraus, the *Booklist* critic describing the memoir as "a sober but ultimately inspiring read." Noting the author's "focus on overcoming adversity and creating positive situations," a *Kirkus Reviews* writer recommended *Rock 'n' Roll Soldier* for both "reluctant readers" and garage-band musicians, while Jon Guttman cited another potential audience. "Filled with personal variations on anecdotes that a good many vets will recognize, *Rock 'n' Roll Soldier* differs from most Vietnam entertainers' memoirs," the critic noted in *Vietnam* magazine; as veterans of the war will quickly realize, Kohler's role as a musician "took him in harm's way more often than did his regular MP duties."

Biographical and Critical Sources

BOOKS

Kohler, Dean Ellis, with Susan VanHecke, *Rock 'n' Roll Soldier: A Memoir*, HarperTeen (New York, NY), 2009.

PERIODICALS

Booklist, July 1, 2009, Daniel Kraus, review of *Rock 'n' Roll Soldier*, p. 49.
Bulletin of the Center for Children's Books, January, 2010, Elizabeth Bush, review of *Rock 'n' Roll Soldier*, p. 203.
Kirkus Reviews, July 1, 2009, review of *Rock 'n' Roll Soldier*.
School Library Journal, September, 2009, Dylan Thomarie, review of *Rock 'n' Roll Soldier*, p. 183.
Vietnam, February, 2010, Jon Guttman, review of *Rock 'n' Roll Soldier*, pp. 61-62.
Voice of Youth Advocates, December, 2009, Leah J. Sparks, review of *Rock 'n' Roll Soldier*, p. 430.

ONLINE

Dean Ellis Kohler Home Page, http://www.deanelliskohler. com (February 15, 2011).

*   *   *

KORMAN, Gordon 1963-

Personal

Born October 23, 1963, in Montreal, Quebec, Canada; son of Charles Isaac (an accountant) and Bernice (a journalist and author) Korman; married Michelle Iserson, 1996; children: Jay, Daisy, Leo. *Education:* New York University, B.F.A., 1985. *Hobbies and other interests:* Music, travel, sports.

Addresses

Home—Long Island, NY. *Agent*—Curtis Brown, Ltd., 10 Astor Pl., New York, NY 10003.

Career

Writer, 1975—.

Member

Writers Union of Canada, Canadian Society of Children's Authors, Illustrators, and Performers, Society of Children's Book Writers and Illustrators.

Awards, Honors

Air Canada Award, Canadian Authors' Association, 1981; Ontario Youth Award, International Year of the Youth Committee of the Ontario Government, 1985, for contributions to children's literature; Children's Choice Award, International Reading Association, 1986, for *I Want to Go Home!*, and 1987, for *Our Man Weston;* Markham Civic Award for the Arts, 1987; American Library Association (ALA) Editors' Choice selection and Best Book citation, both 1988, both for *A Semester in the Life of a Garbage Bag;* ALA Best Book citation, 1991, for *Losing Joe's Place;* Manitoba Young Readers' Choice selection, 1992, for *The Zucchini Warriors;* Our Choice citation, Canadian Children's Book Center, 1992, for *The Twinkie Squad;* numerous readers' choice awards and state reading association prizes.

Writings

FOR CHILDREN

Who Is Bugs Potter?, Scholastic (New York, NY), 1980.
I Want to Go Home!, Scholastic (New York, NY), 1981, reprinted, Scholastic Canada (Markham, Ontario, Canada), 2004.
Our Man Weston, Scholastic (New York, NY), 1982.
Bugs Potter: Live at Nickaninny, Scholastic (New York, NY), 1983.
No Coins, Please, Scholastic (New York, NY), 1984, reprinted, Scholastic Canada (Markham, Ontario, Canada), 2005.
Don't Care High, Scholastic (New York, NY), 1985.
Son of Interflux, Scholastic (New York, NY), 1986.
A Semester in the Life of a Garbage Bag, Scholastic (New York, NY), 1987.
Radio Fifth Grade, Scholastic (New York, NY), 1989, reprinted, 2006.
Losing Joe's Place, Scholastic (New York, NY), 1990.
(With Bernice Korman) *The D-minus Poems of Jeremy Bloom*, Scholastic (New York, NY), 1992.
The Twinkie Squad, Scholastic (New York, NY), 1992.
The Toilet Paper Tigers, Scholastic (New York, NY), 1993.
Why Did the Underwear Cross the Road?, Scholastic (New York, NY), 1994.
The Chicken Doesn't Skate, Scholastic (New York, NY), 1996.
The Last-place Sports Poems of Jeremy Bloom, Scholastic (New York, NY), 1996.

Liar, Liar, Pants on Fire!, illustrated by JoAnn Adinolfi, Scholastic (New York, NY), 1997.

The Sixth-Grade Nickname Game, Scholastic Canada (Toronto, Ontario, Canada), 1998.

No More Dead Dogs, Hyperion (New York, NY), 2000.

Son of the Mob, Scholastic Canada (Markham, Ontario, Canada), 2002.

Hollywood Hustle (sequel to *Son of the Mob*), Hyperion (New York, NY), 2003.

Maxx Comedy: The Funniest Kid in America, Hyperion (New York, NY), 2003.

Jake Reinvented, Hyperion (New York, NY), 2003.

Great Gatsby Novel, Hyperion (New York, NY), 2003.

(With Kathy Burkett) *Clue Me In! The Detective Work of Ethan Flask and Professor Von Offel,* Scholastic (New York, NY), 2003.

Born to Rock, Hyperion (New York, NY), 2006.

(With R.L. Stine and Katherine A. Applegate) *Tales of Suspense for Boys,* Scholastic (New York, NY), 2006.

The Juvie Three, Hyperion (New York, NY), 2008.

Schooled, Hyperion (New York, NY), 2008.

One False Note (book two of multi-author "Thirty-nine Clues" series), Scholastic (New York, NY), 2009.

Pop, Balzer & Bray (New York, NY), 2009.

The Emperor's Code (book eight of multi-author "Thirty-nine Clues" series), Scholastic (New York, NY), 2010.

"MACDONALD HALL" SERIES

This Can't Be Happening at Macdonald Hall!, illustrated by Affie Mohammed, Scholastic (New York, NY), 1977.

Go Jump in the Pool!, illustrated by Lea Daniel, Scholastic (New York, NY), 1979.

Beware the Fish!, illustrated by Lea Daniel, Scholastic (New York, NY), 1980, reprinted, Scholastic Canada (Markham, Ontario, Canada), 2003.

The War with Mr. Wizzle, Scholastic (New York, NY), 1982, published as *The Wizzle War,* Scholastic Canada (Markham, Ontario, Canada), 2003.

The Zucchini Warriors, Scholastic (New York, NY), 1988, reprinted, Scholastic Canada (Markham, Ontario, Canada), 2004.

Macdonald Hall Goes Hollywood, Scholastic (New York, NY), 1991, published as *Lights, Camera, Disaster!,* Scholastic Canada (Markham, Ontario, Canada), 2004.

Something Fishy at Macdonald Hall, Scholastic (New York, NY), 1995, published as *The Joke's on Us,* Scholastic Canada (Toronto, Ontario, Canada), 2004.

"MONDAY NIGHT FOOTBALL CLUB" NOVEL SERIES

Quarterback Exchange: I Was John Elway, Hyperion (New York, NY), 1997.

Running Back Conversion: I Was Barry Sanders, Hyperion (New York, NY), 1997.

The Super Bowl Switch: I Was Dan Marino, Hyperion (New York, NY), 1997.

Heavy Artillery: I Was Junior Seau, Hyperion (New York, NY), 1997.

Ultimate Scoring Machine: I Was Jerry Rice, Hyperion (New York, NY), 1998.

(With James Buckley, Jr., and Brian C. Peterson) *NFL Rules: Bloopers, Pranks, Upsets, and Touchdowns,* Hyperion (New York, NY), 1998.

"NOSE PICKERS" SERIES

Nose Pickers from Outer Space!, illustrated by Victor Vaccaro, Hyperion (New York, NY), 1999.

Planet of the Nose Pickers, illustrated by Victor Vaccaro, Hyperion (New York, NY), 2000.

Your Mummy Is a Nose Picker, illustrated by Victor Vaccaro, Hyperion (New York, NY), 2000.

Invasion of the Nose Pickers, illustrated by Victor Vaccaro, Hyperion (New York, NY), 2001.

The Ultimate Nose-Picker Collection (omnibus), Hyperion (New York, NY), 2006.

"SLAPSHOTS" SERIES

Stars from Mars, Scholastic (New York, NY), 1999.

All-Mars All-Stars, Scholastic (New York, NY), 1999.

The Face-off Phony, Scholastic (New York, NY), 2000.

Cup Crazy, Scholastic (New York, NY), 2000.

"ISLAND" TRILOGY

Shipwreck, Scholastic (New York, NY), 2001.

Survival, Scholastic (New York, NY), 2001.

Escape, Scholastic (New York, NY), 2001.

Island Trilogy (contains *Shipwreck, Survival,* and *Escape*), Scholastic (New York, NY), 2005.

"EVEREST" TRILOGY

The Contest, Scholastic (New York, NY), 2003.

The Climb, Scholastic (New York, NY), 2003.

The Summit, Scholastic (New York, NY), 2003.

"DIVE" TRILOGY

The Discovery, Scholastic (New York, NY), 2003.

The Deep, Scholastic (New York, NY), 2003.

The Danger, Scholastic (New York, NY), 2003.

"ON THE RUN" SERIES

Chasing the Falconers, Scholastic (New York, NY), 2005.

The Fugitive Factor, Scholastic (New York, NY), 2006.

Now You See Them, Now You Don't, Scholastic (New York, NY), 2006.

The Stowaway Solution, Scholastic (New York, NY), 2006.

Public Enemies, Scholastic (New York, NY), 2006.

Hunting the Hunter, Scholastic (New York, NY), 2006.

"KIDNAPPED" TRILOGY

The Abduction, Scholastic (New York, NY), 2006.

The Search, Scholastic (New York, NY), 2006.

The Rescue, Scholastic (New York, NY), 2006.

"SWINDLE" SERIES

Swindle, Scholastic Press (New York, NY), 2008.
Zoobreak, Scholastic Press (New York, NY), 2009.
Framed, Scholastic Press (New York, NY), 2010.

Short stories have appeared in anthologies and magazines, including *From One Experience to Another,* edited by M. Jerry Weiss and Helen S. Weiss, 1997; *Connections,* edited by Donald R. Gallo, 1989; and SCOPE magazine. Creative developer, "Mad Science" series.

Korman's books have been translated into many languages.

Adaptations

The "Monday Night Football Club" series was adapted for the Disney Channel TV series, *The Jersey,* and a series of books have been produced based on that series.

Sidelights

Since publishing his first book when he was only fourteen years old, Gordon Korman has written a slew of best-selling novels for children and young adults. From his "Macdonald Hall" series about rambunctious boarding-school students Boots and Bruno to his "Swindle" series featuring a crime-solving youngster, Korman has "produced wonderfully warm and humorous novels for readers of all ages," wrote *Teacher Librarian* contributor Teri Lesesne. There is a successful "tried-and-true" Korman formula, according to Connie Tyrrell Burns writing in *School Library Journal:* "zany situations; a fast pace; likable, well-drawn characters; contemporary dialogue; and lots of humor."

Korman's slapstick humor, madcap adventures, and high-spirited, rebellious characters have helped make his books popular with school-age readers across Canada and the United States. "Many of Mr. Korman's plots revolve around the frustrations of rambunctious boys forced to submit to stuffy academic authorities," noted Leslie Bennetts in the *New York Times.* From sports stories with a comic edge to classroom tales bordering on the gross, Korman has made a major industry of humorous insurrection and adolescent empowerment.

Additionally, Korman has produced a number of thrilling action tales, including the works in the "Island" and "Dive" trilogies, as well as his "On the Run" series. These titles have proven every bit as popular as his humorous stories. "One of the things that works well in the adventure series is to take a quirky ensemble cast and put them into exciting and dangerous situations," Korman told told *Journal of Adolescent & Adult Literacy* interviewer James Blasingame. "The greater the extent to which these characters are 'everykids', the more likely it will be that readers will ride the adventure right along with them."

Korman was born in Montreal, Quebec, where his father worked as an accountant and his mother wrote an "Erma Bombeck-type column" for a local newspaper,

as he told Bennetts. In elementary and junior high school, Korman was always fond of writing—especially his own brand of zany stories and scenarios. "I wasn't a big reader for some reason," he remarked to Chris Ferns in *Canadian Children's Literature.* "But I always tried to put in creativity where I could: if we had a sentence with all the spelling words for that week, I would try to come up with the stupidest sentences, or the funniest sentences, or the craziest sentences I could think of."

A classroom assignment at the age of twelve developed into Korman's first published work, *This Can't Be Happening at Macdonald Hall!,* and the precocious Korman was only fourteen when his novel was published. A surprising best-seller, *This Can't Be Happening at Macdonald Hall!* set Korman on a course he has held to for over two decades and forty books. He continued writing while a student, finishing a book a year during summer vacations.

Set at a Canadian boarding school, *This Can't Be Happening at Macdonald Hall!* features Bruno Walton and "Boots" Melvin O'Neal. Roommates and best friends, the two get into their fair share of scrapes, usually led by the intrepid Bruno. So effective is the pair at their

Cover of Gordon Korman's humorous chapter book This Can't Be Happening at Macdonald Hall, *which features young sleuths Bruno and Boots.* (Illustration copyright © 1978 by Scholastic Inc. Reproduced by permission of Scholastic Inc.)

pranks that school headmaster Mr. Sturgeon—known fondly to the students as "The Fish"—decides to separate them. The ensuing plot recounts the duo's attempts to get The Fish to reunite them.

Bruno and Boots have made a number of appearances over the years. In *Go Jump in the Pool!,* another roommate, a rich hypochondriac, uses his stock-market wizardry to help raise money for a swimming pool at the school; in *Beware the Fish!* science whiz Drimsdale comes to the rescue when Boots and Bruno try to reverse the declining enrolment at their school. *The War with Mr. Wizzle* features the girls who reside across the road at Miss Scrimmage's Finishing School for Young Ladies. These same girls maintain a high profile in *The Zucchini Warriors,* in which the Macdonald Hall football team secretly recruits a female player to quarterback their pitiful team. When a movie company uses the school for a setting, Bruno tries to become a star in *Macdonald Hall Goes Hollywood,* a book described by a *Publishers Weekly* critic as a "rollicking tale" with "plentiful" laughs.

In his seventh Macdonald Hall outing, *Something Fishy at Macdonald Hall,* Korman's young heroes are upstaged by an anonymous prankster who delights in water balloons and blue dye in the swimming pool. When all fingers initially point to the prankish duo, Bruno and Boots are on the trail of the person trying to frame them. "Fans of the series will delight in another tale of madcap humor, peopled with some of the funniest, most ridiculous adults in middle-grade fiction," Burns concluded in a *School Library Journal* review. Dave Jenkinson, writing in *Quill & Quire,* commented that in *Something Fishy at Macdonald Hall* middle-grade readers "will not only find the usual zany humour they have come to expect from Korman but a well-crafted mystery as well." Jenkinson further noted: "As always, everything comes together in a tumultuous but satisfying conclusion that will leave readers eagerly awaiting Korman's next Macdonald Hall escapade."

Korman's early books relied to a large extent on wildly improbable coincidence and "contrivance of events," as the writer explained to Ferns. *Our Man Weston,* for example, is a wild adventure in which teenager Sidney West foils a spy, saves a high-tech Air Force plane, and solves several other mysteries, including the location of two missing golden retrievers. In the second "Bugs Potter" book, the erstwhile rock drummer is stranded with his family on a wilderness holiday, where he stages a concert and discovers a missing tribe of Native Americans. Korman's complex and comic plots demonstrate that "few writers are as adept at creating fast-paced and hilarious plots," as Peter Carver noted in *Quill & Quire.*

As Korman moved into adolescence and adulthood, receiving a B.F.A. degree in dramatic and visual writing from New York University in 1985, so did his characters, and he began to more fully develop their person-

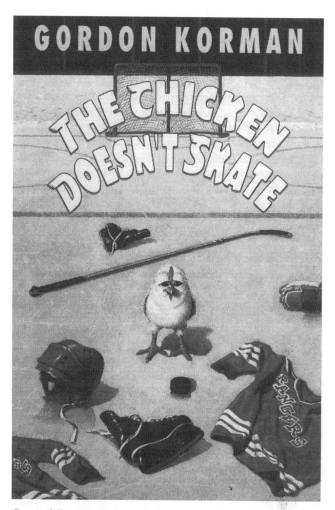

Cover of Korman's humorous elementary-grade novel The Chicken Doesn't Skate, *featuring artwork by René Milot.* (Illustration copyright © 1996 by René Milot. Reproduced by permission of Scholastic, Inc.)

alities and relationships with each other. His slapstick humor, although remaining a significant part of the action in his stories, began to share the stage with realistic depictions of adolescent life. In his 1987 novel, *A Semester in the Life of a Garbage Bag,* for instance, he introduces Raymond Jardine, whose desire to win a school contest (and therefore spend the summer in Greece rather than at his uncle's New Jersey fish-gutting plant) stimulates a chain of events in the life of his English-class partner, Sean Delancey. There is no shortage of absurdity in this novel. Among the characters who become involved in the plot are Sean's grandfather, a yo-yo prodigy, his younger sister, and his rival in romance, the muscular but not-so-bright Steve "Cementhead" Semenski. Along with the caricatures and absurdity, however, there are real teenage emotions and interrelations. Ferns commented in his review of *A Semester in the Life of a Garbage Bag* in *Canadian Children's Literature* that Korman's "lunatic comic inventiveness . . . is accompanied by a perceptive eye for the quirks of adolescent behaviour." The critic added that "the comedy and the observation almost seem to be pulling in different directions," and concluded that, although *A Semester in the Life of a Garbage Bag* finds him stretching into new, not yet mastered territory, "Korman's comic imagination is as fertile as ever."

Radio Fifth Grade, Korman's novel about a student-run radio show, contains the author's customary zany elements: a stubborn parrot, a school bully who insists on radio air time to read his short stories about kittens, and an adviser who is too busy reading pulp science fiction to help students with the show. The book was praised by Todd Morning in *School Library Journal* for its comic value. "This story works well on the level of sheer farce," Morning stated, going on to claim that "Korman is good at creating chaotic, if not always believable, situations." A *Publishers Weekly* critic found value beyond the book's humor, stating that *Radio Fifth Grade* is "feelingly written, and earns a place with the best middle-grade fiction; more than a romp, it has genuine charm."

Losing Joe's Place is the story of Jason Cardone and two friends who, at age sixteen, sublet Jason's brother's Toronto apartment while he is away in Europe. Everything that can go wrong does while the three boys strive to pay their rent each month. Although the story is filled with the farcical characters and chaotic situations for

Cover of Korman's humorous middle-grade novel Zoobreaker, *featuring artwork by Jennifer Taylor.* (Illustration copyright © 2009 by Jennifer Taylor. Reproduced by permission of Scholastic, Inc.)

which Korman is known, it offers more than comedy. Describing Jason, who narrates the tale, Shirley Carmony remarked in *Voice of Youth Advocates* that he "is a lovable adolescent whose hopes and fears are rather typical ones for a 16 year old boy. His humorous viewpoint is a pleasure." Jack Forman concluded in his *School Library Journal* review of *Losing Joe's Place:* "Surprisingly, it's not the quick twists and turns of the farcical plot that keep this very funny story moving. It's Jason's spirited narrative, his self-effacing sense of humor, and his finely tuned ear for the ridiculous that make these unbelievable antics work and create characters from these caricatures."

Korman creates several other characters who, while still battling against authority, also outfox their more successful peers. In *The Twinkie Squad,* for instance, he relates the goings on of a middle schools "Special Discussion Group" for difficult students. When Douglas Fairchild inspires his fellow "Twinkies" to rename and revision their group as the Grand Knights of the Exalted Karpoozi, the students quickly become embroiled in trouble and plots. "Again Korman has used humor to explore and explain the problems of growing up," *Voice of Youth Advocates* contributor Patsy H. Adams remarked. Praising the characters as "well developed and very familiar," Adams added that *The Twinkie Squad* could be "shared by parent, or grandparent and child." Similarly, *The Toilet Paper Tigers* recounts the transformation of a collection of misfits into a championship baseball team. "With their abundant quirks, the cartoonish characters are an engaging lot," wrote a *Publishers Weekly* critic in a review of this work.

More wacky plot elements and rambunctious characters are served up in novels such as *Why Did the Underwear Cross the Road?, The Chicken Doesn't Skate,* and *Nose Pickers from Outer Space* and its sequels. Justin, Jessica, and Margaret are determined to win the Good Deed Contest in *Why Did the Underwear Cross the Road?,* besting their peer competitors by catching car thieves. Reviewing this title in *School Library Journal,* Suzanne Hawley concluded that "Korman's book has a galloping plot full of humor, and young readers are sure to enjoy it." Reviewing the same book in *Quill & Quire,* Phyllis Simon noted that the author "delivers his signature brand of fast-paced humour and frenetic plot-making."

In *The Chicken Doesn't Skate* the action shifts south of the border to a Minnesota school. Milo's science project on food chains features Henrietta, a chicken that becomes the hockey team's mascot in their bid for a winning season. In *Booklist* Bill Ott commented that in his "genuinely funny, refreshingly unpretentious novel," "Korman tells the hilarious story of how a group of kids with little in common . . . are thrown together in the hullabaloo over Henrietta's fate." Zoe Bent is the biggest liar in the third grade in *Liar, Liar, Pants on Fire.* She lies to cover up former lies, and lies even when the truth will suffice. Then a friend convinces Zoe that she has a special gift—a vivid imagination. "The message that everyone is special in their own way is a bit heavy-handed," observed Robin L. Gibson in a *School Library Journal* review of the novel, "but it is, nonetheless, a message that children cannot hear too often."

In *The Sixth Grade Nickname Game* Jeff and Wiley are inseparable friends, born only hours apart and now joined at the hip emotionally and psychically. They love making up nicknames for their schoolmates, but when the new girl, Cassandra, steals both boys' hearts, best friends suddenly become competitors. "Korman is at his amusing best here," wrote Janice M. Del Negro in her review of *The Sixth Grade Nickname Game* for the *Bulletin of the Center for Children's Books*. "This is a funny, fast-paced grade-school romp that is going to cross gender lines with ease," Del Negro concluded. Reviewing the same novel in *Booklist*, Carolyn Phelan wrote that Korman's "story captures the ambience of sixth grade with humor and empathy," while Sheree Haughian noted in *Quill & Quire* that the author "has not lost his gift for satire."

In *Nose Pickers from Outer Space* ten-year-old Devin dismisses exchange student Stan as a real nerd and a nose picker to boot, until he discovers that Stan is actually an alien from the planet Pan on a mission to Earth. The boy's incessant nose picking is actually the activation of a nose computer, as Stan tries to convince his planet that Earth and not Mercury should become the in-spot vacation destination for Pan's inhabitants and thus avoid relocation of the planet to the back of the galactic beyond. "This lightweight sf for middle readers will likely delight Korman fans who usually can't get enough of his slapstick humor, frenzied action, and comic characters," concluded *Booklist* reviewer Karen Hutt in her appraisal of *Nose Pickers from Outer Space*. A contributor to *Publishers Weekly* remarked that "Korman's tongue is in his cheek as often as Stan's finger is in his nose, creating a light and silly caper that will, as the series obviously intends, bring on ample laughs." Intergalactic hijinks continue in *Planet of the Nose Pickers* and *Your Mummy Is a Nose Picker.*

Korman offers his comic take on the crime genre in *Son of the Mob* and its sequel, *Hollywood Hustle,* which center on Vince Luca, seventeen-year-old son of noted Mafia kingpin "Honest" Abe Luca. Although Vince, a gentle soul who longs for romance, does everything in his power to lead a normal life, his father's nefarious business interests often interfere. When he finally meets the girl of his dreams, Kendra Bightly, Vince is crestfallen to learn that Kendra's father is an FBI agent leading an investigation of the Luca family. Korman, noted *Horn Book* critic Peter D. Sieruta, "keeps things light by relating his tale in the first-person voice of a humorously sarcastic yet law-abiding wise guy." *Hollywood Hustle,* a "funny and somewhat over-the-top story," according to *School Library Journal* reviewer Karen Hoth, Vince is now studying film in Los Angeles. An unexpected visit from his mobster brother interrupts

his studies, and then he attends a suspicious union rally at the request of his roommate, Trey, a congressman's son. *Hollywood Hustle* features "lots of action and lots of laughs," according to Paula Rohrlick in *Kliatt.*

In *Born to Rock* an ultra-conservative high schooler with dreams of attending Harvard University discovers that his biological father is King Maggot, the lead singer of an infamous punk band. "What makes the book irresistible is its well-crafted plot, full of fate-reversing twists and bountiful humor," a *Publishers Weekly* contributor observed.

Korman's humorous "Swindle" series focuses on the exploits of Griffin Bing, an energetic problem-solver known to his friends as "The Man with the Plan." In *Swindle,* the debut title, Griffin enlists his schoolmates in an elaborate scheme to recover a rare and valuable baseball card from an unscrupulous collector. Writing in *Booklist,* Thom Barthelmess applauded the "silly, deceptively predictable" narrative. In *Zoobreak* Griffin and his companions rescue a pet monkey from a dishonest zoo owner, and here *Booklist* reviewer Diane Foote reported that "the action is fast and entertaining, with just the right amount of realistic drama to ring true." A missing Super Bowl ring is at the heart of *Framed,* the third installment in the "Swindle" series. "This mystery will draw readers in with its quickly developing plot that combines unconventional characters and situations with believable dialogue and plot twists," Cheryl Ashton commented in *School Library Journal.*

Korman turns from comedy to adventure with his "Island" trilogy, about the survivors of a shipwreck, and his "Everest" trilogy, which chronicles an ascent of the world's tallest mountain. Korman's "Dive" trilogy follows a group of misfit teenagers who are selected for an internship with the prestigious Poseidon Oceanographic Institute. In *The Discovery,* the opening work, Kaz, Dante, Adriana, and Star begin to question their roles on a mysterious research project, as well as the motivations of the other crew members, who seem more interested in finding treasure than identifying underwater caves. The contemporary narrative is interspersed with the story of Samuel Higgins, a cabin boy aboard the *Griffin,* a British privateer ship that prowled the Caribbean in 1665. "I thoroughly enjoyed writing the 1665 storyline," Korman told Blasingame. "I'd always wanted to try historical fiction, and this was kind of 'historical fiction lite.' The trick was placing those scenes in the modern story so that they shed just enough light on what was going on in the hunt for the treasure—without giving too much away." The teens' story continues in *The Deep,* a tale of sabotage beneath the ocean's surface, and concludes with *The Danger.* "Korman has a real winner with these books," declared Blasingame in reviewing the entire "Dive" saga.

Korman admitted to Lesesne that his adventure tales were "a deliberate effort to change styles." Noting that the shift from penning jokes to creating dramatic tension was difficult at first, he observed: "I've come to think that writing something serious is easier than humor, because the need to be funny—to create regular payoffs—isn't there. So it feels like a luxury just to tell the story, without having to worry about laughs." An added benefit of writing the adventure trilogies "is that they taught me to love research, and also to use it as an engine for creativity," the author noted. "That came out of necessity. I don't sail, climb mountains or SCUBA dive. Yet I needed to be able to write convincingly about these topics. So I went on massive reading blitzes, totally immersing myself in those worlds."

Korman's versatility continues to be a hallmark of his literary success. *Jake, Reinvented,* his tribute to F. Scott Fitzgerald's *The Great Gatsby,* concerns a high-school student whose vibrant persona masks a unsavory past. Reviewing the novel in *Kliatt,* Rohrlick described Korman as "an accomplished writer who succeeds in making this plot work in an updated context." In *The Juvie Three* a group of troublemakers hatch a complicated plan to help their amnesiac caregiver, who has removed them from juvenile detention. Jeffrey Hastings, writing in *School Library Journal,* called the work "a celebration of good, youthful intentions and a wholesome and fun treatment of what might otherwise be prohibitively gritty issues."

Raised on a commune by his hippie grandmother, an unconventional teen is forced to attend public school for the first time in *Schooled,* which contains "some memorable moments of comedy, tenderness, and reflection," as Carolyn Phelan noted in *Booklist.* A more somber tale, *Pop,* focuses on the relationship between a budding football star and his mentor, a former professional player suffering from the early onset of Alzheimer's disease. "The football scenes are riveting," a critic in *Kirkus Reviews* maintained, "but the poignant human drama more than holds its own."

With numerous works to his credit, Korman shows no signs of resting on his laurels. "My most worthwhile writing experiences have come when I've been willing to try something new," the author told Lesesne. His popularity with readers shows no signs of waning, critics note, as the author continues to introduce likable characters and craft plots that are blazing fast, making for rapid page-turning and frequent belly laughs. As Korman once told *SATA:* "My books are the kind of stories I wanted to read and couldn't find when I was ten, eleven, and twelve. I think that, no matter what the subject matter, kids' concerns are important, and being a kid isn't just waiting out the time between birth and the age of majority."

Biographical and Critical Sources

BOOKS

Children's Literature Review, Volume 25, Gale (Detroit, MI), 1991.

St. James Guide to Children's Writers, 5th edition, edited by Sara Pendergast and Tom Pendergast, St. James Press (Detroit, MI), 1999.

PERIODICALS

Booklist, November 15, 1996, Bill Ott, review of *The Chicken Doesn't Skate,* p. 588; October 15, 1998, Carolyn Phelan, review of *The Sixth Grade Nickname Game,* p. 422; August 19, 1999, Karen Hutt, review of *Nose Pickers from Outer Space,* p. 2058; November 1, 2002, John Peters, review of *Son of the Mob,* p. 485; June 1, 2003, Kathleen Odean, review of *Maxx Comedy: The Funniest Kid in America,* p. 1777; December 1, 2003, Jennifer Mattson, review of *Jake, Reinvented,* p. 659; May 15, 2005, Carolyn Phelan, review of *Chasing the Falconers,* p. 1658; March 1, 2006, Jennifer Hubert, review of *Born to Rock,* p. 81; August 1, 2006, Hazel Rochman, review of *The Abduction,* p. 78; August, 2007, Carolyn Phelan, review of *Schooled,* p. 71; January 1, 2008, Thom Barthelmess, review of *Swindle,* p. 84; September 1, 2009, Ilene Cooper, review of *Pop,* p. 105; November 1, 2009, Diane Foote, review of *Zoobreak,* p. 49.

Bulletin of the Center for Children's Books, November, 1998, Janice M. Del Negro, review of *The Sixth Grade Nickname Game,* p. 103.

Canadian Children's Literature (annual), number 38, 1985, Chris Ferns, interview with Korman, pp. 54-65; number 52, 1988, Ferns, "Escape from New Jersey," pp. 63-64.

Horn Book, January-February, 2003, Peter D. Sieruta, review of *Son of the Mob,* p. 78.

Journal of Adolescent & Adult Literacy, October, 2002, S. Graber, review of *No More Dead Dogs,* p. 181; September, 2003, T. Ryan Adney, review of *Son of the Mob,* p. 97; May, 2004, James Blasingame, interview with Korman, p. 704, and reviews of *The Discovery,* p. 702, *The Deep,* p. 703, and *The Danger,* p. 707.

Kirkus Reviews, June 1, 2003, review of *Maxx Comedy,* p. 806; September 1, 2004, review of *Hollywood Hustle,* p. 868; January 1, 2008, review of *Swindle;* August 15, 2008, review of *The Juvie Three;* August 15, 2009, review of *Pop.*

Kliatt, January, 2004, Paula Rohrlick, review of *Jake, Reinvented,* p. 8; November, 2004, Paula Rohrlick, review of *Hollywood Hustle,* p. 8; September, 2008, Paula Rohrlick, review of *The Juvie Three,* p. 14.

New York Times, July 24, 1985, Leslie Bennetts, "Gordon Korman: Old-Pro Author of 10 Books at 21," sec. 3, p. 17.

New York Times Book Review, February 14, 2010, Richard Sandomir, review of *Pop,* p. 15.

Publishers Weekly, June 30, 1989, review of *Radio Fifth Grade,* p. 106; March 15, 1991, review of *Macdonald Hall Goes Hollywood,* p. 59; July 26, 1993, review of *The Toilet Paper Tigers,* p. 73; August 2, 1999, review of *Nose Pickers from Outer Space,* p. 85; October 6, 2003, review of *Jake, Reinvented,* p. 86; June 16, 2003, review of *Maxx Comedy,* p. 71; May 2, 2005, review of *Chasing the Falconers,* p. 200; May

8, 2006, review of *Born to Rock*, p. 67; September 1, 2009, review of *Pop*, p. 59.

Quill & Quire, November, 1983, Peter Carver, "From the Gripping Yarn to the Gaping Yawn," p. 24; October, 1994, Phyllis Simon, review of *Why Did the Underwear Cross the Road?*, p. 44; August, 1995, Dave Jenkinson, review of *Something Fishy at Macdonald Hall*, p. 34; January, 1999, Sheree Haughian, review of *The Sixth Grade Nickname Game*, p. 46.

School Library Journal, September, 1989, Todd Morning, review of *Radio Fifth Grade*, p. 252; May, 1990, Jack Forman, review of *Losing Joe's Place*, p. 124; January, 1995, Suzanne Hawley, review of *Why Did the Underwear Cross the Road?*, p. 108; September, 1995, Connie Tyrrell Burns, review of *Something Fishy at Macdonald Hall*, p. 202; November, 1996, Burns, review of *The Chicken Doesn't Skate*, pp. 107-108; September, 1997, Robin L. Gibson, review of *Liar, Liar, Pants on Fire*, p. 185; November, 2002, Diane P. Tuccillo, review of *Son of the Mob*, p. 170; September, 2004, Karen Hoth, review of *Hollywood Hustle*, p. 209; August, 2005, Connie Tyrrell Burns, review of *Chasing the Falconers*, p. 129; September, 2006, Sharon R. Pearce, review of *The Abduction*, p. 209; August, 2007, Lauralyn Persson, review of *Schooled*, p. 118; December, 2008, Jeffrey Hastings, review of *The Juvie Three*, p. 130; November, 2009, Joanna K. Fabicon, review of *Pop*, and Kathy Kirchoefer, review of *Zoobreak*, both p. 113; September, 2010, Cheryl Ashton, review of *Framed*, p. 156.

Teacher Librarian, February, 2004, Teri Lesesne, interview with Korman, p. 45.

Voice of Youth Advocates, June, 1990, Shirley Carmony, review of *Losing Joe's Place*, p. 106; December, 1992, Patsy H. Adams, review of *The Twinkie Squad*, p. 281.

ONLINE

Gordon Korman Home Page, http://www.gordonkorman. com (February 15, 2011).

Scholastic Web site, http://www2.scholastic.com/ (February 15, 2011), "Gordon Korman."*

* * *

KURUSA 1942-

Personal

Born 1942, in Caracas, Venezuela; children: Daneiella, two sons. *Education:* McGill University, B.S. (anthropology).

Addresses

Home—Caracas, Venezuela.

Career

Anthropologist, editor, and author.

Awards, Honors

Horace Mann Book Awards Honor Book selection, 2009, for *The Streets Are Free.*

Writings

La calle es libre, illustrated by Monika Doppert, Ediciones Ekaré (Caracas, Venezuela), 1981, translated by Karen Englander as *The Streets Are Free,* Annick Press (New York, NY), 1995.

(With others) *El rabipelado burlado: Cuento de la tribu Pemon,* illustrated by Vicky Sempere, Editiones Ekaré (Caracas, Venezuela), 1995.

Lom y los nudones, illustrated by Isabel Ferrer, Ediciones Ekaré (Caracas, Venezuela), 2008 translated by Elisa Amado as *Lom and the Gnatters,* Groundwood Books (Toronto, Ontario, Canada), 2009.

Also translator of English texts into Spanish.

Biographical and Critical Sources

PERIODICALS

Kirkus Reviews, September 15, 2009, review of *Lom and the Gnatters.*

Resource Links, February, 2010, Zoe Johnstone, review of *Lom and the Gnatters,* p. 3.

School Library Journal, December, 2009, Kristine M. Casper, review of *Lom and the Gnatters,* p. 86.

ONLINE

Annick Press Web site, http://site.annickpress.com/ (February 15, 2011), "Kurusa."

Ediciones Ekaré Web site, http://www.ekare.com/ve/ (February 15, 2011), "Kurusa."*

L

LEIST, Christina

Personal
Born in Germany; immigrated to Canada. *Education:* University of Applied Sciences (Wiesbaden, Germany), degree (graphic design).

Addresses
Home—Vancouver, British Columbia, Canada. *E-mail*—chris@christinaleist.com.

Career
Illustrator and author of children's books. Worked as an art director in Frankfurt, Germany; freelance graphic designer and illustrator.

Member
Children's Writers and Illustrators of British Columbia Society.

Awards, Honors
ForeWord Book of the Year finalist in picture-book category, 2009, for *Jack the Bear;* Chocolate Lily Award finalist, and Christie Harris Illustrated Children's Literature Prize finalist, both 2010, both for *On My Walk* by Kari-Lynn Winters.

Writings

SELF-ILLUSTRATED

Jack the Bear, Simply Read Books (Vancouver, British Columbia, Canada), 2009.

Christina Leist (Photograph by Chris Spira. Reproduced by permission.)

ILLUSTRATOR

Tifany Stone, *Baaaad Animals,* Tradewind Books (Vancouver, British Columbia, Canada), 2006.
Vi Hughes, *The Graveyard Hounds,* Tradewind Books (Vancouver, British Columbia, Canada), 2008.
Kari-Lynn Winters, *On My Walk,* Tradewind Books (Vancouver, British Columbia, Canada), 2009.

Biographical and Critical Sources

PERIODICALS

Kirkus Reviews, September 15, 2009, review of *Jack the Bear.*

Quill & Quire, November, 2009, Chelsea Donaldson, review of *Jack the Bear.*

Resource Links, April, 2007, Linda Berezowski, review of *Baaaad Animals,* p. 9; December, 2009, Glen Kilback, review of *Jack the Bear,* p. 4; February, 2010, Rachelle Gooden, review of *On My Walk,* p. 61.

ONLINE

Christina Leist Home Page, http://www.christinaleist.com (December 31, 2010).

Tradewinds Books Web site, http://www.tradewindsbooks. com/ (February 15, 2011), "Christina Leist."*

*   *   *

LEWIN, Ted 1935-

Personal

Born May 6, 1935, in Buffalo, NY; son of Sidney (a retail jeweler) and Berenece (a homemaker) Lewin; married Betsy Reilly (an author and illustrator of children's books), 1963. *Education:* Pratt Institute of Art, B.F.A., 1956. *Hobbies and other interests:* Photography, painting, watching birds, travel.

Addresses

Home—Brooklyn, NY. *E-mail*—betsyandted@aol.com.

Career

Professional wrestler, 1952-65; artist and freelance illustrator, 1956—. *Exhibitions:* Solo exhibit at Laboratory of Ornithology, Cornell University, 1978, and Central Park 200 Gallery, New York, NY, 1994; joint exhibition with Betsy Lewin at National Center for Children's Illustrated Literature, Abilene, TX, 2002. *Military service:* U.S. Army, 1958.

Awards, Honors

Mark Twain Award, 1981, for *Soup for President* by Robert Newton Peck; Sandburg Award, 1985, for *The Search for Grissi* by Mary Francis Shura; Books Can Develop Empathy award, 1990, for *Faithful Elephants* by Yukio Tsuchiya; Great Stone Face award, 1991, for *The Secret of the Indian* by Lynne Reid Banks; *Boston Globe/Horn Book* Award, 1991, for *Judy Scuppernong* by Brenda Seabrooke; Hungry Mind Award, 1993, for *Sami and the Time of the Troubles* by Florence Parry Heide and Judith Heide Gilliland; Caldecott Honor Book, American Library Association (ALA), 1993, for

Ted Lewin (Photograph by Ed Tuttle. Reproduced by permission.)

Peppe the Lamplighter by Elisa Bartone; Notable Children's Trade Book in the Field of Social Studies designation, National Council for the Social Studies (NCSS)/ Children's Book Council (CBC), 1997, for *American Too* by Bartone; Best Books of the Year selection, Bank Street College, and Notable Children's Trade Book in the Field of Social Studies designation, NCSS/CBC, 1998, both for *Fair!;* Best Books of the Year selection, Bank Street College, and Notable Children's Trade Book in the Field of Social Studies designation, NCSS/ CBC, 1998, both for *Ali, Child of the Desert* by Jonathan London; Big Crit award for excellence in design, *Critique* magazine, 1998, for signage at Central Park Children's Zoo; Parents' Choice Award, 1999, for *Nilo and the Tortoise;* Top-of-the-List Youth picture book honor, *Booklist,* 1999, for *Barn Savers* by Linda Oatman High; (with Betsy Lewin) Notable Children's Trade Book in the Field of Social Studies designation, NCSS/CBC, 1999, for *The Storytellers;* Notable Book for Children designation, *Smithsonian* magazine, 1999, and Outstanding Science Trade Books for Children designation, National Science Teachers Association (NSTA)/CBC, 2000, both for *Gorilla Walk;* Alumni Achievement Award, Pratt Institute, 2000; (with Betsy Lewin) John Burroughs Award, American Museum of Natural History, and Outstanding Trade Books for Children Award designation, NSTA/CBC, both 2000, both for *Elephant Quest;* (with Betsy Lewin) ALA Notable Book designation, and Bank Street College Best Books selection, both 2009, both for *Horse Song;* (with Betsy Lewin) *Kirkus Reviews* Best Books of the Year designation, 2010, for *Stable.*

Writings

SELF-ILLUSTRATED

World within a World—Everglades, Dodd (New York, NY), 1976.

World within a World—Baja, Dodd (New York, NY), 1978.

World within a World—Pribilofs, Dodd (New York, NY), 1980.

Tiger Trek, Macmillan (New York, NY), 1990.

When the Rivers Go Home, Macmillan (New York, NY), 1992.

Amazon Boy, Macmillan (New York, NY), 1993.

I Was a Teenage Professional Wrestler (memoir), Orchard Books (New York, NY), 1993.

The Reindeer People, Macmillan (New York, NY), 1994.

Sacred River, Houghton (Boston, MA), 1995.

Market!, Lothrop, Lee (New York, NY), 1996.

Fair!, Lothrop, Lee (New York, NY), 1997.

The Storytellers, Lothrop, Lee (New York, NY), 1998.

Touch and Go: Travels of a Children's Book Illustrator, Lothrop, Lee (New York, NY), 1999.

(With wife, Betsy Lewin) *Gorilla Walk,* Lothrop, Lee (New York, NY), 1999.

Nilo and the Tortoise, Scholastic (New York, NY), 1999.

(With Betsy Lewin) *Elephant Quest,* Morrow (New York, NY), 2000.

Red Legs: A Drummer Boy of the Civil War, HarperCollins (New York, NY), 2001.

Big Jimmy's Kum Kau Chinese Take-Out, HarperCollins (New York, NY), 2001.

Tooth and Claw: Animal Adventures in the Wild, Harper-Collins (New York, NY), 2003.

Lost City: The Discovery of Machu Picchu, Philomel Books (New York, NY), 2003.

(With Betsy Lewin) *Top to Bottom Down Under,* Harper-Collins (New York, NY), 2005.

How Much?: Visiting Markets around the World, Harper-Collins (New York, NY), 2006.

At Gleason's Gym, Roaring Brook Press (New Milford, CT), 2007.

(With Betsy Lewin) *Horse Song: The Naadam of Mongolia,* Lee & Low (New York, NY), 2008.

(With Betsy Lewin) *Balarama: A Royal Elephant,* Lee & Low (New York, NY), 2009.

Stable, Roaring Brook Press (New York, NY), 2010.

ILLUSTRATOR

Jack McClellan, Millard Black, and Sid Norris, adapters, *A Blind Man Can!,* Houghton Mifflin (Boston, MA), 1968.

Wyatt Blassingame, *The Look-It-up Book of Presidents,* Random House (New York, NY), 1968.

Jack McClellan, Millard Black, and Sheila Flume Taylor, *Up, out, and Over!,* Houghton Mifflin (Boston, MA), 1969.

George S. Trow, *Meet Robert E. Lee,* Random House (New York, NY), 1969.

Margaret T. Burroughs, *Jasper, the Drummin' Boy,* Follett (New York, NY), 1970.

Janet H. Ervin, *More than Half Way There,* Follett (New York, NY), 1970.

Donald W. Cox, *Pioneers of Ecology,* Hammond, 1971.

Nellie Burchardt, *A Surprise for Carlotta,* Franklin Watts (New York, NY), 1971.

Darrell A. Rolerson, *Mr. Big Britches,* Dodd (New York, NY), 1971.

Gene Smith, *The Visitor,* Cowles, 1971.

Betty Horvath, *Not Enough Indians,* Franklin Watts (New York, NY), 1971.

Maurine H. Gee, *Chicano, Amigo,* Morrow (New York, NY), 1972.

Rose Blue, *Grandma Didn't Wave Back,* Franklin Watts (New York, NY), 1972.

Michael Capizzi, *Getting It All Together,* Delacorte (New York, NY), 1972.

Rose Blue, *A Month of Sundays,* Franklin Watts (New York, NY), 1972.

Rita Micklish, *Sugar Bee,* Delacorte (New York, NY), 1972.

Darrell A. Rolerson, *In Sheep's Clothing,* Dodd (New York, NY), 1972.

Rose Blue, *Nikki 108,* Franklin Watts (New York, NY), 1972.

Charlotte Gantz, *Boy with Three Names,* Houghton Mifflin (Boston, MA), 1973.

William MacKellar, *The Ghost of Grannoch Moor,* Dodd (New York, NY), 1973.

Marjorie M. Prince, *The Cheese Stands Alone,* Houghton Mifflin (Boston, MA), 1973.

Marian Rumsey, *Lion on the Run,* Morrow (New York, NY), 1973.

Darrell A. Rolerson, *A Boy Called Plum,* Dodd (New York, NY), 1974.

Jean Slaughter Doty, *Gabriel,* Macmillan (New York, NY), 1974.

Gene Smith, *The Hayburners,* Delacorte (New York, NY), 1974.

Matt Christopher, *Earthquake,* Little, Brown (Boston, MA), 1975.

Patricia Beatty, *Rufus, Red Rufus,* Morrow (New York, NY), 1975.

Charles Ferry, *Up in Sister Bay,* Houghton Mifflin (Boston, MA), 1975.

Jean Slaughter Doty, *Winter Pony,* Macmillan (New York, NY), 1975.

S.T. Tung, *One Small Dog,* Dodd (New York, NY), 1975.

Rose Blue, *The Preacher's Kid,* Franklin Watts (New York, NY), 1975.

Scott O'Dell, *Zia,* Houghton Mifflin (Boston, MA), 1976.

Lynne Martin, *Puffin, Bird of the Open Seas,* Morrow (New York, NY), 1976.

Laurence Pringle, *Listen to the Crows,* Crowell (New York, NY), 1976.

Patricia Edwards Clyne, *Ghostly Animals of America,* Dodd (New York, NY), 1977.

Mildred Teal, *Bird of Passage,* Little, Brown (Boston, MA), 1977.

Marian Rumsey, *Carolina Hurricane,* Morrow (New York, NY), 1977.

Nigel Gray, *The Deserter,* Harper (New York, NY), 1977.

Robert Newton Peck, *Patooie,* Knopf (New York, NY), 1977.

Philippa Pearce, *The Shadow-Cage, and Other Tales of the Supernatural,* Crowell (New York, NY), 1977.

Helen Hill, Agnes Perkins, and Alethea Helbig, editors, *Straight on till Morning: Poems of the Imaginary World,* Crowell (New York, NY), 1977.

Rose Blue, *The Thirteenth Year: A Bar Mitzvah Story,* Franklin Watts (New York, NY), 1977.

Leslie Norris, *Merlin and the Snake's Egg: Poems,* Viking (New York, NY), 1978.

William MacKellar, *The Silent Bells,* Dodd (New York, NY), 1978.

Robert Newton Peck, *Soup for President,* Knopf (New York, NY), 1978.

William MacKellar, *The Witch of Glen Gowrie,* Dodd (New York, NY), 1978.

Anne E. Crompton, *A Woman's Place,* Little, Brown (Boston, MA), 1978.

Margaret Goff Clark, *Barney and the UFO,* Dodd (New York, NY), 1979.

Patricia Edwards Clyne, *Strange and Supernatural Animals,* Dodd (New York, NY), 1979.

Robert Newton Peck, *Hub,* Knopf (New York, NY), 1979.

David Stemple, *High Ridge Gobbler: A Story of the American Wild Turkey,* Collins (New York, NY), 1979.

Jean Slaughter Doty, *Can I Get There by Candlelight?,* Macmillan (New York, NY), 1980.

Rose Blue, *My Mother, the Witch,* McGraw (New York, NY), 1980.

Margaret Goff Clark, *Barney in Space,* Dodd (New York, NY), 1981.

Francine Jacobs, *Bermuda Petrel: The Bird That Would Not Die,* Morrow (New York, NY), 1981.

Mark Twain, *The Adventures of Tom Sawyer,* Wanderer Books, 1982.

Margaret Goff Clark, *Barney on Mars,* Dodd (New York, NY), 1983.

Eleanor Clymer, *The Horse in the Attic,* Bradbury Press (New York, NY), 1983.

Priscilla Homola, *The Willow Whistle,* Dodd (New York, NY), 1983.

Enid Bagnold, *National Velvet,* Morrow (New York, NY), 1985.

R.R. Knudson, *Babe Didrikson, Athlete of the Century,* Viking Kestrel (New York, NY), 1985.

Mary Francis Shura, *The Search for Grissi,* Dodd (New York, NY), 1985.

Frances Wosmek, *A Brown Bird Singing,* Lothrop, Lee (New York, NY), 1986.

Patricia Reilly Giff, *Mother Teresa, Sister to the Poor,* Viking Kestrel (New York, NY), 1986.

Elizabeth Simpson Smith, *A Dolphin Goes to School: The Story of Squirt, a Trained Dolphin,* Morrow (New York, NY), 1986.

Scott O'Dell, *The Serpent Never Sleeps: A Novel of Jamestown and Pocahontas,* Houghton Mifflin (Boston, MA), 1987.

Susan Saunders, *Margaret Mead: The World Was Her Family,* Viking Kestrel (New York, NY), 1987.

Kathleen V. Kudlinski, *Rachel Carson: Pioneer of Ecology,* Viking Kestrel (New York, NY), 1988.

Yukio Tsuchiya, *Faithful Elephants: A True Story of Animals, People, and War,* translated by Tomoko Tsuchiya Dykes, Houghton Mifflin (Boston, MA), 1988.

Lynne Reid Banks, *The Secret of the Indian,* Doubleday (New York, NY), 1989.

Bruce Coville, editor, *Herds of Thunder, Manes of Gold: A Collection of Horse Stories and Poems,* Doubleday (New York, NY), 1989.

Leon Garfield, *Young Nick and Jubilee,* Delacorte (New York, NY), 1989.

Florence Parry Heide and Judith Heide Gilliland, *The Day of Ahmed's Secret,* Lothrop, Lee (New York, NY), 1990.

Scott O'Dell, *Island of the Blue Dolphins,* Houghton Mifflin (Boston, MA), 1990.

Gregory Patent, *Shanghai Passage,* Clarion (New York, NY), 1990.

Brenda Seabrooke, *Judy Scuppernong,* Cobblehill Books (New York, NY), 1990.

Jane Yolen, *Bird Watch: A Book of Poetry,* Philomel Books (New York, NY), 1990.

Margaret Hodges, *Brother Francis and the Friendly Beasts,* Scribner (New York, NY), 1991.

Megan McDonald, *The Potato Man,* Orchard Books (New York, NY), 1991.

Frances Ward Weller, *I Wonder If I'll See a Whale,* Philomel Books (New York, NY), 1991.

Corinne Demas Bliss, *Matthew's Meadow,* Harcourt (San Diego, CA), 1992.

Florence Parry Heide and Judith Heide Gilliland, *Sami and the Time of the Troubles,* Clarion (New York, NY), 1992.

Megan McDonald, *The Great Pumpkin Switch,* Orchard Books (New York, NY), 1992.

Frances Ward Weller, *Matthew Wheelock's Wall,* Macmillan (New York, NY), 1992.

Elisa Bartone, *Peppe the Lamplighter,* Lothrop, Lee (New York, NY), 1993.

Ann Herbert Scott, *Cowboy Country,* Clarion (New York, NY), 1993.

Sheldon Oberman, *The Always Prayer Shawl,* Boyds Mills Press (Honesdale, PA), 1993.

Louise Borden, *Just in Time for Christmas,* Scholastic (New York, NY), 1994.

Jan Slepian, *Lost Moose,* Putnam (New York, NY), 1995.

Mary Kay Kroeger and Louise Borden, *Paperboy,* Houghton Mifflin (Boston, MA), 1996.

Jane Yolen, *Sea Watch: A Book of Poetry,* Putnam (New York, NY), 1996.

Megan McDonald, *The Great Pumpkin Switch,* Orchard Books (New York, NY), 1996.

Elisa Bartone, *American Too,* Lothrop, Lee (New York, NY), 1996.

Jonathan London, *Ali, Child of the Desert,* Lothrop, Lee (New York, NY), 1997.

Jane Yolen, *The Originals*, Putnam (New York, NY), 1997.

Sheldon Oberman, *The Always Prayer Shawl*, Puffin Books (New York, NY), 1997.

Linda Oatman High, *Barn Savers*, Boyds Mills Press (Honesdale, PA), 1999.

Louise Borden, *A. Lincoln and Me*, Scholastic (New York, NY), 1999.

Faith McNulty, *How Whales Walked into the Sea*, Scholastic (New York, NY), 1999.

Corinne Demas Bliss, *The Disappearing Island*, Simon & Schuster (New York, NY), 2000.

Edward Grimm, *The Doorman*, Orchard Books (New York, NY), 2000.

Linda Oatman High, *Winter Shoes for Shadow Horse*, Boyds Mills Press (Honesdale, PA), 2001.

Tony Johnston, *Sunsets of the West*, Putnam (New York, NY), 2002.

Linda Oatman High, *The Girl on the High-diving Horse: An Adventure in Atlantic City*, Philomel Books (New York, NY), 2003.

T.A. Barron, *High as a Hawk: A Brave Girl's Historic Climb*, Philomel Books (New York, NY), 2004.

Ralph Helfer, *The World's Greatest Elephant*, Philomel Books (New York, NY), 2006.

Eve Bunting, *One Green Apple*, Clarion (New York, NY), 2006.

Dori Chaconas, *Pennies in a Jar*, Peachtree (Atlanta, GA), 2007.

Marion Dane Bauer, *The Longest Night*, Holiday House (New York, NY), 2009.

Illustrations have also appeared in periodicals, including *Boy's Life, Ladies' Home Journal, Seventeen,* and *Reader's Digest.*

Sidelights

Author and illustrator Ted Lewin has been inspired in his career by his lifelong love of nature. Married to fellow author/illustrator and sometime collaborator Betsy Lewin, he creates engaging self-illustrated books for children and young adults, among them *Tiger Trek, Lost City: The Discovery of Machu Picchu, At Gleason's Gym,* and *Stable.* "I am a deeply concerned environmentalist and conservationist," Lewin once noted, adding that both he and his wife travel "to wilderness areas around the world for both graphic and literary material." The result of these travels can bee seen in a list of their collaborative, nature-themed books that includes *Gorilla Walk, Horse Song: The Naadam of Mongolia,* and *Balarama: A Royal Elephant.*

As an author, Lewin has been praised for the poetic quality he brings to his texts, and his plots draw from his extensive knowledge of and concern for wildlife and its habitats throughout the world. As an illustrator, his work is characterized by its realistic detail, and his award-winning paintings have enhanced texts by a wide variety of writers. Praising Lewin's watercolor art for Tony Johnston's *Sunsets of the West,* a *Kirkus Reviews* writer noted that the illustrator's paintings feature "characters and scenery . . . infused with life," while *School*

Library Journal writer Rosalyn Pierini maintained that "prairie and mountain vistas are well served by Lewin's majestic, detailed paintings." Ralph Helfer's *The World's Greatest Elephant,* a true story of a circus elephant named Modoc who befriends a lonely orphan, is brought to life by Lewin in what *Booklist* critic Hazel Rochman described as "stunning . . . depictions of the bond between the lifelong friends, the exhilarating public performances, the wrenching partings, and the loving reunion years later." In Marion Dane Bauer's "stunningly crafted" picture book *The Longest Night* Lewin's large-format illustrations capture the passage of the winter solstice and allow readers to become "a participant in this annual ritual of nature," according to *Booklist* critic Carolyn Phelan

As a young boy growing up in upstate New York, Lewin dreamed of becoming an artist. "Not a policeman, fireman, or doctor—an artist," he recalled in his autobiography, *I Was a Teenage Professional Wrestler.* "I remember working first with a metal-armed copying toy I got for Christmas, then the Magic-Pad, on which you could pull up a flap and make whatever you'd drawn disappear." With the encouragement of his family, Lewin practiced drawing by copying photographs, illus-

Lewin's illustration projects include creating the detailed artwork for Rose Blue's story in **Grandma Didn't Wave Back.** (Franklin Watts, Inc., 1972. Reproduced by permission of the illustrator.)

trations from children's books, and even a portrait of President Harry S Truman, for which he received a personal letter from the White House.

By the time Lewin graduated from high school, he had made plans to study art at Pratt Institute in Brooklyn. Because paying for school and living expenses would be expensive, he established the secondary career that would help support him for almost fifteen years: professional wrestling. Lewin had attended professional matches with his family for many years, and his older brother Donn had become a wrestler after serving in the U.S. Marines during World War II. With the aid of his brother and the many contacts his family had made in the sport over the years, the seventeen year old began wrestling during summers and at night during the school year. In his autobiography, Lewin recalled his dual life, alternating between art classes and wrestling matches: "Every day I had classes in two-dimensional design, three-dimensional design, and figure drawing. Around me, the light-filled, high-ceilinged studio would be electric with concentrated effort. . . . I would see a great play of light and shadow—in a sense, not so different from what I'd seen in the charged, dramatic atmosphere of a wrestling arena. The medium was different, that's all."

"More a series of vignettes than an autobiography," as *Bulletin of the Center for Children's Books* writer Deborah Stevenson described it, *I Was a Teenage Professional Wrestler* details Lewin's involvement with the sport and provides portraits—written and painted—of the many wrestlers he met during his career. "It is a fascinating story that leaves the reader wanting to learn more about both Lewin and the other wrestlers," noted Patrick Jones in the *Voice of Youth Advocates*. In recreating a different era, Lewin describes the wrestlers "quite masterfully in words, then he brings them to life with old black and white photographs, drawings and paintings." *School Library Journal* contributor Todd Morning likewise praised Lewin's "surprisingly funny and affectionate" remembrances, as well as the author's combination of "vivid" artwork and human stories. "The artist's sensibility and eye for detail are always in evidence," the critic concluded. "His talent in this realm is truly formidable."

After earning his bachelor of fine arts degree, Lewin continued wrestling as he slowly built a career as a freelance artist. He began with magazine work, and by the late 1960s had begun illustrating children's books. In 1976 Lewin debuted his own book series, "World within a World," which focuses on wildlife in several regions visited by the author; the series has received high praise for both Lewin's text and his illustrations. The first volume in the series, *World within a World—Everglades*, is based on observations of the plant and animal life in the area made by Lewin over a five-year period. *World within a World—Baja* describes elephant seals and details the annual migration of the California gray whales. Of the volume on the Pribilof Islands,

Detailed paintings such as "Souk in Marrekesh" capture Lewin's impressions during his many travels throughout the world. (Reproduced by permission.)

which highlights the precarious fate of the seals who bear and raise their young on these Alaskan coastal islands, a reviewer from *Booklist* called Lewin's prose "elegant and uncompromising," adding that "the evocation of this small corner of the world is strong."

Many of Lewin's self-authored books are inspired by trips he has made while exploring planet Earth. He describes an outing spent riding on the back of an elephant through one of India's national parks in *Tiger Trek*, while other travel books include *The Reindeer People*, *Sacred River*, and *Tooth and Claw: Animal Adventures in the Wild*. Joan McGrath, reviewing *Tiger Trek* for *School Library Journal*, deemed the book "gorgeous" and "far above the ordinary." A similar journey is documented in *When the Rivers Go Home*, which describes Lewin's trip through a large swamp in central Brazil called the Pantanal. *When the Rivers Go Home* also received praise for its watercolor paintings, a *Kirkus Reviews* writer describing Lewin's work as "lovely" and "evocative." In *Amazon Boy* Lewin's "light-filled pictures, dense with detail, reinforce the theme that the riches of the rain forest must be protected," according to *School Library Journal* contributor Kathleen Odean.

Readers are carried on a trip to the South-American rain forest in Lewin's original picture book **Amazon Boy.** (Reproduced by permission of the illustrator.)

In *The Reindeer People* Lewin introduces readers to Ola, a Sami reindeer herdsman from Lapland, a remote area north of the Arctic Circle. In addition to describing Ola's unique line of work—herding reindeer—the book also describes favorite pastimes of the Sami people—racing reindeer—and a traditional wedding blended with contemporary flavor. "The author's highly descriptive prose is as luxurious as a reindeer coat, and his finely detailed, snapshot-style watercolors will engage readers of any age," enthused a *Publishers Weekly* reviewer. Describing *Sacred River,* based on a trip Lewin made to India, *Horn Book* contributor Maria B. Salvadore wrote that the author's "descriptive, fluid, and straightforward text combines with richly detailed full-color illustrations to describe a pilgrimage to the Ganges River in the Indian city of Benares."

In *Gorilla Walk* the Lewins chronicle their 1997 trip to Uganda to view the mountain gorillas that live there. The book was praised for its "handsome paintings and carefully focused text" by *Horn Book* critic Margaret A. Bush, the critic adding that the work presents "intriguing glimpses of both the rarely seen animals and the ambiguities of ecotourism." *Elephant Quest* also take the couple to Africa, while in *Top to Bottom Down Un-*

der they explore the vast continent of Australia, ranging from Kakadu National Park to Australia's Kangaroo Island. Illustrated with Lewin's paintings and his wife's field sketches, *Top to Bottom Down Under* was praised by *School Library Journal* contributor Patricia Manning as an "eye-catching and informative . . . treat for animal lovers and adventurers alike." Citing Lewin's "striking, realistic" watercolors and noting the inclusion of animal facts, *Booklist* reviewer Karin Snelson also lauded the work, noting that *Top to Bottom Down Under* allows readers to accompany the creative couple on a "contagiously cheerful Aussie expedition."

The Lewins continue to share their around-the-world travels in *Horse Song,* which profiles a young jockey who races horses at Naadam, in the outer reaches of Asia, in an athletic competition that is almost as old as the Olympics. In this summer sporting festival, tribes from throughout the region gather and compete in sports ranging from archery and wrestling to racing half-wild horses. Nine-year-old Tamir is one of these jockeys—all are children because of their small stature—and through their friendship with the boy and his family the Lewins learn how horses are captured, raised, and trained for the Naadam event. In *Horse Song* "the

Lewins give a heart-pounding, moment-by-moment account of Tamir's race," wrote Gillian Engberg in *Booklist,* and their "color-washed sketches and beautiful full-page" illustrations "will truly capture readers' attention." "The book's glory is its art," asserted *Horn Book* critic Johanna Rudge Long, citing Lewin's detailed "desert vistas." Writing in *School Library Journal,* Heide Piehler also praised the book's art, recommending *Horse Song* as "a dynamic view of a culture rarely portrayed in children's books."

Set in Mysore, India, a stopping point of the globe-trotting Lewins, *Balarama* follows the life of a young elephant as it grows up in the Karapur Forest, becomes captured, and is trained to become the star of Mysore's yearly Dasara celebration. Young Balarama eventually takes the place of its predecessor, the elephant Drona, who led the procession of royal elephants for fifteen years until its death in 1997. Reviewing *Balarama* in *Horn Book,* Long deemed the work a "gorgeous" travelogue and added that "pageantry and noble beasts alike are vividly realized in Ted Lewin's signature watercolors." The "pathos and tension" in the Lewins' richly told tale was commended by Paula Willey in *School Library Journal,* while Hazel Rochman noted in *Booklist* that "the combination of compelling travelogue and images is immediate and dramatic."

A perusal of the adventurous author/illustrator's *Tooth and Claw* prompted *Horn Book* critic Danielle J. Ford to exclaim: "Thank goodness Ted Lewin has survived" his travels. Calling Lewin a "gifted storyteller," Ford praised the author's presentation of fourteen "suspenseful, often terrifying, and sometimes quite funny experiences" Lewin and his fellow travelers have had during a life of globe-hopping. Lewin comes face to face with North American grizzly bears, Bengal tigers, African snakes and other grassland creatures, Florida bull sharks, and many other creatures, all told in a travelogue format. Ford praised the work as "outstanding nature storytelling," while in *Kirkus Reviews* a critic explained that, by hauling a rucksack full of drawing supplies with him, Lewin was able to highlight his "fascinating" stories with his "typically wonderful drawings" and "on-site photographs." Echoing other praise, *School Library Journal* critic Pam Spencer Holley noted that *Tooth and Claw* will serve children as "a great read-aloud" for budding naturalists or "simply as a good adventure story."

In addition to narrative accounts, Lewin sometimes weaves his experiences into picture-book texts, such as *Market!* and *Fair!* In *Market!* he creates "paintings so vivid you can almost smell the market scents," according to Susan Dove Lempke in *Booklist.* In the book Lewin describes the various people, products, and atmosphere of six markets—from New York City to Nepal. Similar in focus, *Fair!* presents the many scenes and flavors of a typical country fair, including animal and food contests, games, rides, and fireworks. A *Kirkus Reviews* critic described *Fair!* as a "pulsing, panoramic

examination of a summertime ritual," and a *Publishers Weekly* reviewer asserted that "this visit to the fair [is] worth the price of admission." Lewin's fascination with the Galapagos Islands provided him with the setting for his fictional tale *Nilo and the Tortoise,* about a young boy who is stranded on one of the islands. In *Booklist* Stephanie Zvirin noted that Lewin's pictures once again are the main attraction of the book, capturing "the remoteness and beauty of the exotic place and some of its distinctive wildlife."

Several of Lewin's books focus on history, among them *Red Legs: A Drummer Boy of the Civil War* and *Lost City.* In *Red Legs* a nine-year-old boy accompanies his father to the reenactment of a U.S. Civil War battle where he plays the part of Stephen Benjamin Bertow, a young drummer boy who died during the fight. Noting Lewin's "brief yet stirring text" and evocative watercolors, a *Publishers Weekly* reviewer wrote that *Red Legs* expresses a "true passion for history" that might inspire similar enthusiasm in young readers. The fascinating story of the discovery of an ancient Incan city also proves arresting in Lewin's book about Hiram Bingham's 1911 jungle adventure. Based on Bingham's account of the discovery of the Andean city of Macchu Pichu, *Lost City* follows the explorer' path through the Andes, linking his tale to the dreams of a young Quechua boy that anticipate Bingham's arrival. Lewin "balances a compelling visual chronicle with sure storytell-

Lewin creates the detailed paintings that team up with the sketches by wife Betsy Lewin to illustrate their coauthored picture book **Balarama: A Royal Elephant.** (Lee & Low Books, 2005. Illustration copyright © 2005 by Ted Lewin. Reproduced by permission.)

ing," according to a *Publishers Weekly* critic, while in *Horn Book* Bush called Bingham's "tortuous journey richly rewarded is a good adventure story" brought to life by Lewin's "evocative" watercolor art.

Set in New York City, *At Gleason's Gym* transports readers to the place where famous pugilists such as Muhammad Ali and Jake La Motta once trained. In Lewin's self-illustrated story, a nine-year-old statewide champion boxer named Sugar Boy Younan weighs in at just over 100 pounds. Helped by his father, Sugar Boy works daily at the historic Brooklyn gym in the hopes that he too will achieve a similar measure of fame in the ring. In both pencil drawings and watercolor paintings, Lewin captures the energy of the place, and "sets the scene in fittingly staccato prose," according to a *Publishers Weekly* writer. Calling the book a "glorious tribute" to the many athletes who train at the gym, *Booklist* critic Ilene Cooper cited *At Gleason's Gym* for "text that is both moving and informative and . . . vibrant artwork so realistic that readers can practically smell the sweat."

Even closer to home, *Stable* focuses on Kensington Stables, an historic structure that is only minutes from the Lewins' home in Brooklyn. A remnant of the late nineteenth century, a time before automobiles when horses powered the city, Kensington Stables is one of the few city stables remaining. With each turn of the page, Lewin's book carries readers forward from the time when the clip-clop of horse hooves could be heard on city streets, pulling delivery wagons, carriages, and even water-filled fire engines to the modern world where the Kensington horses transport Sunday riders and equestrians-in-training along the trails of a nearby park. Calling *Stable* "an unusual offering," *Booklist* critic Phelan added that Lewin's book "gives a vivid sense of the passage of time" through paintings that are "beautiful in their use of light and shadow." The author/illustrator's "chatty prose summons the sounds and the sights of the stable," noted a *Publishers Weekly* writer, while in *School Library Journal* Jayne Damron recommended *Stable* for "horse-crazy readers."

Working from photos he shoots during his travels and then projects onto a screen in his studio, Lewin manages to retain much of the original realism and energy of scenes he has witnessed firsthand. A steady producer, he maintains a disciplined work regimen as well. His day begins at eight in the morning and continues without break into the afternoon. While he is at work in the upstairs of his New York brownstone, his wife, Betsy, works in her studio downstairs. In addition to creating the artwork for his own books, Lewin has also illustrated the texts of numerous other writers, among them *Peppe the Lamplighter* by Elisa Bartone, *Paperboy* by Mary Kay Kroeger, and Louise Borden, and *Sea Watch: A Book of Poetry* by Jane Yolen.

A Caldecott honor book, *Peppe the Lamplighter* focuses on a young Italian immigrant living in New York City who takes a job lighting gas lamps to help support his family. "Lewin's masterly watercolors express the swirling energy of the crowded streets as well as the intimate feelings and interactions of individual people," Rochman observed in her *Booklist* review of Barbara's story. Lewin also illustrated *American Too*, in which Bartone continues the young immigrant's adventures in his new country. *Paperboy*, "filled with carefully detailed watercolors," according to *Horn Book* contributor Elizabeth S. Watson, focuses on Willie Brinkman, a young paperboy living in Cincinnati in 1927. After boxing hero Jack Dempsey loses a major prizefight, Willie honors his commitment to sell newspapers proclaiming the defeat, despite his and the neighborhood's shock and disappointment. Rochman, writing in *Booklist,* declared that Lewin's watercolor illustrations here are "more exuberant than the artwork in Lewin's Caldecott Honor Book, *Peppe the Lamplighter.*" For his contribution to Yolen's *Sea Watch, Booklist* reviewer Lauren Peterson noted that "Lewin's trademark watercolors, fresh, realistic, and beautifully rendered, nicely complement the poetry."

About his career, Lewin once commented: "There are still so many stories out there waiting to be found and so many manuscripts by wonderful authors to take me on journeys I might never have made myself."

Biographical and Critical Sources

BOOKS

Lewin, Ted, *I Was a Teenage Professional Wrestler,* Orchard Books (New York, NY), 1993.
Silvey, Anita, editor, *Children's Books and Their Creators,* Houghton (Boston, MA), 1995.
Something about the Author Autobiography Series, Volume 25, Gale (Detroit, MI), 1998.

PERIODICALS

Booklist, January 1, 1981, review of *World within a World—Pribilofs,* p. 625; April 15, 1993, Hazel Rochman, review of *Peppe the Lamplighter,* p. 1522; December 15, 1993, Stephanie Zvirin, review of *The Always Prayer Shawl,* p. 750; October 1, 1994, Julie Corsaro, review of *The Reindeer People,* p. 322; June 1, 1995, Hazel Rochman, review of *Sacred River,* p. 1778; March 15, 1996, Hazel Rochman, review of *Paperboy,* p. 1269; April 15, 1996, Susan Dove Lempke, review of *Market!,* p. 1444; June 1, 1996, Lauren Peterson, review of *Sea Watch: A Book of Poetry,* p. 1716; August, 1996, Hazel Rochman, review of *American Too,* p. 1903; February 1, 1998, Hazel Rochman, review of *The Originals,* p. 917; April, 1998, Susan Dove Lempke, review of *The Storytellers,* p. 1332; May 31, 1999, Stephanie Zvirin, review of *Nilo and the Tortoise,* p. 93; January 1, 2002, Cynthia Turnquest, *Big Jimmy's Kum Kau Chinese Take Out,* p.

866; June 1, 2002, Carolyn Phelan, review of *Sunsets of the West*, p. 1738; January 1, 2003, Carolyn Phelan, review of *Tooth and Claw: Animal Adventures in the West*, p. 882; July, 2003, Gillian Engberg, review of *Lost City: The Discovery of Machu Picchu*, p. 1895; March 1, 2004, Ilene Cooper, review of *As High as a Hawk: A Brave Girl's Historic Climb*, p. 1204; January 1, 2005, Karin Snelson, review of *Top to Bottom Down Under*, p. 866; February 1, 2006, Hazel Rochman, review of *The World's Greatest Elephant*, p. 48, and Carolyn Phelan, review of *How Much? Visiting Markets around the World*, p. 52; June 1, 2006, Jennifer Mattson, review of *One Green Apple*, p. 74; September 1, 2007, Ilene Cooper, review of *At Gleason's Gym*, p. 133; October 1, 2007, Abby Nolan, review of *Pennies in a Jar*, p. 66; May 1, 2008, Gillian Engberg, review of *Horse Song: The Naadam of Mongolia*, p. 88; September 1, 2009, Gillian Engberg, review of *The Longest Night*, p. 98; November 15, 2009, Hazel Rochman, review of *Balarama: A Royal Elephant*, p. 36; October 15, 2010, Carolyn Phelan, review of *Stable*, p. 49.

Bulletin of the Center for Children's Books, June, 1993, Deborah Stevenson, review of *I Was a Teenage Professional Wrestler*, pp. 321-322; April, 1998, Betsy Hearne, review of *The Storytellers*, p. 286; January, 2002, review of *Big Jimmy's Kum Kau Chinese Take Out*, p. 177; September, 2003, Elizabeth Bush, review of *Lost City*, p. 23.

Horn Book, May-June, 1993, Margaret A. Bush, review of *Amazon Boy*, pp. 320-321; January-February 1996, Maria B. Salvadore, review of *Sacred River*, p. 99; September-October, 1996, Elizabeth S. Watson, review of *Paperboy*, p. 581; November-December, 1999, Margaret A. Bush, review of *Gorilla Walk*, p. 758; January 2001, review of *Elephant Quest*, p. 111; March-April, Danielle J. Ford, review of *Tooth and Claw*, p. 226; September-October, 2003, Margaret A. Bush, review of *Lost City*, p. 631; July-August, 2008, Joanna Rudge Long, review of *Horse Song*, p. 46; January-February, 2010, Joanna Rudge Long, review of *Balarama*, p. 102.

Kirkus Reviews, February 15, 1992, review of *When the Rivers Go Home*, pp. 257-258; July 1, 1997, review of *Fair!*, p. 1031; May 15, 1999, review of *Touch and Go*, p. 803; May 15, 2002, review of *Sunsets of the West*, p. 734; February 2, 2003, review of *Tooth and Claw*, p. 235; March 15, 2003, review of *The Girl on the High-diving Horse: An Adventure in Atlantic City*, p. 468; June 1, 2003, review of *Lost City*, p. 807; April 1, 2004, review of *High as a Hawk*, p. 324; February 15, 2005, review of *Top to Bottom Down Under*, p. 231; February 1, 2006, review of *The World's Greatest Elephant*, p. 132; June 1, 2006, review of *One Green Apple*, p. 569; August 15, 2007, review of *Pennies in a Jar*; April 15, 2008, review of *Horse Song*; August 1, 2009, review of *The Longest Night*; August 15, 2009, review of *Balarama*.

New York Times Book Review, January 17, 2010, Julie Just, review of *The Longest Night*, p. 17; October 14, 2007, review of *At Gleason's Gym*, p. 18.

Publishers Weekly, August 10, 1990, review of *The Day of Ahmed's Secret*, p. 444; October 26, 1990, review of *Bird Watch*, p. 71; April 17, 1993, review of *Peppe the Lamplighter*, p. 61; April 26, 1993, review of *Amazon Boy*, p. 78; October 24, 1994, review of *The Reindeer People*, p. 61; August 7, 1995, review of *Sacred River*, p. 460; April 29, 1996, review of *Market!*, p. 72; June 9, 1997, review of *Fair!*, p. 45; June 19, 2000, review of *The Disappearing Island*, p. 79; September 4, 2000, review of *The Doorman*, p. 107; December 11, 2000, review of *A. Lincoln and Me*, p. 86; March 19, 2001, review of *Paperboy*, p. 102; June 18, 2001, review of *Red Legs: A Drummer Boy of the Civil War*, p. 81; February 25, 2002, review of *Big Jimmy's Kum Kau Chinese Take Out*, p. 68; May 13, 2002, review of *Sunsets of the West*, p. 70; January 13, 2003, review of *The Girl on the High-diving Horse*, p. 60; June 2, 2003, review of *Lost City*, p. 51; June 21, 2004, review of *High as a Hawk*, p. 62; April 10, 2006, review of *The World's Greatest Elephant*, p. 71; July 23, 2007, review of *At Gleason's Gym* p. 68; September 17, 2007, review of *Pennies in a Jar*, p. 54; September 7, 2009, review of *Balarama*, p. 46; October 11, 2010, review of *Stable*, p. 44.

School Library Journal, March, 1990, Joan McGrath, review of *Tiger Trek*, p. 208; June, 1993, Kathleen Odean, review of *Amazon Boy*, pp. 80, 83; July, 1993, Barbara Peklo Abrahams, review of *Peppe the Lamplighter*, p. 56; July, 1993, Todd Morning, review of *I Was a Teenage Professional Wrestler*, p. 108; July, 1997, Jackie Hechtkopf, review of *Fair!*, p. 85; July, 2000, Kate McClelland, review of *The Disappearing Island*, p. 70; October 2000, Marianne Saccardi, review of *The Doorman*, p. 126; April, 2002, John Peters, review of *Big Jimmy's Kum Kau Chinese Take Out*, p. 114; July, 2002, Rosalyn Pierini, review of *Sunsets of the West*, p. 94; February, 2003, Carol Schene, review of *The Girl on the High-diving Horse*, p. 112; May, 2003, Pam Spencer Holley, review of *Tooth and Claw*, p. 173; June, 2003, Daryl Grabarek, review of *Lost City*, p. 163; November, 2003, Carol Fazioli, review of *I Was a Teenage Professional Wrestler*, p. 83; May, 2004, Laurie Edwards, review of *High as a Hawk*, p. 101; March, 2005, Patricia Manning, review of *Top to Bottom Down Under*, p. 196; January, 2006, Carol L. MacKay, review of *How Much?*, p. 120; February, 2006, Margaret Bush, review of *The World's Greatest Elephant*, p. 120; June, 2006, Marianne Saccardi, review of *One Green Apple*, p. 107; October, 2007, Joan Kindig, review of *At Gleason's Gym*, p. 121; October, 2007, Rachel Kamin, review of *Pennies in a Jar*, p. 110; June, 2008, Heide Piehler, review of *Horse Song*, p. 127; September 2009, Paula Willey, review of *Balarama*, p. 144; September, 2009, Susan Scheps, review of *The Longest Night*, p. 115; October, 2010, Jayne Damron, review of *Stable*, p. 100.

Social Education, January, 2001, Barbara J. Holt, review of *Faithful Elephants: A True Story of Animals, People, and War*, p. S9.

Voice of Youth Advocates, October, 1993, Patrick Jones, review of *I Was a Teenage Professional Wrestler*, p. 247.

ONLINE

Ted Lewin Home Page, http://www.tedlewin.com (February 15, 2011).

*   *   *

LOPEZ, Antonio Castro
See CASTRO L., Antonio

*   *   *

LOPEZ, Mario 1973-

Personal

Born October 10, 1973, in San Diego, CA; son of Mario (a municipal worker) and Elvia (a telephone clerk) Lopez; partner of Courtney Lane Mazza (a dancer and actress); children: Gia Francesca. *Religion:* Roman Catholic.

Addresses

Home—Burbank, CA.

Career

Actor and author. Television roles include: (as Mario) *Kids Incorporated* (series), 1984-86; (as Hector) *The Deacon Street Deer* (movie), 1986; (as car rental clerk) *The Last Fling,* 1987; (as A.C. Slater) *Saved by the Bell* (series) 1989-93, *Saved by the Bell: The College Years,* 1993-94, and movie spinoffs; (host) *Name Your Adventure,* 1992; (host) *Masters of the Maze,* 1995-96; (as Greg Louganis) *Breaking the Surface: The Greg Louganis Story* (movie), 1997; (as David Ruggles) *Killing Mr. Griffin* (movie), 1997; (as Bobby Cruz) *Pacific Blue* (series), 1998-99; (co-host) *The Other Half,* 2001-02; (co-host) *Pet Star,* 2002; (co-host) *ESPN Hollywood,* 2002; (host) *America's Most Talented Kid,* 2003; (as Antonio) *The Soluna Project* (movie), 2004; (as Dr. Christian Ramirez) *The Bold and the Beautiful* (soap opera), 2006; (as David Martin) *Holiday in Handcuffs* (movie), 2007; (as Marco) *Husband for Hire* (movie), 2008; (weekday host) *Extra,* 2008—; (host) *America's Best Dance Crew,* 2008; (as voice of Zeus the dog) *The Dog Who Saved Christmas* (movie), 2009; (host) *MTV's Top Pop Group;* (co-host) *Dating Factory;* (as voice of Zeus the dog) *The Dog Who Saved Christmas Vacation* (movie), 2010; and (as himself) *Mario Lopez: Saved by the Baby* (reality program), 2010. Guest star on television series, including: (as Tomás) *a.k.a. Pablo,* 1984; (as Mario) *Golden Girls,* 1987; *Resurrection Boulevard; Eve; The Bad Girl's Guide;* (as Dr. Mike Hamoui) *Nip Tuck,* 2006-10; (celebrity guest host) *Extra,* 2006—; (contestant) *Dancing with the Stars,* 2006; and (as police officer) *The George Lopez Show,* 2007. Host of television specials, including *Miss Teen USA,* 1998,

2003, 2007; *Miss America,* 2007, 2009, 2010; and *Miss Universe,* 2007. Film roles include: (as Felipe's friend) *Colors,* 1988; (as Jessie Mata) *Depraved,* 1996; (as Steve) *Fever Lake,* 1998; (as Ryan Murphy) *The Journey: Absolution,* 1997; (as Antonio Lopez) *Eastside,* 1999; (as Coach) *Big Brother Trouble,* 2000; (as Lehman) *A Crack in the Floor,* 2000; (as David Morales; and co-producer) *Outta Time,* 2002; and (as Juan Vallejo) *King Rikki,* 2002. Stage roles include: (as Zach) *A Chorus Line,* produced on Broadway, 2008. Guest speaker and host at celebrity and sporting events; boxing analyst for Top Rank Promotions.

Writings

FOR CHILDREN

(With sister Marissa Lopez Wong) *Mud Tacos!,* illustrated by Maryn Roos, Celebra Children's Books (New York, NY), 2009.

OTHER

(With Jeff O'Connell) *Mario Lopez's Knockout Fitness,* Macmillan (New York, NY), 2008.
(With Jimmy Pena) *Extra Lean: The Fat-burning Plan That Changes the Way You Eat for Life,* New American Library (New York, NY), 2010.
Extra Lean Family, New American Library (New York, NY), 2011.

Sidelights

A veteran of television, film, and Broadway, where he debuted in a revival of *A Chorus Line* in 2008, Mario Lopez is particularly well known to television audiences. While his work as an actor has been ongoing since the mid-1980s, Lopez's appearance as a competitor on television's popular *Dancing with the Stars* series revealed his likeable personality and led to increased visibility and numerous hosting opportunities. In addition to acting, Lopez is also a sports and fitness advocate—he wrestled competitively in high school and now works as a boxing analyst—and he has co authored *Mario Lopez's Knockout Fitness* as well as two cookbooks promoting healthy eating.

Born in San Diego, California, Lopez started working in television in the early 1980s, and his acting career quickly took off. A part as a dancer and drummer on the variety show *Kids Incorporated* beginning in 1984 led to other roles, among them a guest spot on the popular sit-com *Golden Girls.* In1989 Lopez began a five-year stint as A.C. Slater on *Saved by the Bell,* a television comedy series that also spawned several movie-length sequels due to Lopez's popularity among teen audiences. In 1992 he got his first hosting spot on *Name Your Adventure,* an NBC series in which selected teen-

Artist Maryn Roos teams up with celebrity siblings Mario Lopez and Marissa Lopez Wong to create the Latino-themed picture book **Mud Tacos!**. (Illustration copyright © 2009 by Via Mar Productions, Inc. All rights reserved. Used by permission of Celebra Children's Books, a division of Penguin Young Readers Group, a member of Penguin Group (USA) Inc., 345 Hudson Street, New York, NY 10014.)

agers were filmed living out their fantasies, from a job at a cool company to going on the road with their favorite rock band. The job brought Lopez into contact with Olympic champion swimmer Greg Louganis, whom the actor would eventually play in the 1997 television movie *Breaking the Surface: The Greg Louganis Story.*

Other acting opportunities have continued to come Lopez's way, including roles on the daytime soap opera *The Bold and the Beautiful,* co-hosting the television talk show *The Other Half,* and hosting the entertainment program *Extra!* By 2010 he was even starring in his own reality show, *Mario Lopez: Saved by the Baby,* alongside partner Courtney Lane Mazza, an actress and dancer with whom he is raising a daughter. In 2007 Lopez also became the first celebrity to host both the Miss America and Miss Universe pageants.

Working with sister Marissa Lopez Wong, Lopez has also moved into children's publishing with the book *Mud Tacos!,* which was inspired by watching Wong's children at play and also by their own experiences growing up together. In *Mud Tacos!* the coauthors cast much younger versions of themselves in central parts, and as readers watch Marissa and big brother Mario play pretend restaurant and serve up pretend tacos made from flower petals and mud. When the children grow hungry, they join their cousins and grandmother in a trip to the store and back, a trip that ends with a meal of real tacos made by their Nana Lopez. Praising Maryn Roos' colorful cartoon art for *Mud Tacos!,* a *Kirkus Reviews* writer described Wong and Lopez's story as "a simple tale that celebrates the twin pleasures of childhood, food and imagination."

Biographical and Critical Sources

PERIODICALS

Kirkus Reviews, October 1, 2009, review of *Mud Tacos!*
People, June 7, 2010, Caroline Leavitt, Beth Perry, Judith Newman, Kim Hubbard, review of *Extra Lean: The Fat-burning Plan That Changes the Way You Eat for Life,* p. 63.

ONLINE

Mario Lopez Home Page, http://www.mariolopez.net (February 11, 2010).*

* * *

LYONS, Jayne

Personal

Born in Liverpool, England; immigrated to Australia, 2005; married; husband's name Angus; children: Rosie. *Education:* University of London, B.Sc. (geology), 1990, M.Sc. (geology), 1993. *Hobbies and other interests:* Tennis, writing, films, spending time with friends and family.

Addresses

Home—Perth, Western Australia, Australia. *Agent*—Golvan Arts Management, Kew, Victoria, Australia. *E-mail*—jaynelyons100percent@bigpond.com.

Career

Author and geologist. Worked in Scotland as a geologist, until 2004. Presenter at schools and conferences.

Writings

"FREDDY LUPIN" NOVEL SERIES

100 Percent Wolf, illustrated by Victor Rivas, Random House Australia (North Sydney, New South Wales, Australia), 2008, Atheneum Books for Young Readers (New York, NY), 2009.
100 Percent Hero, illustrated by Victor Rivas, Random House Australia (North Sydney, New South Wales, Australia), 2009.

Sidelights

Jayne Lyons is an Australian author whose humorous "Freddy Lupin" novels put a humorous spin on traditional vampire lore. Born in England, Lyons (her last name is a pseudonym) studied geology and worked in

He's SMALL.
He's PINK.
He's GROOMED.
But he's . . .

100% WOLF

by JAYNE LYONS
with illustrations by VICTOR RIVAS

Cover of Jayne Lyons' middle-grade thriller 100 Percent Wolf, *featuring cover art by Victor Rivas.* (Illustration copyright © 2009 by Victor Rivas. Reprinted with the permission of Atheneum Books for Young Readers, an imprint of Simon & Schuster Children's Publishing Division.)

Scotland's oil industry for over a decade. Looking for a change, she eventually relocated to Australia, where she and her family now make their home. The irreverent humor prevalent in Australia may have encouraged Lyons' creative side, because a few years after moving to her new country, Random House Australia published her first book, the elementary-grade novel *100 Percent Wolf.*

When readers meet orphaned Freddy Lupin, the ten-year-old hero of *100 Percent Wolf,* they already suspect that he has transformative powers. When Freddy undergoes his first transformation at Farfang Castle, his Uncle Hotspur anticipates seeing a sleek, strong wolf standing beneath the full moon. When a tiny poodle appears in

Freddy's place, the boy is banned from the werewolf pack; even worse, his mischievous cousins actually dye his fur bright pink! Fortunately, he finds a new friend in Batty, a scruffy abandoned pup that helps Freddy protect the other homeless dogs and keep his fellow werewolves from a relentless wolf-tracker armed with silver bullets. Freddy's adventures continue in *100 Percent Hero,* as he realizes that his parents' idea of summer camp is several weeks learning ballet dancing. Meanwhile, one of Freddy's relatives has been abducted by a local reporter and caged in a zoo, and something evil is lurking outside in the dark. Brought to life in drawings by Victor Rivas, *100 Percent Wolf* "blends humor, suspense, and a lively, mischievous protagonist," according to *Booklist* critic Shelle Rosenfeld. "Freddy has oodles of resilience and courage," wrote a *Kirkus Reviews* writer, and Hayden Bass predicted in *School Library Journal* that "the fast-paced action and numerous fart jokes" Lyons includes in *100 Percent Hero* "will lure young reluctant readers."

Discussing why she enjoys writing for children, Lyons noted on her home page: "I love the fact that [kids] . . . have such great imagination. It gives the writer lots of freedom. If you wrote a book for grown ups about werewolves, they'd be going, yeah, but how does he have time to turn into a wolf, he has to do the washing up, and who cleans up the mess after them? And if a child goes into a wardrobe and discovers another world then they go into it, become a king or queen and have famous adventures. A dad would go to [the hardware store] . . . to get stuff to fix the hole and a mum would start making a packed lunch. That's why children are more fun."

Biographical and Critical Sources

PERIODICALS

Booklist, October 1, 2009, Shelle Rosenfeld, review of *100 Percent Wolf,* p. 41.
Kirkus Reviews, June 15, 2009, review of *100 Percent Wolf.*
School Library Journal, September, 2009, Hayden Bass, review of *100 Percent Wolf,* p. 165.

ONLINE

Jayne Lyons Home Page, http://www.jaynelyons.com (February 15, 2011).*

M

McCLINTOCK, Norah

Personal

Born in Montreal, Quebec, Canada; married. *Education:* McGill University, B.A. (history); graduate study (medieval history). *Hobbies and other interests:* Reading, hiking, biking, long walks, cross-country skiing, going to the movies.

Addresses

Home—Toronto, Ontario, Canada. *E-mail*—nmbooks@web.net.

Career

Mystery writer and editor. Centre for Philanthropy, Toronto, Ontario, Canada, former editor.

Member

Crime Writers of Canada, Canadian Society of Children's Authors, Illustrators, and Performers.

Awards, Honors

Arthur Ellis Award for Best Juvenile Crime Novel, Crime Writers of Canada, 1995, for *Mistaken Identity,* 1997, for *The Body in the Basement,* 1998, for *Sins of the Father,* 2000, for *Scared to Death,* 2002, for *Break and Enter;* White Pine Award nomination, Ontario Library Association, 2000, for *Over the Edge;* Palmares Communication-Jeunesse award, 2001, for *Cadavre au sous-sol* (French translation of *The Body in the Basement*); Canadian Children's Book Centre (CCBC) Our Choice designation, 2003, for *Break and Enter;* White Pine Award nomination, Anthony Award nomination for Young-Adult Mystery, and Manitoba Young Readers' Choice Award shortlist, all 2004, all for *No Escape;* Red Maple Award, Ontario Library Association, 2004, for *Hit and Run;* Red Maple Award nomination, 2005, for *Dead and Gone;* CCBC Our Choice designation, 2007, for both *Last Chance* and *You Can Run;* finalist,

Arthur Ellis Award for Best Juvenile Crime Novel, CCBC Our Choice designation, and Quick Picks for Reluctant Young-Adult Readers selection, American Library Association (ALA), all 2007, all for *Tell;* ALA Quick Picks for Reluctant Young-Adult Readers selection, and CCBC Best Books for Kids and Teens selection, both 2008, both for *Down;* ALA Quick Picks for Reluctant Young-Adult Readers selection, and CCBC Best Books for Kids and Teens selection, both 2008, both for *Bang;* Red Maple Award, 2009, for *Out of the Cold;* finalist, Arthur Ellis Award for Best Juvenile Crime Novel, 2009, for *Dead Silence;* CCBC Best Books for Kids and Teens selection, 2009, for both *Marked* and *Shadow of Doubt;* CCBC Our Choice designation, 2009, for *Dooley Takes the Fall;* CCBC Best Books for Kids and Teens selections, 2010, for both *Back* and *Watch Me;* ALA Quick Picks for Reluctant Young-Adult Readers selection, 2010, for *Taken,* and 2011, for *Picture This.*

Writings

NOVELS

End of the Line, RFP Publications (Montreal, Quebec, Canada), 1981.

Shakespeare and Legs, Scholastic Canada (Richmond Hill, Ontario, Canada), 1987.

Sixty-four, Sixty-five (for children), McClelland & Stewart (Toronto, Ontario, Canada), 1989.

The Stepfather Game, Scholastic Canada (Richmond Hill, Ontario, Canada), 1990, revised as part of the "Chloe and Levesque" series as *The Third Degree* (also see below), 2005.

Jack's Back, Scholastic Canada (Richmond Hill, Ontario, Canada), 1992.

Mistaken Identity, Scholastic Canada (Richmond Hill, Ontario, Canada), 1995.

The Body in the Basement, Scholastic Canada (Toronto, Ontario, Canada), 1997.

Sins of the Father, Scholastic Canada (Toronto, Ontario, Canada), 1998.

Password: Murder, Scholastic Canada (Toronto, Ontario, Canada), 1999.

Snitch (for young adults), Orca Book Publishers (Victoria, British Columbia, Canada), 2005.

Tell (for young adults), Orca Book Publishers (Custer, WA), 2006.

Bang, Orca Book Publishers (Victoria, British Columbia, Canada), 2007.

Down, Orca Book Publishers (Custer, WA), 2007.

Marked, Orca Book Publishers (Custer, WA), 2008.

Watch Me, Orca Book Publishers (Custer, WA), 2008.

Dooley Takes the Fall, Red Deer Press (Markham, Ontario, Canada), 2008.

Homicide Related, Red Deer Press (Markham Ontario, Canada), 2008.

Back, Orca Book Publishers (Custer, WA), 2009.

Picture This, Orca Book Publishers (Custer, WA), 2009.

Taken, Orca Book Publishers (Custer, WA), 2009.

El Soplon, Orca Book Publishers (Custer, WA), 2010.

Masked, Orca Book Publishers (Custer, WA), 2010.

Author's works have been translated into French, Swedish, Norwegian, and German.

"CHLOE AND LEVESQUE" YOUNG-ADULT MYSTERY NOVELS

Over the Edge, Scholastic Canada (Markham, Ontario, Canada), 2000, Kane Miller (Tulsa, OK), 2010.

Double Cross, Scholastic Canada (Markham, Ontario, Canada), 2000, Kane Miller (Tulsa, OK), 2010.

Scared to Death, Scholastic Canada (Markham, Ontario, Canada), 2000, Kane Miller (Tulsa, OK), 2011.

Break and Enter, Scholastic Canada (Toronto, Ontario, Canada), 2002.

No Escape, Scholastic Canada (Markham, Ontario, Canada), 2003.

Not a Trace, Scholastic Canada (Markham, Ontario, Canada), 2005.

"MIKE AND RIEL" YOUNG-ADULT MYSTERY NOVELS

Hit and Run, Scholastic Canada (Markham, Ontario, Canada), 2003.

Truth and Lies, Scholastic Canada (Markham, Ontario, Canada), 2004.

Dead and Gone, Scholastic Canada (Markham, Ontario, Canada), 2004.

Seeing and Believing, Scholastic Canada (Toronto, Ontario, Canada), 2006.

Dead Silence, Scholastic Canada (Toronto, Ontario, Canada), 2008.

"ROBYN HUNTER" YOUNG-ADULT MYSTERY NOVELS

Last Chance, Scholastic Canada (Markham, Ontario, Canada), 2006.

You Can Run, Scholastic Canada (Markham, Ontario, Canada), 2006.

Nothing to Lose, Scholastic Canada (Markham, Ontario, Canada), 2007.

Out of the Cold, Scholastic Canada (Markham, Ontario, Canada), 2007.

Shadow of Doubt, Scholastic Canada (Markham, Ontario, Canada), 2008.

Nowhere to Turn, Scholastic Canada (Markham, Ontario, Canada), 2009.

Change of Heart, Scholastic Canada (Markham, Ontario, Canada), 2009.

In Too Deep, Scholastic Canada (Markham, Ontario, Canada), 2010.

Something to Prove, Scholastic Canada (Markham, Ontario, Canada), 2010.

OTHER

Body, Crime, Suspect: How a Murder Investigation Really Works, illustrated by Paul McCusker, Scholastic Canada (Markham, Ontario, Canada), 2001.

Editor with Rick Blechta) *Dishes to Die For—Again: Crime Writers of Canada Put the Mystery Back into Good Cooking!,* Crime Writers of Canada (Scarborough, Ontario, Canada), 2004.

Sidelights

Norah McClintock is a prolific writer of mystery and suspense novels for young adults. A five-time winner of the Crime Writers of Canada award for Best Juvenile Crime Novel, she peoples her compelling storylines with likable teen characters who find themselves involved in unusual and often challenging relationships. "The great thing about McClintock's books," stated *Resource Links* contributor Teresa Hughes, "is that she writes about young teenagers who have real problems . . . and weaves them into a mystery setting where they play a significant role in the outcome." That element of verisimilitude is important to the author, who remarked to *Canadian Review of Materials* interviewer Dave Jenkinson: "To a certain extent, the characters can do the unexpected, just not a big unexpected. I still try, and I hope I succeed to some extent, to create a real person. Whatever else is happening in terms of the crime, there are other things going on in their life too."

In addition to standalone thrillers such as *The Body in the Basement, Tell,* and *Taken,* McClintock has gained fans through her "Mike and Riel," "Chloe and Levesque," and "Robyn Hunter" mystery series. Noting that her "plots are complicated enough to keep readers in suspense," *Resource Links* reviewer Nadine d'Entremont added in an appraisal of the "Chloe and Levesque" novel *Break and Enter* that McClintock's stories are also "not so intricate that we are left scratching our heads wondering whether it all really works out."

In *Mistaken Identity* McClintock introduces sixteen-year-old Zanny Dugan, a girl who lives an isolated and peripatetic life under the care of her overprotective, single dad. A lengthy stay in the small town of Birk Falls seems to mean the end of their constant moves, that is until Zanny's father is found murdered. The constant family moves relocations were an effort to shake whoever wanted her dad dead, the teen now realizes. But what if the killer is not finished yet? Another relationship between a teen and her father is at the center of *The Body in the Basement,* but this time Tasha Scanlan's dad is accused of murdering his wife. When the body of Tasha's mother turns up in the basement of a demolished building five years after she disappeared, suspicion quickly turns to her husband. With the help of a friend, Tasha must now work to prove her father's innocence, and her search for the truth leads her into her parents' past and ultimately into danger. In *Resource Links,* Margaret Mackey called *The Body in the Basement* an intriguing "pageturner" with a surprise ending in which McClintock weaves together "a competent mixture of mystery and romance."

Focusing on fifteen-year-old Mick Standish, *Sins of the Father* finds a teen forced to deal with his anger toward his alcoholic, recently paroled father, Dan. Deposited at his grandfather's house, Mick begins to suspect that, despite his father's poor track-record for honesty, the man may not have committed his worst offense after all. Now, should the teen attempt to help the parent who has caused him such emotional pain due to his negligence? In *Password: Murder* seventeen-year-old Harley Dankser suffers the loss of his dad in an auto accident in which Harley was driving. Feelings of guilt propel the teen into a mental hospital, where he attempts to deal with nightmares about the accident and his role in his father's death. Meanwhile, Harley's mom has remarried, and his new step dad is his real father's best friend. When Harley returns home to live with the newlyweds, he is haunted by new dreams, this time dreams hinting that the car accident may actually have been murdered.

Aimed at reluctant readers, *Snitch* features two teens who face a moral quandary after they steal some money from a charity organization dedicated to AIDS research. While Scott wanted to give the money back, Josh did not, and now he finds himself forced to go to a dog-training program as a form of court-ordered rehabilitation. While working with the dogs tests Josh's patience, a tumultuous home life provides other challenges. When Scott is beaten by someone wielding a club and Josh is framed for the violent attack, the teen must discover the identity of the real attacker and also learn to control the anger that has made him a convincing scapegoat for the crime. Noting that McClintock presents a realistic character dealing with anger-management issues in *Snitch, Kliatt* reviewer Lisa M. Carlson added that the novel's troubled teen "protagonist is well developed." *Snitch* would be a good choice for reluctant readers—particularly boys—in the opinion of *Resource Links* reviewer Leslie L. Kennedy, the critic going on to praise the novel as "a darn good read from a very talented writer."

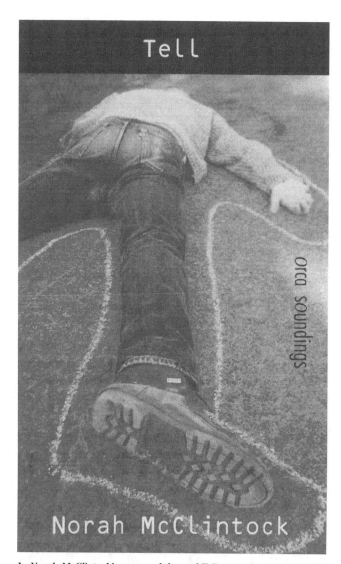

In Norah McClintock's young-adult novel Tell *a teen knows more than he reveals regarding the murder of his stepfather.* (Orca Book Publishers, 2006. Reproduced by permission.)

Reviewing *Tell,* another work for reluctant readers, *Kliatt* critic Sherri Forgash as "a well-written, compelling story" that brings to life "a complicated family relationship." Citing the novel's intriguing plotline about a young poker player and his efforts to discover his stepfather's killer, Linda Aksomitis wrote in *Resource Links* that McClintock's "resolution is a strong one that brings the novel full circle without moralizing." In *Back,* a convicted felon committed to changing his ways faces hatred and discrimination after returning to his neighborhood, where he committed a brutal assault years earlier. "Bullying and revenge are common themes in young adult literature, but . . . McClintock gives these classic themes an updated twist," Shelly Shaffer asserted in the *Journal of Adolescent and Adult Literacy.*

A kidnapped teenager fights for her life in McClintock's *Taken,* "an unflinching depiction of the unforgiving and often brutal realities of the natural world," observed Shaun Smith in *Quill & Quire.* In the novel, Stephanie Rawls, a high-school student, is abducted by a serial killer and left at a remote cabin. After she escapes, Stephanie must make her way back to civilization using the survival skills taught to her by her late grandfather. A *Kirkus Reviews* contributor remarked that Stephanie's "harrowing journey back to safety" in *Taken* "propels this plot-driven, fast-paced tale forward."

McClintock's "Chloe and Levesque" novel series includes the books *Over the Edge, Break and Enter,* and *Not a Trace.* Readers meet Chloe Yan in *Over the Edge,* which finds the teen dealing with a new stepfather and problems over fitting in at the high school in the suburban community where she and her parents now live. Chloe is struggling on both fronts: her stepdad, Louis Levesque, has not only forced the move from Montreal to East Hastings; he is also the chief of police. Fortunately, the teen has found a new group of friends as well as a boyfriend in football star Thomas Rennie. When Levesque asks her to help him in the investigation surrounding the suspicious death of Peter, one of Chloe's classmates, the girl soon discovers that her new friends are not what they appear. In *Double Cross* Chloe sides with an unpopular fellow student who is trying to clear his father of accusations of murder, while in *Scared to Death* she realizes that her best friend, Ross, is a suspect in the mysterious death of a woman who had come to Chloe for help only days before.

More corpses pop up in *Break and Enter,* while in *No Escape* the teen begins to doubt the violent nature of Caleb, a man who has recently returned to town after spending time in prison. When Levesque is shot and the evidence points to Caleb, Chloe takes it upon herself to clear Caleb's name. Noting that McClintock's mysteries are "excellent choices for . . . both avid . . . and reluctant readers," Brenda Dillan wrote in a *Resource Links* review of *No Escape* that the "engaging" series features a "strong [main] character who gets involved in some very interesting situations." Calling *Over the Edge* a "good combination of thriller and mystery," another *Resource Links* contributor maintained that McClintock's suspenseful plot leaves "lots for the reader to discover and think about." In *Not a Trace,* the duo investigates the murder of a contractor hired to build a golf course on a native tribe's ancestral burial grounds. "McClintock unravels the mystery a clue at a time," Kristin Butcher stated in the *Canadian Review of Materials,* "effectively stringing the reader along with intermittent red herrings."

Hit and Run, the first installment in the "Mike and Riel" series, introduces fifteen-year-old Mike, who is living with a disinterested uncle now that his mom is dead and his father has left the scene. While his mother's death had always been thought to be an accident, Mike's new teacher, an ex-cop named John Riel, begs to differ, and he takes Mike into his home as a foster son. A fellow student turns up dead and Mike becomes the chief suspect in *Truth and Lies,* while an unsolved murder and the discovery of a hand-dug grave combine to turn Mike's world upside down in *Dead and Gone.* Praising

McClintock's ability to create realistic characters, Joan Marshall noted in a *Resource Links* appraisal of *Dead and Gone* that Mike's "acute observations of the people around him and his witty, self-deprecating remarks, will keep young teens, especially boys, laughing in recognition." In *Seeing and Believing* Mike comes to the aid of a longtime friend accused of armed robbery. According to *Canadian Review of Materials* critic Thom Knutson, in the novel "McClintock creates a sense of urgency and suspense that drives the well-crafted plot increasingly faster towards its satisfying conclusion."

The sixteen-year-old heroine of the "Robyn Hunter" series finds herself on the wrong side of the law in *Last Chance,* the debut title in that series. Forced to do volunteer work at a local animal shelter, Robyn meets Nick, a troubled teen who is at the shelter working off his own misdemeanor. It seems that Nick has now added car theft and criminal negligence to his list of crimes, but Robyn is not so sure. Her investigation into Nick's background serves as the focus of a novel described by *Resource Links* reviewer Brendan White as "easy to read and hard to put down." In *Out of the Cold,* Robyn looks into the strange death of a homeless man who

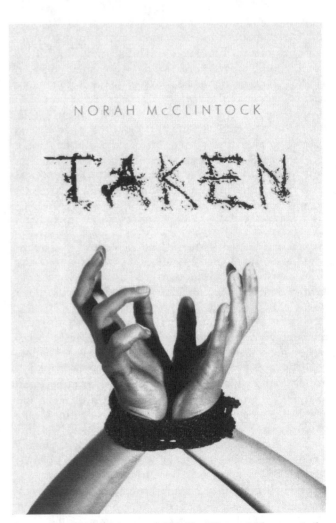

Cover of McClintock's young-adult thriller Taken, *which recounts the experiences of a teenage kidnap victim.* (Orca Book Publishers, 2009. Cover photo by Larry Lilac, GetStock.com. Reproduced by permission.)

was removed from a shelter after an altercation with the young protagonist. Leslie L. Kennedy, writing in *Resource Links* noted that that the "many characters" in *Out of the Cold* are complex enough to keep [readers] interested."

In *Shadow of Doubt* Robyn finds herself drawn to a new beau after Nick unexpectedly leaves town, discovers a poignant secret about her mother's boyfriend, and comes to the assistance of a young teacher who receives a series of threatening messages. In the words of *Canadian Review of Materials* critic Ruth Latta, "Robyn mulls over her teenage romantic experiences in the light of the similar but more complicated relationships of the adults around her. To what extent can we learn from past experience? When are others' experiences relevant to our own lives?" In *Something to Prove,* the final installment in the series, Robyn's stormy relationship with Nick comes to a head as she deals with a new classmate with a haunted past. "McClintock's sophisticated novel shows young people taking on adult responsibilities and experiencing adult emotions," Latta observed.

McClintock introduces a new teenage sleuth, Ryan Dooley, in *Dooley Takes the Fall.* Recently released from juvenile detention, Ryan witnesses a man plunge to his death from a bridge, an apparent suicide. When the deceased's sister expresses disbelief about that conclusion, Ryan agrees to investigate further. Writing in *School Library Journal,* Julianna M. Helt called Ryan "a likable, if somewhat flawed, character" and described *Dooley Takes the Fall* as "an excellently written murder mystery." Ryan makes a return appearance in *Homicide Related,* where readers find him looking into the suspicious deaths of his drug-addicted mother and an old friend. "Patient readers will pull for this resilient teen determined to rise above a tough life," maintained a contributor in *Kirkus Reviews.*

"Sometimes it takes as long to plan a book as it does to actually write it," McClintock explained to Jenkinson in discussing her career as a crime novelist. "I try to stop myself from starting to write it until I know exactly how the story's going to end because, with a mystery, you can get off-track." She further noted, "I spend the time beforehand asking 'What's the crime that actually happened? Who actually did it? How did they do it? How did they manage not to get caught so far? Who are some of the other people who conceivably could have something to hide?' . . . I make sure I have a crime that makes sense and somebody who has done it for a good reason and has managed so far to get away with it. Sometimes that's hard. People don't just go killing people willy-nilly. There has to be some logic to it."

Biographical and Critical Sources

PERIODICALS

Booklist, April 15, 2009, Daniel Kraus, review of *Back,* p. 40; September 15, 2009, Daniel Kraus, review of *Taken,* p. 53; October 15, 2009, Connie Fletcher, review of *Homicide Related,* p. 42.

Canadian Book Review Annual, 2000, review of *Double Cross,* p. 493; 2001, review of *Body, Crime, Suspect: How a Murder Investigation Really Works,* p. 556.

Canadian Children's Literature, spring-summer, 2002, reviews of *Password: Murder, Over the Edge,* and *Double Cross,* all pp. 105-106.

Canadian Review of Materials, December 1, 1995, Leslie Millar, review of *Mistaken Identity;* February 27, 1998, Marsha Kaiserman, review of *The Body in the Basement;* January 1, 1999, Valerie Nielsen, review of *Sins of the Father;* January 21, 2000, Ruth Scales McMahon, review of *Password: Murder;* November 17, 2000, Betsy Fraser, review of *Over the Edge;* April 13, 2001, Betsy Fraser, review of *Double Cross;* June 22, 2001, Betsy Fraser, review of *Scared to Death;* January 4, 2002, Julie Chychota, review of *Body, Crime, Suspect;* April 14, 2006, Kristin Butcher, review of *Not a Trace;* February 2, 2007, Thom Knutson, review of *Seeing and Believing;* June 13, 2008, Ruth Latta, review of *Shadow of Doubt;* September 10, 2010, Ruth Latta, review of *Something to Prove.*

Emergency Librarian, March-April, 1993, Dave Jenkinson, interview with McClintock, pp. 66-69.

Journal of Adolescent and Adult Literacy, November, 2009, Selly Shaffer, review of *Back,* p. 269.

Kirkus Reviews, September 1, 2009, review of *Taken;* October 1, 2009, review of *Homicide Related.*

Kliatt, May, 2006, Lisa M. Carlson, review of *Snitch,* p. 21; November, 2006, Sherrie Forgash Ginsberg, review of *Tell,* p. 22.

Quill & Quire, September, 2009, Shaun Smith, review of *Taken.*

Resource Links, June, 1998, review of *Body in the Basement,* p. 19; October, 2000, review of *Over the Edge,* p. 28; December, 2001, Eva Wilson, review of *Body, Crime, Suspect,* p. 27, and Betty McDougall, review of *Scared to Death,* p. 38; February, 2003, Nadine d'Etremont, review of *Break and Enter,* p. 42; June, 2003, Brenda Dillon, review of *Hit and Run,* p. 28; February, 2004, Brenda Dillon, review of *No Escape,* p. 36; April, 2004, Theresa Hughes, review of *Truth and Lies,* p. 40; February, 2005, Joan Marshall, review of *Dead and Gone,* p. 38; February, 2006, Leslie L. Kennedy, review of *Snitch,* p. 47; June, 2006, Brendan White, review of *Last Chance,* p. 26; October, 2006, Leslie L. Kennedy, review of *Seeing and Believing,* p. 36; December, 2006, Lisa Aksomtis, review of *Tell,* and Teresa Hughes, review of *You Can Run,* both p. 35; April, 2007, Anne Hatcher, review of *Nothing to Lose,* p. 45; June, 2007, Eva Wilson, review of *Bang,* p. 35; December, 2007, Emily Springer, review of *Down,* p. 39; February, 2008, Leslie L. Kennedy, review of *Out of the Cold,* p. 34; December, 2009, Patricia Jermey, review of *Change of Heart,* and Joan Marshall, review of *Homicide Related* both p. 36, and Alison Edwards, review of *Picture This,* and Karen Taylor, review of *Taken,* both p. 37.

School Library Journal, January, 2007, Sadie Mattox, review of *Tell,* p. 132; January, 2009, Julianna M. Helt, review of *Dooley Takes the Fall,* p. 110; December, 2009, Mary-Brook J. Todd, review of *Homicide Related,* and Robyn Zaneski, review of *Taken,* both p. 126.

Voice of Youth Advocates, April, 1992, review of *The Step-father,* p. 33; February, 2006, Teri S. Lesesne, review of *Snitch,* p. 488.

ONLINE

Canadian Review of Materials Web site, http://www. umanitoba.ca/cm/profiles/ (June 9, 2001), Dave Jenkinson, interview with McClintock.
Canadian Society of Children's Authors, Illustrators, and Performers Web site, http://www.canscaip.org/ (February 10, 2011), "Norah McClintock."
Norah McClintock Home Page, http://www.web.net/~nmbooks (February 10, 2011).
Scholastic Canada Web site, http://www.scholastic.ca/ (February 10, 2011), "Norah McClintock.*

* * *

Julie McLaughlin (Reproduced by permission.)

McLAUGHLIN, Julie 1984-

Personal

Born December 4, 1984, in Edmonton, Alberta, Canada. *Education:* Alberta College of Art & Design, bachelor of Design in Visual Communication (illustration). *Hobbies and other interests:* Traveling, picnics in the park, playing board games, drinking wine.

Addresses

Home—Montreal, Quebec, Canada. *E-mail*—julie@whatwouldjuliedraw.com.

Career

Illustrator and graphic artist.

Illustrator

Harriet Rohmer, *Heroes of the Environment: True Stories of People Who Are Helping to Protect Our Planet,* Chronicle Books (San Francisco, CA), 2009.
Smarta små upptäcker nature, Rabén & Sjögren (Stockholm, Sweden), 2011.

Contributor to periodicals, including *Ffwd* and *National Post.*

Biographical and Critical Sources

PERIODICALS

Kirkus Reviews, October 1, 2009, review of *Heroes of the Environment: True Stories of People Who Are Helping to Protect Our Planet.*
School Library Journal, January, 2010, Patricia Ann Owens, review of *Heroes of the Environment,* p. 125.

ONLINE

Julie McLaughlin Home Page, http://www.whatwould juliedraw.com (February 15, 2011).
Julie McLaughlin Web log, http://whatwouldjuliedraw. blogspot.com (February 15, 2011).

* * *

McMENEMY, Sarah 1965-

Personal

Born August 2, 1965, in Welwyn Garden, England; daughter of James McMenemy (an advertising executive) and Gilia Florentin-Lee (a homemaker and artist); children: one son, one daughter. *Education:* Attended Chelsea School of Art, 1983-84; Brighton University, B.A. (illustration), 1987. *Hobbies and other interests:* Dancing, walking, playing the piano, live music, singing.

Addresses

Home—North London, England. *Agent*—Artworks Illustration Agency, 40 Frith St., Soho, London W1D 5LN, England. *E-mail*—sarah@sarahmcmenemy.com.

Career

Illustrator, beginning 1987. Commercial artist, with clients including periodicals, design groups, publishers, and businesses such as Toyota, Kodak, British Airways, Mastercard, Hertz, and Royal Mail. Visiting lecturer at Chelsea School of Art, Central St. Martin's School of Art, Liverpool School of Art, and Bath School of Art. *Exhibitions:* Work exhibited at group shows at Royal Festival Hall, Smiths Gallery, Hardware Gallery, Artworks Gallery, and The Mall Galleries, all London, England; and at Tallberg Taylor Gallery, Paris, France, and Society of Illustrators, New York, NY.

Member

Association of Illustrators.

Writings

SELF-ILLUSTRATED

Waggle, Candlewick Press (Cambridge, MA), 2003.
Jack's New Boat, Candlewick Press (Cambridge, MA), 2005.

McMenemy's work has been translated into Japanese.

ILLUSTRATOR

Bel Mooney, *Big Dog Bonnie,* Walker Books (London, England), 2007.
Jill Davis, *The First Rule of Little Brothers,* Alfred A. Knopf (New York, NY), 2008.
Leslie Kimmelman, *Everybody Bonjours!,* Knopf (New York, NY), 2008.
Bel Mooney, *Best Dog Bonnie,* Walker Books (London, England), 2008.
Bel Mooney, *Bad Dog Bonnie,* Walker Books (London, England), 2008.
Mara Rockliff, *The Busiest Street in Town,* Alfred A. Knopf (New York, NY), 2009.
Sue Stauffacher, *Tillie the Terrible Swede: How One Woman, a Sewing Needle, and a Bicycle Changed History,* Alfred A. Knopf (New York, NY), 2009.
Bel Mooney, *Brave Dog Bonnie,* Walker Books (London, England), 2009.
London: A Three-dimensional Expanding City Skyline, Walker Books (London, England), 2011.

Sidelights

Artist and author Sarah McMenemy lives and works in London, creating lighthearted images to delight young picture-book fans. As an illustrator, McMenemy's work has been a feature of stories by authors such as Bel Mooney, Jill Davis, Mara Rockliff, Leslie Kimmelman, and Sue Stauffacher. In *The First Rule of Little Brothers,* a picture book by Davis that focuses on a relationship between young siblings, the artist's retro-styled "mixed-media vignettes" feature "playful palettes and nimble shapes" set against her characteristic white background, according to a *Publishers Weekly* critic. The pages of Kimmelman's *Everybody Bonjours,* which take readers on a tour of gay Paree, feature what Ilene Cooper described in *Booklist* as "cheery ink-and-watercolor artwork [that] is stylishly rendered," while another reviewer in *Publishers Weekly* cited McMenemy's art as "a stylish yet timeless melange of fauvist whimsy and affectionate reportage." Expanding on her work as a picture-book illustrator, McNemeney's original self-illustrated stories for children include the entertaining *Waggle* as well as *Jack's New Boat.*

McMenemy brings to life the close relationship between a young girl and her high-spirited puppy in *Waggle,* her authorial debut. When Rosie's father brings home a new pet for his daughter, girl and pup become fast friends and find all manner of ways to keep busy. It is Rosie's task to choose a name for her new friend, which she does when she realizes that Waggle's tail never stops moving. Praising McMenemy's simple text and "bright, uncluttered collage illustrations," *Booklist* reviewer Helen Rosenberg described *Waggle* as "a truly satisfying read-aloud," and a *Publishers Weekly* reviewer noted that the author/illustrator's "playful page design and enthusiastic narration" make her "a new talent to watch." "Young readers . . . will instantly adore this doggy dynamo," predicted an enthusiastic *Kirkus Reviews* critic.

Jack's New Boat also features McMenemy's trademark loosely drawn ink-over-collage style. In the story, young Jack is visiting Uncle Jim at the man's coastal home. Jim is a veteran sailor, and he shared his knowledge and love of the sea with the boy through the gift of a handmade toy sailboat. When a spate of stormy weather discourages sailing, Jack puts his boat in the water anyway and learns an important lesson about patience from his loving uncle. Paired with "understated" torn-paper and gouache images in tones of sea blue, brown, and nautical red and navy blue, McNemeny's illustrations "evoke a bygone, unhurried era," according to a *Publishers Weekly* critic, while Jennifer Locke dubbed *Jack's New Boat* a "summery" story in which a "simple and engaging text" is brought to life in "boldly composed" art. Featuring "bold brushstrokes" done in "moody blues," according to a *Kirkus Reviews* writer, McMenemy's tale is "as simple and satisfying as a toy sailboat on a salty sea."

McMenemy once told *SATA:* "I have worked as an illustrator for years, for a largely adult audience, on a broad range of projects from regular magazine columns to packaging, brochures for cars, schools, and hospitals. I've drawn on location in New York and Paris, and made eighteen images to go on large enamel panels in Shadwell Station for the London Underground. So it was a wonderful voyage of discovery and a steep learning curve to write and illustrate a children's book. My agent had shown some pictures and little books that I had done for my own children to Walker Books at the Bologna Book Fair. I met them back in London and we decided to create a picture book together.

"In creating my first book, *Waggle,* it was very satisfying to be able to tell a story that combined the experiences of playing with my children and my own memories of having a puppy as a child. I really wanted to convey the sense of fun and joy that a child and puppy find wherever they are. In creating the artwork for *Waggle* I wanted a sense of freshness and enjoyment, a simplicity of color, line, and movement. Using pure, bold colors was a daily uplifting experience. It was also a challenge to condense all lines and shapes to an es-

Sarah McMenemy's colorful retro-inspired illustration projects include Mara Rockliff's picture book The Busiest Street in Town. (Illustration copyright © 2009 by Sarah McMenemy. Reproduced by permission of Alfred A. Knopf, an imprint of Random House Children's Books, a division of Random House, Inc.)

sential minimum. I relished working as part of a small team with an editor and designer as illustration can be quite a solitary occupation.

"My original inspiration for drawing came from watching my mother drawing plants and pets in the garden. As a child I was fascinated by the ease and fluidity with which her line flowed onto the page. Drawing started to become a stronger theme in my life when, as a teenager and also through college, I generated income drawing façades of elegant Victorian terraced houses where my family lived in North London and also in Philadelphia, Pennsylvania, whilst on an exchange trip there.

"In school I was more drawn to painters than illustrators for inspiration. I loved the graphic work of Toulouse-Lautrec, Bonnard, Picasso, Dufy, and Matisse. I know now that the work of Edward Ardizzone, Eric Ravillious, and David McKee were important influences in my childhood reading. After having my daughter, I became very interested in children's books and quickly found that I had a strong opinion about what I liked. I admire illustrators such as Emma Chichester-Clark, Charlotte Voake, Lucy Cousins, Melanie Walsh, and Patrick Benson. I think the field of children's book illustration is one of the most exciting and vibrant areas of the business at the moment. It is also refreshing that it is not dominated by computer-generated imagery.

"I work at home, in north London. I love going to art exhibitions and having fun with my children. I also love the city of Paris, and have visited it many times. I stayed there once for a few months, in the Bastille area, drawing every day. Inspiration was everywhere I looked!"

Biographical and Critical Sources

PERIODICALS

Booklist, May 15, 2003, Helen Rosenberg, review of *Waggle,* p. 1672; May 1, 2005, Jennifer Locke, review of *Jack's New Boat,* p. 1592; August 1, 2008, Ilene Cooper, review of *Everybody Bonjours!,* p. 68; October 1, 2009, Michael Cart, review of *The Busiest Street in Town,* p. 49.

Chicago Tribune, July 6, 2003, review of *Waggle.*

Kirkus Reviews, May 15, 2003, review of *Waggle,* p. 754; May 15, 2005, review of *Jack's New Boat,* p. 593; March 15, 2008, review of *Everybody Bonjours!;* October 1, 2008, review of *The First Rule of Little Brothers;* September 1, 2009, review of *The Busiest Street in Town.*

New York Times Book Review, November 8, 2009, Rich Cohen, review of *The Busiest Street in Town,* p. 24.

Publishers Weekly, April 23, 2003, review of *Waggle,* p. 60; July 25, 2005, review of *Jack's New Boat,* p. 76; March 24, 2008, review of *Everybody Bonjours!,* p. 70; October 13, 2008, review of *The First Rule of Little Brothers,* p. 54; October 19, 2009, review of *The Busiest Street in Town,* p. 51.

School Library Journal, August, 2003, Carol Schene, review of *Waggle,* p. 138; August, 2005, Linda Staskus, review of *Jack's New Boat,* p. 100; April, 2008, Julie R. Ranelli, review of *Everybody Bonjours!,* p. 114; October, 2009, Ieva Bates, review of *The Busiest Street in Town,* p. 104.

ONLINE

Sarah McMenemy Home Page, http://www.sarahmcmenemy.com (February 15, 2011).

*　　*　　*

MORRISON, Frank 1971-

Personal

Born 1971, in MA; married; wife's name Connie; children: three sons, one daughter.

Addresses

Office—3645 Marketplace Blvd., Ste. 130-121, Eastpoint GA 30344. *E-mail*—morrisonarts@netzero.net.

Career

Illustrator. Gallery of Morrison Arts, Atlanta, OH, then Morrison Graphics, Eastpoint, GA, owner. Clothing designer for Phat Pharm label. Former break dancer and member of traveling dance troupe Sugar Hill Gang. *Exhibitions:* Solo exhibit at Savacaou Gallery, New York, NY, 20 North Gallery, Atlanta, GA, and Schomberg Center for Research in Black Culture, New York Public Library.

Awards, Honors

Coretta Scott King/John Steptoe New Talent Award for Illustration, 2005, for *Jazzy Miz Mozetta* by Brenda C. Roberts; (with others) Image Award in Outstanding Work for Children category, National Association for the Advancement of Colored People, 2009, for *Our Children Can Soar* by Michelle Cook.

Illustrator

Brenda C. Roberts, *Jazzy Miz Mozetta,* Farrar, Straus (New York, NY), 2004.

Debbie A. Taylor, *Sweet Music in Harlem,* Lee & Low (New York, NY), 2004.

Queen Latifah, *Queen of the Scene,* Laura Geringer Books (New York, NY), 2006.

Lissette Noman, *My Feet Are Laughing,* Farrar, Straus (New York, NY), 2006.

Gaylia Taylor, *George Crum and the Saratoga Chip,* Lee & Low (New York, NY), 2006.

Alex Rodriguez, *Out of the Ballpark,* HarperCollins (New York, NY), 2007.

Melanie Turner-Denstaedt, *Grandma's Good Hat,* Farrar, Straus (New York, NY), 2008.

Chris Paul, *Long Shot: Never Too Small to Dream Big,* Simon & Schuster Books for Young Readers (New York, NY), 2009.

Melanie Turner-Denstaedt, *The Hat That Wore Clara B.,* Farrar, Straus & Giroux (New York, NY), 2009.

Pelé, *For the Love of Soccer!,* Disney-Hyperion Books (New York, NY), 2010.

Peter Abrahams, *Quacky Baseball,* HarperCollins Children's Books (New York, NY), 2011.

Muriel Harris Weinstein, *Play, Louis, Play!: The True Story of a Boy and His Horn,* Bloomsbury Books for Young Readers (New York, NY), 2011.

Mary Brigid Barrett, *Shoebox Sam,* Zonderkidz (Grand Rapids, MI), 2011.

Contributor to *Our Children Can Soar: A Celebration of Rosa, Barack, and the Pioneers of Change* by Michelle Cook, Bloomsbury (New York, NY), 2009, and *Manners Mash-up: A Goofy Guide to Good Behavior,* 2011.

"KEENA FORD" READER SERIES BY MELISSA THOMSON

Keena Ford and the Second-grade Mix-up, Dial Books for Young Readers (New York, NY), 2008.

Keena Ford and the Field Trip Mix-up, Dial Books for Young Readers (New York, NY), 2009.

Keena Ford and the Secret Journal Mix-up, Dial Books for Young Readers (New York, NY), 2010.

Sidelights

Winner of the 2005 Coretta Scott King/John Steptoe Award for New Talent in Illustration, Frank Morrison creates paintings that reflect the rich culture of inner-city life. Among Morrison's illustration projects are stories by Peter Abrahams, Melanie Turner-Denstaedt, and celebrity authors ranging from Queen Latifah to sports greats Alex Rodriguez, Chris Paul, and Pelé. He has also creates the entertaining images that enliven Melissa Thomson's "Keena Ford" series of beginning chapter books about a spunky second grader. Morrison's unique style incorporates dark backgrounds and elongated figures rendered using sinuous lines and featuring exaggerated features. He "plays with the human form like a kid with soft taffy," wrote Tahree Lane in a profile of the artist for the *Toledo Blade,* "pulling and stretching faces and limbs in exaggeration of a key characteristic."

A self-educated artist and designer, Morrison was raised in New Jersey and now works out of a studio in Georgia. He was inspired to pursue a career as a painter by studying the work of the "Old Masters" and revisioning their work to reflect a modern urban aesthetic. His first illustration project, Debbie A. Taylor's *Sweet*

Frank Morrison contributes his characteristic stylized art to Chris Paul's inspirational picture book Long Shot: Never Too Small to Dream Big. (Illustration copyright © 2009 by Frank Morrison. Reproduced by permission of Simon & Schuster Books for Young Readers, an imprint of Simon & Schuster Macmillan.)

Music in Harlem, was dubbed "a confident debut" by a *Publishers Weekly* contributor while a *Kirkus Reviews* writer noted that Morrison's "elongated" characters move "against backgrounds that curve, slant, and boogie-woogie—but almost never stay still."

Brenda C. Roberts' *Jazzy Miz Mozetta* was the book that won Morrison his first major award. A *Kirkus Reviews* writer noted that Roberts' story—about a woman who loves to dance—is paired with a "colorful jumble of exaggeratedly long, skinny limbs in dynamic illustrations that dance to the beat of a fresh, rhythmic story." "Morrison captures the linear angles and smooth curves of jazz swing" concluded Mary Elam in a review of the same book for *School Library Journal.*

The determination of young athletes is a focus of several books illustrated by Morrison, among them New Orleans Hornets basketball star Chris Paul's *Long Shot: Too Small to Dream Big,* in which the artist's "kinetic pictures" bring to life an inspiring "tale of determination," according to *Booklist* critic Karen Cruze. In *Out of the Ballpark,* a picture book by New York Yankees third baseman Rodriguez, a boy dreams of becoming a sports star, while in Pelé's *For the Love of Soccer* the noted Brazilian athlete shares his history while also introducing a young player who views Pelé's accomplishments as inspiration. Morrison's "stylized paintings capture the . . . energy" of *Out of the Ballpark,* "and his playfully skewed perspectives keep things light," wrote a *Publishers Weekly* contributor, while in *School*

Library Journal Marilyn Taniguchi noted that Morrison's "action-packed illustrations, in vivid hues, help keep the story moving at a brisk pace." Calling *For the Love of Soccer* "a pithy recap of his illustrious career," John Peters added in his *Booklist* review that Morrison's characters "explode the infectious, winning enthusiasm" of Pelé's tale. "The legendary soccer player composes a stirring ode to his beloved sport," wrote a *Kirkus Reviews* writer, and Morrison's art captures "all the energy" of the globally popular game.

In Lissette Norman's *My Feet Are Laughing* Morrison creates artwork that *Booklist* contributor Hazel Rochman described as "full of swirling curves and angles." It "exhibits versatility, exuding Morrison's characteristic energy as well as capturing the story's more subdued moments," the critic added. Discussing Morrison's work for Queen Latifah's *Queen of the Scene,* about a young African-American girl who excels at all playground activities, *School Library Journal* contributor Mary Hazelton wrote that the illustrator's "elastic-bodied figures are graceful and brazen," making each page of the picture book "spin with movement and action." A *Kirkus Reviews* critic had a similar assessment of the work, writing that "Morrison's illustrations burst with originality, vibrancy and humor" and capture the "upbeat attitude reflected by the story's urban neighborhood setting."

Biographical and Critical Sources

PERIODICALS

Booklist, May 1, 2004, Terry Glover, review of *Sweet Music in Harlem,* p. 1564; April 1, 2006, Linda Perkins, review of *George Crum and the Saratoga Chip,* p. 46, and Hazel Rochman, review of *My Feet Are Laughing,* p. 49; September 1, 2009, Karen Cruze, review of *Long Shot: Never Too Small to Dream Big,* p. 110; July 1, 2010, John Peters, review of *For the Love of Soccer!,* p. 64.

Kirkus Reviews, April 15, 2004, review of *Sweet Music in Harlem,* p. 402; October 1, 2004, Brenda C. Roberts, review of *Jazzy Miz Mozetta,* p. 967; March 15, 2006, Gaylia Taylor, review of *George Crum and the Saratoga Chip,* p. 301; October 1, 2006, review of *Queen of the Scene,* p. 1022; February 1, 2007, review of *Out of the Ballpark,* p. 128; June 15, 2008, review of *Keena Ford and the Second-Grade Mix-up;* June 15, 2009, review of *Keena Ford and the Field Trip Mix-up;* August 15, 2009, review of *Long Shot;* May 1, 2010, review of *For the Love of Soccer!*

New York Times Book Review, July 12, 2009, review of *Keena Ford and the Field Trip Mix-Up.*

Publishers Weekly, May 24, 2004, review of *Sweet Music in Harlem,* p. 61; January 3, 2005, review of *Jazzy Miz Mozetta,* p. 54; October 2, 2006, review of *Queen of the Scene,* p. 61; February 5, 2007, review of *Out of the Ballpark,* p. 58; September 21, 2009, review of *Long Shot,* p. 57.

School Library Journal, July, 2004, Jane Marino, review of *Sweet Music in Harlem,* p. 89; December, 2004, Mary Elam, review of *Jazzy Miz Mozetta,* p. 118; December, 2006, Mary Hazelton, review of *Queen of the Scene,* p. 101; May, 2007, Marilyn Taniguchi, review of *Out of the Ballpark,* p. 107; October, 2008, Sharon R. Pearce, review of *Keena Ford and the Second-Grade Mix-Up,* p. 126; May, 2009, Mary N. Oluonye, review of *The Hat That Wore Clara B.,* p. 90; July, 2009, Debbbie S. Hoskins, review of *Keena Ford and the Field Trip Mix-up,* p. 68; October, 2009, Sara Paulson-Yarovoy, review of *Long Shot,* p. 101; July, 2010, Blair Christolon, review of *For the Love of Soccer!,* p. 75.

Toldedo Blade, February 1, 2007, Tahree Lane, "Atlanta Artist Plays with the Human Form."

ONLINE

Frank Morrison Home Page, http://www.morrisongraphics.com (February 15, 2011).*

N

NAIYOMAH, Wilson Kimeli 1977-

Personal

Born 1977, in Enoosaen, Kenya. *Education:* University of Oregon, B.S.; Stanford University, degree; University of Queensland, postgraduate study at Rotary Center for International Studies, beginning 2010.

Addresses

Home—Queensland, Australia.

Career

Peacemaker and author Former Maasai warrior. Speaker at gatherings throughout the world, including at U.S. Library of Congress National Book Festival, 2010, and National Press Club.

Awards, Honors

Named Rotary International World Peace fellow, beginning 2009.

Writings

(Coauthor) Carmen Agra Deedy, *Fourteen Cows for America,* illustrated by Thomas Gonzalez, Peachtree Publishers (Atlanta, GA), 2009.

Author's work has been translated into Spanish.

Sidelights

Wilson Kimeli Naiyomah is a Kenyan who created a unique bridge between diverse cultures through his skill as a storyteller. In his efforts to explain the tragedy suffered by a Western city to Africans with no knowledge of life beyond their rural tribal village, he inspired a compassionate gesture that was ultimately recognized by the U.S. State Department and written up in the *New York Times.* Carmen Agra Deedy, a children's author, was inspired to contact Naiyomah after reading the newspaper's account, and the children's book *Fourteen Cows for America* was the result.

A member of the Wasinkishu clan, Naiyomah was born in the Kenyan village of Enoosaen, where he was raised in the nomadic Maasai warrior tradition. Recognizing Naiyomah's potential, tribal elders worked together to send the young man the United States to gain the education that would allow him to improve life for his people. After graduating from the University of Oregon, Naiyomah enrolled at Stanford University, intending to pursue a medical degree. However, the man's career plans changed after a chance visit to the United Nations building in Manhattan on September 11th, 2001. On that day the Kenyan witnessed, first hand, the terror, the tragedy, and the spread of sorrow that occurred following the terrorist attacks that brought down the twin towers.

When Naiyomah returned to Kenya six months later and spoke of witnessing this tragedy, few in his village could comprehend the scope of destruction. In telling his story, he helps them visualize building taller than trees, the acrid smoke, the bravery of both survivors and rescuers, and the sadness of those who had lost friends and loved ones. When Naiyomah requested their blessing on his family's cow—a highly valued possession that is considered by the Maasai to be a sacred symbol of life—as a way of honoring those who had been touched by this tragedy, the elders of Enoosaen responded with a similar gesture. Their gift of fourteen cows to the people of America was acknowledged by State Department officials and—because it was not feasible for the creatures to be shipped halfway across the earth—these cattle and their offspring remain honored in Naiyomah's village, where relations between the elders and the United States has been strengthened to the benefit of both cultures. For Naiyomah, the response to his story, as captured with Deedy's help in *Fourteen Cows for America*, inspired him to pursue work on behalf of world peace, and he began postgraduate work at the Rotary Center for International Studies at the University of Queensland, Brisbane, Australia, in early 2010.

In reviewing *Fourteen Cows for America, Booklist* contributor Ilene Cooper recommended the work, writing that Deedy's text and Naiyomah's endnote combine with "the glowing mixed-media illustrations [by Thomas Gonzalez to] show empathy and connections across communities." A *Publishers Weekly* critic praised the story as a "lyrical account" that "avoids specifics" of the actual attack on New York City, and Rebecca Dash observed in her *School Library Journal* review that,

while the book's themes may be too abstract for very young children, Naiyomah's endnote "provides a fitting conclusion to this breathtaking chronicle." For the *Publishers Weekly* reviewer, the text of *Fourteen Cows for America* is enriched by Gonzalez' "luminous" colored-pencil and pastel images, which capture both "vivid native dress and sweeping African landscapes."

Asked to describe the qualities of a Maasai warrior in an interview for the Children's Literature Web site, Naioymah explained: "To be a Maasai warrior means your life belongs to society, not to your individual family. You are always ready to put your life on the line to defend any community you find yourself in. Your home is the earth; your people are those around you. You never eat at your parent's house without another warrior or a child to share the food with. You should not be selfish with your life or your food."

Carmen Agra Deedy recounts Wilson Kimeli Naiyomah's story of community in the picture book **Fourteen Cows for America,** *featuring artwork by* ***Thomas Gonzalez.*** (Peachtree Publishers, 2009. Illustration © 2009 by Thomas Gonzalez. Reproduced by permission.)

Biographical and Critical Sources

PERIODICALS

Booklist, July 1, 2009, Hazel Rochman, review of *Fourteen Cows for America,* p. 57.

Childhood Education, winter, 2009, Anne Hannibal, review of *Fourteen Cows for America,* p. 118.

Kirkus Reviews, July 1, 2009, review of *Fourteen Cows for America.*

New York Times, June 3, 2002, Marc Lacey, review of *Fourteen Cows for America.*

New York Times Book Review, November 8, 2009, Nicholas D. Kristof, review of *Fourteen Cows for America,* p. 15.

Publishers Weekly, August 3, 2009, review of *Fourteen Cows for America,* p. 45.

School Library Journal, August, 2009, Rebecca Dash, review of *Fourteen Cows for America,* p. 89.

Washington Post, May 4, 1996, Stephen Buckley, "It Takes a Village to Make a Doctor: Maasai Tribesmen, Who Once Revered the Warrior, Help a Student."

ONLINE

BBC News Web site, http://news.bbc.co.uk/ (September 12, 2006), Ruth Nesoba, "New Home for U.S. Maasai Cattle."

Children's Literature Web site, http://www.childrenslit.com/ (February 15, 2011), "Wilson Kimeli Naiyomah."

Rotary International Web site, http://www.rotary.org/ (July 29, 2009), Ryan Hyland "Maasai Warrior Hopes to Work for Diplomacy"; (September 17, 2009) "Wilson Kimeli Naiyomah: From Maasai Warrior to Peace Fellow."*

*   *   *

NAYERI, Dina
(Dina Nayeri Viergutz)

Personal

Born in Iran; married. *Education:* Princeton University, B.S. (economics; summa cum laude), 2001; Harvard University, M.B.A., 2006, M.Ed., 2007. *Hobbies and other interests:* Cooking, travel, writing.

Addresses

Home—Amsterdam, Netherlands. *Agent*—Anderson Literary Management, 12 W. 19th St., 2nd Fl., New York, NY 10011.

Career

Author and school counselor. McKinsey & Co., New York, NY, strategy consultant, c. 2001-03; Saks Fifth Avenue, New York, NY, former project manager.

Writings

"ANOTHER" YOUNG-ADULT SERIES; WITH BROTHER DANIEL NAYERI

Another Faust, Candlewick Press (Somerville, MA), 2009.
Another Pan, Candlewick Press (Somerville, MA), 2010.
Another Jeykll, Candlewick Press (Somerville, MA), 2010.

Adaptations

Another Faust was adapted for audiobook, read by Katherine Kellgren, Brilliance Audio, 2009.

Sidelights

Dina Nayeri collaborates with her brother, writer and editor Daniel Nayeri, on the novels *Another Faust, Another Pan,* and *Another Jeykll.* Geared for teen readers, the books are part of the Nayeris' "Another" series, in which elements from literary classics weave their way into the lives of students at an elite New York City prep school. The Nayeris' stories are liberally salted with literary references that take curious readers to the output of writers ranging from James Barrie, Johann Wolfgang von Goethe, and Lord Byron to Nathaniel Hawthorne, Robert Louis Stevenson, and Laura Ingalls Wilder. they also tap many layers of world history.

Nayeri was born in Iran but fled with her family when she was eight years old for religious reasons. The Nayeris lived as refugees until they moved to the United States three years later. Driven to succeed academically, Dina Nayeri earned an economics degree at Princeton University and went on to earn advanced degrees in both business and higher education while working in the business sector. While completing her M.B.A. at Harvard University, she realized that there might not be another opportunity to pursue her dream of writing a novel. She contacted her brother, who was then working for a New York City publisher, and during a two-week stint the siblings expanded her idea into an outline and completed the manuscript over the next twelve months. When the novel was finally released as *Another Faust,* it had already been expanded from one story into a series, and Nayeri had made the shift to full-time author.

In *Another Faust* the Nayeris follow the story of five kidnaped ten year olds who were selected for their special talents, kidnaped, and groomed in avarice and ambition by the mysterious Madame Nicola Vileroy. Now age fifteen, they emerge from seclusion and arrive at Manhattan's exclusive Marlowe School, where Madame has enrolled them. Trained to cheat, lie, and steal without any moral quibbles, the five soulless Fausts—Valentin, Victoria, Christian, and twins Bella and Bice—quickly take control and begin to pursue their endless ambitions, until secrets are revealed that cause them to see the true consequences of acquiescing to their driven natures. "Telling the story from alternate viewpoints

Cover of Dina and Daniel Nayeri's prep-school thriller **Another Faust,** *a story with literary origins that features artwork by Scott Nobles.* (Jacket photograph copyright © 2010 by Scott Nobles. Reproduced by permission of Candlewick Press, Somerville, MA.)

keeps the action moving," noted *Booklist* contributor Shauna Yusko, and a *Publishers Weekly* critic dubbed the Nayeris' prose "clever and stylish." Noting the references to Goethe's *Faust* that appear throughout the novel, Hayden Bass added in *School Library Journal* that the "well-timed twists" in *Another Faust* will attract "fans of dark contemporary fantasy."

J.M. Barrie's perennial favorite *Peter Pan* is the Nayeris' jumping-off point in *Another Pan*. This time the Marlowe School counts Wendy and John Darling among its students. The siblings know that their admission is a result of their Egyptologist father's place on the school's faculty; most of the other students are wealthy and look down on the poorer Darlings, even though Wendy is dating the popular Connor Wirth. Then a new student, Peter, arrives, aided by the sinister Madame Vileroy and bringing with him the mysterious *Book of Gates*. Wendy and John are seduced by his stories of magic, only to find themselves trapped in an underworld containing an ancient mystery. Captain Hook, the Lost Boys, and teenage romance mix with Egyptian myths, mystical pyramids, and the lure of eternal youth in the Nayeris' intriguing story. In *Booklist* Shauna Yusko predicted of *Another Pan* that "this unique twist on a classic story

should find even wider appreciation" than the siblings' debut, and Sue Giffard asserted in her *School Library Journal* review that "the authors succeed in creating a sense of danger that builds to a suspenseful climax."

Discussing her collaborative writing career with brother Daniel during an interview for the Candlewick Press Web site, Nayeri explained their decision to focus on a young-adult readership: "We wanted to write a story that explored all the things we desperately wanted when we were teenagers. So first came the teenage characters, and it grew from there." "Writing with two people is actually a lot harder than writing alone," she added. "Before each of our books, we've actually had to spend weeks discussing the voice and the tone (with sample paragraphs and scenes), so that when we begin writing, we can both be shooting for the same mark. Then we divide up the chapters and write a draft, and each person gets to thoroughly edit the other person's chapter. We do that a couple more times until the voice is smooth. I can't imagine being able to pull it off with a non-family member."

"Our series is about retellings," Nayeri added in discussing the "Another" books, "but at the end of the day it is also about rediscovering all the wonderful literature that is already available to teens. It's about empowering young adults to add their own mark to the literary world. I hope this series leads readers to experiment with their own writing."

Biographical and Critical Sources

PERIODICALS

Booklist, September 15, 2009, Shauna Yusko, review of *Another Faust,* p. 49.
Bulletin of the Center for Children's Books, October, 2009, Karen Coats, review of *Another Faust,* p. 76.
Publishers Weekly, August 3, 2009, review of *Another Faust,* p. 46.
School Library Journal, September, 2009, Hayden Bass, review of *Another Faust,* p. 168.
Voice of Youth Advocates, August, 2009, Jennifer Miskec, review of *Another Faust,* p. 241.

ONLINE

Anderson Literary Management Web site, http://www.andersonliterary.com/ (February 15, 2011).
Candlewick Press Web site, http://www.candlewick.com/ (February 15, 2011), interview with Daniel and Dina Nayeri.
Dina and Daniel Nayeri Home Page, http://www.anotherfaust.com (February 15, 2011).*

* * *

NGUYEN, Vincent

Personal

Born in TX. *Education:* School of Visual Arts (New York, NY), B.F.A. (illustration).

Addresses

Home and office—Hoboken, NJ. *Agent*—Shannon Associates, 333 W. 57th St., Ste. 809, New York, NY 10019.

Career

Illustrator and animation artist. Blue Sky Studios, White Plains, NY, animator and concept artist; Twentieth Century-Fox, member of art department.

Member

Society of Illustrators.

Illustrator

(With Joe Bartos) Mark Shulman, *Some Ducks,* Barron's Educational (Hauppauge, NY), 2003.

Gwyn Borcherding, *The Good That I Should: Romans 7 for Kids,* Concordia Publishing House (St. Louis, MO), 2004.

Mark Shulman, *Stella the Star,* Walker & Company (New York, NY), 2004.

Karen Hill, *A Sky Full of Praise,* Little Simon Inspirations (New York, NY), 2005.

Mark Shulman, *Louis and the Dodo,* Sterling Publishing (New York, NY), 2005.

Sally Derby, *Whoosh Went the Wind!,* Marshall Cavendish (New York, NY), 2006.

Steven Kroll, *Jungle Bullies,* Marshall Cavendish (New York, NY), 2006.

Mark Shulman, *Not Another Tea Party,* Sterling Publishing (New York, NY), 2006.

Eric A. Kimmel, *Little Britches and the Rattlers,* Marshall Cavendish (New York, NY), 2008.

Karen Rostoker-Gruber, *Bandit,* Marshall Cavendish (New York, NY), 2008.

Mark Shulman, *Gorilla Garage,* Marshall Cavendish Children (Tarrytown, NY), 2009.

Debbie Macomber and Mary Lou Carney, *The Truly Terribly Horrible Sweater . . . That Grandma Knit,* Harper (New York, NY), 2009.

Karen Rostoker-Gruber, *Bandit's Surprise,* Marshall Cavendish (New York, NY), 2010.

Eileen Spinelli, *Buzz,* Simon & Schuster Books for Young Readers (New York, NY), 2010.

Donita K. Paul and Evangeline Denmark, *The Dragon and the Turtle,* Waterbrook Press (Colorado Springs, CO), 2010.

Sidelights

A graduate of New York City's School of Visual Arts, Vincent Nguyen works as a concept artist for animated films produced at both Blue Sky Studios and Twentieth Century-Fox. In addition to creating art for motion pictures, Nguyen's colorful art has also been featured in children's books such as *Whoosh Went the Wind!* by Sally Derby, *Stella and the Star* and *Gorilla Garage* by Mark Shulman, *Little Britches and the Rattlers* by prolific writer Eric A. Kimmel, and Eileen Spinelli's simply titled *Buzz.* Reviewing *Buzz,* the tale of a tiny bumblebee that overcomes its fears in order to help a

friend in trouble, *Booklist* critic Julie Cummins praised Nguyen's "delightful mixed-media illustrations" for capturing the upbeat nature of Spinelli's story, while his "digitally enhanced" watercolor-and-pencil art for Kimmel's folksy retelling of "Little Black Sambo" help make that picture book "a rattling fun tale," according to a *Kirkus Reviews* writer.

Nguyen's background as an animation artist has helped to shape his style as an illustrator. His picture-book projects often include lively action and provide a unique and unlikely point of view. For instance, in capturing the fabricated adventures of a young boy who is always late for school in *Whoosh Went the Wind!,* Nguyen assembles an array of illustrations that portray the story's imaginative young protagonist scaling mountains and depict dandelions flurrying in the wind and chickens and roosters flying about. In a review of *Whoosh Went the Wind!* for *School Library Journal,* Rebecca Sheridan remarked that Nguyen's "acrylic and charcoal illustrations . . . carry the action and add to the story's energy." Julie Cummins in her review for *Booklist* noted that, much like his work for film, Nguyen's picture-book images "effectively use perspective to generate the melee."

In *Stella the Star* Nguyen adds his unique viewpoint to a title that highlights a little girl experiencing her first

Vincent Nguyen creates the colorful artwork for Sally Derby's adventure-filled picture book **Whoosh Went the Wind!** (Marshall Cavendish Children, 2006. Illustration copyright © 2006 by Vincent Nguyen. Reproduced by permission.)

turn on stage in a school play as her proud parents look on. In praise of the collaboration between author and artist, *Booklist* reviewer Ilene Cooper wrote that the story's "welcomingly theatrical" illustrations will attract young readers. In *Not Another Tea Party* Shulman describes an unusual assemblage of guests that end up seated around the table at young Hilary's afternoon tea, and the artist's "quirky and appealing illustrations" add humor to the tale, according to a *Kirkus Reviews* writer.

A knitting project gone awry takes center stage in Debbie Macomber and Mary Lou Carney's *The Truly Terribly Horrible Sweater . . . That Grandma Knit*. Like many children, Cameron has a doting grandmother who also dabbles with crafts. For his birthday, the boy receives a hand-knit, rainbow-striped sweater that he knows will make him the subject of taunting should he wear it to school. Every attempt to hide the sweater fails, and only when the boy models the garment for its maker does he appreciate the true value of Grandma's gift. Complete with knitting instructions, *The Truly Terribly Horrible Sweater . . . That Grandma Knit* features illustrations that "pick up a considerable amount of energy and beauty" as the story moves into an imaginative realm.

Bringing to life *Bandit* and *Bandit's Surprise,* two picture books by Karen Rostoker-Gruber, Nguyen captures the antics of a frisky orange tiger kitten who shares a home with a girl named Michelle. In *Bandit* the kitty finds its household in an uproar as Michele's family prepares to move to a new home, and even when its toys are scattered around the new house the cat continues to view its former house as home. "What might have been just a story of everyday experiences is elevated by terrific art," asserted Cooper in *Booklist,* and Kara Schaff Dean commented in *School Library Journal* that the "attractive Pop Art style" of Nguyen's digitized images evokes "the comic-book and newsprint look of artist Roy Lichtenstein."

Bandit's Surprise finds the orange tabby forced to share Michelle's affections with a new kitten, the insufferable Mitzy, whose constant antics prompt the older cat to leave home. Praising the author's "well-paced story," Gillian Engberg added of Bandit's second outing that Nguyen's "polished, simply shaded drawings" "add to the book's read-aloud appeal." In *School Library Journal* Carrie Rogers-Whitehead commended the "laughout-loud dialogue" in *Bandit's Surprise,* adding that the

book's "clever" images feature kitty characters with the "humanlike expressions [that] give feeling to the text."

Biographical and Critical Sources

PERIODICALS

Booklinks, July, 2005, Pat Scales, review of *Stella the Star,* p. 35; November, 2006, Barbara Chatton, review of *Whoosh Went the Wind!,* p. 58.

Booklist, April 15, 2004, Ilene Cooper, review of *Stella the Star,* p. 1449; October 15, 2006, Julie Cummins, review of *Whoosh Went the Wind!,* p. 54; May 15, 2008, Ilene Cooper, review of *Bandit,* p. 46; September 15, 2008, Ian Chipman, review of *Little Britches and the Rattlers,* p. 57; April 1. 2010, Gillian Engberg, review of *Bandit's Surprise,* p. 45; June 1, 2010, Julie Cummins, review of *Buzz,* p. 90.

Kirkus Reviews, December 1, 2005, review of *Louis and the Dodo,* p. 1280; July 15, 2006, review of *Whoosh Went the Wind!,* p. 721; October 15, 2006, review of *Not Another Tea Party,* p. 1080; July 15, 2008, review of *Little Britches and the Rattlers;* February 1, 2009, review of *Gorilla Garage;* October 1, 2009, review of *The Truly Terrible Horrible Sweater. . . That Grandma Knit.*

Publishers Weekly, January 2, 2006, review of *Louis and the Dodo,* p. 61; October 19, 2009, review of *The Truly Terrible Horrible Sweater . . . That Grandma Knit,* p. 50; June 28, 2010, review of *Buzz,* p. 127.

School Library Journal, May, 2004, Maryann H. Owen, review of *Stella the Star,* p. 124; January, 2006, Amy Lilien-Harper, review of *Louis and the Dodo,* p. 113; October, 2006, Rebecca Sheridan, review of *Whoosh Went the Wind!,* p. 109; November, 2006, M. Casper, review of *Jungle Bullies,* p. 98; May, 2008, Kara Schaff Dean, review of *Bandit,* p. 107; September, 2008, Linda M. Kenton, review of *Little Britches and the Rattlers,* p. 152; March, 2009, Martha Simpson, review of *Gorilla Garage,* p. 128; November, 2009, Kathleen Finn, review of *The Truly Terribly Horrible Sweater . . . That Grandma Knit,* p. 84; June, 2010, Marianne Saccardi, review of *Buzz,* p. 84.

ONLINE

Children's Bookwatch Web site, http://www.midwestbook review.com/ (October 1, 2006), review of *Whoosh Went the Wind!*

Shannon Associates Web site, http://www.shannonassociates.com/ (February 15, 2011), "Vincent Nguyen."*

P-R

PENNER, Lucille Recht 1942-

Personal
Born 1942, in New York, NY. *Education:* Barnard College, degree.

Addresses
Home—Tucson, AZ.

Career
Author of children's nonfiction.

Writings

FOR CHILDREN

Dinosaur Babies, illustrated by Peter Barrett, Random House (New York, NY), 1991.

Celebration: The Story of American Holidays, illustrated by Ib Ohlsson, Maxwell Macmillan International (New York, NY), 1993.

A Native American Feast, Simon & Schuster Books for Young Readers (New York, NY), 1994.

S-S-S-Snakes!, illustrated by Peter Barrett, Random House (New York, NY), 1994.

The True Story of Pocahontas, illustrated by Pamela Johnson, Random House (New York, NY), 1994.

Sitting Bull, illustrated by Will Williams, Grosset & Dunlap (New York, NY), 1995.

The Little Women Book: Games, Recipes, Crafts, and Other Homemade Pleasures, illustrated by Diane de-Groat, Random House (New York, NY), 1995.

Cowboys, illustrated by Ben Carter, Grosset & Dunlap (New York, NY), 1996.

Monster Bugs, illustrated by Pamela Johnson, Random House (New York, NY), 1996.

The Pilgrims at Plymouth, illustrated by S.D. Schindler, Random House (New York, NY), 1996.

The Statue of Liberty, illustrated by Jada Rowland, Random House (New York, NY), 1996.

Twisters!, illustrated by Kazushige Nitta, Random House (New York, NY), 1996, illustrated by Allen Garns, Random House (New York, NY), 2009.

Baby Elephant, illustrated by Betina Ogden, Grosset & Dunlap (New York, NY), 1997.

The Teddy Bear Book, illustrated by Jody Wheeler, Random House (New York, NY), 1997.

Westward Ho!: The Story of the Pioneers, illustrated by Bryn Barnard, Random House (New York, NY), 1997.

The Liberty Tree: The Beginning of the American Revolution, illustrated by David Wenzel, Random House (New York, NY), 1998.

Big Birds, illustrated by Bryn Barnard, Random House (New York, NY), 2000.

Clean Sweep Campers ("Math Matters" series), illustrated by Paige Billin-Frye, Kane Press (New York, NY), 2000.

Lights Out! ("Math Matters" series), illustrated by Jerry Smath, Kane Press (New York, NY), 2000.

Where's That Bone? ("Math Matters" series), illustrated by Lynn Adams, Kane Press (New York, NY), 2000.

Ice Wreck ("Road to Reading" series), illustrated by David La Fleur, Golden Books (New York, NY), 2001.

Slowpoke, illustrated by Gioia Fiammenghi, Kane Press (New York, NY), 2001.

Sam's Sneaker Squares ("Math Matters" series), illustrated by Ron Fritz, Kane Press (New York, NY), 2002.

X Marks the Spot! ("Math Matters" series), illustrated by Jerry Smath, Kane Press (New York, NY), 2002.

Bears on the Brain ("Science Solves It!" series), illustrated by Lynn Adams, Kane Press (New York, NY), 2003.

Dragons, illustrated by Peter Scott, Random House (New York, NY), 2004.

Unicorns, illustrated by Mel Grant, Random House (New York, NY), 2005.

Mermaids, illustrated by Mel Grant, Random House (New York, NY), 2008.

Monsters, illustrated by Allen Douglas, Random House (New York, NY), 2009.

OTHER

The Colonial Cookbook, Hastings House (New York, NY), 1976.

The Honey Book, Hastings House (New York, NY), 1980.

The Thanksgiving Book, Hastings House (New York, NY), 1985.

Eating the Plates: A Pilgrim Book of Food and Manners, Maxwell Macmillan International (New York, NY), 1991.

The Tea Party Book: With Menus, Recipes, Decorations, and Favors to Make, illustrated by Jody Wheeler, Random House (New York, NY), 1993.

Sidelights

Lucille Recht Penner began her career writing history-themed cookbooks such as *The Colonial Cookbook, The Thanksgiving Book, A Native American Feast,* and *Eating the Plates: A Pilgrim Book of Food and Manners.* In more recent years she has focused on beginning readers, creating standalone books such as *Ice Wreck, Dragons,* and *Twisters!* in addition to contributing to several nonfiction book series. Reviewing *Twisters!,* which features artwork by Nitta Kazushige, *Booklist* critic Ilene Cooper predicted that "the heart-stopping terrors that twisters engender will entice new readers." Gillian Engberg noted in the same periodical that Penner's text in *Ice Wreck* brings British Arctic explorer Ernest Shackleton's "heart pounding expedition" aboard the ill-fated sailing ship *Endurance* "vividly to life."

Penner was born in New York City and attended Barnard College. Her first book, *The Colonial Cookbook,* was published in 1976, and was followed by several

Lucille Recht Penner presents an illustrated study of some of the world's most unusual creatures of legend in her book Mermaids, *which features artwork by Mel Grant.* (Stepping Stone Books, 2008. Illustration copyright © 2008 by Mel Grant. Used by permission of Random House Children's Books, a division of Random House, Inc.)

other cookery-themed children's books before she began to focus almost exclusively on the beginning-reader market. Reviewing another early work, *A Native American Feast,* Mary Harris Veeder explained in *Booklist* that Penner goes beyond merely describing the foods eaten by North American Indian tribes and "details the hard work involved in finding and preparing food."

In her contributions to the "Math Matters" series, Penner mixes an entertaining story with a problem or mystery that can be solved with basic math skills. In *Slowpoke,* for example, a boy attempts to curb his habit of dawdling by running to each destination, tallying up the minutes he save for use in pursuing a favorite pastime. A little girl helps her pet dog Bingo learn to map the locations where he buries his prize bones in Penner's story for *Where's That Bone? Lights Out!,* another "Math Matters" story featuring illustrations by Jerry Smath, finds a little girl staying up past her bedtime, hoping to be the last one in her city block to turn her light out. In *Clean-Sweep Campers,* which pairs Penner's text with colorful art by Paige Billin-Frye, readers visit Annie at summer camp and learn how she and her bunk-mates devised a way to keep their cabin tidy using fractions and a bit of teamwork. In *School Library Journal* Maura Bresnahan praised *Where's That Bone?* as an entertaining "backyard adventure" studded with "'position words'" (adverbs and prepositions) and "lively, colorful illustrations" by Lynn Adams. Lucinda Snyder Whitehurst, commenting on the "Math Matters" series in *School Library Journal,* noted that "the stories hold interest" and "are true to their purpose" in illustrating the many ways that math involves itself in everyday life.

Penner taps into children's interest in magic and fantasy in her series of chapter books that includes *Dragons, Monsters, Mermaids,* and *Unicorns.* In *Dragons* she begins by introducing the earliest stories to feature a flying lizard creature, drawing from Chinese, Central American, and European myths and legends as she traces these mythical creatures forward through time to such present-day incarnations as the Loch Ness monster. A similar approach is taken in *Monsters,* but this time Penner also focuses on the universal need of human societies to create these fearsome beings. In *Unicorns* her text is paired with drawings by Mel Grant and leads from myths and legends to the many ways that white-coated horses and ponies and even goats have been costumed to look like the legendary long-horned unicorn. Creating a nonfiction book "about a fantastical topic is a great way to interest fantasy fans," noted *Booklist* critic Diane Foote in her positive review of *Dragons,* and a *Kirkus Reviews* writer dubbed *Monsters* "a good introduction to folklore for young fantasy lovers."

Biographical and Critical Sources

PERIODICALS

Booklist, November 1, 1994, Mary Harris Veeder, review of *A Native American Feast,* p. 494; November 15,

1996, Ilene Cooper, review of *Twisters!*, p. 597; July, 2001, Gillian Engberg, review of *Ice Wreck*, p. 2002; April 15, 2002, Carolyn Phelan, review of *Sam's Sneaker Squares*, p. 1408; August, 2004, Diane Foote, review of *Dragons*, p. 1926.

Kirkus Reviews, October 15, 2005, review of *Unicorns*, p. 1144; July 1, 2009, review of *Monsters*.

School Library Journal, June, 2000, Lucinda Snyder Whitehurst, review of *Lights Out!*, p. 111; February, 2001, Maura Bresnahan, review of *Where's That Bone?*, p. 104; February, 2001, Holy T. Sneeringer, review of *Clean-Sweep Campers*, p. 92; February, 2002, Wendy S. Carroll, review of *Slowpoke*, p. 110; October, 2003, Karen Land, review of *Buried in the Backyard*, p. 125.*

*   *   *

REYNOLDS, Peter H. 1961-

Personal

Born March 16, 1961, in Weston, Ontario, Canada; son of Keith H. (a treasurer) and Hazel E. (a bookkeeper) Reynolds; children: Sarah. *Education:* Attended Fitchburg State College, 1978-83, and Massachusetts College of Art, 1979-80.

Addresses

Office—The Blue Bunny, 577 High St., Dedham, MA 02026. *Agent*—Pippin Properties, 155 E. 38th St., Ste. 2H, New York, NY 10016; info@pippinproperties.com.

Career

Author, illustrator, and entrepreneur. Tom Snyder Productions, Cambridge, MA, vice president and creative director, 1983-96; FableVision Studios, Boston, MA, cofounder (with brother, Paul Reynolds) and creative director, 1996—; Blue Bunny (books and toy store), Dedham, MA, co-owner. Dedham Square Circle (civic development group), cofounder, beginning 2005; Creative Journey Retreat, founder and organizer; speaker at events. *Exhibitions:* Work exhibited at Danforth Museum of Art, Framingham, MA, 2009; and Katonah Museum of Art Learning Center Katonah, NY, 2011.

Member

International Society for Technology in Education.

Awards, Honors

Media and Methods Excellence in Education Award, *Parenting* magazine award, Parents' Choice Award, Educom Distinguished Software award, and Technology and Learning Award of Excellence, all for work on Tom Snyder Productions projects; Telly Award second place, ASIFA-East, and BDA International Design Silver Award, both for *The Blue Shoe;* Distinguished Alumni Award, Fitchburg State College, 1999; ASIFA-East third-place honor, and ASIFA-Hollywood Annie nomination, both 1999, both for film *Living Forever;* National Education Association Top 100 Books listee, 2000, and Silver award, Nautilus Book Award, 2010, both for *The North Star;* named Shaper of the Future 2000, *Converge* magazine; Children's Choice selection, International Reading Association/Children's Book Council (IRA/CBC), Notable Children's Book designation, American Library Association, and Oppenheim Toy Portfolio Gold Award, all c. 2001, all for *Judy Moody Gets Famous!* by Megan McDonald; Christopher Award, Oppenheim Toy Portfolio Platinum Award, Irma S. and James H. Black Honor Book designation, Bank Street College of Education, Chicago Public Library Best Book designation, and Chapman Award for Best Classroom Read-aloud, all 2004, and La-Belle Prize, 2007, all for *The Dot;* Best Books for Children and Teens designation, Chicago Public Library, 2005, for *Stink* by McDonald; Children's Choice selection, IRA/CBC, 2005, for *Judy Moody Declares Independence* by McDonald; Literary Lights for Children Award, Associates of the Boston Public Library, 2007; L.H.D., Fitchburg State College, 2007; Best of the Best selection, Chicago Public Library, 2009, for *Judy Moody and Stink: The Mad, Mad, Mad, Mad Treasure Hunt* by McDonald.

Writings

SELF-ILLUSTRATED

Fizz and Martina in the Incredible Not-for-Profit Pet Resort Mystery, Tom Snyder Productions (Watertown, MA), 1993.

The North Star, FableVision Press (Watertown, MA), 1997, revised, Candlewick Press (Somerville, MA), 2009.

(With Sue Pandiani) *North Star Inspiration for the Classroom*, FableVision Press (Watertown, MA), 1999.

Sydney's Star, Simon & Schuster (New York, NY), 2001.

The Dot, Candlewick Press (Cambridge, MA), 2003.

Ish, Candlewick Press (Cambridge, MA), 2004.

So Few of Me, Candlewick Press (New York, NY), 2006.

My Very Big Little World, Atheneum (New York, NY), 2006.

The Best Kid in the World, Atheneum (New York, NY), 2006.

Rose's Garden, Candlewick Press (Somerville, MA), 2009.

Has created more than twenty interactive children's stories for the online service Prodigy, including *The Three Wolf Architects, The Adventures of Pewter Pan, Snow White and the Seven Accounts, Hilary and the Beast,* and *The Gingerbread Channel.*

ILLUSTRATOR

Megan McDonald, *Judy Moody*, Candlewick Press (Cambridge, MA), 1999.

Donald H. Graves, *The Portfolio Standard,* Heinemann (Portsmouth, NH), 2000.

Tobi Tobias, *Serendipity,* Simon & Schuster (New York, NY), 2000.

Megan McDonald, *Judy Moody Gets Famous!,* Candlewick Press (Cambridge, MA), 2001.

Megan McDonald, *Judy Moody Saves the World,* Candlewick Press (Cambridge, MA), 2002.

Ellen Potter, *Olivia Kidney,* Philomel Books (New York, NY), 2003.

Megan McDonald, *Judy Moody Predicts the Future,* Candlewick Press (Cambridge, MA), 2003.

Megan McDonald, *Judy Moody, M.D.: The Doctor Is In!,* Candlewick Press (Cambridge, MA), 2004.

Megan McDonald, *Judy Moody Declares Independence,* Candlewick Press (Cambridge, MA), 2005.

Ellen Potter, *Olivia Kidney and the Exit Academy,* Philomel Books (New York, NY), 2005.

Megan McDonald, *Stink: The Incredible Shrinking Kid,* Candlewick Press (Cambridge, MA), 2005.

Megan McDonald, *Judy Moody's Double-Rare Way-Not-Boring Book of Fun Stuff to Do,* Candlewick Press (Cambridge, MA), 2005.

Megan McDonald, *Judy Moody: Around the World in 8 1/2 Days,* Candlewick Press (Cambridge, MA), 2006.

Megan McDonald, *Stink and the Incredible Super-galactic Jawbreaker,* Candlewick Press (Cambridge, MA), 2006.

Megan McDonald, *Stink and the World's Worst Super-stinky Sneakers,* Candlewick Press (Cambridge, MA), 2007.

Megan McDonald, *Judy Moody and Stink: The Holly Joliday,* Candlewick Press (Cambridge, MA), 2007.

Alison McGhee, *Someday,* Atheneum (New York, NY), 2007.

Megan McDonald, *Judy Moody Goes to College,* Candlewick Press (Cambridge, MA), 2008.

Alison McGhee, *Little Boy,* Atheneum (New York, NY), 2008.

Megan McDonald, *Stink and the Great Guinea Pig Express,* Candlewick Press (Cambridge, MA), 2008.

Megan McDonald, *Judy Moody and Stink: The Mad, Mad, Mad, Mad Treasure Hunt,* Candlewick Press (Somerville, MA), 2009.

Jess M. Brallier, *Tess's Tree,* Harper (New York, NY), 2009.

Bob Raczka, *Guyku: A Year of Haiku for Boys,* Houghton Mifflin (Boston, MA), 2010.

Megan McDonald, *Judy Moody's Way Wacky Uber Awesome Book of More Fun Stuff to Do,* Candlewick Press (Somerville, MA), 2010.

Megan McDonald, *Judy Moody, Girl Detective,* Candlewick Press (Somerville, MA), 2010.

Megan McDonald, *Stink: Solar System Superhero,* Candlewick Press (Somerville, MA), 2010.

Megan McDonald, *Stink-o-pedia: Super Stink-y Stuff from A to Zzzzz,* Candlewick Press (Somerville, MA), 2010.

Sean Taylor, *Huck Runs Amuck,* Dial Books (New York, NY), 2011.

Contributor to *Knock, Knock!,* by Saxton Freymann, Dial (New York, NY), 2007. Also illustrator of texts and book covers for other children's books.

OTHER

Sharon Emerson, *Peter H. Reynolds and FableVision Present Zebrafish,* illustrated by Renee Kurilla, Atheneum Books for Young Readers (New York, NY), 2010.

Adaptations

The Dot was adapted for video, Weston Woods, 2004; *Ish* was adapted for video, Weston Woods, 2005.

Sidelights

An author, illustrator, designer, filmmaker, and motivational speaker, Peter H. Reynolds has garnered critical acclaim for such inspiring picture books as *The Dot, Ish,* and *Rose's Garden.* Reynolds, who has also earned accolades as the illustrator of Megan McDonald's best-selling "Judy Moody" series of chapter books, is also the cofounder, with twin brother Paul Reynolds, of FableVision Studios, an educational media company. "Nothing irks me more than seeing a person's creativity get shut down," he remarked on the Candlewick Press Web site. "Through my books, I want to help give kids—and grown-up kids—the vocabulary to protect their exploration, in art, writing, and thinking."

Reynolds began his career in advertising but quickly moved on to become a pivotal player in Tom Snyder Productions, one of the early computer software companies specializing in educational products. As creative director, author, and/or artist, of the firm Reynolds created short films, public-service announcements, interactive software programs, and online stories, all with a goal of encouraging creativity in young people while making learning fun. His view of life as a journey of learning is detailed in *The North Star,* a 1997 work that has also inspired a guidebook for teachers interested in bringing the North Star approach into their classrooms. Praising Reynolds' work revising the inspiring book for a new century, *Booklist* critic Randall Enos predicted of *The North Star* that readers "will enjoy this simple tale of a quintessential quest."

In *The Dot* Reynolds focuses on Vashti, a young girl who seems to have no natural artistic ability. However, when she completes a drawing assignment by marking her paper with one single dot, Vashti's clever art teacher expresses enthusiasm, asks the girl to sign her work, and hangs it prominently in the classroom. Soon, Vashti is making all sizes, colors, and patterns of dots, and when a little boy has the same frustration over a lack of drawing skill the girl takes on the role of encouraging teacher in reaction to his own simple, unschooled mark. A similar tale is the focus of *Ish,* in which Ramon loves to draw anywhere and anytime, until teasing from his older brother makes the boy yield to his inner critic. Discarding drawing after drawing, he soon discovers that his little sister sees something special in Ramon's un-realistic pictures, giving the budding artist renewed confidence.

Cover of Peter H. Reynolds' award-winning picture book The Dot, *in which the author shows that creativity can take many forms.* (Candlewick Press, 2003. Illustration © 2003 by Peter H. Reynolds. Reproduced by permission of Candlewick Press, Inc., Cambridge, MA.)

Calling *The Dot* "simplicity itself," Ilene Cooper added in her *Booklist* review that Reynolds' "small book carries a big message." According to *School Library Journal* reviewer Kathy Krasniewicz, in *The Dot* Reynolds pairs spare, gestured images rendered in "fluid pen-and-ink, watercolor, and tea" with a simple text to recount a journey "of self-expression, artistic experimentation, and success." A *Kirkus Reviews* writer predicted that *Ish* "may speak to formerly artistic young readers who are selling their own abilities short," while a *Publishers Weekly* contributor noted that the author/illustrator's "minimalist pen-and-ink illustrations" bring to life the book's "tidy lesson in the importance of . . . drawing . . . outside the box and believing in one's own abilities despite others' reactions." As Cooper noted in *Booklist,* the "great emotion and warmth" in *Ish* will appeal to young children, while the *Kirkus Reviews* writer concluded that Reynolds' book "will encourage other little artists."

Reynolds packs a message relevant to adults as well as children in *So Few of Me.* Poor Leo is a busy young boy, and when he wishes the wish of all very-busy people—that there was another "him" to help get everything on his to-do list completed—the wish actually comes to pass. Soon ten Leos crowd each page, each one rushing to get something done. All those Leos need supervision, however, and after a time the original boy decides that perhaps one Leo is quite enough. Citing Reynolds' characteristic simple line-and-wash art, a *Kirkus Reviews* writer noted that the book's "spare portraits glow amid backgrounds that are softly colored yet clearly defined and set against crisp, white space." According to a *Publishers Weekly* contributor, *So Few of Me* is "an engaging and eye-opening tale for over-programmed kids and the adults who set their schedules."

Both *My Very Big Little World* and *The Best Kid in the World* highlight the relationship between Sugarloaf and Spoke, two siblings in a close-knit family, as they deal with typical events and feelings. In *My Very Big Little World* readers meet toddler Sugarloaf, who lives in the shadow of her likeable older brother Spoke. Sibling jealousy is the focus of *The Best Kid in the World,* which finds Sugarloaf jealous after Spoke returns home from school with a special medal acknowledging his helpfulness. Praising Reynolds' "clear, simple sentences" in her *School Library Journal* review of *The Best Kid in the World,* Linda L. Watkins added that the author/illustrator's "breezy watercolor illustrations depict the child's undertakings with humor and charm." A *Kirkus Reviews* writer concluded of *The Best Kid in the World* that Reynolds' "watercolor characters are delightfully expressive."

Dedicated to Rose Fitzgerald Kennedy, the mother of U.S. President John F. Kennedy, *Rose's Garden* follows the adventures of a young girl who sails around the world in a teapot collecting seeds, then uses them to transforms a blighted urban area into a wondrous oasis. Reynolds's illustrations "explode with color and joy as the garden evolves and people come to enjoy it," Anne Beier commented in *School Library Journal,* and a *Publishers Weekly* reviewer observed that Reynolds' "fable emphasizes that having faith (and patience) can pay off big."

In addition to his original stories, Reynolds has also illustrated texts by other writers. Working with McDonald on her "Judy Moody" series, he helped introduce a likeable new heroine to budding readers. In *Judy Moody* the titular third grader approaches the first day of school with some trepidation, and things only get worse when she finds herself assigned to a seat next to a boy well known for his habit of eating paste. McDonald's ability to capture both the way children think and the way they talk makes for an entertaining read, remarked Shelle Rosenfeld in a review of *Judy Moody* for *Booklist,* the critic adding that children will "also like the witty, detailed drawings." Janice M. Del Negro, writing in the *Bulletin of the Center for Children's Books,* similarly commented that "each chapter is amiably illustrated with . . . full-page and spot art that extends the friendly feeling of the humorous text."

As the "Judy Moody" series plays out, Judy is joined by her seven-year-old sibling Stinky Moody. A number of reviewers noted Reynolds' contributions to the success of the books, *Horn Book* contributor Roger Sutton maintaining that his illustrations in *Judy Moody and Stink: The Holly Joliday* "spread the Christmas cheer." Writing in *Booklist,* Carolyn Phelan applauded the "expression and verve" evident in Reynolds' black-and-white drawings for *Judy Moody Goes to College,* and a *Kirkus Reviews* critic acknowledged that the "cheerful cartoon illustrations add to the appeal" of *Stink and the World's Worst Super-stinky Sneakers.*

Reynolds demonstrates the intricacies involved in multi-tasking in his engaging self-illustrated picture book **So Few of Me.** (Copyright © 2006 by Peter H. Reynolds. Reproduced by permission of Candlewick Press, Somerville, MA.)

Reynolds has also contributed art to Alison McGhee's *Someday* and Tobi Tobias's *Serendipity*, the latter a picture book that defines the tongue-twisting word of the title with both humor and sentimentality, according to critics. In *Serendipity* "Reynolds provides sweet-natured and airy watercolor and ink cartoons," asserted a reviewer in *Publishers Weekly*, while Sue Sherif wrote in *School Library Journal* that "teachers will undoubtedly use [*Serendipity*] . . . as a starting point for writing exercises." Reynolds' ink-and-watercolor images for *Someday* "have the same soft sentimentality" as McGhee's story, noted Carolyn Janssen in *School Library Journal*, and a *Publishers Weekly* contributor also highlighted the positive contribution made by Reynolds' "spare, wispy pen-and-ink and watercolor" art.

Reynolds and McGhee have also collaborated on *Little Boy*, a work that celebrates the simple joys of childhood. "The artwork bursts with energy," Linda M. Kenton remarked in her *School Library Journal* review of this work, and Phelan maintained that the "sensitive ink drawings" in *Little Boy* "will beguile children and grown-ups alike."

A youngster channels her grief over the loss of a cherished old tree by organizing a memorial in *Tess's Tree*, a story by Jess M. Brallier that also features Reynolds' art. According to *School Library Journal* reviewer Linda Ludke, the artist's "fluid ink and watercolor illustrations poignantly convey the story's emotions," and a *Publishers Weekly* critic similarly noted that the "spare, emotive illustrations" in *Tess's Tree* "illuminate the story's messages about cycles of life and the importance of mourning." Bob Raczka offers a lively and humorous look at outdoor play in his poetry collection *Guyku: A Year of Haiku for Boys*. Reynolds's illustrations, wrote Joan Kindig in *School Library Journal*, "mirror the simplicity of each entry and capture the expressions of the boys and their adventures honestly."

Through his children's books and his work at Fable-Vision, Reynolds continues to inspire youngsters. As he remarked on the Pippin Properties Web site, "When I visit students in schools they ask me what my hobbies are. I say thinking, dreaming. If my art and stories can help inspire others to do the same, I'll feel my life had meaning."

Biographical and Critical Sources

PERIODICALS

Booklist, July, 2000, Shelle Rosenfeld, review of *Judy Moody*, pp. 2028, 2030; December 15, 2001, Todd Morning, review of *Sydney's Star*, p. 741; November 1, 2003, Ilene Cooper, review of *The Dot*, p. 513; November 1, 2004, Ilene Cooper, review of *Ish*, p. 498; April 15, 2007, Carolyn Phelan, review of *Stink and the World's Worst Super Stinky Sneakers*, p. 49; November 15, 2007, Hazel Rochman, review of *Judy Moody and Stink: The Holly Joliday*, p. 38; March 1, 2008, Carolyn Phelan, review of *Stink and the Great Guinea Pig Express*, p. 70; June 1, 2008, Carolyn Phelan, review of *Little Boy*, p. 89; September 1, 2008, Carolyn Phelan, review of *Judy Moody Goes to College*, p. 90; June 1, 2009, Randall Enos, review of *The North Star*, p. 76; July 1, 2009, Carolyn Phelan, review of *Judy Moody and Stink: The Mad, Mad, Mad, Mad Treasure Hunt*, p. 58; January 1, 2010, Hazel Rochman, review of *Stink: Solar System Superhero*, p. 86; March 15, 2010, Francisca Goldsmith, review of *Zebrafish*, p. 62; June 1, 2010, Daniel Kraus, review of *Guyku: A Year of Haiku for Boys*, p. 84.

Bulletin of the Center for Children's Books, May, 2000, Janice M. Del Negro, review of *Judy Moody*, pp. 324-325.

Horn Book, September, 2001, review of *Judy Moody Gets Famous!*, p. 589; November-December, 2007, Roger Sutton, review of *Judy Moody and Stink: The Holly Joliday*, p. 632.

Kirkus Reviews, October 1, 2001, review of *Sydney's Star*, p. 1432; October 1, 2003, review of *The Dot*, p. 1229; July 15, 2004, review of *Ish*, p. 693; August 1, 2006, review of *So Few of Me*, p. 795; March 1, 2007, review of *Stink and the World's Worst Super-stinky Sneakers*, p. 228; August 1, 2007, review of *Knock, Knock!*; March 15, 2008, review of *Little Boy*; August 1, 2009, review of *Tess's Tree*; October 15, 2009, review of *Rose's Garden*; April 15, 2010, review of *Zebrafish*.

Publishers Weekly, April 17, 2000, review of *Judy Moody*, p. 81; August 28, 2000, review of *Serendipity*, p. 82; July 30, 2001, review of *Judy Moody Gets Famous!*, p. 85; November 12, 2001, review of *Sydney's Star*, p. 59; October 20, 2003, review of *The Dot*, p. 54; October 11, 2004, review of *Ish*, p. 79; October 16, 2006, review of *So Few of Me*, p. 51; February 12, 2007, review of *Someday*, p. 84; March 24, 2008, review of *Little Boy*, p. 69; September 21, 2009, review of *Tess's Tree*, p. 55; November 2, 2009, review of *Rose's Garden*, p. 50; April 5, 2010, review of *Zebrafish*, p. 64.

School Library Journal, July, 2000, Janie Schomberg, review of *Judy Moody*, p. 83; Sue Sherif, November, 2000, review of *Serendipity*, p. 135; October, 2001, Sharon R. Pearce, review of *Judy Moody Gets Famous!*, p. 124; December, 2001, Maryann H. Owen, review of *Sydney's Star*, p. 110; November, 2003, Kathy Krasniewicz, review of *The Dot*, p. 114; July, 2004, Lisa Gangemi Kropp, review of *The Dot*, p. 44; January, 2005, Shawn Brommer, review of *Ish*, p. 97; May, 2005, Caroline Ward, review of *Olivia Kidney and the Exit Academy*, 138; July, 2006, Sharon Rawlins, review of *The Dot*, p. 86; August, 2006, Linda L. Walkins, review of *The Best Kid in the World*, p. 96; December, 2006, review of *So Few of Me*, p. 114; March, 2007, Carolyn Janssen, review of *Someday*, p. 176; May, 2007, Elaine Lesh Morgan, review of *Stink and the World's Worst Super-stinky Sneakers*, p. 102; October, 2007, Teri Markson, review of *Judy Moody and Stink: The Holly Joliday*, p. 101; March, 2008, Bethany A. Lafferty, review of *Sink and the Great*

Guinea Pig, p. 172; June, 2008, Linda M. Kenton, review of *Little Boy,* p. 110; May, 2009, Kirsten Cutler, review of *The North Star,* p. 86; August, 2009, Madigan McGillicuddy, review of *Judy Moody and Stink: The Mad, Mad, Mad, Mad Treasure Hunt,* p. 80; December, 2009, Anne Beier, review of *Rose's Garden,* p. 90; February, 2010, Linda Ludke, review of *Tess's Tree,* p. 76 and Elizabeth Swistock, review of *Stink: Solar System Superhero,* p. 90; May, 2010, Janet Weber, review of *Zebrafish,* p. 139; August, 2010, Amelia Jenkins, review of *Judy Moody, Girl Detective,* p. 80; September, 2010, Joan Kindig, review of *Guyku,* p. 139.

ONLINE

Candlewick Press Web site, http://www.candlewick.com/ (February 10, 2011), "Peter H. Reynolds."

Digital MASS Web site, http://www.boston.com/ (April, 2000), Tim Allik, "Peter Reynolds, FableVision: He Hasn't Forgotten the 'Little' People."

FableVision Web site, http://www.fablevision.com/ (February 2, 2002), "Peter Reynolds."

Peter H. Reynolds Home Page, http://www.peterhreynolds. com (February 10, 2011).

Peter H. Reynolds Web log, http://stellarcafe.blogspot.com/ (February 10, 2011).

Pippin Properties Web site, http://www.pippinproperties. com/ (February 10, 2011), "Peter H. Reynolds."*

*   *   *

RIGG, Sharon
See CREECH, Sharon

*   *   *

RIOUX, Jo
(Jo-Anne Rioux)

Personal

Born in Ottawa, Ontario, Canada. *Education:* Sheridan College, degree.

Addresses

Home—Ottawa, Ontario, Canada. *E-mail*—jorioux@ gmail.com.

Career

Illustrator.

Awards, Honors

Comics for Kids Award nomination, Joe Schuster Awards, 2010, for *Lake Monster Mix-up* by Mary Labatt.

Illustrator

(As Jo-Anne Rioux) Nancy Yi Fan, *Sword Quest,* Harper-Collins (New York, NY), 2008.

"SAM AND FRIENDS MYSTERY" NOVEL SERIES BY MARY LABATT

Lake Monster Mix-up, Kids Can Press (Toronto, Ontario, Canada), 2009.
Dracula Madness, Kids Can Press (Toronto, Ontario, Canada), 2009.
Mummy Mayhem, Kids Can Press (Toronto, Ontario, Canada), 2010.
Witches' Brew, Kids Can Press (Toronto, Ontario, Canada), 2011.

Sidelights

Canadian artist Jo Rioux has been a fan of comic books since she was a child, expanding her interest to Japanese-style *manga* (cartoons) by the time she reached high school. Although many would bemoan a steady diet of comics in favor of books, for Rioux this literary diet led to her interest in art and a career as an illustrator. Her manga-inspired illustrations, a mix of traditional line drawings and digital "painting", appear in Nancy Yi Fan's fantasy novel *Sword Quest* as well as in Mary Labatt's multi-volume "Sam and Friends Mystery" graphic-novel series. In many cases "comics stand almost completely on their art and visual design," Rioux noted in an interview for the Open Book Toronto Web site, "and some others shine simply through their storytelling and dialogue. Personally though, I think an AWESOME comic needs good pacing and a compelling storyline. The art should serve the story and not distract from it."

Labatt's "Sam and Friends Mystery" graphic-novel series, features adaptations of longer novels and includes *Lake Monster Mix-up, Dracula Madness,* and *Witches' Brew.* Sam, an Old English sheepdog, loves a good mystery, and when her owners move to the small town of Woodford she meets ten-year-old neighbor Jennie. When Jennie is given the job of walking Sam for her owners, the girl quickly realizes that she has the ability to sense the shaggy-haired dog's thoughts. In *Dracula Madness* Jennie takes Sam and best friend Beth to one of Woodford's scariest house, where the owner is suspected of being a vampire. *Lake Monster Mix-up* finds the sleuthing sheepdog unhappy about an upcoming family vacation to Sagawa Lake, but while sniffing around the lakeside cabin she discovers an old diary that sends the three sleuths on a new adventure. In *Mummy Mahem,* the third "Sam and Friends Mystery" story, the sheepdog worries about an ancient curse and turns to Jennie and Beth to help root out the source of the evil.

Reviewing *Dracula Madness* in the *Canadian Review of Materials,* Gregory Bryan suggested that Labatt's story might be too weak "to sustain interest" among the

Jo Rioux's illustration projects include creating the artwork for Mary Labatt's graphic novel **Dracula Madness.** (Illustration © 2009 by Jo Rioux. Used by permission of Kids Can Press Ltd., Toronto.)

book's intended readership. Nonetheless, Bryan dubbed Rioux's cartoon illustrations "strong," adding that her images "have depth and texture and are generally pleasing to the eye," and Kat Kan wrote in *Booklist* that the book's "simple yet expressive art . . . stays just on the lighter side of spooky." The "excellent body language, sufficient dollops of realistic detail, and good comic timing and expression" in Rioux's illustrations for *Lake Monster Mix-up* add to a "successful" easy-reading graphic novel, according to *School Library Journal* critic Benjamin Russell, and in a *Kirkus Reviews* writer commended the artist's creation of sequential "panels, which ably mix the styles of manga and Western comics."

Biographical and Critical Sources

PERIODICALS

Booklist, March 1, 2009, Kat Kan, review of *Dracula Madness,* p. 62.
Canadian Review of Materials, June 12, 2009, Gregory Bryan, review of *Dracula Madness.*
Kirkus Reviews, January 15, 2009, review of *Dracula Madness;* July 1, 2009, review of *Lake Monster Mix-Up.*
School Library Journal, June, 2008, Robyn Gioia, review of *Sword Quest,* p. 138; March, 2009, Travis Jonker, review of *Dracula Madness,* p. 172; November, 2009, Benjamin Russell, review of *Lake Monster Mix-Up,* p. 139.

ONLINE

Jo Rioux Home Page, http://www.jorioux.com (February 15, 2011).
Open Book Toronto Web site, http://www.openbooktoronto. com/ (May 31, 2010), "Jo Rioux."*

*   *   *

RIOUX, Jo-Anne
See RIOUX, Jo

*   *   *

RYDER, Joanne 1946-

Personal

Born September 16, 1946, in Lake Hiawatha, NJ; daughter of Raymond (a chemist) and Dorothy (a homemaker) Ryder; married Laurence Yep (an author). *Education:* Marquette University, B.A. (journalism), 1968; graduate study at University of Chicago, 1968-69. *Hobbies and other interests:* Travel, gardening, reading and listening to poetry, hiking.

Addresses

Home—Pacific Grove, CA.

Career

Writer and editor. Harper & Row Publishers, Inc., New York, NY, editor of children's books, 1970-80; full-time writer, beginning 1980. Lecturer at schools and conferences. Docent at San Francisco Zoo.

Member

Society of Children's Book Writers and Illustrators, California Academy of Sciences, San Francisco Zoological Society.

Awards, Honors

Children's Book Showcase selection, 1977, for *Simon Underground;* New Jersey Author's Award, New Jersey Institute of Technology, 1978, for *Fireflies,* and 1980, for both *Fog in the Meadow* and *Snail in the Woods;* Outstanding Science Trade Book of the Year designation, National Science Teachers Association (NSTA), 1979, and Children's Choice Book honor, Children's Book Council/International Reading Association, 1980, both for *Fog in the Meadow;* Parents Choice designation, *Parents'* magazine, and New York Academy of Sciences Children's Science Book Award in younger category, both 1982, and Golden Sower Award nomination, Nebraska Library Association, 1984, all for *The Snail's Spell;* Outstanding Book of the Year designation, National Council of Teachers of English, and Outstanding Science Trade Book of the Year designation, NSTA, both 1985, and Outstanding Book of the Year designation, Bank Street College School of Education, all for *Inside Turtle's Shell, and Other Poems of the Field;* Outstanding Science Trade Book designation, NSTA, and Children's Book Medal, Commonwealth Club of Northern California, both 1988, both for *Step into the Night;* Outstanding Science Trade Book designation, NSTA, 1989, for *Where Butterflies Grow;* Eva L. Gordon Award for Excellence in Writing for Children, American Nature Study Society, 1995, for body of work; Favorite Book Contest winner, Aspen School (Los Alamos, NM), 1996, for *The Bear on the Moon;* Black-eyed Susan Award nomination, Maryland Education Media Organization, 1996, for *Without Words;* Pick of the Lists selection, American Booksellers Association, 1997, for *Night Gliders;* Henry Bergh Award for Children's Poetry, American Society for the Prevention of Cruelty to Animals, 2000, for *Each Living Thing;* Best Book citation, *Parents'* magazine, 2004, for *Won't You Be My Kissaroo?*

Writings

FOR CHILDREN

Simon Underground, illustrated by John Schoenherr, Harper (New York, NY), 1976.

A Wet and Sandy Day, illustrated by Donald Carrick, Harper (New York, NY), 1977.

Fireflies, illustrated by Don Bolognese, Harper (New York, NY), 1977.

Fog in the Meadow, illustrated by Gail Owens, Harper (New York, NY), 1979.

(With Harold S. Feinberg) *Snail in the Woods,* illustrated by Jo Polseno, Harper (New York, NY), 1979.

The Spider's Dance, illustrated by Robert Blake, Harper (New York, NY), 1981.

Beach Party, illustrated by Diane Stanley, Frederick Warne (New York, NY), 1982.

The Snail's Spell, illustrated by Lynne Cherry, Frederick Warne (New York, NY), 1982.

The Incredible Space Machines, illustrated by Gerry Daly, Random House (New York, NY), 1982.

C-3PO's Book about Robots, illustrated by John Gampert, Random House (New York, NY), 1983.

The Evening Walk, illustrated by Julie Durrell, Western Publishing (Racine, WI), 1985.

Inside Turtle's Shell, and Other Poems of the Field, illustrated by Susan Bonners, Macmillan (New York, NY), 1985.

The Night Flight, illustrated by Amy Schwartz, Four Winds Press (New York, NY), 1985.

Old Friends, New Friends, illustrated by Jane Chambless-Rigie, Western Publishing (Racine, WI), 1986.

Animals in the Woods, illustrated by Lisa Bonforte, Western Publishing (Racine, WI), 1987, published as *Animals in the Wild,* 1989.

Chipmunk Song, illustrated by Lynne Cherry, Lodestar (New York, NY), 1987.

My Little Golden Book about Cats, illustrated by Dora Leder, Western Publishing (Racine, WI), 1988.

Puppies Are Special Friends, illustrated by James Spence, Western Publishing (Racine, WI), 1988.

(Adaptor) Hardie Gramatky, *Little Toot,* illustrated by Larry Ross, Platt, 1988.

(Adaptor) Charles Dickens, *A Christmas Carol,* illustrated by John O'Brien, Platt, 1989.

Under the Moon: Just Right for 3's and 4's, illustrated by Cheryl Harness, Random House (New York, NY), 1989.

Where Butterflies Grow, illustrated by Lynne Cherry, Lodestar (New York, NY), 1989.

The Bear on the Moon, illustrated by Carol Lacey, Morrow (New York, NY), 1991.

Hello, Tree!, illustrated by Michael Hays, Lodestar (New York, NY), 1991.

When the Woods Hum, illustrated by Catherine Stock, Morrow (New York, NY), 1991.

Dancers in the Garden, illustrations by Judith Lopez, Sierra Club (San Francisco, CA), 1992.

Turtle Time, illustrated by Julie Downing, Knopf (New York, NY), 1992.

The Goodbye Walk, illustrated by Deborah Haeffele, Lodestar (New York, NY), 1993.

One Small Fish, illustrated by Carol Schwartz, Morrow (New York, NY), 1993.

(Adaptor) Felix Salten, *Walt Disney's Bambi,* Disney Press (New York, NY), 1993.

(Adaptor) Felix Salten, *Walt Disney's Bambi's Forest: A Year in the Life of the Forest,* illustrated by David Pacheco and Jesse Clay, Disney Press (New York, NY), 1994.

My Father's Hands, illustrated by Mark Graham, Morrow (New York, NY), 1994.

A House by the Sea, illustrated by Melissa Sweet, Morrow (New York, NY), 1994.

Without Words (poems), photographs by Barbara Sonneborn, Sierra Club Books for Children (San Francisco, CA), 1995.

Bears out There, illustrated by Jo Ellen McAllister-Stammen, Atheneum (New York, NY), 1995.

Night Gliders, illustrated by Melissa Bay Mathias, Bridge-Water Books (Mahwah, NJ), 1996.

Earthdance, illustrated by Norman Gorbaty, Holt (New York, NY), 1996.

Winter White, illustrated by Carol Lacey, Morrow (New York, NY), 1996.

Pondwater Faces, illustrated by Susan Ford, Chronicle Books (San Francisco, CA), 1997.

Rainbow Wings, illustrated by Victor Lee, Morrow (New York, NY), 2000.

Each Living Thing, illustrated by Ashley Wolff, Harcourt, 2000.

Fawn in the Grass, illustrated by Keiko Narahashi, Henry Holt (New York, NY), 2000.

The Waterfall's Gift, illustrated by Richard Jesse Watson, Sierra Club (San Francisco, CA), 2000.

Little Panda: The World Welcomes Hua Mei at the San Diego Zoo, Simon & Schuster (New York, NY), 2001.

A Fawn in the Grass, illustrated by Keiko Narahashi, Henry Holt (New York, NY), 2001.

Mouse Tail Moon, illustrated by Maggie Kneen, Henry Holt (New York, NY), 2002.

Big Bear Ball, illustrated by Steven Kellogg, HarperCollins (New York, NY), 2002.

Wild Birds, illustrated by Susan Estelle Kwas, HarperCollins (New York, NY), 2003.

Come along, Kitten, illustrated by Susan Winter, Simon & Schuster (New York, NY), 2003.

Won't You Be My Kissaroo?, illustrated by Melissa Sweet, Harcourt (Orlando, FL), 2004.

My Mother's Voice, illustrated by Peter Catalanotto, HarperCollins (New York, NY), 2006.

A Pair of Polar Bears: Twin Cubs Find a Home at the San Diego Zoo, Simon & Schuster Books for Young Readers (New York, NY), 2006.

Bear of My Heart, illustrated by Margie Moore, Simon & Schuster Books for Young Readers (New York, NY), 2006.

Won't You Be My Hugaroo?, illustrated by Melissa Sweet, Harcourt (Orlando, FL), 2006.

Dance by the Light of the Moon, illustrated by Guy Francis, Hyperion Books for Children (New York, NY), 2007.

Toad by the Road: A Year in the Life of These Amazing Amphibians, illustrated by Maggie Kneen, Henry Holt (New York, NY), 2007.

Panda Kindergarten, photographs by Katherine Feng, HarperCollins (New York, NY), 2009.

"NIGHT AND MORNING" SERIES

Step into the Night, illustrated by Dennis Nolan, Four Winds Press (New York, NY), 1988.

Mockingbird Morning, illustrated by Dennis Nolan, Four Winds Press (New York, NY), 1989.

Under Your Feet, illustrated by Dennis Nolan, Four Winds Press (New York, NY), 1990.

"JUST FOR A DAY" SERIES

White Bear, Ice Bear, illustrated by Michael Rothman, Morrow (New York, NY), 1989.

Catching the Wind, illustrated by Michael Rothman, Morrow (New York, NY), 1989.

Lizard in the Sun, illustrated by Michael Rothman, Morrow (New York, NY), 1990.

Winter Whale, illustrated by Michael Rothman, Morrow (New York, NY), 1991.

Sea Elf, illustrated by Michael Rothman, Morrow (New York, NY), 1993.

Jaguar in the Rain Forest, illustrated by Michael Rothman, Morrow (New York, NY), 1996.

Shark in the Sea, illustrated by Michael Rothman, Morrow (New York, NY), 1997.

Tyrannosaurus Time, illustrated by Michael Rothman, Morrow (New York, NY), 1999.

"FIRST GRADE IS THE BEST" SERIES

Hello, First Grade, illustrated by Betsy Lewin, Troll Associates (Mahwah, NJ), 1993.

First-Grade Ladybugs, illustrated by Betsy Lewin, Troll Associates (Mahwah, NJ), 1993.

First-Grade Valentines, illustrated by Betsy Lewin, Troll Associates (Mahwah, NJ), 1993.

First-Grade Elves, illustrated by Betsy Lewin, Troll Associates (Mahwah, NJ), 1994.

OTHER

Contributor to periodicals.

Ryder's papers are housed in a permanent collection at the Cooperative Children's Book Center, School of Education, University of Wisconsin, Madison.

Sidelights

Joanne Ryder creates picture books for readers in the primary grades that are praised for combining poetry, fantasy, and science in a particularly original and appealing manner. A prolific, popular writer, she introduces young readers to the life cycles and habits of a variety of creatures, ranging from insects and birds to dinosaurs and whales, through the context of imaginary play. Ryder invites children to become the creatures that she profiles by identifying with her young male and female protagonists, who imagine what it would be like to be an animal, bird, or insect. In her works she encourages readers—to whom she often refers in the second person—to transform themselves and to take on new points of view, challenging them to see the world from an unusual perspective while also heightening their awareness of, and appreciation for, the natural world.

In addition to contributing to the "Just for a Day," "First Grade Is the Best," and "Night and Morning" series, Ryder has also created numerous well-received standalone stories, among them *Fog in the Meadow, The Snail's Spell, The Bear on the Moon, Each Living Thing,* and *Bear of My Heart.* During the course of her career she has worked with such notable illustrators as John Schoenherr, Donald Carrick, Diane Stanley, Lynne Cherry, Don Bolognese, Any Schwartz, Betsy Lewin, Dennis Nolan, Michael Rothman, and Ashley Wolff, and her books are often praised for their union of text and illustration.

Born in Lake Hiawatha, New Jersey, Ryder was attracted to nature from an early age. Her birthplace was, as the author once described it in an interview with *SATA,* "a small, rural town." For her parents, who were both born and bred in New York City, Lake Hiawatha was "'the country'—very different from the crowded

A tiny kitten's exploration of a new garden world is the subject of Joanne Ryder's engaging **Come Along, Little Kitten,** *featuring pencil drawings by* **Susan Winter.** (Illustration copyright © 2003 Susan Winter. Reprinted with the permission of Simon & Schuster Books for Young Readers, an imprint of Simon & Schuster Children's Publishing Division.)

city they knew. For me, it was a wonderful place to explore, full of treasures to discover. There were just a few houses on our street, but there were woods all around. . . . I loved living there and playing outdoors. There were always animals around to observe and encounter." As she recalled, "One of my earliest memories is trying to follow a butterfly darting across the road and being scolded by a neighbor for running into the street." While growing up, Ryder cared for an assortment of pets, including chickens, hamsters, ducks, rabbits, and fish.

Ryder's parents were also fascinated by nature and by living in the country—"probably," their daughter surmised, "because they had spent all their lives in the city." Mother Dorothy taught Joanne "to watch sunsets and to take time to stop and enjoy special moments in nature," once stopping her chores to sit for hours and observe a flock of migrating spring warblers that had stopped to rest in a nearby tree. "My mother loved nature's grand displays—sunsets, ocean walks, spring

trees all in bloom," Ryder recalled. She weaves her memories of her mother into her picture book *My Mother's Voice,* a story illustrated by Peter Catalanotto that *Booklist* critic John Peters praised as a "lyrical" story that "will strike a responsive chord in many children."

In contrast to her mother, Ryder's father Raymond Ryder, a chemist, "liked to pick things up and examine them. He was the one who introduced me to nature up close and made the discoveries we shared very personal ones." Raymond Ryder also liked to tend his garden, and he would often call his daughter to come and see the interesting creatures that enhabited it. Ryder remembered that if her father "could catch it, he would cup the tiny creature in his hands and wait until I ran to him. Then he would open his fingers and show me whatever it was he had found—a beetle, a snail, a fuzzy caterpillar. Then gently he would let me hold it, and I could feel it move, wiggle, or crawl—even breathe—as I held it in my hand." She continued, "My father's excitement was easy to catch. As he pointed out amazing features of each animal, I could see that, even though it had a few more legs or less legs than I was used to; it was rather marvelous. So tiny, hidden animals became very much a part of my world, as real to me as the people I knew."

Ryder's father also helped her "appreciate what it might be like to be another creature, someone wonderfully different," as she commented on the HarperChildren's Web site. In my books, I try to share with my readers the experience of being 'shape changers.' We imagine together how it would feel to be someone new—a huge, furry polar bear running on an ice-covered sea, a lean lizard changing colors in the hot sun, . . . a jaguar prowling in a lush tropical rain forest, and a great white shark gliding towards its prey." Ryder and her father sometimes went for walks in the woods or to a nearby waterfall. Because of these walks, Ryder once recalled to *SATA,* it "felt natural for me to feel comfortable and part of the world around me."

When the Woods Hum, her semi-autobiographical picture book, describes how a father introduces his daughter to the periodical cicadas, insects that appear once every seventeen years; at the end of the story, the protagonist, now a grown woman, introduces the cicadas to her son. Her picture book *My Father's Hands* is also

Ryder's imaginative bedtime picture book **The Night Flight** *features colorful artwork by Amy Schwartz.* (Illustration copyright © 1985 by Amy Schwartz. All rights reserved. Reprinted with the permission of Simon & Schuster Books for Young Readers, an imprint of Simon & Schuster Children's Publishing Division.)

based on her close relationship with her father and on how he opened the natural world to her.

Just before her fifth birthday, Ryder and her family moved to the same Brooklyn, New York, apartment building where her mother had grown up. At first, it "was a bit of a shock for me to live where there were so many people all around. But the city seemed also to be a magical land, full of special places for me." Ryder enjoyed going to the park and to museums; in addition, the city provided lots of opportunities for her to use her imagination. She noted in *SATA:* "Every day on my way to school, I passed an old stone lion. I believed he could understand my thoughts, and I would tell him secrets. He was one of my first friends in the city. I also began to have lovely dreams at night in which I could fly over the tall trees outside my home." Ryder would later use these childhood memories as the basis for her picture book *Night Flight.*

When she was almost seven, Ryder and her family moved again, this time to New Hyde Park, on Long Island. At about that time, she learned to read and began to enjoy books, "especially adventures about dogs and cats," as she noted on the HarperChildren's Web site. Soon she was writing her own animal stories as well as poetry. "Though I've always had trouble spelling words correctly, my parents and teachers encouraged me to keep on writing even when I made mistakes," Ryder once told *SATA.* "I liked playing with words and making them up. I wrote about animals and everyday things—and also about imaginary people and creatures." Ryder became a voracious reader, borrowing multiple titles from her local library. "Reading so much," she noted, "made it easier for me to write. Since I enjoyed imagining other author's worlds, it seemed natural for me to create stories and worlds of my own."

By age ten, Ryder began to think seriously about being a writer and started her first book, the fantasy "The Marvelous Adventures of Georgus Amaryllis the Third." In high school she edited the school newspaper, and at Marquette University in Wisconsin she studied journalism and edited the college literary magazine. At Marquette, Ryder met the man who she would soon marry: Laurence Yep, an aspiring author who has become a well-respected writer of books for children and young people.

After receiving her bachelor's degree in journalism in 1968, Ryder studied library science at the University of Chicago for a year before moving to New York City to spend ten years working at Harper & Row as an editor of children's books. "During the day, I worked on other people's books," Ryder recalled. "Then at night, I worked on my own stories."

In 1976 she produced her first picture book. *Simon Underground* describes the activities of a mole named Simon from fall to spring, taking young readers into the creature's subterranean world and describing his in-

Ryder introduces young readers to a fascinating creature in **Panda Kindergarten,** *a work featuring color photographs by Dr. Katherine Feng.* (Photographs copyright © 2009 by Dr. Katherine Feng/Globio.org/Minden Pictures. Used by permission of HarperCollins Children's Books, a division of HarperCollins Publishers.)

stincts and sensations. Writing in the *St. James Guide to Children's Writers,* Christine Doyle Stott stated that *Simon Underground* "exquisitely combines scientific accuracy with poetic expression. Young readers not only learn abstract facts about a mole, they are brought into such close contact with the details of its life that they must actively consider what it feels like, smells like, looks like, sounds like, to be a mole."

In 1985 Ryder produced her first book of verse, *Inside Turtle's Shell, and Other Poems of the Field.* She imagines a day in a field and pond from dawn to evening, and profiles the creatures that inhabit each place in short poems focusing on their essential qualities. The poems also form a picture of two turtles, one who has turned one hundred years old, and one who has recently been born, facts that the reader learns gradually. Writing in *School Library Journal,* Ruth M. McConnell noted of the work that, "with pithy delicacy touched with humor, the author . . . distills her perceptions of nature into a series of free-verse vignettes with the punch of haiku." Citing the "quiet beauty" of the poems in *Inside Turtle's Shell, and Other Poems of the Field,* Carolyn Phelan concluded in *Booklist* that Ryder "offers a collection of poetry concise, precise, and immediate." Zena Sutherland, writing in the *Bulletin of the Center for Children's Books,* added that Ryder's poems "have a quiet tenderness and empathy" before concluding that most of the poems "are brief, some almost as compressed as haiku; most have delicate imagery; all are evocative."

Another volume of poetry by Ryder, *Without Words,* is brought to life in photographs by Barbara Sonneborn

and illustrates the bonds that humans share with animals. Author and photographer depict children and adults touching, holding, and playing with such animals as tigers, snakes, dolphins, chimpanzees, and elephants. A critic in *School Library Journal* wrote of this work that Ryder's "expressive poems are at the same time simple and thought-provoking."

In Ryder's autobiographical picture book *Night Flight* Anna plays in the city park near her home during the day. She enjoys riding Alexander, the stone lion, and hopes that the skittish goldfish in the pond will take bread from her hand. At night, Anna dreams that she is flying over the rooftops to the park. She rides Alexander, now running free, and becomes friends with the goldfish and pigeons. When she goes to the park the next day; the goldfish eat from her hands as she calls them by name. Reviewing *Night Flight* in *Booklist,* Ilene Cooper stated that "Ryder's lyrical text, which paints its own word pictures, meets its match with [Amy] Schwartz's vibrant, brilliantly colored illustrations." As Anne E. Mulherkar wrote in *School Library Journal,* both author and illustrator "stretch their capabilities and children's imaginations in *Night Flight.*"

Ryder's other fictional tales for children include *Big Bear Ball, Come Along, Kitten,* and the companion picture books *Won't You Be My Kissaroo?* and *Won't You Be My Hugaroo? Big Bear Ball,* geared for pre-school and early elementary children, shows a forest full of bears throwing a wild party to celebrate the full moon. At first their loud antics annoy the other woodland creatures, who are trying to sleep, but eventually the neighboring creatures decide to get out of bed and join in the fun. "Ryder's light-footed rhymes set the celebratory pace," Ellen Mandel noted in *Booklist,* and her story's festive atmosphere is reflected in illustrator Steven Kellogg's brightly colored watercolors. "This team has outdone itself," Wanda Meyers-Hines declared in *School Library Journal,* dubbing *Big Bear Ball* "an absolute must for every library."

Come Along, Kitten is a quieter story told in simple rhymes designed for very young children. In Ryder's tale a young, headstrong kitten goes out to explore the world under the protection of a big, older dog. The kitten chases bumblebees and crickets and spies on mice, all with the encouragement of its canine guardian. "Preschoolers will identify with the curious kitten" and its need for both freedom and security, Lauren Peterson commented in *Booklist,* and Sandra Kitain similarly concluded in *School Library Journal* that *Come Along, Kitten* "will have broad appeal with the preschool set."

Featuring artwork by Melissa Sweet, *Won't You Be My Kissaroo?* and *Won't You Be My Hugaroo?* focus on the loving care adults give to children. Like *Come Along, Kitten, Won't You Be My Kissaroo?* is written in Ryder's trademark "tender rhyming couplets," as a *Publishers Weekly* critic described them. In this story a young lamb wakes up on its birthday to special birthday kisses and the titular question from its mother. As the day progresses, the lamb sees many other young animals, including a puppy and a bear cub, getting kisses from their own parents. In *Won't You Be My Hugaroo?* Ryder again employs rhyming couplets to illustrate the many ways that animals can provide physical reassurance to their young. *Won't You Be My Kissaroo?* is "a feel-good choice for sharing one-on-one or with a group," Kathy Krasniewicz commented in *School Library Journal*, while in *Booklist* Shelle Rosenfeld wrote that the "bouncy rhymes and child-friendly vocabulary" in *Won't You Be My Hugaroo?* pair with Sweet's softly tinted mixed-media art to create a picture book that is "a joy to read and view."

Ryder takes a more energetic approach to rhyme in *Dance by the Light of the Moon,* with its text moving to the tune of the popular nineteenth-century song "Buffalo Gals, Won't You Come out Tonight." As illustrator Guy Francis shows in what Rosenfeld described as "colorful, patterned art" full of "witty details," all the animals in Farmer Snow's barnyard are putting on the Ritz and tuning up for a night full of music and dancing. "A foot-tapping read," according to Rosenfeld, *Dance by the Light of the Moon* was described by *School Library Journal* critic Kathleen Whalin as "an exuberant animal fantasy" in which "the rhymes dance, and so do Francis's paintings." Although remarking on the historical nature of the song at the basis of Ryder's story, a *Kirkus Reviews* critic maintained that "kids will enjoy" *Dance by the Light of the Moon* "without knowing the song or its origin."

Many of Ryder's books are notable for teaching children about the natural world, particularly the many animals that inhabit it. In some of these books, including *The Snail's Spell* and *The Chipmunk's Song,* her child protagonists become small enough to accompany animals and observe their behavior first-hand. The first of her "Just for a Day" books, *White Bear, Ice Bear,* takes this concept a step further: like the other books in the series, the main characters actually transform into animals. As the boy morphs into a polar bear in an Arctic landscape, Ryder also defines the adaptive characteristics that allow the bear to survive in this beautiful but brutal environment: heavy fur, protective coloration, strong claws, padded soles, and an advanced sense of smell. The boy/bear also tracks a seal for food, but it escapes before the kill. At the end of the book, the boy returns to his normal state after he smells his supper. Writing in *Booklist,* Carolyn Phelan commented that in *White Bear, Ice Bear* "Ryder shifts points of view so smoothly that the boy's transformations seem quite natural" and "leads readers into deeper sympathy for their fellow creatures." In *School Library Journal* Patricia Manning called the work "rich, empathic, and eye-pleasing," while Anne Rose concluded her *Appraisal* review by noting that *White Bear, Ice Bear* is "challenging while remaining inviting for younger readers."

In subsequent volumes of her "Just for a Day" series Ryder continues the formula of having her young boy

and girl characters shape-shift into various species of creatures; the author outlines the habits of such animals as a goose, a lizard, a whale, and a jaguar. In *A Shark in the Sea* she deals openly with the predatory habits of her animal subject. After the boy of the story dives into the ocean off the California coast and imagines himself to be a great white shark, Ryder shows the actual shark hunting and killing a young seal while also fighting off a competitor that attempts to steal its feast. Reviewing *A Shark in the Sea,* Phelan concluded that the author "captures the feeling of 'otherness,' a different environment, a different kind of body for a different way of moving, and a different way of survival. Although the story may sound slightly sensational, the treatment remains matter-of-fact."

Brought to life in detailed art by Maggy Kneen, *Toad by the Road: A Year in the Life of These Amazing Amphibians* deals imaginatively with a common creature as Ryder sets to rhyme twenty-six views of life and the passage of the four seasons from a toad's perspective. With a brief poem on each page, the author mixes what Phelan described as "a scientist's curiosity about details . . . and a poet's ability to imagine," making the lowly toad both "humble" and "amazing," according to the critic. "Written with simple language, rhythmic repetition, and flowing rhymes," in the view of *School Library Journal* critic Joy Fleishhacker, Ryder's "poems read aloud beautifully; they consistently mix interesting toad trivia with whimsy" while Knee's finely crafted illustrations are "realistic yet pleasingly soft-looking." The mix of "solid information and pleasing poetry" served up in *Toad by the Road* results in a "charming" introduction . . . to the world of toads," concluded a *Kirkus Reviews* writer.

In *Tyrannosaurus Time,* another "Just for a Day" story, two children uncover a fossil and suddenly find themselves looking at a prehistoric world through the eyes of a T-Rex. Set amid a prehistoric landscape that will eventually become the western United States, the story builds in drama as the dinosaur searches for food and kills a triceratops; in the process, readers learn about the habitat of the beast and are presented with scientific information on theories about why dinosaurs became extinct. Ellen Mandel, writing in *Booklist,* praised Ryder's "lyrical, even mystical prose. . . . Melding poetic intensity with gripping visualization of the action, the book offers a memorable depiction of prehistoric life." Although a *Kirkus Reviews* critic warned that "not all children will be ready for the gory conclusion," the writer concluded, that "for readers already familiar with such realistic aspects of the dinosaurs' lives, [*Tyrannosaurus Time*] . . . is a must-have." Reviewers have generally commended Ryder's approach in the "Just for a Day" series; for example, Carolyn Phelan, reviewing *Lizard in the Sun* for *Booklist,* called the series "consciousness-expanding."

As well as being respected as a writer, Ryder is acknowledged as a conservationist. Two of her works,

Earthdance and *Each Living Thing,* stand as significant examples of why she has achieved this reputation. *Earthdance* is a poem that asks young readers to imagine that they are the Earth, which is personified through strong physical imagery. Ryder asks her audience to see themselves turning in space, feeling things growing and oceans shifting, and she suggests that, when taken together, the people, animals, seas, rivers, mountains, and forests of the Earth form a brightly colored quilt. A *Kirkus Reviews* contributor commented that in *Earthdance* Ryder beckons readers "to join in a cosmic appreciation of the earth and all it holds" by combining "powerful, pulsing graphics [by Norman Gorbaty] and a valuable, almost incantatory, message." As Lisa Mahoney wrote in the *Bulletin of the Center for Children's Books,* the author's "strong verbs, internal rhyme, and alliteration add force and music to her poetry."

Each Living Thing depicts a group of multicultural children who observe life in seven different habitats, including a park and the seashore, over the course of a day. In this work, which has as its theme the importance of respecting nature, Ryder asks children to be aware of animals and their needs and to take care of them—or to just let them be. She shows how animals fit into our surroundings while discouraging the notion that some animals—alligators, bats, bees, bears, snakes, and spiders, among others—are our enemies. Writing in *School Library Journal,* Susan Marie Pitard called *Each Living Thing* a "remarkable marriage of spare, poetic text and luminous, detailed paintings" by Ashley Wolff. In its ability to raise concerns about the environment in an engaging manner, the book serves as a "wonderful choice for sharing . . . [and] for learning to honor each living thing," the critic added.

Ryder again encourages her audience to explore their natural surroundings in *A Fawn in the Grass.* Her text, which consists of an extended poem, focuses on a young child's solitary walk through a meadow and recounts the animals he encounters along his way. While the little boy passes through this natural environment, he leaves its inhabitants undisturbed during his travels. Thus the fawn of the title is there when he enters the meadow and is there when the child come back. "Though never stated explicitly," noted a *Publishers Weekly* reviewer, *A Fawn in the Grass* "underscores the message that nature is full of beauty, grace, and unexpected pleasures." Similarly, *Booklist* critic Hazel Rochman felt that Ryder successfully presents a "child's-eye view of the amazing natural world, the things you can see when you are quiet, still, alone, and very close."

Mouse Tail Moon and *Wild Birds* teach children about specific animals that they are likely to encounter: field mice in the former title and common North American birds, including geese, robins, finches, blue jays, sparrows, and starlings, in the latter. *Mouse Tail Moon* contains eighteen brief poems written from the perspective of a white-tail mouse as it goes about a typical night of searching for food and avoiding foxes, housecats, and other predators. "Teachers in the early elementary grades will find this book useful both as poetry and as literature that effectively integrates interesting factual information," commented a *Kirkus Reviews* contributor. In *Booklist* Phelan also praised the book as poetry, noting its "natural rhythms and unforced rhymes."

Using what Cooper described as a "brief, almost haiku-like text," Ryder's *Little Panda: The World Welcomes Hua Mei at the San Diego Zoo* focuses on a specific animal: a panda cub that was born at the San Diego Zoo in 1999. This tiny cub, named Hua Mei, was the first panda to be born in captivity and survive for more than a few days. Similar in focus, *A Pair of Polar Bears: Twin Cubs Find a Home at the San Diego Zoo* follows Kalluk and Tatqiq as they move from their isolated and protected environment out into the zoo's prepared habitat with its wading pool, sandy spot for dirt baths, scheduled mealtimes, and crowds of interested human onlookers. *Little Panda* "is an engaging book [that] will complement any curriculum about animal extinction and environmental responsibility," according to Tina Hudak in *School Library Journal,* while *Booklist* critic Jennifer Mattson dubbed *A Pair of Polar Bears* "a poignant zoo drama [that] offers rewarding browsing for animal enthusiasts."

The Conservation and Research Center for the Giant Panda, located in China's Wolong Nature Preserve, is explored by Ryder in *Panda Kindergarten,* which pairs her study of sixteen young cubs with photographs by Katherine Feng. The basics of the zoo-controlled panda lifestyle—from infanthood with their mother to the cubs' gradual introduction to others of their kind and the selection of which of them will be returned to the wild and which will remain at the preserve to bear offspring—is contrasted with the "activities . . . of children as they play, explore their world, eat, and nap," observed *Booklist* critic Linda Perkins. Ryder also contrasts the treatment of the zoo-raised pandas with the life of a panda raised in the wild, and Feng's colorful photos supplement her fact-filled text with "a high cuteness factor," according to *School Library Journal* critic Nancy Call. Discussing the work in *Horn Book,* Janet Hamilton predicted that the "engaging" approach Ryder takes in *Panda Kindergarten* will make the book "a sure hit at story-time."

Ryder, who now lives in Pacific Grove, California, enjoys visiting schools and sharing her experiences as a writer. For preschoolers and first graders, she uses animal puppets to help illustrate her concepts of changing shape. For older students, she utilizes a personal slide show about her life as an author. She has also written and talked about her career. "My language is poetic, full of images, sounds, and sensations to help readers slip into a new skin, a new shape," Ryder noted. "My father helped me discover the wonders hidden all around me, and in my books I try to share my own discoveries with children." In *SATA,* Ryder also once commented:

"For a person who enjoys thinking in images and writing poems, writing picture books is a good life and a joyful way to make a living."

Biographical and Critical Sources

BOOKS

Children's Literature Review, Volume 37, Gale (Detroit, MI), 1996.

St. James Guide to Children's Writers, 5th edition, edited by Tom Pendergast and Sara Pendergast, St. James Press (Detroit, MI), 1999.

PERIODICALS

Appraisal, summer, 1990, John R. Pancella, review of *Where Butterflies Grow,* p. 48; autumn, 1989, Anne Rose, review of *White Bear, Ice Bear,* p. 57.

Booklist, April 15, 1985, Carolyn Phelan, review of *Inside Turtle's Shell,* p. 1200; November 1, 1985, Ilene Cooper, review of *Night Flight,* pp. 413-414; March 15, 1989, Carolyn Phelan, review of *White Bear, Ice Bear,* p. 1304; March 1, 1990, Carolyn Phelan, review of *Lizard in the Sun,* p. 1348; March 1, 1997, Carolyn Phelan, review of *Shark in the Sea,* p. 1173; September 1, 1999, Ellen Mandel, review of *Tyrannosaurus Time,* p. 142; May 1, 2000, Susan Dove Lempke, review of *Rainbow Wings,* p. 1679; March 1, 2001, Hazel Rochman, review of *A Fawn in the Grass,* p. 1288; April 15, 2001, Ilene Cooper, review of *Little Panda: The World Welcomes Hua Mei at the San Diego Zoo,* p. 1562; May 1, 2002, Ellen Mandel, review of *Big Bear Tall,* p. 1536; January 1, 2003, Carolyn Phelan, review of *Mouse Tail Moon,* p. 900; September 1, 2003, Lauren Peterson, review of *Come Along, Kitten,* p. 130; June 1, 2004, Lauren Peterson, review of *Won't You Be My Kissaroo?,* p. 1748; February 1, 2006, Jennifer Mattson, review of *A Pair of Polar Bears: Twin Cubs Find a Home at the San Diego Zoo,* p. 52; March 1, 2006, Shelle Rosenfeld, review of *Won't You Be My Hugaroo?* p. 101; April 15, 2006, John Peters, review of *My Mother's Voice,* p. 55; January 1, 2007, Shelle Rosenfeld, review of *Dance by the Light of the Moon,* p. 116; April 1, 2007, Carolyn Phelan, review of *Toad by the Road: A Year in the Life of These Amazing Amphibians,* p. 51; June 1, 2009, Linda Perkins, review of *Panda Kindergarten,* p. 58.

Bulletin of the Center for Children's Books, June, 1985, Zena Sutherland, review of *Inside Turtle's Shell,* p. 194; July, 1996, Lisa Mahoney, review of *Earthdance,* p. 385; April, 1997, Elizabeth Bush, review of *Shark in the Sea,* p. 295.

Childhood Education, spring, 2002, review of *Little Panda,* p. 172.

Horn Book, May, 2001, Lolly Robinson, review of *Little Panda,* p. 351; September-October, 2009, Janet Hamilton, review of *Panda Kindergarten,* p. 583.

Kirkus Reviews, April 1, 1996, review of *Earthdance,* p. 536; July 1, 1999, review of *Tyrannosaurus Time,* p. 1058; October 1, 2002, review of *Mouse Tail Moon,* p. 1479; February 1, 2003, review of *Wild Birds,* p. 238.

Publishers Weekly, March 19, 2001, reviews of *A Fawn in the Grass,* p. 98, and *The San Diego Panda,* p. 102; April 29, 2002, review of *Big Bear Ball,* p. 68; December 16, 2002, review of *Wild Birds,* p. 65; July 7, 2003, review of *Come along, Kitten,* p. 70; May 17, 2004, review of *Won't You Be My Kissaroo?,* p. 49; January 1, 2006, review of *A Pair of Polar Bears,* p. 44; February 15, 2006, review of *Won't You Be My Hugaroo?,* p. 190; March 1, 2006, review of *My Mother's Voice,* p. 238; December 1, 2006, review of *Dance by the Light of the Moon,* p. 1226; December 1, 2006, review of *Bear of My Heart,* p. 1225; March 1, 2007, review of *Toad by the Road,* p. 230; June 15, 2009, review of *Panda Kindergarten.*

School Library Journal, April, 1985, Ruth M. McConnell, review of *Inside Turtle's Shell,* p. 82; November, 1985, Anne E. Mulherkar, review of *Night Flight,* p. 77; April, 1989, Patricia Manning, review of *White Bear, Ice Bear,* p. 90; June, 1995, review of *Without Words,* p. 104; April, 1997, Helen Rosenberg, review of *Shark in the Sea,* p. 116; April, 2000, Susan Marie Pitard, review of *Each Living Thing,* p. 113; May, 2000, Joy Fleischhacker, review of *Rainbow Wings,* p. 153; May, 2001, Ellen A. Greever, review of *A Fawn in the Grass,* p. 134; July, 2001, Tina Hudak, review of *Little Panda,* p. 98; August, 2001, Holly T. Sneeringer, review of *The Waterfall's Gift,* p. 160; June, 2002, Wanda Meyers-Hines, review of *Big Bear Ball,* p. 110; February, 2003, Dona Ratterree, review of *Mouse Tail Moon,* p. 137; March, 2003, Susan Scheps, review of *Wild Birds,* p. 206; July, 2003, Sandra Kitain, review of *Come Along, Kitten,* p. 105; June, 2004, Kathy Krasniewicz, review of *Won't You Be My Kissaroo?,* p. 119; March, 2006, Wendy Woodfill, review of *A Pair of Polar Bears,* p. 214; April, 2006, Wanda Meyers-Hines, review of *My Mother's Voice,* p. 116; January, 2007, Kathleen Whalin, review of *Dance by the Light of the Moon,* p. 108; February, 2007, Kara Schaff Dean, review of *Bear of My Heart,* p. 96; April, 2007, Joy Fleishhacker, review of *Toad by the Road,* p. 126; August, 2009, Nancy Call, review of *Panda Kindergarten,* p. 92.

Sierra, May, 2001, review of *The Waterfall's Gift,* p. 83.

ONLINE

Balkin Buddies Web site, http://www.balkinbuddies.com/ (February 11, 2011), "Joanne Ryder."

HarperChildren's Web site, http://www.harperchildren's. com/ (July 6, 2005), "Joanne Ryder."

Penguin/Putnam Web site, http://www.penguin/putnam. com/ (November 27, 2000), "Joanne Ryder."*

S

SCANLON, Elizabeth Garton
See SCANLON, Liz Garton

*   *   *

SCANLON, Liz Garton
(Elizabeth Garton Scanlon)

Personal

Born in CO; married; children: daughters. *Education:* Master's degree. *Hobbies and other interests:* Travel, yoga, running, walking her dog.

Addresses

Home—Austin, TX. *Agent*—Erin Murphy Literary Agency, 2700 Woodlands Village, No. 300-458, Flagstaff, AZ 86001-7127. *E-mail*—liz@lizgartonscanlon. com.

Career

Author of books for children. IBM, former corporate copywriter; Austin Community College, teacher.

Member

Society of Children's Book Writers and Illustrators (Austin, TX, chapter), Texas Writers' League, Texas Library Association.

Awards, Honors

New York Times Best Book selection, and Parents' Choice Gold Award, both 2009, and Caldecott Honor designation, and Indies Choice Honor designation, both 2010, all for *All the World.*

Writings

(As Elizabeth Garton Scanlon) *A Sock Is a Pocket for Your Toes: A Pocket Book,* illustrated by Robin Preiss Glasser, HarperCollins (New York, NY), 2004.

All the World, illustrated by Marla Frazee, Beach Lane Books (New York, NY), 2009.
Noodle & Lou, illustrated by Arthur Howard, Beach Lane Books (New York, NY), 2011.

Sidelights

Liz Garton Scanlon began her career as a children's author as soon as she began her own family, as the presence of infants and toddlers sparked songs and poems and numerous trips to the library. Scanlon's first book, *A Sock Is a Pocket for Your Toes: A Pocket Book,* has been followed by the award-winning *All the World* as well as by *Noodle & Lou,* which introduces the close friendship between a blue bird and a tiny brown worm. "For ages I didn't know that it was the writing life I was settling into," the author explained to online interviewer Cynthia Leitich Smith in reflecting on her pre-picture-book career. "I wrote letters and poems and political rants. I read like a fiend. I slept with my thesaurus. But I didn't know what any of that had to do with my big-picture life. I went from degree to degree and from job to job with a scary sense of disconnect. . . . The writing life can be fantastically nebulous, so much so that I didn't know I was in it 'til I was in it. Now, I'd say that it's been a calling more than a choice, and maybe what I love the most are the shifting borders, the flexibility, the dynamic space it makes for a changeling like me."

Illustrated by Robin Preiss Glasser, *A Sock Is a Pocket for Your Toes* features a rhyming text that re-envisions the nature of a pocket, transforming it from a sewn-on patch to a container that might hold anything from a scoop of ice cream (a cone) to a beacon of light (a star). Scanlon also uses a rhyming text in *All the World,* in which readers can follow the linking chain of life as a family's day of activities—going to the beach, visiting a farmer's market, and enjoying dinner at a small restaurant—are related to a larger word. Artist Marla Frazee contributes what a *Publishers Weekly* contributor described as "blithesome watercolor and pencil-streaked illustrations" which capture Scanlon's "larger goal: to

Marla Frazee's artwork captures Liz Garton Scanlon's story in the life-affirming picture book **All the World.** (Illustration copyright © 2009 by Marla Frazee. Reprinted with the permission of Beach Lane Books, an imprint of Simon & Schuster Children's Publishing Division.)

show the world's connectivity." "Charming illustrations and lyrical rhyming couplets speak volumes in celebration of the world and humankind," wrote *School Library Journal* contributor Maryann H. Owen, and in *Booklist* Daniel Kraus cited the "pleasing rhythm" of Scanlon's text as it moves "from normal-life specifics all the way to more existential concepts." *All the World* received a Caldecott Honor designation in addition to several other picture-book awards.

Biographical and Critical Sources

PERIODICALS

Booklist, July 1, 2009, Daniel Kraus, review of *All the World*, p. 64.
Horn Book, September-October, 2009, Jennifer M. Brabander, review of *All the World*, p. 546.
Kirkus Reviews, August 15, 2009, review of *All the World*.
Publishers Weekly, August 24, 2009, review of *All the World*, p. 59.

School Library Journal, August, 2009, Maryann H. Owen, review of *All the World*, p. 92.

ONLINE

Cynthia Leitich Smith Web log, http://cynthialeitichsmith. blogspot.com/ (February, 2007), interview with Scanlon.
Liz Garton Scanlon Home Page, http://www.lizgarton scanlon.com (January 1, 2010).
Liz Garton Scanlon Web log, http://liz-scanlon.livejournal. com (February 15, 2011).

*   *   *

SCOTT, Jane Wooster 1939-

Personal

Born 1939, in Havertown, PA; married Vernon Scott (a journalist); children: Vernon IV, Ashley. *Education:* Attended college.

Addresses

Home—Sun Valley, ID.

Career

Artist and illustrator. Former model and actress; producer and host of *Hollywood Diary* (talk show), Los Angeles, CA, in 1960s; painter, 1971—. *Exhibitions:* Work exhibited at galleries in Los Angeles, CA, and New York, NY. Works included in permanent collections at the White House, Washington, DC, and in private collections throughout the United States.

Awards, Honors

Named "Most Reproduced Artist in America" by *Guinness Book of World Records.*

Writings

(Self-illustrated) *An American Jubilee: The Art of Jane Wooster Scott,* Cross River Press (New York, NY), 1993.

(Self-illustrated) *Simple Joys: The Folk Art of Jane Wooster Scott,* Courage Books (Philadelphia, PA), 2006.

Deborah Raffin, *Mitzi's World: Seek and Discover More than 150 Details in 15 Works of Folk Art,* Abrams Books for Young Readers (New York, NY), 2009.

Sidelights

Jane Wooster Scott, an internationally renowned artist whose work has drawn comparisons to that of American primitivist Grandma Moses, offers bucolic images of turn-of-the-twentieth-century America in her detailed and brightly colored paintings. Surprisingly, the talented Scott, whose shows have been sponsored by such Hollywood luminaries as Paul Newman, Gene Kelly, and Henry Fonda, never planned on a career as a painter and has achieved her great success despite having no formal training. Asked to describe the popularity of her works, she told *People* contributor Eleanor Hoover: "What I paint gives people a good feeling about an easier time and way of living."

Among Jane Wooster Scott's many creative projects are the detailed folk-art seek-and-find images in Deborah Raffin's picture book **Mitzi's World.**
(Abrams Books for Young Readers, 2009. Illustration copyright © 2009 Jane Wooster Scott. Reproduced by permission.)

A Pennsylvania native, Scott long harbored dreams of becoming a movie star and ventured to California at the age of eighteen. Within a year, she was producing and hosting her own talk show in Los Angeles, where she met her husband, Vernon Scott. While raising her children, Scott took up painting as a hobby, and when a family friend asked for a Grandma Moses-style painting to hang over her fireplace, Scott copied one of the great artist's works, signing it "Grandma Wooster." Talking to *Celeb Life* interviewer Elizabeth Klein, the artist joked, "I wonder if my girlfriend had said, what I really need is a Picasso over the fireplace, that's what I'd be doing."

Scott's work eventually came to the attention of comedian Jonathan Winters, himself an artist, who invited her to exhibit her paintings at the Ankrum Gallery; she sold all forty in one hour. Soon, her work began appearing in national magazines, and exhibitions in Los Angeles and New York City helped Scott attract a loyal following, especially among celebrities. (She has earned commissions from Arnold Schwarzenegger and Ronald and Nancy Reagan, among others.) The painter also licenses her work for calendars, greeting cards, commemorative plates, and puzzles; after one of her Christmas scenes appeared on a multi-state lottery ticket, she was cited by the Guinness Book of World Records as the "Most Reproduced Artist in America."

Scott's painting has also graced the pages of *Mitzi's World: Seek and Discover More than 150 Details in 15 Works of Folk Art,* a picture book featuring a text by Deborah Raffin. In the work, young readers are encouraged to explore a host of charming scenes from country life—including a county fair, a veterinarian's office, and an ice-skating rink—with the assistance of Mitzi, the black-and-white dog that appears in each painting. "Classic Americana scenes depict rolling hills and quaint villages," noted a critic in *Kirkus Reviews,* and Lisa Glasscock observed in *School Library Journal* that Scott's pictures "exhibit a broad spectrum of color."

Biographical and Critical Sources

PERIODICALS

Art Business News, November, 2002, Kevin Lo, "Americana Mama: Artist Jane Wooster Scott Left Hollywood behind for Family Life and to Capture American Ideals in Her Paintings," p. 64.

Celeb Life, fall, 2008, Elizabeth Klein, "Sometimes Your Dream Finds You: Jane Wooster Scott's Story," p. 116.

Christian Science Monitor, June 23, 2000, "Modern 'Grandma Moses' Captures Life in Simpler Times," p. 16.

Kirkus Reviews, September 1, 2009, review of *Mitzi's World: Seek and Discover More than 150 Details in 15 Works of Folk Art.*

School Library Journal, September, 2009, Lisa Glasscock, review of *Mitzi's World,* p. 146.

People, December 12, 1977, Eleanor Hoover, "Jane Wooster Scott Is the Improbable Grandma Moses of Hollywood Hills."

Time, April 3, 2000, Michele Orecklin, "You May Already Be a Collector," p. 99.

ONLINE

Jane Wooster Scott Graphics Web site, http://www.woosterscott.com (February 10, 2011).*

* * *

SENIR, Mirik
See SNIR, Mirik

* * *

SLADE, Suzanne 1964-

Personal

Born 1964; married; children: two. *Education:* B.S. (mechanical engineering). *Hobbies and other interests:* In-line skating.

Addresses

Home—Libertyville, IL. *E-mail*—slade357-author@yahoo.com.

Career

Author of books for children. McDonnell Douglas, CA, former test engineer on Delta IV rockets; Ford, IN, designer of automobile brake boosters until 1993. Presenter at schools.

Member

Society of Children's Book Writers and Illustrators (co-representative of Chicago chapter).

Awards, Honors

Amelia Bloomer Recommended Titles listee, 2008, for *Susan B. Anthony;* Teacher's Choice designation, *Learning* magazine, 2011, for *What's New at the Zoo?;* Blueberry Award, 2010, for *From Seed to Apple Tree.*

Writings

PICTURE BOOKS

Animals Are Sleeping, illustrated by Gary Phillips, Sylvan Dell (Mount Pleasant, SC), 2008.

Suzanne Slade (Reproduced by permission.)

What's New at the Zoo?: An Animal Adding Adventure, illustrated by Joan Waites, Sylvan Dell (Mount Pleasant, SC), 2009.

What's the Difference?: An Endangered Animal Subtraction Story, illustrated by Joan Waites, Sylvan Dell (Mount Pleasant, SC), 2010.

Climbing Lincoln's Steps: The African-American Journey, illustrated by Colin Bootman, Albert Whitman (Chicago, IL), 2010.

Multiply on the Fly, illustrated by Erin E. Hunter, Sylvan Dell (Mount Pleasant, SC), 2011.

JUVENILE BIOGRAPHIES

Frederick Douglass: Writer, Speaker, and Opponent of Slavery, illustrated by Robert McGuire, Picture Window Books (Minneapolis, MN), 2007.

Susan B. Anthony: Fighter for Freedom and Equality, illustrated by Craig Orback, Picture Window Books (Minneapolis, MN), 2007.

Albert Einstein: Scientist and Genius, illustrated by Jolene Schultz, Picture Window Books (Minneapolis, MN), 2008.

Booker T. Washington: Teacher, Speaker, and Leader, illustrated by Siri Weber Feeney, Picture Window Books (Minneapolis, MN), 2008.

Cesar Chavez: Champion and Voice of Farm Workers, illustrated by Jeffrey Thompson, Picture Window Books (Minneapolis, MN), 2008.

Jackie Robinson: Hero and Athlete, illustrated by Thomas Spence, Picture Window Books (Minneapolis, MN), 2008.

Martha Washington: First Lady of the United States, illustrated by Frances Moore, Picture Window Books (Minneapolis, MN), 2008.

Sojourner Truth: Preacher for Freedom and Equality, illustrated by Natascha Alex Blanks, Picture Window Books (Minneapolis, MN), 2008.

SERIES NONFICTION; FOR CHILDREN

Adopted: The Ultimate Teen Guide, Scarecrow Press (Lanham, MD), 2007.

Atoms and Chemical Reactions, PowerKids Press (New York, NY), 2007.

Elements and the Periodic Table, PowerKids Press (New York, NY), 2007.

Elements in Living Organisms, PowerKids Press (New York, NY), 2007.

Looking at Atoms and Molecules, PowerKids Press (New York, NY), 2007.

States of Matter, PowerKids Press (New York, NY), 2007.

The Carbon Cycle, PowerKids Press (New York, NY), 2007.

The Four Seasons, PowerKids Press (New York, NY), 2007.

The Nitrogen Cycle, PowerKids Press (New York, NY), 2007.

The Phases of the Moon, PowerKids Press (New York, NY), 2007.

The Rock Cycle, PowerKids Press (New York, NY), 2007.

The Structure of Atoms, PowerKids Press (New York, NY), 2007.

Water on the Move, PowerKids Press (New York, NY), 2007.

Let's Go Camping, PowerKids Press (New York, NY), 2007.

Let's Go Canoeing and Kayaking, PowerKids Press (New York, NY), 2007.

Let's Go Fishing, PowerKids Press (New York, NY), 2007.

Let's Go Hiking, PowerKids Press (New York, NY), 2007.

Let's Go Hunting, PowerKids Press (New York, NY), 2007.

Let's Go Snowboarding, PowerKids Press (New York, NY), 2007.

A Look at Jupiter, PowerKids Press (New York, NY), 2008.

A Look at Neptune, PowerKids Press (New York, NY), 2008.

A Look at Saturn, PowerKids Press (New York, NY), 2008.

A Look at Uranus, PowerKids Press (New York, NY), 2008.

What Do You Know about Animal Adaptations?, PowerKids Press (New York, NY), 2008.

What Do You Know about Food Chains and Food Webs?, PowerKids Press (New York, NY), 2008.

What Do You Know about Fossils?, PowerKids Press (New York, NY), 2008.

What Do You Know about Life Cycles?, PowerKids Press (New York, NY), 2008.

What Do You Know about Plant Life?, PowerKids Press (New York, NY), 2008.

What Do You Know about World Habitats?, PowerKids Press (New York, NY), 2008.

Ants ("Backyard Bugs" series), PowerKids Press (New York, NY), 2008.

Bees ("Backyard Bugs" series), PowerKids Press (New York, NY), 2008.

Butterflies ("Backyard Bugs" series), PowerKids Press (New York, NY), 2008.

Dragonflies ("Backyard Bugs" series), PowerKids Press (New York, NY), 2008.

Grasshoppers ("Backyard Bugs" series), PowerKids Press (New York, NY), 2008.

Ladybugs ("Backyard Bugs" series), PowerKids Press (New York, NY), 2008.

Feel the G's: The Science of Gravity and G-forces, Compass Point Books (Mankato, MN), 2009.

Fencing for Fun!, Compass Point Books (Minneapolis, MN), 2009.

From Caterpillar to Butterfly, illustrated by Jeff Yesh, Picture Window Books (Minneapolis, MN), 2009.

From Egg to Snake, illustrated by Jeff Yesh, Picture Window Books (Minneapolis, MN), 2009.

From Pup to Rat, illustrated by Jeff Yesh, Picture Window Books (Minneapolis, MN), 2009.

From Puppy to Dog, illustrated by Jeff Yesh, Picture Window Books (Minneapolis, MN), 2009.

From Seed to Apple Tree, illustrated by Jeff Yesh, Picture Window Books (Minneapolis, MN), 2009.

From Seed to Pine Tree, illustrated by Jeff Yesh, Picture Window Books (Minneapolis, MN), 2009.

From Tadpole to Frog, illustrated by Jeff Yesh, Picture Window Books (Minneapolis, MN), 2009.

Do All Bugs Have Wings?, and Other Questions Kids Have about Bugs, illustrated by Cary Pillo, Picture Window Books (Minneapolis, MN), 2010.

How Do Tornadoes Form?, and Other Questions Kids Have about Weather, illustrated by Cary Pillo, Picture Window Books (Mankato, MN), 2010.

Who Invented Basketball?, and Other Questions Kids Have about Sports, illustrated by Cary Pillo, Picture Window Books (Minneapolis, MN), 2010.

Why Do Dogs Drool?, and Other Questions Kids Have about Dogs, illustrated by Cary Pillo, Picture Window Books (Minneapolis, MN), 2010.

Basketball: How It Works, Capstone Press (Mankato, MN), 2010.

Birds: Winged and Feathered Animals, illustrated by Kristin Kest, Picture Window Books (Minneapolis, MN), 2010.

Fish: Finned and Gilled Animals, illustrated by Kristin Kest, Picture Window Books (Minneapolis, MN), 2010.

Insects: Six-legged Animals, illustrated by Rosiland Solomon, Picture Window Books (Minneapolis, MN), 2010.

What Can We Do about Endangered Animals?, PowerKids Press (New York, NY), 2010.

What Can We Do about Pollution?, PowerKids Press (New York, NY), 2010.

What Can We Do about the Energy Crisis?, PowerKids Press (New York, NY), 2010.

What If There Were No Bees?: A Book about the Grassland Ecosystem, illustrated by Carol Schwartz, Picture Window Books (Mankato, MN), 2010.

A Dollar Bill's Journey, illustrated by Susan Swan, Picture Window Books (Mankato, MN), 2011.

A Plastic Bottle's Journey, illustrated by Nadine Wickenden, Picture Window Books (Mankato, MN), 2011.

A Raindrop's Journey, illustrated by Holli Conger, Picture Window Books (Mankato, MN), 2011.

What If There Were No Gray Wolves?: A Book about the Temperate Forest Ecosystem, illustrated by Carol Schwartz, Picture Window Books (Mankato, MN), 2011.

What If There Were No Lemmings?: A Book about the Tundra Ecosystem, illustrated by Carol Schwartz, Picture Window Books (Mankato, MN), 2011.

What If There Were No Sea Otters?: A Book about the Ocean Ecosystem, illustrated by Carol Schwartz, Picture Window Books (Mankato, MN), 2011.

Sidelights

A prolific author who specializes in nonfiction, Suzanne Slade produces informative books for a range of reading levels and focuses on everything from animals and nature to science, sports, and history. Many of her works are part of larger series chock full of illustrations and designed for young researchers. Slade has contributed to many series, including the "Following the Life Cycle," "Kids' Questions," and "What Would You Know About. . ." books. In *Adopted: The Ultimate Teen Guide,* which is part of the "It Happened to Me" series, she draws from her own experience while adopting a child and produces what *School Library Journal* contributor Deborah Vose praised as an "exhaustive guide" in which "Slade's writing reflects her sensitivity toward all parties involved in adoption."

While growing up, Slade enjoyed science and math. During family vacations on the island of Tortola, the lack of technology inspired her to explore and record her finds in illustrated journals. In college she majored in mechanical engineering, and then worked for several years testing rockets and designing automotive braking systems. After Slade and her husband started their family by adopting their first child, a baby daughter, she left her job and was soon introduced to the world of picture books. When the time was right, she began to see how her interest in science might fit the needs of picture-book publishers and she enrolled at a writing class at a local college. Although her first efforts generated dozens of rejection letters, Slade persevered and

Joan Waites creates the artwork for Slade's nature-themed concept book **What's New at the Zoo?: An Animal Adding Adventure.** (Sylvan Dell Publishing, 2009. Illustration copyright © 2009 by Joan Waites. Reproduced by permission.)

eventually received her first book contract. She often shares her story of persistence during school author visits as she encourages children not to give up on their dreams.

Illustrated by Gary R. Phillips, Slade's picture book *Animals Are Sleeping* presents a fascinating look at the diverse behaviors exhibited by creatures settling down for a good rest, and her "calming and peaceful text" contain "enough factual and interesting information to keep young minds engaged," according to *School Library Journal* critic Lisa Gangemi Kropp. *What's New at the Zoo?: An Animal Adding Adventure* pairs Slade's text with artwork by Joan Waites into what Alyson Low described in the same periodical as a "fun introduction to early math skills and basic animal facts." "Slade slyly sneaks in some great vocabulary," observed a *Kirkus Reviews* writer in discussing *What's New at the Zoo?*, "working the animal baby names into each verse" of her engaging rhyming text. The sequel to this title, *What's the Difference?: An Animal Subtraction Story*, provides young readers with subtraction practice while sharing important ways that people can make a difference and help endangered animals.

Slade uses the Lincoln Memorial in Washington, DC, as a vehicle to follow the history of black civil rights in America in her picture book *Climbing Lincoln's Steps: The African-American Journey*. Featuring illustrations by award-winning artist Colin Bootman, the book begins its narrative in 1863, as President Abraham Lincoln signed the Emancipation Proclamation that ended slavery in the United States. From there, readers follow Slade's trail to 1922 and the construction of the memorial, its use as a stage for noted opera singer Marian Anderson in 1939, and as the eventual backdrop to a famous speech by civil rights leader Dr. Martin Luther King, Jr. In *School Library Journal* Barbara Auerbach praised *Climbing Lincoln's Steps* as an "attractive, accessible" introduction to an important epoch in twentieth-century history and dubbed Bootman's detailed water-color illustrations "striking."

Biographical and Critical Sources

PERIODICALS

Booklist, June 1, 2007, Ilene Cooper, review of *Susan B. Anthony: Fighter for Freedom and Equality*, p. 94; August 1, 2009, John Peters, review of *What's New at the Zoo?: An Animal Adding Adventure*, p. 75; June 1, 2010, Carolyn Phelan, review of *What's the Difference?: An Endangered Animal Subtraction Story*, p. 87.

Kirkus Reviews, June 15, 2009, review of *What's New at the Zoo?*

School Library Journal, February, 2007, Maren Ostergard, review of *Mixtures and Compounds*, p. 140; August, 2007, Sarah O'Holla, review of *Frederick Douglas:*

Writer, Speaker, and Opponent of Slavery, p. 103; October, 2007, Michael Giller, review of *Let's Go Camping*, p. 185; November, 2007, Deborah Vose, review of *Adopted: The Ultimate Teen Guide*, p. 154; March, 2008, Karey Wehner, review of *Ants*, p. 190; June, 2008, Lisa Gangemi Kropp, review of *Animals Are Sleeping*, p. 131; September, 2009, Alyson Low, review of *What's New at the Zoo?*, p. 148; June, 2010, Stacy Dillon, review of *What's the Difference?*, p. 91; August, 2010, Barbara Auerbach, review of *Climbing Lincoln's Steps: The African American Journey*, p. 91.

Reference & Research Book News, November, 2007, review of *Adopted*.

ONLINE

Suzanne Slade Home Page, http://www.suzanneslade.com (February 15, 2011).

                    *   *   *

SNIR, Mirik 1948-
(Mirik Senir)

Personal

Born 1948, in Israel; married Israel Snir; children: nine. *Education:* College degree (education). *Religion:* Jewish.

Addresses

Home—Israel. *E-mail*—info@mirik-snir.com.

Career

Educator, author, and translator. Teacher of special education and in elementary schools; freelance writer, beginning 1982. Presenter at schools and teacher conferences throughout the world.

Awards, Honors

Gold Award, National Parenting Publications Awards, 2009, for *When I First Held You*; Israeli Prime Minister award.

Writings

Galgalim, illustrated by Dani Kerman, Sifriyat po'alim (Tel Aviv, Israel), 1982.

Yaldah ahat amrah, illustrated by Avner Galili, ha-Kibuts ha-me'uhad (Tel Aviv, Israel), 1984.

Leshonot ketanim, illustrated by Shelomit Zohar, Sifriyat Ma'ariv (Tel Aviv, Israel), 1987.

Miryam v'Ha-yam, illustrated by Gil-Li Alon Kuri'el, ha-Kibuts ha-me'uhad (Tel Aviv, Israel), 1993.

Kulam omrim shalom, ha-Kibuts ha-me'uhad (Tel Aviv, Israel), 1993.

Mirik Snir (Reproduced by permission.)

Parah parparah, ha-Kibuts ha-me'uhad (Tel Aviv, Israel), 1993.
'Amos, bakbuk ve-khos, ha-Kibuts ha-me'uhad (Tel Aviv, Israel), 1993.
Ani veha-mishpahah sheli, ha-Kibuts ha-me'uhad (Tel Aviv, Israel), 1995.
Salat-tov-tari, ha-Kibuts ha-me'uhad (Tel Aviv, Israel), 1995.
When I First Held You: A Lullaby from Israel, translated from the Hebrew by Mary Jane Shubow, illustrated by daughter, Eleyor Snir, Kar-Ben Publishing (Minneapolis, MN), 2009.

Author of numerous other books published in Hebrew, including the "My Little Library" and "I Have a Song" series. Translator, from the Yiddish, of stories by Kadia Molodovsky and other writers.

Snir's work has been translated into several languages, including Spanish.

Sidelights

Israeli author Mirik Snir focuses her time on writing for children, from infancy to literacy. Her books expose young readers to literature and poetry, while also introducing them to a rich language from infancy. Snir's original stories encourage children to attempt independent reading at a very young age, and they are also use by those learning Hebrew as a second language in Israel as well as abroad. *When I First Held You: A Lullaby from Israel,* Snir's first book to be translated from the Hebrew into English, features illustrations by the author's daughter, artist Eleyor Snir.

"I hope my stories will be kept in the heart of children and adults forever," Snir commented to *SATA.* "When I write I know my book will be read by two: a child and a parent. My mission is to voice children's issues to parents, teachers, and educators.

"Love of the written word, however important as it may seem, is not an end in itself but the glorious route to loving all of humanity. I believe with all my heart that language builds a relationship whose crowning point is love. The opposite of a relationship through language is silence: uncommunicativeness from which stems violence. Deficient and poor communication in childhood is liable to take a violent expression later on, whereas a language rich with understanding and trust-building strengthens love in the world."

Biographical and Critical Sources

PERIODICALS

Kirkus Reviews, August 15, 2009, review of *When I First Held You: A Lullaby from Israel.*
Publishers Weekly, October 5, 2009, review of *When I First Held You,* p. 46.
School Library Journal, November, 2009, Heidi Estrin, review of *When I First Held You,* p. 89.

ONLINE

Mirik Snir Home Page, http://www.mirik-snir.com (January 1, 2010).
San Diego Jewish World Web log, http://sdjewishworld.wordpress.com/ (November 14, 2009), Jennie Starr, "Mirik Snir, Israeli Children's Author, Guest Teaches in San Diego."

*   *   *

SNYDER, Zilpha Keatley 1927-

Personal

Born May 11, 1927, in Lemoore, CA; daughter of William Solon (a rancher and driller) and Dessa J. Keatley; married Larry Allan Snyder (a professor of music), June 18, 1950; children: Susan Melissa, Douglas; foster children: Ben. *Education:* Whittier College, B.A., 1948; additional study at University of California, Berkeley, 1958-60. *Politics:* Democrat. *Religion:* Episcopalian. *Hobbies and other interests:* Reading, writing, travel.

Zilpha Keatley Snyder (Reproduced by permission.)

Addresses

Home—Mill Valley, CA. *E-mail*—zilpha@zksnyder.com.

Career

Writer. Public school teacher at Washington School, Berkeley, CA, and in New York, Washington, and Alaska, 1948-62; University of California, Berkeley, master teacher and demonstrator for education classes, 1959-61; lecturer.

Awards, Honors

Notable Book selections, American Library Association, 1964, for *Season of Ponies,* 1967, for *The Egypt Game,* 1971, for *The Headless Cupid,* 1972, for *The Witches of Worm,* 1990, for *Libby on Wednesday,* 1981, for *A Fabulous Creature;* Lewis Carroll Shelf Award, and Spring Book Festival first prize, both 1967, Newbery Honor Book designation, 1968, and George G. Stone Recognition of Merit, Claremont Graduate School, 1973, all for *The Egypt Game;* Christopher Medal, 1970, for *The Changeling;* William Allen White Award, Newbery Honor Hook designation, and Christopher Medal, all 1972, and Hans Christian Andersen International honor list, International Board on Books for Young People, 1974, all for *The Headless Cupid;* Outstanding Book selection, *New York Times,* 1972, and National Book Award finalist and Newbery honor book, both 1973, all for *The Witches of Worm;* Outstanding Book selection, *New York Times,* 1981, for *A Fabulous Creature;* PEN

Literary Award, 1983, and Parents' Choice Award, Parents' Choice Foundation, both for *The Birds of Summer; Blair's Nightmare* included on state awards master lists in Missouri, Texas, Nebraska, the Pacific Northwest, and New Mexico, c. 1984; Bay Area Book Reviewers Award, 1988, for *And Condors Danced;* New Mexico State Award, 1989-90, and Notable Trade Books in the Language Arts selection, National Council of Teachers of English, both 1985, both for *The Changing Maze; Libby on Wednesday* included on Virginia State Book Award master list, c, 1991; Mythopoeic Society Award finalist, and state award master-list inclusions in Missouri, Illinois, and Utah, all 1991, all for *Song of the Gargoyle;* Best Books designation, New York Public Library, CLA Beatty Award, and Book of the Year for Children selection, Child Study Children's Book Committee, all 1994, all for *Cat Running;* California Young Readers' Medal nomination, 1994-95, for *Fool's Gold;* Texas Bluebonnet Award master list inclusion, 1996, for *The Trespassers;* honorary D.H.L., Whittier College, 1998; inclusion on state master lists in Texas, Nebraska, Vermont, New Mexico, and South Carolina, 1999-2000, for *Gib Rides Home;* Parents' Choice Foundation Silver Medal, 2004, for *The Unseen;* Mark Twain Readers' Award nomination, 2007, for *The Treasures of Weatherby.*

Writings

FOR CHILDREN

Season of Ponies, illustrated by Alton Raible, Atheneum (New York, NY), 1964.

The Velvet Room, illustrated by Alton Raible, Atheneum (New York, NY), 1965.

Black and Blue Magic, illustrated by Gene Holtan, Atheneum (New York, NY), 1966.

The Egypt Game, illustrated by Alton Raible, Atheneum (New York, NY), 1967.

Eyes in the Fishbowl, illustrated by Alton Raible, Atheneum (New York, NY), 1968.

Today Is Saturday (poetry), photographs by John Arms, Atheneum (New York, NY), 1969.

The Changeling, illustrated by Alton Raible, Atheneum (New York, NY), 1970.

The Headless Cupid, illustrated by Alton Raible, Atheneum (New York, NY), 1971, reprinted, Yearling Book (New York, NY), 2005.

The Witches of Worm, illustrated by Alton Raible, Atheneum (New York, NY), 1972, reprinted, Yearling Book (New York, NY), 2005.

The Princess and the Giants (picture book), illustrated by Beatrice Darwin, Atheneum (New York, NY), 1973.

The Truth about Stone Hollow, illustrated by Alton Raible, Atheneum (New York, NY), 1974, published as *The Ghosts of Stone Hollow,* Lutterworth (London, England), 1978.

Below the Root (first volume in the "Green-sky" trilogy), illustrated by Alton Raible, Atheneum (New York, NY), 1975, reprinted, 1992.

And All Between (second volume in the "Green-sky" trilogy), illustrated by Alton Raible, Atheneum (New York, NY), 1976, reprinted, 1992.

Until the Celebration (third volume in the "Green-sky" trilogy), illustrated by Alton Raible, Atheneum (New York, NY), 1977, reprinted, 1992.

The Famous Stanley Kidnapping Case, illustrated by Alton Raible, Atheneum (New York, NY), 1979.

Come on, Patsy (picture book), illustrated by Margot Zemach, Atheneum (New York, NY), 1982.

Blair's Nightmare, Atheneum (New York, NY), 1984.

The Changing Maze (picture book), illustrated by Charles Mikolaycak, Macmillan (New York, NY), 1985.

The Three Men, Harper (New York, NY), 1986.

And Condors Danced, Delacorte (New York, NY), 1987.

Squeak Saves the Day, and Other Tooley Tales, illustrated by Leslie Morrill, Delacorte (New York, NY), 1988.

Janie's Private Eyes, Delacorte (New York, NY), 1989.

Libby on Wednesday, Delacorte (New York, NY), 1990.

Song of the Gargoyle, Delacorte (New York, NY), 1991.

Fool's Gold, Delacorte (New York, NY), 1993.

Cat Running, Delacorte (New York, NY), 1994.

The Trespassers, Delacorte (New York, NY), 1994.

Castle Court Kids (series; includes *The Diamond War, The Box and the Bone, Ghost Invasion,* and *Secret Weapons*), Yearling (New York, NY), 1995.

The Gypsy Game, Delacorte (New York, NY), 1997.

Gib Rides Home, Delacorte (New York, NY), 1998.

The Runaways, Delacorte (New York, NY), 1999.

Gib and the Gray Ghost, Delacorte (New York, NY), 2000.

Spyhole Secrets, Delacorte (New York, NY), 2001.

The Ghosts of Rathburn Park, Delacorte (New York, NY), 2002.

The Magic Nation Thing, Delacorte (New York, NY), 2005.

The Treasures of Weatherby, Atheneum Books for Young Readers (New York, NY), 2007.

The Bronze Pen, Atheneum Books for Young Readers (New York, NY), 2008.

William S. and the Great Escape, Atheneum Books for Young Readers (New York, NY), 2009.

NOVELS; FOR YOUNG ADULTS

A Fabulous Creature, Atheneum (New York, NY), 1981.

The Birds of Summer, Atheneum (New York, NY), 1983.

The Unseen, Delacorte (New York, NY), 2004.

OTHER

Heirs of Darkness (adult novel), Atheneum (New York, NY), 1978.

Author's books have been translated into thirteen languages. Short stories included in anthologies.

Author's manuscripts are housed in the Kerlan Collection, University of Minnesota at Minneapolis.

Adaptations

Black and Blue Magic was adapted as a filmstrip with audiotape by Pied Piper, 1975. *The Egypt Game* was recorded by Miller-Brody, 1975, and produced as a filmstrip and audiotape by Piped Piper. *The Headless Cupid* was recorded for *Newbery Award Cassette* stories by Miller-Brody, 1976, and produced as a filmstrip with audiotape by Pied Piper, 1980. *The Witches of Worm* was recorded by Miller-Brody, 1978. *Below the Root* was adapted as a computer game by Spinnaker Software/Windham Classics, 1985. *Cat Running, The Egypt Game, Song of the Gargoyle, The Witches of Worm, The Headless Cupid, Gib Rides Home, Gib and the Gray Ghost, Spyhole Secrets,* and *The Ghosts of Rathburn Park* were adapted as audiobooks by Recorded Books.

Sidelights

Three-time Newbery Honor Book recipient Zilpha Keatley Snyder is noted for creating middle-grade novels full of wonder, mystery, and suspense. Addressing topics from magic to dysfunctional families and from murder to witchcraft, Snyder's works range in genre from fantasy to mainstream fiction and usually focus on a female protagonist. Her elegant but whimsical and tightly plotted prose appeals to readers of all ages. In addition to the majority of her work written for juvenile readers, Snyder has also written two young adult novels, an adult Gothic novel, and poetry. Newbery Honor books from Snyder include *The Egypt Game, The Headless Cupid,* and *The Witches of Worm,* while the list of her other award-winning titles is a lengthy one: *The Changeling, A Fabulous Creature, The Birds of Summer, And Condors Danced, The Changing Maze, Blair's Nightmare, Song of the Gargoyle, Cat Running,* and *The Unseen,* among others.

Snyder was born in Lemoore, California, in 1927, the daughter of a rancher and oil driller. Growing up in the Depression era, she and her friends found entertainment by developing fantasy games and play. She also formed a love for books and for the fantasy worlds they create. Skipping a grade in elementary school, Snyder found herself out of sync with the older children in her class and retreated further into books and fantasy. From high school on, she determined to become a writer and harbored romantic dreams of living in a New York City garret after graduating from Whittier College. However, marriage and family, as well as her career teaching elementary school, intervened until her late thirties and publication of Snyder's first novel, *Season of Ponies.*

Published in 1964, *Season of Ponies* drew on Snyder's lifelong love for horses. The story of a young and lonely girl living with two aunts whose boredom is mitigated by the arrival of magical ponies, the novel features many trademark Snyder elements. Zena Sutherland, writing in the *Bulletin of the Center for Children's Literature,* neatly summed up the Snyder effect: "A story that is written on two levels—realistic and fanciful."

From that first novel, Snyder has gone on to develop her characteristic style, creating stories that are heavily inspired and infused with her own childhood experiences. They feature lonely, reclusive young girls and meld a strong element of the supernatural or of mystery to an outwardly realistic tale.

One of Snyder's most highly regarded early books, *The Egypt Game,* was published in 1967. In this work, April and Melanie turn a vacant lot into a pretend ancient Egypt for their fantasy games, but their play turns nasty when a child-killer stalks April. Using a multiracial cast of urban characters, Snyder created "one the controversial books of the [1960s]," in the opinion of *Bulletin of the Center for Children's Books* contributor Sutherland. "It is strong in characterization, the dialogue is superb, the plot is original. . . . *The Egypt Game* is a distinguished book," Sutherland concluded.

Snyder produced a sequel three decades later in *The Gypsy Game,* which continues the story of April and Melanie and introduces Melanie's little brother, Marshall. This time out the children are playing gypsies, having grown weary with playing ancient Egyptians. In the process, they try to figure out why

Cover of Snyder's middle-grade novel Cat Running, *featuring artwork by Robert Hunt.* (Cover copyright © 1996 by Yearling. Used by permission of Yearling, an imprint of Random House Children's Books, a division of Random House, Inc.)

their friend Toby has disappeared. Deborah Stevenson noted in the *Bulletin of the Center for Children's Books* that "the multicultural and age-diverse gang of characters retains much of its original charm," while Jennifer M. Brabander commented in her *Horn Book* review of *The Gypsy Game* that readers who responded to the exotic costumes and rites of *The Egypt Game* "will find themselves drawn to and intrigued by the jewelry, colorful clothes, and fortune-telling in this adventure."

Another pair of youthful protagonists appears in *The Changeling,* a book that traces the growth of Ivy and Martha from age seven to their early teens. "It will be comforting to children to hear they can grow up without necessarily turning into those dull creatures known as 'grown-ups,'" noted Jean Fritz in the *New York Times Book Review.* In *The Witches of Worm,* another novel by Snyder, a lonely young girl finds solace in the company of animals. When she befriends a stray cat, she becomes convinced that the animal is possessed by a witch. Elizabeth Minot Graves, writing in *Commonweal,* called *The Witches of Worm* "a haunting story of the mind and ritual, as well as of misunderstanding, anger, loneliness and friendship." Of Snyder's *The Headless Cupid,* Barbara Sherrard-Smith noted in *Children's Book Review* that "this most readable and enjoyable book races along absorbingly," while Graves commented in *Commonweal* that it "pokes fun in a discerning way at the current interest in the occult and its beaded young practitioners, at the same time leaving an avenue open to a belief in ghosts and poltergeist."

With *The Headless Cupid* Snyder began a quartet of novels about the Stanley siblings: five stepbrothers and stepsisters who get involved in dangerous and often comic situations. All four novels are told from the character David's point of view. These children also make appearances in *The Famous Stanley Kidnapping Case, Blair's Nightmare,* and *Janie's Private Eyes.* In the award-winning *Blair's Nightmare,* the Stanley kids want to keep a dog that Blair has found and also try to discover if a group of escaped convicts have come to their locale. Felice Buckvar, writing in the *New York Times Book Review,* concluded that "there is enough mystery to keep the reader turning the pages and enough realism to illustrate the theme," while Kathleen Brachman wrote of *Blair's Nightmare* in *School Library Journal* that "this will delight Snyder's fans and earn her new ones."

Another group of interlocking books, Snyder's "Green-Sky" science-fiction trilogy, comprises *Below the Root, And All Between,* and *Until the Celebration.* The trio of books deals with themes from violence and human nature to the morality of the actions that governments take. Set in an arboreal world located far above the forest floor, the books feature young Raamo and Genaa and their mission to liberate the Erdlings, a race long ago captured among the roots below. "This is intellectual fantasy in that the ideas are in complete control,"

Cover of Snyder's elementary-grade novel The Unseen, *featuring artwork by Tim Jessell.* (Illustration copyright © 2004 by Tim Jessell. Used by permission of Delacorte Press, an imprint of Random House Children's Books, a division of Random House, Inc.)

noted a *Kirkus Reviews* critic of *Until the Celebration,* "but throughout the trilogy they always come embodied in well-paced action."

Of Snyder's young-adult novels, *Birds of Summer* remains the most popular, and "just as timely today as it was in 1983," according to Hazel K. Davis, writing in the *St. James Guide to Young Adult Writers.* In this novel, fifteen-year-old Summer has to deal not only with her budding sexuality, but also with a hippie mother, Oriole, who is still tripping from her days on a commune. Living in a run-down trailer while on welfare, memries of the glory days of sex, drugs, and rock and roll are a hiding place for Oriole, leaving Summer to determine how to make her own way in the world. Reviewing *Birds of Summer* for the *Voice of Youth Advocates,* Eleanor Klopp concluded: "What a joy to find a truly heroic heroine in a book whose plot alone will endear it."

Not one to write the same book over and over, Snyder turns from contemporary novels to history with *And Condors Danced,* a novel set in turn-of-the-twentieth-century southern California. Young Carly's mother is

dying and the family's citrus farm is threatened with a water-rights issue in a story that "vividly captures the daily life of the farming community of Santa Luisa . . . before the automobile superseded the horse and buggy," according to Wendy Martin in the *New York Times Book Review.*

Sticking with historical settings, Snyder focuses on life in a small California town during the Depression years in *Cat Running,* on an orphanage at the turn of the twentieth century in *Gib Rides Home,* and on a lonely desert town in the 1950s in *The Runaways.* In *Cat Running,* eleven-year-old Cat Kinsey builds a secret hideaway as a refuge from her unhappy home life, and soon finds friendship with a family of "Okies" who have lost their home in the widescale drought known as the Dust Bowl. In so doing, Cat comes smack up against her family's intolerance and bigotry. *Booklist* critic Stephanie Zvirin asserted that Snyder illustrates "Cat's change from self-absorbed child to caring young woman with energy and enough verisimilitude to keep readers pleasantly involved." Roger Sutton concluded in his *Bulletin of the Center for Children's Books* review of *Cat Running* that Snyder's "honorable, prickly heroine" is part of "a girls'-book tradition that stretches from Alcott's Jo March to Cynthia Voigt's Dicey."

In *The Runaways* Dani O'Donnell, twelve years old and bored, hates the desert town of Rattler Springs, Nevada, where she is now living. Her mother works at the local bookstore and Dani spends most of her time with Stormy, a troubled nine-year-old dyslexic boy. She dreams of running away and heading back to the coastal town where she used to live, but her plans are complicated with the arrival of young Pixie and her geologist parents. GraceAnne A. DeCandido, reviewing *The Runaways* in *Booklist,* called Stormy "an unforgettable portrait of a child whose life is heartbreakingly complicated." In *Publishers Weekly* a critic observed that even "minor characters . . . seem to have lives off the page" in Snyder's atmospheric novel of longing and regret.

Drawing on her father's stories of his childhood in a Nebraska orphanage, Snyder describes the plight of orphans living a century ago in *Gib Rides Home* and *Gib and the Gray Ghost.* Gib Whittaker manages to keep an optimistic outlook despite harsh treatment at the Lovell House Home for Orphaned and Abandoned Boys. When adopted by the wealthy Thornton family, he thinks he has finally found a loving family, only to discover that he has actually been sent into a sort of bondage, "farmed out" to be a farm hand. Susan Dove Lempke wrote in *Booklist* that Snyder's "deft pacing and characterization, along with a background rich in sensory detail . . . make [*Gib Rides Home*] . . . a touching, satisfying tribute to Snyder's father and to all children who face difficult lives with courage." *Gib and the Gray Ghost* continues the story of Gib Whittaker, finding him leaving the orphanage for good and returning to work with the Thornton family again. While working on the ranch, he attends school and makes new friends, including

Livy Thornton. He also trains a horse named Gray Ghost, who mysteriously showed up at the ranch during a snowstorm. Lauralyn Persson, writing in *School Library Journal*, found Gib to be "a sympathetic and appealing character," and *Booklist* critic Kay Weisman praised "Snyder's strong characterizations, compelling story, and rich setting details."

Snyder introduces readers to a troubled eleven-year-old girl named Hallie in *Spyhole Secrets*. When Hallie's father is killed in a traffic accident, she and her mother move to a new house. Hallie misses her father and hates the new home she must live in and the new school she now attends. Lonely and bored, she discovers a peephole in the attic where she can look across at the teen-aged girl next door. The girl fascinates her because she seems to be undergoing tragic events that Hallie cannot quite understand. She nicknames the girl "Rapunzel" because of her long blonde hair. When Hallie befriends "Rapunzel's" younger brother, Zachary, she begins to learn more about the enigmatic girl in the window, a process that takes her out of her own depressive state. Shelle Rosenfeld, writing in *Booklist*, called *Spyhole Secrets* "an absorbing book with many intriguing issues," while a critic for *Publishers Weekly* praised the "realism and power of Snyder's writing."

Mysteries involving strange or paranormal elements are a feature of Snyder's novels *The Ghosts of Rathburn Park*, *The Treasures of Weatherby*, and *William S. and the Great Escape*. In *The Ghosts of Rathburn Park* the Hamilton family has just moved to Timber City. At the annual Fourth of July picnic young Matt hears about the great fire that consumed the town years before and about the ghosts that are said to still haunt Rayburn Park. After Matt sees a dog in the woods that no one else is able to see, he meets a strange girl, Amelia, who dresses in clothes from the nineteenth century. Together they explore an old church, the local swamp, and the Rathburn mansion, where the town's oldest family lives. Kathryn Kosiorek, writing in *School Library Journal*, called *The Ghosts of Rathburn Park* a "skillfully told story," while a *Publishers Weekly* critic asserted that Snyder's "gifts for fashioning lifelike and sympathetic characters are as pronounced as ever."

Unpleasant relatives provide the central conflict in *The Treasures of Weatherby*, as twelve-year-old Harleigh J. Weatherby IV is determined to break free of his powerlessness in the face of both teasing classmates and a controlling great aunt and uncle. When he meets a strange girl named Allegra, Harleigh begins to explore the history of his family's mansion and the maze that surrounds it. When the preteens unearth a Weatherby family secret their discovery leads to a plot to abscond with the family's secret treasure. Writing in *Kirkus Reviews*, a critic recommended *The Treasures of Weatherby* as a "quick, yet multi-layered mystery that incorporates themes of good vs. evil, peer acceptance, self-esteem and confidence," while in *Booklist* Carolyn Phelan praised Snyder's story for "its distinctive pleasures and unusual characters."

For the four children in *William S. and the Great Escape*, home is where their favorite aunt is. Their effort to escape from an abusive older stepbrother and a disinterested dad are helped by a schoolmate who, like oldest sibling William, is a fan of Shakespearean drama. Set during the late 1930s, *William S. and the Great Escape* was described by *School Library Journal* contributor Marie Orlando as "an engrossing read" featuring scenes of Shakespeare's *The Tempest* that serve as "an accessible introduction to the play." "Snyder lightens the potentially tragic feel of this tale by keeping the focus on the children's hope for a better future," wrote a *Kirkus Reviews* writer in describing the same novel, while in *Booklist* Ilene Cooper cited *William S. and the Great Escape* for its "openhearted characters" and "clever twist."

In *The Unseen* Snyder introduces Xandra Hobson, a twelve year old who enjoys exploring the woods and taking in orphaned animals. One day Xandra rescues a bird that mysteriously disappears the next day, leaving only a white feather behind. Friend Belinda claims that the feather is magical and can lead the two girls into unknown worlds. As they explore the feather's potential for bestowing special powers, Xandra unwittingly betrays her friend. Saleena L. Davidson, writing in the *School Library Journal*, called *The Unseen* "a wonderful ride into fantasy," while Phelan asserted in *Booklist* that Snyder's "well-grounded fantasy" has a "satisfying conclusion."

Like *The Unseen*, *The Bronze Pen* also focuses on a child's use of transformative power, but in this case it comes through a preteen's creativity. Audrey loves to write stories, and the twelve year old's dream is to earn enough money from her writing to support her parents so that her mom can stay home and care for her ill father. When she receives a bronze pen from a stranger, Audrey sets to work on a new story and soon discovers that the powers she yo gives her fictional heroine have become hers as well. "Audrey is an appealing kid and her thoughts and actions are interesting and believable," wrote Eva Mitnick in a *School Library Journal* review of *The Bronze Pen*, and a *Kirkus Reviews* writer called Snyder's subtle fantasy "a solid, slightly old-fashioned inquiry into the power of the pen, the limits of hope and the necessity of dreams." According to a *Publishers Weekly* critic, *The Bronze Pen* "showcases [Snyder's] . . . gift for characterization" in her portrayal of a likeable young girl.

Throughout almost five decades of writing, Snyder has continued to grow as a writer and to entertain as well as inform. Her many works have spanned the timeline and bridged genres, blending fantasy and history, realism and the supernatural, suspense and humor. A primary ingredient in each Snyder story is a compelling plot. "I still begin a story by indulging in what has always been for me a form of self-entertainment," Snyder wrote in *The Writer*. "I look for a character or characters and a beginning situation that cries out to be explored and embellished. . . . This beginning situation must be something that connects directly to my long-established urge to find excitement, mystery, and high emotion in the midst of even the most prosaic circumstances."

Biographical and Critical Sources

BOOKS

American Women Writers, 2nd edition, St. James Press (Detroit, MI), 2000.

Beacham's Guide to Literature for Young Adults, Volume 1, Beacham Publishing (Osprey, FL), 1990.

Carpenter, Humphrey and Mari Prichard, *The Oxford Companion to Children's Literature*, Oxford University Press (Oxford, England), 1984.

Children's Literature Review, Volume 31, Gale (Detroit, MI), 1994.

Contemporary Literary Criticism, Volume 17, Gale (Detroit, MI), 1981.

Hopkins, Lee Bennett, *More Books by More People: Interviews with Sixty-five Authors of Books for Children*, Citation Press (New York, NY), 1974.

Legends in Their Own Time, Prentice Hall (New York, NY), 1994.

Silvey, Anita, editor, *Children's Books and Their Creators*, Houghton (Boston, MA), 1995.

St. James Guide to Young-Adult Writers, 2nd edition, St. James Press (Detroit, MI), 1999.

PERIODICALS

Booklist, February 1, 1991, Ilene Cooper, review of *Song of the Gargoyle*, p. 1127; September 1, 1994, Stephanie Zvirin, review of *Cat Running*, p. 44; February 1, 1997, Ilene Cooper, review of *The Gypsy Game*, p. 942; January 1, 1998, Susan Dove Lempke, review of *Gib Rides Home*, p. 816; January 1, 1999, GraceAnne A. DeCandido, review of *The Runaways*, p. 879; January 1, 2000, Kay Weisman, review of *Gib and the Gray Ghost*, p. 912; May 1, 2001, Shelle Rosenfeld, review of *Spyhole Secrets*, p. 1612; March 1, 2004, Carolyn Phelan, review of *The Unseen*, p. 1190; May 1, 2005, Gillian Engberg, review of *The Magic Nation Thing*, p. 1584; December 1, 2006, Carolyn Phelan, review of *The Treasures of Weatherby*, p. 50; February 15, 2008, Jennifer Mattson, review of *The Bronze Pen*, p. 82; July 1, 2009, Ilene Cooper, review of *William S. and the Great Escape*, p. 61.

Bulletin of the Center for Children's Books, September, 1964, Zena Sutherland, review of *Season of Ponies*, p. 20; May 13, 1967, Zena Sutherland, review of *The Egypt Game*, pp. 55-56; January, 1995, Roger Sutton, review of *Cat Running*, p. 178; February, 1997, Deborah Stevenson, review of *The Gypsy Game*, p. 223.

Childhood Education, winter, 2008, D. Thomas Markle, review of *The Treasures of Weatherby*, p. 127.

Children's Book Review, October, 1973, Barbara Sherrard-Smith, review of *The Headless Cupid*, p. 146.

Commonweal, November 19, 1971, Elizabeth Minot Graves, "The Year of the Witch," pp. 179-182; November 17, 1972, Elizabeth Minot Graves, review of *The Witches of Worm*, p. 157.

Horn Book, March-April, 1997, Jennifer M. Brabander, review of *The Gypsy Game*, p. 204; March-April, 1998, Susan P. Bloom, review of *Gib Rides Home*, p. 224; May, 2000, review of *Gib and the Gray Ghost*, p. 321.

Kirkus Reviews, February 1, 1977, review of *Until the Celebration*, p. 95; September 15, 2002, review of *The Ghosts of Rathburn Park*, p. 1401; March 15, 2004, review of *The Unseen*, p. 277; July 1, 2005, review of *The Magic Nation Thing*, p. 744; November 15, 2006, review of *The Treasures of Weatherby*, p. 1178; February 1, 2008, review of *The Bronze Pen*; August 1, 2009, review of *William S. and the Great Escape*.

New York Times Book Review, December 13, 1970, Jean Fritz, review of *The Changeling*, p. 26; December 10, 1972, Jean Fritz, review of *The Witches of Worm*, pp. 8, 10; July 8, 1984, Felice Buckvar, review of *Blair's Nightmare*, p. 15; December 27, 1987, Wendy Martin, review of *And Condors Danced*, p. 17.

Publishers Weekly, January 20, 1997, review of *The Gypsy Game*, p. 402; January 18, 1999, review of *The Runaways*, p. 340; August 30, 1999, review of *Gib Rides Home*, p. 86; July 2, 2001, review of *Spyhole Secrets*, p. 76; October 21, 2002, review of *The Ghosts of Rathburn Park*, p. 76; November 20, 2006, review of *The Treasures of Weatherby*, p. 59; March 24, 2008, review of *The Bronze Pen*, p. 70; October 5, 2009, review of *William S. and the Great Escape*, p. 49.

School Library Journal, August, 1984, Kathleen Brachman, review of *Blair's Nightmare*, pp. 77-78; February, 1997, Lisa Dennis, review of *The Gypsy Game*, p. 106; January, 1998, Janet Hilbun, review of *Gib Rides Home*, p. 114; March, 1999, Susan Oliver, review of *The Runaways*, p. 215; March, 2000, Lauralyn Persson, review of *Gib and the Gray Ghost*, p. 242; June, 2001, Ellen Fader, review of *Spyhole Secrets*, p. 156; October, 2001, Veronica Schwartz, review of *Gib and the Gray Ghost*, p. 89; September, 2002, Kathryn Kosiorek, review of *The Ghosts of Rathburn Park*, p. 234; August, 2003, Cheryl Preisendorfer, review of *The Ghosts of Rathburn Park*, p. 70; April, 2004, Saleena L. Davidson, review of *The Unseen*, p. 162; September, 2005, Elizabeth Bird, review of *The Magic Nation Thing*, p. 214; February, 2007, Robyn Gioia, review of *The Treasures of Weatherby*, p. 128; March, 2008, Eva Mitnick, review of *The Bronze Pen*, p. 210; October, 2009, Marie Orlando, review of *William S. and the Great Escape*, p. 136.

Voice of Youth Advocates, October, 1983, Eleanor Klopp, review of *Birds of Summer*, pp. 208-209.

Writer, July, 1993, Zilpha Keatley Snyder, "To Be a Storyteller."

ONLINE

Zilpha Keatley Snyder Home Page, http://www.zksnyder. com (February 15, 2011).

OTHER

A Talk with Zilpha Keatley Snyder (videotape), Tim Podell
   Productions, 1998.

*   *   *

SPRINGER, Kristina

Personal

Married; husband's name Athens; children: Teegan,
Maya, London, Gavin. *Education:* Attended Northern
Illinois University; Illinois State University, B.A.
(English education); DePaul University, M.A. (writing).

Addresses

Agent—Levine Greenberg Literary Agency, 307 7th
Ave., Ste. 2407, New York, NY 10001. *E-mail*—
kristina@kristinaspringer.com.

Career

Writer. Technical writer for five years; DePaul University, Chicago, IL, technical writing instructor; freelance
writer, 2000—.

Awards, Honors

Society of School Librarians International Book Award,
2010, for *The Espressologist.*

Writings

NOVELS

The Espressologist, Farrar, Straus & Giroux (New York,
   NY), 2009.
My Fake Boyfriend Is Better than Yours, Farrar, Straus &
   Giroux (New York, NY), 2010.

Former columnist for *Relationship101.com.* Contributor
to Web sites, including *AbsoluteWrite.com, Writing-
World.com, pregnancyandbaby.com, sheknows.com,* and
CoolChyck.com. Contributor to periodicals, including
Writer's Digest.

Sidelights

Kristina Springer, a technical writer-turned-fiction
writer, is the author of the young-adult novels *The
Espressologist* and *My Fake Boyfriend Is Better than
Yours.* "I still don't know how I did this. I never thought
I'd be good at writing fiction," Springer remarked in a
BookPage online interview with Linda M. Castellitto.
"Maybe I just found the right genre and age group. My
natural voice must be the teen voice."

Springer's debut title, *The Espressologist,* focuses on a
barista's uncanny ability to identify her customers' romantic interests based on their coffee preferences and
was drawn from the author's own experiences. "When
we were dating, my husband and I would go to coffee
shops to hang out and people-watch," the author recalled to Castellitto. "After a while, it occurred to me
that I could tell what people will order." The novel focuses on Jane Turner, a seventeen year old who, armed
with a notebook that catalogs her patrons' drink orders
and personality traits, discovers a gift for matchmaking.
Known as the "espressologist," Jane works wonders for
a host of single customers, but she has less success with
her own love life. "Springer has created a lovable, na-
ive young woman in Jane," Melissa Moore noted in
School Library Journal, and *Booklist* reviewer Courtney Jones described the work as "the fluffiest kind of
escapist chick-lit, best enjoyed over the holidays with a
hot drink."

My Fake Boyfriend Is Better than Yours, dubbed a "very
funny and strongly realistic novel" by a *Publishers
Weekly* critic, finds a seventh grader learning a valuable
lesson while engaging in a game of one-upsmanship.
After losing touch with Sienna over the summer, Tori is
shocked to learn that her best friend has undergone a
dramatic transformation: Sienna returns from her
Florida vacation tanned, beautiful, and boasting of a
wonderful boyfriend. Suspicious of Sienna's tale and
jealous of her friend's newfound popularity, Tori claims
to have a beau of her own and this bit of fiction sparks
a heated competition between the girls. "Tori is a well-
rounded character, both likable and relatable," Kimberly Castle observed in *School Library Journal,* and
Shelle Rosenfeld commented in *Booklist* that in *My
Fake Boyfriend Is Better than Yours* Springer "incorporates issues that readers will appreciate, especially the
importance of honesty, trust, and self-appreciation."

Biographical and Critical Sources

PERIODICALS

Booklist, October 15, 2009, Courtney Jones, review of *The
   Espressologist,* p. 59; September 15, 2010, Shelle
   Rosenfeld, review of *My Fake Boyfriend Is Better
   than Yours,* p. 73.
Bulletin of the Center for Children's Books, January, 2010,
   Karen Coats, review of *The Espressologist,* p. 218.
Kirkus Reviews, August 15, 2009, review of *The
   Espressologist.*
Publishers Weekly, August 30, 2010, review of *My Fake
   Boyfriend Is Better than Yours,* p. 54.
School Library Journal, September, 2009, Melissa Moore,
   review of *The Espressologist,* p. 174; August, 2010,
   Kimberly Castle, review of *My Fake Boyfriend Is Bet-
   ter than Yours,* p. 113.

ONLINE

BookPage Web site, http://www.bookpage.com/ (November, 2009), Linda M. Castellitto, review of *The
   Espressologist.*

Kristina Springer Home Page, http://www.kristinaspringer.
com (February 10, 2011).*

*   *   *

STARMER, Aaron 1976-

Personal

Born 1976, in CA; married Catharine Wells. *Education:*
Drew University, B.A. (English), 1998; New York University, M.A. (cinema studies), 2000. *Hobbies and other
interests:* Running.

Addresses

Home—Hoboken, NJ. *E-mail*—drajwells@gmail.com.

Career

Author and editor. Longitude Books (online publisher),
Web site editor, 1999-2007; Micato Safaris, operations
director, 2007-09, school sponsorship program coordinator of America Share (nonprofit), 2009; freelance author beginning 2009.

Writings

(With Catharine Wells and Timothy Starmer) *The Best in
Tent Camping—New York State: A Guide for Car
Campers Who Hate RV's, Concrete Slabs, and Loud
Portable Stereos,* Menasha Ridge Press (Birmingham,
AL), 2007.

Dweeb: Burgers, Beasts, and Brainwashed Bullies, illustrated by Andy Rash, Delacorte Press (New York,
NY), 2009.

The Only Ones (young-adult novel), Delacorte Press (New
York, NY), 2011.

Contributor to *Mountain Man Dance Moves: The Mc-
Sweeney's Book of Lists,* 2006, and *The Unofficial Guide
to New York City,* Wiley, 2010.

Sidelights

Aaron Starmer turned to writing after earning an advanced degree in cinema studies and working as Web
editor for an online publisher specializing in travel
books for the international set. Joined by his brother
Tim Starmer and wife Catharine Starmer, he shared his
interest in low-eco-impact travel in *The Best in Tent
Camping—New York State: A Guide for Car Campers
Who Hate RV's, Concrete Slabs, and Loud Portable
Stereos.* Turning to a younger readership allowed
Starmer to indulge his wit and his imagination. His
middle-grade novel *Dweeb: Burgers, Beasts, and Brainwashed Bullies* is enlivened by a quirky humor, while
his futuristic young-adult novel *The Only Ones* imagines a world where only a few people remain on Earth,
each one with a particular gift that will help to recon-
struct some semblance of human society.

Cover of Aaron Starmer's middle-grade novel Dweeb Burgers, Beasts,
and Brainwashed Bullies, *featuring artwork by Andy Rash.* (Jacket art ©
2009 Andy Rash. Used by permission of Delacorte Press, an imprint of Random House
Children's Books, a division of Random House, Inc.)

Enlivened by Andy Rash's illustrations and set in New
Jersey, *Dweeb* introduces five bright but socially inept
eighth graders: Bijay, Denton, Eddie, Elijah, and
Wendell. When the time for standardized testing comes
around, the five classmates are trapped in the school
basement by their school's vice principal. They decide
to team up to figure out why, but first they have to escape from their subterranean prison. Plans to develop
super-teen DNA and efforts to transform the school
lunchroom into a fast-food heaven also figure in Starmer's quirky tale, which *School Library Journal* critic
Robin Henry recommended as a "fun . . . break from
the often-heavy realistic fiction" that predominates in
the Y-A genre. In *Booklist* Andrew Medlar noted the
wry humor in Starmer's story, predicting that "there are
undoubtedly those who will find companionship and
commiseration" in the "dweebishness" of the story's
unusual heroes.

Biographical and Critical Sources

PERIODICALS

Booklist, October 15, 2009, Andrew Medlar, review of *Dweeb: Burgers, Beasts, and Brainwashed Bullies,* p. 64.
Bulletin of the Center for Children's Books, January, 2010, Karen Coats, review of *Dweeb,* p. 219.
Kirkus Reviews, September 15, 2009, review of *Dweeb.*
School Library Journal, November, 2009, Robin Henry, review of *Dweeb,* p. 122.

ONLINE

Aaron Starmer Home Page, http://www.aaronstarmer.com (February 15, 2011).

*   *   *

STOUT, Shawn K.

Personal

Born in MD; married. *Education:* Towson University, B.A.; Vermont College of Fine Arts, M.F.A., 2009.

Addresses

Home—Frederick, MD. *Agent*—Sarah Davies, Greenhouse Literacy Agency, 11308 Lapham Dr., Oakton, VA 22124. *E-mail*—shawn@shawnkstout.com.

Career

Writer. Worked variously as a dog-treat baker, retail sales clerk, health communications manager, and research editor.

Shawn K. Stout (Photograph by Tom Clark. Reproduced by permission.)

The young heroine in Stout's Fiona Finkelstein, Big-time Ballerina! *comes to life in Angela Martini's pastel-tined art.* (Aladdin, 2009. Illustration copyright © 2009 by Angela Martini. Reproduced by permission of the illustrator.)

Writings

Fiona Finkelstein, Big-time Ballerina!!, illustrated by Angela Martini, Aladdin (New York, NY), 2009.
Fiona Finkelstein Meets Her Match!!, illustrated by Angela Martini, Aladdin (New York, NY), 2010.

Sidelights

Shawn K. Stout drew on personal experience, including ten years of dance lessons, for her debut work of fiction, *Fiona Finkelstein, Big-time Ballerina!!,* a middle-grade novel about an aspiring performer with a bad case of nerves. "I think there is a little bit of me in every character I create, for better or worse," Stout admitted on her home page. "Definitely, Fiona and I share self-conscious personalities—overly aware of ourselves and how people see us. With or without a tutu, I am more comfortable by myself than in a room full of people I don't know."

In *Fiona Finkelstein, Big-time Ballerina!!* Stout introduces her protagonist, a lively grade schooler living in Ordinary, Maryland. Fiona comes from a family of high achievers: her father is a television meteorologist and her often-absent mother is a soap opera star. Although she dreams of becoming a prima ballerina, Fiona suffers from crippling bouts of stage fright, earning the nickname "Vomitstein" during one regrettable appearance. When the girl lands a role in her company's performance of *The Nutcracker,* she relies on the help of her good pal, Cleo, as well as a boost from her dad to gain some much-needed confidence. "Stout gives her heroine's story an abundance of gentle humor and friendship," a critic in *Kirkus Reviews* noted, while *Booklist* critic Shelle Rosenfeld similarly observed of *Fiona Finkelstein, Big-time Ballerina!!* that the author's "peppy, engaging narrative relates [Fiona's] challenges and successes with humor and sympathy."

Biographical and Critical Sources

PERIODICALS

Booklist, September 15, 2009, Shelle Rosenfeld, review of *Fiona Finkelstein, Big-time Ballerina!!*, p. 54.

Kirkus Reviews, August 15, 2009, review of *Fiona Finkelstein, Big-time Ballerina!!*.

School Library Journal, January, 2010, Kate Neff, review of *Fiona Finkelstein, Big-Time Ballerina!!*, p. 82.

ONLINE

Shawn K. Stout Home Page, http://www.shawnkstout.com (February 10, 2011).

Simon & Schuster Web site, http://www.simonandschuster. com/ (February 10, 2011), "Shawn K. Stout Revealed."

T-V

THOMAS, Jan 1958-

Personal
Born 1958.

Addresses
Home—Sorroco, NM. *E-mail*—www@janthomasbooks.com.

Career
Writer and illustrator.

Writings

SELF-ILLUSTRATED

What Will Fat Cat Sit On?, Harcourt (Orlando, FL), 2007.
A Birthday for Cow!, Harcourt (Orlando, FL), 2008.
In the Doghouse, Harcourt (Orlando, FL), 2008.
Can You Make a Scary Face?, Beach Lane Books (New York, NY), 2009.
Rhyming Dust Bunnies, Atheneum (New York, NY), 2009.
Here Comes the Big, Mean Dust Bunny!, Beach Lane Books (New York, NY), 2009.
Pumpkin Trouble, Harper (New York, NY), 2011.

ILLUSTRATOR

Mem Fox, *Let's Count Goats!*, Beach Lane Books (New York, NY), 2010.

Sidelights
In the picture books created by author and illustrator Jan Thomas, readers meet entertaining animal characters that come to life in colorful, large-scale cartoon art. In Thomas's humorously titled *What Will Fat Cat Sit On?*, for instance, a group of farmyard animals are less concerned about where Fat Cat will sit than which of them will wind up beneath him! A *Publishers Weekly* critic praised the work as "a rollicking and highly promising debut," while a contributor to *Kirkus Reviews* characterized *What Will Fat Cat Sit On?* as a book "toddlers and new readers will reach for again and again." Other books by Thomas that can also be placed in the "reach for again and again" category include *A Birthday for Cow!*, *In the Doghouse*, *Can You Make a Scary Face?*, and *Rhyming Dust Bunnies.*

Pig and Mouse bake a cake for Cow in *A Birthday for Cow!*, and their efforts must also include preventing a persistent Duck from adding an unwanted turnip to the recipe. Thomas's "riotous read-aloud is guaranteed to have them rolling in the aisles," predicted a contributor to *Kirkus Reviews*, while G. Alyssa Parkinson noted in *School Library Journal* that the "whimsical story" comes to life in the author's "simple language." Mouse, Duck, and Pig find themselves entering new territory when Cow kicks a ball far afield in *In the Doghouse*, and here a *Kirkus Reviews* writer observed that Thomas's "successful use of repetition [is] . . . realized through succinct sentences" that make the story accessible to just-beginning readers.

Thomas ranges far afield of the farmyard in casting the animal characters that star in both *Rhyming Dust Bunnies* and *Here Comes the Big, Mean Dust Bunny!* The four fluffy creatures that star in *Rhyming Dust Bunnies* are having fun finding words that rhyme with "car" when one of their number veers from the script to announce an emergency: the approach of their arch-enemy, the broom-wielding homeowner. Out of the dustpan and back at their usual haunts in *Here Comes the Big, Mean Dust Bunny!*, the resilient household critters have their rhyming game spoiled by a dusty grey dustbunny. A guest appearance from the overweight star of Thomas's picture-book debut, *What Will Fat Cat Sit On?* adds additional humor to the quirky tale. Large-scale illustrations and high-level "silliness . . . combine for a party-hearty mood" in *Rhyming Dust Bunnies*, according to a

Jan Thomas creates the fearsome—but also humorous—characters in her cartoon art for **Here Comes the Big, Mean Dust Bunny!** (Copyright © 2009 by Jan Thomas. Reprinted with the permission of Beach Lane Books, an imprint of Simon & Schuster Children's Publishing Division.)

Publishers Weekly critic, while a *Kirkus Reviews* critic noted that the story's "dynamic quartet of dust bunnies . . . have quite the flair for rhyming words." "Thomas doesn't simply fulfill children's expectations," asserted Weitz in her *School Library Journal* review of the same work. "True to form, she adds funny and thrilling surprises up to the absorbing end of the tale." *Hear Comes the Big, Mean Dust Bunny!* "is simplicity at its best," asserted Ieva Bats in the same periodical, and a *Kirkus Reviews* writer noted that "Thomas's signature digital illustrations" for the book "utilize stark dark lines and bright color splashes with a quirky exuberance."

Featuring what a *Publishers Weekly* critic characterized as a "cheerleading narration, bold cartoons and flourescent backdrops," *Can You Make a Scary Face?* is a book better suited to pre-play storyhours than bedtime reading. In an energizing text, readers are encouraged to wriggle, blow, and dance as if to dislodge a tiny, tickling insect. A different palette of vibrant colors is introduced with each turn of the page as the demands of a dictatorial ladybug rev up both the story's energy and silliness. A good way "to encourage lively activity and imaginative games," in the opinion of *School Library Journal* contributor Susan Weitz, *Can You Make a Scary Face?* leads readers along on a trail of speech bubbles and highly contrasted digital images that culminates in what a *Kirkus Reviews* writer described as "a whopper of a twist."

Biographical and Critical Sources

PERIODICALS

Christian Science Monitor, November 20, 2007, Jenny Sawyer, review of *What Will Fat Cat Sit On?,* p. 16.

Childhood Education spring, 2010, Lauren Roth, review of *Can You Make a Scary Face?,* p. 178.
Horn Book, November-December, 2008, Jennifer M. Brabander, review of *The Doghouse,* p. 695.
Kirkus Reviews, August 1, 2007, review of *What Will Fat Cat Sit On?*; March 1, 2008, review of *A Birthday for Cow!*; August 1, 2008, review of *The Doghouse;* November 15, 2008, review of *Rhyming Dust Bunnies;* July 15, 2009, review of *Can You Make a Scary Face?;* October 1, 2009, review of *Here Comes the Big, Mean Dust Bunny!*
Publishers Weekly, September 10, 2007, review of *What Will Fat Cat Sit On?,* p. 59; December 1, 2008, review of *Rhyming Dust Bunnies,* p. 45; August, 2009, review of *Can You Make a Scary Face?,* p. 44.
School Library Journal, December, 2007, Blair Christolon, review of *What Will Fat Cat Sit On?,* p. 101; June, 2008, G. Alyssa Parkinson, review of *A Birthday for Cow!,* p. 114; October, 2008, Ieva Bates, review of *The Doghouse,* p. 126; February, 2009, Susan Weitz, review of *Rhyming Dust Bunnies,* p. 87; August, 2009, Susan Weitz, review of *Can You Make a Scary Face?,* p. 85; November, 2009, Ieva Bates, review of *Here Comes the Big, Mean Dust Bunny!,* p. 90.

ONLINE

Jan Thomas Home Page, http://www.janthomasbooks.com (February 18, 2009).*

*   *   *

TOBIN, James

Personal

Married; children: two daughters. *Education:* University of Michigan, Ph.D.

Addresses

Home—Ann Arbor, MI. *Agent*—Fletcher & Parry, 121 E. 17th St., New York, NY 10003. *E-mail*—jetobin@comcast.net.

Career

Journalist and author. *Detroit News,* Detroit, MI, reporter, 1986-98; freelance writer, 1998—.

Awards, Honors

Two Pulitzer Prize nomination, Columbia University; National Book Critics Circle Award, 1997, for *Ernie Pyle's War;* J. Anthony Lukas Work-in-Progress Award, 2000, for *To Conquer the Air.*

Writings

Ernie Pyle's War: America's Eyewitness to World War II, Free Press (New York, NY), 1997.

Great Projects: The Epic Story of Building America, from the Taming of the Mississippi to the Invention of the Internet, Free Press (New York, NY), 2001.

To Conquer the Air: The Wright Brothers and the Great Race for Flight, Free Press (New York, NY), 2003, published as *First to Fly: The Unlikely Triumph of Wilbur and Orville Wright,* John Murray (London, England), 2003,

(Editor with Michelle Ferrari) *Reporting America at War: An Oral History,* Hyperion (New York, NY), 2003.

Sue MacDonald Had a Book, illustrated by Dave Coverly, Henry Holt (New York, NY), 2009.

Adaptations

Great Project was adapted as a television series for the Public Broadcasting System, produced by Great Projects Film Company, 2002.

Sidelights

In his work as a journalist for the *Detroit News,* James Tobin was nominated twice for a Pulitzer prize. After publishing his first book, the award-winning *Ernie Pyle's War: America's Eyewitness to World War II,* in 1997, Tobin left journalism to follow his interest in history as an independent writer. In addition to nonfiction works such as *Great Projects: The Epic Story of Building America, from the Taming of the Mississippi to the Invention of the Internet* and *To Conquer the Air: The Wright Brothers and the Great Race for Flight,* he has also entertained young readers with *Sue MacDonald Had a Book,* a story illustrated by Dave Coverly. Praised as a "lively spin" on the well-known farmyard rhyme in which a vowel recitation serves as the refrain by *Booklist* critic Hazel Rochman, *Sue MacDonald Had a Book* features a "simple, chanting text." A *Publishers Weekly* critic predicted that the combination of "cartoony illustrations and smart verse" in *Sue MacDonald Had a Book* "make for an engaging read-aloud—or sing-along.

In *Ernie Pyle's War* Tobin presents what *New York Time Book Review* contributor Malcolm W. Browne characterized as "undoubtedly the best biography of Ernie Pyle ever written." The work documents the professional and personal life of Pyle, a journalist who became the most famous war correspondent of World War II. Born to an Indiana farm family in 1900, Pyle left Indiana University to accept a reporting position with the *LaPorte Herald* and eventually joined the *Washington Daily News.* While covering the war as a correspondent for Scripps-Howard newspapers, he became known for his columns depicting the bravery of the frontline soldier. By the time of his death, on April 18, 1945 while covering the invasion of Okinawa in the Pacific theatre, Pyle had become a best-selling author and the winner of a Pulitzer prize. *Ernie Pyle's War* "is a balanced tribute to the quintessential war correspondent," wrote a *Kirkus Reviews* contributor discussing Tobin's biography, and in *Booklist* Margaret Flanagan dubbed it "a respectful and insightful biography of a giant among journalists."

Tobin's story in *To Conquer the Air* spans a crucial decade in the early history of manned flight. He balances a chronology of the efforts of Ohio natives Wilbur and Orville Wright to perfect their flying machine. While the Wrights studied the aeronautics of gliders and incorporated glider physics with a simple motor to achieve propulsion, fellow American Samuel Langley focused on lift through steam power, and in 1896 his fledgling efforts—funded by the U.S. War Department—achieved success. Praising the book in *National Geographic Adventure,* a reviewer praised *To Conquer the Air* as "detailed, well written, and told with the grace of a symphony conductor making with his wand one grand and glorious whole out of many melodies." "Tobin is stunningly effective in presenting the intertwining lives of the [Wright] brothers and an amazing cast of friends and competitors," wrote a *Publishers Weekly* critic, while a *Kirkus Reviews* critic asserted that Tobin's "meticulous account of the grinding, day-to-day advances and setbacks," in the Wright brothers' work is "also infected with the sheer wonder of taking wing."

Tobin turns to other American achievements in *Great Projects,* which accompanied a documentary television series and chronicles those Americans who inspired eight of the ground-breaking engineering accomplishments produced since the nation's founding. The George Washington Bridge, the Hoover Dam, Thomas Edison's electrical street lighting, Boston's Big Dig, and even the information superhighway, the Internet: these are just some of the accomplishments covered in Tobin's volume, and the vision, tenacity, setbacks, and ultimate achievement are set forth in the author's compelling narrative. The author's "clearly written, nontechnical narratives are lively and comprehensive and form a colorful mosaic" of engineering accomplishments, according to *Library Journal* contributor John E. Hodgkins, and Gilbert Taylor dubbed *Great Projects* "a winning testament to American ingenuity" in his *Booklist* review. Noting the many photographs and other illustrations that bring to life Tobin's text, a *Publishers Weekly* critic described the book's "thematic scope" as "ambitious" and added that the author "brings it all together in a grand pattern that reveals how the seemingly impossible can move from a personal vision to a reality."

Biographical and Critical Sources

PERIODICALS

Air & Space Power Journal, spring, 2005, Michael Pierson, review of *Ernie Pyle's War: America's Eyewitness to World War II,* p. 119.

American History, April, 2002, Joseph P. Ritz, review of *Great Projects: The Epic Story of Building America, from the Taming of the Mississippi to the Invention of the Internet,* and interview with Tobin, both p. 70.

Booklist, June 1-15, 1997, Margaret Flanagan, review of *Ernie Pyle's War,* p. 1621; September 1, 2001, Gilbert Taylor, review of *Great Projects,* p. 28; March 1,

2003, Gilbert Taylor, review of *To Conquer the Air: The Wright Brothers and the Great Race for Flight,* p. 1132; October 15, 2003, Roland Green, review of *Reporting America at War,* p. 359; July 1, 2009, Hazel Rochman, review of *Sue MacDonald Had a Book,* p. 69.

Contemporary Review, October, 2003, review of *First to Fly: The Unlikely Triumph of Wilbur and Orville Wright,* p. 253.

Kirkus Reviews, March 15, 1997, review of *Ernie Pyle's War,* p. 451; January 15, 2003, review of *To Conquer the Air,* p. 134; June 15, 2009, review of *Sue MacDonald Had a Book.*

Library Journal, October 15, 2001, John E. Hodgkins, review of *Great Projects,* p. 94; March 15, 2003, John Carver Edwards, review of *To Conquer the Air,* p. 98.

National Geographic Adventure, April, 2003, review of *To Conquer the Air,* p. 44.

New York Times Book Review, June 8, 1997, Malcolm W. Browne, review of *Ernie Pyle's War,* p. 34.

Nieman Reports, winter, 1997, Jack Foisie, review of *Ernie Pyle's War,* p. 77.

Publishers Weekly, September 3, 2001, review of *Great Projects,* p. 78; February 17, 2003, review of *To Conquer the Air,* p. 65; August 18, 2003, review of *Reporting America at War,* p. 66; June 15, 2009, review of *Sue MacDonald Had a Book,* p. 48.

School Library Journal, June, 2009, Mary Jean Smith, review of *Sue MacDonald Had a Book,* p. 101.

ONLINE

Detroit News Online, http://www.detnews.com/ (July 20, 1999), "James Tobin."*

* * *

VELASQUEZ, Eric 1961-

Personal

Born 1961, in New York, NY. *Education:* School of Visual Arts, B.F.A., 1983; studied with Harvey Dinnerstein at Art Student's League, 1984.

Addresses

Home and office—Hartsdale, NY.

Career

Illustrator and author.

Member

Art Student's League.

Awards, Honors

Coretta Scott King/John Steptoe Award for New Talent, 1999, for *The Piano Man;* Carter G. Woodson Award, National Council for the Social Studies/Children's Book

Council, 2001, for *The Sound That Jazz Makes;* Pura Belpré Illustrator Award, ALSC/American Library Association, 2011, for *Grandma's Gift.*

Writings

SELF-ILLUSTRATED

Grandma's Records, Walker & Company (New York, NY), 2001.

Grandma's Gift, Walker & Company (New York, NY), 2010.

ILLUSTRATOR

Beverley Naidoo, *Journey to Jo'burg: A South African Story,* Lippincott (Philadelphia, PA), 1985.

Lesley Koplow, *Tanya and the Tobo Man: A Story for Children Entering Therapy/Tanya y el hombre Tobo: Una historia para niños que empiezan terapia,* Spanish translation by Alexander Contos, Magination Press (New York, NY), 1991.

Gary Soto, *The Skirt,* Delacorte (New York, NY), 1992, reprinted, 2008.

Eleanora E. Tate, *Front Porch Stories at the One-Room School,* Bantam (New York, NY), 1992.

Kim L. Siegelson, *The Terrible, Wonderful Tellin' at Hog Hammock,* HarperCollins (New York, NY), 1996.

Gary Soto, *Off and Running,* Delacorte (New York, NY), 1996.

Debbi Chocolate, *The Piano Man,* Walker & Company (New York, NY), 1998.

Sharon Shavers Gayle, *Escape!: A Story of the Underground Railroad,* Soundprints (Norwalk, CT), 1999.

Carole Boston Weatherford, *The Sound That Jazz Makes,* Walker & Company (New York, NY), 2000.

David "Panama" Francis and Bob Reiser, *David Gets His Drum,* Marshall Cavendish (New York, NY), 2002.

Jim Haskins, *Champion: The Story of Muhammad Ali,* Walker & Company (New York, NY), 2002.

Candice Ransom, *Liberty Street,* Walker & Company (New York, NY), 2003.

Sharon Shavers Gayle, *Emma's Escape: A Story of America's Underground Railroad,* Soundprints (Norwalk, CT), 2003.

Linda Walvoord, *Rosetta, Rosetta, Sit by Me!,* Marshall Cavendish (New York, NY), 2004.

Kathleen Krull, *Houdini: World's Greatest Mystery Man and Escape King,* Walker & Company (New York, NY), 2005.

Charisse K. Richardson, *The Real Lucky Charm,* Dial Books (New York, NY), 2005.

Angela Johnson, *A Sweet Smell of Roses,* Simon & Schuster (New York, NY), 2005.

Regina Hanson, *A Season for Mangoes,* Clarion Books (New York, NY), 2005.

Nikki Grimes, *Voices of Christmas,* Zonderkidz (Grand Rapids, MI), 2006.

Carole Boston Weatherford, *Jesse Owens: The Fastest Man Alive,* Walker & Company (New York, NY), 2006.

Hugh Brewster, *The Other Mozart: The Life of the Famous Chevalier de Saint-George,* Abrams Books (New York, NY), 2007.

Carole Boston Weatherford, *I, Matthew Henson: Polar Explorer,* Walker & Company (New York, NY), 2008.

Carole Boston Weatherford, *Racing against the Odds: Wendell Scott, African American Stock-Car Champion,* Marshall Cavendish (New York, NY), 2008.

Addie K. Boswell, *The Rain Stomper,* Marshall Cavendish (New York, NY), 2008.

Traci Dant, *Some Kind of Love: A Family Reunion in Poems,* Marshall Cavendish (New York, NY), 2010.

Cheryl Willis Hudson, *My Friend Maya Loves to Dance,* 2010.

Angela Farris Watkins, *My Uncle Martin's Big Heart,* Harry Abrams (New York, NY), 2010.

Also illustrator of book covers, including "Encyclopedia Brown" series, "You Be the Jury" series, "Ghost Writers" series, and "Apple Classics" series.

Sidelights

During his career as a freelance illustrator, Eric Velasquez has provided the images for hundreds of book covers as well as creating artwork to accompany picture-books texts by authors such as Nikki Grimes, Patricia C. McKissack, Carole Boston Weatherford, and Cheryl Willis Hudson. Many of his illustration projects feature characters of diverse ethnicities, and his awards include the Coretta Scott King/John Steptoe Award for New Talent and the Pura Belpré Illustrator Award from the American Library Association Reviewing the picture book *My Friend Maya Loves to Dance,* Mary N. Oluonye wrote in *School Library Journal* that Velas-

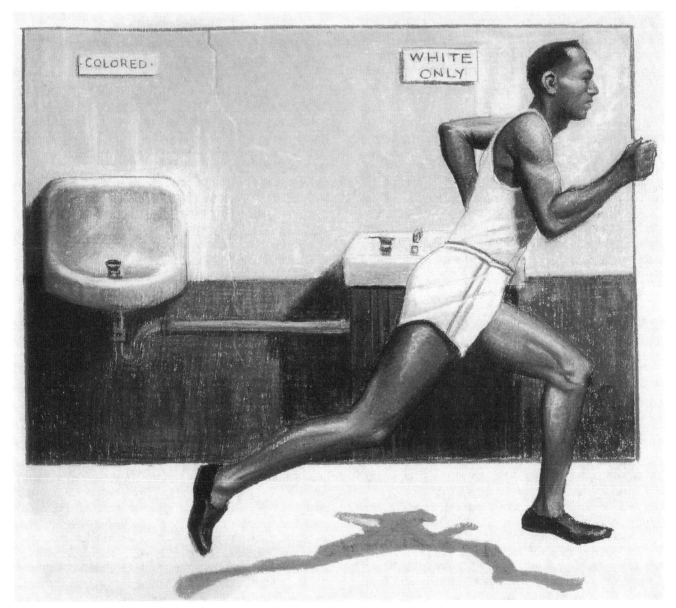

Eric Velasquez captured the life of a phenomenal twentieth-century athlete in his illustrations for Carole Boston Weatherford's **Jesse Owens: The Fastest Man Alive.** (Walker & Company, 2007. Illustration © 2007 by Eric Velasquez. All rights reserved. Reproduced by permission.)

quez's "fluid" oil paintings depicting "a willowy, long-limbed" young dancer effectively capture the lyricism in Hudson's "simple, sweet story about music, dance, and friendship."

Growing up in New York City's Spanish Harlem neighborhood, Velasquez was greatly influenced by his grandmother's love of music and his father's love of film. Meanwhile, his mother encouraged her son's interest in drawing and sketching. His unique style, which involves applying oils to textured watercolor paper, brings a light to his images that captures the emotional depth of each of his subjects. "Becoming an artist was a natural choice for me," Velasquez once stated. "I have never thought of being anything else."

Velasquez made his picture-book debut in 1985, serving as the illustrator for Beverley Naidoo's *Journey to Jo'burg: A South African Story.* He subsequently collaborated with Debbi Chocolate on *The Piano Man,* a tribute to an African-American musician who shares his music with family and friends as he grows increasingly elderly. Velasquez's "subtle characterization of faces gives warmth and individuality to the main characters," observed *Booklist* reviewer Carolyn Phelan in a review of Chocolate's story.

Angela Johnson's *A Sweet Smell of Roses* follows two young girls as they join a civil rights march led by Dr. Martin Luther King, Jr. Here "Velasquez's red-accented pencil illustrations capture the sweep and emotion of the march," Martha V. Parravano stated in *Horn Book.* Set in Jamaica, Regina Hanson's *A Season for Mangoes* focuses on a youngster's memories of her late grandmother during an all-night "sit-up," a type of wake. "Rich, naturalistic, full-color oil paintings fill the pages," observed Nancy Palmer in her *School Library Journal* review of *A Season for Mangoes.* "They reflect emotions well, succeeding most often in their close-up, almost portrait-like faces."

Weatherford's award-winning *The Sound That Jazz Makes* traces the evolution of an American musical form through the musicians who contributed to its development. Here Velasquez contributes "portraits [that] emphasize the dignity and pride of his subjects," according to a *Publishers Weekly* contributor. Author and artist team up again on the picture-book biographies *Jesse Owens: The Fastest Man Alive, I, Matthew Henson: Polar Explorer,* and *Racing against the Odds: Wendell Scott, African American Stock-Car Champion.* In reviewing *Jesse Owens,* a biography of the famed sprinter who won four gold medals at the 1936 Olympic Games, Velasquez's "pleasingly grainy pastels easily convey the movement and speed, determination and triumph at the core of Owens's uplifting story," according to a *Publishers Weekly* critic. *I, Matthew Henson,* Weatherford's portrait of the African-American adventurer who journeyed to the North Pole with Robert Peary, features "full-spread pastel illustrations" that "use a palette of white, gray, pale blue, and brown to show the vast, icy landscape," noted a *Kirkus Reviews* writer.

In addition to his work with Weatherford, Velasquez has illustrated several other critically acclaimed biographies. *Champion: The Story of Muhammad Ali,* a work by Jim Haskins, explores the life of the boxing legend. "Velasquez's lush oils dominate the page in monumental fashion," a *Kirkus Reviews* critic stated of this work. "They frequently appear as montages or in sequences of stop-action frames, for a truly cinematic effect." Celebrated illusionist, stunt performer, and escape artist Harry Houdini is the subject of Kathleen Krull's *Houdini: World's Greatest Mystery Man and Escape King.* In the words of *School Library Journal* critic Heide Piehler, "Velasquez's impressive framed, posed oil paintings portray the magician's intensity and sense of showmanship." In *The Other Mozart: The Life of the Famous Chevalier de Saint-George* author Hugh Brewster looks at an accomplished eighteenth-century French composer who was born into slavery in Guadeloupe. According to *Booklist* reviewer Gillian Engberg, "Velasquez's arresting full-page portraits" for Brewster's profile "will captivate many young readers."

In addition to illustrating texts for other writers, Velasquez has also created several original picture books that are inspired by memories of a beloved relative. In *Grandma's Records* he recalls a special concert he attended with his grandmother, a woman who supported his dream of becoming an artist. He continues his illustrated ode to his grandmother in *Grandma's Gift,* which recalls a winter spent with his abuelita in her apartment in New York City's Puerto Rican neighborhood. In addition to cooking traditional holiday treats, the two treat themselves to a trip to the Metropolitan Museum of Art, where the young Velasquez is impressed by the paintings of Diego Velasquez, the sixteenth-century Spanish painter who shares his surname. "Velasquez's touching yet simply told memoir of this tender relationship is lovingly captured in his illustrations," wrote Alicia Eames in her *School Library Journal* review of *Grandma's Records.* Virginia Walter wrote in the same periodical that *Grandma's Gift* "transport[s] readers to another time and place and expertly capture[s] the characters' personalities and emotions."

Velasquez discussed his illustration process in an online interview with *The Brown Bookshelf.* "After reading the manuscript several times I begin to do my rough thumbnail storyboard sketches," he explained. "Next I begin to research the story in terms of costumes, location, books, etc. Basically I try and learn everything I can about the subject within the time I have." Creating the book "dummy", a mock-up of the 32-page picture book, "involves cutting up the manuscript and pasting it down next to the corresponding images. I submit the book dummy to the publisher for approval. Sometimes there are changes at this stage. Next I find models and costumes, then I set up a photo shoot." Now is the point at which Velasquez creates the images readers will see: "First I create a detailed drawing of the image then I paint on top of it using oil paint." Velasquez's perspective on an illustrator's greatest challenge? "Finding your voice in the story without overshadowing the text."

Velasquez's illustration projects include Cheryl Willis Hudson's engaging story in **My Friend Maya Loves to Dance.** (Abrams Books for Young Readers, 2010. Illustration copyright © 2010 by Eric A. Velasquez. Reproduced by permission.)

Biographical and Critical Sources

PERIODICALS

American Music Teacher, June-July, 2007, Diane Higgins, review of *The Other Mozart: The Life of the Famous Chevalier de Saint-George,* p. 97.

Booklist, February 15, 1998, Carolyn Phelan, review of *The Piano Man,* p. 1018; September 1, 2005, Ilene Cooper, review of *The Real Lucky Charm,* p. 119; February 1, 2007, Gillian Engberg, review of *The Other Mozart,* p. 56; February 1, 2008, Hazel Rochman, review of *I, Matthew Henson: Polar Explorer,* p. 56; September 1, 2008, Hazel Rochman, review of *The Rain Stomper,* p. 107; September 9, 2009, John Peters, review of *Racing against the Odds: The Story of Wendell Scott, Stock-Car Racing's African-American*

Champion, p. 108; November 15, 2009, Ilene Cooper, review of *Voices of Christmas,* p. 45; April 1, 2010, Carolyn Phelan, review of *My Friend Maya Loves to Dance,* p. 47; April 1, 2010, Hazel Rochman, review of *Some Kind of Love: A Family Reunion in Poems,* p. 44; September 1, 2010, Hazel Rochman, review of *My Uncle Martin's Big Heart,* p. 94; November 15, 2010, Andrew Meldar, review of *Grandma's Gift,* p. 51.

Bulletin of the Center for Children's Books, December, 2009, Elizabeth Bush, review of *Voices of Christmas,* p. 155; May, 2010, Deborah Stevenson, review of *Some Kind of Love,* p. 376.

Horn Book, January-February, 2005, Martha V. Parravano, review of *A Sweet Smell of Roses,* p. 79; March-April, 2008, Kathleen Isaacs, review of *I, Matthew Henson,* p. 231; November-December, Claire E. Gross, review of *Voices of Christmas,* p. 641.

Kirkus Reviews, April 15, 2002, review of *Champion: The Story of Muhammad Ali,* p. 569; March 1, 2005, review of *Houdini: World's Greatest Mystery Man and Escape King,* p. 289; April 1, 2005, review of *A Season for Mangoes,* p. 417; December 1, 2006, review of *Jesse Owens: The Fastest Man Alive,* p. 1226; December 15, 2006, review of *The Other Mozart,* p. 1265; December 1, 2007, review of *I, Matthew Henson;* August 15, 2008, review of *The Rain Stomper;* September 15, 2009, review of *Voices of Christmas.*

Publishers Weekly, November 24, 1997, review of *The Piano Man,* p. 73; May 15, 2000, review of *The Sound That Jazz Makes,* p. 115; January 3, 2005, review of *A Sweet Smell of Roses,* p. 55; January 1, 2007, reviews of *The Other Mozart* and *Jesse Owens,* both p. 49; January 28, 2008, review of *I, Matthew Henson,* p. 67; October 26, 2009, review of *Voices of Christmas,* p. 57; August 30, 2010, review of *My Uncle Martin's Big Heart,* p. 50.

School Library Journal, July, 2000, Ginny Gustin, review of *The Sound That Jazz Makes,* p. 99; September, 2001, Alicia Eames, review of *Grandma's Records,* p. 207; July, 2002, Alicia Eames, review of *Champion,* p. 136; November, 2004, Tracy Bell, review of *Rosetta, Rosetta, Sit by Me!,* p. 120; April, 2005, Heide Piehler, review of *Houdini,* p. 124; May, 2005, Nancy Palmer, review of *A Season for Mangoes,* p. 84; October, 2005, Mary N. Oluonye, review of *The Real Lucky Charm,* p. 126; March, 2007, Suzanne Myers Harold, review of *Jesse Owens,* p. 236; June, 2007, Emily R. Brown, review of *The Other Mozart,* p. 166; January, 2008, Barbara Auerbach, review of *I, Matthew Henson,* p. 112; September, 2008, Mary N. Oluonye, review of *The Rain Stomper,* p. 138; October, 2009, Eva Mitnick, review of *Voices of Christmas,* p. 80; May, 2010, Julie Roach, review of *Some Kind of Love,* p. 96; June, 2010, Mary N. Oluonye, review of *My Friend Maya Loves to Dance,* p. 74; October, 2010, Virginia Walter, review of *Grandma's Gift,* p. 77, and Mary N. Oluonye, review of *My Uncle Martin's Big Heart,* p. 104.

ONLINE

Brown Bookshelf Web site, http://thebrownbookshelf.com/ (February 16, 2010), "Eric Velasquez."*

*   *   *

**VENNER, Grace Chang
See CHANG, Grace**

*   *   *

**VIERGUTZ, Dina Nayeri
See NAYERI, Dina**

W-Y

WARD, Jennifer 1963-

Personal

Born December 4, 1963; daughter of Paul (an economics professor) and Charlene Sultan; married; children: Kelly. *Education:* University of Arizona, B.A.

Addresses

Home—IL. *Agent*—Stefanie Von Borstel, Full Circle Literary, 7676 Hazard Center Dr., Ste. 500, San Diego, CA 92108.

Career

Writer and educator. Former teacher in Tucson, AZ, elementary schools for over ten years.

Member

Society of Children's Book Writers and Illustrators, Society of Southwestern Authors.

Awards, Honors

Parents' Choice Award, Parents' Choice Foundation, c. 2000, for *Somewhere in the Ocean;* Media and Partnership Award, Association for Public Lands, 2006, for *The Little Creek;* Izaack Walton League of America Award, Teachers' Choice Award, Pick of the Lists selection, American Booksellers Association, and Giverny Award, all 2009, all for *Forest Bright, Forest Night;* Growing Good Kids—Excellence in Children's Literature Award, 2010, for *The Busy Tree;* numerous state association honors.

Writings

(With T.J. Marsh) *Way out in the Desert,* illustrated by Kenneth J. Spengler, Northland Publishing (Flagstaff, AZ), 1998.

(With T.J. Marsh) *Somewhere in the Ocean,* illustrated by Kenneth J. Spengler, Northland Publishing (Flagstaff, AZ), 2000.

Over in the Garden, illustrated by Kenneth J. Spengler, Northland Publishing (Flagstaff, AZ), 2002.

The Seed and the Giant Saguaro, Northland Publishing (Flagstaff, AZ), 2003.

Forest Bright, Forest Night, illustrated by Jamichael Henterly, Dawn Publications (Nevada City, CA), 2005.

The Little Creek, illustrated by Julie Scott, Western National Parks Association (Tucson, AZ), 2005.

Because You Are My Baby, illustrated by Sylvia Long, Rising Moon (Flagstaff, AZ), 2007.

There Was a Coyote Who Swallowed a Flea, illustrated by Steve Gray, Rising Moon (Flagstaff, AZ), 2007.

Way up in the Arctic, illustrated by Kenneth J. Spengler, Rising Moon (Flagstaff, AZ), 2007.

I Love Dirt!: Fifty-two Activities to Help You and Your Kids Discover the Wonders of Nature, illustrated by Susie Ghahremani, Trumpeter Books (Boston, MA), 2008.

Let's Go Outside!: Outdoor Activities and Projects to Get You and Your Kids Closer to Nature, illustrated by Susie Ghahremani, Trumpeter Books (Boston, MA), 2009.

The Busy Tree, illustrated by Lisa Falkenstern, Marshall Cavendish (New York, NY), 2009.

There Was an Old Monkey Who Swallowed a Frog, illustrated by Steve Gray, Marshall Cavendish (New York, NY), 2010.

Sidelights

An elementary school teacher-turned-author, Jennifer Ward explores the wonders of the natural world in books for young readers that have earned praise for their poetic narratives and touches of humor. A number of Ward's titles are musical counting books, all set to the tune of the traditional song "Over in the Meadow" and illustrated by Kenneth J. Spengler. In each of these books, she showcases ten animals found in a specific habitat; *Way out in the Desert,* for example, features horned toads, hummingbirds, rattlesnakes, Gila mon-

The engaging star of Jennifer Ward's picture book There Was an Old Monkey Who Swallowed a Frog *comes to life in Steve Gray's quirky art.* (Marshall Cavendish Children, 2010. Illustration copyright © 2010 by Steve Gray. Reproduced by permission.)

sters, jackrabbits, and road runners, while *Somewhere in the Ocean* focuses on clown fish, hermit crabs, tiger sharks, and other sea-dwelling creatures. *Way up in the Arctic,* a "particularly timely ecological romp," according to *School Library Journal* critic Susan Moorhead, examines beluga whales, lemmings, and fox cubs. Besides teaching counting, the books also include other activities for children: Spengler's double-page spreads each contain a picture of the relevant numeral hidden in the illustration, and all of Ward's books conclude with an appendix of "Fun Facts" about the animals mentioned in the volume. The finished product, as *School Library Journal* contributor Mollie Bynum wrote of *Way out in the Desert,* is "absolutely delightful."

In *Forest Bright, Forest Night* Ward employs an unusual "flip-the-book" format to highlight the differences between nocturnal creatures and their diurnal counterparts. Writing in *School Library Journal,* Pamela K. Bomboy described the work as a "fun introduction to nature." A host of desert animals care for their offspring in *Because You Are My Baby,* which features illustrations by Sylvia Long. Susan E. Murray, writing in *School Library Journal,* applauded the combination of rhythmic text and art, stating that the pictures "ex-

tend Ward's verses from being just about the animal world to being about all mothers." In *The Busy Tree,* a work told in rhyming couplets, Ward explores the incredible variety of spiders, woodpeckers, chipmunks, and other creatures that make an oak tree their home. In her descriptions of this small ecosystem, she uses "simple-seeming phrases that sneakily introduce good vocabulary," according to a *Kirkus Reviews* critic.

Ward joins with illustrator Steve Gray on a pair of tales designed to tickle children's funny bones: *There Was a Coyote Who Swallowed a Flea* and *There Was an Old Monkey Who Swallowed a Frog.* In the former, a variation on the childhood favorite "There Was an Old Lady," a hungry desert dweller devours everything in its path, from a tiny flea to a prickly cactus. Set in the rainforest, *There Was an Old Monkey Who Swallowed a Frog* earned praise for its "over-the-top comic scenario," in the words of a *Kirkus Reviews* contributor.

Ward once told *SATA:* "I began my career writing for children with a simple but passionate love of children's literature combined with a desire to write.

"My career as a writer literally fell into my lap. My first manuscript submitted for publication, *Way out in the Desert,* was accepted by the first publisher it was sent to. It was critically acclaimed and picked up by the Scholastic market and later released in a board book format. As many know, the road to publication is usually not that simple or quick. Call it beginner's luck!

"I believe writers should write about what they know and what they love. I love nature and animals and thus find them easy subjects to write about. I write every day and am disciplined about it, even if it's just a few words.

"If I could offer advice to aspiring writers or illustrators, it would be to read a lot of children's books. Consistently. Also, the professional organization Society of Children's Book Writers and Illustrators offers tremendous resources for writers and illustrators of all levels, from aspiring, yet unpublished, to advanced and well known. If you're serious about wanting to write for children, follow your dream!"

Biographical and Critical Sources

PERIODICALS

Booklist, April 1, 2000, Carolyn Phelan, review of *Somewhere in the Ocean,* p. 1472; September 1, 2009, Hazel Rochman, review of *The Busy Tree,* p. 96; March 15, 2010, Hazel Rochman, review of *There Was an Old Monkey Who Swallowed a Frog,* p. 45.

Childhood Education, fall, 2002, Elizabeth Bacon and Patricia A. Crawford, review of *Over in the Garden,* p. 53.

Kirkus Reviews, August 15, 2009, review of *The Busy Tree;* March 1, 2010, review of *There Was an Old Monkey Who Swallowed a Frog*

Library Journal, February 15, 2008, Julianne J. Smith, review of *I Love Dirt!: Fifty-two Activities to Help You and Your Kids Discover the Wonders of Nature,* p. 127.

Natural Life, September-October, 2008, Wendy Priesnitz, review of *I Love Dirt!,* p. 56.

Publishers Weekly, March 20, 2000, review of *Somewhere in the Ocean,* p. 94; March 4, 2002, review of *Over in the Garden,* p. 78; February 22, 2010, review of *There Was an Old Monkey Who Swallowed a Frog,* p. 66.

School Library Journal, June, 1998, Mollie Bynum, review of *Way out in the Desert,* p. 115; July, 2000, Lisa Gangemi Kropp, review of *Somewhere in the Ocean,* p. 90; August, 2002, Susan Scheps, review of *Over in the Garden,* p. 172; October, 2005, Pamela K. Bomboy, review of *Forest Bright, Forest Night,* p. 146; November, 2007, Susan Moorhead, review of *Way up in the Arctic,* p. 102; March, 2008, Susan E. Murray, review of *Because You Are My Baby,* p. 179; September, 2009, Susan Scheps, review of *The Busy Tree,* p. 137.

ONLINE

Jennifer Ward Home Page, http://www.jenniferwardbooks. com (February 10, 2011).*

WEATHERFORD, Carole Boston 1956-

Personal

Born February 13, 1956, in Baltimore, MD; daughter of Joseph Alexander and Carolyn Virginia Boston; married Ronald Jeffrey Weatherford (a minister), February 2, 1985; children: one daughter, one son. *Education:* American University, B.A., 1977; University of Baltimore, M.A. (publication design), 1982; University of North Carolina—Greensboro, M.F.A. *Politics:* Democrat. *Religion:* Methodist. *Hobbies and other interests:* Travel, beadwork, sewing, visiting museums and parks, jazz music.

Addresses

Home and office—3313 Sparrowhawk Dr., High Point, NC 27265-9350. *E-mail*—weathfd@earthlink.net.

Career

Educator and author. English teacher at public schools in Baltimore, MD, 1978; American Red Cross, Baltimore, MD, field representative in Blood Services Department, 1978-79; *Black Arts Review* (radio talk show), creator, producer, and host, 1979; Art Litho Co., Baltimore, account executive, 1981; National Bar Association, Washington, DC, director of communications, 1981-85; B & C Associates, Inc., High Point, NC, vice president and creative director, 1985-88; freelance writer and publicist, beginning 1988; Fayetteville State University, Fayetteville, NC, professor, 2002—. Presenter at schools.

Member

North Carolina Writers Network (vice president, 1996-97), Phi Kappa Phi, Delta Sigma Theta, Alpha Kappa Alpha.

Awards, Honors

North Carolina Writers Network Black Writers Speak Competition winner, 1991, and Harperprints Chapbook Competition winner, 1995, both for *The Tan Chanteuse;* North Carolina Arts Council fellowship, 1995; Carter G. Woodson Book Award in elementary category, National Council for the Social Studies, 2001, for *The Sound That Jazz Makes;* AAUW-North Carolina Juvenile Literature Award, 2002, for *Remember the Bridge;* North Carolina Children's Book Award finalist, Bank Street College Best Children's Book designation, and North Carolina Juvenile Literature Award, all 2002, all for *Freedom on the Menu;* Bank Street College Best Children's Book designation, 2003, for *Sidewalk Chalk;* Furious Flower Poetry Prize, James Madison University; International Reading Association (IRA) Notable Book for a Global Society designation, 2005, for *A Negro League Scrapbook;* Golden Kite Honor designation, Society of Children's Book Writers and Illustrators, and National Association for the Advancement of Colored

People Image Award nomination, both 2006, both for *Dear Mr. Rosenwald;* IRA/Children's Book Council (CBC) Teachers' Choice designation; National Council on the Social Studies Notable Children's Trade Book designation, American Library Association Notable Book designation, IRA Notable Book for a Global Society designation, and New York Public Library One Hundred Books for Reading and Sharing designation, all 2006, all for *Moses;* Lee Bennett Hopkins Poetry Award, and Jane Addams Children's Literature Honor designation, both 2007, and Jefferson Cup Award, 2008, all for *Birmingham, 1963;* Bank Street College Best Children's Book designation, 2007, for *Champions on the Bench;* Coretta Scott King Author Honor designation, 2008, for *Becoming Billie Holiday;* North Carolina Award for Literature, 2010.

Writings

FOR CHILDREN

My Favorite Toy, Writers and Readers Publishing (New York, NY), 1994.

Juneteenth Jamboree, illustrated by Yvonne Buchanan, Lee & Low Books (New York, NY), 1995.

Me and My Family Tree, illustrated by Michelle Mills, Black Butterfly (New York, NY), 1996.

Grandma and Me, illustrated by Michelle Mills, Black Butterfly (New York, NY), 1996.

Mighty Menfolk, illustrated by Michelle Mills, Black Butterfly (New York, NY), 1996.

The Sound That Jazz Makes (poetry), illustrated by Eric A. Velasquez, Walker (New York, NY), 2000.

The African-American Struggle for Legal Equality in American History, Enslow Publishers (Berkeley Heights, NJ), 2000.

Princeville: The 500-Year Flood, illustrated by Douglas Alvord, Coastal Carolina Press (Wilmington, NC), 2001.

Sidewalk Chalk: Poems of the City, illustrated by Dimitrea Tokunbo, Wordsong/Boyds Mills Press (Honesdale, PA), 2001.

Jazz Baby, illustrated by Laura Freeman, Lee & Low Books (New York, NY), 2002.

Remember the Bridge: Poems of a People, Philomel (New York, NY), 2002.

Great African-American Lawyers: Raising the Bar of Freedom, Enslow Publishers (Berkeley Heights, NJ), 2003.

Freedom on the Menu: The Greensboro Sit-Ins, illustrated by Jerome Lagarrigue, Dial Books for Young Readers (New York, NY), 2005.

A Negro League Scrapbook, Boyds Mills Press (Honesdale, PA), 2005.

Jesse Owens: The Fastest Man Alive, illustrated by Eric A. Velasquez, Walker & Co. (New York, NY), 2006.

Dear Mr. Rosenwald, illustrated by R. Gregory Christie, Scholastic Press (New York, NY), 2006.

Birmingham, 1963, Wordsong (Honesdale, PA), 2007.

Champions on the Bench: The 1955 Cannon Street YMCA All-Stars, illustrated by Leonard Jenkins, Dial Books for Young Readers (New York, NY), 2007.

Before John Was a Jazz Giant: A Song of John Coltrane, illustrated by Sean Qualls, Henry Holt (New York, NY), 2008.

I, Matthew Henson, illustrated by Eric A. Velasquez, Walker (New York, NY), 2008.

Becoming Billie Holiday, illustrated by Floyd Cooper, Wordsong (Honesdale, PA), 2008.

The Library Ghost, illustrated by Lee White, Upstart Books (Fort Atkinson, WI), 2008.

First Pooch: The Obamas Pick a Pet, illustrated by Amy Bates, Marshall Cavendish (New York, NY), 2009.

Racing against the Odds: The Story of Wendell Scott, Stock-Car Racing's African-American Champion, illustrated by Eric A. Velasquez, Marshall Cavendish (Tarrytown, NY), 2009.

Michelle Obama: First Mom, illustrated by Robert T. Barrett, Marshall Cavendish (New York, NY), 2010.

Obama: Only in America, illustrated by Robert T. Barrett, Marshall Cavendish (New York, NY), 2010.

Oprah: The Little Speaker, illustrated by London Ladd, Marshall Cavendish (New York, NY), 2010.

The Beatitudes: From Slavery to Civil Rights, illustrated by Tim Ladwig, Eerdmans Books for Young Readers (Grand Rapids MI), 2010.

OTHER

The Tan Chanteuse (poetry; for adults), 1995.

Sink or Swim: African-American Lifesavers of the Outer Banks (audiobook), Coastal Carolina Press (Wilmington, NC), 1999.

(With husband, Ronald Jeffrey Weatherford) *Somebody's Knocking at Your Door: AIDS and the African-American Church,* Haworth Pastoral Press (Binghamton, NY), 1999.

The Tar Baby on the Soapbox, Longleaf Press at Methodist College, 1999.

The Carolina Parakeet: America's Lost Parrot in Art and Memory (nonfiction), Avian Publications, 2005.

Contributor of articles and poetry to magazines and newspapers, including *Essence, Christian Science Monitor,* and the *Washington Post.*

Sidelights

The writings of North Carolina writer Carole Boston Weatherford, which include both fiction and nonfiction, were described as "remarkably forthright celebrations" and "a colorful assembly of African American tradition, pride, and love" by Heather Ross Miller in her *African American Review* appraisal of Weatherford's picture book *Juneteenth Jamboree. Juneteenth Jamboree* is characteristic of much of Weatherford's writing in its focus on important moments in African-American history as well as the importance of perseverance, family ties, and closely held tradition. Among her other award-winning titles for younger children are the picture books

The Sound That Jazz Makes, A Negro League Scrapbook, Freedom on the Menu: The Greensboro Sit-ins, Remember the Bridge: Poems of a People, Moses: When Harriet Tubman Led Her People to Freedom, Dear Mr. Rosenwald, and *Becoming Billie Holiday,* the last which earned Weatherford a Coretta Scott King Author honor.

Juneteenth Jamboree revolves around the traditional celebration of that day in 1865 when Texas slaves finally got word of their emancipation. In Weatherford's story, young Cassandra has recently moved to Texas and has never heard of "Juneteenth," despite the fact that it became a legal holiday in that state in 1980. She witnesses the elaborate preparations with the eyes of a newcomer and feels the excitement rising in her community without understanding, at first, what it means. Gradually, Cassandra learns the significance of this historic celebration, its importance to African-Americans amplified by the jubilant crowds, the parades and dances, and the picnics that bring the black community together. "Weatherford does an excellent job" of introducing the reader to an unusual regional holiday, commented Carol Jones Collins in her *School Library Journal* review of *Juneteenth Jamboree,* while in *Publishers Weekly* a contributor remarked that the "enthusiastic text allows readers to discover—and celebrate—the holiday along with Cassandra."

Featuring illustrations by Dimitrea Tokunbo, *Sidewalk Chalk: Poems of the City* is an expression of pride, according to a reviewer for the *Bulletin of the Center for Children's Books.* In twenty vignettes Weatherford celebrates the city as a child might experience it. Her poems evoke the spirit of the neighborhood and the daily activities of the people who live there: jumping rope on a sidewalk, getting a haircut, or going to the Laundromat or to church. "The overall tone of the collection is upbeat and positive," remarked *Booklist* contributor Kathy Broderick in her review of *Sidewalk Chalk,* and the *Bulletin of the Center for Children's Books* critic dubbed the author's verses "vivid snapshots of city life."

A fan of jazz music, Weatherford shares her knowledge of this genre and its history in her books *Jazz Baby, The Sound That Jazz Makes, Becoming Billie Holiday,* and *Before John Was a Jazz Giant: A Song of John Coltrane.* A celebration in rhyme of American music, *The Sound That Jazz Makes* tracks the roots of this uniquely American musical form into African-American history. Weatherford's short poem pairs with paintings by award-winning artist Eric A. Velasquez and lead readers on a musical journey from the drumbeats of Africa to the sound of rap music reverberating through city streets. Poet and illustrator range in their focus from the work-chants of the cotton fields to the plaintive laments of the blues echoing through the Mississippi delta, to the celebrations of gospel, the sweet rhythms of the swing era, and the bold harmonies of the nightclubs of Harlem. According to *Booklist* contributor Bill Ott, Weatherford's poems "possess a flowing rhythm that younger readers will respond to eagerly." Although a *Publishers Weekly* reviewer found the book's rhymes to be "at odds with" the rhythms of jazz music, in *Black Issues Book Review* Khafre Abif described *The Sound That Jazz Makes* as "a soft poetic journey of rhythm" in which the "words are as seamless as the rhythm's growth" from primitive drumbeats into one of the most far-reaching musical movements of modern times.

Illustrated by Sean Qualls, *Before John Was a Jazz Giant* pairs what *Booklist* contributor Rochman described as Weatherford's "lyrical words" and Qualls' "beautiful illustrations" to capture the life of famed jazz musician John Coltrane. Raised in the south during the 1930s, Coltrane was inspired by home-grown musicians as well as by musical recordings, and he punctuated this music with the rhythmic sounds of everyday life and nature in his career as a saxophonist. *Before John Was a Jazz Giant* will likely appeal to "contemporary children, who will recognize the music in their daily lives," according to Rochman, while a *Kirkus Reviews* writer noted that the author's "compressed poetic homage to Coltrane's early influences relays biographical details through metaphors evoking sound." Praising the "evocative poem" in *Before John Was a Jazz Giant, School Library Journal* critic Joyce Adams Burner added that Weatherford's "redolent voice" is "as smooth and vivid as jazz itself."

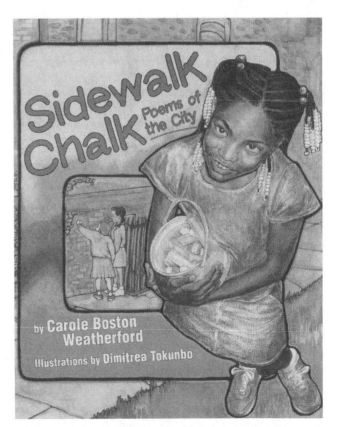

Cover of Carole Boston Weatherford's Sidewalk Chalk, *a poetry collection featuring artwork by Dimitrea Tokunbo.* (Wordsong/Boyds Mills Press, Inc., 2001. Illustration © 2001 by Dimitrea Tokunbo. All rights reserved. Reproduced by permission.)

In the dozens of poems included in *Becoming Billie Holiday* Weatherford focuses on one of the preeminent jazz singers of the early twentieth century. Born in Baltimore and raised in New York's Harlem neighborhood by her single mom, Holiday suffered abuse as a child but showed a talent for singing. As a teen she performed under the name Lady Day and eventually toured the country with Artie Shaw's band despite the racism of her day. Although Holiday's later life was fraught with turmoil due to her drug addiction, Weatherford's poems in *Becoming Billie Holiday* capture the determination of the singer as a child and young woman. She creates what *Booklist* critic John Peters described as a "proud, clear-voiced testimonial" to perseverance that is narrated, in verse, in "the renowned jazz singer's own voice." In *School Library Journal* Paula Willey remarked on the "brilliant" decision by the poet to title each of her verses after one of Holiday's songs, which technique "provides readers with a haunting built-in sound track" to the woman's life story. Praising both Weatherford's "evocative" verses and Cooper's distinguished paintings for the book, a *Kirkus Reviews* contributor reflected the view of many contributors in dubbing *Becoming Billie Holiday* "a remarkable tribute [that is] well worthy of its subject."

Weatherford draws on the story of black athletes to illustrate the importance of determination and personal growth in books such as *Jesse Owens: Fastest Man Alive, Champions on the Bench: The 1955 Cannon Street YMCA All-Stars,* and *A Negro League Scrapbook.* In *Champions on the Bench* readers meet a young baseball player whose talented team is in the running for the 1955 Little League World Series playoff until their white opponents refuse to meet them on the playing field. Praised by *School Library Journal* critic Marilyn Taniguchi as "an engaging overview, richly augmented by archival photographs," *A Negro League Scrapbook* provides a visual history of the Negro Leagues from 1887 to 1947, when Jackie Robinson became the first black

player to sign with the majors. In *Booklist* GraceAnne A. DeCandido noted that Weatherford "lightly fictionalizes" the true story that inspired *Champions on the Bench* while Leonard Jenkins' "dramatic paintings . . . capture the joy of baseball and the boys' frustration." Also praising the book, Mary Hazelton concluded in *School Library Journal* that *Champions on the Bench* presents "a powerful story, well told."

Weatherford moves from the baseball diamond to the 1936 Olympic Games in Berlin, Germany for *Jesse Owens,* which a *Publishers Weekly* praised as a "poetic tribute" to the American athlete's "remarkable performance" during wartime. Man's push for speed is also the focus of *Racing against the Odds: The Story of Wendell Scott, Stock-Car Racing's African-American Champion,* as Weatherford's free-verse text pairs with Velasquez's art to illuminate the story of the first African American to win a NASCAR race. In *Booklist* Peters described *Racing against the Odds* as a example of "pervasive racial discrimination and harassment overcome by quiet, stubborn endurance," and Patricia Manning predicted in *School Library Journal* that the book "will add a welcome dimension to sports collections." In *Kirkus Reviews* a reviewer dubbed *Racing against the Odds* "eye-opening, exhilarating and inspiring."

In addition to athletics, African Americans have made notable strides in other areas of endeavor, and Weatherford focuses on these in several other picture books. In *Oprah: The Little Speaker,* illustrated by London Ladd, she follows the life of talk-show host Oprah Winfrey from Winfrey's impoverished childhood and growing determination through her meteoric rise to fame. Another collaboration with Velasquez, Weatherford's *I, Matthew Henson: Polar Explorer,* "draws much of its power from what it leaves unsaid," according to a *Publishers Weekly* critic. Henson began as a cabin boy at age thirteen, and rose through the ranks to become an assistant to Captain Robert Peary on his historic 1909 expedition to the North Pole. The book's evocative narration gives the black explorer "an ennobling distance," the *Publishers Weekly* critic added, and Barbara Auerbach wrote in *School Library Journal* that Weatherford's prose "sparse, poetic language" "effectively captures [her] . . . subject's determination." Praising *I, Matthew Henson* in *Kirkus Reviews,* a contributor described the book as "lovely and inspiring," while *Horn Book* critic Kathleen Isaacs wrote that "Velasquez's striking pastels" pair well with Weatherford's "spare, poetic language."

Moving to more-recent history, Weatherford focuses on the First Family of the United States in a series of picture books that include *First Pooch: The Obamas Pick a Pet,* illustrated by Amy Bates, and *Michelle Obama: First Mom* and *Obama: Only in America,* both illustrated by Robert T. Barrett. A "brief, lighthearted chronicle of the Obama family's search for a suitable puppy," according to *Booklist* critic Randall Enos, *First Pooch* shares the happiness of Malia and Sasha Obama

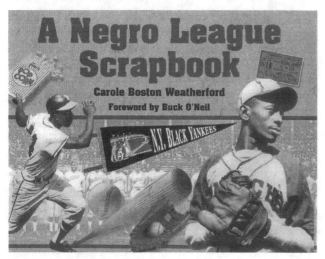

Weatherford captures an important epoch of baseball history in her well-illustrated **A Negro League Scrapbook.** (Boyds Mills Press, 2005. Reproduced by permission.)

An influential advocate of black education is commemorated in R. Gregory Christie's artwork for Weatherford's **Dear Mr. Rosenwald.** (Illustration copyright © 2006 by R. Gregory Christie. Reproduced by permission of Scholastic, Inc.)

upon the arrival of their new pup and also describes an interesting roster of past presidential pets. Both "adulatory" and full of facts, according to Cooper, *Obama* profiles the first black president of the United States, while *Michele Obama* follows the career of a mother and children's advocate.

Weatherford moves from black culture to history in books such as *Freedom on the Menu, Moses, Birmingham, 1963* and *Dear Mr. Rosenwald.* Segregation and the civil-rights movement is the subject of *Freedom on the Menu,* a picture book based on a true story that took place near Weatherford's childhood home. The book's story follows eight-year-old Connie as she experiences segregation at a downtown Greensboro lunch counter, then watches as her older siblings band with other blacks and take the seats at the counter that have been denied to them as a result of the town's Jim Crow laws. Former slave turned abolitionist Harriet Tubman is the focus of *Moses,* which profiles Tubman's courageous work helping escaped slaves travel north on the Underground Railway in the years leading up to the U.S. Civil War. Reviewing *Freedom on the Menu* in *Publishers Weekly,* a critic described the book as "a fresh and affecting interpretation of a pivotal event in the civil rights movement," while another reviewer in the same periodical likened Weatherford's three-tier narrative in *Moses* to "a wholly engrossing dramatic play."

Focusing on one of the pivotal events of the civil rights movement, *Birmingham, 1963* describes the firebombing of Birmingham, Alabama's 16th Street Baptist Church, an act of arson in which many people were injured and four young girls were killed. As captured in Weatherford's fictional eyewitness testimony, the men responsible for the fire remained free for over four decades before they were brought to justice, despite the nationwide outrage inspired by their racist actions.

A collaboration with artist R. Gregory Christie, *Dear Mr. Rosenwald* was inspired by the memories of Weatherford's mother, who attended one of the many "Rosenwald" schools that were established throughout the rural south during the 1920s, thanks to the donations of Sears, Roebuck & Company president Julius Rosenwald and the hard work of many small-town residents. In the story, ten-year-old Ovella, whose father works as a sharecropper, watches as the residents of her poor community work together to earn matching funds and invest time and hard work in a new town school. Reviewing the book in *Publishers Weekly,* a contributor dubbed *Dear Mr. Rosenwald* "a heartening sliver of American history," while in Rochman cited Weatherford's "clear free verse" and Christie's "exuberant gouache and colored-pencil illustrations."

Weatherford views African-American history on a broader scale in *Remember the Bridge,* a poetic celebration of men and women from America's earliest days through to the twentieth century, as well as in *The Beatitudes: From Slavery to Civil Rights.* Illustrated by Tim Ladwig, *The Beatitudes* frames the journey of African Americans from slavery through the civil rights era with the biblical Sermon on the Mount. A contributor to *Kirkus Reviews* claimed that *Remember the Bridge* "brilliantly summarizes . . . a complete timeline" of history and its closing poem, "I Am the Bridge," evokes "a bridge toward understanding and acceptance." "Ladwig's elegant watercolors . . . lend a dreamlike quality to the stirring depictions" in Weatherford's words, according to Courtney Jones in *Booklist,* and Barbara Elleman wrote in *School Library Journal* that Weatherford's "verses, short and meaningful, carry forth a poignant message."

Biographical and Critical Sources

PERIODICALS

African American Review, spring, 1998, Heather Ross Miller, reviews of *The Tan Chanteuse* and *Juneteenth Jamboree,* both pp. 169-171.

American Visions, December-January, 1995, Yolanda Robinson Coles, review of *Juneteenth Jamboree,* p. 37.

Black Issues Book Review, September, 2000, Khafre Abif, review of *The Sound That Jazz Makes,* p. 81.

Booklist, December 15, 1999, Carolyn Phelan, review of *Sink or Swim: African-American Lifesavers of the Outer Banks,* pp. 783-784; August, 2000, Bill Ott, re-

Weatherford focuses on a well-known polar exploration in her picture book I, Matthew Henson: Polar Explorer, *featuring artwork by Eric A. Velasquez.* (Walker & Company, 2008. Illustration copyright © 2008 by Eric A. Velasquez. Reproduced by permission.)

view of *The Sound That Jazz Makes,* p. 2133; September 15, 2001, Kathy Broderick, review of *Sidewalk Chalk: Poems of the City,* p. 224; February 15, 2002, Kay Weisman, review of *Princeville: The 500-Year Flood,* p. 1014, and Gillian Engberg, review of *Remember the Bridge: Poems of a People,* p. 1030; February 15, 2003, Gillian Engberg, review of *Great African-American Lawyers: Raising the Bar of Freedom,* p. 1080; February 1, 2005, GraceAnne A. DeCandido, review of *A Negro League Scrapbook,* p. 976, and Carolyn Phelan, review of *Freedom on the Menu: The Greensboro Sit-ins,* p. 980; October 1, 2006, Hazel Rochman, review of *Dear Mr. Rosenwald,* p. 61; February 1, 2007, GraceAnne A. DeCandido, review of *Champions on the Bench: The Cannon Street YMCA All-Stars,* p. 61; February 1, 2008, Hazel Rochman, review of *Before John Was a Jazz Giant: A Song of John Coltrane,* p. 60; October 1, 2008, John Peters, review of *Becoming Billie Holiday,* p. 35; September 1, 2009, John Peters, review of *Racing against the Odds: The Story of Wendell Scott, Stock-Car Racing's African-American Champion,* p. 108; November 15, 2009, Randall Enos, review of *First Pooch: The Obamas Pick a Pet,* p. 41; February 1, 2010, Courtney Jones, review of *The Beatitudes: From Slavery to Civil Rights,* p. 56; March 15, 2010, Julie Cummins, review of *Oprah: The Little Speaker,* p. 44; May 1, 2010, Ilene Cooper, review of *Obama: Only in America,* p. 81.

Bulletin of the Center for Children's Books, October, 2001, review of *Sidewalk Chalk,* p. 81; May, 2002, review of *Remember the Bridge,* p. 344; February, 2005, Karen Coats, review of *Freedom on the Menu,* p. 268; October, 2006, Deborah Stevenson, review of *Dear Mr. Rosenwald,* p. 53; November, 2006, Karen Coats, review of *Moses: When Harriet Tubman Led Her People to Freedom,* p. 148; January, 2007, Elizabeth Bush, review of *Champions on the Bench,* p. 233.

Canadian Review of Materials, March, 2001, AnnMarie Hamar, review of *The Sound That Jazz Makes,* p. 23.

Georgia Review, summer, 1997, Ted Kooser, review of *The Tan Chanteuse,* p. 375.

Horn Book, January-February, 2005, Joanna Rudge Long, review of *Freedom on the Menu,* p. 87; November-December, 2006, Michelle H. Martin, review of *Moses,* p. 737; March-April, 2008, Kathleen Isaacs, review of *I, Matthew Henson: Polar Explorer,* p. 231; May-June, 2008, Susan Dove Lempke, review of *Before John Was a Jazz Giant,* p. 342.

Kirkus Reviews, December 1, 2001, review of *Remember the Bridge,* p. 1691; December 15, 2004, review of *Freedom on the Menu,* p. 1211; March 1, 2005, review of *A Negro League Scrapbook,* p. 297; August 15, 2006, review of *Dear Mr. Rosenwald,* p. 853; September 1, 2006, review of *Moses,* p. 914; December 1, 2006, review of *Jesse Owens,* p. 1226; December 1, 2007, review of *I, Matthew Henson;* March 15, 2008, review of *Before John Was a Jazz Giant;* September 1, 2008, review of *Becoming Billie Holiday;* October 1, 2009, review of *Racing against the Odds;* December 15, 2009, review of *The Beatitudes.*

New York Times Book Review, February 11, 2007, Rebecca Zerkin, review of *Moses,* p. 17; February 18, 2007, review of *Moses: When Harriet Tubman Led Her People to Freedom,* p. 26.

Publishers Weekly, October 30, 1995, review of *Juneteenth Jamboree,* p. 61; May 15, 2000, review of *The Sound That Jazz Makes,* p. 115; September 17, 2001, review of *Sidewalk Chalk,* p. 82; December 24, 2001, review of *Remember the Bridge,* p. 62; January 3, 2005, review of *Freedom on the Menu,* p. 55; July 31, 2006, review of *Moses,* p. 78; October 23, 2006, review of *Dear Mr. Rosenwald,* p. 51; December 11, 2006, review of *Champions on the Bench,* p. 69; January 1, 2007, review of *Jesse Owens: Fastest Man Alive,* p. 49; January 28, 2008, review of *I, Matthew Henson,* p. 67.

School Library Journal, January, 1996, Carol Jones Collins, review of *Juneteenth Jamboree,* p. 97; July, 2000, Ginny Gustin, review of *The Sound That Jazz Makes,* p. 99; January, 2002, review of *Sidewalk Chalk,* p. 127; June, 2002, Marge Loch-Woulters, review of *Jazz Baby,* p. 114; March, 2005, Marilyn Taniguchi, review of *A Negro League Scrapbook,* p. 236; April, 2005, Mary N. Oluonye, review of *Freedom on the Menu,* p. 115; August, 2005, Blair Christolon, review of *Freedom on the Menu,* p. 50; October, 2006, Margaret Bush, review of *Moses,* and Catherine Threadgill, review of *Dear Mr. Rosenwald,* both p. 129; January, 2007, Mary Hazelton, review of *Champions of the Bench,* p. 110; March, 2007, Suzanne Myers Harold, review of *Jesse Owens,* p. 236; January, 2008, Rick Margolis, "She Shall Overcome: Poet Carole Boston Weatherford Writes about the Struggle for Equality," p. 33, and Barbara Auerbach, review of *I, Matthew Henson,* p. 112; April, 2008, Joyce Adams Burner, review of *Before John Was a Jazz Giant,* p. 138; October, 2008, Paula Willey, review of *Becoming Billie Holiday,* p. 176; November, 2009, Patricia Manning, review of *Racing against the Odds,* p. 97; December, 2009, Fay Lynn Van Vleck, review of *First Pooch,* p. 100; March, 2010, Barbara Elleman, review of *The Beatitudes,* p. 145; April, 2010, Donna Cardon, review of *Oprah,* p. 149, and Stacy Dillon, review of *Obama,* p. 183.

Winston-Salem Journal, March 1, 2007, review of *When Harriet Tubman Led Her People to Freedom.*

Voice of Youth Advocates, August, 2002, review of *Remember the Bridge,* p. 213.

ONLINE

Carole Boston Weatherford Home Page, http://www.carole weatherford.com (February 15, 2011).

*   *   *

WILLEY, Margaret 1950-

Personal

Born November 5, 1950, in Chicago, IL; daughter of Foster (an artist) and Barbara Willey; married Richard Joanisse, 1980; children: one daughter. *Education:* Grand Valley State College, B.Ph., B.A., 1975; Bowling Green State University, B.F.A., 1979.

Addresses

Home—Grand Haven, MI. *E-mail*—margwilley@ hotmail.com.

Career
Writer.

Member
Authors Guild.

Awards, Honors
American Library Association (ALA) Best Books for Young Adults designation, 1983, for *The Bigger Book of Lydia,* 1986, for *Finding David Dolores,* 1988, for *If Not for You,* and 1990, for *Saving Lenny;* creative artist grant, Michigan Arts Council, 1984, 1988, 1995; Recommended Books for Reluctant YA Readers selection, Young Adult Services Division/ALA, 1989, for *If Not for You;* Best of the Best for Children selection, ALA, 1993, for *David Dolores;* Charlotte Zolotow Award, 2002, for *Clever Beatrice;* Anne Izard Storytellers' Choice Award, 2005, for *Clever Beatrice and the Best Little Pony;* Green Earth Book Awards Honor designation, 2010, for *The Summer of Silk Moths.*

Writings

YOUNG-ADULT NOVELS

The Bigger Book of Lydia, Harper (New York, NY), 1983.
Finding David Dolores, Harper (New York, NY), 1986.
If Not for You, Harper (New York, NY), 1988.
Saving Lenny, Bantam (New York, NY), 1990.
The Melinda Zone, Bantam (New York, NY), 1993.
Facing the Music, Delacorte Press (New York, NY), 1996.
A Summer of Silk Moths, Flux (Woodbury, MN), 2009.

Contributor of short fiction to literary journals and to periodicals, including *Redbook* and *Good Housekeeping.*

PICTURE BOOKS

Thanksgiving with Me, illustrated by Lloyd Bloom, Laura Geringer Book (New York, NY), 1998.
The Three Bears and Goldilocks, illustrated by Heather M. Solomon, Atheneum Books for Young Readers (New York, NY), 2008.

"CLEVER BEATRICE" PICTURE-BOOK SERIES; ILLUSTRATED BY HEATHER M. SOLOMON

Clever Beatrice: An Upper Peninsula Conte, Atheneum Books for Young Readers (New York, NY), 2001.
Clever Beatrice and the Best Little Pony, Atheneum Books for Young Readers (New York, NY), 2004.
A Clever Beatrice Christmas, Atheneum Books for Young Readers (New York, NY), 2006.

Sidelights
Michigan author Margaret Willey has earned praise for both her teen novels and her picture books for younger children. In novels that include *The Bigger Book of Ly-dia, Finding David Dolores, Facing the Music, The Melinda Zone,* and *A Summer of Silk Moths,* Willey features characters with what Jan Tyler described in *Twentieth-Century Young-Adult Writers* as "distinctly drawn personalities with a wide range of conflicts: problems with parents; troubles with boyfriends; breeches of loyalty between best friends; school woes; and particularly, always, the struggle to find and to be oneself." In contrast to her teen novels, Willey's stories for children are characterized for their lighthearted themes and the delightful illustrations of collaborator Heather M. Solomon. She introduces an engaging folk-tale character named Clever Beatrice in a sequence of illustrated tales set in the north woods of French Canada, and she returns to a similar setting in her humorous retelling *The Three Bears and Goldilocks.* Reviewing Willey's version of "Goldilocks and the Three Bears" for *Booklist,* Janice Del Negro concluded that the author's "lively" text combines with Solomon's "expressive images" to "shake the dust from this old tale and make it shiny new."

Cover of Margaret Willey's young-adult novel Facing the Music, *featuring artwork by Jana Leon.* (Laurel-Leaf Books, 1997. Used by permission of Delacorte Press, an imprint of Random House Children's Books, a division of Random House, Inc.)

Willey's first teen novel, *The Bigger Book of Lydia,* focuses on bullying and the value of close friends. For Lydia, a small stature and meek nature have made her the target of school bullies, while Michelle hides a secret: to control her weight she has become anorexic. When the two outcasts become friends and learn to trust each other, they are able to work together to confront their own problems. The friendship in *Saving Lenny* is a romantic one, and for Jesse her loyalties to her new boyfriend, Lenny, keep her in the relationship even when it becomes clear that she cannot help him with his clinical depression. In *Finding David Dolores* Willey explores a different kind of friendship as an impressionable thirteen year old seeks clues to her own true self through her relationships with others, including an aloof older teen and a classmate whose rebellious nature hides a troubled home life. For *New York Times Book Review* contributor Ann Turner, *Finding David Dolores* rewards teen readers with "an engrossing, fast-paced story of an intense friendship and how it goes awry."

For the fifteen year old that Willey introduces in *The Melinda Zone,* friends are the problem. Melinda's parents divorced years ago, and she has never felt the reassurance of a stable home. When she has the chance to spend the summer with a relative, the teen takes the opportunity to stay in one place and enjoy making decisions independent of her parents' demands. Reviewing the novel, a *Publishers Weekly* commended *The Melinda Zone,* writing that it takes a "forthright" approach to "the emotional grip of divorce on children" while also gaining teen appeal through its inclusion of a "satisfying teen romance."

A teen's experiences in a garage band are the focus of *Facing the Music.* Music has always been a refuge for Lisa Franklin, especially since her mother died just when she was beginning her teen years and needed the woman most. Lisa's older brother Mark also enjoys music and has joined a rock band with a group of his friends. When band member Danny asks Lisa to be their front singer, she agrees and the experience help her build self-confidence while also inspiring a romantic interest in Danny. Lisa's talent as a vocalist is hard to argue with, but her romantic entanglement with Danny ultimately causes tensions between brother and sister in a story that *Booklist* contributor Anne O'Malley described as "a powerful novel of adolescent joy and defeat" that also features a "wonderfully realistic portrayal of the adolescent psyche." "Willey focuses more on the growth of characters than the formulation of neat resolutions," asserted a *Publishers Weekly* critic in noting the realism of *Facing the Music.*

As Willey noted on her home page, *A Summer of Silk Moths* was inspired by a favorite childhood read: Gene Stratton Porter's *A Girl of the Limberlost.* "Both stories feature a fatherless but fearless girl and a moth collection," the author noted, although Willey's story exchanges Stratton's Indiana setting for the riverside town

Cover of Willey's teen novel A Summer of Silk Moths, *featuring artwork by Nenad Jakesevic.* (Cover illustration © 2009 by Nenad Jakesevic. Reproduced by permission of Flux, an imprint of Llewellyn Publications.)

of Buchanan, Michigan. The North American silk moth referenced in the title of *A Summer of Silk Moths* represents "creativity, mystery, dream life, and regeneration," according to Willey, and through her story she shares her "long-standing belief that damaged children can find emotional healing in the natural world." Seventeen-year-old Pete is working with Abe McMichaels to create a nature preserve built to honor Abe's naturalist brother Paul, who was killed years earlier. When Nora, a teen runaway, appears at the preserve and explains that she is Paul's daughter, Pete is intrigued by her secretive nature. While they share their interest in nature, Paul also befriends Nora, helping her to deal with her problematic family and build a healthy relationship with her estranged uncle. In *School Library Journal* Wendy E. Dunn praised Willey's characters as "engaging and engrossing" and added that "well-written descriptions of rural Michigan" contribute to the "gradually unfolding" mystery at the core of *A Summer of Silk Moths.* In *Kirkus Reviews* a critic recommended Willey novel as a "thoughtful, complex and moving story about loss and discovery of identity, love and the ability to change and the restorative powers of nature."

Willey turns to younger readers in her series of books that include *Clever Beatrice: An Upper Peninsula Conte, Clever Beatrice and the Best Little Pony,* and *A Clever Beatrice Christmas.* When readers first meets the titular character in *Clever Beatrice,* the little girl is determined to help her poor family earn enough money to buy food. Because she is too young to work in the lumber camps that are the only employers in the area, the spunky Beatrice marches off to the home of a wealthy but gullible giant, ultimately using her sprightly intelligence to trick him out of a sack full of gold. In *Clever Beatrice and the Best Little Pony* someone is riding Beatrice's pony in the dark of night, and the girl is undaunted when she is told that it may be a mischievous elf-like *lutin.* Willey take on a holiday focus in *A Clever Beatrice Christmas,* which finds the clever girl outsmarting herself when she brashly promises to visit the North Pole and bring back a curl from the beard of Father Christmas himself. *Clever Beatrice* "is spiced with a singsong dialect and sparkles with . . . brash, good-humored improbability," noted *Booklist* contributor Gillian Engberg, and Carolyn Phelan wrote in the same periodical that *Clever Beatrice and the Best Little Pony* benefits from a "well-crafted, smoothly written story" that is "well suited to reading aloud." In *Kirkus Reviews* a contributor made special note of Solomon's "carefully researched" illustrations for the series, writing that in *A Clever Beatrice Christmas* she illuminates the traditions of French-speaking Canada in her "muted, folk-art style." Commenting on the series' positive contribution to the folk-tale genre, another *Kirkus Reviews* writer noted of *Clever Beatrice and the Best Little Pony:* "Willey's telling is superb, and Solomon's watercolor illustrations . . . evok[e] . . . the village life of yesteryear."

Biographical and Critical Sources

BOOKS

Twentieth-Century Young-Adult Writers, St. James Press (Detroit, MI), 1994, pp. 708-709.

PERIODICALS

Booklist, January 15, 1993, review of *The Bigger Book of Lydia;* March 15, 1996, Anne O'Malley, review of *Facing the Music,* p. 1253; September 1 1998, Ilene Cooper, review of *Thanksgiving with Me,* p. 135; July, 2001, Gillian Engberg, review of *Clever Beatrice: An Upper Peninsula Conte,* p. 2015; February 1, 2005, Carolyn Phelan, review of *Clever Beatrice and the Best Little Pony,* p. 964; October 15, 2006, Carolyn Phelan, review of *A Clever Beatrice Christmas,* p. 55; November 1, 2008, Janice Del Negro, review of *The Three Bears and Goldilocks,* p. 50.

Horn Book, November-December, 2001, Martha V. Parravano, review of *Clever Beatrice,* p. 763; September-October, 2004, Martha P. Parravano, review of *Clever Beatrice and the Best Little Pony,* p. 577; November-December, 2006, Martha V. Parravano, review of *A Clever Beatrice Christmas,* p. 694; September-October, 2008, Joanna Rudge Long, review of *The Three Bears and Goldilocks,* p. 574.

Kirkus Reviews, November 1, 1983, review of *The Bigger Book of Lydia,* p. 210; January 1, 1993, review of *The Melinda Zone,* p. 69; September 1, 2001, review of *Clever Beatrice,* p. 1303; August 1, 2004, review of *Clever Beatrice and the Best Little Pony,* p. 750; November 1, 2006, review of *A Clever Beatrice Christmas,* p. 1135; August 15. 2008, review of *The Three Bears and Goldilocks;* October 1, 2009, review of *A Summer of Silk Moths.*

New York Times Book Review, October 12, 1986, Ann Turner, review of *Finding David Dolores.*

Publishers Weekly, December 9, 1983, review of *The Bigger Book of Lydia,* p. 50; January 19, 1990, review of *Saving Lenny,* p. 111; January 18, 1993, review of *The Melinda Zone,* p. 470; February 26, 1996, review of *Facing the Music,* p. 106; July 30, 2001, review of *Clever Beatrice,* p. 84.

School Library Journal, December 1983, review of *The Bigger Book of Lydia,* p. 78; March 1993, review of *The Melinda Zone,* p. 224; October, 2001, Rosalyn Pierini, review of *Clever Beatrice,* p. 147; November, 2004, Linda M. Kenton, review of *Clever Beatrice and the Best Little Pony,* p. 132; October, 2006, Lisa Falk, review of *A Clever Beatrice Christmas,* p. 101; August, 2008, Susan Scheps, review of *The Three Bears and Goldilocks,* p. 106; January, 2010, Wendy E. Dunn, review of *A Summer of Silk Moths,* p. 116.

Voice of Youth Advocates, April, 1984, review of *The Bigger Book of Lydia,* p. 36.

ONLINE

Margaret Willey Home Page, http://www.margaretwilley. com (February 15, 2011).

Margaret Willey Web Log, http://www.mothsandmetamor phoses.com (February 15, 2011).*

*   *   *

WONG, Marissa Lopez

Personal

Born in Chula Vista, CA; daughter of Mario (a municipal worker) and Elvia (a telephone clerk) Lopez; married Kailee Wong (a professional football player); children: Makai, Lalia, Mailee. *Education:* Degree (criminal justice).

Addresses

Home—Houston, TX.

Career

Author. Formerly worked in probation. Speaker at conferences.

Writings

(With brother, Mario Lopez) *Mud Tacos!,* illustrated by Maryn Roos, Celebra Children's Books (New York, NY), 2009.

Biographical and Critical Sources

PERIODICALS

Houston Chronicle, November 28, 2009, review of *Mud Tacos!,* p. 2.
Kirkus Reviews, October 1, 2009, review of *Mud Tacos!*

ONLINE

Momlogic Web site, http://www.momlogic.com/ (November 3, 2009), interview with Wong.*

*   *   *

WORTIS, Edward Irving
See AVI

*   *   *

XUAN, YongSheng 1952-

Personal

Born July 24, 1952, in Shanghai, China; immigrated to Canada, 1990; son of Xing Kang (a civil engineer) and Bing Xian (Tang) Xuan; married Rong Rong Gu (a restaurant manager); children: Faye Lee. *Education:* Attended Central Institute of Culture (QiDong, China), 1970-73; Central University of Arts and Crafts (Beijing, China), Fine Arts and Crafts certificate, 1985-86; attended University of Regina (Saskachewan, Canada), 1993-94.

Addresses

Home—5883 Sherbrooke St., Vancouver, British Columbia V5W 3N1, Canada.

Career

QiDong Arts Factory of China, QiDong, JianShu, China, art designer, 1973-78; Industrial Arts Institute of China, Nan Tong, JianShu, master art designer and director, 1978-90; Burant Cabinet and Mill Work, Regina, Saskatchewan, Canada, woodwork designer and carver, 1990-93; Benchmark Mould, Ltd., Windsor, Ontario, Canada, art director and master engraver and finisher, 1994-96; Ford City Business District, Windsor, muralist, 1998—. Freelance artist and illustrator, beginning

YongSheng Xuan (Photograph by ZhiFu Wang. Reproduced by permission.)

1981. *Exhibitions:* Solo art exhibitions staged at Art Gallery of Shanghai, China, 1985; and in Regina, Saskatchewan, Canada. Work included in Society of Illustrators' Original Art Exhibit, New York, NY, 1999.

Member

Chinese Arts and Crafts Association.

Awards, Honors

Parents' Choice storybook recommendation, Parents' Choice Foundation, 1998, for *The Laziest Boy in the World* by Lensey Namioka; Notable Children's Trade Book in the Field of Social Studies selection, National Council for Social Studies/Children's Book Council, 1999, for *Ten Suns* by Eric A. Kimmel.

Writings

SELF-ILLUSTRATED

The Dragon Lover and Other Chinese Proverbs, Shen's Books (Auburn, CA), 1999.

Contributor to publications, including *Beijing Esperanto, YuNan Science,Beijing Arts and Crafts, Beijing Traditional Arts, JianShu Traditional Arts, Sinorama,* and *Cricket.*

ILLUSTRATOR

Eric A. Kimmel, reteller, *Ten Suns: A Chinese Legend,* Holiday House (New York, NY), 1998.

Lensey Namioka, *The Laziest Boy in the World,* Holiday House (New York, NY), 1998.

Eric A. Kimmel, reteller, *The Rooster's Antlers: A Story of the Chinese Zodiac,* Holiday House (New York, NY), 1999.

Marianne Carus, editor, *That's Ghosts for You: Thirteen Scary Stories,* Front Street/Cricket (Chicago, IL), 2000.

Ying Chang Compestine, *The Story of Chopsticks,* Holiday House (New York, NY), 2001.

Ying Chang Compestine, *The Story of Noodles,* Holiday House (New York, NY), 2002.

Ying Chang Compestine, *The Story of Paper,* Holiday House (New York, NY), 2003.

Ying Chang Compestine, *The Story of Kites,* Holiday House (New York, NY), 2003.

Ying Chang Compestine, *D Is for Dragon Dance,* Holiday House (New York, NY), 2006.

Illustrator of books published in China.

Adaptations

Sidelights

Chinese artist and illustrator YongSheng Xuan has been widely praised for his ability to bridge cultural gaps with a unique and compelling style. His illustration work includes the award-winning titles *The Laziest Boy in the World,* written by Lensey Namioka, and *Ten Suns: A Chinese Legend,* adapted and retold by Eric A. Kimmel. Xuan has worked with Ying Chang Compestine on several books and is the author and illustrator of *The Dragon Lover and Other Chinese Proverbs.* His art also appears in *That's Ghosts for You: Thirteen Scary Stories,* a collection of tales that were originally published in *Cricket* magazine. According to Elaine Baran Black in her *School Library Journal* review of *That's Ghosts for You,* "Xuan's black-and-white paper-cut illustrations set off the stories beautifully."

Xuan was born in Shanghai, China, in 1952, and as a teenager he studied under famed Chinese sculptor Zhang Chenren. Xuan later worked as an art designer and professional artist, and eventually took advanced fine arts and crafts classes at the Central Arts and Crafts University in Beijing, considered one of the highest art institutes in China.

In 1981 Xuan began contributing artwork to a variety of publications and magazines in China, Japan, Taiwan, and the United States. Since that time his illustrations, paintings, and paper cuts have appeared in *Beijing Arts and Crafts, Sinorama, Cricket,* and many other periodicals.

Xuan and his family immigrated to Canada in 1990. He worked for several years as a woodwork designer and cabinetmaker in Regina, Saskatchewan, then as art director and master engraver at a production company in Windsor, Ontario. All the while, he continued to contribute his work to children's magazines.

In 1998 Xuan illustrated his first English-language picture book, *Ten Suns,* retold by Eric A. Kimmel. One of the oldest Chinese legends, *Ten Suns* tells the story of the emperor of the eastern sky, Di Jun, and his ten sons, who are also suns. Each day one of the emperor's sons takes his turn walking across the sky from east to west. After many years they tire of following the path alone, and one day, despite their father's warnings, all ten sons make the journey across the sky together. Their combined heat scorches the land—crops wither and die, forests burst into flame, and the seas boil. To save the earth and its people, Emperor Di Jun sends the Archer of Heaven to find the suns and shoot all but one from the sky. A *Kirkus Reviews* contributor called Xuan's illustrations "magical" and "as richly crafted and detailed as fine embroidery on Chinese silk."

Xuan's artwork is also a feature of Lensey Namioka's story *The Laziest Boy in the World,* which tells the story of young Xiaolong, who as a baby is so lazy that he almost never kicks or cries. As he grows older, Xiaolong becomes increasingly spoiled and lazy, until he does not even want to play. When a thief breaks into his home, Xiaolong is finally moved to take action. He thwarts the villain and discovers the satisfaction of a job well done. *Booklist* critic Karen Morgan praised *The Laziest Boy in the World* as "both fun to read and visually appealing."

The Dragon Lover and Other Chinese Proverbs, published in 1999, was Xuan's first self-illustrated picture book. Written in both English and Chinese, the book includes five traditional Chinese proverbs: "The Lazy Farmer," "The Crane and the Clam," "The Musician and the Water Buffalo," "An Old Horse," and "The Dragon Lover." Each story is illustrated with intricate Chinese-style paper cuts that *Booklist* reviewer Kay Weisman called "striking" and "remarkable."

Xuan began his collaboration with Compestine in *The Story of Chopsticks,* published in 2001. A folktale retelling, the work introduces Kuai, a hungry boy with so many older brothers that he is never able to reach the best pieces of food at family meals before his brothers eat them. Kuai solves his problem by inventing chopsticks. "Xuan's richly colored traditional Chinese cut paper illustrations lend authenticity" to the tale, according to a *Kirkus Reviews* contributor. Noting the black strips of paper used to outline the shapes in Xuan's art, Carolyn Phelan wrote in *Booklist* that, "like the hues in a stained glass window," the colors in each image are "all the more brilliant for their proximity to black."

The brothers from *The Story of Chopsticks* return in other books by Compestine, including *The Story of Noodles, The Story of Paper,* and *The Story of Kites.* In each, the resourceful siblings invent the title object, making life better for everyone in their village and the empire to boot. "The boys' humorous exploits are brought to life in Xuan's illustrations," a *Kirkus Reviews* contributor wrote of *The Story of Noodles,* while Gillian Engberg concluded in *Booklist* that the "action, noise, and humor" in *The Story of Kites* is "nicely captured in the detailed, cut-paper illustrations that resemble stained glass."

D Is for Dragon Dance, another book by Compestine, celebrates aspects of the Chinese New Year. While Rachel G. Payne questioned the work's effectiveness as an alphabet primer, the *School Library Journal* critic asserted that Xuan's "art makes up for the patchy text and depicts the vibrancy and color of the [Chinese New Year] celebrations." A *Kirkus Reviews* contributor called "the jewel-like paintings" in the book "engaging," and Stephanie Zvirin commented in *Booklist* that Xuan's art in *D Is for Dragon Dance* "is cheerful and bright, rather stylistic, with appealing repetitive details that will draw kids right in."

Biographical and Critical Sources

PERIODICALS

Booklist, May 1, 1998, review of *Ten Suns: A Chinese Legend,* p. 496; November 1, 1998, Karen Morgan, review of *The Laziest Boy in the World,* p. 504; May 15, 1999, Kay Weisman, review of *The Dragon Lover and Other Chinese Proverbs,* p. 1700; December 1, 2000, Roger Leslie, review of *That's Ghosts for You: 13 Scary Stories,* p. 713; January 1, 2002, Carolyn Phelan, review of *The Story of Chopsticks,* p. 863; November 1, 2002, John Peters, review of *The Story of Noodles,* p. 505; April 15, 2003, Gillian Engberg, review of *The Story of Kites,* p. 1476; December, 15, 2003, Gillian Engberg, review of *The Story of Paper,* p. 752; February 1, 2006, Stephanie Zvirin, *D Is for Dragon Dance,* p. 51.

Bulletin of the Center for Children's Books, July, 1999, *Ten Suns,* review of p. 1804.

Childhood Education, fall, 2003, Teresa Boarder, review of *The Story of Kites,* p. 39.

Kirkus Reviews, April 1, 1998, review of *Ten Suns,* p. 496; October 1, 2001, review of *The Story of Chopsticks,* p. 1420; October 1, 2002, review of *The Story of Noodles,* p. 1464; April 15, 2003, review of *The Story of Kites,* p. 605; December 15, 2005, review of *D Is for Dragon Dance,* p. 1320.

Publishers Weekly, May 5, 2003, review of *The Story of Chopsticks,* p. 224.

School Library Journal, May, 1998, review of *Ten Suns,* p. 134; December, 2000, Elaine Baran Black, review of *That's Ghosts for You,* p. 142; December, 2001, Margaret A. Chang, review of *The Story of Chopsticks,* p. 97; November, 2002, Laurie Edwards, review of *The Story of Noodles,* p. 119; May, 2003, Barbara Scotto, review of *The Story of Kites,* p. 110; November, 2003, Laurie Edwards, review of *The Story of Paper,* p. 90; March, 2006, Rachel G. Payne, review of *D Is for Dragon Dance,* p. 185.

Autobiography Feature

YongSheng Xuan

I was born into an ordinary intellectual's family in Shanghai, China. My father was a civil engineer, and my mother a housewife. After the Communists took over China, my parents were classified as "alien-class elements" belonging to the so-called "black four groups," and our inherited properties were confiscated by the Communist government for the fact that my parents were both from "rich families." When I was four or five, my father had to go far away from Shanghai to the mountainous areas in Fujian Province to build highways and bridges. The financial conditions of my family went from bad to worse. My childhood was half spent in hunger. Only when there was a holiday could we have a full meal with rationed pork. I have a brother one year my junior and a sister nine years younger. Every day after school, my job was to help Mother do house chores and look after my brother and sister. We couldn't afford toys, so we made our own. I cut a piece of cardboard into an oval shape with two holes, attached a string, brush painted it as the face of an eagle, and let my brother wear it to play hawk-and-chicken with me. When my sister cried, I would fold candy wrappers into flowers or birds to make her laugh. Chinese chess was made of bottle caps. We were most excited during the Chinese New Year when Mother often took us to the countryside in Qidong County on the north shore of the Yangtze River after a day's ride in a boat to spend the festival with our maternal grandparents.

My grandparents were both Buddhists. They prayed every morning and evening. After they finished their work in the fields, they would make paper sacrificial offerings for funerals for their neighbors, friends, relatives, and villagers. They cut colorful paper and cardboard to make houses, furniture, barrows, trunks, farm tools, water pails, coins, gold ingots, etc. After gluing and tying, they all looked so real and delicate. Those three-dimensional offerings were first framed with reed and bamboo and covered with colored paper. Then all kinds of pictures, birds, animals, symmetrical or continuous patterns cut out with scissors were pasted on them. My grandfather was a well-known folk art craftsman among the villages far and near.

I would spend hours watching my grandfather work. Often I was so fascinated that I couldn't help offering to help. Every time he would say to me, "Xiao Long (Little Dragon, my infant name because I was born in the year of the dragon), you are still a child. When you

YongSheng Xuan (right) with his younger brother, Shanghai, China, 1959. (Courtesy of YongSheng Xuan.)

grow up, you can help me. Now go to Grandma and have some dumplings." When he had some time, he would make a rabbit lantern or a kite for us. To this day, I remember those handicrafts Grandpa made. Years later when I grew to be an adult and became a professional folk art researcher, I visited many old folk art craftsmen but never met anyone that matched my grandpa's talents. What a pity!

Grandma was always warm and kind. She taught us how to make dumplings, but I didn't like to make the same boring dumplings over and over again. Instead, I'd sculpt the sticky rice dough into little dogs, goats, fish, or birds. Grandma allowed me to put them into the steamer. When time was up and the steamer was opened, my brother, sister, and cousins would fight over my "craft works." That was my proudest time!

All children seem to love animals. My pets during my childhood were crickets and silkworms. When it was dark, my brother and I would go with other children in the countryside who were our age to look for crickets in the grass with the help of a flashlight. We put our catches into a bamboo pipe with a few grains of rice before sealing it with some cloth. Returning home, we would release the crickets into a big paper box and stir them with green bristle grass. Before long, they would start fighting each other like crazy. Eventually, one would retreat and try to run away, and that was the loser. I once had a big cricket named "the Unbeatable."

Somehow one day it died in the bamboo pipe. I was sad for quite a few days and buried it in a corner of the school ground.

We had a headache over the problem of feeding the silkworms that moved with us to Shanghai. Where could we find mulberry trees, the leaves of which were the food for the silkworms? On Sunday, my brother and I would walk for two hours to Hongkou Park. We could not afford the entrance tickets, so we walked around and found a lower part of the wall. We climbed in and finally found some mulberry trees. Picking flowers and plants was prohibited, but how could we watch the silkworms die? We looked around and saw nobody. We hurried to pick up some leaves, stuff them into our schoolbags, and run. When we saw the silkworms hungrily eat the food we got them through our adventure, nothing could make us happier. We witnessed the silkworms spit out silk, make cocoons, transform to chrysalides and then moths, lay eggs . . . indeed, their whole life cycle.

Those childhood experiences all remained in my memory and fused into my conception of illustrations for children's books in recent years. For example, the experience with the silkworms helped me in creating the cover of the November 1999 issue of *Cricket* with its theme of silk fabrication. I once received a letter from twelve-year-old Beverly Klozkin forwarded to me by *Cricket*. She wrote: "The artist who drew the front cover is fantastic. Maybe you should ask him to do further covers. I really liked it." The young reader's praise was the greatest encouragement for me. I was deeply moved and sent through the press to her a paper-cut dragon to wish her a happy and lucky Year of the Dragon.

My father, being an architect designer, knew a little about art himself. Occasionally, he would draw grids on a piece of paper to make a portrait or something else. But I remember him most for his storytelling. Although he was rarely home, he made the most of his little time with us, telling us Chinese classic stories such as *The Three Kingdoms, The Marsh,* and *The Shrine of Gods.* He also told us about world classics such as *The Count of Monte Cristo.* I only partially understood his stories but became fascinated by "picture storybooks for children"—the comics.

Different from those in North America, Chinese comics were not about action heroes with superhuman strength and their adventures, they were stories adapted from Chinese and world classics, novels, and movies. They were not limited to children's topics but covered a wide range of interests. Artists' illustrations added vivid pictures to make them very interesting. Thus the readers were not only children but also adults. The books were small in size, only five inches by four inches. The covers were usually in color but the content pages were mainly of black-and-white line drawings.

During the 1950s there were not many radios available in Shanghai (nor the whole country of China), no television, and movies were too expensive to attend. Read-

Xuan's award-winning woodcut print "The Lights on a Fishery," 1971. (Courtesy of YongSheng Xuan.)

Xuan with his parents, wife Rong Rong, and daughter Faye Lee at the Shanghai Art Gallery, 1986. (Courtesy of YongSheng Xuan.)

ing comics, therefore, became the favorite pastime for children. Shanghai was the largest comics producer. Everywhere in Shanghai, comics stalls could be seen. Everyday after school, I would rush to those stalls, searching round and round with the three cents Mother had given me for breakfast in my hand. Three cents were enough only for reading three comics, and they were the cost for a full stomach, so I was very careful with my choices.

As time went by, I saved the "kowtow" money given to me at Chinese New Year by adults and the pocket money from my parents to buy some secondhand comics for repeated reading. I was deeply attracted to the rich contents and beautiful illustrations. I began to copy them in pencil. I couldn't afford paper, so sheets from used notebooks after the work was erased became my painting paper. Maybe it is safe to say that those comics were my earliest art teachers and marked the very beginning of my art career.

When I was seven or eight years old, I was the best at drawing among the forty-five students in my class. By

the time I finished grade school, I was a "famous painter" in my school. But my parents discouraged me from becoming a painter, just as later I persuaded my daughter, Faye Lee (officially Feli on her passport), to give up her wish for literature and art and choose an engineer's career, because the road for a successful artist is so much harder than that of an engineer. I dared not resist my parents' wishes, so I could only copy the illustrations from comics by hiding them in my bed after my family went to sleep. After a few months, I accumulated a pile of my "artwork" and I picked out the best to put on the wall. My brother was usually the only visitor at my "art exhibition" and the only critic.

*

In 1966, the Cultural Revolution began. Schools were closed. I was only fourteen and in high school then. It was supposed to be the golden time for studying, but I had to idle away time at home. Because my grandfather was named an enemy of the Communist government, even though he had died long ago, I was affected as his grandson. I was barred from joining the Red Guards and any social activities. During the Cultural Revolution, my father was imprisoned in Fujian Province for more than three years and stripped of his salary, thanks to the status of my grandfather and my aunt (my father's elder sister, who went to Taiwan before the Communists' takeover). My mother almost collapsed under the enormous economic and mental pressures, and was forced to bed by illness for a long time. I had to sell our personal belongings to buy food to keep the family from starving.

But poverty and discrimination did not deter me from my ever growing interest in art. By pure chance, I met Mr. Zhang Chongren, a famous sculptor who had graduated from the Belgium Royal Academy of Arts during the 1930s. He was my first mentor. He had sculpted for Chiang Kai-shek, leader of the Nationalist Party of China. Mr. Chongren was also a faithful Christian. The Red Guards regarded him as an alien element much like my family. He was denounced and jailed, his home searched, and properties confiscated more than once.

I visited him very cautiously to avoid his neighbors' suspicion. He taught me how to draw and sculpt. After I went home, I would practice portrait sketching from life with a few friends with the same interests. Our models were mostly children. Some days we would be lucky to find two or three children, but when we were not so lucky we would look in a mirror to sketch our own images. My home at 185 Jiangxi Road, north of Shanghai, soon became our art studio.

With things so hard, I didn't have money for art supplies. I collected waste metals, old newspapers, and magazines to sell for money to buy pens, ink, and paper. But I never got enough money to buy clay or plaster, the materials for sculpture. One day I rode a bicycle to a suburb of Shanghai dozens of li (a Chinese measure of distance that equates to half of a kilometer) away to dig up some clay to practice sculpture. The clay contained too much sand to be useable. To poverty and politics, I lost a dream.

During those school-less days, I picked up another hobby: kung fu. The traditional Chinese martial art of Shaolin boxing fascinated me. Every morning, I would go to Waitan Park to learn kung fu from a master who was a retired guard from a bank. I remember the first time I went home from practice, I couldn't walk for quite a few days from pain. After three to four years, I learned the basics of kung fu. Emphasizing the combination of strength and delicacy, the Chinese martial arts enlightened me with my painting. Making a feint to the east and attacking in the west, hiding your power as if there is none, freedom to advance or retreat—they were the essence of painting also. Had the painting art not attracted me more, I might have become Jackie Chan the Second today. Who knows?

During the 1960s, Mao Zedong's portraits were everywhere in China. They were seen from buildings on bou-

Xuan with a fellow artist at the Nantong Research Institute, creating sculpture later exhibited in the Cultural Palace of Nationalities in Beijing, 1986. (Courtesy of YongSheng Xuan.)

levards and small streets alike, just like Khomeini of Iran in later years. I was recommended by a neighbor to paint a giant portrait of Mao, fifteen feet by ten feet, at the gate of a factory. It took me more than three months to finish. My reward was a daily free lunch and the left-over oil painting brushes and oil colors, but I was very happy about that. After the portrait was finished, many people in my neighborhood spread the news: a teenage boy independently painted a giant Mao Zedong portrait.

But Mao did not appreciate what I did for him. Eventually I was sent with many other youths to the countryside to be a "new farmer" and receive reeducation from the lower-and middle-class peasants. Every day as the peasants did, we went to the fields at sunrise and came back home at sunset, with a scorching sun above us and burning heat under our feet. A hard day's work could only earn us a few dimes, just enough to keep us alive. For my mere existence, I had to carry out the primitive, repetitious labor.

I continued my pursuit of art using every bit of my spare time to practice painting, no matter if it was hot summer or cold winter. Finally I passed the exam with excellent marks to be accepted by the Cultural Center of Qidong County training class for professional painters of pictures from graven plates. Aside from learning some basic techniques of fine arts and making pictures from engraved plates, we three students and four teachers spent time sketching in the cotton fields or visiting workers in the local farm machinery factory.

What interested me most was the Lusi Fishery in Qidong County. I visited the fishery many times to sketch, interview, and experience life on the sea. I was charmed by the boundless ocean, the simple but honest fishermen, and the fishing boats tossed by the waves, struggling in the stormy sea. When night fell, the fishermen returned with full boats, unloaded the catch of the day, and quietly berthed in the harbor. After a day's hard work, the fishermen would cook, drink, chat, and play cards, Chinese chess, or some musical instruments against a background of hundreds of lights from their fishing boats. What a beautiful scene of happy fishermen! So natural, so tranquil! It triggered my strong desire to reproduce it. I made the composite in my head and finished the sketch in a relatively short time and named it "The Lights on a Fishery."

When the draft was submitted for approval, I was ordered to change the fishermen under the fishing lights to be studying Mao's works. I had no choice but to comply. Looking at the painting, which has a strong political overcast, I now feel that it also reflects the real life of that particular period of Chinese history.

During this period, I created many black-and-white as well as color pictures from graven plates. Some were selected to be published in magazines or newspapers and displayed at municipal, provincial, and national art exhibits. But this watercolor-block painting "The Lights on a Fishery" was my most successful work. I was only nineteen that year. It was later selected to be one of the representative pieces of Chinese modern art from graven plates to be exhibited abroad in countries such as Australia and Yugoslavia. It was also included in an album of paintings and won many awards.

I lived in Qidong County for a whole ten years. Besides creating pictures from graven plates at the Cultural Center, I also worked in a few handicraft factories designing wood sculpture, carving bamboo, creating batiks on blue cloth, crafting fans and imitations of antiques, etc. Every year I would apply and take the entrance exam for a formal academy of fine arts; every time I did very well with the exam, but for the reasons mentioned before, I could not pass the political examination of the government and was shut out of the door of universities.

As I almost lost all hope, I met Rong Rong Gu, a girl with a very similar family background to mine. Her father was a lawyer who also was classified as an enemy

The author/illustrator welcoming his wife and daughter at the Regina Airport, Saskatchewan, 1990. (Courtesy of YongSheng Xuan.)

Teaching Chinese art in an elementary school classroom in Regina, 1990. (Courtesy of YongSheng Xuan.)

by the government due to "historical problems." She also was a student driven to the countryside from the city. The differences between us were that I was good with thinking in images, using my hands, but I was reticent. In contrast, Rong Rong was talkative and eloquent, had no taste for art but a good sense of logic and a brain for mathematics. Above all, she was understanding and kind.

I was deeply hurt by the refusals of universities again and again. And as misfortune never strikes just once, I injured my head at work and had dozens of stitches and was hospitalized. Rong Rong came to look after me. With so much in common, love grew between us. Two years later, she became my wife. We have quite different personalities. During the twenty-plus years we have been married, we have had many quarrels, but after the storm, either she or I would reach out for reconciliation. A Chinese proverb says, "A harmonious home is the source of all successes." More often, my wife and I would complement each other in dealing with family problems or making family decisions, big or small. The saying "Half of the success of a man can be traced to a woman" is very true in our case.

*

After Mao Zedong died in 1976, Deng Xiaoping announced the end of the Cultural Revolution. The fate of

our families, as for many ordinary Chinese families, gradually changed. I was transferred to work in the Nantong Municipal Research Institute of Arts and Crafts as a full-time professional designer of handicrafts and painter. This was a big step forward in my art career. I once had been a fan of comics but now was a story writer and illustrator myself.

My work also included paper cutting, woodcarving, creating china and porcelain objects, interior decoration, etc. In the early 1980s, China opened up her door to the world. Modern Western artistic concepts also landed in China. I was the happiest to have realized my decade-long dream: to enter the study and research class of one of the highest creative-art education institutions in China—the Central University of Arts and Crafts of China. To make up for lost time, my classmates and I had to work extremely hard. After classes, I studied by myself for four to five hours. We finished the usual three years' work for university students in just over a year. I was fortunate to receive the teaching and guidance of many Chinese legendary artists, such as Wu Guanzhong, Bai Xueshi, and Zhang Ting.

Because of the earlier influence from Mr. Zhang Chongren, I was particularly fond of three-dimensional sculpture. For practice after classes, I went with a few classmates and teachers to the "Capitals of Chinese

Porcelain"—Shenhou Town of Henan Province and Lusi of Jiangsu Province—where I created many modern porcelain artworks and ceramic color picture plates. In 1986, my modern porcelain artworks were displayed at the Shanghai Art Gallery. The exhibit received broad favorable comments. The Shanghai television and radio stations made special reports on the show. A few newspapers and magazines published commentaries. In 1988 a few artists from the Nantong Research Institute and I had a joint art show in the Cultural Palace of Nationalities in Beijing. The period between 1979 to 1989 was the harvest time in my art career. I made breakthroughs in modern ceramic crafts, paper cuttings, woodcarving, handicraft design, comic-book illustration, pure artistic painting, and art theories, etc. I had formed my own art style with nutrients from a variety of art forms.

After China's opening up, I made many friends from Japan, Western Germany, the United States, Canada, Hong Kong, and Taiwan. Professor Ken Mitchell, dean of the English literature department at the University of Regina in Saskatchewan, Canada, was one of them. He was a guest professor at the China Institute of Diplomacy in Beijing. Besides teaching, he was also a productive writer. His award-winning play *Gone the Burning Sun,* a story about Canadian surgeon Dr. Norman Bethune, who came to China during the Japanese invasion to help with the fight and died at work, was on tour across China then. After visiting the art exhibit of our work at the Cultural Palace of Nationalities, Professor Mitchell invited me to design a poster for the play. I finished the work within a very short time in the form of an oil painting from graven plate. It came as a surprise that, before the play was performed, somebody took the poster for his or her private collection. After the tour was over, even Professor Mitchell himself didn't have a copy of it. Later I made a few more copies for him especially. He was deeply moved, and we became good friends.

At the beginning of 1989, Professor Mitchell acted as my sponsor to visit Canada. The paperwork was done so fast and smoothly that I was not fully prepared in my mind. Before that, I had published some art theory work, illustrations, wood carving, and paper cuttings in Japanese trade magazines. A well-known professor and the president of a Japanese applied art university had sponsored me to study in Japan. I studied Japanese in my spare time. I had also studied some Russian in my high-school years, but I couldn't even read the English alphabet! I was very hesitant to take the step, considering the nearly twenty years' foundation I had laid in the art circle of China, and most of all leaving a home and family behind.

My wife gave me enormous support at the time. She encouraged me to go out and open my eyes, saying that the vast world outside was necessary to broaden the views of an artist. So, at the age of thirty-eight, I, an English illiterate, stepped on the land of North America with two suitcases and 1,000 U.S. dollars my wife had

carefully sewn into my shirt. Soon I had to choose between two paths: to study at the University of Regina as I had desired or to work and make a living. How I wished I could choose the first path! But the realities of having to start English from zero and being penniless forced me to give up the idea of studying for a master's degree. I found a job making cabinets in a small furniture factory. With my training in woodcarving, I designed some special carved furniture and restored some antique furniture in addition to my routine production work. After hours, I went to high schools to demonstrate and teach Chinese arts, especially paper cutting. The children's eagerness to learn, expressions of surprise, liveliness, and naivete reminded me of my own childhood and my own daughter. I love children, and I especially love my only daughter. But because I was so busy with my work all the time, I did not have the opportunity to teach her my own art. I did not even keep her company or take care of her. I still blame myself for that today.

After I lived a lonely life for seven months in Canada, my wife and daughter came to join me in Regina. Regina is in the cold zone even by Canadian standards. We were very unused to the freezing weather there, but my daughter was much more adaptable to the new environment than we. With her talent in language, she soon acted as our English interpreter. To save money, we could only rent a basement apartment. Before long, my wife found a job sewing and altering clothing. Often we both worked sixty hours a week and studied English at night. After awhile we did not have to worry about our living. During the first two years of our most difficult times, we received help and support from many friends. Among them were my sponsor Professor Mitchell as well as Professor Wilfred Dube, fine arts professor Joe Fafard, and Professor Pantis. Professor Dube often came to help us with our English, introduced me to friends in the art circle, and even gave financial help to me and other Chinese students who shared the same house with me. They helped me overcome the initial barrier of "illiteracy and nonrelevancy" in North America. I would like to take this opportunity to most sincerely thank all the friends who have helped us!

As soon as I didn't have to worry about food, I began climbing the heights of art. I strongly wished to integrate my art into the mainstream of North America although I knew very well that it was not easy to enter the art world here. But that didn't stop me from trying. I held personal art exhibitions at the university, art shops, and the music conservatory in Regina, and painting exhibits in Calgary. I also went to universities, high schools, and grade schools to teach paper cutting. At multicultural festivals, I displayed rich and colorful Chinese folk art and craft, and demonstrated how they were made. I often frequented public libraries. I was surprised to find that picture books for children made up a good portion of every library's collection. Many parents brought their children to read in the libraries. It

Cut-paper illustration from Dragon Lover, *the first book Xuan both wrote and illustrated, 1999.* (Courtesy of YongSheng Xuan.)

reminded me that I had been a comics, or picture book, illustrator back in China, so I decided to send out my art portfolio.

My daughter helped me translate my resume into English. I sorted and made copies and pictures of many of my creative artworks together with reference materials. Addresses and phone numbers were taken down from children's books found in the library, and I sent out all my portfolio packages. Some were like stones thrown into the sea without any response; some were returned with the remarks, "For the time being, we don't have stories that match your artistic style. We will contact you when the opportunity comes." Finally, the art director of *Cricket* magazine, Mr. Ron McCutchan, replied to me, saying that they would let me have a try. Shortly after that, he gave me my first assignment: to illustrate a short poem, "New Sounds." Because of the tremendous differences Western and Eastern arts in the operations of art publishing, and my limited ability to communicate in English, Mr. Mc-Cutchan spent a great deal of time with me explaining every little detail, including the choice of papers, layout of illustrations, correct sizes, and ratios, etc. His help enabled me to complete the illustration, a color paper-cut mosaic which achieved a rather good artistic effect. At later art exhibitions, its originals would sell well for collections. (When I make paper cuttings, I can stack five to seven pieces of Chinese rice paper together and make five to seven originals at the same time.)

There is a Chinese proverb: Everything is hard at the beginning. If I may say that I have achieved some success in illustrating for children's books in North America, it is partly attributable to Mr. McCutchan's help. I will be forever grateful for his kindness, sincerity, and patience. It is a pity that we have been exchanging letters, sketches, and phone calls for seven years, but we haven't yet met even once! Since 1993, I have illustrated for *Cricket* many times including some interiors, some title pages, and some front covers. Most of the stories were from Asian countries such as China, Japan, and Korea. Only one was from North America: a little poem named "Snowball Wind."

In the fall of 1994, by chance, I found a full-time position to adjust and carve molds. So our family moved from central Canada to the city of Windsor in southeast Ontario. I was skillful in wood carving, etc., so the precise and delicate manual job was just my cup of tea. The pay and benefits were good, too. Day in and day out, I drove in the morning to work and came home in the evening. Gradually I became tired of the noncreative, repetitious, and mechanical work. It reminded me of my time in the Chinese countryside. The comparison does not fundamentally overshoot the mark except for the difference of living standards. I now felt I was in the "foreign" countryside, working just for a living. I dreamed of devoting more time to my creative art. Finally, I sent my resignation letter to my boss in the mold company, but he insisted on my staying. Not until later when the company was closed due to some business problems did I have time to myself to pursue art.

My wife always understood and supported my wish to pursue my art career. After due consideration, we used all our savings to buy a house on Ottawa Street in Windsor, a commercial area. We lived upstairs and opened an art shop downstairs, selling oil paintings, porcelain picture plates, watercolors, acrylic paintings, etc. Most were my own works. There were also some handicrafts, antiques, and homemade jewels. I designed and decorated the shop myself, and the whole family worked hard on it. The shop looked elegant and unique, but business was too slow.

We suffered some shoplifting. After a year, we had to shut the store down and rent out the space. We analyzed our failure afterwards and came to the conclusion that we didn't do good marketing research and lacked deep understanding of North American culture. Windsor is an industrial "blue-collar" city with mainly auto and mold companies. The development of an art market must follow a thorough investigation of the local residents' needs before it can succeed.

In 1996, with the art shop, I not only sold some of my own works, but also painted some oil paintings and portraits to customers' orders. I also rewrote and illustrated eighteen Chinese proverbial stories for the *Sinorama* pictorial magazine of Taiwan. The magazine is an official publication in seventeen languages and is distributed all over the world. In the United States and Canada, it is available even in the libraries of the average small city. The stories were well received after publication. I often got letters from readers. Singapore's number-one newspaper, *Straight Times,* reprinted the series. The publisher of Shen's Books obtained my mailing address and phone number from *Sinorama,* and soon they signed a publishing contract with me to write and illustrate the picture book *The Dragon Lover and Other Chinese Proverbs,* whose bilingual edition in Chinese and English was published in 1999. I used five different paper-cutting techniques to illustrate the five stories in the book. In the whole process of composition, I tried to incorporate traditional Chinese art into modern Western art. The first English-language draft of the book was translated by my daughter Faye Lee. I hope North American children, including North American Chinese children, like the book.

At the end of 1996, Regina Griffin, the chief editor of Holiday House, called me from New York. She said that she often saw my illustrations in *Cricket* and that Holiday House loved my works very much. She asked me if I would like to illustrate their children's book *Ten Suns,* which was already in their publishing plan. I was delighted to accept the assignment. *Ten Suns* is a Chinese fairy story based on the legend of "Houyi Shooting the Suns" from the ancient classic book *Shanghai Jing.* The story, known to every Chinese family, was adapted by the famous North American writer and professor Mr. Eric A. Kimmel. The adapted story was more to the taste of North American children of mainstream families, and it distanced itself somewhat from the original flavor of Chinese culture. So I made some recommendations to the adapted story and did my best during my creation of the artwork to take advantage of my familiarity with the cultural background to make the story more Chinese while being acceptable by North American readers.

While I was creating the illustrations for *Ten Suns*, I emphasized the feeling of sunlight and the bright and lively colors that children love. I used a "dry painting method" of watercolor together with lines drawn by watercolor pens, pencils, and crayons. Since the publication of the book, reviews have appeared even to this day. *Ten Suns* was named the Notable Children's Trade Book in the Field of Social Studies for 1999.

The second assignment that Holiday House gave me was *The Laziest Boy in the World.* This is a very popular story among the Chinese. I heard the story as a boy from my mother. In today's China, such "lazy boys" are found in many Chinese families, where the "one-child family policy" has created a new generation of "little emperors." I dedicated the book to my daughter, who is also the only child in the family, but she is the opposite of Xiao Long in the story. She was a tomboy from early age, restless and mischievous. She liked to climb trees and play in the dirt. She could buy herself breakfast and walk one and one-half miles to school when she was

only six. She came to Canada with us at the age of twelve and soon became our helper with the English language. In 1996, she passed the strict basic physical training and various tests to join the Canadian naval reserve, and now she is also a full-time, third-year electrical engineering student at the University of Windsor. Like Xiao Long, she hates to tidy up her room; her books, clothes, and socks are everywhere; she'd rather eat instant noodles everyday than take the time to cook. But she still climbs—rocks and mountains, that is. In addition, she is learning to be a pilot, climbing the heights of the sky.

The historical background of the story in *The Laziest Boy in the World* was impossible to trace. After a long time of considering, I used the Qing Dynasty, the last feudal dynasty in China, as its background. For the illustrations in the book I used acrylic paint on Chinese rice paper because I felt this combination could better imbue the pictures with local flavor, expose the inner world of the figures, and add more humor. The book received even more reviews after publication and won the 1998 Parents' Choice Award.

The third assignment Holiday House gave me was *The Rooster's Antlers,* a story originating from the well-known Chinese zodiac, the twelve animals symbolizing

Xuan and his wife "at our own gallery," the Head to Hand Arts and Crafts Store in Windsor, Canada, 1999. (Courtesy of YongSheng Xuan.)

twelve years in continuous cycles. Each year is represented by one animal. The symbol for the year 2000 is "dragon." For a child born in this year, dragon is his/her guardian animal. I decided to use color paper cuts, at which I am best. Compared with any children's book I had illustrated before, I spent three times as many hours on this one. I carefully deliberated and studied the expressions, colors, and layout of each animal. After painstaking cutting, the pasting and inlaying also required great patience. After the first draft, I was not satisfied with a few of them. So I started over again. When I looked at the final product of my hard work, my joy was beyond expression.

After the sample book was sent to me, I was very disappointed because the photographs did not capture the unique three-dimensional shadowy effect of the paper cuts. It was quite different from the originals. However, I was glad that the original art of the book was selected to participate in the Society of Illustrators' Original Art 99 Exhibition.

I lived in Windsor for five years. Other than running our art shop, I held personal art exhibitions at the Art's Centre-Gallery in Leamington, Ontario, and the art gallery of the Taiwan Center for Culture and Arts in Toronto. They caught media attention. The number of visitors was not as high as I expected, but the sale of my work was good. Windsor is only a river across from Detroit. I was fortunate to be invited by the Detroit Institute of Arts to perform paper cutting at the annual multicultural festival. I explained to the amazed audience the brief history of Chinese paper cuts, the invention of paper, and the techniques of paper cutting. When the audience saw my large-scale, framed, original works, many couldn't believe that they were handcut until they saw with their own eyes how they were made. They would utter, "This is amazing!" The curious children threw out endless questions. Some people proposed to collect my paper cut work. I was deeply moved. Here was I, an ordinary artist from China, and my paper cuts were being appreciated by so many people in the first-class Detroit art gallery where world-famous artists have their works on display. It really made me very confident that Chinese art would be understood and appreciated by more and more North American friends.

In 1998, I participated in the Windsor Drouillard Road project. The Windsor municipal government initiated the project to reflect the historic scene where the first Ford automobile was born. Together with a few other artists, we created some huge frescoes on the origin and development of Ford Motor Company. I especially liked one of them: "The Burning Furnace." I hope someday to adapt it to a large-scale oil painting. I regard visual arts as the goal of my life, but from time to time I also have to compromise with my daily needs. The closure of my art shop was because of financial reasons. Experience tells me that it is not easy to keep art alive and developing if the artist does not have basic security for his daily life.

At work on illustrations for Sinorama magazine, Michigan, 1999. (Courtesy of YongSheng Xuan.)

I have been in North America for ten whole years now. I have always been busy, but I have not achieved the goal of supporting my family solely on the income from my artwork. My wife was a businesswoman in China. Since coming to North America, her expertise has not been given a chance to play. She always wanted to do something here. Then she suggested to me that we operate a restaurant. It would give her a chance to do what she was good at, and if the business was OK, I wouldn't have to worry about making a living and could become a true freelance artist.

After more than two years' market research, we chose Michigan to be our target market and eventually bought an over-seventy-year-old American restaurant, Ann Sayles Dining Room, in Royal Oak. The customers of this restaurant are mainly middle-aged and elderly people. Many friends asked us why we did not open a Chinese restaurant, but chose a Western one whose cultural background was so different from ours and whose customers were much more difficult to serve. My wife and I both believe that we should try to merge into the mainstream of the North American society now that we live here. We should learn from and familiarize ourselves with their culture, which includes their food and beverage. A restaurant is a showcase for this aspect of the culture. It would provide an opportunity to explore this society and gain more raw materials and inspiration for my creative art.

Another reason was that both my wife and I believed in a Chinese virtue: respect for the elderly. When I was creating picture books for children, my mind often wandered back to my own innocent and happy childhood. When we first stepped into Ann Sayles Dining Room, we saw one elderly couple after another walking haltingly into the restaurant, holding each other's arms. My wife and I were deeply touched by the scene. Everybody follows the steps from their childhood to old age through life's decades of happiness and sorrow. I couldn't help associating the children I created in my books with the hobbling elderly in front of me. The former reflected our past, and the latter foretold our future. At the same time, they reminded me of our parents half a world away. We would love them as our parents. If we have some money in the future, we will invest it all into the renovation of the restaurant and enrich our menu of offerings. In the near future, we will add a special art corridor in our restaurant to offer them enjoyment from the taste of food, the vision of art, to the sound of music.

Art will be the pursuit of my whole life. Be it in the sun-scorched farm fields, in the sawdust-flying furniture shop, in the deafening mold factory, or by the steaming-hot furnace, art has always accompanied me. Starting in 2000, there have been more and more invitations for me to contribute. The series of eighteen stories based on the Chinese classic novel *The Marsh* with watercolor illustrations, which was contracted through *Sinorama* magazine, is under way. Two books contracted with Holiday House are in initial composition. The picture story "Firecracker Master" for *Cricket* has just been finished. While writing this autobiography, I received a letter from *Cricket* again. *Cricket* has begun a line of books including an anthology of scary stories coming up for the fall of 2000. The anthology *That's Ghosts for You* will feature stories from a wide range of countries: India, the British Isles, Appalachia, the American Southwest, Japan, and contemporary North America). They have given the assignment to me. I plan to use cut paper for the thirteen interior illustrations. This is high visibility, being their first anthology in the book line and playing off the *Cricket* reputation. So far the jacket sketches have been appraised five times and the interior sketches three times. These are record numbers in my book illustration history, but I patiently revise and retouch the sketches again and again. The creation of a good piece of art always goes through repeated deliberation and polishings.

This year will be critical both for my business and my art. I may be worn out, have no time to rest or accompany my daughter on a vacation, but more children will be able to read my stories and enjoy my illustrations. That is truly my greatest pleasure and happiness.

*

Xuan contributed the following update to his autobiographical essay in 2009:

One month into taking over Ann Sayles Dining Room, Holiday House signed me to four more books: *The Story*

of Chopsticks, The Story of Noodles, The Story of Kites, and *The Story of Paper*. They were a series of humorous stories about inventions that were very symbolic of Chinese culture. The stories described the innovative, clever, and innocent spirit of children.

Managing the restaurant was far more demanding than we ever expected. I held down the fort in the kitchen while my wife was managing everything front house. We worked twelve-hour days on top of my four book obligations. I brainstormed and worked on the sketches in between making dinner rolls and fixing a broken-down freezer. I decided to use Chinese paper cutting to tell these folk-inspired tales.

Tragedy also hit before we started this business. Jessica Yin Lei was not only a friend of my daughter, but also our families had been friends for a long time. She was a smart and exceptional kid. Christmas Eve of 1999, her family went on a vacation to California. En route, the van carrying the entire family got into a head-on collision. The accident was fatal for Jessica and her mother. The news shook the community and was extremely painful and devastating for our family. A year later, the high school that Jessica and my daughter had attended set up a scholarship in Jessica's name. I wanted to create a bronze sculpture in her honour. Using my memories of Jessica and photos and other material given to me by her family, I started creating a clay model. This was all done in the small space by the bar in the restaurant. When I was called to take care of kitchen issues, I would cover the clay model in a wet cloth.

After two years, I finally finished the bronze sculpture of Jessica, and it is now permanently displayed at the high school. Along with that, I completed the four-book

Bronze sculpture of Jessica Yin Lei. (Courtesy of YongSheng Xuan.)

series, the fifth book *That's Ghosts for You,* twenty or so magazine illustrations, and various Detroit Institute of Arts live demonstrations. I consider these two years my hardest years. There was always a shortage of both time and sleep. However, I felt a great sense of accomplishment in my art work and of course, took pride in running my own business.

My daughter Faye Lee also graduated from university as an electrical engineer during those two years. My wife and I attended her graduation ceremony in the fall of 2001. Watching her dressed in her graduation gown, we were very happy and proud. I can't help but feel I wasn't a good father. Because of my busy schedule, I didn't care for her enough in her daily life, education, career, or even her emotional life. My responsibility should have been more than just to meet her material needs.

Faye Lee's new boyfriend also attended the ceremony. He is a handsome kid of English descent. They met while serving as naval reservists in the Canadian Armed Forces. My wife and I had always hoped our daughter would find someone who shared the same culture and life style as us. However, it did not take long before Greg's laid-back personality, wonderful sense of humour, and most of all, his commitment to our daughter won us over. Now they are getting married this summer. Almost twenty years ago, a new immigrant family with 2,000 dollars in their pocket and a dream for a new life arrived in North America. Twenty years later, we are once again a family with a brand new member. We hope there will be more new members to come. That will be the biggest reward from our journey to the West.

In the next few years we sold Ann Sayles Dining Room and bought a microbrewery named Sports Brew Pub in Wyandotte, Michigan. It was a very different place and customer base than Ann Sayles. The pub made nine different kinds of beer. It lit up whenever there was a major sports event going on. The pub allowed us to experience a very American way of life: enjoying a nice cold beer with friends while cheering on their favorite sports team. The management of the pub was easier and less hectic than Ann Sayles since we had two managers. I now had more time to dedicate to my work. I signed another book, *D Is for Dragon Dance,* with Holiday House. I wanted to have a very different and out-of-the-box concept for this book, so I experimented with various techniques and textures. Finally, it was the mixture of acrylic, sandy-textured watercolour, and paper cutting that gave the best effect. The book did better than I had ever expected: Holiday House published a paperback and hardcover version, and the book was also picked up by Scholastic, Inc.

Once upon a time I felt strong and didn't think anything could stop me. After years of long days and irregular work schedules, the inevitable caught up to me. During work on *D Is for Dragon Dance,* I found out that I had early-stage prostate cancer. Cancer was a

Family portrait in front of the pyramids in Egypt, December, 2006.
(Courtesy of YongSheng Xuan.)

very scary word and the news was tough on my family and me. However, I was extremely lucky that the disease was discovered at a very early stage, and that a simple surgery to freeze the cancer cells would send me back to good health. I think my younger years of practicing martial arts really helped me during the recovery.

After my recovery, we needed a big vacation. It had been a long while since the family had gone on a vacation together. My wife and I sold the Sports Brew Pub and made Egypt our first stop. Like China, Egypt is an ancient country full of history and mysticism. We landed in Cairo in the late afternoon and had dinner by the Nile river. The cool December breeze, with its musky scent of the desert, was unforgettable. Feluccas sailed by on the sparkles of the sun-touched Nile. I looked at the excited faces of my wife, daughter, and future son-in-law, and felt fortunate and privileged in life.

Over the next eighteen days, we ducked our heads inside the Pyramids, walked between the towering gods of Abu Simbel, swam in the Red Sea, touched the Burning Bush, climbed Mount Sinai in the middle of the night to catch the sunrise, and so much more. From the point of view of an artist, I was always very proud of what my ancestors had accomplished throughout 5,000 years of history. However, the ancient Egyptians were far more advanced and sophisticated than I ever thought. The Chinese reflected their culture and religion by being meticulously detailed and elegant in their artworks. The Egyptians were very different. They were bold and grand in everything they did. Tombs were built so high that they touched the heavens, and hieroglyphs were carved so deep into the temple walls that no amount of time can tarnish their beauty and meanings. Egypt is a fascinating and inspirational country with so much to give. I feel that every artist, or person aspiring to be an artist, should go there to discover one of the oldest cultures and civilizations in the world.

The vacation turned into self-exploration for me as an artist. I really wanted to become re-educated and re-immersed in all different types of art styles. I wanted to draw inspiration through maximum exposure for all my senses. Therefore, I made my second stop New York City. My family and I had been to New York a few times on vacation, but this time I decided to explore the city and its vast art culture on my own for two weeks. I made my return to the Metropolitan Museum of Art a priority. I feasted on what the museum had to offer. I went back for three days straight. On the fourth day and the next three days, I toured the Museum of Modern Art. The second week, my days consisted of visiting the art districts, underground art galleries and studios, and an international art exposition.

Exploring New York's art and culture was like walking through history. All styles of art are located in close proximity to each other: Renaissance art, impressionism, cubism, abstract art, pop art, and even graffiti. I really don't think two weeks were enough to take everything in. Through its past, I believe I see the next generation's art style: more blending of styles and techniques, the East meets the West, the North meets the South. Each country would still maintain its own identity; however, the globalization of our world is creating a distinctive art style that seems both exotic and recognizable.

New York was certainly an intense journey for me. Now I had to go back to where I came from. I left China twenty years ago. Back then, art was merely a tool to express strictly ideological ideas and concepts. Today, the influences and scenes in Chinese art have changed so much, and I felt completely estranged from them. Chinese artists now have more creative freedom: the content of art has become much more liberated and edgy; the concept of art has become a hip status symbol; and the market for art is hopping and alive. This is a huge step forward for artists and art communities in China.

My wife and I touched down in my hometown of Shanghai first. We were lost amongst the tall buildings, highways, and cars. After a short visit with family, I

"Gaze" July 2007. (Courtesy of YongSheng Xuan.)

was excited to head to Beijing, the epicentre for Chinese culture and arts. Not to mention, Beijing was where I spent my university days.

It is said that the number of professional artists who have come from all over China to settle in Beijing exceeds ten thousand. There are now galleries and art organizations from Europe, North America, Hong Kong, Taiwan, and Southeast Asia occupying the art market in Beijing. It has also attracted the attention of international collectors and business investors in the same fashion that the stock and real-estate markets have generated tremendous enthusiasm.

I reconnected with my former classmate and good friend Zhang QuXian who now lives in Beijing. He is now a prominent artist and is doing well selling his artwork. I counted on QuXian to re-introduce me into the Chinese art community. I accompanied him to the Chinese Painting and Artists Nominate Exhibition, which was sponsored by the local Cultural Centre and Imperial Art Academy in GanSu province. The exhibition was held in the cities of Jinchang, Duhuang, and Juchan and included a couple of live demonstrations. The invited artists had all of their trip expenses covered by the sponsors during this tour. They were also rewarded 10,000 yen for their attendance. In return, each artist donated two pieces of his or her work for the exhibition as well as the pieces that were created during the live demonstrations. Artists came from all over the country, including fifty famous artists and professors, and brought in over 400 art pieces.

"My wife and I in QingHuang Island, China," May 2007. (Courtesy of YongSheng Xuan.)

I asked QuXian what would happen to these artworks and why they put on these exhibition tours. He said: first, to promote and improve arts and culture in these cities; second, the pieces would be used as gifts for building relationships with other cities or organizations; and third, some of these artworks would become collectible items for the local government agencies and cultural centres. China's new cultural-exchange movement widened my eyes and it really gave artists both moral encouragement and material reward.

One of the activities during this exhibition was visiting the Dunhuang Caves, which was very important for me. The Dunhuang Caves were built in 1800 BCE and had gone through all kinds of difficulties. In recent years, the surrounding desert has been coming closer to the caves. The government and international organizations are paying a good deal of attention to this, and are making every effort to arrest its advance. When I stood in one of the dark caves and gazed at the beautiful Buddhist statues, Buddhist frescoes, carved stones, clay sculptures, and temple architecture from different periods, it reminded me of the temples and statues I had visited in Egypt.

A few days after I returned to Beijing, another former classmate, Gong WeiMin, offered to drive me to a famous art community called Song Zhuang. Located in the outer suburbs of Beijing, this community was home to a group of artists who had rebelled against government art and traditional ideas. Some of them rented farm houses and others had built their own studios. It was similar to the artist lofts found in downtown Manhattan.

My wife and I stayed in Beijing for almost seventy days. While I felt the beating pulse of the heart of the art community in China, I also sensed a darker side. In the pursuit for fame and money, artists compromised their artistic integrity. Their work had become uninspired copies of the original creations; even so, the pieces were still being sold at the same price and in the same quantity. I believe that art items and original artistic creations are two totally different things. Currently, art items are in abundance, but original artistic creations are rare. I hope this condition will reverse itself soon.

This was a vacation after all. When my wife and I finally left Beijing, we visited dozens more cities such as Nin Xian, Tai Wan, Hong Kong, Shen Zhen, and others.

Coming back from our year-long hiatus abroad, my wife and I decided to continue to live a laid-back life. I spent my days in deep contemplation, living what might be considered a vagabond life and going so far as to cut

"Working in my studio in Windsor, Ontario" 2008 (Photograph by ZhiFu Wang. Reproduced by permission.)

off contact with my publisher and with my teaching life. However, I felt regenerated. I started thinking about creating something that was distinctively my style, my originality. I began brush painting and writing. I was familiar with brush writing, but hadn't done it in a long time. My oil painting and traditional Chinese painting skills returned faster than I imagined they would. I just wanted to paint. I felt restless if I hadn't painted in a week.

Life is a bit of a funny thing. Just when I became so involved in my work again, life managed to pull me back. In the summer of 2008, my wife and I were visiting friends in North Carolina. As we drove, a van pulled into our lane and hit us head-on. My wife bruised just about every inch of her body. I fractured my collar bone, cracked two other ribs and sustained an injury to my liver. There was water in my thoracic cavity. We were told by doctors and friends alike that we escaped death by sheer luck. My daughter Faye flew to North Carolina immediately to be by our side on her thirtieth birthday. As I looked at her worried face, I could hardly imagine that my wife and I had come so close to never seeing her turn thirty, get married, and have children.

Before the accident, my wife and I had debated whether to move to the West Coast to be closer to Faye. I had wanted to stay on the East Coast to be closer to New York and Toronto. I can't help but feel a bit foolish now. My artwork will always be important to me. However, I couldn't do it, or have the inspiration to do it, without my family by my side. I am so lucky that they love me and keep me grounded. Now my wife, daughter, future son-in-law, and I live in beautiful Vancouver, British Columbia, where I find my inspiration everyday and all around me.

*   *   *

YAYO 1961-
(Diego Herrera)

Personal

Born 1961, in Mesitas del Colegio, Colombia; immigrated to Canada, 1987; children: one son. *Education:* Studied advertising, marketing, and commercial art.

Addresses

Home—Montréal, Québec, Canada. *Agent*—Wanda Nowak, Creative Illustrators Agency, 231 E. 76th St., Ste. 5D, New York, NY 10021. *E-mail*—yayo@yayoart. com.

Career

Illustrator and cartoonist. Presenter at schools. *Exhibitions:* Work exhibited at Maison de la culture Plateau Mont-Royal, Montréal, Québec, Canada, 2008.

Member

Communication-Jeunesse, Association des créateurs et intervenants de la bande dessinée, Association des illustrateurs et illustratrices du Québec.

Awards, Honors

Mr. Christie Book Prize, 1995, for *Au lit, princesse Émilie* by Pierrette Dubé; Governor General's Award, 1998, for *Le chasseur d'arc-en-ciel.*

Writings

SELF-ILLUSTRATED

Humor Grafico, Centro Colombo Americano (Bogotá, Colombia), 1989.
Le carton de Yayo (cartoon collection), Éditions du Phylactère (Montréal, Québec, Canada), 1990.
Zoo-illogique, Éditions du Phylactère (Montréal, Québec, Canada), 1991.
Rêverire, Zone Convective (Montréal, Québec, Canada), 1996.
Le chasseur d'arc-en-ciel, Les 400 Coups (Laval, Québec, Canada), 1998.
Humoro sapiens, Les 400 Coups (Montréal, Québec, Canada), 2008.

Creator of comic strip "Le Monde de Yayo," for *L'Actualité* magazine, beginning late 1980s.

ILLUSTRATOR

Daniel Sernine, *La fresque aux trois démons,* Hurtubise (LaSalle, Québec, Canada), 1991.
Jean Coué, *Les 80 palmier d'Abbar Ben Badis,* Hurtubise (LaSalle, Québec, Canada), 1992.
Grégoire Horveno, *Mamie blues,* Hurtubise (LaSalle, Québec, Canada), 1993.
Jacques Delval, *L'inconnu,* Hurtubise (LaSalle, Québec, Canada), 1993.
Hélène Vachon, *Le sixième arrêt,* Éditions Héritage (Saint-Lambert, Québec, Canada), 1995.
Hélène Vachon, *Mon plus proche voisin,* Éditions Héritage (Saint-Lambert, Québec, Canada), 1995.
Pierrette Dubé, *Au lit, princesse Émilie!,* Saint-Hubert, Québec, Canada), 1995.
Hélène Vachon, *Mon ami Godefroy,* Éditions Héritage (Saint-Lambert, Québec, Canada), 1996.
Jacinthe Gaulin, *Mon p'tit frère,* Éditions Héritage (Saint-Lambert, Québec, Canada), 1996.
Hélène Vachon, *Le cinéma de Somerset,* Domenique et cie. (Saint-Lambert, Québec, Canada), 1997.
Denice Skrepcinski, Melissa Stock, and Lois Lyles, *Silly Celebrations!: Activities for the Strangest Holidays You've Never Heard Of,* Aladdin (New York, NY), 1998.
Francis Pelletier, *Si,* Les 400 Coups (Laval, Québec, Canada), 1998.

Hélène Vachon, *Le délire de Somerset,* Domenique et cie. (Saint-Lambert, Québec, Canada), 1999.

Cécile Gagnon, *Petits contes de ruse et de malice,* Les 400 Coups (Laval, Québec, Canada), 1999.

Évelyne Wilwerth, *La veste noire,* Hurtubise (Montréal, Québec, Canada), 2001.

Hélène Vachon, *L'oiseau de passage,* Domenique et cie. (Saint-Lambert, Québec, Canada), 2001.

Brenda Silsbe, *A Tree Is Just a Tree?,* Advanced Global Distribution Services (San Diego, CA), 2001.

Sheree Fitch, *If I Had a Million Onions,* Tradewind Books (Vancouver, British Columbia, Canada), 2005.

Teresa Bateman, *Keeper of Soles,* Holiday House (New York, NY), 2006.

Charlotte Foltz Jones, *The King Who Barked: Real Animals Who Ruled,* Holiday House (New York, NY), 2009.

Lee Bennett Hopkins, selector, *I Am the Book: Poems,* Holiday House (New York, NY), 2010.

Lesley Simpson, *The Hug,* Annick Press (Toronto, Ontario, Canada), 2010.

Sidelights

Yayo is the pen name of Diego Herrera, a Colombia-born artist whose work is characterized by a sophisticated humor that highlights life's wry moments. Now living in Canada, where his cartoon strip "Le Monde de Yayo" has appeared in the back pages of the magazine *L'Actualité* since the late 1980s, Yayo has won several awards for his work as an illustrator of books by authors such as Hélène Vachon, Pierrette Dubé, Jacques Delval, Teresa Bateman, and Brenda Silsbe. His cartoon art has been collected in several anthologies, among them *Zoo-illogique, Rêveries,* and *Humoro sapiens.* Reviewing *The King Who Barked: Real Animals Who Ruled,* a story anthology by Charlotte Foltz Jones that casts a range of animals in positions of political power, a *Kirkus Reviews* critic wrote that Yayo's brightly colored acrylic images "add to the whimsy and fun" of the story. "Animal lovers will find this a fascinating diversion," added Marily Taniguchi in her *School Library Journal* review of the book, the critic adding that "Yayo's acrylic-on-canvas paintings capture the topsy-turvy spirit of the tales and add playful details."

Yayo's other picture-book projects include Silsbe's *A Tree Is Just a Tree?,* a story that describes the important interrelationship among trees, people, and animals. The book's repetitive poetic text contains less than ninety words, making it an appropriate storytime offering for very young children, while its thoughtful message will also resonate with older readers. Praising Silsbe's story as "refreshingly light-hearted," Gillian Richardson added in *Resource Links* that Yayo's "whimsical illustrations . . . successfully extend the text" by imaginatively weaving trees and their textures into each image. The book's sequenced images "hold the reader's attention and tell their own story as many are paintings within paintings," observed L.M. Sykes in the *Canadian Review of Materials,* and they "present a variety of tree types during different seasons of the year."

Yayo's artwork captures the fun in Lesley Simpson's friendship-forming picture book **The Hug.** *(Annick Press, 2010. © 2010 Yayo (art). Reproduced by permission.)*

The illustrations Yayo contributes to Bateman's picture book *Keeper of Soles* also attracted critical praise. An entertaining story that combines a play on words with a new take on the timeless story of a man attempting to thwart Death personified, *Keeper of Soles* features what a *Publishers Weekly* critic described as "acrylic paintings brushed in warm, smudged colors" into which "Yayo tucks dry jokes into nearly every corner." Noting that the artist plays with perspective to "add interest and momentum, *School Library Journal* critic Wendy Lukehart added that *Keeper of Soles* is "witty and urbane, yet full of child appeal."

"To draw a single drawing or an illustration is like writing a poem or a verse," Yayo noted in discussing the difference between cartooning and writing with blogger Talleen Hacikyan. "When you write a children's picture book or a comic, it's another way to narrate. It's like going on a long trip. I used to draw thoughts and feelings, now I'm also writing them. You have to use other tools to express feelings and thoughts in words. The sources of inspiration and the use of creativity remain the same. The more I write the more I respect writers' work."

Biographical and Critical Sources

PERIODICALS

Booklist, March 1, 2006, Michael Cart, review of *Keeper of Soles,* p. 99.

Horn Book, May-June, 2006, Sarah Ellis, review of *Keeper of Soles,* p. 288.

Kirkus Reviews, January 15, 2006, review of *If I Had a Million Onions,* p. 84; January 15, 2006, review of *Keeper of Soles,* p. 82; August 1, 2009, review of *The King Who Barked: Real Animals Who Ruled.*

Publishers Weekly, February 27, 2006, review of *Keeper of Soles,* p. 61.

Resource Links, December, 2001, Gillian Richardson, review of *A Tree Is Just a Tree?,* p. 11.

School Library Journal, February, 2006, Adriane Pettit, review of *If I Had a Million Onions,* p. 21; April, 2006, Wendy Lukehart, review of *Keeper of Soles,* p. 96; June, 2006, Kathleen Whalin, review of *If I Had a Million Onions,* p. 174; September, 2009, Marilyn Paniguchi, review of *The King Who Barked,* p. 142.

ONLINE

Bibliothèque et Archives Canada Web site, http://www.collectionscanada.gc.ca/ (February 15, 2011), "Yayo."

Illustration Québec Web site, http://www.illustration quebec.com/ (February 15, 2011), "Yayo."

Talleen Hacikyan's Art Web log, http://talleen.unblog.fr/ (September 29, 2008), interview with Yayo.*